PIRḲÊ DE RABBI ELIEZER

(THE CHAPTERS OF RABBI ELIEZER THE GREAT) ACCORDING TO THE TEXT OF THE MANUSCRIPT BELONGING TO ABRAHAM EPSTEIN OF VIENNA

TRANSLATED AND ANNOTATED
WITH INTRODUCTION AND INDICES
BY

GERALD FRIEDLANDER

SEPHER-HERMON PRESS
New York

TO

ADOLPH BÜCHLER, Ph.D.

PRINCIPAL OF THE JEWS' COLLEGE, LONDON

PIRKE DE RABBI ELIEZER
First edition: London, 1916
Second edition: New York, 1965
Third edition: New York, 1970
Fourth edition: New York, 1981
THE JUDAIC STUDIES LIBRARY, no.
SEPHER-HERMON PRESS, Inc.
LCC No. 80-54592
ISBN 0-87203-095-4

PREFACE

My thanks are due to Dr. A. Marmorstein for much general help in the course of my work. He has verified all the Rabbinic quotations in the notes and has added many additional references. I have further to express my gratitude to Dr. Büchler for valuable counsel in the preparation of the translation and also for reading and correcting the proof-sheets. I dedicate this book to him as a mark of gratitude for a series of kindnesses shown to me during many years. It is mainly owing to his inspiration and encouragement that I have ventured to offer this effort as a contribution to Jewish literature.

G. F.

GENERAL CONTENTS

GENERAL CONTENTS

INTRODUCTION

§ 1. Short Account of the Book and its History

The book usually designated פרקי דר׳ אליעזר, *Pirkê de Rabbi Eliezer* (*Chapters of Rabbi Eliezer*), is not the least important of the Rabbinic Pseudepigrapha. The attention recently given to the study of the Apocrypha and Pseudepigrapha has, to a certain extent, been limited by the neglect of the Rabbinic side of the subject. The only Hebrew works translated in the magnificent Oxford edition of the *Apocrypha and Pseudepigrapha* are the *Pirkê Aboth* and the *Fragments of a Zadokite Work*. The selection of these two books is singularly unfortunate, since neither belongs to the Pseudepigrapha proper. More appropriate would have been the inclusion in the afore-mentioned *corpus* of such works as the *Othijoth de Rabbi 'Aḳiba* or the *Pirkê de Rabbi Eliezer*, now presented, for the first time, in an English translation.

The name of the writer of the book is unknown. The putative author is Rabbi Eliezer, son of Hyrḳanos, who lived in the latter half of the first century C.E. and in the first decades of the second century. He was famous on account of his great erudition, but in spite of his reputation as a scholar he was ultimately excommunicated. Was it on account of this very fact that the actual writer of our book deliberately selected the name of this famous master in Israel as its supposed author? In many respects the book is polemical and unorthodox—polemical in opposing doctrines and traditions current in certain circles in former times, unorthodox in revealing certain mysteries which were reputed to have been taught in the school of Rabban Jochanan ben Ẓakkai, the teacher of our Rabbi Eliezer. Did our author deem it dangerous to expose his own identity? Did he not run the risk of being placed under the ban for the daring displayed in writing his book? What name was more honoured, in spite of the excommunication which had made it so prominent, than Rabbi Eliezer the Great, who is quoted in Mishnah and Talmud more frequently than any one of his contemporaries?

The book enjoyed considerable popularity in Jewish circles in former days, for there are more than two dozen editions. There is also a Latin version with an elaborate commentary by Vorstius (1644), indicating a certain interest in the book even in non-Jewish circles. The first edition was printed in Constantinople in 1514, the second edition appeared in Venice, 1544, the third edition was published in Sabbioneta in 1567. Later editions of value are those of Amsterdam and Prague. The folio edition of Rabbi David Luria (Vilna, 1837) is the best extant. His critical commentary is a mine of valuable information which has been constantly laid under contribution in the preparation of the notes in the present volume. The editions of Brode and Einhorn have also been consulted.

The text adopted for translation is a valuable unedited MS. belonging to Abraham Epstein of Vienna. This treasure contains not only the entire work as printed in the various editions, but a small section of the last chapter which has never been printed. Wertheimer's *Bottê Midrashoth*, iii. pp. 29–34, contains a parallel text to the last chapter, but not as complete as our MS. text. The MS. is probably the work of a Spanish scribe of the twelfth or thirteenth century. It was formerly the property of N. Coronel. In very many instances the text preserved in the MS. is superior to that contained in the printed editions. The MS. used by the editor of the *editio princeps* was fairly accurate, as this text is on the whole correct and consecutive. This edition was used by the editor of the beautiful second edition, in which some of the errors incidental to a first edition have been rectified. This text has been used by all subsequent editors and was adopted by Vorstius for his Latin version.

In addition to Epstein's MS., the present writer has used an old MS. fragment of the astronomical chapters (VI.–VIII.) belonging to the Rev. Dr. M. Gaster, and also his MS. (9), which, however, is incomplete. Several fragments from the Cairo Genizah belonging to Mr. Elkan N. Adler, M.A., have been collated. The Genizah fragments belonging to the Cambridge University have been copied by Dr. A. Marmorstein and his transcript has been used. The MSS. of the Bodleian Library, Oxford, have also been collated. The fragment MS. in the British Museum, edited by Horowitz, has likewise been consulted.

In the printed texts there are fiftv-four chapters, whereas in our MS. there are only fifty-three chapters, due to the fact that the last two are combined into one. In its present form the book is undoubtedly incomplete. In all the editions the last chapter breaks off in the middle of a sentence. The MSS. referred to in the *Jewish Encyclopedia* (x. p. 59b) have not been available.

§ 2. Plan and Contents of the Book

The book, as we now know it, is, in all probability, a composite work, consisting of three originally distinct sections. The object of one of these parts was to describe in detail the " ten descents " from heaven to earth, which God is said in Holy Scripture to have made in the past. The books of old told of the Ascension of Isaiah, as well as of the Assumption of Moses and other worthies; our book essayed the more sacred task of revealing the ten Divine descents on earth. The purpose of the Pistis Sophia is somewhat similar, of course from the standpoint of the Christian gnostic. The last chapter in our book deals with the eighth descent. The missing part of the work is claimed to be preserved in the text published by M. Friedmann in the *Pseudo-Tanna de bê Elijahu.* The authenticity of this material has, however, not been established thus far.

Another section incorporated in our present work professed to give a detailed account of Rabbinic mysticism, more particularly the ancient mysteries of the Creation (Ma'aseh Bereshith), the Divine Chariot (Ma'aseh Merkabah), as well as the secret of the Calendar (Sôd Ha-'Ibbur) and the secret of the Redemption (Sôd Ge'ullah). The mysteries of the heaven above, the earth beneath, and the waters under the earth are all revealed. Paradise and Gehenna, this world and the new world, are all explored. We hear of the Ministering Angels, Sammael and the angels "who fell from their holy place in heaven," and also concerning Leviathan and Behemoth. The life hereafter, the resurrection of the dead, and the Messianic Age are discussed. The doctrine of the "Last Things," usually known as Eschatology, is not entirely forgotten.

The possibility of a third book in our work is to be detected in the fragment of a Midrash on the *Shemoneh 'Esreh* (the Jewish prayer *par excellence*), which is contained in the latter part of the "Chapters." Whether the three chapters (VI.–VIII.) dealing with the Calendar are an integral part of the section previously discussed or whether they belong to the actual *Pirḳê de Rabbi Eliezer* is a moot point, which cannot be decided off-hand. The result of the combination of the different sections may be seen in the repetition of several narratives (*e.g.* the creation of Adam), in obvious contradictions (*e.g.* Chapter III. and Chapter XVIII.; Chapter XXX. and Chapter XXXI., on the question of the difference between the ages of Isaac and Ishmael), and finally in the absence of consecutive order in the arrangement of the material. Likewise the order in which the different chapters are arranged is a further proof of the composite nature of the entire book. Moreover, the first two chapters form an independent section which has been prefixed for the purpose of providing a preface in order to justify the authorship attributed to Rabbi Eliezer. The two chapters are entirely biographical, setting forth the call of Rabbi Eliezer. Our contention as to the relation of these two chapters towards the rest of the book, as we now know it, seems to be supported by the fact that the MS. of the first part of our book in the British Museum begins at Chapter III. of the printed text. The same fact applies to the portion of our book which has been incorporated by R. Asher Ha-Levi in his *Sepher Ha-Zikhronoth* (Bodleian MS. Heb. d. 11, No. 2797). Dr. Marmorstein finds in MS. Adler (522, p. 143b), Chapter XLIV. quoted. This corresponds to Chapter XLII. in the printed texts. Again, on p. 79a, Chapter XLI. is mentioned, corresponding to Chapter XXXIX. in our text. In Gaster MS. (9) ten anciently written chapters have been inserted which are all enumerated as though the book began with Chapter III. This clearly shows that in some MSS. the first two chapters were missing, and, as we have suggested, did not form part of the original work.

Chapters III.–XI. deal with the work of the Creation.

Chapters XII.–XX. refer to Adam and Eve.

Chapters XXI. and XXII. give the story of Cain, Abel, and the other descendants of Adam and Eve.

Chapters XXIII. and XXIV. contain the history of Noah and his sons and the narrative of the Flood.

Chapter XXV. sets forth the sin and doom of Sodom.

Chapters XXVI.–XXXI. cover the life story of Abraham, including the story of the 'Aḳedah (or the binding of Isaac).

Chapters XXXII. and XXXIII. deal with the life of Isaac.

Chapter XXXIV. is devoted to an account of the resurrection of the dead.

Chapters XXXV.–XXXVII. present the story of Jacob's life.

Chapters XXXVIII. and XXXIX. refer to Joseph.

Chapter XL. discusses the signs given by God to Moses.

Chapter XLI. is concerned with the revelation on Sinai.

Chapters XLII. and XLIII. (which are evidently out of place) contain the narrative of the Exodus (which should precede the story of the revelation on Sinai).

Chapter XLIV. unfolds the history of Amalek.

Chapters XLV.–XLVII. set forth the story of the Golden Calf.

Chapter XLVIII. resumes the subject of the Exodus.

Chapters XLIX. and L. give the story of Haman and Mordecai.

Chapter LI. is eschatological.

Chapter LII. describes the wonders of old.

Chapter LIII. reverts to the history of Israel in the wilderness, *e.g.* the "Brazen" Serpent and Miriam.

In the second half of the book we see the fragment of the Midrash on the *Shemoneh 'Esreh*, furnishing a series of links connecting the various sections of this part of the book. Thus the first benediction is referred to in Chapter XXVII. in connection with Abraham. The second benediction occurs in Chapters XXXI. and XXXIV., in connection with Isaac. The third in Chapter XXXV. (Jacob), the fourth in Chapter XL. (Moses), the fifth in Chapter XLIII. in connection with Manasseh and Nineveh, the sixth in Chapter XLVI. in connection with Israel in the wilderness, the seventh in Chapter LI. (Messianic), and the eighth in Chapters LII. and LIII. (Miriam). The fact that only eight descents and only eight benedictions are dealt with in the book is noteworthy, and points to the present incomplete condition of the work.

§ 3. Our Book in Jewish and Christian Literature

The book is usually known by the title *Pirḳê de Rabbi Eliezer*. Our MS. uses this designation, adding "Ha-Gadol" ("the Great"). The first to quote our book are the Geonim or Rabbis of Babylon, see *Siddur* of Rab ʿAmram (*c.* 850 C.E.), p. 32a. Machẓor Vitry (ed. S. Hurwitz), p. 117, quotes our book by the title "Peraḳim" ("The Chapters"). In the Tosaphoth to Kethuboth, 99a, R. Tam calls it "Haggadath de Rabbi Eliezer ben Hyrḳanos." The ʿArukh terms it "Baraitha de Rabbi Eliezer." Dr. Marmorstein finds our book mentioned in Midrash Ha-Chêfêz (B.M. 2351, p. 89b) under the title of "Mishnah de R. Eliezer"; the same designation occurs in a bookseller's catalogue of the twelfth to thirteenth century, see *J.Q.R.* xiii. p. 53.

The usual title *Pirḳê de Rabbi Eliezer* is employed by Rashi (*e.g.* on Gen. xxvii. 9; Deut. xii. 17; Jonah i. 7), Jehudah Ha-Levi (Khazari iii. 65 and iv. 29), and Maimonides (Moreh Nebukhim i. 70 and ii. 26). For further references see the excellent chapter on our book in Zunz, *Gottesdienstliche Vorträge der Juden* (2nd ed.), p. 283, note *f*.

In addition to the writers and books mentioned in the previous paragraphs, quotations from our book are to be found in R. Achai Gaon in She'eltoth, in Naṭronai Gaon in Chemdah Genuẓah No. 93, in R. Moses of Coucy's *S.M.G.*, in Halakhoth Gedoloth (ed. Hildesheimer, p. 5), in Midrash Haggadol (ed. Schechter), Midrash Agadah (ed. Buber), Jalḳuṭ Shimʿoni, Jalḳuṭ Makhiri, Midrash Sekhel Ṭob (ed. Buber), also in the commentaries on the Pentateuch by R. Bechai and Nachmanides, as well as in the latter's Torath Ha-Adam, and many other books too numerous to mention.

In addition to the bibliography to be found in the *Jewish Encyclopedia* (x. p. 60a) and in Wolff, *Bibl. Hebr.* i. p. 173, iii. p. 110, and iv. p. 1032, the following references have been furnished by Dr. Marmorstein:

Ẓakuto, *Juchasin*, p. 52b (the first to cast a doubt on the authorship of R. Eliezer).

'Azariah de Rossi, *Meor 'Enayim*, ch. xliii.

Rapoport, in *Kerem Chemed*, vii. p. 41.

Steinschneider, *Polemische und Apologetische Literatur*, p. 339; *Z.D.M.G.* xxviii. 640; *H.B.* v. 15 and 120, viii. 7, and ix. 3.

The periodicals *Keneseth Ha-Gedolah*, i. 165; *Ha-Maggid*, xii. nos. 26 ff.; *R.É.J.* liv. 66; *M.G.W.J.*, 1893, p. 253; *J.Q.R.* iv. 622, and *J.Q.R.* (new series) i. pp. 64 f.

Graetz, *M.G.W.J.*, 1859, p. 207; *H.B.* xiv. 7; *Geschichte*, iv. p. 223; and *Z.D.M.G.* xxviii. 645.

Epstein, *Eldad*, p. 76; and

Chwolson, *Ssabier*, i. p. 98.

§ 4. *P.R.E.* and Talmud, Targum, Midrash, Ẓohar, and Liturgy

The fact that with two exceptions all the names of the Rabbis quoted in our book are Palestinian teachers has been duly noted by scholars, see *J.E.* x. p. 59a. Equally remarkable is the fact that the direct quotations from the Talmud are to be found in the Palestinian Talmud only. The inference to be drawn from this circumstance is that the author was probably a Palestinian. Again, there is a very close connection between the Palestinian Targum to the Pentateuch, usually known as the Pseudo-Jonathan ben Uẓẓiel, and our author.

The present writer inclines to the view that our book was one of the sources used by this Targumist. There is also evidence which goes to show that the author of the Second Targum to Esther used our book. Likewise there is reason to believe that the Ẓohar has used many of the interpretations and doctrines which are to be found in our work. In all probability a similar statement applies to the Book of Jashar.

On the other hand, our author has laid Genesis Rabbah under contribution. In the notes attention will be drawn to some of the parallels to be found in Talmudic and Midrashic literature.

The question of interdependence arises in connection with the *Baraitha de Sh'muel.* The date 776 C.E. is mentioned in this work, and shortly after this date the work was most probably written. Have we, however, the original *Baraitha*? Was our book used by the writer of this *Baraitha*? Were the two works originally united in one book? Are we to believe, as Dr. Gaster seems to urge in his valuable Introduction to *Jeraḥmeel*, that the three astronomical chapters (VI.–VIII.) are part of the original *Baraitha*? These problems must remain for the present unsolved. The views of Zunz on this question will be referred to in the notes. On the entire problem Bornstein's note on pp. 177 f. in Sokolow's Jubilee Volume (1904) should be consulted. A similar unsolved problem arises in connection with the Sepher Jezirah; some of the points of contact between this book and *P.R.E.* will be mentioned in the notes.

Many of the Midrashic explanations and legends contained in our book have been utilized by the Payeṭanim (liturgical poets) whose poems have enriched the liturgy of the Synagogue. The commentary to the Machẓor by Heidenheim draws attention to many parallels in our book.

Recent investigation has proved that the date hitherto assigned to Ḳalir must be altered to an earlier period (*c.* seventh century). According to Zunz, *G.V.* (p. 290) Ḳalir used *P.R.E.* in his liturgical compositions, and if this be so, he must have had an earlier form of our book than has come down to us.

The Jozeroth as well as the daily and Sabbath liturgy of the Synagogue point to the direct influence exerted by our book. One instance will illustrate this point. The Ḳedushah of the Mussaph for Sabbath and Holyday is to be found in its earliest form in our book (see p. 26 and cf. *M.G.W.J.*, 1887, pp. 550 ff.). Does this fact enable us to determine the provenance of our "Chapters"? Dr. Büchler has pointed out to the present writer that the phrase on p. 169, "Through me will all the righteous crown Thee with a crown of sovereignty," shows that the author knew the special form of the Ḳedushah of the mystics known as the "Joredê Merkabah," discussed by P. Bloch in *M.G.W.J.*, 1893 (37), p. 310, and by Dr. Büchler in *R.É.J.* liii. p. 220.

In connection with this subject, it is interesting to note that the tenth chapter seems to be a homily for the Day of Atonement. According to Horowitz, *Beth 'Eḳed Ha-Hagadoth*, p. 21, Chapter XXX., which has been incorporated in the Midrash of the Ten Kings, was also written for liturgical purposes, probably as a Midrash for the Sabbath preceding the 9th of Ab. Possibly Chapters XXV. and XXVI. were homilies for the New Year. The sections from Chapters III., IV., V., VI., IX., and XI. dealing with the Creation and Adam, which are preserved in the B.M. MS. 27089 and printed by Horowitz, *Sammlung kleiner Midraschim*, i. pp. 4 ff., may have served a liturgical purpose in connection with the New Year, because according to our author Adam was created on the New Year. Similar Midrashic sections are—(1) Chapter XLII., for Sabbath Shirah or for the seventh Day of Passover; (2) Chapter XLI., for Pentecost; (3) Chapter IV., dealing with the Cherubim and the Divine Throne for Pentecost (the Haphṭarah being Ezek. i.); and (4) Chapter XXXIII., for the Intermediate Sabbath in Passover (the Haphṭarah being Ezek. xxxvii.). Several chapters are also to be regarded as Midrashim to the weekly Portion (Sedra). Finally, Chapter XLIV. and Chapter XLIX. are probably Midrashim for Sabbath Ẓakhôr, whilst Chapter L. is a Midrashic reading for Purim. Chapter XXXI., which deals with the 'Aḳedah, may have been a homily for the New Year or for Sabbath Vayêra. Chapter XXXIII. was most likely the Midrash to the Haphṭarah for Sabbath Vayêra.

§ 5. *P.R.E.* and the Pseudepigrapha and Apocrypha

Among the most valuable writings in the second volume of the Oxford edition of the *Apocrypha and Pseudepigrapha* are Jubilees, the two Books of Enoch, the Testaments of the XII Patriarchs, 4 Ezra, and the Books of Adam and Eve. With all these books there are points of contact in the *Pirḳê de R. Eliezer*. For instance, the

Biblical narrative covered by our book agrees to a considerable extent with the material dealt with by the Book of Jubilees. We shall find frequent occasion in the notes to refer not only to the points of similarity between the two works, but also to several points of dissimilarity. There seems to be reasonable ground for assuming that the author of our book was acquainted not only with Jubilees, but also with the pseudepigraphic Books of Enoch (Ethiopic and Slavonic), and very probably with the Testaments of the XII Patriarchs, or with the sources of these books.

Jubilees and our book are alike in being practically Midrashic paraphrases and expansions of the narratives contained in the Book of Genesis and part of the Book of Exodus. Our book contains more than this, but it is a later compilation. Both books deal with the Calendar (see Jubilees vi. 28–33), and in this respect they recall the Books of Enoch (Eth. Enoch lxxii.–lxxxii.). In all these books we have chapters setting forth the story of the Creation (Maʿaseh Bereshith). The mysteries and secrets contained in some of the above-mentioned books of the Pseudepigrapha reappear in our book. The past is recalled and the future revealed. The nature of God, angels, and man is unfolded. We read of sin and grace, repentance and atonement, good and evil, life and death, Paradise and Gehenna, Satan and Messiah. The same anthropomorphic expressions occur in all this literature and reappear in our book. The Index will enable the reader to find easily in our book its teaching on all these points.

Our book does not merely re-echo the esoteric doctrines of Apocalypse, it occasionally dares to speak with its own voice and at times deliberately modifies the teaching of the old Pseudepigrapha. For instance, the Calendar doctrines set forth in Jubilees and part of the Enoch literature are rejected and opposed. The Calendar section in our book is of more than passing interest, because it may indicate—(1) The probable date when our book was written, (2) its provenance, and (3) the motive for its composition. According to S. Poznański (Hastings' *Ency. of Religion and Ethics*, iii. 117) the probable date is in the period of the Geonim (*c.* 800), its origin was in Babylon, and the purpose of the book was to oppose factions or sects who at this period had their individual calendars. Reference should be made to the *J.Q.R.* x. 152–161 for the discussion on the Calendar disputes in the days of Sa'adiah (892–942), see also *J.Q.R.* xiv. pp. 37 ff. and (new series) v. 4, pp. 543 ff.

The various forms of the Calendar, which were probably the occasion of attack or defence, *e.g.* the systems set forth in Jubilees and the Books of Enoch, as well as the calendars of the Samaritans and Karaites, and the systems elaborated in the Rabbinic and Patristic literature and also in the Hellenistic Jewish writings, would have to be carefully considered before we can be in a position to formulate the purpose of the Calendar in our book.

To revert to the Book of Jubilees in relation to our book, the following passages in the former seem to have some connection with our text.

Jub. i. 29 refers to the renewal of the heavens and the earth (cf. *ibid.* iv. 26 and xxiii. 26–28, and Charles' note on p. 10 of his edition of Jubilees); Chapter LI. (pp. 410 ff.) in our book is devoted to this theme.

In Jub. i. and ii. reference is made to the intercourse between Moses and the angels; the same subject reappears in our book (Chapter XLVI. pp. 361 f.), where we also read of "letters and tablets for healing" (p. 362) given to Moses by the angels, this is similar to Jub. x. 12, 13.

According to Jub. ii. 17–21, when the Israelites observe the Sabbath, they resemble the angels; this belief reappears in our book (Chapter XLVI. p. 364), except for the fact that Sabbath is replaced by the Day of Atonement (*i.e.* the Sabbath of Sabbaths).

Very striking is the passage in Jub. ii. dealing with the selection of Israel to keep the Sabbath and the nature of the Sabbath observance, "eating, drinking, and blessing God" (ii. 21). This must be compared with *P.R.E.* xix. p. 138: "The Holy One, blessed be He, blessed and hallowed the Sabbath day, and *Israel* is bound only to keep and to hallow the Sabbath day. . . . Whosoever says the benediction and sanctification over the wine on the eves of Sabbaths." Jub. ii. 29, 30, should also be compared with *P.R.E.*, *loc. cit.*

Both books protest against the exposure of the person; thus in Jub. iii. 31 and vii. 20 this ordinance is laid down in connection with Noah, whilst in our book, xxii. p. 160, this sin is one of the causes of the flood.

The offering brought by Noah, according to Jub. vi. 3, consisted of an ox, a goat, a sheep, kids, salt, a turtle-dove, and the young of a dove; in our book, xxiii. p. 171, this reappears as "ox, a sheep, a turtle-dove, and pigeons."

Jub. vi. 17 f. lays great stress on the importance of the festival of Pentecost, even attributing its institution to Noah and the patriarchs; our book varies this by connecting the institution of Passover with Adam and the patriarchs (pp. 153, 236).

Jub. vi. 23–29 dwells on the importance of the New Moon; this occurs also in our book, p. 410.

Jub. vii. 2, 35 ff., xvi. 20–31, and xxi. 7–17 refers to the age of the patriarchs various laws other than the seven precepts of the sons of Noah. This tendency is followed by our book, which mentions Sha'atnez (p. 154; see Lev. xix. 19), Sabbath (p. 142), Habdalah (pp. 145 f.), and the wedding benediction (pp. 89 f.) in connection with the life of Adam.

Noah divides the earth among his three sons (Jub. viii. 11). Dr. Charles (*in loc.*) refers to Beer, who quotes *P.R.E.* xxiv. The actual text in Jub. viii. 11–30 should be compared with the last paragraph in *P.R.E.* xxiii. (pp. 172 f.), which might reasonably be looked upon as a condensed version of the twenty verses in Jubilees. Thus the first sentence in *P.R.E.* (*loc. cit.*) reads: "Noah brought his sons and *his grandsons*, and he blessed them with their (several) settlements, and he gave them as an inheritance all the earth." Jubilees (viii. 11) reads: "And he called his sons, and they drew nigh to him, they and *their children*, and he divided the earth into the lots, which his three sons were to take in possession." Shem receives according to Jubilees (viii. 12) "the middle of the earth," and according to *P.R.E.* (*loc. cit.*) he inherits "the habitable land." Ham receives "beyond the Gihon . . . and it extends towards the west to the sea of 'Atêl, and it extends . . . till it reaches the sea of Mâ'ûk" (Jub. viii. 22). Dr. Charles (*in loc.*) thinks that Mâ'ûk is a distortion of Ὠκεανός, the great ocean stream. *P.R.E.* (*loc. cit.*) reads: "He blessed Ham and his sons . . . and he gave them as an inheritance the coast of the sea." Japhet's portion is Northern Asia, Europe, and five great islands (Jub. viii. 25–29a); and according to *P.R.E.* (*loc. cit.*) he receives "for an inheritance the desert and its fields."

Both books agree (Jub. xii. 26, *P.R.E.* p. 188) in saying that Abraham spoke Hebrew, the holy language of the Creation. In both books Satan (or Sammael in *P.R.E.*, Mastema in Jubilees) plays a striking part, he is a chief or prince (see Jub. xvii. 16 and xlviii. 2, and *P.R.E.* p. 92). Jub. x. 11 identifies Satan and Mastema; a parallel to this section of Jubilees (x. 8–11) is to be found in our book (p. 363 f.). According to Jub. iii. 17 the serpent alone was the cause of the fall of Eve; our author (p. 92), following other legends, describes Sammael as using the serpent in his plot against Eve. In Jub. xviii. 9, 12, Mastema is put to shame at the sacrifice of Isaac; this legend reappears in *P.R.E.* (pp. 228, 233 f.), according to which Sammael attempts to hinder Abraham.

The fundamental importance of circumcision is insisted upon in both books (Jub. xv. 11 ff. and *P.R.E.* xxix.), and they both refer to the serious neglect of the rite (Jub. xv. 33 f. and *P.R.E.* pp. 212 ff.). According to Jub. xv. 30–32 and *P.R.E.* p. 177, Israel alone is subject to God, whilst the nations of the world are subject to the dominion of the angels. Both books, Jub. xvii. 17 and *P.R.E.* pp. 187 ff., refer to the ten trials of Abraham. Again, both books (Jub. xxi. 17; *P.R.E.* pp. 61, 212) lay stress on the duty of covering the blood with dust. They also agree (Jub. xxii. 16; *P.R.E.* pp. 208, 301) in ordaining restrictions as to the food of non-Jews. Isaac's oath to the Philistines (Jub. xxiv. 25, 33) reappears in our book, pp. 278 f. Jub. xxxii. 2 f. has a close parallel in our book (p. 284), about the story of the choice of Levi as the tithe devoted to God.

There is considerable agreement in both books on Angelology and Demonology. Both books teach the eternal validity of the Law, older than creation and coming from the custody of the angels in heaven.

On the other hand, there are many divergent teachings. We have already referred to the Calendar. According to Jub. i. 27 (see Charles' ed. p. lxiv f.) an angel reveals the Law to Moses; our author (p. 320) opposes this doctrine, which was taught in Hellenistic Jewish and Christian circles (see LXX to Deut. xxxiii. 2 and Acts of the Apostles vii. 53, and cf. Josephus quoted in the Westminster N.T. ed. of Acts, *loc. cit.*). In *P.R.E.* (*loc. cit.* and pp. 324 f. and 327) God alone gives the Law, although myriads of ministering angels are present. Jub. ii. 2–3 fixes the first day for the creation of the angels, our book (p. 20) gives the second day. According to Jub. ii. 7 the garden of Eden was created on the third day, whereas in our book (p. 11) it belongs to the premundane creation. Jub. iv. 15, 22, identifies the angels of the Lord who descended on the earth with the Watchers who sinned with the daughters of men. This interpretation of the "sons of Elohim" is accepted by our author (p. 160), who qualifies it by adding that the Israelites are also called "sons of God" (p. 161). Dr. Charles (*Jubilees*, pp. 33 ff., note 14) refers to the Christian interpretation of "the sons of God" as indicating "the good among mankind, the descendants of Seth, and the daughters of men to be the descendants of Cain." Our author (p. 158 f.) tells us that, "all the generations of the righteous arose from Seth," whereas "from Cain arose and were descended all the generations of the wicked." Jub. v. 7 teaches that the sons of the angels who rebelled against God slew one another with the sword, but our author (p. 162) varies this by letting them perish in the flood. In Jub. xii. 14, Haran, the brother of Abraham, is burnt in the fire, whereas according to our book (p. 188) it is Abraham who is cast into the fire and rescued by Divine interposition.

In Jub. xix. 11 the marriage of Abraham with Keturah is spoken of as his third marriage, "for Hagar had died before Sarah"; this is contradicted by our author (p. 219), who identifies Keturah and Hagar. Jub. xxx. 2 ff. gives the praise of Simeon and Levi in connection with the punishment which they inflicted upon Shechem; this is omitted in our book (pp. 288 f.), which speaks of Jacob cursing the wrath of his sons, "and he also cursed their sword in the Greek language"; Jubilees (xxx. 25) adds, "And he reproached them because they had put the city to the sword and he feared those who dwelt in the land." In Jub. xxxiv. 12, 18 f., the institution of the Day of Atonement is connected with the sale of Joseph; this view is controverted by our book (p. 204) by associating the Day with Abraham. In Jub. xxxviii. 2, Jacob is represented as slaying Esau; our author (p. 309) varies this tradition by referring the incident to the action of Chushim, the son of Dan, a deaf mute, on the occasion of the burial of Jacob. Jub. xl. 10 rejects the legend which formed the basis of the Hellenistic Jewish romance dealing with the history of Asenath (see Hastings' *Bible Dict.* i. 162), according to which Asenath was of the house of Israel; our book (pp. 272 f., 287 f.) adopts this legend, and states that she was the daughter of Dinah. Our book differs from Jubilees by omitting the sins of Reuben and Judah and by enunciating the doctrine of the resurrection. There are many other points of connection between the two books, some of which will be indicated in the notes.

The most valuable contribution to the study of Jubilees in its relation to the Midrashim is B. Beer's *Das Buch der Jubiläen* (1856). This was amplified by a second essay by the same author. These important pioneer works are indispensable. Dr. Marmorstein has a chapter on "Jubilees and Pal. Targum" in his *Studien zum Pseud-Jonathan Targum* (1905), pp. 22–26. Dr. Kohler's article on Jubilees in *J.E.* vii. pp. 301 ff. should also be consulted in this connection.

Ethiopic Enoch, usually known as 1 Enoch, also contains many ideas which seem to be repeated or reflected in our book. The notes contain the references to many of these similar thoughts. Some of the most interesting points of contact are the following:

1 Enoch vi. 2: "The angels" are "the children of heaven"; cf. *P.R.E.* p. 161: "Whilst they (the angels) were still in their holy place in heaven, these were called *the sons of God.*"

— vi. 4: "Let us all swear an oath and all bind ourselves by mutual imprecations," cf. *P.R.E.* (p. 293), which reads: "Let us swear among ourselves . . . and they proclaimed the ban" (חרם).

— vii. 1–5: "And all the others together with them took unto themselves wives . . . and they began to go in unto them . . . and they bare great giants . . .

who consumed all the acquisitions of men. The giants turned against them and devoured mankind . . . and drunk the blood." Cf. *P.R.E.* (pp. 160 f.): "The angels . . . took wives from amongst them . . . from them were born the giants . . . who stretched forth their hands to all (kinds of) robbery and violence, and shedding of blood."

1 Enoch viii. 1, 2: "And the beautifying of the eyelids . . . and they committed fornication, and they were led astray"; cf. *P.R.E.* (p. 160): "their eyes painted like harlots, and they went astray after them."

— ix. 1: "Michael, Uriel, Raphael, and Gabriel"; cf. *P.R.E.* (p. 22): "Michael . . . Gabriel . . . Uriel . . . and Raphael."

— ix. 1, 2 and x. 2: "Much blood being shed upon the earth, and all lawlessness being wrought upon the earth. . . . The earth made without inhabitant cries the voice of their crying up to the gates of heaven . . . and a deluge is about to come"; cf. *P.R.E.*, *loc. cit.* and also p. 162: "Behold, we will restrain ourselves from multiplying and increasing, so as not to produce the offspring of the children of men. . . . They said, If He bring from heaven the waters of the flood."

— x. 4: "Bind Azazel . . . and make an opening in the desert . . . and cast him therein"; cf. *P.R.E.* p. 363: "and the lot for Azazel was the goat as a sin offering" (cf. Charles' note on p. 22 of *Jubilees*).

— xii. 4 (and cf. xv. 3): "The Watchers of the heaven who have left the high heaven, the holy eternal place"; cf. *P.R.E.* p. 160: "The angels who fell from their holy place in heaven," cf. *ibid.* pp. 46, 92, and 194.

— xiv. 9 ff.: "Crystals . . . and fiery cherubim between them, (that house) was hot as fire and cold as ice . . . fear covered me and tremblings gat hold upon me . . . and I looked and saw therein a lofty throne, its appearance was as crystal, and the wheels thereof as the shining sun, and there was the vision of the Cherubim. And from underneath the throne came streams of flaming fire so that I could not look thereon. And the Great Glory sat thereon. None of the angels could enter and could behold His face. . . . The flaming fire was round about Him . . . ten thousand times ten thousand (angels stood) before Him." Cf. ***P.R.E.***, Chapter IV. (pp. 21–25), where we read of the "crystal . . . and the fiery ministering angels and the Shekhinah of the Holy One . . . sitting on a throne high and exalted. The appearance of His *Glory* is like the colour of amber (or crystal). One half (of His Glory) is fire and the other half is hail . . . and a veil is spread before Him, and the seven angels . . . minister before Him. . . . Fire is flashing continually around His throne, and the Chajjôth (around the throne) . . . are the Cherubim . . . the whirling wheels of the Chariot, lightnings . . . go forth. . . . The Chajjôth . . . do not know the place of His Glory . . . a river of fire arises and goes forth before Him. . . . The Seraphim . . . cover their face so as not to behold the presence of the Shekhinah."

1 Enoch xvii. 5 refers to the river of fire, cf. ***P.R.E.*** pp. 25 and 412.

— xviii. 2: "And I saw the Corner Stone of the Earth," cf. ***P.R.E.*** p. 71: "and he saw there the Foundation Stone," and cf. *ibid.* p. 266.

— xviii. 5: "The firmament of the heaven above," cf. ***P.R.E.*** p. 21: "The firmament which is above the head of the four Chajjôth."

— xviii. 8: "And the summit of the throne was of sapphire," cf. ***P.R.E.*** p. 23: "And the likeness of His throne is like a sapphire throne." [1]

— xx. 2–8: here the Seven Archangels are mentioned; ***P.R.E.*** p. 23 refers to "the seven angels, which were created first, (who) minister before God." Four of these seven angels mentioned in 1 Enoch are Uriel, Raphael, Michael, and Gabriel; these four names occur also in ***P.R.E.*** p. 22; cf. also 1 Enoch xl. 9.

— xxv. 5: "Its fruit shall be good for the elect: it shall be transplanted to the holy place, to the temple of the Lord," cf. ***P.R.E.*** p. 418 f.

— xxv. 6: "And they shall live a long life on earth . . . and in their days shall no sorrow or plague or torment

[1] Cf. Ezek. i. 26.

or calamity touch them"; cf. *P.R.E.* pp. 411 f. and 418, for a similar expression and idea.

1 Enoch xxvi. 1: "The middle of the earth," cf. *P.R.E.* p. 266, for parallel expression.

— xxxii. 1: Seven mountains are referred to, cf. *P.R.E.* p. 71.

— xxxiii. 2: "The ends of the earth whereon the heavens rest," cf. *P.R.E.* p. 16.

— xxxiv. 3: The north is described, cf. *P.R.E.* p. 17.

— xxxvi. 1: "I went to the south to the ends of the earth . . . and thence there come dew, rain, and wind"; *P.R.E.* p. 17 reads: "From the quarter facing south the dews of blessing and the rains of blessing go forth to the world."

— xxxvi. 4: "That they might praise His work," cf. *P.R.E.* pp. 8 f.

— xxxvii. 2: "It had been good for them if they had not been born," cf. *P.R.E.* pp. 104 f.

— xxxvii. 4: "Has caused His light to appear on the face of the holy," cf. *P.R.E.* p. 7.

— xxxix. 7: "And all the righteous . . . shall be strong as fiery lights," cf. *P.R.E.* p. 21.

— xxxix. 11: "He knows before the world was created what is for ever," cf. *P.R.E.* p. 11.

Cf. 1 Enoch xxxix. 12–13 and *P.R.E.* p. 26, on the trisagion.

1 Enoch xl. 1: "And on the four sides of the Lord of Spirits I saw four presences," cf. *P.R.E.* pp. 22 f.

— xli. 7: "The one (sun) holding a position opposite to the other," cf. *P.R.E.* p. 44.

— xlv. 4, 5: "I will transform the heaven . . . and I will transform the earth," cf. *P.R.E.* pp. 410 ff.

— xlvii. 3: "The books of the living," cf. *P.R.E.* p. 104 (note 6).

— xlviii. 3: "Yea before the sun . . . his name was named," cf. *P.R.E.* pp. 12 and 233.

— li. 1: "The earth shall give back that which has been entrusted to it," cf. *P.R.E.* pp. 258 and 335.

— lii. 7: "None shall be saved, either by gold or by silver," cf. *P.R.E.* pp. 256 f.

— liv. 6: "And cast them into the burning furnace," cf. *P.R.E.* p. 103.

— liv. 8: "The waters shall be joined with the waters, that

which is above the heavens is the masculine and the water which is beneath the earth is the feminine," cf. *P.R.E.* p. 167.

1 Enoch lv. 2: "This shall be a pledge of good faith between Me and them for ever as long as heaven is above the earth," cf. *P.R.E.* p. 172.

— lvi. 7: "And they shall begin to fight among themselves," cf. *P.R.E.* p. 62.

— lviii. 3: "The righteous shall be in the light of the sun . . . the days of their life shall be unending," cf. *P.R.E.* pp. 21, 412, and 418.

— lx. 4: "Michael sent another angel . . . and he raised me up . . . and my spirit returned," cf. *P.R.E.* p. 325.

— lx. 7: "Leviathan," cf. *P.R.E.* pp. 63 f. and 70.

— lx. 8: "Behemoth," cf. *P.R.E.* pp. 75 f.

— lx. 20: "The waters are for those who dwell on the earth, for they are nourishment for the earth," cf. *P.R.E.* p. 87

— lxi. 5: "Those who have been destroyed by the desert, and those who have been devoured by the beasts, and those who have been devoured by the fish of the sea, that they may return," cf. *P.R.E.* p. 249.

— lxii. 2: "The word of his mouth slays all the sinners," cf. *P.R.E.* p. 379.

— lxii. 16: "They shall have been clothed with garments of glory," cf. *P.R.E.* p. 98.

— lxv. 7: "How silver is produced from the dust of the earth," cf. *P.R.E.* p. 181.

— lxvii. 8: "And those waters . . . shall serve for the healing of the body," cf. *P.R.E.* p. 418.

— lxix. 6: "And he led astray Eve," cf. *P.R.E.* pp. 92, 94 f., and 150 f.

— lxix. 11: "For men were created exactly like the angels," cf. *P.R.E.* pp. 85, 151, and 378.

— lxix. 18: "The sea was created, and as its foundation He set for it the sand against the time of its anger," cf. *P.R.E.* pp. 27 f.

— lxx. 3: "He set me between the two winds, between the north and the west, where the angels took the cords to measure," cf. *P.R.E.* p. 416 f.

— lxxi. 4: "The ends of the heaven," cf. *P.R.E.* p. 16.

1 Enoch lxxi. 15: "The world to come," cf. *P.R.E.* pp. 112, 228, and 230.

— lxxi. 15: "Since the creation of the world," cf. *P.R.E.* p. 420.

— lxxii. 1: "Till the new creation," cf. *P.R.E.* p. 411.

— lxxii. 2: "The portals which are in the east," cf. *P.R.E.* pp. 37 ff.

— lxxii. 3: "The leaders of the stars," cf. *P.R.E.* p. 34.

— lxxii. 3: "Windows," cf. *P.R.E.* pp. 37 ff.

— lxxii. 5: "The chariot on which he (*i.e.* the sun) ascends," cf. *P.R.E.* p. 40.

— lxxii. 14: "The day becomes double the night," cf. *P.R.E.* p. 322.

— lxxii. 37: "But as regards size they are both equal," cf. *P.R.E.* p. 31.

— lxxv. 1: "And the leaders render service," cf. *P.R.E.* p. 34.

— lxxvii. 1–3 refers to the four quarters of the world, cf. *P.R.E.* p. 17.

— lxxvii. 4: "Seven mountains," cf. *P.R.E.* p. 71.

— lxxvii. 5: "Seven rivers," cf. *P.R.E.* pp. 140 f.

— lxxviii. 3: "The size . . . of both is alike," cf. *P.R.E.* p. 31.

— lxxviii. 12: "She becomes full moon exactly on the day when the sun sets in the west," cf. *P.R.E.* pp. 50 f.

— lxxxii. 1: "So preserve the books . . . and see that thou deliver them to the generations of the world," cf. *P.R.E.* pp. 52 f.

— lxxxix. 9: "One was white . . . one . . . red, and one black," cf. *P.R.E.* pp. 172 f.

— lxxxix. 59: "And he called seventy shepherds," cf. *P.R.E.* pp. 67, 176 f., and 221.

— xci. 16: "All the powers of the heavens shall give sevenfold light," cf. *P.R.E.* p. 412.

— xciii. 11: "Who is there of all the children of men that is able to hear the voice of the Holy One?" etc., cf. *P.R.E.* p. 9.

— xcviii. 9: "Wherefore do not hope to live, ye sinners . . . for ye have no ransom," cf. *P.R.E.* pp. 256 and 416.

1 Enoch c. 1: "And brothers, one with another shall fall in death," cf. *P.R.E.* pp. 220 f.

— ci. 6: "Has He not set limits to the doings (of the sea) and confined it throughout by the sand?" cf. *P.R.E.* pp. 27 f.

— civ. 1: "Remember you for good," cf. *P.R.E.* p. 2.

— cvi. 2: "And when he opened his eyes, he lighted up the whole house like the sun, and the whole house was very bright," cf. *P.R.E.* p. 7.

— cvi. 5: "Resembling the sons of the God of heaven . . . sprung from the angels," cf. *P.R.E.* p. 161.

The similar phrases and ideas which occur in *P.R.E.* and in the Book of the Secrets of Enoch, usually known as the Slavonic Enoch, are noteworthy. Many of the following references are given in the notes on our book:

Slav. Enoch iv. 1: "The rulers of the orders of the stars," cf. *P.R.E.* p. 34.

— iv. 1: "Angels who rule the stars and their heavenly service," cf. *P.R.E.* pp. 34 and 46.

— v. 1: "The treasuries of the snow and ice," cf. *P.R.E.* p. 17.

— vi.: "The treasuries of the dew," cf. *P.R.E.* pp. 17, 236.

— x. 3: "The angels terrible and without pity," cf. *P.R.E.* p. 103.

— xi. 3: "The chariot of the sun," cf. *P.R.E.* p. 40.

— xi. 4: "Angels go with the sun, each angel has six wings," cf. *P.R.E.* p. 40.

— xii. 2: "Their wings were like those of angels, each with twelve," cf. *P.R.E.* p. 92.

— xiii. 2: "Six . . . gates, each gate having sixty-one stadia," cf. *P.R.E.* p. 37.

— xiv. 2: "Angels take his (*i.e.* the sun's) crown," cf. *P.R.E.* p. 40.

— xvi. 8: "And seven (months) are computed to the circle of the moon during a revolution of nineteen years," cf. *P.R.E.* p. 57.

— xviii. 4 and 5: "The Watchers with their prince Satanail, . . . and of them there went three to the earth from the throne of God . . . and took unto themselves wives

. . . and the giants were born and . . . there was much wickedness," cf. *P.R.E.* pp. 160 f.

Slav. Enoch xix. 1: "Seven bands of angels . . . superintend the good or evil condition of the world," cf. *P.R.E.* pp. 103 f.

— xix. 3: "They hold in subjection all living things both in heaven and earth," cf. *P.R.E.* pp. 48 f.

— xix. 6: "Seven Cherubim . . . and they rejoice before the Lord at His footstool" (cf. Rev. iv. 6). See *P.R.E.* p. 23.

— xx. 3: "The Lord from afar sitting on His lofty throne," cf. *P.R.E.* p. 22.

— xxi. 1: "The six-winged creatures overshadow all His throne, singing: Holy, Holy, Holy, Lord God of Sabaoth! heaven and earth are full of Thy glory," cf. *P.R.E.* pp. 25 f.

— xxii. 6: "Michael, the chief captain, lifted me up and brought me before the face of the Lord," cf. *P.R.E.* p. 284.

— xxiii. 6: "366 books," cf. *P.R.E.* pp. 37 and 165.

— xxiv. 3: "Nor have (My angels) understood My infinite creation," cf. *P.R.E.* p. 25.

— xxiv. 4: "For before anything which is visible existed, I alone held my course," cf. *P.R.E.* p. 10.

— xxiv. 5: "And I planned to lay the foundations," cf. *P.R.E.* p. 10.

— xxv. 4: "And I made for Myself a throne, and sat upon it," cf. *P.R.E.* p. 11.

— xxviii. 4: "I gathered the sea . . . and I restrained it with a yoke," cf. *P.R.E.* pp. 27 f.

— xxix. 3: "From the fire I made the ranks of the spiritual hosts, ten thousand angels . . . and their garment is a burning flame," cf. *P.R.E.* pp. 21 and 25.

— xxix. 5: "And I hurled (Satanail) from the heights with his angels," cf. *P.R.E.* pp. 99 and 193 f.

— xxx. 11: "And I placed (Adam) upon the earth, like a second angel, in an honourable, great, and glorious way," cf. *P.R.E.* pp. 85 and 89.

— xxx. 12: "And I made him a ruler to rule upon the earth," cf. *P.R.E.* pp. 79 and 86.

— xxx. 15: "And I showed him the two ways, the light and

the darkness, and I said unto him: 'This is good and this is evil,'" cf. *P.R.E.* p. 102.

Slav. Enoch xxxi. 1: "And I made a garden in Eden . . . and (I ordained) that he should observe the law and keep the instruction," cf. *P.R.E.* pp. 84 f.

— xxxi. 2: "And I made for him the heavens open that he should perceive the angels singing the song of triumph," cf. *P.R.E.* pp. 89 f.

— xxxi. 3: "And the devil took thought, as if wishing to make another world, because things were subservient to Adam on earth, to rule it and have lordship over it," cf. *P.R.E.* pp. 91 f.

— xxxi. 4: "He became Satan after he left the heavens," cf. *P.R.E.* pp. 92 and 193 f.

— xxxi. 6: "He conceived designs against Adam; in such a manner he entered and deceived Eve. But he did not touch Adam"; cf. *P.R.E.* pp. 92, 94 and 150 f.

— xl. 2: "The heavens and the end of them," cf. *P.R.E.* p. 16.

— xl. 6: "I have laid down the four seasons, and from the seasons I made four circles, and in the circles I placed the years," cf. *P.R.E.* p. 35.

— xl. 12: "The lowest hell," cf. *P.R.E.* pp. 340 f.

— xli. 2: "Blessed is the man who was not born," cf. *P.R.E.* pp. 104 f.

— xlii. 1: "The guardians of the gates of hell," cf. *P.R.E.* p. 103.

— xlii. 3: "Rest has been prepared for the just," cf. *P.R.E.* pp. 128, 255 (note 4).

— xlii. 4: "Blessed is he who turns from the unstable path of this vain world, and walks by the righteous path which leads to eternal life," cf. *P.R.E.* p. 103.

— xliv. 1: "God made man with His own hands," cf. *P.R.E.* p. 148.

— xliv. 3: "If a man spits at the face of another," cf. *P.R.E.* p. 434.

— xlviii. 1, 2: "I gave (the sun) 182 thrones when he goes on a short day, and also 182 thrones when he goes on a long day, and he has two thrones on which he rests," cf. *P.R.E.* p. 37.

— xlviii. 2: "From the month Sivan after seventeen days

he descends to the month Thevan (? Kislev) and from the 17th day of Thevad (? Ṭebeth) he ascends," cf. *P.R.E.* p. 38.

Slav. Enoch l. 2: "Ye shall inherit the endless life that is to come," cf. *P.R.E.* p. 137.

— l. 5: "Whoever shall spend gold or silver for the sake of a brother shall receive abundant treasure in the day of judgment," cf. *P.R.E.* p. 238.

— lii. 11: "Blessed is he who establishes peace and love," cf. *P.R.E.* pp. 102 f.

— lii. 12: "Cursed is he who troubles those who are at peace," cf. *P.R.E.* pp. 310 f.

— liii. 1: "For there is no person there to help any man who has sinned," cf. *P.R.E.* pp. 104 f. and 341.

– lviii. 1: "In those days when the Lord came upon the earth for the sake of Adam," cf. *P.R.E.* p. 89.

— lix. 5: "If any one does an injury to an animal secretly, it is an evil custom," cf. *P.R.E.* p. 291.

— lxi. 2: "Mansions: good for the good, evil for the evil," cf. *P.R.E.* pp. 104 f. and 255.

— lxii. 2: "If he let the appointed time pass and does not perform the works, he is not blessed, for there is no repentance after death," cf. *P.R.E.* p. 341.

— lxiii. 1: "When a man . . . feeds the hungry, he gets a recompense from God," cf. *P.R.E.* pp. 181 f.

— lxv. 3: "The Lord contemplated the world for the sake of man, and made all the creation for his sake," cf. *P.R.E.* pp. 29 and 86 f.

— lxv. 9: "There shall be . . . no sickness nor anxiety," cf. *P.R.E.* pp. 411 f.

— lxvi. 6: "They (the just) shall be seven times brighter than the sun," cf. *P.R.E.* p. 412.

Appendix, p. 90 (iii. 17): At the birth of Melchizedek, "the child was complete in its body like one of three years old; and spake with its lips and blessed the Lord"; cf. *P.R.E.* p. 161.

— p. 91 (iii. 35): "The middle of the earth where Adam was created," cf. *P.R.E.* p. 143.

— — (iii. 36): "As Adam buried his son Abel there, . . . wherefore he lay unburied . . . till he saw a bird called a jackdaw burying its fledgling"; cf. *P.R.E.* p. 156.

Testaments of the Twelve Patriarchs, and P.R.E.

Test. Reuben v. 5–7: "Command your wives and daughters that they adorn not their heads and faces . . . for thus they allured the Watchers who were before the flood . . . and the women gave birth to giants"; cf. *P.R.E.* pp. 160 f.

Test. Simeon ii. 8: "His God . . sent forth His angel and delivered" (Joseph), cf. *P.R.E.* p. 292.

— ii. 10: "When Reuben heard (of the sale of Joseph) he was grieved, for he wished to restore him to his father," cf. *P.R.E.* pp. 292 f.

— iv. 4: "Now Joseph . . . had the Spirit of God within him," cf. *P.R.E.* p. 305.

— v. 3: "Then shall perish the seed of Canaan, and a remnant shall not be unto Amalek," cf. *P.R.E.* p. 347.

Test. Levi ii. 7: "And I saw there a great sea hanging between" (the first and second heaven), cf. *P.R.E.* pp. 16 and 39.

— ii. 10: "The redemption of Israel," cf. *P.R.E.* pp. 62 and 72.

— iii. 4: "In the highest (heaven) of all dwelleth the Great Glory," cf. *P.R.E.* p. 22.

— iii. 5: "And in . . . it are the angels of the presence of the Lord, who minister," cf. *P.R.E.* p. 22.

— iii. 9: "When, therefore, the Lord looketh upon all creation, the heavens and the earth and the abysses are shaken," cf. *P.R.E.* pp. 23 ff.

— iv. 2: (Levi) to be "a servant and a minister of His presence," cf. *P.R.E.* p. 284.

— v. 1, 3: "The angel opened to me the gates of heaven and I saw . . . upon a throne of glory the Most High . . . then the angel brought me down to the earth"; cf. *P.R.E.* pp. 22 and 284.

— vi. 8: "They sought to do to . . . Rebecca as they had done to Dinah," cf. *P.R.E.* pp. 110 f.

— viii. 3, 4: "When we came to Bethel, my father Jacob saw a vision concerning me, that I should be their priest unto God . . . and he paid tithes of all to the Lord through me"; cf. *P.R.E.* pp. 283 f.

Test. Levi xiii. 5, 6: "Work righteousness . . . upon the earth, that ye may have a treasure in heaven, and *sow* good things in your souls, that ye may find them in your life"; cf. *P.R.E.* p. 238.

— xvi. 4: "And your holy places shall be laid waste . . . and ye shall have no place that is clean," cf. *P.R.E.* p. 221.

— xviii. 9, 11: "Sin shall come to an end, and the lawless shall cease to do evil. . . . And he shall give to the saints to eat from the tree of life," cf. *P.R.E.* pp. 411 and 418.

Test. Judah vii. 7: (And the Canaanites) "besought my father (Jacob) and he made peace with them," cf. *P.R.E.* pp. 279 f.

— ix. 2, 3: "Esau, the brother of my father, came upon us with a mighty and strong people, and Jacob smote Esau with an arrow and he was taken up wounded on Mount Seir"; cf. *P.R.E.* pp. 309 f.

— xxii. 2 and cf. Test. Naph. viii. 2: "Until the salvation of Israel shall come," cf. *P.R.E.* pp. 62 and 72.

— xxiii. 2 ff.: Messianic woes are described, cf. *P.R.E.* pp. 62 and 221 f.

— xxiii. 4: "And they shall make some of you eunuchs," cf. *P.R.E.* p. 426.

— xxiv. 4: Messiah called "branch," cf. *P.R.E.* p. 384.

— xxv. 4: "They who have died in grief shall arise in joy, and they who were poor for the Lord's sake shall awake to life," cf. *P.R.E.* p. 252.

Test. Zebulun i. 5, 6: "For I covenanted with my brethren not to tell my father what had been done . . . because they had all agreed, that if any one should declare the secret, he should be slain," cf. *P.R.E.* p. 293.

— iii. 2: (They) "took the price of Joseph and bought sandals for themselves," cf. *P.R.E.* p. 293.

— iv. 5: "Reuben's sorrow," cf. *P.R.E.* p. 293.

— ix. 4: "Be not ye, therefore, divided into two heads, for everything which the Lord made hath but one head"; cf. *P.R.E.* p. 333.

Test. Dan. ii. 2, 3: "For anger is blindness . . . though it be a prophet of the Lord, he disobeyeth him," cf. *P.R.E.* p. 373.

Test. Dan. iv. 7 : " When the soul is . . . disturbed, the Lord departeth from it," cf. *P.R.E.*, *loc. cit.*

— v. 6 : " Your prince is Satan," cf. *P.R.E.* p. 92.

— v. 12 : " And the saints shall rest in Eden," cf. *P.R.E.* pp. 58 and 128.

— vi. 4 : " On the day on which Israel shall repent, the kingdom of the enemy shall be brought to an end, for the very angel of peace[1] shall strengthen Israel " ; cf. *P.R.E.* p. 344.

In Test. Naphtali i. 11, 12, Zilpah and Bilhah are sisters, cf. *P.R.E.* p. 271.

Test. Naphtali ii. 1 : " I was swift on my feet like the deer," cf. *P.R.E.* p. 309.

— iii. 4 : " Sodom, which changed the order of nature," cf. *P.R.E.* pp. 181 ff.

— iii. 5 : " The Watchers, . . . whom the Lord cursed at the flood, on whose account He made the earth without inhabitant and fruitless," cf. *P.R.E.* p. 162.

— v. 6, 7 : " A bull . . . with two great horns . . . and Joseph came and seized him, and ascended up with him on high," cf. *P.R.E.* p. 131.

— v. 8 : " Assyrians, Medes, Persians, Syrians shall possess in captivity the twelve tribes of Israel," cf. *P.R.E.* pp. 128, 201 f., and 265.

— vii. 4 : " To declare that Joseph had been sold, but I feared my brethren," cf. *P.R.E.* p. 293.

— viii. 5 : " For a good work there is a good remembrance before God," cf. *P.R.E.* pp. 290 and 309.

Test. Gad i. 6, 7 : " Joseph told our father that the sons of Zilpah and Bilhah were slaying the best of the flock . . . for he saw that I had delivered a lamb out of the mouth of the bear . . . and had slain the lamb, being grieved concerning it that it could not live " ; cf. *P.R.E.* p. 291.

— ii. 3 : " Therefore I and Simeon sold him to the Ishmaelites for thirty pieces of gold," cf. *P.R.E.* pp. 292 f.

— v. 10 : " For by what things a man transgresseth, by the same also is he punished," cf. *P.R.E.* pp. 185 and 331 f.

[1] Elijah = Phineas.

Test. Gad vii. 4: "Though a man became rich by evil means, even as Esau, the brother of my father," cf. *P.R.E.* p. 290.

— vii. 5: "The unrepentant is reserved for eternal punishment," cf. *P.R.E.* p. 105.

Test. Asher i. 3: "Two ways hath God given to the sons of men," cf. *P.R.E.* p. 102.

— vii. 4, 5, 6: "For the latter end of men do show their righteousness (or unrighteousness), when they meet the angels of the Lord and of Satan. For when the soul departs troubled, it is tormented by the evil spirit . . . but if he is peaceful with joy he meeteth the angel of peace, and he leadeth him into eternal life"; cf. *P.R.E.* pp. 103 ff., 255.

— vii. 1: "Sodom which . . . perished for ever," cf. *P.R.E.* p. 186.

Test. Joseph ii. 1: "The God of Israel my father delivered me (Joseph) from the burning flame," cf. *P.R.E.* p. 305.

— ii. 7: "In ten temptations He showed me approved," cf. *P.R.E.* p. 187.

— iii. 3: "But I remembered the words of my father" (and sinned not with the Egyptian woman); cf. *P.R.E.* p. 305.

— iii. 7: "Because she had no male child she pretended to regard me as a son, and so I prayed to the Lord, and she bare a male child," cf. *P.R.E.* p. 288.

— vi. 6: "The God of my father hath revealed unto me by His angel thy wickedness," cf. *P.R.E.* p. 305.

— x. 2: "The Lord will dwell among you, because He loveth chastity," cf. *P.R.E.* pp. 305 f.

Test. Benjamin iv. 1: "That ye also may wear crowns of glory," cf. *P.R.E.* pp. 367 f.

The Greek Apocalypse of Baruch or 3 Baruch contains several phrases and ideas common to *P.R.E.*

Both books profess to reveal the mysteries of God, thus 3 Baruch ii. 1 refers to the firmament and "where there was a river"; cf. *P.R.E.* p. 16, and see also *A. and P.* ii. p. 534.

3 Baruch iii. 5, 6: "A woman making bricks . . . brought

forth while she was making bricks . . . and the Lord appeared to them," cf. *P.R.E.* pp. 385 f.

3 Baruch iv. 6 and v. 2: "Dragon . . . also drinks about a cubit from the sea, which does not sink at all"; cf. *P.R.E.* pp. 75 f., and see *A. and P.* p. 535, note 3.

— iv. 8: "Tree which led Adam astray . . . which Sammael planted," cf. *P.R.E.* p. 95.

— iv. 10: "The flood . . . removed without the bounds (of Paradise) the shoot of the vine and cast it outside," cf. *P.R.E.* p. 170.

— iv. 11: (Noah) "found also the shoot of the vine," cf. *P.R.E., loc. cit.*

— iv. 16: (Adam) "was divested of the glory of God," *P.R.E.* p. 98.

— vi. 1, 2, and vii. 4: "The sun . . . chariot . . . crown of fire," cf. *P.R.E.* p. 40.

— vi. 5: "Expanding his wings receives its fiery rays," cf. *P.R.E.* pp. 25 and 40.

— vi. 7: "On his right wing very large letters," cf. *P.R.E.* p. 40.

— ix. 7: "Sammael when he took the serpent as a garment," cf. *P.R.E.* p. 92.

— xiv. 2: "Michael . . . presenting the merits of men to God," cf. *P.R.E.* p. 386.

The (Syriac) Apocalypse of Baruch, and P.R.E.

Baruch iv. 3: (The city) "which was prepared beforehand here from the time when I took counsel to make Paradise," cf. *P.R.E.* p. 14, note 10.

— iv. 3: "And showed (Paradise) to Adam before he sinned," cf. *P.R.E.* p. 128.

— vi. 9: "Jerusalem . . . is again (to be) restored for ever," cf. *P.R.E.* p. 414.

— x. 6: "Blessed is he who was not born," cf. *P.R.E.* pp. 104 f.

— xi. 4: "The righteous sleep in the earth," cf. *P.R.E.* p. 260.

— xiv. 18: (Man) "was by no means made on account of the world, but the world on account of him . . .

on account of the righteous has this world come," cf. *P.R.E.* pp. 62 f., 76, and 86 f.

Baruch xvii. 2: "Adam . . . lived nine hundred and thirty years," cf. *P.R.E.* p. 128, and see Gen. v. 5.

— xviii. 2: "Darkness of Adam," cf. *P.R.E.* p. 144.

— xxi. 6: "The holy living creatures . . . which Thou didst make from the beginning, of flame and fire, which stand around Thy throne," cf. *P.R.E.* pp. 21 and 23 f.

— xxiv. 2: "Who has been long-suffering towards all those born that sin and are righteous," cf. *P.R.E.* p. 76.

— xxviii. 2: "For the measure and reckoning of that time are two parts weeks of seven weeks," cf. *P.R.E.* pp. 62 and 200 f.

— xxix. 4: "And Behemoth will be revealed from his place, and Leviathan will ascend from the sea . . . then they will be for food for all that are left," cf. *P.R.E.* pp. 70, 72, and 76.

— xxix. 7: "The dew of health," cf. *P.R.E.* pp. 238 and 260.

— xxx. 2: "The treasuries will be opened in which is preserved the number of the souls of the righteous," cf. *P.R.E.* pp. 255 and 259.

— xxxii. 4: (The building of Zion) "must be renewed afterwards in glory, and it will be perfected for evermore," cf. *P.R.E.* p. 414.

— xxxix. 7: "The *principate* of My Messiah will be revealed," cf. *P.R.E.* p. 83.

— xlviii. 46: "For Thou didst of old command the dust to produce Adam," cf. *P.R.E.* pp. 76 ff.

— l. 2: "For the earth will then assuredly restore the dead, which it now receives, in order to preserve them, making no change in their form, but as it has received so will it restore them"; cf. *P.R.E.* p. 258.

— li. 3: "Their splendour will be glorified in changes, and the form of their face will be turned into the light of their beauty," cf. *P.R.E.* p. 412.

— li. 11: "The living creatures which are beneath the throne," cf. *P.R.E.* pp. 23 f.

— lvii. 2: "At that time (in the days of Abraham and Isaac) the unwritten law was named amongst them," cf. *P.R.E.* p. 223.

Baruch lix. 3: "And those who were under the throne of the Mighty One were perturbed, when He was taking Moses unto Himself," cf. *P.R.E.* pp. 361 and 365.

— lix. 5–7: "He showed to him . . . the suppression of anger and the multitude of long-suffering . . . wisdom . . . understanding . . . and knowledge," cf. *P.R.E.* pp. 76 and 365 f.

— lix. 10: "The mouth of Gehenna," cf. *P.R.E.* pp. 29, 71, and 432.

— lxiv. 8: "When (Manasseh) was cast into the brazen horse," cf. *P.R.E.* p. 340, note 1.

— lxxiii. 2: "Then healing will descend in dew," cf. *P.R.E.* p. 260.

— lxxv. 4: "Who is able to recount the thoughts of Thy mind?" cf. *P.R.E.* p. 9.

The Book of Wisdom, and P.R.E.

Book of Wisdom i. 13: "Nor hath (God) pleasure in the destruction of them that live," cf. *P.R.E.* p. 104.

— ii. 13: (Having) "knowledge of God, and calleth himself the Lord's child," cf. *P.R.E.* p. 161.

— ii. 18 and cf. v. 5: "For if the righteous be God's son," cf. *P.R.E.* p. 161.

— ii. 22: "Yea, they know not the mysteries of God," cf. *P.R.E.* p. 9.

— ii. 24: "But through the Devil's envy came death into the world," cf. *P.R.E.* p. 100.

— iii. 7, 8: "And in the day of their inspection they shall shine forth . . . and their Lord shall be King for ever," cf. *P.R.E.* pp. 83 and 260.

— iv. 4: "For even if in their shoots they blossom for a season, standing unstably they shall be shaken by the wind, and be rooted out by the violence of the winds," cf. *P.R.E.* p. 132.

— v. 15: "But the righteous live for ever," cf. *P.R.E.* pp. 104 and 260.

— vii. 18, 19: "The turn of the solstices and the changes of seasons, the cycles of years and the positions of the stars," cf. *P.R.E.* p. 52.

— ix. 2: "And through Thy wisdom didst form man to

have rule over the creatures made by Thee," cf. *P.R.E.* p. 79.

Book of Wisdom ix. 6: "For though one be perfect among the sons of men, if the wisdom from Thee be lacking, he shall be accounted for naught," cf. *P.R.E.* p. 129.

— ix. 8: "The holy Tabernacle which Thou preparedst from the beginning," cf. *P.R.E.* p. 12.

— ix. 9, 10: "And with Thee is wisdom that knoweth Thy works, and was present when Thou madest the world. . . . Send her forth out of the holy heavens. And despatch her from the throne of Thy glory," cf. *P.R.E.* p. 12.

— x. 1, 2: "She it was that protected the first formed father of the world throughout, created alone as he was, and rescued him from his own transgression, and gave him strength to rule over all things"; cf. *P.R.E.* pp. 79 and 127.

— x. 4: "Through whom (Cain's descendants) when the earth was drowned," cf. *P.R.E.* p. 162, and cf. Josephus, *Ant.* i. 2. 2.

— x. 5: "She also, when the nations were confounded in a conspiracy of wickedness, found the just man and preserved him blameless unto God, yea, and kept him firm against pity for a son"; cf. *P.R.E.* pp. 176 and 224, and Jerome, *Quaest. Heb. in Gen.*, quoted by Deane *in loc.*

— x. 7: "And plants that bear fruit of bloom that never ripeneth; a pillar of salt standing as a memorial of an unbelieving soul," cf. *P.R.E.* p. 186.

— x. 10: Wisdom guided "in straight paths"; and showed "to him (Jacob) God's kingdom and gave him knowledge of holy things"; cf. *P.R.E.* p. 265.

— x. 12: "She preserved him throughout from enemies, and made him safe from liers in wait, yea, and a sore conflict she decided for him"; cf. *P.R.E.* pp. 309 f.

— x. 13, 14: "She deserted not a righteous one that was sold, but delivered him from sin . . . until she brought him the sceptre of a kingdom," cf. *P.R.E.* p. 305.

— x. 19: "But their enemies did she drown, and cast them up out of the depths of the abyss," cf. *P.R.E.* p. 332.

Book of Wisdom xi. 16: "That they might know that by what things a man sinneth, thereby he is punished," cf. *P.R.E.* p. 332.

— xi. 23: "Thou hast mercy on all because Thou hast power over all, and dost overlook the faults of men in order to their repentance," cf. *P.R.E.* p. 76.

— xi. 24: "Thou cherishest all things that are and abhorrest nothing which Thou madest, for Thou never wouldst have formed anything in hatred thereof," cf. *P.R.E.* p. 76.

— xii. 10: "But executing judgment upon them by little and little Thou gavest them a place of repentance," cf. *P.R.E.* p. 10.

— xii. 19: "And madest Thy sons to be of good hope that Thou grantest for sins repentance," cf. *P.R.E.* p. 10.

— xiv. 6: "For in the beginning also, when the haughty giants perished," cf. *P.R.E.* p. 161.

— xiv. 15: "For a father afflicted with untimely grief, having made an image of a child quickly reft away, now honoured as a god him which was then a dead human being, and enjoined on his dependants mysteries and initiations"; cf. *P.R.E.* pp. 273 f.

— xvi. 7 (and cf. *ibid.* 12): "For he that turned towards it was not saved by that which was beheld, but through Thee, the preserver of all," cf. *P.R.E.* p. 437.

— xviii. 6: "That night was known beforehand to our fathers, that knowing surely on what oaths they trusted they might be cheered," cf. *P.R.E.* p. 195.

— xviii. 16: (The Logos) "bearing as a sharp sword Thine irrevocable commandment," cf. *P.R.E.* p. 367.

— xviii. 22: "And he (Aaron) overcame the wrath . . . but by word he subdued the chastiser, appealing to the oaths and covenants of the fathers," cf. *P.R.E.* p. 357 f.

— xviii. 25: "To these the destroyer yielded," cf. *P.R.E.*, *loc. cit.*

— xix. 8: Cf. *P.R.E.* p. 330, note 7.

The Book of Adam and Eve, and P.R.E.

"The Book of Adam and Eve," also called the "Conflict of Adam and Eve with Satan," offers many passages which seem to recall phrases and thoughts in our book. The quotations given refer to the edition of Malan.

Book of Adam and Eve I. i.: "Water that encompasses the world and reaches unto the borders of heaven," cf. *P.R.E.* pp. 16, 39.

— I. i.: "To dwell there in a cave," cf. *P.R.E.* p. 148.

— I. iv. and I. xxiii.: "When Adam looked at his flesh that was altered," cf. *P.R.E.* pp. 98, 147.

— I. v., xi., and xii.: "From light into this darkness," cf. *P.R.E.* p. 144.

— I. v.: "Thou art (He) who made us both in one day," cf. *P.R.E.* p. 78.

— I. vi.: "If only you had not transgressed My commandment and had kept My law" (in the Garden), cf. *P.R.E.* p. 85.

— I. vi.: "The wicked Satan who continued not in his first estate . . . so that I hurled him down from heaven," cf. *P.R.E.* pp. 99, 193.

— I. vii.: "Thou madest them all (*i.e.* the beasts) subject to me," cf. *P.R.E.* p. 79.

— I. vii.: "The beasts did obeisance to Adam," cf. *P.R.E.* p. 79.

— I. x.: "While thou wast under My command and wast a bright angel," cf. *P.R.E.* pp. 85, 98.

— I. xiii.: The first dark night is described, cf. *P.R.E.* p. 144.

— I. xiii.: "Thou didst not keep one day My commandment," cf. *P.R.E.* p. 125.

— I. xvii.: "Wriggling on its breast on the ground by reason of the curse that fell upon it from God." cf. *P.R.E.* p. 99.

— I. xvii.: "Aforetime the serpent was the most exalted of all beasts," cf. *P.R.E.* p. 92.

— I. xxii.: "We did transgress Thy commandment, and forsook Thy law, and sought to become gods like unto Thee when Satan the enemy deceived us"; cf. *P.R.E.* p. 94.

Book of Adam and Eve I. xxiii.: "Adam and Eve . . . offered upon the altar as an offering unto God," cf. *P.R.E.* p. 171, note 8.

— I. xxiv.: "God accepted their offering and showed them mercy," cf. *P.R.E.* p. 147.

— I. xxv.: "And thereby it will be made known that Thou art a merciful God," cf. *P.R.E.* p. 147.

— I. xxvii.: "And he shed light into the cave," cf. *P.R.E.* p. 144.

— I. xxvii.: "Angels filled with light and sent . . . to keep us," cf. *P.R.E.*, *loc. cit.*

— I. xxvii.: "Satan was hidden in the serpent," cf. *P.R.E.* p. 93.

— I. xxix.: God sends Michael to fetch golden rods to be with Adam in the cave, and to "shine forth with light in the night around him and put an end to his fear of the darkness," cf. *P.R.E.* p. 144.

— I. xxx.: "Gabriel fetches for Adam from Paradise sweet-smelling incense," cf. *P.R.E.* p. 146, note 7.

— I. xxxi.: Cave of Treasures, (so called) by reason of the bodies of righteous men that were in it, cf. *P.R.E.* p. 148.

— I. xxxii.: "On the eighth day . . . Eve went down into the water . . . Adam also went down into the water," cf. *P.R.E.* p. 147.

— I. xxxiii.: "They fasted in the water," cf. *P.R.E.*, *loc. cit.*

— I. xxxiv.: "Their bodies were lean," cf. *P.R.E.* p. 147.

— I. xxxiv.: "Thou . . . didst create me out of . . . dust . . . and didst bring me into the garden at the third hour, on a Friday," cf. *P.R.E.* pp. 78 f., 84, 128.

— I. xxxvii.: "We transgressed Thy commandment at the sixth hour of Friday, we were stripped of the bright nature we had, and did not continue in the garden after our transgression, more than three hours. On *the evening* Thou madest us come out of it"; cf. *P.R.E.* pp. 94, 98, 125.

— I. xxxviii.: "Thy righteous seed," cf. *P.R.E.* p. 336.

— I. xliv.: "See this fire of which we have a portion in us," cf. *P.R.E.* pp. 20, 88.

— I. xlviii.: "Satan called to his hosts . . . and said to them, 'Ye know that this Adam, whom God created out of the dust, is he who has taken our kingdom. Come, let us gather together and kill him'"; cf. *P.R.E.* pp. 91 f.

Book of Adam and Eve I. xlviii.: "Spread over us like a tent," cf. *P.R.E.* p. 16.

— I. li.: "And bound (Satan) by the side of those skins until Adam and Eve came near," cf. *P.R.E.* p. 99.

— I. li. and cf. lvii.: "This is (Satan) who was hidden in the serpent, and who deceived you, and stripped you of the garment of light and glory in which you were. This is he who promised you majesty and divinity"; cf. *P.R.E.* pp. 93 f., 98.

— I. lv.: "You (angels) do not serve me as you were wont," cf. *P.R.E.* pp. 89, 125.

— I. lv.: "(Satan) gathered together his hosts, and made war with us (angels). And if it had not been for God's strength that was with us, we could not have prevailed against him to hurl him down from heaven"; cf. *P.R.E.* pp. 193 f.

— I. lvi.: "A day of rest as I gave thee," cf. *P.R.E.* pp. 125 f.

— I. lvi.: "And God commanded His angels to escort Adam (and Eve) to the cave with joy. . . . And the angels took up Adam and Eve and brought them . . . with songs and psalms until they brought them to the cave"; cf. *P.R.E.* pp. 89 f.

— I. lix.: "See (Satan) is lord and master of all thou (Adam) hast," cf. *P.R.E.* p. 93.

— I. lx.: Apparition of Satan as an old man described, cf. *P.R.E.* p. 234.

— I. lxii., lxix., lxxii.: "But Satan, the wicked, was envious," cf. *P.R.E.* p. 91.

— I. lxii.: "Then Satan went away ashamed of not having wrought out his design," cf. *P.R.E.* p. 233.

— I. lxvii. (and cf. lxxii.): (Adam and Eve) "may, perhaps, deny God, and He (will) destroy them. So shall we be rid of them"; cf. *P.R.E.* p. 91.

— I. lxviii. (I. lxxv. and II. xviii.): "They offered . . . on the altar they had built at first," cf. *P.R.E.* p. 227, note 2.

— I. lxxiii. and II. iii.: Angels arrange *the wedding* of Adam and Eve; "the *wedding*," cf. *P.R.E.* pp. 89 f.

Book of Adam and Eve I. lxxiv.: (Eve) "brought forth her first-born son, and with him a daughter," cf. *P.R.E.* p. 152.

— I. lxxv.: (Eve) "brought forth another son and daughter," cf. *P.R.E.*, *loc. cit.* and p. 154.

— I. lxxv.: "After the birth of these, Eve ceased from child-bearing," cf. *P.R.E.* p. 152, note 11.

— I. lxxv.: "Cain, moved by Satan to kill Abel on account of the twin-sister of the former," cf. *P.R.E.* p. 154.

— I. lxxix.: "Cain took a large stone, and smote his brother with it upon the head," cf. *P.R.E.*, *loc. cit.*

— I. lxxix.: "The earth, when the blood of . . . Abel fell upon it, trembled," cf. *P.R.E.* pp. 155 f.

— I. lxxix.: "Cain began at once to dig the earth (wherein to lay) his brother . . . he . . . cast his brother into the pit (he made) . . . but the earth would not receive him; but it threw him up at once"; cf. *P.R.E.*, *loc. cit.*

— I. lxxix.: "God (said) to Cain, 'Where is thy brother?' . . . in mercy . . . to try and make him repent," cf. *P.R.E.*, *loc. cit.*

— II. i.: (Adam and Eve) "found (Abel) lying on the earth, and beasts around him," cf. *P.R.E.* p. 156.

— II. i.: "Adam . . . laid him in the Cave of Treasures," cf. *P.R.E.*, *loc. cit.*

— II. i.: "They placed a lamp (in the Cave of Treasures) to burn, by night and by day, before the body of Abel," cf. *P.R.E.* p. 275.

— II. viii. and II. xxi.: Adam directs his body to be placed in the Cave of Treasures, and finally to be buried in the middle of the earth, cf. *P.R.E.* pp. 78, 148, 266.

— II. viii. and II. x., xi.: Seth's children are to be kept apart from those of Cain, cf. *P.R.E.* pp. 158 f.

— II. ix.: Adam came out of the garden on Friday at the ninth hour, cf. *P.R.E.* p. 125.

— II. ix.: Adam's body was in the cave and "in front of him a lamp-stand (was) kept burning," cf. *P.R.E.* p. 275.

— II. ix.: "The altar upon which Adam offered," cf. *P.R.E.* p. 227, note 2.

— II. xi., III. iv.: The children of Seth are named "children of God" or "angels of God," by reason of their purity; cf. *P.R.E.* pp. 158 f., 161.

Book of Adam and Eve II. xvii.: "The land, north of the garden, which God created before the world," cf. *P.R.E.* p. 11.

— II. xvii.: "The chosen garments," cf. *P.R.E.* pp. 175, 178.

— II. xviii.: "The fathers themselves were praying for his deliverance," cf. *P.R.E.* pp. 310 f., 432 f.

— II. xx. deals with the immorality of the children of Cain, cf. *P.R.E.* pp. 159 f.

— II. xx.: Genun misleads the children of Seth, cf. *P.R.E.* p. 377.

— II. xx.: "And when they looked at the daughters of Cain, at their beautiful figure and at their hands and feet dyed with colour, and tattooed in ornaments on their faces, the fire of sin was kindled in them," . . . and they committed abominations; cf. *P.R.E.* pp. 159 f.

— III. ii.: (Noah) builds the ark in the presence of the children of Cain, that "they may see thee working at it; and if they will not repent, they shall perish," cf. *P.R.E.* pp. 161, 165.

— III. ii.: "The first storey shall be for lions, and beasts, animals and ostriches all together. The second storey shall be for birds and creeping things.

"And the third storey shall be for thee and thy wife, and for thy sons and their wives.

"And make in the ark wells for water, and openings to them . . . and thou shall line these wells with lead"; cf. *P.R.E.* p. 165.

— III. v.: God made Adam king over His works, cf. *P.R.E.* pp. 79 f.

— III. v.: "To watch over the body of our father Adam, for it is a body of great value before God," cf. *P.R.E.* p. 148.

— III. vii. (viii. and xi.): "Thy wife, and the wives of thy sons, shall be on the western side of the ark; and they and their wives shall not come together"; cf. *P.R.E.* p. 169.

— III. viii.: "All the animals shall be gathered unto thee," cf. *P.R.E.* p. 166.

— III. ix.: "An angel of God sat upon the ark," cf. *P.R.E.* p. 167.

— III. xi.: When the flood was over, they (men and women

in the ark) "came together, the husband with his wife," cf. *P.R.E.* p. 169.

Book of Adam and Eve III. xiii.: "Noah took a root of vine and planted it, and dressed it until it yielded fruit," cf. *P.R.E.* p. 170.

— III. xiv.: Noah divides the earth among (his sons), cf. *P.R.E.* pp. 172 f.

— III. xvii.: "The house full of light," cf. *P.R.E.* pp. 166 f.

— III. xvii.: "And (lest) they hang on to the body of Adam," cf. *P.R.E.* p. 148.

— III. xxiii.: "*One of the first kings* that ever reigned on the earth, whose name was Nimrud, a giant," cf. *P.R.E.* p. 80.

— III. xxiv.: "Satan entered into the idol of gold," cf. *P.R.E.* p. 355.

— III. xxv.: Nimrod sacrifices victims to the fire, cf. *P.R.E.* pp. 188, 420.

— IV. ii.: (Pharaoh) "gave to Sarah, Hagar the Egyptian," cf. *P.R.E.* p. 190.

— IV. ii. refers to Ishmael as being thirteen years older than Isaac, cf. *P.R.E.* p. 217, note 3.

— IV. ii. states that Isaac was fourteen years old when put on the altar, cf. *P.R.E.* p. 225.

— IV. iii.: "Jerusalem that means the middle of the earth," cf. *P.R.E.* p. 266.

— IV. v.: "And this Naasson was great among the sons of Judah," cf. *P.R.E.* p. 331, note 1.

— IV. ix.: Lion-proselytes and Samar[itans], cf. *P.R.E.* p. 299.

— IV. xi.: "The fire . . . is the Divine fire that was all the time in the house of God," cf. *P.R.E.* p. 429.

Dr. Ginzberg's article on the Book of Adam and Eve in the first volume of the *Jewish Encyclopedia* should be read, and the notes on the Books of Adam and Eve in *A. and P.* ii. might be consulted. Many of the references to similar phrases and ideas given in this Introduction are not repeated in the notes to *P.R.E.*

The Apocalypse of Abraham (see *P.R.E.* pp. 70, 76) should also be read as a side-light to our book. Thus, the interpretation of "Ur of the Chaldees" as the fire of the Chaldees is common to both. The attempt of Azazel to disturb

Abraham when offering his sacrifice to God is somewhat similar to the attempt of Sammael to hinder Abraham's sacrifice of the ram instead of Isaac. The "unclean bird" which swoops down upon the carcasses, as well as "the vision" of Abraham between the pieces, beholding the world in its future career, reappear in our book. Both writings refer to the Divine throne and the Cherubim as well as to the revelation of the secrets of the deep (Leviathan). Sammael (or Azazel) had twelve wings according to our book and the Apocalypse. Dr. Ginzberg, in his interesting article on the Apocalypse in the *J.E.* i. 92, refers to Chapters IX., XIII., XX., XXI., and XXVIII. of the *Pirḳê de Rabbi Eliezer.*

For parallel or similar expressions and teaching in—

(*a*) 4 Ezra, see pp. 11, 60, 63, 70, 87, 136, 198, 202, 257 ff., 260, 350, and 357.

(*b*) Ascension of Isaiah, see pp. 17, 21, 92, and 245.

(*c*) Assumption of Moses, see pp. 11, 63, 194, 266, 339, 344, 357, 393, and 412.

We have by no means exhausted the material in the foregoing paragraphs. Such books as *Schatzhöhle, Kebra Nagast,* and the Book of the Bee, not to mention the Koran and its famous commentaries, contain much material in common with our "Chapters." Philo and Ecclesiasticus also offer several interesting parallels.

It is not by any means definitely established that our author actually copied any of the afore-mentioned books. What is maintained, however, is the existence of some sort of literary connection between *P.R.E.* and these books. This may be explained by the existence of compositions based on the Pseudepigrapha or used by the authors of this class of literature. The link is missing and it would be extremely hazardous to do more than point out the existence of similar ideas and occasionally actual parallel phrases. It must not be forgotten that many of the ideas common to the Midrashim and the Pseudepigrapha were, so to say, common property, floating traditions which were recorded not only in Enoch or Jubilees, but also in the Books of Adam and Eve, and later in our book, and later still in such compositions as the Book of the Bee.

One lesson seems to be driven home from our study,

and that is the impossibility of properly understanding the Apocryphal and Pseudepigraphic writings without the assistance of the teaching of Rabbinics. So also *vice versa*, we must illustrate Rabbinical literature by the teaching of the Apocrypha and Pseudepigrapha.

§ 6. *P.R.E.* and Patristic Literature

Ginzberg, Goldfahn, Graetz, Kohler, Rahmer, and others have discussed various aspects of Patristic literature in connection with Midrashic teaching. This field of inquiry is by no means exhausted. Very many interesting parallels to some of the teaching in our " Chapters " are to be found in the writings of the Church Fathers. It would be advantageous to read the Patristic literature in the light of Midrashic exegesis and interpretation and *vice versa*. One or two instances will explain this standpoint.

The Statutes of the Apostles (ed. Horner), § 70, p. 215, direct that " seven days should be kept for a memorial of the living and the dead." This rule will be appreciated if compared with the Jewish institution of the " seven days of mourning " (see *P.R.E.* p. 115). Again, the 48th statute directs prayers to be said five times daily (*op. cit.* pp. 182 f.). This rule should be illustrated by the Rabbinic custom of praying thrice daily (see *P.R.E.* p. 110).

Vorstius and many scholars after him have not disguised their profound contempt for the legends contained in our " Chapters " and in other Midrashic writings. This attitude must give place to a more sympathetic understanding of the fact that Midrash exists not only in the works of the Rabbis but also in the New Testament and in Patristic literature. Many legends preserved in our " Chapters " are also to be found in the interesting volumes of the " Ante-Nicene Christian Library." Many of these parallels are mentioned in the notes to our " Chapters."

§ 7. Date and Origin of *P.R.E.*

A few historical and literary clues, disclosed by a careful study of our book, enable us to fix the date of its final redaction. This is probably either the second or the third decade of the ninth century. This late date does not, however, indicate that most of the material at the disposal of the redactor did not belong to a much earlier period. We have already mentioned 776 C.E. in connection with the *Baraitha de R. Sh'muel*, and if this treatise proved to be an independent work, which has been partially incorporated into our book, we can safely assert that the three astronomical chapters belong to a date at least half a century prior to the final redaction of the book. The Creation legends, which go back to the Books of Enoch and Jubilees as well as to the Books of Adam and Eve, contain material which is earlier than the first century C.E. Again, the legends dealing with the Flood have elements in common with traditions preserved by Hippolytus, whose activity was in the first decades of the third century (*c.* 200–236). Jean Gagnier, who was at Oxford in the eighteenth century, drew attention to a parallel in Hippolytus to *P.R.E.*, duly noted by Fabricius in his stately edition of the writings of the Church Father.

Scholars are by no means agreed as to the locality whence *P.R.E.* emanated. The latest opinion is that of Dr. Samuel Krauss, who refers to it as a Byzantine production, see *Studien zur Byzantinisch-Jüdischen Geschichte* (1914), pp. 145 f. M. Grünbaum in his learned book, *Neue Beiträge zur Semitischen Sagenkunde* (1893), inclines to the view that *P.R.E.* was written in an Arabian atmosphere. There are clear indications of contact with Mohammedan material (cf. *P.R.E.* xxx.), the names Fatimah (p. 219) and 'Ayeshah (p. 218) as wives of Ishmael occur and betray Islamic influence. In Chapter XXX. (pp. 221 f.) two brothers who are reigning simultaneously are indicated; Graetz has long ago pointed to this passage as referring to the two sons of Harun al-Rashid, Alemin and Elmamum, who ruled in the early years of the ninth century. Müller has drawn attention to the Minhagim or religious customs which are peculiar to our book, and as a result of his investigation he is of opinion that *P.R.E.* is a Palestinian production. There are many subsidiary points which seem to support this view. The fact already mentioned, that the direct quotations from the Talmud are only from the Palestinian recension; and the use made of another Palestinian work, Genesis

Rabbah, seem to support a Palestinian origin. There are striking references to the Holy Land, its privileges and superiority, which point to a Palestinian authorship. On the other hand, there are reasons for regarding Babylon as the home of *P.R.E.* Dr. Büchler's studies dealing with the ban, which will be quoted in the notes (pp. 301 f.), seem to point to Babylon as the source whence our book came. Other lines of inquiry, *e.g.* the punishment inflicted on a woman guilty of immorality (see p. 100), point in the same direction. It is extremely difficult to decide in a question of this kind, especially when eminent authorities hold such divergent views. It is right to point out that the views of Graetz referred to on pp. 221 f. have been refuted by Steinschneider (see note on p. 222). Likewise his theory (*Geschichte*, v. p. 446) that our book in Chapter XXX. is indebted to the Secrets of R. Simeon ben Jochai in connection with the misrule of the Ishmaelites, has been controverted by Horowitz, *Beth 'Eḳed Ha-Hagadoth*, p. 24. Both, however, agree that the date of the composition of our book is about 750 C.E.

§ 8. Polemical Tendency in *P.R.E.*

Apparently there is no direct reference to Christianity. On the other hand, there are several allusions to Islam as the "Fourth Kingdom" destined to persecute the Chosen People prior to the dawn of the Messianic Kingdom. There are also several echoes from the old controversies which the ancient teachers in Israel waged against the Gnostics (cf. pp. 17, 79 f.). One of the set purposes of part of the work is to combat certain teachings contained in some of the Pseudepigrapha, especially in the Book of Jubilees. It is noteworthy that the Cairo Geniẓah has restored to us Aramaic fragments based on the Book of Jubilees and also on the Testaments of the XII Patriarchs. The Ẓohar refers to a book of Enoch (Lev. 10a) which seems to have been in Aramaic. We believe we have established the fact that there is close connection between our "Chapters" and the afore-mentioned pseudepigraphic books.

Our author lays great stress on the doctrine of the resurrection of the body (cf. pp. 228, 249 f.). This may be directed against the teaching set forth in many of the pseudepigraphic and apocryphal books, which deny the physical resurrection.

On page 254 he opposes, as the Talmud, the destruction of fruit-bearing trees (see Krauss in השילח, 1908, xix. 28 ff.; and *T.A.* ii. p. 205).

There may be a polemical interest in the description of the Teraphim (pp. 273 f.), possibly the worship of relics is attacked here. The belief in the possibility of the Deity having physical offspring (see p. 85, note 10) is opposed. Celibacy (p. 89, note 2) seems to be regarded with disfavour, and possibly divorce (see p. 219) is likewise disapproved.

§ 9. Theology of *P.R.E.*

The note struck in the first two chapters, proclaiming the supreme value of the Torah, the Law of God, is in harmony with the teaching in the rest of the book. The Law belongs to the premundane creation (p. 11), it was with God at the Creation (p. 12), even consulted by the Divine Architect when He was planning the Universe (*ibid.*) and creating man (p. 76). The Torah had its home in heaven and was entrusted to Israel because the other nations refused to accept its teaching (p. 319). Some of the precepts of the Torah were kept in heaven by God and the Angels (pp. 137 f.), and also by Adam and the patriarchs (pp. 126, 143, 204) prior to the revelation on Sinai.

The love or goodness of God impelled Him to the creation of man (p. 76). The belief in original sin is not countenanced (pp. 158 f.). Moral evil was brought into the world by Sammael (p. 158) and the offspring of the fallen angels (pp. 160 f.). The angelology in our book is interesting on account of its connection with the Pseudepigrapha. Michael, Sammael (with whom Azazel is identified), demons and merciful angels, the fall of the angels, Cherubim, Chajjôth, Seraphim, and the heavenly host, are all dealt with. The Index will enable the reader to find our author's views on this theme.

The ethical tone is excellently expressed in the chapter on the Two Ways (pp. 102 f.). The duty of loving service is set forth in two chapters (pp. 106 ff.) and in many passages throughout the book. The sacredness of human life (pp. 176, 386) is emphasized. The day of judgment and retribution is not forgotten (p. 416). The value of repentance is dealt with in a special chapter (pp. 337 ff.). There are chapters devoted to eschatology (pp. 410 ff.) and the resurrection (pp. 252 ff.). For references to God, Shekhinah, the Divine throne, Messiah, Leviathan and Behemoth, Gehenna and Paradise, the future world and death, the reader can consult the Index.

The quotations from the O.T. are given according to the chapters and verses in the Revised Version. This translation has frequently been modified in order to express the Haggadic interpretation of our author. The quotations in the original are rarely given in full, but in order to understand the teaching in question the entire verse should be read. To facilitate reference the source of every Biblical quotation is given, a labour already done by Vorstius and Luria. The headings at the head of each chapter have been added by the present writer. Most of the printed editions contain a summary of the contents of each chapter. The method of transliteration adopted has not been uniformly followed, especially when a name is well known by reason of appearing in the Revised Version, *e.g.* Eliezer. The R.V. names have generally been retained. The letter ח is represented by *ch*, ט by *ṭ*, כ by *kh*, כּ by *k*, ק by *ḳ*, ז by *ẓ*, צ by *z*, ע by ‘.

ABBREVIATIONS EMPLOYED IN NOTES

A.T. = Altes Testament.
A.N.C.L. = Ante-Nicene Christian Library.
Apoc. = Apocalypse.
A. and P. = Apocrypha and Pseudepigrapha, ed. Charles (Oxford).
A.R.W. = Archiv für Religionswissenschaft.
Bacher, T. = Bacher's Agada der Tannaiten.
Bacher, Terminologie = Bacher's Die älteste Terminologie der jüdischen Schriftauslegung.
B.H.M. = Beth Ha-Midrash.
B.M. = British Museum.
C. = column.
C.E. = Common Era.
Comm. = Commentary.
C.W. = Cohn, Wendland.
D.B. = Dictionary of the Bible.
d. R. = de Rabbi.
ed. = edition.
eds. = editions.
Enc. Bib. = Encyclopædia Biblica.
E.T. = English Translation.
Eth. = Ethiopic.
Geiger, Was hat Mohammed = Geiger's Was hat Mohammed aus dem Judentume aufgenommen?
Ginzberg, Die Haggada = Ginzberg's Die Haggada bei dem Kirchenvätern.
Grünbaum, Beiträge = Grünbaum's Neue Beiträge zur Semitischen Sagenkunde.
G.T. = German Translation.
G.V. = Die Gottesdienstlichen Vorträge.
I.C.C. = International Critical Commentary.
Jahrbücher = Jahrbücher für jüdische Geschichte.
J.E. = Jewish Encyclopedia.
J.Q.R. = Jewish Quarterly Review.
Lazarus, Ethik = Lazarus' Die Ethik des Judentums.
LXX = Septuagint Version.
M. = Mangey.
Monatsschrift = Monatsschrift für Geschichte und Wissenschaft des Judentums.
MS. = Manuscript.
M.T. = Massoretic text.
N.H.W.B. = Neuhebräisches Wörterbuch.
N.T. = New Testament.
O.T. = Old Testament.
p., pp. = page, pages.
Pal. Targum = Palestinian Targum (Pseudo-Jonathan).
Pesh. = Peshitta.
P.R.E. = Pirḳê de Rabbi Eliezer.
R. = Rabbi or Rabban.
Rab. = Rabbah.
Real-Ency. s. = Real Encyclopädie Supplementband.
R.É.J. = Revue des Études Juives.
R.V. = Revised Version.
Schechter, Aspects = Schechter's Aspects of Rabbinic Theology.
Schürer = Schürer's Geschichte des jüdischen Volkes.

Singer = Authorized Daily Prayer Book.

Slav. = Slavonic.

T. = Testament.

T.A. = Talmudische Archäologie (Krauss).

Targ. = Targum.

T.B. = Babylonian Talmud.

T.D. = Targum Dictionary.

Test. XII Pat. = Testaments of the Twelve Patriarchs.

T.J. = Talmud of Jerusalem (Palestinian Talmud).

Z.A.T.W. = Zeitschrift für die A.T. Wissenschaft.

Z.D.M.G. = Zeitschrift der Deutschen Morgenländischen Gesellschaft.

Z.f.N.T. Wissensch = Zeitschrift für die Neutestamentliche Wissenschaft.

Zur Gesch. = Zur Geschichte (Zunz).

THE CHAPTERS OF RABBI ELIEZER THE GREAT[1]

CHAPTER I

RABBI ELIEZER AND THE TORAH[2] [1B. i.]

THE following befell Rabbi Eliezer, son of Hyrḳanos. His father had many ploughmen[3] who were ploughing arable ground,[4] whereas he was ploughing a stony plot; he sat down and wept. His father said to him: O my son! Why

[1] Also called "Baraitha of Rabbi Eliezer"; see *supra*, Introduction, and cf. Zunz, *G.V.*, p. 283, Weiss, *Dor Dor veDorshav*, iii. p. 290, and Hamburger, *Real-Ency*. s. II. i. pp. 162 ff., on the *P.R.E.* The first two chapters are probably a later addition to the Midrash contained in the rest of the "Chapters." They form a very good introduction to this pseudepigraphic book, which was attributed to the famous teacher, Rabbi Eliezer the Great. The third chapter opens with the name of Rabbi Eliezer. The MS. fragment of our book in the British Museum which Horowitz has edited in his *Sammlung Kleiner Midraschim*, i. 4 ff., begins with the third chapter. The same fact obtains in some of the fragments contained in the Bodleian Library. For the biography of Rabbi Eliezer ben Hyrḳanos see Bacher, T. i. pp. 96 ff., and *J.E.* v. 113 ff., where a bibliography is added. Our "Chapters" contain about twenty dicta attributed to R. Eliezer; see Bacher, *op. cit.* pp. 122 f., who considers all these sayings as pseudepigraphic. The subject-matter of the first two chapters of our book is to be found in Aboth d. R. Nathan (*a*) vi., (*b*) xiii., Jalḳuṭ, Gen. § 72, and Gen. Rab. xlii. (in the new edition of Theodor, ch. xli., where further parallels are given in the notes on p. 397). Various recensions of the first two chapters have been published by Horowitz, *Beth 'Eḳed Ha-Hagadoth*, pp. 7 ff.

[2] The headings to the chapters have been added by the translator. The numbers in the square brackets after the headings indicate the pages and columns of the MS.

[3] Gen. Rab. xlii. 1 and Jalkut, Gen., *loc. cit.*, read: "his brethren were ploughing in the plain, whereas he was ploughing on the mountain." The 1st and 2nd eds. omit the word "many."

[4] Lit. "were ploughing upon the surface of the *furrow*." Cf. Ps. cxxix. 3 for the word "furrows."

dost thou weep? Art thou perchance distressed because thou dost plough a stony plot? In the past thou hast ploughed a stony plot,[1] now behold thou shalt plough with us arable soil.[2] He sat down on the arable ground and wept. His father said to him: But why dost thou weep? Art thou perchance distressed because thou art ploughing the arable land? He replied to him: No. (Hyrḳanos) said to him: Why dost thou weep? He answered him: I weep only because I desire to learn Torah.[3] (Hyrḳanos) said to him: Verily thou art twenty-eight years old [4]—yet dost thou desire to learn Torah? Nay, go, take thee a wife and beget sons and thou wilt take them to the school.[5] He fasted two weeks [6] not tasting || anything, until Elijah [7]—may he be remembered for good [8]—appeared to him and said to him: Son of Hyrḳanos! Why dost thou weep? He replied to him: Because I desire to learn Torah. (Elijah) said to him: If thou desirest to learn Torah get thee up to Jerusalem to Rabban Jochanan ben Zakkai.[9] He arose and went up to Jerusalem to R. Jochanan ben Ẓakkai and sat down and wept. (R. Jochanan) said to him: Why dost thou weep? He answered him: Because I wish to learn

[1] These words are omitted in the 1st and 2nd eds.

[2] This would be easier labour. At this point the MS. adds the second letter of the Hebrew alphabet to signify the beginning of the second paragraph. The 1st and 2nd eds. omit "with us."

[3] Torah is not merely the written word of God, but also its oral interpretation. The term sums up all that is implied by Religion and Ethics.

[4] Aboth d. R. Nathan (*a*) vi. reads "22 years," and cf. *ibid.* (*b*) xiii.

[5] Thy merit will be accounted as though thou didst study the Torah; see T.B. Ḳiddushin, 30a, for this doctrine. The second paragraph in MS. ends here.

[6] "He was distressed for three weeks" is the reading in Aboth d. R. Nathan (*b*) xiii. On "weeks" see Krauss, *T.A.* ii. pp. 422 f.; and note 784.

[7] On Elijah in Rabbinical literature see *J.E.* v. 122 ff. In our work the Elijah story and legends are treated at considerable length. In Christian books Elijah also appears; see Mark ix. 4 ff. and Matt. xvii. 11. In the Gospel of Barnabas (124a) Elijah rebukes a man for weeping. See also Coptic Apocrypha, ed. Budge, p. 265, for a further parallel. Elijah is the "comforter" in Jewish and Christian literature, and in this capacity he is the forerunner of the Messiah.

[8] On this expression see Zunz, *Zur Gesch.* pp. 321 ff.

[9] The greatest teacher of his day, who preserved Judaism in spite of the overthrow of the Jewish State by the Romans, in the year 70 C.E. For his biography see Bacher, T. i. pp. 22 ff., and *J.E.* vii. 214 ff. Graetz, *Geschichte der Juden*, iv. pp. 11 ff., Schürer, ii. 366 ff., and Schlatter's biography should be consulted.

Torah. (R. Jochanan) said to him: Whose son art thou? But he did not tell him.

(R. Jochanan) asked him: Hast thou never learnt [1] to read the Shema',[2] or the Tephillah,[3] or the Grace after meals? [4] He replied to him: No. He arose [5] and (R. Jochanan) taught him the three (prayers).[6] (Again) he sat down and wept. (R. Jochanan) said to him: My son, why dost thou weep? He replied: Because I desire to learn Torah.[7] He (thereupon) taught him two rules (of the Law) [8] every day of the week, and on the Sabbath [9] (Eliezer) repeated them and assimilated them.[10] He kept a fast for eight days without tasting anything until the odour of his mouth attracted the attention of R. Jochanan ben Ẓakkai, who directed him to withdraw from his presence. He sat down and wept. (R. Jochanan) said to him: My son, why dost thou weep? He rejoined: Because thou didst make me withdraw from thy presence just as a man makes his fellow withdraw, when the latter is afflicted with leprosy. (R. Jochanan) said to him: My son, just as || the odour of thy mouth has ascended before me, so may the savour of the statutes of the Torah ascend from thy mouth to Heaven.[11] He said to him: My son! Whose son art thou?

[1] Aboth d. R. Nathan (*b*) xiii. reads: "Didst thou never go to school?"

[2] The "Shema'" is the Jewish confession of faith. It is set forth in Deut. vi. 4–9, etc.; see Singer, pp. 40 ff., and *J.E.* xi. 266.

[3] The "Tephillah" or "Shemoneh 'Esreh," the Jewish prayer *par excellence*, is to be found in Singer, pp. 44 ff.; see *R.É.J.* xix. pp. 17 ff., and *J.E.* xi. 270 ff. Our "Chapters" deal with the subject-matter of the "Shemoneh 'Esreh"; cf. Zunz, *G.V.*, p. 285, and S. Sachs in "Ha-Techiyah," pp. 21 f. On the question as to the relation between Sirach and the "Shemoneh 'Esreh" see Oesterley's edition of *Ecclesiasticus*, pp. 232 and 349 f.

[4] The Geniẓah Fragment has: "the reading of the Grace after meals." On Grace after meals see Singer, pp. 280 ff., and *J.E.* vi. 61 f.

[5] The student stood whilst learning; see T.B. Megillah, 21a. The 1st and 2nd eds. read: "He said, Stand, and I will teach thee the three (prayers)."

[6] In the MS. the fourth paragraph begins here.

[7] And not merely prayers.

[8] "Halakhoth," *i.e.* laws to be observed by the Jews, based upon the Torah. Thus, according to Matt. xii. 1–8, Jesus discusses Halakhah. The final decisions become Halakhoth; cf. Mark vii. 5 and Luke xi. 40 f. See Bacher, *Terminologie*, i. *s.v.* הלכה, pp. 42 f.

[9] The first two editions omit "on the Sabbath."

[10] In the MS. this is the end of the fourth paragraph.

[11] In Aboth d. R. Nathan (*b*) xiii. the reading is: "So may the teaching of thy mouth go forth from one end of the world to the other."

He replied: I am the son of Hyrḳanos. Then said (R. Jochanan): Art thou not the son of one of the great men of the world,[1] and thou didst not tell me? By thy life! he continued, This day shalt thou eat with me.[2] (Eliezer) answered: I have eaten already with my host.[3] (R. Jochanan) asked: Who is thy host? He replied: R. Joshua ben Chananjah [4] and R. José the Priest.[5]

(R. Jochanan) sent to inquire of his hosts, saying to them: Did Eliezer eat with you this day? They answered: No; moreover has he not fasted eight days without tasting any food? [6] R. Joshua ben Chananjah and R. José the Priest [7] went and said [8] to R. Jochanan ben Ẓakkai: Verily during the last eight days (Eliezer) has not partaken of any food.[9]

1 Hyrḳanos was a very wealthy man.

2 In MS. the sixth paragraph begins here.

3 *Akhsania* (ξενία), hospitality, lodging, host. According to Aboth d. R. Nathan (*a*) vi., Eliezer was silent when R. Jochanan asked him whether he had partaken of food.

4 See Bacher, T. i. pp. 123 ff., and *J.E.* vii. 290 ff.

5 See Bacher, T. i. pp. 67 ff., and *J.E.* vii. 243 ff.

6 Here begins the seventh paragraph in the MS. The Geniẓah Fragment continues: "Moreover."

7 Aboth d. R. Nathan (*b*) xiii. adds: "R. Simeon ben Nathaniel."

8 Some of the old printed editions read here: "Has he not been without food for the last eight days?" Luria, *in loc.*, thinks that the last clause was spoken by R. Jochanan to the Rabbis who visited him, telling them that Eliezer had not eaten at his table. Aboth d. R. Nathan (*loc. cit.*) refers to R. Jochanan's grief at this neglect, which might have cost Eliezer's life.

9 The Geniẓah Fragment adds: "And he compelled him to eat and to drink, and on the morrow" (also).

CHAPTER II

R. ELIEZER AND HIS BRETHREN [2A. i.]

THE sons of Hyrḳanos said to their father: Get thee up to Jerusalem and vow that thy son Eliezer should not enjoy any of thy possessions.[1] He went up to Jerusalem to disinherit him, and it happened that a festival was being celebrated there by R. Jochanan ben Ẓakkai. All the magnates of the district were dining with him; (such as) Ben Zizith Hakkeseth,[2] Nicodemus ben Gorion,[3] and Ben Kalba S'bu'a.[4] ||

Why was his name called Ben Zizith Hakkeseth? Because he reclined at table in a higher position than the other magnates of Jerusalem.[5] Concerning Nicodemus ben Gorion, people said that he had (stored) provisions containing 3 S'ah[6] of fine flour for every inhabitant of Jerusalem. When the

[1] Lit. "and ban thy son Eliezer from thy possessions." The Geniẓah Fragment reads: "to put him in the ban." The brothers claimed that Eliezer should be disinherited because he had left his old father without permission. For a parallel text see Gen. Rab. xlii. (ed. Theodor, p. 398), Aboth d. R. Nathan (*a*) vi. Was it the custom to resort to the Synhedrion in order to disinherit one's son?

[2] See Lam. Rab. i. 5 (31), Eccles. Rab. to Eccles. vii. 11, and T.B. Giṭṭin, 56a. According to the Talmud (*loc. cit.*) the name Ben Zizith Hakkeseth was due to his intercourse (*Kisê, i.e.* seat) with the great men of Rome.

[3] See *J.E.* ix. 300, where the reference to T.B. Ta'anith should be emended to 20a.

[4] Ben Kalba S'bu'a, this name is the result of a pun. According to T.B. Giṭṭin, *loc. cit.*, anyone who came to him even as hungry as a dog (*keleb*) was dismissed fully satisfied (*sab'a*).

[5] T.B. Giṭṭin, *loc. cit.*, gives another explanation of this name, due to the tradition that the fringes (*Zizith*) of the man's garments were hanging over the cushions of his seat. The 'Arukh (ed. Kohut, vii. 40a, *s.v.*) appears to have had a text of our passage in accordance with the Talmudic reading, but unlike our text.

[6] S'ah, a dry measure, the size of which is held to equal 12·148 litres or 10·696 qts. The Geniẓah Fragment reads "three years" instead of "three S'ah."

zealots [1] arose and burnt all the storehouses, they measured and found that he had had provisions for three years for every inhabitant in Jerusalem.[2] Concerning Ben Kalba S'bu'a it was told that he had a house measuring 4 Kors [3] with roofs covered with gold.[4] The people said (to R. Jochanan): Behold, the father of R. Eliezer has arrived. He bade them saying: Prepare a place for him, and seat him next to us.[5] (R. Jochanan) fixed his gaze [6] on R. Eliezer, saying to him,[7] Tell us some words [8] of the Torah. (R. Eliezer) answered him saying: Rabbi! [9] I will tell thee a parable. To what is the matter like? To this well which cannot yield more water than the amount which it has drawn (from the earth); likewise am I unable to speak words of the Torah in excess of what I have received from thee.[10]

(R. Jochanan) said to him, I will (also) tell thee a parable. To what is the matter like? To this fountain which is bubbling and sending forth its water, and it is able to effect a discharge more powerful || than what it secretes; in like manner art thou able to speak words of the Torah in excess of what Moses [11] received at Sinai. (R. Jochanan) continued: Lest thou shouldst feel ashamed on my account, behold I

[1] On the Zealots or Sicarii see Josephus, *Wars*, iv. 3. 9 ff.

[2] This passage is missing in the printed editions, but it occurs in the Genizah Fragment.

[3] The Kor is assumed by Gesenius (Oxford ed. p. 499) to be the same as the Chomer, which was thirty times the S'ah. On these measures see *Enc. Bib.* iv. 5294 ff.

[4] The first printed editions read: "gardens crushed with gold." Luria reads: "he had a palace with an area covering 4 Kors, all the beams were overlaid with gold." He thinks that the text should read: "he had a palace covering 4 Kors with treasuries containing gold." The MS. seems to have preserved the true reading, which is also the reading in the Genizah Fragment.

[5] The 1st and 2nd eds. read: "They prepared a place for him and seated him next to him" (*i.e.* R. Jochanan). The Genizah Fragment reads: "and seat him next to yourselves; they prepared a place for him and placed him next to him" (R. Jochanan). In the MS. the first paragraph ends here.

[6] For this expression see T.B. Synhedrin, 11a: "the sages fixed their gaze upon Hillel the Elder."

[7] The Genizah Fragment adds: "O my son!"

[8] Lit. "One word."

[9] Perhaps "Rabban" would be more correct. The MS. uses an abbreviation.

[10] See Aboth ii. 10, where Eliezer is described as a "plastered cistern which loses not a drop," and cf. Taylor's note on p. 34 of his (2nd) edition of Aboth. The second paragraph ends here in the MS.

[11] The 1st and 2nd eds. read, "they received."

will arise and go away from thee. Rabban Jochanan ben Ẓakkai arose and went outside. (Thereupon) R. Eliezer sat down and expounded.[1] His face shone like the light of the sun and his effulgence beamed forth like that of Moses,[2] so that no one knew whether it was day or night.[3] They went and said to Rabban Jochanan ben Ẓakkai: Come and see R. Eliezer sitting and expounding, his face shining like the light of the sun and his effulgence beaming like that of Moses, so that no one knows whether it be day or night.[4] He came from (his place) behind him [5] and kissed him on his head, saying to him: Happy are ye, Abraham, Isaac, and Jacob, because this one has come forth from your loins.

Hyrḳanos his father said: To whom does (R. Jochanan) speak thus? The people answered: To Eliezer thy son. He said to them: (R. Jochanan) should not have spoken in that manner, but (in this wise), "Happy am I because he has come forth from my loins." Whilst R. Eliezer was sitting and expounding, his father was standing upon his feet. When || (Eliezer) saw his father standing upon his feet, he became agitated and said to him: My father! be seated, for I cannot utter the words of the Torah when thou art standing on thy feet.[6] (Hyrḳanos) replied to him: My son, it was not for this reason that I came, but my intention was to disinherit thee. Now that I have come and I have

[1] According to Gen. Rab. XLII. i., the text of Eliezer's exposition was Ps. xxxvii. 14, "The wicked have drawn out the sword, and have bent their bow; to cast down the poor and needy, to slay such as be upright in the way." The brothers of Eliezer might possibly be described in the terms of this text.

[2] The reference is to Ex. xxxiv. 35, "And the skin of Moses' face shone." See also Eccles. viii. 1.

[3] The third paragraph ends here.

[4] This sentence is wanting in the printed editions. There seems to be some confusion in the text. The MS. concludes here the fourth paragraph.

[5] According to Aboth d. R. Nathan (*b*) xiii. R. Jochanan had gone forth from the assembly so as not to embarrass R. Eliezer. While Eliezer is expounding, R. Joshua and R. Simeon ben Nathaniel leave the assembly to find R. Jochanan, to whom they say, "Come and see! R. Eliezer is sitting and expounding things more profoundly than (the things) told to Moses at Sinai." For another instance of kissing by the same teacher see T.B. Chagigah, 14b.

[6] It would be disrespectful for a son to sit in the presence of his parent, who would be standing; cf. T.B. Ḳiddushin, 33b, where this theme is discussed.

witnessed all this praise; behold thy brothers are disinherited and their portion is given to thee as a gift.[1]

(Eliezer) replied: Verily I am not equal to one of them.[2] If I had asked the Holy One, blessed be He, for land, it would be possible for Him to give this to me, as it is said, "The earth is the Lord's, and the fulness thereof" (Ps. xxiv. 1). Had I asked the Holy One, blessed be He, for silver and gold, He could have given them to me, as it is said, "The silver is mine, and the gold is mine"[3] (Hag. ii. 8). But I asked the Holy One, blessed be He, that I might be worthy (to learn the) Torah only, as it is said, "Therefore I esteem all precepts concerning all things to be right; and I hate every false way" (Ps. cxix. 128).

[1] The fifth paragraph ends here in the MS.

[2] This section to the end of the chapter is to be found in Jalkuṭ Makhiri to Psalms (Ps. cxix.), § 77, with slight variations in the reading. The last sentence reads: "But I prayed to Him only that I might be found worthy, as it is said, 'Therefore I esteem all precepts,'" etc.

[3] The 1st ed. and subsequent editions continue the rest of the verse, but a strange error has crept into their texts; they read "amar" instead of "n'um," which is the actual reading in Haggai. This error is also in the Talmud (B.) Ḳiddushin, 82b.

CHAPTER III[1]

PREMUNDANE CREATION, AND THE WORK OF THE FIRST DAY

[2B. ii.]

R. ELIEZER[2] BEN HYRḲANOS opened[3] (his discourse with the text), "Who can utter the mighty acts of the Lord, or[4] shew forth all his praise?" (Ps. cvi. 2).[5] Is there any man[6] who can utter the mighty acts of the Holy One, blessed be He, or who can shew forth all His praise?[7] Not even the ministering angels[8] are able to narrate (the Divine praise). But to investigate a part of His mighty deeds with reference to what He has done, and what He will do in the future (is permissible), so that His name should be exalted among His creatures, whom He has

[1] This is probably the beginning of the Baraitha or Pirḳê de R. Eliezer. The Chronicles of Jeraḥmeel begin with this section of our work. The following chapters up to Chapter XI. form a treatise dealing with Ma'aseh Bereshith (The Work of the Creation) and Ma'aseh Merkabah (The theme of God's Chariot). Cosmological and theosophical themes were favourite ones in the school of R. Eliezer's famous teacher, R. Jochanan ben Ẓakkai; see T.B. Chagigah, 14b, for the story of R. Jochanan ben Ẓakkai listening to R. Elaẓar ben 'Arakh expounding the Ma'aseh Merkabah.

[2] This gives the title to the book.

[3] *i.e.* explained (the text).

[4] The Venice edition and several later editions are at variance with the actual text of the psalm by adding "and who," which is not in the Biblical quotation. The quotation is correctly given in B.M. MS. and in the first printed text (Constantinople, 1514).

[5] See Jalḳuṭ, *in loc.*

[6] The printed editions add: "in the world."

[7] See T.B. Megillah, 18a, for the view that the one who utters the praise of God to excess will be taken from the world, based on Job xxxvii. 20. Cf. Slav. Enoch xxiv. 3.

[8] The ministering angels are identified by Siphrê (Deut. § 306, end) with "the sons of Elohim" of Job i. 6, and they are probably to be identified with "the angels of sanctification" mentioned in the Book of Jubilees ii. 2, 18; cf. Eth. Enoch lxi. 10 ff. For "the heavenly host praising God" see Luke ii. 13, and for angelology see *J.E.* i. 583 ff.

created, from one end of the world || to the other, as it is said, "One generation to another shall laud thy works" (*ibid.* cxlv. 4).[1]

Before the world was created, the Holy One, blessed be He, with His Name[2] alone existed, and the thought arose in Him to create the world. He began to trace (the foundations of)[3] the world before Himself, but it would not stand. They[4] told a parable, To what is the matter like? To a king who wishes to build a palace[5] for himself. If he had not traced in the earth its foundations, its exits and its entrances,[6] he does not begin to build.[7] Likewise the Holy One, blessed be He, was tracing (the plans of) the world before Himself, but it did not remain standing until He created repentance.[8]

Seven things[9] were created before the world was created.

[1] Our text has been used by Jalkuṭ, Psalms, § 864. Here ends the first paragraph in MS.

[2] On the Tetragrammaton see Nestle, *Z.D.M.G.* xxxii.; Fürst, *ibid.* xxxiii.; and Nager, *ibid.* xxxv. The printed editions read here: "The Holy One, blessed be He, and His great Name." On "God and His Name" see D. H. Joël's *die Religionsphilosophie des Sohar*, p. 235.

[3] The words in brackets are based on B.M. MS., which reads: "He traced its foundations, its exits and entrances, on the earth, but it did not stand firm until He created repentance, because seven (things) were created before the world."

[4] *i.e.* the Rabbis.

[5] *Palṭin*=παλάτιον, *palatium*, palace.

[6] The phraseology is based on Ezek. xliii. 11. The printed editions reverse the order and read: "its entrances and its exits."

[7] The architect's plans must be prepared prior to the erection of the building. What holds good for our earthly experience is assumed to have its counterpart in the experience of the Creator. Philo (*de Mundi opific.* 4. i. M. 4, C.W. i. p. 4, § 19) offers a good parallel to the idea of preparing plans prior to the Creation; see also Gen. Rab. I. i. and my *Rabbinic Philosophy and Ethics*, p. 4.

[8] Repentance is the sole condition whereby harmony, divine and human, can obtain, cf. Wisdom xii. 10, 19. On the subject of Repentance see *J.E.* x. 376 ff. Lazarus, *Ethik*, i. pp. 44 f., and Schechter, *Aspects*, see index, *s.v.* "Repentance" and "Penitence," and cf. my *Grace of God*, pp. 30 ff. The second paragraph in the MS. ends here.

[9] This passage is borrowed from T.B. Pesachim, 54a, or T.B. Nedarim, 39b, the order being varied by Repentance coming after the Torah. See also Jalkuṭ on Jeremiah, § 298, and cf. Gen. Rab. i. 4 (Theodor, p. 6 note, *in loc.*) and Tanna de bê Elijahu Rab. xxxi. p. 160, where only six subjects are enumerated. Friedmann (note 33, *in loc.*) points out that by comparing the various readings in Talmud and Midrash we find that there were nine premundane things, cf. Ẓohar, Lev. 34b. It is important to bear in mind, in reading Gen. Rab. i. 4, that of the six premundane things some were actually created and some were only ideally present in the mind of the Creator. The Torah and the Throne of Glory were created, but the patriarchs, Israel, the Temple,

They are: The Torah, Gehinnom, the Garden of Eden,[1] the Throne of Glory, the Temple, Repentance, and the Name of the Messiah.

Whence do we know that this applies to the Torah? Because it is said, "The Lord possessed me [2] in the beginning of his way, before his works *of old*" (Prov. viii. 22). "Of old"[3] means before the world was created.[4] Whence do we know this with regard to the Garden of Eden? Because it is said, "And the Lord God planted a garden *of old*"[5] (Gen. ii. 8). "*Of old*," whilst as yet the world had not been created. Whence do we know this with reference to the Throne of Glory?[6] Because it is said, "Thy throne is established *of old*" (Ps. xciii. 2). "Of old," whilst as yet the world had not been created. Whence do we know

and the Name of the Messiah were only in the thought of God. In the Book of Enoch (Ethiopic) xlviii. 3, the Messiah is said to have had his name named *before* the sun and the signs were created; see my *Hellenism and Christianity*, pp. 15 ff., on the question of the pre-existence of the Messiah, and cf. Assumption of Moses i. 14.

[1] The "Garden of Eden" is usually rendered by the term Paradise. The fact that Gehenna is in juxtaposition to "Gan Eden" would lead one to infer that Paradise was referred to in this context. Our author is probably opposing the view that the Garden of Eden was created on the "third day"; see Jubilees ii. 7.

[2] The verse might be rendered: "The Lord formed me as the beginning of his way." The reference is to Wisdom, which is here personified; see *Hellenism and Christianity*, pp. 64 ff. Christianity under the influence of Alexandrian Jewish thought identified Wisdom with its Messiah, whilst Palestinian Judaism identified Wisdom with the Torah.

[3] The 1st ed. and later editions derive the inference from the word "*before*."

[4] "Whence do we know this with reference to Gehinnom? Because it is said, 'For a Topheth is prepared *of old*' (Isa. xxx. 33). 'Of old' means whilst yet the world had not been created." This paragraph is omitted by the MS., but it occurs in the 1st ed. Topheth was a place in the Hinnom Valley (*i.e.* Ge-henna or Ge-Hinnom) where the hateful and cruel Moloch abominations had been perpetrated; see W. R. Smith, *Religion of the Semites*, p. 357. The Tanna de bê Elijahu Rab., *loc. cit.*, says: "Topheth is nought else but Gehinnom." See also Schwally, *Z.A.T.W.*, 1890, pp. 212 ff.

[5] See R.V. *in loc.* Our Midrashic passage occurs as follows in the Pal. Targum of Gen. ii. 8: "And a garden from the Eden of the just was planted by the Word of the Lord God before the creation of the world." This Haggadah appears also in Jerome; see Diestel, *Geschichte des A.T. in der Christlichen Kirche*, p. 102, and Rahmer, *Die Hebräischen Traditionen in den Werken des Hieronymus*, p. 17. See also 4 Ezra iii. 6, which states: "And thou leddest him (Adam) into Paradise, which thy right hand did plant *before ever* the earth came forward." On Paradise see *J.E.* ix. pp. 516 f.

[6] The Throne of Glory as premundane occurs in Slavonic Enoch xxv. 4, where God says, "And I made for myself a throne . . . and I said to the light," etc.; see LXX Prov. viii. 27.

that Repentance (was premundane)? Because it is said, "*Before* the mountains were brought forth, or ever thou hadst formed the earth and the world" (*ibid.* xc. 2);[1] and then in close proximity (we read), "Thou turnest man to contrition" (*ibid.* 3). "Before," *i.e.* before || the world was created. Whence do we know this with regard to the Temple? Because it is said, "A glorious throne, set on high *from the beginning*, is the place of our *sanctuary*" (Jer. xvii. 12). "From the beginning," whilst as yet the world had not been created.[2] Whence we do know that the name of the Messiah (was premundane)? Because it is said, "His name shall endure for ever; before the sun Yinnôn was his name" (Ps. lxxii. 17).[3] "Yinnôn," before the world had been created. Another verse says, "But thou, Bethlehem Ephrathah,[4] which art to be least among the thousands of Judah, from thee shall he come forth unto me who is to be ruler over Israel; whose ancestry belongs to the *past*, even to the days of old[5]" (Mic. v. 2). "The past,"[6] whilst as yet the world had not been created.

Forthwith[7] the Holy One, blessed be He, took counsel with the Torah whose name is Tushijah (Stability or Wisdom) with reference to the creation of the world. (The Torah) replied and said to Him: Sovereign of the worlds!

[1] The translation in the Revised Version might be consulted, in order to see how the Midrashic point of view, based on a literal translation, agrees with or differs from the ordinary interpretation. In the 1st ed. this section follows that dealing with the Temple.

[2] The premundane or Heavenly Temple was known to the writer of the Epistle to the Hebrews, ix. 11, who speaks of the "greater and more perfect tabernacle, not made with hands, that is to say, *not of this creation.*" See Wisdom ix. 8, and Odes of Solomon iv. 3. Maimonides, *Guide* I. ix., discusses our theme. See also Menorath Ha-Maor, Introduction to the fourth book, where we are cautioned not to take the words in this passage in their literal meaning.

[3] The R.V. reads: "His name shall be continued as long as (or, "before") the sun." For Yinnôn as a Messianic name see T.B. Synhedrin, 98b, and *infra*, p. 233. The Midrashic interpretation in our text occurs already in LXX, *in loc.*: "His name endures *before* the sun."

[4] The rest of the quotation is missing in the MS.

[5] This quotation, a second one to justify the idea that the name of the Messiah was premundane, is omitted by the Menorath Ha-Maor, *loc. cit.* It is not given by the Talmud. On this verse in Micah see *Hellenism and Christianity*, pp. 5 f.

[6] "The past" is the same word which was rendered "of old" (Gen. ii. 8) quoted above.

[7] In the MS. the fourth paragraph begins here. On the theme see Wisdom ix. 9 f.

if there be no host for the king [1] and if there be no camp for the king, over whom does he rule? If there be no people to praise the king, where is the honour of the king? The Holy One, blessed be He, heard this and it pleased Him. The Torah spake: The Holy One, blessed be He, took counsel with me concerning the creation of the world, as it is said, "Counsel is mine, and sound knowledge; [2] I am understanding; I have might" (Prov. viii. 14). Hence they [3] say, Every government which has no counsellors is not a proper government.[4] Whence do we know this? From the government of the House of David which employed counsellors, as it is said, "And Jonathan David's uncle [5] was a counsellor, a man of understanding, and a scribe" (1 Chron. xxvii. 32). If the government of the House of David had counsellors, how much more so should other people act likewise. This is of benefit to them, as it is said, "But he that hearkeneth unto counsel is wise" (Prov. xii. 15), || and (Scripture) says, "But in the multitude of counsellors there is safety" (*ibid.* xi. 14).

Eight [6] things were created on the first day, namely,

[1] This is quoted in Ginzberg's *Geonica*, ii. p. 88.

[2] The idea of Wisdom or the Torah being with God prior to the Creation is generally assumed to be expressed in the famous passage verses 22–31 of this eighth chapter of Proverbs. This is, however, a mistaken view; see *Hellenism and Christianity*, pp. 65 ff. The source is rather to be found in the LXX Prov. viii. 30. Our Midrashic passage is based on Gen. Rab. I. i.; see also Jalkuṭ on Prov. viii. 14, § 941, and see Bacher, P. i. p. 107 (note), who refers to the parallel in Philo.

[3] The 1st ed. reads: "The wise men."

[4] Might one infer from this passage that the writer of *P.R.E.* was living in a land where the régime was not conducted in accordance with the rule laid down? Perhaps the reference is to the rule of the Mohammedans in Palestine, Egypt, or Babylon.

[5] The 1st and 2nd eds. have the reading "the son of David." This is an error.

[6] The fifth paragraph in the MS. begins here. These eight things are almost identical with the seven things enumerated in Jubilees ii. 2, if "the abysses" of the latter correspond to the "Chaos and Void" of our text. See Jeraḥmeel i. 3, which is based on our text. This suggested identification seems to be warranted by the fact that Philo (*loc. cit.* 7) agrees with the enumeration in our text and Jubilees in the following six objects of creation: heaven, earth, darkness, water, spirit, and light. As the seventh object created on the first day he gives the abyss. This is also the reading in the Midrash Tadsheh vi., where Tehomoth=abyss. It seems that Philo knew a cosmology which was known to Jubilees, to Midrash Tadsheh, and to our author; see Charles, *Jubilees*, pp. 11 f. T.B. Chagigah, 12a, which gives appropriate quotations to support the view enunciated, enumerates ten things as being created on the first day. Neither the Talmud nor *P.R.E.*

Heaven, Earth, Light, Darkness, Tohu (Chaos), Bohu (Void), Wind (or Spirit), and Water, as it is said, "And the *wind* of God was moving upon the face of the *waters*" (Gen. i. 2).[1]

mention Tehomoth, which is the equivalent to abyss, but they both have Tohu and Bohu.

[1] רוח can mean *wind* or *spirit*; Gen. i. 2 might be rendered, "And a mighty wind." Is there any ancient Rabbinic authority for the translation in the R.V., "the spirit of God"? See Bacher, T. i. p. 424, and cf. Philo, ed. Cohn, G.T. i. p. 36, n. 3. The following section first appeared in the 2nd ed. (Venice, 1544) of *P.R.E.*:

"Some (wise men) say that day and night also,[1] as it is said, 'And there was evening and morning, one day' (Gen. i. 5).

"Eight things were created on the second day, namely, the Well,[2] the Manna,[3] the Rod,[4] the Rainbow,[5] the art of writing, the written characters,[6] the Garments,[7] and the destroying spirits.[8]

"Ten things arose in the thought (of the Creator),[9] namely, Jerusalem,[10] the spirits of the patriarchs,[11] the paths of the righteous,[12]

---

[1] This is based on T.B. Chagigah, *loc. cit.*, which refers to the "measure of the day and the measure of the night"; cf. Jubilees ii. 2.

[2] For the Well, see Num. xxi. 16 ff.; see also Pirkê Aboth v. 9, with Taylor's note, p. 84. Cf. Pal. Targum, Num. xxii. 28. There seems to be considerable confusion here, because, according to Aboth (*loc. cit.*), all the things enumerated in our text except the Garments were created at twilight just before the first Sabbath. This tradition is recorded by our book, *infra*, pp. 124 f.; see also T.B. Pesachim, *loc. cit.*

[3] On the Manna, see *Rabbinic Philosophy and Ethics*, pp. 185 ff.

[4] On the Rod, see Ex. iv. 17, and cf. Abrahams, *The Rod of Moses*, the Book of Jashar, lxvii., and *infra*, p. 312.

[5] On the Rainbow, see Gen. ix. 13.

[6] On the art of writing and the characters of the script, see Löw, *Graphische Requisiten und Erzeugnisse bei den Juden*, p. 3 and note 9, where we learn that the text should be rendered, "the writing and the instrument employed in writing." The writing on the tablets is mentioned in Ex. xxxii. 16.

[7] The Garments were those worn by Adam and Eve; see Gen. iii. 21, and the Book of Jashar, vii.; the subject will arise in a later section of our book. The Church also has its legends dealing with the seamless tunic of its Founder.

[8] On the Mazzikin or evil spirits, see *J.E.* iv. 514 ff., and cf. T.B. Pesachim, *loc. cit.*, and Siphrê, Deut. § 355, n. 10, for the source of the entire paragraph.

[9] Here again we have a text which is faulty, inasmuch as Gehenna and the Temple were reckoned among the premundane creation. The writer has confused the tradition about the ten things created on the eve of the first Sabbath at twilight with the premundane creation. See Pal. Targ. Gen. ii. 2 and Aboth v. 9.

[10] The ideal heavenly Jerusalem of the O.T. (see Isa. xlix. 16) is known also to the writers of the New Testament; see Gal. iv. 26 and Rev. iii. 12. The Jerahmeel MS. reads: "the *place* of the Temple." See also Apoc. Baruch iv. 3, and Test. XII Pat., Dan v. 12.

[11] See Hos. ix. 10, where the emphasis is to be put on the words "first season" according to Gen. Rab. i. 4.

[12] For the expression see Prov. iv. 18, and cf. Gen. Rab. ii. 5.

Whence were the heavens created? From the light of the garment with which He was robed.[1] He took (of this light) and stretched it like a garment and (the heavens) began to extend continually until He caused them to hear, "It is sufficient."[2] Therefore is He called God Almighty (*El Shaddai*), who said to the world:[3] "*It is sufficient,*" and it stood (firm). Whence do we know that the heavens were created from the light of His garment? Because it is said, "Who coverest thyself with light as with a garment; who stretchest out the heavens like a curtain" (Ps. civ. 2).[4]

Whence was the earth created? He took of the snow[5]

Gehinnom,[1] the waters of the Flood,[2] the second tables of the Law,[3] the Sabbath,[4] the Temple,[5] the Ark,[6] and the light of the world to come."[7]

This reading occurs in Jeraḥmeel i. 3, 4, but not in the B.M. MS. of *P.R.E.* The latter continues: "Whence was the water created? From the light of the garment of the Holy One, blessed be He. Light signifies nought else but water, as it is said, 'He spreadeth abroad the cloud of his light'" (Job xxxvii. 11).

[1] See Ex. Rab. L. i. The idea of this Midrash is that God created the heavens without any help from any intermediary. God alone is the Creator. "The light of His robe" means His will or favour. The world has been created by Divine love and favour for the benefit of mankind, the children of the Heavenly Father.

[2] See T.B. Chagigah, *loc. cit.*, "This is what Resh Laḳish also said: What is the meaning of the words 'I am God Almighty' (*Shaddai*)? It means I am He who (*Sha*) said to the world, 'It is sufficient' (*dai*)."

[3] The printed editions read: "to the heavens."

[4] The second half of the verse is omitted in the MS. The fifth paragraph ends here. Cf. also Ps. cii. 25, 26. The Church Fathers discussed the creation narrative in much the same way as our author: thus Athanasius in his exposition of the 103rd Psalm (corresponding to the Hebrew 104th Psalm) refers to the formation of the heavens in the terms of the Old Testament writers; see also Basil, *Hexæmeron*, iii.

[5] See D. H. Joël, *op. cit.* pp. 321 ff., where a full discussion of this passage is given and the views of Maimonides and the theories of the Cabbalists are examined.

---

[1] On the fire of Gehenna see *infra*, p. 20. Luria suggests that the text should be emended so as to read, "the paths of the wicked," to correspond with the expression "paths of the righteous."

[2] In the days of Noah; see Gen. Rab. ii. 3.

[3] See Ex. xxxiv. 1: "Hew thee two tables of stone like unto *the first*." The first tables were of heavenly origin (cf. *ibid.* xxxii. 16), so also the second.

[4] Jubilees ii. 30 offers a parallel to our text, "We kept Sabbath in the heavens before it was made known to any flesh to keep Sabbath thereon on the earth."

[5] See 1 Kings viii. 13, and cf. *supra*, p. 12, note 2.

[6] Of the Sanctuary; see Num. Rab. iv. 13. According to the Midrash, the Ark represents the Throne of Glory.

[7] See T.B. Chagigah, *loc. cit.*, and *Rabbinic Philosophy and Ethics*, p. 8 and note 3.

(or ice) which was beneath His Throne of Glory and threw it upon the waters, and the waters became congealed so that the dust of the earth was formed, as it is said, "He saith to the snow, Be thou earth" (Job xxxvii. 6).[1]

The hooks [2] of the heavens are fixed in the waters of the ocean.[3] The waters of the ocean are situated between the ends of the heavens and the ends of the earth. The ends of the heavens are spread out over the waters of the ocean, as it is said, "Who layeth the beams of his chambers [4] in the waters" (Ps. civ. 3).[5]

The dome (or inside shape) of the heavens ascends upwards like a tub,[6] (that is to say) like a tent (*denda*) which is spread out [7] with its extremities (fixed) || downwards [8] and its dome stretching upwards so that people can sit beneath it and their feet stand on the earth, whilst all of them are inside the tent; in like wise are the heavens, their extremities are (fixed) downwards and their dome stretches upwards

[1] See Tanchuma (Buber) Miḳez, 16. Our text seems to be based upon T.J. Chagigah, ii. 1. 77a, according to which the world was originally "Water in water." Then God made the water into snow (or ice); see Ps. cxlvii. 16, 17. This psalm in verse 15 speaks of God sending out "his commandment upon (the) earth; his word runneth very swiftly"—pointing to the word of creation. See Bacher, P. iii. 218. The verse quoted from Job (xxxvii. 6) is rendered by the R.V., "He saith to the snow, Fall thou on the earth." See also Sepher Jezirah i. 11 for a parallel. See Isa. xl. 12 for the reference to the "dust of the earth," and cf. T.B. Joma, 54b; Maimonides, *Guide*, ii., xxvi., and Midrash Kônen, ed. Jellinek, *B.H.M.* ii. p. 24. This concludes the seventh paragraph. The sixth paragraph is not marked in the MS.

[2] Ḳurḳos (κίρκος), ring or hook. The heaven's being compared with a curtain are assumed to have hooks or rings wherewith they may be fastened; see Tosaphoth Chagigah, 12a, catchword "From the end." The 'Arukh (ed. Kohut, vii. 215b) quotes our text.

[3] Oḳeanos (ὠκεανός). The Church Fathers dwell on the relation between the Ocean and the world; thus Chrysostomus, *Homilies on the Epistle to the Romans* (xxviii.), quotes Ps. civ. 6 in this connection. Cf. Augustine, *de Civitate Dei*, xii. 12. John of Damascus, *On the Orthodox Faith*, ii. 9, tells us, "The Ocean flows around the entire earth like a river." See Test. Levi ii. 7, "And I entered from the first heaven, and I saw there a great sea hanging." Cf. also Jubilees ii. 4.

[4] *i.e.* the heavens.

[5] The eighth paragraph ends here.

[6] Or, basket. The MS. uses the word *denda* (tent), which occurs again, *infra*, p. 323; this points to Spain as the home of the scribe who wrote our MS. On the "tent" see T.J. Berakhoth, 2c, d, and Baraitha d. Shemuel, i. The word which is translated by "tub" occurs only in our MS.

[7] The MS. adds: "like a tent."

[8] The 1st ed. reads "upwards"; in this paragraph there are several variants in the MSS. and the printed texts.

and all creatures dwell beneath them as in a tent, as it is said, "And he spreadeth them out as a tent to dwell in" (Isa. xl. 22).[1]

Four quarters[2] have been created in the world; the quarter facing the east, that facing the south, that facing the west and that facing the north. From the quarter facing the east the light goeth forth to the world.[3] From the quarter facing south the dews of blessing and the rains of blessing[4] go forth to the world.[5] From the quarter facing west[6] where are the treasuries[7] of snow and the treasuries of hail, and thence come forth into the world cold and heat and rains. From the quarter facing north darkness goeth forth into the world. The quarter facing north He created, but He did not complete it, for He said, Anyone who says: I am a God, let him come and complete this quarter which I have left (incomplete) and all will know that he is a God.[8]

There (in the north) is the abode of the destroying spirits, earthquakes, winds, demons, lightnings and thunders; thence evil issues forth into the world, as it is said, "Out of the north evil shall break forth upon all the inhabitants of the earth" (Jer. i. 14).[9] Some say by ten Sayings was

[1] This verse is also applied by Basil, *op. cit.* i. 8, in his account of the form of the heavens.

[2] רוח (as in Ezek. xlii. 16–20) = direction or quarter of the world; wind would not be appropriate here. Gaster, Jerahmeel i. 7, renders the word "wind" and also "corner." On the four quarters see Ethiopic Enoch lxxvii. 1, Num. Rab. ii. 10, and Pesikta Rabbathi, § xlvi. p. 188a.

[3] See T.B. Baba Bathra, 25a, b.

[4] See Ezek. xxxiv. 26.

[5] The rains which are not a blessing come from the north; see *infra*, note 9.

[6] Eth. Enoch lxxvii. 2: "And the west quarter is named the diminished, because there all the luminaries of the heaven wane and go down." In Num. Rab., *loc. cit.*, the reading is slightly different: "In the west are the treasuries of snow, and the treasuries of hail, cold, and heat go forth to the world . . . from the north cometh forth darkness to the world."

[7] See T.B. Chagigah, 12b, and cf. Eth. Enoch xli. 3 ff. The conception rests on Job xxxviii. 22. All the powers of nature were supposed to dwell in their respective chambers or to be stored up in treasuries.

[8] This seems to point to polemics. Probably the Gnostic doctrine of the Demiurge is attacked here. For other polemics in our book, see *infra*, pp. 79, 85 f., and 252. See also Ascension of Isaiah iv. 6.

[9] In the MS. the tenth paragraph ends here. Cf. Jubilees ii. 2. Origen, *de Principiis*, ii. viii. 3, quotes Jer. i. 14, and identifies the

the world created[1] || and in three (Divine attributes) are these (ten Sayings) comprised,[2] as it is said, "The Lord by wisdom founded the earth; by understanding he established the heavens, by his knowledge the depths were broken up" (Prov. iii. 19, 20). By these three (attributes) was the Tabernacle made, as it is said, "And I have filled him with the spirit of God, with wisdom, with understanding, and with knowledge" (Ex. xxxi. 3). Likewise with these three (attributes) was the Temple made, as it is said, "He[3] was the son of a widow woman of the tribe of Naphtali, and his father was a man of Tyre, a worker in brass; and he was filled with wisdom and understanding and knowledge" (1 Kings vii. 14). By these three attributes it will be rebuilt in the future, as it is said, "Through wisdom is an house[4] builded; and by understanding it is established; and by knowledge are the chambers filled" (Prov. xxiv. 3, 4).

With these three attributes will the Holy One, blessed be He, give three good gifts to Israel in the future, as it is

"north" with "the cold north wind," which is the "Devil." For Rabbinic references to the winds see T.B. Baba Bathra, *loc. cit.*; and cf. Num. Rab., *loc. cit.*, as a parallel to our text. Jeraḥmeel MS. omits the rest of this chapter.

[1] Our text reappears in the Ẓohar, Lev. 11a. See Pirḳê Aboth v. 1, and Taylor's note, p. 78 of his 2nd edition. Cf. T.B. Rosh Ha-Shanah, 32a, where the first verse of Genesis is reckoned as one of the ten sayings owing to verse 6 of Ps. xxxiii. The Venice edition adds the following, namely: (1) "And God said, Let there be light" (Gen. i. 3). (2) "And God said, Let there be a firmament" (*ibid.* 6). (3) "And God said, Let the waters be gathered together" (*ibid.* 9). (4) "And God said, Let the earth put forth grass" (*ibid.* 11). (5) "And God said, Let there be luminaries" (*ibid.* 14). (6) "And God said, Let the waters bring forth abundantly" (*ibid.* 20). (7) "And God said, Let the earth bring forth" (*ibid.* 24). (8) "And God said, Let us make man" (*ibid.* 26). (9) "And God said, Behold, I have given you" (*ibid.* 29). (10) "And God[1] said, It is not good that the man should be alone" (*ibid.* ii. 18).

[2] Perhaps the translation should be: By three (Divine attributes) were (the works of creation) completed. The Venice edition adds: "And they are, Wisdom, Understanding, and Knowledge." On these three attributes see T.B. Berakhoth, 55a, and Midrash Shocher Ṭob, Ps. l. 1, and Buber's note (4), where the sources are given. This Midrash may help us to understand our text: "With three names did the Holy One, blessed be He, create His world, corresponding to the three good attributes through which the world was created."

[3] Hiram, the builder of Solomon's Temple.

[4] The *House* is a common designation of the Temple, see Jastrow, *Targum Dictionary*, p. 168a.

---

[1] The Hebrew text in Genesis reads, "Lord God."

said, "For the Lord will give[1] wisdom, out of his mouth cometh knowledge and understanding" (*ibid.* ii. 6).[2] It is not said, "The Lord has given wisdom." These three attributes will be given[3] to King Messiah, as it is said, "And the spirit of the Lord shall rest upon him, the spirit of wisdom and understanding, the spirit of counsel and might, the spirit of knowledge and of the fear of the Lord" (Isa. xi. 2).[4]

[1] The next sentence should precede the rest of the quotation if we follow the order of the words in the MS. It is omitted in the printed editions.

[2] See Jalḳuṭ, Prov. § 935, where attention is drawn to the verb "will give" in the imperfect tense indicating the future. This point is lost sight of in the R.V.; see also Ex. Rab. xli. 3, and cf. T.B. Berakhoth, 5a.

[3] The 1st ed. adds "in double measure"; this has been adopted by later editions.

[4] This famous passage from Isaiah is quoted by Justin Martyr in his *Dialogue with Trypho*, lxxxvii., as referring to the Messiah.

CHAPTER IV

THE CREATION ON THE SECOND DAY [4A. i.]

ON the second day [1] the Holy One, blessed be He, created the firmament,[2] the angels,[3] fire for flesh and blood,[4] and the fire of Gehinnom.[5] Were not heaven and earth created on the first day, as it is said, "In the beginning God created [6] the heaven and the earth" (Gen. i. 1)? Which firmament

[1] See Jalkuṭ, Gen. § 5, and Jalkuṭ, Ezek. § 338.

[2] According to Jubilees ii. 4, the firmament *only* was created on the second day; see Slav. Enoch xxvi.–xxvii.

[3] In Gen. Rab. i. 3 and iii. 8, the question is discussed as to which day of the week of creation were the angels called into being. According to R. Jochanan it was the second day, as in our text, whereas according to R. Chanina it was the fifth day. Theodor (*in loc.*) gives the various parallel sources in notes 7 and 8. See also Pal. Targum on Gen. i. 26, where the creation of the angels is also assigned to the second day, as in Slavonic Enoch xxix. 1 ff. In Jubilees ii. 2 this event is said to have been on the *first* day; see Charles' note 2 on pp. 12 f. Our book opposes this view. The Church Fathers sometimes held this view; see Epiphanius, *adv. Hær.* lxv. 4. The Rabbis were fully aware of the teaching that God was assisted at the creation by angels or the Messiah, and in order to oppose such doctrine the creation of the angels was fixed on the second or fifth day; cf. Ex. Rab. xv. 22.

[4] See T.B. Pesachim, 54a, and Gen. Rab. xi. 2 for the view that this fire was created at the termination of the first Sabbath. As the angels are often of fire (cf. Rev. xiv. 18), both angels and fire are held by our author to have been created on the second day. This view is held in spite of the statement that *light* was created on the first day.

[5] The fire of Gehenna is mentioned in the New Testament; see Matt. v. 22, and cf. Rev. xx. 10. See also Eth. Enoch xc. 24 and 26, the Apocalypse of Baruch lix. 10, 11, and the Apocalypse of Peter for an account of Gehenna. The 21st book of Augustine's *de Civitate Dei* is devoted to this theme. The Rabbis came to the conclusion that the fire of Gehenna must have been created on the second day, because the Scripture does not say with reference to this day "and it was good," which, however, does occur in the story of the other five days of creation; see T.B. Pesachim, 54a, Ex. Rab. xv. 22, and Jalkuṭ, Gen. § 15.

[6] The MS. omits the rest of the verse; it is given in the 1st ed. and subsequent editions.

was created on the second day? Rabbi Eliezer said: || It was the firmament which is above the heads of the four Chajjôth (living creatures),[1] (as it is said[2]), "And over the head of the Chajjôth there was the likeness of a firmament, like the colour of the terrible crystal"[3] (Ezek. i. 22). What is the meaning of (the expression), "like the colour of the terrible crystal"? It means like precious stones and pearls; it illuminates all the heavens like a lamp which is illuminating[4] the whole house and like the sun which is shining with maximum intensity at noonday, as it is said, "The light dwelleth with him" (Dan. ii. 22);[5] and like this in the future will the righteous shed light,[6] as it is said, "And they that be wise shall shine as the brightness of the firmament" (*ibid.* xii. 3).[7] Were it not for that firmament the world would be engulfed by the waters above it and below it;[8] but (the firmament) divides the waters (above) from the waters (below), as it is said, "And God said, Let there be a firmament in the midst of the waters, (and let it divide the waters from the waters)"[9] (Gen. i. 6), it illuminates[10] between the waters above and the waters below.[11]

(As for) the angels created on the second[12] day, when they are sent (as messengers) by His word they are changed into winds, and when they minister before Him they are changed into fire, as it is said, "Who

[1] On the Chajjôth, see T.B. Chagigah, 13a, and Hastings' *Dictionary of the Bible*, iii. 128 f. The Chajjôth are to be identified with the "creature" of Rev. iv. 7. Do they correspond with the angels of the presence of Jubilees ii. 2? The firmament implies the division between the upper and lower waters; see Midrash Kônen (Jellinek, *B.H.M.* ii. p. 25).

[2] "As it is said" occurs in the printed texts.

[3] Or "ice."

[4] This is also the reading in B.M. MS. See also Jalkuṭ to Ezek. *loc. cit.*, and cf. Eth. Enoch xiv. 9 ff.

[5] The second paragraph in MS. begins here.

[6] Cf. Matt. xiii. 43, Eth. Enoch xxxix. 7 f., and Ascension of Isaiah viii. 22.

[7] This section is quoted by Tosaphoth, T.B. Baba Bathra, 8b, catchword, "Umazdiḳê."

[8] Perhaps the translation should be: "by the waters, for above it are waters and beneath it are waters." This is practically the text in the printed editions. See Pal. Targum, Gen. i. 6.

[9] This part of the verse in brackets is wanting in the MS.

[10] The 1st ed. reads: "it divides."

[11] The second paragraph ends here.

[12] B.M. MS. reads: "first day."

maketh his angels winds; his ministers a flaming fire" (Ps. civ. 4).[1]

Four [2] classes of ministering angels minister and utter praise [3] before the Holy One, blessed be He: the first camp (led by) Michael [4] on His right, the second camp (led by) Gabriel [5] on His left, the third camp || (led by) Uriel [6] before Him, and the fourth camp (led by) Raphael [7] behind Him; and the Shekhinah of the Holy One, blessed be He, is in the centre. He [8] is sitting on a throne high and exalted.[9] His throne is high and suspended above in the air. The appearance of His Glory is like the colour of amber.[10] And the adornment of a crown is on His head, and the Ineffable Name [11] is upon His forehead.[12] One half (of His glory) is fire the other half is hail,[13] at His right hand is life and at His

[1] This verse is quoted by many of the Church Fathers in order to describe the nature of the angels; see John of Damascus, *op. cit.* ii. 3. The MS. quotes only the first half of the verse. The entire verse is given by the first editions. The third paragraph ends here.

[2] The New Testament refers to the four living creatures before God's throne; see Rev. iv. 6. The whole of this chapter is a parallel to our text.

[3] The printed texts omit "minister and."

[4] The Midrash here has given rise to a passage in the Hebrew prayer-book; see Singer, p. 297. See also Num. Rab. ii. 10, Midrash Kônen, p. 27, and Pesiḳta Rabbathi, § xlvi. p. 188a. On Michael see the valuable monograph by Leuken, and *J.E.* viii. 535 ff. As parallels to our text see Targum to Job xxv. 2, and Eth. Enoch xl. 9 and lxxi. 8 f., which mentions the four archangels in the following order: Michael, Raphael, Gabriel, and Phanuel; in this Book of Enoch (ix. 1) the angel Uriel appears to be the same as Phanuel. In the N.T. we find Michael and Gabriel mentioned. The B.M. MS. reads here Gabriel in place of Michael, and Michael instead of Gabriel.

[5] See *J.E.* v. 540 f.

[6] See *J.E.* xii. 383.

[7] See *J.E.* x. 317 f.

[8] *i.e.* God.

[9] This sentence is omitted by the B.M. MS. The words are found in the Sabbath Morning Liturgy, Singer, p. 126, last two lines. See Eth. Enoch xiv. 18.

[10] The B.M. MS. adds: "One-half thereof is fire and the other half is hail." In our MS. the fourth paragraph ends here. The 1st ed., followed by subsequent editions, adds: "As it is said: 'And I saw as the colour of amber'" (Ezek. i. 27).

[11] The 1st ed. reads: "A crown is set on His head, and the diadem of the Ineffable Name is upon His forehead." On the *Shem Hammephorash* or "Ineffable Name" see G. Klein, *Der älteste Christliche Katechismus*, pp. 44 ff., and *supra*, p. 10, note 2.

[12] This passage is the source for the words: "Upon His forehead is impressed the glory of His holy name" in the Hymn of Glory; see Singer, p. 79. The Venice edition adds: "and His eyes run to and fro throughout the whole earth."

[13] Fire and hail represent the two divine attributes of justice and love; see Ẓohar, Gen. 186a, and cf. Eth. Enoch xiv. 20. The B.M. MS. omits these words in this context.

left is death. He has a sceptre of fire in His hand and a veil[1] is spread before Him, and His eyes run to and fro throughout the whole earth,[2] and the seven angels,[3] which were created first,[4] minister before Him within the veil, and this (veil) is called Pargod.[5] His footstool is like fire and hail.[6] Fire is flashing continually around His throne,[7] righteousness and judgment are the foundation of His throne.[8] And the likeness of His throne is like a sapphire throne with four legs,[9] and the four holy Chajjôth are fixed to each leg, each one[10] has four faces and each one

[1] See Coptic Apocrypha, p. 90, and Eth. Enoch xiv. 21.

[2] Cf. 2 Chron. xvi. 9.

[3] The seven angels or archangels are referred to in the Book of Enoch (Eth.), ch. xx.; see Charles' notes, *in loc.*, for further references.

[4] The printed texts read: "Since the beginning." Does our book here agree with Jubilees ii. 2?

[5] פרגוד (Παραγαῦδος); see T.B. Berakhoth, 18b, and T.B. Chagigah, 15a, the veil which separates the Shekhinah from the angels; see Rashi on T.B. Jebamoth, 63b, catchword, גוף (body). The B.M. MS. reads here: "The seven angels which were created at the beginning, minister before the veil which is spread before Him." See Coptic Apoc., p. 254, Eth. Enoch xc. 21; Rev. iv. 5; and T.B. Baba Mezi'a, 59a.

[6] The Footstool of God represents Divine Justice and Love, which in their turn are symbolised by fire and hail; cf. Lam. ii. 1, "He did not remember his *footstool* in the day of his *anger*." The 1st ed. of our text reads: "His footstool is fire and hail flashing around His throne." See Slav. Enoch xxxvii. 1.

[7] See Ps. xcvii. 3. Origen, *contra Celsum*, iv. 13, discusses the fiery nature of God.

[8] The Venice and Sabbioneta editions insert the following: "and the seven clouds of glory[1] surround it. And the whirling Ophan[2] and the Cherub and the Chajjah (living creature) are uttering praise before Him."[3]

[9] Cf. T.B. Chagigah, 13a.

[10] See Ezek. x. 14. On the Cherubim see Maimonides, *Guide*, iii. 1 ff. and cf. *ibid.* ch. xlv., and Hastings' *Dictionary of the Bible*, i. 377 ff., where the N.T. and Patristic references are given. Speaking generally, the Patristic literature has much more to say concerning angels, good and bad, than Rabbinic literature. This can be easily seen by comparing the references in Eisenmenger's *Entdecktes Judentum* or in Weber's *Jüdische Theologie* on the one hand and the index to Thalhofer's *Bibliothek der Kirchenväter*, i. pp. 226–229, on the other. The state-

---

[1] On the seven clouds of glory, see Mekhilta, 24b, based on Ps. cv. 39, and cf. *J.E.* iv. 123. The number 7 is in harmony with the notion of 7 heavens, 7 rivers around the Holy Land, the 7 planets (T.B. Baba Bathra, 74b), 7 portals to Gehenna, the 7 archangels, etc.; and cf. *infra*, p. 140. Eth. Enoch lxxvii. 4–8 speaks of 7 mountains, 7 rivers, and 7 islands. See also Ps. xcvii. 2.

[2] Ophan (or wheel) occurs in Ezek. x. 13; this is identified by *P.R.E.* with the Galgal (גלגל) or whirling wheel.

[3] See Ezek. i. 24 and iii. 12 f. with Targum. The B.M. MS. adds here: "They are the Cherubim."

has four wings, as it is said, "And every one had four faces and four wings" (Ezek. i. 6), and these (Chajjôth) are the Cherubim.

When[1] He || speaks towards the west He speaks between the two Cherubim with the face of the ox, when He speaks towards the north He speaks between the two Cherubim with the face of an eagle.

Over against them[2] are the Ophanim (Wheels) and the Whirling Wheels of the Chariot,[3] and when He looketh

ment on the subject in Hastings' *Dictionary of Christ and the Gospels*, i. 57, "The Jews believed all that the N.T. says of angels, but they also believed much more," needs revision. The Church is more concerned with angels in its liturgy and ritual than the Synagogue.

[1] The first editions add the following: "when He speaks towards the east He speaks between the two Cherubim with the face of a man, and when He speaks towards the south He speaks between the two Cherubim with the face of a lion." See Ezek. i. 10. The scheme indicated seems to be as follows:—

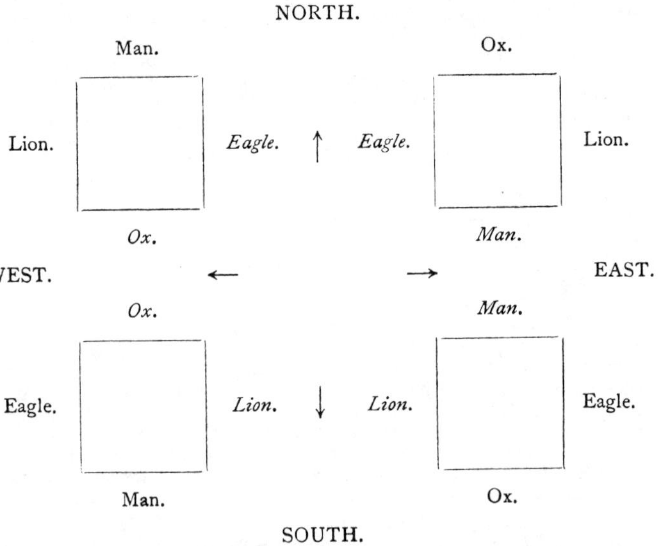

[2] The Cherubim.

[3] The Merkabah (מרכבה) or Chariot is described in Ezek. i. and x. See T.B. Chagigah, 14b, Maimonides, *Guide*, iii. 1–7, and cf. Ecclus. xlix. 8, and *J.E.* viii. 498 ff. The mystery of the Chariot is also referred to by Eth. Enoch xiv. 18, and Origen, *contra Celsum*, vi. 18. See also Hastings' *Dictionary of the Bible*, i. 377 f. and v. 644. The Venice edition adds: "When He sits He is upon the throne high and exalted."

upon the earth His chariots are upon the Ophanim, and owing to the noise caused by the whirling wheels of the Chariot—lightnings and thunder go forth into the world.[1] When He dwells [2] in heaven He rideth upon a swift cloud.[3] When He hastens He flies upon the wings of the wind, as it is said, " And he rode upon a cherub, and did fly; yea, he flew swiftly upon the wings of the wind " (Ps. xviii. 10).

The Chajjôth stand next to the throne of His glory and they do not know the place of His glory.[4] The Chajjôth stand in awe and dread,[5] in fear and trembling, and from the perspiration of their faces a river of fire arises and goes forth [6] before Him, as it is said, " A fiery stream issued and came forth from before him . . ." (Dan. vii. 10). And the wings of Gallizur [7] the angel, who stands next to the Chajjôth, (are spread forth) so that the fire which consumes the fire of the angels should not burn (them). Two Seraphim stand, one on His right and one on His left, each one has six wings,[8] with twain they cover their face [9] so as not to behold the presence of the Shekhinah, with twain they cover their feet so that they should not be seen before the presence of the Shekhinah, || so that the standing of the foot of the calf [10] might be forgotten. With twain do they fly,

[1] See Ps. lxxvii. 18.

[2] This is omitted in the Cambridge Genizah and in the first editions.

[3] The Venice edition adds: " as it is said, ' And he rode upon a cherub, and did fly ' " (Ps. xviii. 10). A more appropriate quotation would be: " Behold, the Lord rideth upon a swift cloud " (Isa. xix. 1).

[4] This is wanting in the Oxford MS. (d. 35).

[5] A parallel text with deviations occurs in Singer, pp. 38 and 130. See also Liturgy, Second Day of New Year, ed. Heidenheim, p. 36a.

[6] See T.B. Chagigah, 13b; cf. Eth. Enoch lxxi. 6 and xiv. 18f.: " And I looked and saw a lofty throne; its appearance was as *crystal*, and *the wheels* thereof as the shining sun, and there was the vision of *cherubim*. And from underneath the throne came *streams of flaming fire*, so that I could not look thereon." The N.T. speaks of the heavenly throne; see Rev. i. 4, iii. 21, iv. 2; cf. Gen. Rab. lxxviii. 1.

[7] The whole of this sentence is missing in the printed texts. Gallizur, as the name of an angel, occurs in Pesiḳta Rabbathi, § xx. p. 97b; Jeraḥmeel, lii. 8; and Liturgy, Eighth Day of Solemn Assembly, ed. Heidenheim, p. 20b.

[8] The B.M. MS. adds here: " as it is said, ' Above him stood the Seraphim; each one had six wings ' " (Isa. vi. 2).

[9] Our text agrees with the B.M. MS., and this reading has been preserved in Jalḳuṭ on Isaiah, § 404; see also Lev. Rab. xxvii. 3, and Tanchuma, Emor, § viii. The 1st and 2nd eds. read: " With twain does each one cover his face."

[10] The foot of the Cherub was like that of the calf (see Ezek. i. 7); this might recall the sin of the Golden Calf. See T.B. Chagigah, *loc. cit.*

praising and reverencing, and they sanctify.[1] One answers and another calls,[2] one calls and another answers, and they say, "Holy, Holy, Holy, is the Lord of Hosts; the whole earth is full of his glory" (Isa. vi. 3).[3]

The Chajjôth stand at the side of the throne of His glory and they do not know the place of His glory;[4] they respond and say in every place where His glory[5] is, "Blessed be the glory of the Lord from his place" (Ezek. iii. 12). Israel,[6] a nation unique on the earth,[7] declares daily[8] the unity of His great Name, saying, "Hear, O Israel: the Lord is our God, the Lord is one" (Deut. vi. 4). He answers His people Israel and says to them, I am the Lord your God who has delivered[9] you from every trouble.[10]

[1] These words are similar to the first words of the Ḳedushah (Sanctification); see Singer, p. 160, and cf. Ps. lxxxix. 7. The Sephardic Liturgy is somewhat different, its phraseology for this part of the Prayer Book being probably based on Isa. xxix. 23. For the Ḳedushah see Ezek. xxxvi. 23; Isa. vi. 3; Ex. Rab. xv. 6, and Lev. Rab. ii. 8. The Venice edition adds: "His Great Name." The B.M. MS. reads here: "And they stand near the throne of His glory and do not know the place of His glory, as it is said, 'Blessed be the glory of the Lord from his place' (Ezek. iii. 12), and the Chajjôth stand in awe and dread," etc., as above.

[2] See Jalḳuṭ on Isaiah, *loc. cit.*, and T.B. Chullin, 91b, for the angelic sanctification. The Oxford MS. (d. 35) reads: "One calls and they all reply and say."

[3] This is the end of the 7th section in the MS. On the theme see Slav. Enoch xxi. 1.

[4] The reading seems to be corrupt, and should run: "The Chajjôth respond and say," etc. The first part of the sentence has already been given at the beginning of the preceding paragraph.

[5] On the "Glory" see Abelson, *The Immanence of God in Rabbinic Literature*, p. 380 ff. The *Place* of God's glory is identified by *P.R.E.* with the Shekhinah; see *infra*, p. 225, note 9, and cf. Eth. Enoch xxxix. 12–14.

[6] The 9th section in the MS. begins here.

[7] These words occur in the 'Amidah for Sabbath afternoon; see Singer, p. 175.

[8] The Oxford MS. (d. 35) adds: "continually every day twice."

[9] The Oxford MS. (d. 35) reads: "who redeems."

[10] The many parallels in our text to Eth. Enoch xiv. 9–22, and Slav. Enoch xxi. 1 and xxii. 1–3 are noteworthy, and point to the influence which the pseudepigraphic books have had upon our author. The latter part of this chapter is of importance in connection with the liturgy of the Synagogue. We note how the threefold responses of the Ḳedushah are set forth here as the responses of (1) the angels, (2) Israel, and (3) God; compare Singer, pp. 160 f. The writer of the MS. did not end the chapter here, but continued with the next chapter. A later scribe has added in the margin, "Chapter V.," thus agreeing with other MSS. and the printed editions. Our chapter should be compared with the Merkabah Midrashim in the first two volumes of Wertheimer's *Bottê Midrashoth*.

CHAPTER V

THE GATHERING OF THE WATERS [5A. i.]

On the third day [1] all the earth was flat like a plain and the waters covered the surface of all the earth. When the word of the Almighty [2] was uttered, "Let the waters be gathered together" (Gen. i. 9), the mountains and hills arose from the ends of the earth and they were scattered [3] over the surface of all the earth, and valleys were formed over the inner parts of the earth; and the waters were rolled together and gathered into the valleys, as it is said, "And the gathering together of the waters he called seas" (*ibid.* 10).[4] Forthwith the waters became proud [5] and they arose to cover the earth as at first, when the Holy One, blessed be He, rebuked them || and subdued them,[6] and placed them beneath the soles of His feet,[7] and measured them with

[1] Of the week of creation. Our Book agrees here with the Book of Jubilees, which states: "And on the third day He commanded the waters to pass from off the face of the whole earth" (ii. 5). Cf. Ps. civ. 6, according to which the mountains were beneath the water, the surface of which was like a plain.

[2] Jalkut, Gen. § 8, reads: "The Holy One, blessed be He."

[3] The gathering of the waters revealed the hills and valleys which had hitherto been covered by the water.

[4] In the MS. the tenth paragraph (of the fourth chapter) is marked here. For a parallel text see Wertheimer, *op. cit.*, i. p. 6.

[5] The Oxford MS. (d. 35) reads: "The waters became insolent and attempted to ascend to Heaven as at first until He rebuked and subdued them and placed them beneath the soles of His feet, as it is said: 'Who maketh a way in the sea, and a path in the mighty waters'" (Isa. xliii. 16). The first editions agree with our MS.

[6] See Ps. civ. 7, Job xxxviii. 8–10, and Prov. viii. 29. Eth. Enoch offers a parallel: "the sea was created, and as its foundation He set for it *the sand against the time of anger*, and it dare not pass beyond it from the creation of the world unto eternity" (lxix. 18).

[7] See Job ix. 8, Ps. lxxvii. 19, and Shocher Ṭob, Ps. xciii. 5, where our text is preserved; cf. Midrash Kônen, p. 25. The 1st ed. (*P.R.E.*) reads: "and He subdued them beneath the ends of His feet." The

the hollow of His hand[1] that they should neither decrease nor increase. He made the sand as the boundary of the sea, just like a man who makes a fence for his vineyard. When they rise and see the sand before them they return to their former place,[2] as it is said, "Fear ye not me? saith the Lord[3]: will ye not tremble at my presence, which have placed the sand for the bound of the sea?" (Jer. v. 22).

Before the waters were gathered together the depths[4] were created. These are the depths which are beneath the earth; for the earth is spread[5] upon the water like a ship which floats in the midst of the sea, so likewise is the earth spread out over the water, as it is said, "To him that spread forth the earth above the waters . . ." (Ps. cxxxvi. 6). He opened an entrance to the Garden of Eden[6] because thence were planted upon the face of all

Midrash should be compared with Tanchuma, Chuḳḳath, § 1, and see T.B. Baba Bathra, 74b. The subject has been discussed by Jampel in the *Monatsschrift*, 1912, p. 148.

[1] See Isa. xl. 12.

[2] See *Rabbinic Philosophy and Ethics*, p. 10.

[3] The second half of the verse is not given in the MS., which reads "etc."

[4] The Venice edition adds the words "the luminaries" before the words "the depths." This is clearly a mistake.

[5] Jalḳuṭ Makhiri to Psalms (Ps. cxxxvi. 11) reads: "the earth floats upon the depths." The text of this section in the Jalḳuṭ is more correct than the printed editions of *P.R.E.*

[6] This agrees with the Book of Adam and Eve (ed. Malan) I. i.: "And to the north of the garden there is a sea of water." See Jalḳuṭ Makhiri (*loc. cit.*) for a parallel to our text. The Venice edition differs slightly from the 1st ed. and reads: "The entrance to the Garden of Eden opened therein and He brought forth thence plants upon the face of all the earth." This 5th chapter is devoted to the account of the creation on the third day. Thus far we find the following things enumerated: (1) the gathering of the waters, (2) the appearance of the mountains and hills, (3) the transference of the plants and trees from the Garden of Eden, and we shall have (4) an account of the mists and clouds which water the face of the earth. The Book of Jubilees seems to offer a parallel: (1) "And the dry land appeared, and on that day He created for them (2) all the seas according to their separate gathering-places, and all the rivers, and the gathering of the waters in the mountains and on all the earth and all the lakes, (3) and all the dew of the earth, (4) and the seed which is sown, and all sprouting things, and fruit-bearing trees, and trees of the wood, and the Garden of Eden in Eden, and all (plants after their kind). These four great works God created on the third day" (ii. 6, 7). It seems strange that both books in connection with the third day refer to the Garden of Eden, especially as our book has already dealt with this as one of the pre-mundane creations. According to Gen. Rab. xv. 3 the Garden of Eden was created *before* the creation *of man*, who was created on the sixth

the earth all kinds of trees yielding fruit according to their kind, and all kinds of herbs and grass [1] thereof, and in them (was seed), as it is said, "Wherein is the seed thereof, upon the earth" (Gen. i. 11).

He prepared a table for the creatures whilst as yet they were not created,[2] as it is said, "Thou preparest a table before me" (Ps. xxiii. 5). All the fountains arise from the depths to give water to all creatures.[3] Rabbi Joshua said: The diameter [4] of the earth is equal to a journey of sixty years,[5] and one of the depths which is near to Gehinnom bubbles with water and produces water [6] for the delight of the sons of man.

Rabbi Jehudah ‖ said: Once every month ducts [7] rise from the depths to irrigate the face of all the earth, as it is said, "And there went up a *mist* from the earth and watered [8] the whole face of the ground" (Gen. ii. 6).[9] The clouds cause the seas to hear the sound of their waterspouts,[10] and the seas cause the depths to hear the sound of their waterspouts, and the deep calls to the deep to bring up waters to give them to the clouds, as it is said, "Deep

day, whereas Eden was created on the third day. This tradition is preserved in Slavonic Enoch (A and B) xxx. 1 and in the Book of Adam and Eve (ed. Malan), *loc. cit.*

[1] The Venice edition adds: "He planted thereof, and in them was their seed upon the earth."

[2] The reading in the first editions is: "whilst as yet the world was not created." This "table" is not one of the premundane creations; see T.B. Synhedrin, 38a, based on Prov. ix. 1–3, and cf. Lev. Rab. xi. 1. Gregory, Bishop of Nyssa in the fourth century C.E., has a similar Midrash in his work *de Hominis opificio*, 2; see also Slav. Enoch (B) xxx. 1.

[3] See Ps. civ. 10–13.

[4] On this theme see T.B. Pesachim, 94a, and Gen. Rab. iv. 5, and see Theodor's notes on p. 29 of his edition for further parallels.

[5] Oxford MS. (2835, c. 27) reads "five hundred years"; cf. T.J. Berakhoth, 2c; T.B. Chagigah, 12a, and Gen. Rab. vi. 6.

[6] The 1st ed. reads: "and produces delight for the sons of man." On the subject referred to in the text see T.B. Sabbath, 39a.

[7] Our text is preserved in Jalḳuṭ to Psalms (Ps. xlii. § 744). On "Silonoth" (ducts) see Jastrow, T.D. 979b. Gaster, Jerahmeel ii. 5, renders here "rivulets ascend from the depths," etc.

[8] The rest of the verse is not given by the MS., which reads "etc."

[9] The LXX renders this verse: "But a *fountain* ascended out of the earth"; see *Hellenism and Christianity*, p. 25 note.

[10] See Jalḳuṭ Makhiri, Psalms (Ps. xlii. 16), where our text occurs with variant readings; thus, instead of "Zinôrôthiham," which means "their splashing," or "duct," or "spout," we find "Kinôrôthiham" ("their harps").

calleth unto deep at the sound of thy waterspouts" (Ps. xlii. 7).[1]

The clouds draw water from the depths, as it is said, "He causeth the vapours to ascend from the ends[2] of the earth" (*ibid.* cxxxv. 7), and in every place where the King commands them,[3] there they cause rain (to fall), and forthwith the earth becomes fruitful and yields produce like a widow who becomes pregnant through debauchery.[4] But when the Holy One, blessed be He, desires to bless the produce of the earth,[5] and to give provision to the creatures,[6] He opens the good treasuries in heaven and sends rain upon the earth, namely, the fructifying rain,[7] and forthwith the earth becomes fruitful like a bride who conceives from her first husband and produces offspring of blessing, as it is said, "The Lord shall open unto thee his good treasury the heaven"[8] (Deut. xxviii. 12).

[1] See T.B. Ta'anith, 25b, for the application of this verse in connection with the water ceremonies on the Feast of Tabernacles.

[2] Where originally the water was.

[3] See Job xxxvii. 11–13. The rain illustrates the working of Divine Providence; cf. Jer. xiv. 22.

[4] This rain would not be the rain of blessing, cf. T.B. Ta'anith, 6b.

[5] See Ps. lxv. 9, 10, and cf. T.B. Ta'anith, 8b.

[6] This phrase does not occur in the 1st ed. See Ps. cxxxii. 15.

[7] The rain from heaven is full of vitalizing power; see *infra*, pp. 63 and 167. The actual expression in our context is "the masculine waters." Eth. Enoch liv. 8 offers a parallel: "And all the waters shall be joined with the waters, that which is above the heavens is the *masculine*, and the water which is beneath the earth is *feminine*." See Charles' interesting note (8) on p. 107 of his edition, where he quotes T.J. Berakhoth, ix. 2, "the upper water is male and the lower water is female."

[8] The verse continues: "To give the rain of thy land in its season and to bless all the work of thy hand." This is given in the B.M. MS. The 1st ed. and later editions add: "and it is written, 'For as a young man marrieth a virgin, so shall thy sons marry thee'[1] (Isa. lxii. 5), and it is written, 'For as the rain cometh down, and the snow from heaven,[2] . . . and watereth the earth, and maketh it bring forth and bud, and giveth seed to the sower and bread to the eater'" (*ibid.* lv. 10).

---

[1] See T.B. Mo'ed Ḳaṭan, 2a, where this verse is explained as in our context. On "rain" see Hastings' *Dictionary of the Bible*, iv. 195 f., and Krauss, *Talmudische Archäologie*, ii. 149 f. Interesting references to rain occur in Eth. Enoch apart from the quotation given in note above, namely, lx. 21 ff., and in the previous verse "the chambers of the rain" are mentioned.

[2] The latter part of the verse is not given by the printed texts, which merely add "etc."

CHAPTER VI[1]

THE PLANETS; THE COURSE OF THE SUN [5B. i.]

ON the fourth day He connected together[2] the two luminaries,[3] of which one was not greater (in size) than the other.[4] They were equal[5] as regards their height,[6] || qualities,[7] and illuminating powers,[8] as it is said, "And God made *the two great* lights" (Gen. i. 16). Rivalry ensued between them, one said to the other, I am bigger than thou art. The other rejoined, I am bigger than thou art.

What did the Holy One, blessed be He, do,[9] so that there should be peace between them? He made the one larger and the other smaller,[10] as it is said, "The *greater* light to rule the day,[11] and the *lesser* light to rule the night and the stars he also made" (*ibid.*).[12]

[1] In our MS. the fifth chapter begins here.

[2] The B.M. MS. reads here "created." The word in the printed texts means "associated" or "joined." On the legend see Gen. Rab. vi. 3 and T.B. Chullin, 60b, which is translated in *Rabbinic Philosophy and Ethics*, pp. 12 f.; and see Pal. Targum, Gen. i. 16.

[3] The first editions read: "the two great luminaries."

[4] This legend occurs in Eth. Enoch lxxii. 37, "but as regards size they are both equal," and cf. Slavonic Enoch xvi. 7. Our text reads (if taken quite literally): "This one was not greater than that one, and that one was not greater than this one."

[5] The equality was implied in the words of the Scripture, "the two great lights." The Oxford MS. (d. 35) reads: "but the two of them were equal as though they were one."

[6] Above the earth, or firmament. [7] *e.g.* they have the same shape.

[8] The Pal. Targ. Gen. i. 16 offers a parallel here.

[9] The B.M. MS. adds: "to restore peace between them. He made the one smaller because it had slandered its companion." See Gen. Rab. vi. 3.

[10] See T.B. Chullin, *loc. cit.*, and cf. 3 Baruch ix. 7. The Midrash is also preserved in the Machzor Vitry, p. 154, reading of the Sabbath morning liturgy. Cf. Singer, p. 129. See also Baer's '*Abodath Israel*, p. 212, note, for the reading in the Ṭur: "and He diminished (והקטין) the figure of the moon."

[11] The MS. does not give the second half of the verse, it merely reads "etc."

[12] See *Rabbinic Philosophy and Ethics*, pp. 12 f.

All the stars minister[1] to the seven planets,[2] and their names are: Sun, Venus, Mercury, the Moon, Saturn, Jupiter, Mars.[3] The mnemonic of their service is KZNSh ChLM, by night; ChLM KZNSh by day and KLSh ZMChN for the hours of the night; ChNKL ShZM for the hours of the day.[4] On the first day Mercury and the Sun, on the second day Jupiter and the Moon, on the third day Venus and Mars, on the fourth day Saturn and Mercury, on the fifth day the Sun and Jupiter, on the sixth day the Moon and Venus, on the seventh day Mars and Saturn.[5]

[1] The word in the text may mean *serve*, or *minister to the needs of*, or *to be in attendance on others*, or *to be placed over*, hence to influence, or rule.

[2] Lit. "Stars of the hours." The 1st ed. reads, "the seven stars and all the hours," but subsequent editions read, "the seven stars of the hours." The first editions give the names in the following order: Mercury, the Moon, Saturn, Jupiter, Mars, Sun, and Venus. These editions continue: "And they minister to the seven days of the week." The idea implied is that each planet influences the world for one hour by day and by night. Thus—

							SUNDAY MORNING—		
At 6 o'clock, SATURDAY NIGHT (when the first day of the week begins), MERCURY (K) rules, and again at					1 a.m.	SUNDAY MORNING.	The SUN (Ch) rules at		6 a.m.
SATURDAY,	7 p.m.,	the MOON (L)	rules,	and at	2 ,,		VENUS (N)	,,	7 ,,
,,	8 ,,	SATURN (Sh)	,,	,,	3 ,,		MERCURY (K)	,,	8 ,,
,,	9 ,,	JUPITER (Z)	,,	,,	4 ,,		MOON (L)	,,	9 ,,
,,	10 ,,	MARS (M)	,,	,,	5 ,,		SATURN (Sh)	,,	10 ,,
,,	11 ,,	the SUN (Ch)	,,	,,	6 ,,		JUPITER (Z)	,,	11 ,,
,,	12 ,,	VENUS (N)	,,	,,	7 ,,		MARS (M)	,,	12 noon.

At 6 p.m.	SUNDAY, JUPITER (Z)	rules,	and at	6 a.m.	MONDAY, the MOON (L)	rules.
,,	MONDAY, VENUS (N)	,,	,,	,,	TUESDAY, MARS (M)	,,
,,	TUESDAY, SATURN (Sh)	,,	,,	,,	WEDNESDAY, MERCURY (K)	,,
,,	WEDNESDAY, the SUN (Ch)	,,	,,	,,	THURSDAY, JUPITER (Z)	,,
,,	THURSDAY, the MOON (L)	,,	,,	,,	FRIDAY, VENUS (N)	,,
,,	FRIDAY, MARS (M)	,,	,,	,,	SATURDAY, SATURN (Sh)	,,

The Jewish day begins at 6 p.m. (*i.e.* six hours earlier than the usual time in vogue in this country). For full explanation see Rashi on T.B. Berakhoth, 59b, and on T.B. 'Erubin, 56a. The seven planets are mentioned in the Sepher Jezirah iv. 7 by the same names as in our text. See also Baraitha d. Shemuel, ch. iii.

[3] The seven planets in the order of the text are represented by the following letters: Ch (Sun), N (Venus), K (Mercury), L (Moon), Sh (Saturn), Z (Jupiter), M (Mars). The letters represent the Hebrew names of the planets.

[4] The whole of this sentence is missing in the printed editions.

[5] The seven planets were believed to move in seven different orbits; see Philo, *op. cit.* 38, i. M. 27, C.W. i. 112. Origen, *contra Celsum*, vi. 21, speaks of "the spheres of the planets." In the next chapter of Origen we hear of the mysteries of Mithras, and in connection with the rites of this cult the seven planets are mentioned. The order is as follows: Saturn, Venus, Jupiter, Mercury, Mars, the Moon, the Sun. This is exactly the reverse order of the mnemonic in our text for the service of the planets by day. In chapter xxxi. Origen deals with the "ruling

All of them minister to the twelve constellations [1] which correspond to the twelve months. The constellations are: Aries, Taurus, Gemini, Cancer, Leo, Virgo, Libra, Scorpio, Sagittarius, Capricornus, Aquarius, and Pisces.[2] All the constellations minister to [3] the days of the sun.[4] Now the days of the solar month are 30 days, 10 hours and a half,[5]

spirits" accepted by the teaching of the Gnostics; these "ruling spirits" are the seven planets. The system has fortunately been preserved in the *Pistis Sophia* (ed. Mead), pp. 360 ff. The Church Father John of Damascus, in his *Doctrine of Faith*, ii. 7, also mentions the seven planets. See also Hippolytus, *Philosophumena*, iv. 6 ff.

[1] *i.e.* the Zodiac. On this subject see John of Damascus, *loc. cit.*, and cf. *J.E.* iv. 244 f. Slavonic Enoch xxx. reads: "The sun that he should go according to each sign of the Zodiac; and the course of the moon through the twelve signs of the Zodiac," and see Eth. Enoch lxxiii.–lxxiv.

[2] The first editions add: "These (*i.e.* the constellations) were created in the work of the Creation to rule the world, and thus are their ordinances. And these seven servants [1] were created, and He placed them in the firmament of the heavens." [2] Our MS. agrees here with the Oxford MS. (d. 35)

[3] Perhaps the word should be rendered "serve"; see *supra*, p. 32, note 1. Gaster's Jeraḥmeel iv. 2 has "rules" in reference to the sun, and "serves" in connection with the other planets.

[4] Does this mean that the constellations influence the months, there being twelve constellations corresponding to the twelve months? Perhaps the reference is to the fact that the sun is in each constellation for 30 days, 10 hours, 30 minutes (*i.e.* a solar month). The Oxford MS. (d. 35) reads, "the days of the solar year." The Venice edition reads: "the days of the solar month." According to John of Damascus (*loc. cit.*)—

The sun enters		Aries	on	March 21st.
,,	,,	Taurus	,,	April 23rd.
,,	,,	Gemini	,,	May 24th.
,,	,,	Cancer	,,	June 24th.
,,	,,	Leo	,,	July 25th.
,,	,,	Virgo	,,	August 25th.
,,	,,	Libra	,,	September 25th.
,,	,,	Scorpio	,,	October 25th.
,,	,,	Sagittarius	,,	November 25th.
,,	,,	Capricornus	,,	December 25th.
,,	,,	Aquarius	,,	January 25th.
,,	,,	Pisces	,,	February 24th.

The 1st ed. adds "Sun, Moon, Mars, Mercury, Venus, Saturn. Sun, Moon, Saturn, and Mercury minister to each constellation 30 (days) 4 hours like an attendant, and just as the Sun and Moon and Mercury enter simultaneously." The text is evidently corrupt.

[5] The 1st ed. adds here: "and during the days of the lunar month two constellations serve for four days and eight hours." The meaning is not evident. 4 days, 8 hours $\times$ 7 = 30 days, 8 hours.

---

[1] *i.e.* the planets.
[2] Each one in its own orbit.

and each constellation ministers to the || days of the solar month for two days and a half, so that two constellations (minister for) five days.[1] The chief [2] which begins at the beginning of the solar month is the same chief which completes [3] at the end of the solar month; the one which opens is the one which closes.[4]

The great cycle of the sun is 28 years,[5] and therein are seven small cycles each of four years.[6] The number of days of the solar year [7] is 365 and a quarter of a day. The seasons [8] of the solar year are four, each season (consisting of) 91 days 7½ hours. The beginnings of the cycles of the seasons are the 4th, 2nd, 7th, 5th, 3rd, 1st, and 6th (days).[9] Between each cycle there are 5 days and 6 (hours).[10]

[1] The sense to be conveyed seems to be that in a solar month every 2½ days is under the influence of a constellation, the last 10½ hours being reckoned as part of the service of the constellation which is next in order to that constellation which was placed over the last 2½ days of the month. We shall see that each constellation is served by the Moon for 2½ days, or, as John of Damascus says (*loc. cit.*), " The Moon passes through the twelve constellations in each month."

[2] *i.e.* the constellation.

[3] This would then mean that the next constellation begins its influence at the beginning of the next solar month.

[4] It seems that the last 10½ hours of the solar month are under the influence of the constellation which ruled at the beginning of that month.

[5] See T.B. Berakhoth, *loc. cit.*; T.B. Sabbath, 129b, with Rashi.

[6] The order of the planets which begin the seven small cycles respectively is Saturn, Jupiter, Mars, the Sun, Venus, Mercury, and the Moon, a cycle of four years being supposed to elapse between the beginning of the rule of each of these planets.

[7] 1st ed. reads " solar years," the later texts read " the sun."

[8] Teḳuphah; see Jewish Calendar, 1915–16, edited by the present writer, pp. 31, 35, etc., for the Teḳuphah. The word means " turn," or " cycle "; cf. Ex. xxxiv. 22 and Ps. xix. 6. It means in our book season, or (1) vernal equinox, or (2) the summer solstice, or (3) the autumnal equinox, or (4) the winter solstice. See Rashi on T.B. Berakhoth, *loc. cit.* where we learn that the first Teḳuphah of Nisan at the Creation was on the fourth day (Wednesday). Can Jubilees i. 14 and ii. 9 refer to Teḳuphah? See Pal. Targ. Gen. i. 14, which reads: " And God said: Let there be lights in the expanse of the heavens, to distinguish between the day and the night; and let them be for signs and seasons for festivals and for the numbering by them of the calculation of the days and for the sanctification by them of new moons and new years, (for) intercalations of months and intercalations of years and Teḳuphoth of the Sun and the Molad of the Moon and cycles." Etheridge's version (*The Targums*, i. p. 159) is inaccurate.

[9] The seven days respectively of the seven small cycles. The Oxford MS. (d. 35) reads: " The Teḳuphoth are at the beginning of the night of the fourth day, the beginning of the night of the second day " . . . concluding with " the beginning of the night of the sixth day."

[10] Is the text faulty here? The interval of five days is apparent from the preceding sentence in the text.

The Tekuphoth (*i.e.* seasons) of the small cycle are four in each year, some of them (last) 91 days 7½ hours and some last 92 days.[1] The first year of the cycle (of four years) has its Tekuphah in Nisan at 6 p.m.; in the second year at 12 p.m.; in the third year at 6 a.m.; in the fourth year at 12 a.m.[2]

The four beginnings of the Tekuphah of the four months of Nisan [3] commence at the beginning of the night,[4] at midnight, at the beginning of the day,[5] and at noon (respectively). The rest of the other (days of the) || Teḳuphoth are as follows: ẒCh; GYCh; VACh; ṬDCh.[6]

The first Teḳuphah of Nisan [7] took place at the beginning

[1] This means that the year equals 4 × 91 days, 7½ hours = 365¼ days. The Oxford MS. (d. 35) reads: "Some of them (last) 91 days and some of them 92 days." This reading seems preferable to our text and seems to point to 366 days in the year, *i.e.* two seasons of 91 days each and two of 92 days each. Luria rejects the reading, "Some of them (last) 92 days."

[2] Luria's reading in the latter part of Note 22, *in loc.*, has been adopted, as the MS. text seems to be unintelligible. The MS. reads: The first year of the cycle is A–G (1st and 3rd letters of the Hebrew alphabet); the second year is B–B (2nd letter of Hebrew alphabet); the third year is GAD (3rd, 1st, and 4th letters); the fourth year is DD. The reading adopted for the translation gives the following abbreviations: A–A, B–V, G–A, D–V, where the first letters of each set refer to the 1st, 2nd, 3rd, and 4th years (of the small cycle) respectively; the 2nd letters indicate the hours when the Teḳuphoth of Nisan in the four years begin, namely: 6 p.m. (A), 12 p.m. (V), 6 a.m. (A), and 12 a.m. (V).

[3] In each cycle of four years.

[4] The Jewish day consists of night, lasting 12 hours, which begins at 6 p.m., and day, lasting 12 hours and commencing at 6 a.m.

[5] *i.e.* 6 a.m.

[6] ZCh = 7th and 8th letters of Hebrew alphabet.
GYCh = 3rd, 10th, and 8th letters of Hebrew alphabet.
VACh = 6th, 1st, and 8th letters of Hebrew alphabet.
TDCh = 9th, 4th, and 8th letters of Hebrew alphabet.
Ch (8th letter) is an abbreviation for the word (חצי) meaning "half." The abbreviations mean:—

When the Teḳuphah of Nisan is the 1st hour (A) of the night, *i.e.* at 6 p.m., the Teḳuphah of Tammuẓ is 7½ hours (ẒCh) later, *i.e.* 1.30 a.m. The Teḳuphah of Tishri is at 3 hours of the day (G), *i.e.* 9 a.m., and the Teḳuphah of Tebeth is 10½ hours of the day (YCh), *i.e.* 4.30 p.m. Again, when the Teḳuphah of Nisan is the 6th hour, *i.e.* midnight (V), the Teḳuphah of Tammuz is 1½ hour of the day (ACh), *i.e.* 7.30 a.m., and the Teḳuphah of Tishri is 9 hours of the day (Ṭ), *i.e.* 3 p.m., and the Teḳuphah of Ṭebeth is 4½ hours of the following night (DCh), *i.e.* at 10.30 p.m.[1]

[7] At the era of the Creation.

---

[1] See T.B. 'Erubin, *loc. cit.*

(of the hours) of Saturn.[1] The Teḳuphah of Tammuz (took place) at the middle (of the hours) of Saturn.[2] The Tekuphah of Tishri (occurred) at the beginning of the hours of Jupiter.[3] The Tekuphah of Ṭebeth (took place) at the middle (of the hours) of Jupiter.[4] And thus with all the other Teḳuphoth, which occur at the beginning of the hours or at the middle of the hours.[5]

The first cycle[6] took place at the beginning of the hour of Saturn, (and the names of the Planets of the hours are) Saturn, Jupiter, Mars, the Sun, Venus, Mercury, and the Moon. The second cycle occurred in the hour (of the Planet) which is in front of it,[7] (*i.e.*) at the beginning of the hour of Jupiter. The third cycle occurred at the beginning of the hour of Mars. The fourth cycle entered at the beginning of the hour of the Sun. The fifth cycle entered at the beginning of the hour of Venus. The sixth cycle entered at the beginning of the hour of Mercury. The seventh cycle entered at the beginning (of the hour) of the Moon. (At) the end of seven hours,[8] at the end of seven cycles,

[1] Saturn is the planet for the eve of the fourth day at 6 o'clock p.m. on Tuesday. See *supra*, p. 32, note 2.

[2] 7½ hours later is still the hour of Saturn; this would be at 1.30 a.m. Wednesday.

[3] 7½ hours later is the hour of Jupiter at 9 a.m. Wednesday.

[4] 7½ hours later is still in Jupiter at 4.30 p.m. Wednesday afternoon.

[5] This refers to the service of the planets over the hours, as can be seen from the notes above; the two Tekuphoth are either at the beginning or at the middle of the hours.

[6] Of the seven Teḳuphoth cycles referred to above, the first begins on the fourth day, *i.e.* Wednesday (which commences on Tuesday at 6 p.m., which is the hour of Saturn).

[7] In reference to the position of its orbit around the earth as centre. In this connection the position of the planets is as follows: nearest to the earth we have the Moon, Mercury, Venus, the Sun, Mars, Jupiter, Saturn.

[8] It has been suggested by R. Elijah of Vilna that this reference to the seven hours should be omitted. Perhaps the reading should be "At the end of the seven planets of the hours," *i.e.* the cycle recommences with Saturn. The Teḳuphoth of Nisan are as follows:—

		1	2	3	4	years.
1.	Wednesday	6.0 p.m.				
	Thursday		12.0 p.m.			
	Friday			6.0 a.m.		
	Saturday				12.0 a.m.	

		5	6	7	8	years.
2.	Monday	6.0 p.m.				
	Tuesday		12.0 p.m.			
	Wednesday			6.0 a.m.		
	Thursday				12.0 a.m.	

at the end of 35 days [1] of the great cycle of 28 years, the Teḳuphah cycle returns (*i.e.* begins again) at the beginning of the fourth day [2] in the hour of Saturn in the hour when it was created.

In 366 (degrees) [3] the sun rises and declines, it rises 183 (degrees) || in the east, and it declines 183 (degrees) in the west corresponding to the 365 [4] days of the solar year. (The sun) goes forth through 366 [5] apertures and enters by

The third cycle falls on Saturday, Sunday, Monday, and Tuesday at 6 and 12 p.m. and 6 and 12 a.m. respectively in the 9th, 10th, 11th, and 12th years respectively.

The fourth cycle falls on Thursday, Friday, Saturday, and Sunday at 6 and 12 p.m. and 6 and 12 a.m. respectively in the 13th, 14th, 15th, and 16th years respectively.

The fifth cycle falls on Tuesday, Wednesday, Thursday, and Friday at 6 and 12 p.m. and 6 and 12 a.m. respectively in the 17th, 18th, 19th, and 20th years respectively.

The sixth cycle falls on Sunday, Monday, Tuesday, and Wednesday at 6 and 12 p.m. and 6 and 12 a.m. respectively in the 21st, 22nd, 23rd, and 24th years respectively.

The seventh cycle falls on Friday, Saturday, Sunday, and Monday at 6 and 12 p.m. and 6 and 12 a.m. respectively in the 25th, 26th, 27th, and 28th years respectively.

It must be borne in mind that the first two Teḳuphoth of every cycle are p.m., and therefore the actual English day in these cases is nominally one day earlier than the Jewish day.

[1] This is also the reading of the 1st ed. Later editions are faulty, and read "65 days." The number 35 is due to 7 × 5 days, the latter being the interval between each small cycle of four years, during which there are 16 Tekuphoth, and each Teḳuphah is 7½ hours' interval later than its predecessor. 7 = the number of cycles.

[2] Tuesday evening at six o'clock, when the fourth day (Wednesday) of the Hebrew week begins.

[3] "Degrees" according to the reading in the first two editions. The 1st ed. reads "365 degrees."

[4] In the MS. a later writer has written "6" above the "5." The first editions read, "according to the days of the solar year."

[5] The printed texts read 366 apertures. According to T.J. Rosh Ha-Shanah ii. 5, 58a, l. 41 ff., "The Holy One, blessed be He, created 365 windows for the service of the world: 182 in the east and 182 in the west and one in the centre of the firmament, whence it came forth at the beginning at the Creation." See also Ex. Rab. xv. 22: "The Holy One, blessed be He, created 365 windows in the firmament, 183 on the east and 182 on the west." The Jalkut on 1 Kings, §185, compares the knops mentioned in 1 Kings vii. 24 to "the 365 windows which are in the east and in the west, for the sun rises in one in the east and sets in one in the west." This section of the Jalḳuṭ is taken from the Midrash Tadsheh (cf. Epstein, Midrash Tadsheh, p. xvi). Further parallels are to be found in Buber's Shocher Ṭob, Ps. xix. 11, and Jalḳuṭ on Psalms (xix.), § 673, and on Eccles. § 967. The astronomical theories of our book are not in agreement with the Rabbinical system set forth in the Talmud and Midrashim. It seems that our author held the view that the solar year had 366 days. Each half-year the sun passes through 91, plus 91, plus 1 apertures, or in one year through 366

the east; 90 days[1] it is in the south (east) quarter, 91 days in the north (east) quarter and one aperture is in the middle[2] and its name is Nogah.[3]

(At) the Teḳuphah of Tishri[4] (the sun) begins from the aperture of Nogah and goes through its revolutions towards the south quarter, through one aperture after another until it reaches the aperture of Bilgah.[5] (At) the Teḳuphah of Ṭebeth (the sun) begins from the aperture of Bilgah[5] and continues its course, returning backward through one aperture after another until it reaches the aperture of Ta'alumah,[6] through which the light goes forth,[7] as it is said, "*And the thing that is hid* bringeth he forth to light" (Job xxviii. 11). (At) the Teḳuphah of Nisan (the sun) begins from the aperture of Ta'alumah,[8] and it[9] goes to the north quarter through one aperture after another until it reaches the aperture No'aman.[10] (At) the Teḳuphah of Tammuẓ (the sun) begins from the aperture No'aman and goes on its course, returning backwards through aperture after aperture until it reaches the aperture Cheder[11] whence the whirlwind goes forth, as it is said, "Out of *the chamber*

apertures. Now we find a parallel teaching in the Slavonic Enoch xiii. 2: "And I saw the six great gates open, each gate having sixty-one stadia." Thus far Text B.; see Charles' ed., p. 15, and cf. Eth. Enoch lxxii. 2 ff. on the course of the sun. Here also "windows" are mentioned. The whole of this chapter should be read in comparison with our text. Eth. Enoch adopts the strange calculation that the solar year has 364 days, though he was acquainted with the year of 365¼ days. Does our book attempt a new solution? or, as I venture to suggest, did our author borrow from Slavonic Enoch? This seems the most probable view.

[1] The first editions read 91 days. This agrees with the Oxford MSS. (d. 35) and (O. 167) and also Gaster's MS.

[2] This aperture separates the 91 N.E. windows from the 91 S.E. windows, and the sum total equals 183, which agrees with our text: "it rises 183 (degrees) in the east."

[3] נוגה, or "Venus." The word means light. The Venice edition reads "the aperture Nogah."

[4] About the time of the autumnal equinox; see *J.E.* xii. 76 f. The Teḳuphah Tishri falls now on October 7th, about 14 days after the equinox.

[5] The first editions read (שבתאי) "Saturn."

[6] Or "darkness." See Targum on Job xxviii. 11.

[7] The quotation is not given by the Oxford MS. (d. 35).

[8] The first editions add: "through which the light goeth forth."

[9] The sun.

[10] Or "pleasantness." Nature is at her best at this period of the year. The MS. reads "Nô'aman," the first two editions read "Na'amôn."

[11] Or "secret chamber."

cometh the storm[1] and cold out of the scattering winds" (*ibid.* xxxvii. 9).

Through these apertures which are in the east (the sun) || goes forth and opposite to them[2] in the west (the sun) sets. The Shekhinah is always in the west.[3] (The sun) sets and worships[4] before the King of Kings, the Holy One, blessed be He, saying: Lord of all worlds! I have done according to all that Thou hast commanded me.[5]

The aperture which is in the midst of the firmament is named M'ẓarim[6] and (the sun) does not go forth or set[7] therein except once in its great cycle;[8] (thereon) it goes through it as on the day when it was created.[9] At night the sun is in the west.[10] At the Teḳuphah of Tishri and at the Teḳuphah of Ṭebeth the sun goes on its course in the south quarter and in the waters of the Ocean[11] (which are) between the ends of the heavens and the ends of the earth where it is submerged.[12] For the night is long and the way is long[13] until (the sun) reaches the aperture which is in the east, (even) the aperture through which it desires to go forth,[14] as it is said, "It goeth toward the south, and turneth

[1] The MS. omits the second half of the verse, substituting "etc."

[2] The apertures on the east.

[3] See T.B. Baba Bathra, 25a, and T.B. Synhedrin, 91b.

[4] Lit. "bows down."

[5] See Deut. xxvi. 14 for phraseology.

[6] Or "scattering winds." See Job xxxvii. 9 and Targum, *in loc.*

[7] Lit. "does not go in or go out."

[8] *i.e.* once in twenty-eight years.

[9] The 1st ed. reads: "on the day when the world was created, on the day when it was created."

[10] *i.e.* when it sets. The Prague edition reads here: "on the day it was created at night and in the west."

[11] See John of Damascus, *op. cit.* ii. 9, with reference to the ocean which surrounds the earth.

[12] Or "where it sets."

[13] To traverse half of the west, the north, and half of the east. The apparent risings of the sun are all in the east from the point of view of the spectator on the earth; half the year the rising is south of the earth's equator, the other half of the year this is north of the equator; thus the setting in the west corresponds to the rising, and accounts for the "long way" after setting in the winter.

[14] At its next rising. The following reading is given by the first two editions: "At the Teḳuphoth of Nisan and Tammuẓ the sun goes forth on its course to the north quarter to the waters of the Ocean which are between the ends of the heavens and the ends of the earth; for the night is short and the way is short (after sunset) until it reaches the apertures which are in the east through which it desires to go forth."

about unto the north" (Eccles. i. 6).[1] It goes to the south at the Tekuphah of Tishri and at the Teḳuphah of Ṭebeth, and turns to the north at the Teḳuphah of Nisan and at the Teḳuphah of Tammuz. It goes on its course for six months in the south quarter, and for six months in the north quarter, and owing to its circuits the sun[2] returns to the aperture which is in the east. The sun has three letters of (God's) Name written upon his heart,[3] and the angels lead him;[4] such || as lead him by day do not lead him by night, and such as lead him by night do not lead him by day. The sun rides in a chariot and rises, crowned as a bridegroom,[5] as it is said, "Which is as a bridegroom coming out of his chamber, and rejoiceth as a strong man to run his course" (Ps. xix. 5). The sun's rays and face, which are turned downwards (to the earth), are of hail;[6] and were it not for the hail which quenches the flames of fire[7] the world would be consumed by fire, as it is said, "And there is nothing hid from the heat thereof" (*ibid.* 6). In winter (the sun) turns the upper (half of) his face downwards,[8] and were it not for the fire which warms the face of hail the world could not endure because of the ice (cold), as it is said, "Who can stand before his cold?" (*ibid.* cxlvii. 17). These are the ends of the ways of the sun.[9]

[1] Ecclesiastes refers to the wind here, but our text applies this to the sun. See the Targum to this verse of Ecclesiastes.

[2] Lit. wind or quarter. See previous note.

[3] See Jeraḥmeel iii. 4: "Three letters of the Ineffable Name of God are written upon the heart of the sun." The sun has three different terms in Hebrew.

[4] Slav. Enoch xiv. 2–4 says: "When he (the sun) goes out by the Western gate four hundred *angels* take his *crown* and bring it to the Lord. And the sun revolves in his *chariot* . . . and when he comes near the east . . . the four hundred angels bring his crown and crown him." There is probably some connection between this passage and *P.R.E.* Eth. Enoch refers to the sun's chariot (lxxii. 5). See also 3 Baruch, ch. vi. 1 f. ed. Charles, *Apocrypha and Pseudepigrapha*, ii. p. 536. This Apocalypse of Baruch offers also other parallels to our Midrash, see Introduction, and cf. *J.E.* ii. 550.

[5] The first editions add: "and he goeth forth and rejoiceth like a strong man."

[6] The 1st ed. reads: "The sun's rays and face which look downwards are of fire and his rays and face which look upwards are of hail." The Venice edition adds "to the earth" after "downwards." See Eth. Enoch iv.

[7] The first editions read: "his face of fire."

[8] The first editions read: "the lower (half of) his face upwards, and were it not for the fire which warms the hail."

[9] Compare with our text Eth. Enoch lxxxii. 15–20.

CHAPTER VII[1]

THE COURSE OF THE MOON [7A. i.]

RABBAN JOCHANAN BEN ẒAKKAI, Rabban Gamaliel, R. Ishmael, R. Elaẓar ben 'Arakh, R. Eliezer ben Hyrḳanos, and R. 'Aḳiba[2] were expounding[3] (the laws of) the Molad[4] of the moon. They said:[5] The Holy One, blessed be He, spake one word and the heavens were created[6] as the residence of the Throne of His Glory,[7] as it is said, "By the *word* of the Lord were the heavens made" (Ps. xxxiii. 6). But in connection with the (creation of the) host of heaven He laboured with great labour.[8] || What did the Holy One, blessed be He, do? He blew with His mouth the wind of the breath[9] of life[10] and all the host of heaven were created,[11] as it is said, "And *all* the host of them by the *breath* of his mouth" (*ibid.*).

All the stars and constellations[12] were created at the

[1] In MS. this is ch. vi.

[2] On Rabban Gamaliel ii. see *J.E.* v. 560 ff.; on R. Ishmael see Bacher, T. i. 232 ff., and *J.E.* vi. 648 ff.; on R. Elaẓar b. 'Arakh see *J.E.* v. 96 f.; for life of R. 'Aḳiba see Bacher, T. i. 263 ff. It is difficult to understand how R. 'Aḳiba or R. Ishmael could have discussed Torah with Rabban Jochanan b. Ẓakkai.

[3] The first editions read: "were sitting and expounding."

[4] Molad is the conjunction of Moon and Sun; see Schwarz, *Der jüdische Kalender*, pp. 58 f.

[5] The margin of the MS. has, "and all of them" (said).

[6] Cf. Isa. xlv. 12. See Othijoth d. R. 'Aḳiba, third paragraph of letter Resh, ed. Jellinek, *B.H.M.* iii. p. 46, and compare John i. 3, where the Logos or Word is the Creator.

[7] The first editions read: "His Kingdom."

[8] The first editions read: "great labour is mentioned, as it is said, 'And all the host of them by the *breath* of his mouth' (*ibid.*)."

[9] Breath implies more than a mere word.

[10] The first editions read: "He blew with the wind of the breath of His mouth."

[11] "Simultaneously" is added by the first editions.

[12] "And the two luminaries" is added by the first editions.

beginning of [1] the night of the fourth [2] day, one (luminary) did not precede the other except by the period of two-thirds of an hour. Therefore every motion [3] of the sun (is done) with deliberation, and every motion of the moon is (done) quickly.[4] The distance covered by the sun in thirteen days and a fifth [5] is covered by the moon in one day,[6] and (the distance) covered by the sun all the days of the year, the moon traverses (the same distance) in forty-one days.[7] All the days serve for the beginning of the Molad of the (new) moon; (for the following series [8]) the days are reckoned backward; at the beginning of the night of the fourth day [9] the beginning of the Molad (new moon) was

[1] 6 p.m.

[2] Tuesday evening at 6 p.m., when the fourth day began.

[3] Lit. "action."

[4] Since the sun was created just before the moon the latter hastens to overtake the former.

[5] Oxford MS. (d. 35) reads: "12 days."

[6] The text of the printed editions is hopelessly corrupt. They state: "The distance covered by the sun all the days of the year is traversed by the moon in one day."

[7] The 1st ed. reads: "28 days." The Venice text reads: "30 days," which seems to be more correct than "41 days" of our MS. Our author seems to treat numbers without any regard to the exact amount. By treating fractions as though they were whole numbers, we may find an explanation of the difficulty which has already occurred in the previous chapter; perhaps the 365¼ days of the year were described as 366 so as to avoid the fraction. The text should probably read thus: "The distance covered by the sun in 12 days is covered by the moon in 1 day, and (the distance) covered by the sun all the days of the year, the moon traverses in 30 days." See, however, T.J. Rosh Ha-Shanah ii. 5, p. 58a, which is possibly the source of our text here. The lunar month according to the Hebrew astronomers was said to be 29 days, 12 hours, and $\frac{793}{1080}$ parts of an hour (1 minute=18 parts). Our book sometimes treats this as a whole number by saying, "the month has 30 days," or we find the more exact reference to 29 days, 12 hours, and 40 minutes, neglecting the 4 minutes, 3⅓ seconds, which really belong to the sum total. On the entire subject of the Calendar see the valuable article by S. Poznański in Hastings' *Encyclopædia of Religion and Ethics*, iii. 17 ff.

[8] The series of the small cycles of three years in which the Molad of the next cycle falls on the day which was anterior to that on which the previous Molad fell. The calculation is based on the length of the lunar month being reckoned as measuring 29 days, 12 hours, 40 minutes, so that in one year the surplus over the complete week equals 4 days, 8 hours (since each lunar month has 4 complete weeks and 1 day, 12 hours and 40 minutes; and this surplus multiplied by 12 equals 18 days, 8 hours, *i.e.* 4 days, 8 hours beyond the two weeks), and in three years we have a surplus of 13 days (two weeks less one day); therefore the day of the next series to the one in question will be one day earlier than the preceding series; see Schwarz, *op. cit.* p. 23, and Lewisohn, *Geschichte und System des jüdischen Kalenderwesens*, p. 25, note 84.

[9] Tuesday, at 6 p.m.

in the hour of Saturn;[1] and the mnemonic is ShNZ KMLChSh. After three years of the small cycle the day[2] of the next cycle (reverts to) the beginning of the night of the third day, and the beginning of the Molad (new moon) is in the hour of Venus. After three years of the small cycle the day[2] of the next cycle (reverts to) the beginning of the night of the second day, the beginning of the Molad is in the hour of Jupiter. After three years of the small cycle the day[2] of the next cycle (reverts to) the beginning of the night of the first day, the beginning of the Molad || is in the hour of Mercury.[3] After three years of the small cycle the day[2] of the next cycle (reverts to) the beginning of the night of the Sabbath, the beginning of the Molad is in the hour of Mars. After three years of the small cycle the day[2] of the next cycle (reverts to) the beginning of the night of the sixth day, the beginning of the Molad is in the hour of the Moon. After three years of the small cycle the day[2] of the next cycle (reverts to) the beginning of the night of the fifth day, the beginning of the Molad is in the hour of the Sun. After three years of the small cycle the day[2] of the next cycle (reverts to) the beginning of the night of the fourth day, the beginning of the Molad reverts to the hour of Saturn as in the hour when it was created.

The great cycle of the moon is 21 years; it has 7 small cycles each containing 3 years.[4] The total of the days of the lunar month is 29½ days, 40 minutes, and 73 parts.[5] Each constellation serves the days of the lunar month for 2 days and 8 hours; three constellations serve for 7 days. The chief[6] which begins on the new moon (of the lunar month) is the same which concludes at the end of the lunar month.[7] The moon becomes new at every

[1] See *supra*, p. 32, note 2. Saturn is represented by Sh.

[2] Of the Molad at the beginning of the new cycle.

[3] The MS. reads: "Kôkhab Chamah," which is not the usual appellation for Mercury; see Zunz, *Gesammelte Schriften*, iii. p. 243.

[4] The first editions add: "Each constellation ministers to the days of the lunar month."

[5] As we have seen, 1 hour=1080 parts, therefore 73 parts=$4\frac{1}{18}$ minutes. Luria holds that the expression "73 parts" is an interpolation. See T.B. Rosh Ha-Shanah, 25a, on the question of the duration of a lunar month, which agrees with our text.

[6] The constellation.

[7] The twelve constellations serve or influence 28 days of the lunar month; the remaining 1½ days, etc., are under the influence of the constellation which presided at the beginning of the month.

Molad, once at night and the next time[1] by day, || and this is their sign: "And it was evening and it was morning" (Gen. i. 5). Between one Molad and (the corresponding) Molad in the ensuing year (there elapse) 4 days, 8 hours, and 876 parts.[2]

From one small cycle to the next cycle (elapse) 13 days, 2619 parts.[3] When[4] the sun goes in the south quarter, the moon goes in the north quarter, and when the sun goes in the north quarter[5] the moon goes in the south quarter. All the hours serve for the beginning of the Molad of the moon in a retrospective order, according to the order "ShLKNChM and Z."[6] In the first year at the beginning of the night of the fourth day the beginning of the Molad (conjunction of the moon) is in the hour of Saturn (Sh). In the second year[7] the beginning of the conjunction of the

[1] Lit. "once."

[2] The first editions read: "4 days, 8 hours, and 873 parts." This is incorrect. Luria reads: "4 days and 8 hours." The basis of his assumption, which is unwarranted, is the theory that the lunar month =4 weeks and *1 day, 12 hours, and 40 minutes*, and this surplus multiplied by 12 =18 days, 8 hours, *i.e.* 2 weeks and 4 days, 8 hours. Again this surplus multiplied by 3 (the small cycle) =13 days exactly. Our MS. is quite correct; see Hastings' *Encyclopædia of Religion and Ethics*, iv. p. 120. The 1st and 2nd eds. add: "the difference between a great cycle and a small cycle is only 13 days."[1]

[3] This means 13 days, 2 hours, 25½ minutes.

[4] The text in the printed edition reads: "In the west at the time." The reference is probably to the relation between the position of the sun and moon (1) in the winter and (2) at the beginning of the conjunction of the moon and sun. See T.B. Rosh Ha-Shanah, 24a, with Rashi's commentary at top of page.

[5] In the summer the sun is more in the north than in the winter, and the moon is in conjunction in the south-west, and in the summer its position is south of the sun at its conjunction.

[6] The 1st ed. omits this mnemonic.

[7] "In the hour following" is found in some of the late editions. The difference between one year and the next in this connection is taken to be 4 days, 8 hours; if the first Molad were at 6 p.m. Tuesday, in the next year it will be 4 days, 8 hours later, *i.e.* Sunday 2 a.m., which is the hour of the moon. The following table will summarize the text:—

The beginning of the Molad	at	6 p.m. Tuesday	in the hour of	Saturn.
,,	,,	2 a.m. Sunday	,,	the Moon.
,,	,,	10 a.m. Thursday	,,	Mercury.
,,	,,	6 p.m. Monday	,,	Venus.
,,	,,	2 a.m. Saturday	,,	the Sun.
,,	,,	10 a.m. Wednesday	,,	Mars.
,,	,,	6 p.m. Sunday	,,	Jupiter.

[1] This is the interval between each small cycle, neglecting the fractions.

moon is in the hour of the Moon (L). In the third year, in the following hour, the beginning of the conjunction of the moon is in the hour of Mercury (K).[1] In the fourth year the beginning of the conjunction of the moon is in the hour of Venus (N). In the fifth year, in the hour following, the beginning of the conjunction of the moon is in the hour of the Sun (Ch). In the sixth year the beginning of the conjunction of the moon is in the hour of Mars (M). In the seventh year, in the hour following, the beginning of the conjunction of the moon is || in the hour of Jupiter (Z) in the hour following.[2] The third and fifth years are like the seventh. In like manner for three times these hours serve at the conjunction of the moon retrospectively until the (expiration of) the 21 years of the cycle.

All the constellations serve the moon by night from the four corners of the world:[3] 3 in the north, 3 in the south, 3 in the east, and 3 in the west. All the hours[4] serve the moon by night from the four corners of the world: 2 in the south, 2 in the north, 2 in the east, and 2 in the west. In the hour in which it began to serve in the

Speaking of the sun and moon, Eth. Enoch says (lxxviii. 5): "And they set and enter the portals of the west, and make their revolutions to the north and come forth through the eastern portals on the face of the heaven." The old Jewish belief as to the relation between the motion of the sun and moon was as follows: According to Rashi (T.B. Rosh Ha-Shanah, *loc. cit.*) the conjunction of every Molad (new moon) takes place when the moon is in the south-west corner of its orbit.

In winter since the sun does not traverse the west in the daytime save when it sets, therefore the moon is in the west before the sun gets there, because the moon during the first half of the lunar month goes to the north, whilst the sun revolves in the south.

In summer the sun goes over the greater part of the west in the daytime; and as it is then revolving in the north it is there before the moon, for then the moon is chiefly in the south. Where the sun sets there the moon rises.

[1] See *supra*, p. 43, note 3.

[2] "In the hour following" and the next sentence do not occur in the printed texts.

[3] See Jalkuṭ, Ex. § 418, and Jalkuṭ, 1 Kings, § 185, according to the latter passage, "The twelve constellations (*i.e.* the Zodiac) through which the world is ruled, three turn to the north . . . Aries, Leo, and Sagittarius; Taurus, Virgo, and Capricornus are turned to the west; Gemini, Libra, and Aquarius are turned to the south; Cancer, Scorpio, and Pisces are turned to the east." An entirely different order is given in the Jalkuṭ on Exodus, *loc. cit.* Cf. T.B. Pesachim, 94a, and see Eth. Enoch lxxii. 2 ff.

[4] *i.e.* the stars of the hours or the seven planets. This sentence is wanting in the 1st ed.

south, (therein) it finishes in the west;[1] and so with all its circuits.

All the great[2] luminaries of the stars[3] are situated in the south except Ursa Major,[4] which is placed in the north. All the Mazzikin[5] which move in the firmament and the angels[6] who fell[7] from their holy place (even) from heaven,[8] (when) they ascend to hear the (Divine) Word behind the veil[9] they are pursued[10] with a rod of fire, and they return[11] to their place.[12]

10 days, 21 hours, and 204 parts are the excess of the days of the solar year over the days of the lunar year;[13] and

[1] The eight hours refer to the length of the shortest night according to our book; see *infra*, p. 322. The seven planets are placed thus: two in the south, two in the north, two in the east, and the seventh planet in the west; in addition, the first planet which served in the south serves at the end of the night (8th hour) in the west.

[2] The 1st ed. reads "small."

[3] The expression is borrowed from Ezek. xxxii. 8. The seven planets are not referred to in this connection. The Pal. Targum, Ex. xl. 4, "And thou shalt bring in the lamp-stand on the south side, because thence are the paths of the sun and moon, and the pathways of the luminaries."

[4] עגלה, "waggon." The constellation Taurus of the Zodiac or Ursa Major as a star is probably implied; see Rashi on T.B. Berakhoth, 58b.

[5] See *supra*, p. 14, note 8.

[6] The fall of the angels recalls Jude 6; Jubilees v. 6, 7; Slav. Enoch xviii.; Eth. Enoch vi.–xvi., xix., and lxxxvi.; Test. XII Pat. (Reuben, v. 6, 7), and Fragments of a Zadokite Work (ed. Schechter, iii. 18). See *infra*, pp. 99 and 160. The fall of the angels is a favourite subject with the Church Fathers, *e.g.* Athenagoras, *Embassy*, xxiv.; Justin Martyr, *Second Apology*, v.; and *Dialogue with Trypho*, lxxix.

[7] The first editions add: "from their greatness."

[8] The first editions add: "in the days of the generation of Enosh." This view opposes the doctrine of the Book of Jubilees v. 6–9, which holds that the fall of the angels took place in the days of Noah. Cf. Eth. Enoch vi. 4–6. On the "generation of Enosh" see *Rabbinic Philosophy and Ethics*, pp. 37, 193, and 248; Jeraḥmeel xxiv. 9, xxvi. 20; Pal. Targum, Gen. iv. 26. On the "fall of the angels" see Gen. Rab. xxvi. 7; Pal. Targum, Gen. vi. 4; Jeraḥmeel xxv., and Gaster's Introduction, p. lxxiii, for further parallels. In Christian literature this legend also occurs; see *The Clementine Homilies*, xiii.

[9] See *supra*, p. 23, note 5.

[10] 1st ed. reads: "they are separated."

[11] The first editions add: "backwards."

[12] This is missing in the 1st ed.

[13] The 204 parts = 11⅓ minutes; Luria holds that this is a later addition to our text. On the astronomical question see Gen. Rab. xxxiii. 7. Our reading has been used by the Pal. Targum, Gen. i. 16 (see Ginsburger, *Pseudo-Jonathan*, p. 2, note 8). The Slavonic Enoch says, "And there remain 11 days over, which belong to the solar circle of the whole year" (xvi. 5). According to Eth. Enoch lxxviii. 15, 16, the lunar year has 354 days and the solar year has 364 days, thus

the intercalation is introduced to equalize the days of the solar || year with the days of the lunar year.[1] The sun and the moon begin (their courses) at the new moon of Nisan, the sun goes before the moon at its Tekuphah;[2] and Aries begins to serve before it by day, and all the constellations serve thereafter[3] according to their order. The moon goes in the opposite direction[4] and Aries begins to serve before it[5] by night, and all the constellations serve thereafter according to their order, until the year of the small cycle, until the year of intercalation (comes round). (When) the intercalated month comes round it supersedes (or thrusts aside) the new moon (of Nisan) and remains at the new moon of Shebaṭ,[6] and so on until the twelve[7] intercalated months

the difference between them amounts to 10 days. Jubilees vi. 32–36 holds that the moon "comes in from year to year 10 days too soon."

[1] On the intercalation see *infra*, Chapter VIII. p. 57.

[2] According to Giḳaṭilla's *Ginnath Egôz* (ed. Hanau), p. 50b, the text should read: "The sun goes before the moon according to her ordinance."

[3] Lit. "after it," *i.e.* after Aries.

[4] Lit. "backwards."

[5] The MS. reads "before him," *i.e.* the sun. The first printed editions read: "before her," *i.e.* the moon.

[6] The intercalated month is always interposed between Adar and Nisan, so as to ensure the fall of the Passover in the early spring. The first printed editions read here, "Adar," which appears to be the correct reading. The Venice edition adds: "and thus is it until the year of the small cycle[1] comes round; (when) the intercalated month comes it displaces the new moon and remains at the new moon of Ṭebeth."[2]

[7] The text is questioned by Luria and others. If instead of "12" we read "7" then we have the cycle of 19 years with 7 intercalated months, which will be presently considered. Luria thinks that "the sun and moon are equal at the commencement of the eve of the fourth day in the hour of Saturn," as "when they were created" only applies at the end of the cycle of 84 years. This number is obtained by multiplying 12 (the number of the constellations) by 7 (the number of the planets); or by multiplying the solar cycle of 28 years by 3; or by multiplying the lunar cycle of 21 years by 4; possibly this 84-year cycle was intended to be used for astrological purposes.

---

[1] This small cycle is not the same as we have already discussed, namely, the 3-years cycle; it is the small cycle of intercalation which will be explained in Chapter VIII.

[2] The 1st ed. reads "Shebaṭ." At the second intercalation when the month is interposed before Nisan the intercalated month will be at the new moon of the month before Adar (*i.e.* Shebaṭ) if considered in relation to the first year of the intercalation; and in the next year when the intercalation takes place the intercalated month before Nisan will really begin at the new moon of the month before Shebaṭ (*i.e.* Ṭebeth) if considered in relation to the first year of the series. Thus after 12 years the intercalated month would again begin at the new moon of Adar. This is probably the meaning of the text which speaks of "12 intercalated months."

(come round) when the sun and the moon are equal (again) at the commencement of the eve of the fourth day in the hour of Saturn in the hour when they were created. Between each Molad (conjunction of the moon and sun) there are only 36 hours, 40 minutes, and 73[1] minims (parts).

The moon does not disappear from the firmament save for the twinkling of an eye; even though there were a full thread (of light) surrounding it in the east and in the west,[2] the eye has not the power to see the moon until eight large[3] hours (have elapsed). (The large hours) are two hours for each (large) hour, either at the beginning of the Molad (conjunction) of the moon or at the end of the Molad of the moon.

The number of the days of the lunar year is 354 days, a third of a day, and 876 minims.[4] || All the hours of a lunar month are 708 hours and 40 minutes; all the hours of a lunar year are 8504 hours.[5]

All the constellations serve the Molad of the moon and also the generations[6] of the children of men;[7] upon them

[1] The "73 minims" must be considered as an interpolation; see *supra*, p. 43, note 5.

[2] That is, at the beginning and end of the Molad; see T.B. Rosh Ha-Shanah, 20b, Rashi, *in loc.*

[3] The large hour equals two ordinary hours, as is explained in the next line of the text. This passage explaining the large hour is not in the printed editions. According to T.B. Rosh Ha-Shanah, *loc. cit.*, the Palestinian Jews were unable to discern the moon at the Molad, for 6 hours after and 18 hours before the Molad; in Babylon the reverse rule obtained. The reading "6 hours" in this Talmudic passage seems to Luria to be the appropriate reading in our text. Assuming, however, that our text is correct, we might argue that Palestine could not be the place where our book arose.

[4] 876 minims equal $48\frac{2}{3}$ minutes. There is evidently something amiss here, because the next sentence tells us that the lunar month has 708 hours and 40 minutes, which means that the lunar month equals 29 days, 12 hours, and 40 minutes. On this basis the lunar year has 354 days, 8 hours. Must we assume that the "876 minims" are an interpolation? This figure equals $48\frac{2}{3}$ minutes, which in one lunar month equal $4\frac{1}{18}$ minutes or 73 minims.

[5] 8504 hours = 12 times 29 days, 12 hours, and 40 minutes.

[6] Or, "history."

[7] The knowledge of the influence of the stars and planets on terrestrial affairs or, in other words, astrology was believed to enable men to know the future. Our book bases this on the text, which is quoted in this paragraph; also Gen. v. 1, which was read as follows: "This is the calculation of the generations of man." See also Job xxxviii. 19, "Where is the way to the dwelling of light. . . . And that thou shouldst discern the paths to the house thereof? Thou knowest for thou wast then born." The sun, moon, and the planets are referred to in this chapter, showing that they have some connection with the time

the world stands, and everyone who is wise and understands, he understands the Molad of the moon and the generations of the children of men, and concerning them the text says, "And let them be for signs,[1] and for seasons" (*ibid.* 14). The *signs* of the hours shall not depart from serving the sun by day and the moon by night.

In three cycles of the sun or in four cycles of the moon[2] there are 84 years, which are one hour[3] of the day of the Holy One, blessed be He. When the sun and moon become equal[4] at the beginning of the eve of the fourth day and at the hour of Saturn in the hour when they were created, and in the hour when the flames of the moon reach the sun by day at the degree (or ascent) of 60 (degrees), it passes therein and extinguishes its light; and in the hour when the flames of the sun reach the moon at night in the degree (or ascent) of 40 (degrees), it passes through it and extinguishes its light.[5]

Rabbi Nehorai said: It is the decree of the King[6] that when Israel sins || and fails to intercalate the year as is becoming, the Holy One, blessed be He, acts in His mercy at the time when the flame of the sun reaches the moon by night at 40 degrees (or ascents), then the Holy One, blessed

and duration of life. Slav. Enoch xix. 2 says, "And these orders arrange and study the revolutions of the stars, and the changes of the moon, and revolutions of the sun, and superintend the good and evil condition of the world." The N.T. also implies a belief in the doctrines of astrology, *e.g.* Matt. ii. 9; see Jeremias, *Babylonisches im N.T.*, p. 52. This book of Jeremias is the best book on N.T. astrology; for astrology among the Jews see Löw, *Gesammelte Schriften*, ii. 115 ff.

[1] The first editions add the next word in the verse, "and for seasons"; this is wanting in our MS.

[2] The lunar cycle referred to here consists of 21 years, as stated *supra*, p. 43. The solar cycle consists of 28 years, see *supra*, p. 34.

[3] God's day equals 1000 years, therefore 1 hour (reckoning 12 hours to the day) equals 83⅓ years. The third part of the year is reckoned as a whole year. This is another instance of the use of fractions as whole numbers, which seems to be a characteristic of our author. The Church Fathers use this idea of God's day lasting 1000 years; see Justin Martyr, *Dialogue with Trypho*, lxxxi., and Irenæus, *adv. Hær.* v. 28. 3; and cf. Slavonic Enoch xxxiii. 1 f.

[4] That is, they begin their courses as at the Creation.

[5] This refers to the eclipses. It is not clear what the 60 or 40 degrees or ascents mean here.

[6] The first editions read: "The decree of the King is made public by a word." See Jalkuṭ, Jer. § 285. Instead of the reading "by a word" Luria suggests the reading "in the world," referring to the eclipses which are visible over a large portion of the world.

be He, makes the moon dim and hides one of the Synhedrion.[1] When Israel does the will of the Holy One, blessed be He, in His great mercy He makes the sun dim and He sends forth His anger upon the nations of the world,[2] as it is said, "Thus saith the Lord, Learn not the way of the *nations*, and be not dismayed at the signs of heaven,[3] for the *nations* are dismayed at them" (Jer. x. 2).[4] Just as the moon's light does not rule over the sun's light[5] by day, nor does the sun's light rule over the moon's light[6] by night, likewise the calculation of the moon does not rule by day nor does the calculation of the sun (obtain) by night,[7] and the one does not trespass on the boundary of the other.[8]

The dwelling of the moon is between cloud and thick darkness[9] made like two dishes turned one over the other,[10] and when it is the conjunction of the moon these two clouds turn in the east quarter[11] and (the moon) goes forth from between them[12] like a ram's horn.[13] On the first night (is revealed) one measure (of light), on the second night

[1] Cf. T.B. Synhedrin, 37a, and Cant. Rab. on Cant. vii. 3. Here "to hide" means to conceal in the future life; this, in other words, is a warning not to neglect the intercalation. According to the Jesod 'Olam iii. 17 the moon is the "chief" of the Synhedrion, which dies at the eclipse by being *hidden*. For eclipse in N.T. see Luke xxiii. 44, 45.

[2] The first editions read here also "the nations of the world." Later editions read: "worshippers of idols."

[3] The first editions continue the verse.

[4] Some of the old editions read here: "the nations (or according to the Prague edition 'the worshippers of idols') are dismayed, but not Israel." See Pseudo-Seder Elijahu Ẓuṭṭa (ed. Friedmann, p. 10 and note 40) on the eclipses, where the Talmudic and Midrashic sources are fully given. The astronomical question is treated at length in Israeli's Jesod 'Olam, *loc. cit.*; see also Maimonides, Hilkhoth Kiddush Ha-Chodesh.

[5] According to Slavonic Enoch xvi. 7 the moon shines with her own light.

[6] See T.B. Chullin, 60b. When the sun is invisible the moon shines.

[7] The first editions read: "We do not count the calculation of the sun at night, nor the calculation of the moon by day."

[8] See, however, Gen. Rab. vi. 3 for the opposite opinion. According to Lev. Rab. xxvi. 4 the sun and moon borrow light from one another.

[9] This is based on Job xxxviii. 9. On the text see Buber's introduction to Sepher Ha-Orah, p. 119.

[10] The first printed editions insert here: "and (the moon) goes forth from between them."

[11] The first printed editions read: "turn their faces to the west quarter."

[12] See Singer, p. 128: "bringing forth the sun from his place, and the moon from her dwelling."

[13] At rising.

the second measure, and so on until the half of the month when the moon is fully revealed, and from the middle of the month these two clouds turn their faces in the west quarter.[1] The corner (*i.e.* crescent) of the moon with which it comes forth first,[2] (the same) begins to enter and is covered therein by the two (clouds) on the first night [3] (by) one measure, on the second night (by) a second measure, and so on to the end of the month until || it is entirely covered. And whence do we know that it is placed between two clouds? Because it is said, "When I made the cloud the garment thereof, and thick darkness [4] a swaddlingband for it" (Job xxxviii. 9). And whence do we know that it becomes entirely covered? Because it is said, "Blow ye the trumpet in the new moon, *at the covering*,[5] on our solemn feast day" (Ps. lxxxi. 3). "At the covering," on the day when it is entirely covered, blow ye the trumpet in the new moon.[6]

[1] This is also the reading of the 1st ed. The Venice edition reads: "in the quarter of the east."

[2] See Jalkuṭ Makhiri, Ps. lxxxi. 14, pp. 25a, b, and Jalkut, Job xxxviii. 9, § 923.

[3] After full moon.

[4] The first editions give the next word of the text, whereas our MS. has "etc."

[5] "Covering"; see 'Arukh (ed. Kohut), iv. p. 266a, which has a different text of our passage. For further reference to the sun and moon see T.J. Berakhoth i. 1.; T.J. Rosh Ha-Shanah II. 5. 58a; Shocher Tob (Ps. xix.), pp. 168 f.; Pesikta de R. Kahana, P. Ha-Chodesh, 41b f.; and Ex. Rab. xv. 22.

[6] This verse of Ps. lxxxi. 3 is applied by the Liturgy (see Singer, p. 115) and by the Midrashim (*e.g.* Shocher Ṭob, Ps. lxxxi. § 5) to the New Year. The fact that the Shophar (ram's horn) was mentioned a few lines previously seems to point to this section as forming part of a Midrash for the New Year.

CHAPTER VIII[1]

THE PRINCIPLE OF INTERCALATION [9A. i.]

On the 28th of Ellul the sun and the moon were created.[2] The number of years, months, days, nights,[3] terms, seasons, cycles, and intercalation were before the Holy One, blessed be He,[4] and He intercalated the years and afterwards He delivered the (calculations) to the first man in the garden of Eden,[5] as it is said, "This is the calculation [6] for the generations of Adam" (Gen. v. 1), the calculation of the world is therein for the generations of the children of Adam.

Adam handed on the tradition to Enoch,[7] who was initiated in the principle of intercalation, and he intercalated the year, as it is said, "And Enoch walked with God" (*ibid.* 22). Enoch walked in the ways of the calculation concerning the world which God had delivered to Adam.

[1] This is ch. vii. in the MS. The printed editions present a good deal of the material in this chapter in a different order to that of our MS.

[2] See T.B. Rosh Ha-Shanah, 11a and 27a, for the view of R. Eliezer that the world was created in Tishri. The heavenly bodies were created on Ellul the 28th. The work of creation began on the 25th of Ellul, see also Lev. Rab. xxix. 1. In the preceding chapters the assumption was that the Creation took place in Nisan, cf. *supra*, pp. 35 f., 47. This opinion has also the support of the Talmud B. Rosh Ha-Shanah, 12a. Part of this chapter is quoted in the "Megillah of Abiathar," edited by Schechter in *J.Q.R.* xiv. pp. 463 ff.

[3] The first editions add: "hours." Cf. Wisdom vii. 18 f.

[4] See Gen. Rab. iii. 7 as to the calculations prior to the Creation.

[5] In a holy place; for, according to our book, the Garden of Eden was near Mount Moriah in Palestine. See *infra*, p. 143.

[6] See *supra*, p. 48, note 7, and cf. T.J. Rosh Ha-Shanah i. 3. 57b and Pesiḳta de R. Kahana P. Ha-Chodesh, p. 43b.

[7] The mention of Enoch in connection with the Calendar is significant, suggesting an acquaintance with the Calendar systems associated with Enoch in the pseudepigraphic literature. The fact that according to the O.T. Enoch lived 365 years is also noteworthy in this connection.

And Enoch delivered the principle of intercalation to Noah,[1] and he was initiated in the principle of intercalation, and he intercalated the year, as it is said,[2] "While the earth remaineth,[3] seed-time and harvest, and cold and heat, and summer and winter" (*ibid.* viii. 22). "Seed-time" refers to the Teḳuphah of Tishri,[4] "harvest" refers to the Tekuphah of Nisan, "cold" refers to the Teḳuphah of Tebeth, and "heat" refers to the Teḳuphah of Tammuẓ; "summer" is in its season and "winter" is in its season.[5]

The counting of the sun is *by day* || and the counting of the moon is *by night*, "*they shall not cease*." [6]

Noah handed on the tradition to Shem, and he was initiated in the principle of intercalation; he intercalated the years and he was called a priest, as it is said, "And Melchizedek [7] king of Salem . . . was a priest of God Most High" (*ibid.* xiv. 18). Was Shem the son of Noah a priest? But because he was the first-born, and because he ministered to his God by day and by night, therefore was he called a priest.[8] Shem delivered the tradition to Abraham; he was initiated in the principle of intercalation and he intercalated the year, and he (also) was called priest, as it is said, "The

[1] This should probably read "Methuselah," and the text should continue, "who handed it on to Noah."

[2] Luria's text here needs correction.

[3] The rest of the verse is given by the first editions.

[4] Pal. Targum of this verse reads: "During all the days of the earth, (there shall be) sowing at the Teḳuphah of Tishri, and harvest at the Teḳuphah of Nisan, cold at the Teḳuphah of Tebeth and warmth at the Teḳuphah of Tammuz, and summer and winter, and days and night shall not fail." Teḳuphah means not only season, but also the time of solstice and equinox according to the season.

[5] The "Megillah of Abiathar," p. 463, adds: "summer in its season and winter in its season."

[6] This section is based on the text "day and night shall not cease" (Gen. viii. 22).

[7] Melchizedek is identified by our book with Shem. According to T.B. Nedarim, 32b, the priestly office held by Melchizedek's successors passed to those of Abraham; see Beer, *Buch der Jubiläen*, p. 74. The question of the identification of Shem with Melchizedek occurs in the Talmud (*loc. cit.* in this note), and see Buber's note 18 on p. 30 of the Midrash Agadah, cf. also Pal. Targum and Jer. Targum on Gen. xiv. 18, and Gen. Rab. xliii. 6 and lvi. 9. See also the note of Charles in his ed. of *Jubilees*, p. 101. A considerable part of this section of our text occurs in Jalkut Makhiri, Ps. cx. 16, but the quotation from Gen. xiv. 18 is omitted. There are other variations in the text.

[8] The verse from Gen. xiv. 18 occurs here in the printed editions, and not above as in our MS.

Lord hath sworn, and will not repent,[1] Thou art a priest for ever after the order[2] of Melchizedek" (Ps. cx. 4). Whence do we know that Shem delivered the tradition to Abraham? Because it is said, "After the order of Melchizedek" (*ibid.*). Abraham delivered the tradition to Isaac, and he was initiated in the principle of intercalation, and he intercalated the year after the death of our father Abraham, as it is said, "And it came to pass after the death of Abraham, that God blessed Isaac his son" (Gen. xxv. 11), because he had been initiated in the principle of intercalation and had intercalated the year (therefore) He blessed him with the blessing of eternity.[3] Isaac gave to Jacob[4] all the blessings and delivered to him the principle of intercalation. When Jacob went out of the (Holy) Land, he attempted to intercalate the year outside the (Holy) Land. The Holy One, blessed be He, said to him: Jacob! Thou hast no authority to intercalate the year outside the land (of Israel); behold, Isaac thy father is in the (Holy) Land,[5] he will intercalate the year, as it is said, "And God appeared unto Jacob again, || when he came from Paddan-Aram, and blessed him" (*ibid.* xxxv. 9). Why "again"? Because the first time He was revealed to him, He prevented him from intercalating the year outside the (Holy) Land; but when he came to the (Holy) Land the Holy One, blessed

[1] The rest of the verse is not given by the MS., which merely adds "etc."

[2] Cf. Heb. v. 6 ff., on this theme. The Hebrew דברתי might suggest the meaning of "ruling"; the Oxford *Gesenius*, p. 184, renders the word: "after the order," or "manner of." Is it merely a coincidence that the Test. XII Pat., Benj. x. 6, mentions the same names as in our text and in the same order?—"Then shall ye see Enoch, Noah, and Shem, and Abraham, and Isaac, and Jacob."

[3] Or "of the world."

[4] See Jalkuṭ Makhiri, Pss. *loc. cit.*, which reads: "And Isaac handed on to Jacob all the blessings, and handed to him the principle of intercalation," confirming the accuracy of the text of our MS. The printed editions read: "Isaac delivered the tradition to Jacob, and he was initiated in the principle of intercalation, and he intercalated the year."

[5] Although Isaac was blind, nevertheless the duty of intercalating the year devolved upon him and not upon Jacob when absent from the Holy Land. The Church offers a parallel to the subject-matter of our text in the famous controversy as to the right calculation for Easter; see the epistle sent to Pope Hilarus by Victorius in the fifth century. In this letter we have several references to the lunar cycle of 84 years which also occurs in our book. (For text see Thalhofer's *Bibliothek der Kirchenväter*, Die Briefe der Päpste, vi. pp. 16–30; cf. also Ideler, *Handbuch der Chronologie*, II, p. 276, and see also "The Paschal Canon of Anatolius of Alexandria," in *A.N.C.L.* xiv. pp. 411 ff.)

be He, said to him: Jacob! Arise, intercalate the year, as it is said, " And God appeared unto Jacob *again*, . . . and blessed him " (*ibid.*), because he was initiated in the principle of the intercalation, and He blessed him (with) the blessing of the world.[1]

Jacob delivered to Joseph and his brethren the principle of intercalation, and they intercalated the year in the land of Egypt. (When) Joseph and his brethren died, the intercalations ceased from Israel in Egypt, as it is said, " And Joseph died, and all his brethren, and all that generation " (Ex. i. 6). Just as the intercalations were diminished from the Israelites in the land[2] of Egypt, likewise in the future will the intercalations be diminished at the end of the fourth kingdom[3] until Elijah, be he remembered for good, shall come.[4] Just as the Holy One, blessed be He, was revealed to Moses and Aaron in Egypt, likewise in the future will He be revealed to them[5] at the end of the fourth kingdom,[6] as it is said, " And the Lord spake unto Moses and Aaron in the land of Egypt *saying*,[7] This month shall be unto you the beginning of months " (*ibid.* xii. 1, 2). What is the significance of the word " saying " ? Say to them,[8] Till now[9] the principle of intercalation was with Me, henceforth it is your right to intercalate thereby the year.[10] Thus were the

[1] *i.e.* the revelation of the Divine Name El Shaddai. " When I suspend judgment concerning man's sins, I am called El Shaddai," says the Midrash Tanchuma, Shemoth, § xx., and cf. *infra*, pp. 264 ff. In the first editions here follows the section beginning with the words: " Hence the (Sages) have said."

[2] The first editions read : " the Egyptian bondage."

[3] The first editions read here: " bondage of the fourth kingdom."

[4] The first editions read : " until King Messiah shall come." This sign, due to the ignorance which will obtain in the period just before the advent of the Messiah, is to be compared with the " woes of the Messianic age " in Jubilees xxiii. 19: " For they have forgotten commandment, and covenant, and feasts, and months, and Sabbaths, and jubilees."

[5] The Venice ed. reads: " to us."

[6] Some editions read " exile," or " bondage."

[7] The MS. does not continue the verse; the first editions add: "This month shall be unto you."

[8] The first editions add : " to Israel."

[9] From the death of Joseph during the period of bondage.

[10] See Pesikta de R. Kahana, *loc. cit.*, which reads: "it (the principle of intercalation) is delivered unto you." See also T.J. Rosh Ha-Shanah i. 13. 57d and Ex. Rab. xv. 2. The order of the narrative here in the MS. differs from that of the printed texts. On the astronomical knowledge of Moses, see Clement of Alexandria, *Strom.* I. xxiii., and cf. Acts vii. 22.

Israelites wont to intercalate the year in the (Holy) Land. When they were exiled to Babylon || they intercalated the year through those who were left in the (Holy) Land. When they were all exiled and there were not any (Jews) left in the (Holy) Land,[1] they intercalated the year in Babylon. (When) Ezra and all the community with him [2] went (to Palestine), Ezekiel [3] wished to intercalate the year in Babylon; (then) the Holy One, blessed be He, said to him: Ezekiel! Thou hast no authority to intercalate the year outside the Land; behold, Israel thy brethren,[4] they will intercalate the year,[5] as it is said, "Son of man, when the house of Israel dwell in their *own* land" (Ezek. xxxvi. 17). Hence (the Sages) have said, Even when the righteous and the wise are outside the Land, and the keeper of sheep and herds are in the Land, they do not intercalate the year [6] except through the keeper of sheep and herds in the Land. Even when prophets are outside the Land and the ignorant [7] are in the Land they do not intercalate the year except through the ignorant who are in the land (of Israel),[8] as it is said, "Son of man, when the house of Israel dwell in their *own* land" (*ibid.*) it is their duty to intercalate the year.

On account of three things [9] is the year intercalated, on account of trees, grass, and the seasons (Teḳuphoth). If two of these (signs) be available and not the third,

[1] After the murder of Gedaliah; see T.B. Sabbath, 145b, and Seder 'Olam Rab. xxvii. p. 62a. The Land = Palestine.

[2] This is based on Ezra ii. 1; cf. T.B. 'Arakhin, 13a and 32a.

[3] On the question whether Ezekiel could have been a contemporary of Ezra, see Rashi on Ezek. xxix. (end), and cf. *infra*, p. 249. The special privileges attached to the Holy Land are noteworthy in considering the provenance of our book.

[4] *i.e.* your brethren in the land of Israel, see 2 Kings xxv. 22 and Jer. xliii. 5.

[5] The order of narrative in our MS. differs from that of the printed texts.

[6] This passage if rendered literally reads: "Even the righteous and the wise outside the Land and the keeper of sheep and herds in the Land, then the year is intercalated only by the keeper of sheep and herds." See T.B. Synhedrin, 18b and 26a, for instances of intercalation by shepherds. Cf. the narrative of the Magi and the Star in Matt. ii. 1 ff.

[7] Or "commoners" (הדיוט = ἰδιώτης), see T.B. Nedarim, 78a. For an instance of intercalation outside Palestine see T.B. Berakhoth, 63a, and cf. Tosaphoth on Jebamoth, 115a.

[8] The printed editions differ from our MS. here with reference to the arrangement of the material.

[9] The first editions read: "signs." This is also the reading in the Oxford MS. (d. 35). See *Rabbinic Philosophy and Ethics*, p. 221, note 3.

they do not intercalate the year, (that is to say) neither because of the trees nor because of the grass. If one (sign)[1] be available and the other two be absent, they do not intercalate the year on account of the Teḳuphoth.[2] If the Tekuphah of Tebeth had occurred on the 20th[3] day of || the month or later, they intercalate the year; but till the 20th day of the month Tebeth or earlier they do not intercalate the year.

The cycle of intercalation is 19 years, and there are 7 small cycles[4] therein; some of these are (separated by) 3 years, some (by) 2 years, others (are separated by) 3 or 2 years, or (by) 3, 3, and 3 years (the order of the cycles being): 3rd, 6th, 8th, 11th, 14th, 17th, and 19th years. There are two (sets) of three years' cycles.[5]

[1] *i.e.* the Teḳuphah. Luria thinks that the reading should be as follows: "If two signs be available and not the third we intercalate on account of the presence of the trees and the grass; if one sign be available and the other two be absent we do not intercalate on account of the Teḳuphah" (see T.B. Synhedrin, 12a, b, and cf. T.B. Rosh Ha-Shanah, 21a).

[2] "This is an error," says Luria; "it should be the 16th"; see T.B. Rosh Ha-Shanah, *loc. cit.*, and T.B. Synhedrin, 13a: for if the Teḳuphah of Tebeth fell on the 21st of Tebeth, then the Teḳuphah of Nisan would be on the 24th of Nisan (91 days' interval), which is the day after Passover, accordingly Passover would not be in Abib (the Teḳuphah in Nisan), and therefore Adar Shêni should be intercalated. The reading in our text (the 20th) is approved by Schwarz (*Der jüdische Kalender*, p. 36, note 3). The "Megillah of Abiathar" (*op. cit.* p. 471) reads: "If the Teḳuphah of Ṭebeth had occurred from half (of the month) and later they intercalate the year, but till half (of the month) and earlier they do not intercalate the year." The printed editions read: "If the Teḳuphah had occurred by the 20th day of the month or earlier they intercalate the year; but from the 20th day of the month or later they do not intercalate the year." This is clearly wrong. The correct reading is preserved by our MS., which is confirmed by the Oxford MS. (d. 35). On this subject see Maimonides, Kiddush Ha-Chodesh iv. 2, Schürer, i. (3rd ed.), pp. 752 ff.; F. K. Ginzel, *Handbuch der Mathematischen und Technischen Chronologie*, ii. p. 67; and L. Wreschner, *Samaritanische Traditionen*, p. 10. In the past year (5675) the Teḳuphah of Ṭebeth fell on Wednesday, January 6, 1915, at 10.30 p.m., *i.e.* the fifth day of the Hebrew week, the 21st of Ṭebeth, and the Teḳuphah of Nisan fell on Thursday, April 8, 1915, at 6 a.m., *i.e.* the 24th of Nisan, *after* the termination of the Passover festival. The rule in our text does not apply now in actual practice. See Jozeroth, ed. Arnheim, p. 73.

[3] The first editions read: "they intercalate the year on account of the Teḳuphoth." This reading agrees with "Megillah of Abiathar," p. 469.

[4] Of intercalated years.

[5] Our text has the following order of years, 3rd, 6th (the 3rd after the preceding year of intercalation), the 8th (*i.e.* two years after the preceding year), 11th (again three years' interval), 14th (again three years' interval), 17th (three years' interval), and the 19th year (two

The intercalation takes place in the presence of three;[1] Rabbi Eliezer says that ten (men are required), as it is said, "God standeth in the congregation[2] of God"[3] (Ps. lxxxii. 1), and if they become less[4] than ten, since they are diminished they place a scroll of the Torah before them,[5] and they are seated in a circle in the court-room,[6] and the greatest (among them) sits first,[7] and the least sits last; and they direct their gaze downwards[8] to the earth and (then) they stand and spread out their hands[9] before their Father who is in heaven, and the chief of the assembly[10] proclaims[11] the name (of God), and they

years' interval). On this question see Ginzel, *op. cit.* pp. 75 f.; and cf. Jesod 'Olam iv. ii. p. 63b, and the works on the Calendar by Lewisohn, p. 40, and Schwarz, p. 78. According to the Oxford MS. (d. 35) the text should read thus: the 3rd, 5th, 8th, 11th, 14th, 16th, and 19th, agreeing with the cycle of Meton the Greek astronomer, with the exception that the latter has the 13th year instead of the 14th year.

[1] Men who know the principle of intercalation.

[2] The "congregation" consists of ten, the Minyan; this is derived from the use of the word "congregation" in connection with the ten spies who brought a false report to Moses in the wilderness (Num. xiv. 27). The Oxford MS. (d. 35) reads here: "'In the congregation of God.' 'Congregation' means only ten (men), as it is said: 'How long shall I bear with this evil congregation,'" etc. (Num. xiv. 27). See "Megillah of Abiathar," pp. 469 f.

[3] Or "in the congregation of the mighty." For the occasions when a Minyan is necessary, see Mishnah Megillah iv. 3, tractate Sopherim x. 8, and *infra*, pp. 127 f. The Talmud B. Synhedrin, 70b, also requires ten men at the intercalation, and cf. Ex. Rab. xv. 20.

[4] *e.g.* if one or more of the ten men go away, see T.B. Berakhoth, 47b. Luria thinks that the text is corrupt, reading "when they had deliberated" instead of "if they become less." The MSS. do not support this suggested emendation.

[5] To read therein the section dealing with the Calendar (Ex. xii. 1 f.).

[6] Such as was used by the Synhedrion at Jerusalem; see T.B. Synhedrin, 35b, 36b, and Sopherim xix. 9.

[7] See T.B. Baba Bathra, 120b, for order of procedure; for a Biblical parallel see Gen. xliii. 33. The text means literally: "And they sit, the greatest according to his greatness, and the least according to his littleness."

[8] See Lev. ix. 24 for "falling on the face," and see Ezek. li. 28.

[9] See Lam. iii. 41; Targ. Onkelos on Gen. xiv. 22, and cf. T.B. Jebamoth, 105b.

[10] The "Rosh Yeshibah" points to Palestine or to the schools of the Geonim in Babylon, or to the Academies in Egypt; see *J.Q.R.* xiv. p. 450, note 1.

[11] *i.e.* the benediction on reading the Torah; see Singer, p. 68. It probably means that the Ineffable Name was pronounced. The "Megillah of Abiathar," p. 469, recounts how the Ineffable Name was mentioned with "sanctification, greater than that of the Day of Atonement when the High Priest pronounced it seven times."

hear a Bath Kol[1] (saying) the following words,[2] "And the Lord spake unto Moses and Aaron . . . saying,[3] This month shall be unto you" (Ex. xii. 1, 2).

If, owing to the iniquity of the generation, they do not hear anything at all;[4] then, if one may say so,[5] He is unable to let His glory abide among them. Happy were they who stood in that place[6] in that hour,[7] as it is said, "Happy is the people who know the joyful sound:[8] they walk, O Lord, in the light of thy countenance" (Ps. lxxxix. 15); in the light of the countenance of the Holy One, blessed be He, they walk.[9]

On the New Moon of Nisan || the Holy One, blessed be He, was revealed to Moses and Aaron in the land of Egypt, and it was the 15th[10] year of the great cycle of the moon, the 16th year of the cycle of intercalation,[11] (and He said): "henceforward the counting devolves on you."[12]

[1] The Heavenly Voice; see Mark i. 11, and cf. *Rabbinic Philosophy and Ethics*, p. 195, note 4.

[2] Lit. "according to this expression." The Oxford MS. (d. 35) adds: "as it is said."

[3] The MS. does not continue the quotation.

[4] R. Eliezer was permitted to hear the Bath Ḳol. See T.B. Baba Mezi'a, 59b, and T.B. Sotah, 48b. In later times this privilege was withdrawn because of the sins of the people.

[5] On this term see Bacher, *Terminologie*, i. pp. 72 f.

[6] *i.e.* the court-room of the Synhedrion. The reference is to the good days of old, long before our book was written.

[7] When the intercalation took place; this was at night. According to the "Megillah of Abiathar," p. 471, the intercalation took place by day; see T.B. Synhedrin, 11b.

[8] *i.e.* the Teru'ah or trumpet blast. The various features of this ceremony have a parallel in the ceremonies of the Ban mentioned *infra*, p. 301. Are we dealing with a Geonic institution?

[9] Luria infers from our narrative that the Shophar was sounded at the intercalation ceremony; see T.B. Synhedrin, *loc. cit.*, and Tosephta Synhedrin ii. 7 ff., p. 417, on this ceremony.

[10] Luria corrects this and reads "the 12th." On the date of the Exodus see Seder 'Olam Rab. v. pp. 11b f.

[11] Of 19 years.

[12] See the "Megillah of Abiathar," p. 464. On the important question as to the probable origin of *P.R.E.* in connection with the intercalation, see *J.Q.R.* (New Series) i. pp. 64 f.

CHAPTER IX[1]

THE CREATION AND WONDERS OF THE FIFTH DAY [10A. ii.]

On the fifth day[2] He caused the waters to bring forth abundantly all kinds of winged fowls, male and female, unclean and clean. By two signs[3] are they declared to be clean, by the crop, and by the craw peeling off. Rabbi Eliezer said: (Another sign was) also by the projecting toe of the claw. Two kinds of birds have been chosen for the offering of a burnt sacrifice,[4] namely, the turtle-dove and the young pigeon.

He[5] caused the waters to bring forth abundantly all kinds of fish, male and female, unclean and clean. By two signs are they declared to be clean, by the fins and by their scales;[6] and if they do not have them (*i.e.* both signs) they are unclean.

On the fifth day He caused the waters to bring forth abundantly all kinds of locusts,[7] male and female, clean and unclean. By two signs are they declared to be clean: by their long legs with which they jump,[8] and by the wings which cover the entire body, such are clean. Such (living things) as were brought forth from the water, namely, fish

[1] In our MS. this is ch. viii.

[2] For the creation on the fifth day see Gen. i. 20–23; 4 Ezra vi. 47 ff.; Jubilees ii. 11, 12; Slav. Enoch xxx. 7. Our book reckons three kinds of living things created on the fifth day: birds, fish, and locusts; in Jubilees, *loc. cit.*, three kinds: great sea monsters, fish, and birds are also enumerated.

[3] On the signs see T.B. Chullin, 59a, 61a and 62a; Tosephta Chullin iii. 22, p. 505, and Pal. Targum on Lev. xi. 13.

[4] This agrees with Luria's reading; the printed texts read: "an offering and a burnt-offering."

[5] The Venice edition adds: "On the fifth day." The 1st ed. omits this and the following words up to "male."

[6] On fish see Lev. xi. 9, 10, 12, and T.B. Chullin, 66b.

[7] See T.B. Chullin, 59a and 65 a, b.

[8] The first editions add: "upon the earth." See Lev. xi. 20–23.

and locusts,[1] are (eaten) without (being subject to the laws of) Shechiṭah[2] (with the ritual slaughtering), but the bird cannot be eaten unless (it be killed) by (the method of) Shechiṭah. Such creatures which have been created from the earth[3] || have their blood covered with earth, and such as have been created from the water must have their blood poured out like water.[4]

[1] Dr. Charles is mistaken in stating that in the "Pirke R. Eliezer ix. it is said that locusts are not created from water" (*Fragments of a Zadokite Work*, p. 31). Just the opposite theory is advocated by our work. The Zadokite Fragment taught that the elements of fire and water were to be found in the composition of the locusts, hence they are to be killed by fire or by water; see Schechter, *op. cit.*, p. 51, note 24, who points out that according to Rabbinic law, the locust requires no killing at all; see Maimonides, Mishneh Torah, Hilkhoth Shechiṭah, ch. i. 1, and Ṭur Joreh Di'ah, 13. The importance of this Halakhah will be appreciated if we are able to fix the date and home of our book. The question has been critically discussed by Dr. Büchler in the *J.Q.R.* (New Series) iii. (1913) pp. 442 f.; see *J.Q.R.* (New Series) iv. pp. 460 ff., where Jubilees v. 30 is cited as bearing on the question. Cf. also Wreschner, *op. cit.* p. 52.

[2] The first editions read: "are eaten, for they are not (killed) by Shechiṭah." For the ritual slaughter of animals by the knife see T.B. Chullin, 27a. This method probably obtained among the early Christians, see Acts xv. 20 and 29, xxi. 25; for further references see Preuschen, *N.T. Dict.* s.v. πνικτός, c. 933.

[3] The MS. actually reads "water," but the text was here originally "earth." The Oxford MS. (d. 35) reads: "Such as were created from the earth have their blood poured out like water, and such as swarmed from the water have their blood covered by the dust." As the parchment of our MS. has been damaged by the erasure, an attempt has also been made to change the word "water" (in the next line) into "earth."

[4] Luria reads: "Such as have been created from the water may have their blood consumed like water, and such as have been created from the earth, their blood is prohibited to be consumed: the exception is the fowl; for although it has been created from the water its blood is prohibited to be consumed, and, moreover, it requires that the blood which falls upon the earth when it is killed must be covered by dust." The traditional text found in our MS. as well as in the first editions is probably correct in view of the unusual Halakhah (or Law) preserved in the *Fragments of a Zadokite Work* (ed. Charles), xiv. 13: "Nor shall fish be eaten unless they are split alive and their blood was shed." Dr Schechter thinks that this rule was "directed against the Rabbinic opinion permitting the eating of the blood of the fish. See Sifra, 39a, and Kerithoth, 20b." See, further, T.B. Chullin, 27b, "where," says Dr. Schechter, "we have a homily to the effect that cattle have to be killed in a certain way because they were created out of the dry land (earth); fish, again, require no killing, being created out of the water; whilst birds, which were created out of alluvial mud (a combination of water and earth), occupy also, with regard to their ritual killing, a middle place between cattle and fish. The notion was that the mode of killing is in some way connected with the element out of which the animal in question was created." See Wreschner, *op. cit.* p. 54. The 1st ed. reads: "its blood is poured out on the earth." The Venice edition agrees with our MS.

Rabbi Eliezer said: Not only concerning the water does the Scripture say that "the waters should bring forth abundantly" (Gen. i. 20), but also concerning the birds [1] which are compared with water, as it is said, "And the uproar of many peoples, which roar like the roaring of the seas" (Isa. xvii. 12), and just as the waters brought forth abundantly on the fifth day, likewise in the future will the nations of the world swarm in the fifth world,[2] and they will fight one another to destroy [3] (one another), as it is said, "And they were broken in pieces, nation against nation, and city against city; [4] for God did vex them with all adversity" (2 Chron. xv. 6). What is written (immediately) afterwards? The Salvation of Israel (is mentioned), as it is said,[5] "But be ye strong; and your hands shall not be slack" (*ibid.* 7).

All rivers flowing on the earth,[6] as soon as they flow on the earth, they are blessed and good and sweet. There is some benefit to the world through them; [7] (when) they flow into the sea they are bad,[8] cursed, and bitter, and they are of no benefit to the world. Why are they similar to Israel? For when the Israelites rely upon the protection of their Creator and do His will, they are blessed and good and sweet, and there is some benefit to the world through them,

[1] The Oxford MS. (d. 35) and the first editions read: "nations of the world."

[2] Is the fifth world the fifth kingdom, *i.e.* the kingdom of the Messiah? Or, is the "fifth world" another way of saying the "fifth era" or "day" of the world? This would be the period 5000 A.M. to 6000 C.E. (*i.e.* 1240–2240 C.E.). Our reading is also preserved in the 1st ed. In the Venice edition the word "fifth" is omitted.

[3] See T.B. 'Abodah Ẓarah, 4a, T.B. Synhedrin, 97b, and Ẓohar, Gen. 46b and 119a, for the wars of the Messianic Age, which were supposed to begin about the end of the fiftieth century A.M.; cf. *infra*, pp. 198–203; and see Rev. xvi. 14 for the internecine strife of the nations.

[4] The first two editions have erred here in a strange manner: they *both* quote as a Scripture text the words: "And I will set nation against nation, kingdom against kingdom, for God did vex them with all adversity." The last clause is part of the quotation from 2 Chron. xv. 6, the first part of this verse being accurately given by our MS. Where do we find the words: "And I will set nation against nation, kingdom against kingdom"? Might one suggest Matt. xxiv. 7, based on Isa. xix. 2 and 2 Chron. xv. 6, as a parallel? See also 4 Ezra xiii. 31.

[5] See Isa. lxii. 11 and Ps. xiv. 7.

[6] The Venice edition omits "flowing on the earth"; the 1st ed. agrees with our text.

[7] Cf. Recognitions of Clement viii. 24 and John of Damascus, *op. cit.* ii. 9.

[8] Luria suggests the reading: "they are cursed, evil."

and for their sake[1] the world stands. (When) the men of Israel depart from their Creator and trust in the statutes of the nations,[2] they are bad, accursed, and bitter, || and there is no benefit in them for the world. Just as the waters of the rivers (are) the food of the waters of the sea,[3] so are (the sinners destined to be) fuel for Gehinnom. All the rains that descend into the sea are (as) seed for (all creatures) in them,[4] and thereby the fish are fed.[5]

On the fifth day the waters in Egypt[6] were changed into blood. On the fifth day our forefathers went forth from Egypt.[7] On the same (*i.e.* fifth) day the waters of the Jordan stood still before the ark of the Covenant of God.[8] On the same (*i.e.* fifth) day Hezekiah stopped the fountains which were in Jerusalem, as it is said, "This same[9] Hezekiah also stopped the upper spring of the waters of Gihon" (*ibid.* xxxii. 30).[10]

On the fifth day He brought forth from the water the Leviathan,[11] the flying serpent, and its dwelling is in the

[1] See Jer. x. 2, 3, and Assumption of Moses i. 12. A parallel to our text is given by 4 Ezra iv. 55, 59, vii. 11.

[2] Cf. Matt. v. 13, 14.

[3] The river water is absorbed by the salt water and thereby the composition of the sea water is modified; see Gen. Rab. v. 3 on this problem.

[4] *i.e.* the sea. Cf. *supra*, p. 30, the rain is the male element in water; see Shocher Tob, Ps. cxlvi. § 3, p. 268a.

[5] The first editions read: "become fruitful."

[6] See Seder 'Olam Rab. iii., and cf. Mishnah 'Edujoth ii. 10 for the duration of the Plagues. Our book (*infra*, p. 330) states that the day of departure was on the third day; on this point see T.B. Sabbath, 87b. Luria thinks that the text should be emended thus: "On the fifth day the sea was divided when our fathers went forth from Egypt."

[7] The reading of our text is preserved in Jalkut, Jonah, § 550, as follows: "It was taught in a Baraitha that R. Eliezer said, On the fifth day the waters of Egypt were turned into blood, on that day our fathers went forth from Egypt; on that day the waters of the Jordan stood still before the ark of the Lord, on that day Hezekiah stopped all the fountains; on the fifth day Jonah fled before God." See first sentence in next chapter of our book.

[8] See Josh. iii. 15, 16; Tosaphoth in Menachoth, 30a, catchword: "From here onwards," refers to the day when Jericho fell; cf. Seder 'Olam Rab. xi.; see Ratner's ed. p. 24a, note 24, for the parallels, and see in our book, *infra*, pp. 423 f.

[9] The printed editions are incorrect here.

[10] On Hezekiah see Aboth de R. Nathan (*a*) ii. pp. 6a, b; and cf. T.B. Berakhoth, 5b, T.B. Pesachim, 56a, and in our book, *infra*, pp. 424 ff.

[11] The Leviathan is the "flying serpent." See Isa. xxvii. 1, and Gen. Rab. vii. 4 with Theodor's note, *in loc.*; 4 Ezra vi. 49 ff. (ed. Box, p. 92); Eth. Enoch lxix. 7 f.; and cf. *Monatsschrift*, lxiii. p. 20. Our book holds the view that the Leviathan was created on the fifth

lowest waters; and between its fins [1] rests the middle bar of the earth.[2] All the great sea monsters in the sea are the food for the Leviathan. Every day [3] it opens its mouth, and the great sea monster destined to be eaten that day (tries) to escape and flee, but it enters the mouth of the Leviathan; and the Holy One, blessed be He, plays with it, as it is said, "This is the Leviathan, whom thou hast created to play with him" [4] (Ps. civ. 26).

Rabbi Mana [5] said: Such creatures which have been created from the earth increase and multiply on the earth, and such which have been brought forth from the water increase and multiply in the water, except all kinds of winged birds, for their creation was || from the water, yet they increase and multiply on the earth, as it is said, "And let the fowl multiply in the earth" (Gen. i. 22). Such as were brought forth from the water increase and multiply by the egg; [6] and such as were created from the earth increase and multiply by fœtus (*i.e.* living offspring).[7]

day, and Behemoth on the sixth day; see *infra*, p. 75; and see also T.B. Baba Bathra, 74b, 75a; Pal. Targum on Gen. i. 21. On Behemoth see Pesikta de R. Kahana vi. p. 58a; Lev. Rab. xxii. 10; Num. Rab. xxi. 18, and Tanchuma, Nizabim, § iv.

[1] The first editions read: "its two fins."

[2] See *infra*, p. 71.

[3] The first editions read here: "And the Holy One, blessed be He, plays with it every day." This part of the sentence is out of place, as it occurs again a few lines farther on in these editions. Our MS. is quite correct here.

[4] The R.V. renders: "whom thou hast formed to take his pastime therein." See Job xli. 5, and cf. Jalkuṭ on Job, § 927.

[5] The first editions read: "Meir."

[6] The 1st ed. reads here: "in the water" instead of "by the egg."

[7] See Basil, *op. cit.* vii. 2; and John of Damascus, *op. cit.* ii. 9, for the creation of and from the water; cf. T.B. Chullin, 27b, Bechoroth, 8a, Pal. Targum on Gen. i. 20, and Midrash Agadah, p. 3. Luria (note 43) suggests an emendation of the text as follows: "Such as *were created* from the water increase and multiply by living offspring" (*e.g.* whales); whereas such as were *brought forth* from the water are hatched from the egg" (*e.g.* the duck). The 1st ed. reads: "multiply on the earth." Does the 1st ed. here preserve the true reading?

CHAPTER X[1]

THE HISTORY OF JONAH [11A. i.]

ON the fifth day Jonah[2] fled before his God. Why did he flee? Because on the first occasion when (God) sent him to restore the border of Israel, his words were fulfilled, as it is said, "And he restored the border of Israel[3] from the entering in of Hamath" (2 Kings xiv. 25).[4] On the second occasion (God) sent him to Jerusalem to (prophesy that He would) destroy it. But[5] the Holy One, blessed be He, did according to the abundance of His tender mercy and repented of the evil (decree), and He did not destroy it;[6] thereupon[7] they called him a lying prophet.[8] On the third occasion[9] (God) sent him against Nineveh[10] to destroy it. Jonah argued with himself, saying, I know that the nations

[1] In our MS. this is marked as ch. ix. Jalkuṭ Makhiri, Jonah, ed. Greenup, pp. 6 ff., contains selections from *P.R.E.* here.

[2] The story of Jonah belongs to the series of events which happened on a Thursday; moreover, the Leviathan mentioned in connection with the story was created on the fifth day. See Jalkut, Jonah, § 550, and *supra*, pp. 63 f.

[3] In the MS. the quotation ends here. The first two editions continue as in our translation.

[4] The Oxford MS. (d. 35) continues this verse: "unto the sea of Arabah, according to the word of the Lord, the God of Israel, which he spake by the hand of his servant Jonah, the son of Amittai the prophet, who was of Gathhepher." In spite of the sins of Israel, this prophecy of Jonah was fulfilled. Jonah is only once referred to in the apocryphal literature, 3 Macc. vi. 8; see LXX text of Tobit xiv. 4.

[5] The first editions add: "because they repented."

[6] It is assumed by our Midrash that this prophecy is referred to by Jonah (iv. 2), "Was not this my *saying* when I was yet in *my country* . . . for I knew that thou art a gracious God . . . and repentest thee of the evil." See T.B. Synhedrin, 89b.

[7] The first editions add "Israel."

[8] See 2 Kings ix. 4, 11, 12. The prophet mentioned in these verses is Jonah, according to Rashi and Kimchi, *in loc.*

[9] See T.B. Jebamoth, 98a.

[10] The first editions read: "to Nineveh."

are nigh to repentance,[1] now they will repent and the Holy One, blessed be He, will direct His anger against Israel. And is it not enough for me that Israel should call me a lying prophet; but shall also the nations of the world (do likewise)? Therefore, behold, I will escape from His presence to a place where His glory is not declared. (If) I ascend above the heavens, it is said,[2] "Above the heavens is his glory" (Ps. cxiii. 4). (If) above the earth,[3] (it is said), "The whole earth is full of his glory" (Isa. vi. 3); behold, I will escape to the sea,[4] to a place || where His glory is not proclaimed. Jonah went down to Joppa, but he did not find there a ship in which he could embark, for the ship in which Jonah might have embarked was two days' journey away from Joppa,[5] in order to test[6] Jonah. What did the Holy One, blessed be He, do? He sent against it a mighty tempest on the sea and brought it back to Joppa. Then Jonah saw and rejoiced in his heart, saying, Now I know that my ways will prosper before me.

He said to the (sailors), We[7] will embark with you. They replied to him, Behold, we are going to the islands

[1] See *infra*, pp. 342 f., and Mekhilta Bô, 1, p. 2; T.J. Synhedrin xi. 7, 30b; Tanchuma Vajiḳra, § vii. This is an excellent dictum. The non-Jews are easily turned to repentance. The first editions read: "this nation is nigh to repentance."

[2] The Venice edition reads: "it is said that His glory is there, as it is said."

[3] The Venice edition reads: "Above the earth? It is said that His glory is there, as it is said." For similar questions see Chrysostomus, *Homily on Repentance*, 3.

[4] In the first editions the word (לים) "to the sea" is replaced by (לי) "for myself."

[5] This addition to the Biblical narrative is preserved in the Midrash Jonah (in Jellinek's *Beth Ha-Midrash*, i. pp. 96–105), and see the Ẓohar, Gen. 121a, b, for further embellishment. This Midrash, as well as our chapter, undoubtedly formed one of the Homilies for the service of the Day of Atonement, the Book of Jonah forming the lesson from the Prophets for the afternoon service of that day. This point is of importance in our estimate of the probable use which our book was intended to render. Was it a book for the Synagogue? Was it intended to supply Midrashic material for the preacher in his public discourses? As far as this 10th Chapter is concerned, the answer is in the affirmative. We shall find further evidence to support this view in the course of our study of this book.

[6] Perhaps the text should read: "In order to test Jonah what did the Holy One, blessed be He, do?"

[7] The MS. reads: "*we* will embark." The 1st and 2nd eds. read: "I will embark."

of the sea, to Tarshish.[1] He said to them, We[2] will go with you. Now (this) is the custom on all ships that when a man disembarks therefrom he pays his fare; but Jonah, in the joy of his heart, paid his fare in advance,[3] as it is said, "But Jonah rose up to flee unto Tarshish from the presence of the Lord; and he went down to Joppa and found a ship going to Tarshish; so he paid the fare thereof, and went down into it,[4] to go with them" (Jonah i. 3).

They had travelled one day's journey, and a mighty tempest[5] on the sea arose against them on their right hand and on their left hand; but the movement[6] of all the ships passing[7] to and fro was peaceful in a quiet sea, but the ship into which Jonah had embarked was in great peril of shipwreck, as it is said, "But the Lord sent out a great wind into the sea, and there was a mighty tempest in the sea, so[8] that the ship was like || to be broken" (*ibid.* 4).

Rabbi Chanina[9] said: (Men) of the seventy languages[10]

[1] Ibn Ezra on Jonah i. 3 tells us on the authority of Sa'adiah that Tarshish is Tarsus; he also gives another opinion that Tunis in Africa is the port referred to. For other views, see Gesenius (Oxford edition), pp. 1076 f.

[2] The MS. reads also here: "*we* will embark." The 1st and 2nd eds. read: "I will embark."

[3] See T.B. Nedarim, 38a, according to which Jonah pays the fares of all on board. See *J.E.* vii. 226 f. for the story of Jonah in Rabbinical literature.

[4] Our MS. ends the quotation here, but adds "etc." The first editions add "etc." after "Joppa."

[5] According to the Midrash Kônen, p. 25, at the creation of the world God stipulated with the sea that it should not suffer Jonah to sail to Tarshish.

[6] Lit. "way."

[7] The versions in Tanchuma Vajiḳra, § viii., and Jalḳuṭ Jonah, *loc. cit.*, differ somewhat. Our text is, however, the source whence the Midrashim have drawn their material. Ḳimchi on Jonah i. 7 remarks: "I have found in the Pirḳê R. Eliezer, A great tempest arose against them on the sea, and on their right hand and on their left hand all the ships were passing to and fro in peace in the tranquillity of the sea; and the ship into which Jonah had embarked was in great distress so that one thought that it would be broken in pieces." See Gen. Rab. xxiv. 4 with reference to the wind sent to hinder Jonah; cf. Lev. Rab. xv. 1 on same point.

[8] The first editions omit the preceding part of the quotation.

[9] The first editions read "Chananjah."

[10] The seventy nations of humanity have each one a representative on board. The ship is a type of the world, which only can find its salvation through the willing martyrdom of the Hebrew, who, although he be inoffensive in his conduct with his fellow-men of all nationalities, is nevertheless quite willing to allow himself to be doomed to destruction in order to relieve his fellow-men of their threatened ruin. This

were there on the ship, and each one had his god in his hand, (each one) saying:[1] And the God who shall reply and deliver us from this trouble, He shall be God.[2] They arose and every one called upon the name of his god, but it availed nought.[3] Now Jonah, because of the anguish of his soul, was slumbering and asleep. The captain of the ship came to him, saying, Behold, we are standing betwixt death and life, and thou art slumbering and sleeping; of what people art thou? He answered them, "I am an Hebrew" (*ibid.* 9). (The captain) said to him, Have we not heard that the God of the Hebrews is great? Arise, call upon thy God, perhaps He will work (salvation) for us according to all His miracles which He did for you at the Reed Sea. He answered them,[4] It is on my account that this misfortune has befallen you; take me up and cast me into the sea and the sea will become calm unto you, as it is said, "And he said unto them, Take me up, and cast me forth into the sea; so shall the sea be calm unto you" (*ibid.* 12).

Rabbi Simeon said: The men would not consent to throw Jonah into the sea; but they cast lots among themselves and the lot fell upon Jonah.[5] What did they do? They took all their utensils which were in the ship, and cast them into the sea[6] in order to lighten it for their (safety), but it availed nought. || They wanted to return[7] to the dry land, but they were unable, as it is said, "Nevertheless the men

universalistic aspect of the mission of the Hebrew is familiar to the student of the Bible. Abraham, Moses, and the suffering servant of God, who is none other than Israel, represent this teaching, which our book enforces. The basis for the Midrashic idea of the seventy nations is afforded by comparing the text of Jonah i. 5, which says, "*And every man* cried unto his God," with the text in Mic. iv. 5, "For *all the people* will walk *every man* in the name of his God."

[1] The first two editions read here: "as it is said, 'Then the mariners were afraid, and cried every man unto his God'" (Jonah i. 5). The Venice edition adds: "They bowed down saying, Let each man call on the name of his God."

[2] Cf. Elijah's appeal on Mount Carmel, 1 Kings xviii. 24.

[3] See Targum, Jonah i. 5.

[4] The first editions add: "I will not hide from you that."

[5] The first editions add here: "as it is said, 'So they cast lots, and the lot fell upon Jonah'" (Jonah i. 7).

[6] See Targum, Jonah, *loc. cit.*, and Midrash Jonah (ed. Jellinek), p. 97.

[7] The reading in our MS. is in agreement with the reading of the Tanchuma (*loc. cit.*) and Jalkuṭ, Jonah, *loc. cit.* The printed texts read, "they wanted to row hard," instead of our reading.

rowed hard to get them back to the land; but they could not" (*ibid.* 13).[1] What did they do? They took Jonah and they stood on the side of the ship, saying, God of the world! O Lord! Do not lay upon us innocent blood, for we do not know what sort of person is this man; and he says deliberately,[2] On my account has this misfortune befallen you.[3]

They took him (and cast him into the sea) up to his knee-joints, and the sea-storm abated. They took him up again to themselves and the sea became agitated again against them.[4] They cast him in (again) up to his neck, and the sea-storm abated. Once more they lifted him up in their midst and the sea was again agitated against them, until they cast him in entirely and forthwith the sea-storm abated,[5] as it is said, "So they took up Jonah, and cast him forth into the sea: and the sea ceased from her raging" (*ibid.* 15).

"And the Lord had prepared a great fish to swallow up Jonah" (*ibid.* 17).[6] Rabbi Tarphon said: That fish was specially appointed from the six days of Creation [7] to swallow up Jonah, as it is said, "And the Lord *had* prepared a great fish to swallow up Jonah" (*ibid.*). He entered its mouth just as a man enters the great synagogue, and he stood (therein). The two eyes of the fish were like windows [8] of glass giving light to Jonah.

Rabbi Meir said: || One pearl was suspended inside the

[1] This quotation is missing in the first two editions.

[2] Lit. "with his mouth." The prayer of the sailors here should be compared with the text in Jonah i. 14. The first editions read: "he said to them."

[3] The first editions add: "take me and cast me into the sea. Forthwith."

[4] The first editions add: "they cast him (into the sea) up to his navel,[1] and the sea-storm abated. Again they took him up among themselves, and the sea again was agitated against them."

[5] The quotation is not given by the first editions; the last clause is wanting in the MS., being replaced by "etc."

[6] This quotation occurs here only in the MS. Its presence suggests the probability of our context being part of a Midrash.

[7] See Gen. Rab. v. 5 and T.B. Bechoroth, 8a.

[8] Our MS. reads "*ampumeth.*" According to Jastrow, *T.D.* 78a, this stands for *ôphsejanioth*, "glass windows." This represents ὀψιανός (obsidian), a stone used as glass, see *infra*, p. 330. See 'Arukh, ed. Kohut, i. 24b. Does the "Great Synagogue" refer to the famous Synagogue of Alexandria?

---

[1] See T.B. Soṭah, 45b.

belly of the fish and it gave illumination to Jonah, like this sun which shines with its might at noon; and it showed to Jonah all that was in the sea and in the depths,[1] as it is said, "Light is sown for the righteous" (Ps. xcvii. 11).

The fish said to Jonah, Dost thou not know that my day had arrived to be devoured in the midst of Leviathan's mouth? Jonah replied, Take me beside it, and I will deliver thee and myself from its mouth. It brought him next to the Leviathan. (Jonah) said to the Leviathan, On thy account have I descended to see thy abode in the sea, for, moreover, in the future will I descend and put a rope in thy tongue,[2] and I will bring thee up and prepare[3] thee for the great feast of the righteous.[4] (Jonah) showed it the seal of our father[5] Abraham (saying),[6] Look at the Covenant (seal), and Leviathan saw it and fled before Jonah a distance of two days' journey. (Jonah) said to it (*i.e.* the fish), Behold, I have saved thee from the mouth of Leviathan, show me what is in the sea and in the depths. It showed him the great river of the waters of the Ocean,[7] as it is said, "The deep was round about me" (Jonah ii. 5), and it showed him the paths of the Reed Sea[8] through which Israel passed, as it is said, "The reeds were wrapped about my head" (*ibid.*); and it showed him the place whence the waves of the sea and its billows flow,[9] as it is said, "All || thy waves and thy billows passed over me" (*ibid.* 3); and

[1] The first editions read here: "and concerning him (*i.e.* Jonah) the Scripture says." The Zohar, Exodus, 48a, offers a parallel to this sentence.

[2] See Job xl. 25 (in Heb.=R.V. xli. 1).

[3] The first editions read: "to sacrifice."

[4] The feast of the righteous in the Messianic age is referred to by Jesus in Matt. xxvi. 29; see also T.B. Baba Bathra, 74a, T.B. Chagigah, 14b, and Aboth iv. 16, and cf. T.B. Sabbath, 153a. The "secret chambers of Leviathan" are referred to in Cant. Rab. i. 4; Eth. Enoch lx. 7–9 describes the Leviathan and the Behemoth; see also 4 Ezra vi. 49–52, and Apoc. Baruch xxix. 4. For further references see Charles' note on p. 115 of his ed. of Eth. Enoch, and *J.E.* viii. 37 f.; see also Volz, *Jüdische Eschatologie*, pp. 351 and 365, and Jellinek, *Beth Ha-Midrash*, vi. pp. 150 f., on "Leviathan Banquet."

[5] The first editions omit "our father."

[6] The Venice edition reads: "he said."

[7] The river of the waters of the ocean means the water which was supposed to surround the earth; see 3 Baruch ii. 1, Apoc. Pauli xxi., xxxi., Eth. Enoch xvii. 5 f., Test. Abraham (*A.N.C.L.* extra vol.), viii. p. 191.

[8] See *infra*, p. 330, and cf. *J.Q.R.* v. pp. 151 f.

[9] This is the reading in Tanchuma Vajiḳra, § viii., and Jalḳuṭ, Jonah, § 550.

it showed him the pillars of the earth in its foundations, as it is said, "The earth with her bars *for the world* were by me" (*ibid.* 6);[1] and it showed him the lowest Sheol,[2] as it is said, "Yet hast thou brought up my life from destruction,[3] O Lord, my God" (*ibid.*); and it showed him Gehinnom,[4] as it is said, "Out of the belly of Sheol I cried,[5] and thou didst hear my voice" (*ibid.* 2); and it showed him (what was) beneath the Temple of God, as it is said, "(I went down) to the bottom of the mountains"[6] (*ibid.* 6). Hence we may learn that Jerusalem stands upon seven (hills[7]), and he saw there the Eben Shethiyah[8] (Foundation Stone) fixed in the depths.[9] He saw there the sons of Korah[10] standing and praying over it. They[11] said to Jonah, Behold thou dost stand beneath the Temple of God, pray and thou wilt be answered. Forthwith Jonah said to the fish, Stand in the place where thou art standing, because I wish to pray. The fish stood (still), and Jonah began to pray before the Holy One, blessed be He, and he said: Sovereign of all the

[1] Cf. Ps. civ. 5 and T.B. Chagigah, 12b.

[2] The Venice edition reads "Gehinnom." See T.B. 'Erubin, 19a. According to the Midrash Kônen, p. 30, "there is one gate to Gehinnom in the sea of Tarshish."

[3] The last words of the quotation do not occur in the MS., but the first editions give them.

[4] The first editions read: "the lowest Sheol." The lowest region in Gehenna; see *infra*, pp. 340 f., 343, 432 f. On the theories about Gehenna see Jellinek, *Beth Ha-Midrash*, i. pp. 147–149; Jerahmeel ix. 11, xiii. 5, xiv. 1 ff.; Eth. Enoch lxiii. 10, with Charles' note, *in loc.*

[5] The first editions give the last words of this quotation, which are missing in the MS.

[6] The roots of the seven mountains in Jerusalem whereon the Temple rested. The mountains are designated in the O.T. as follows: Mount Zion, Mount Moriah, The Holy Mount, The Mount of my Holy Beauty, The Mount of the House of the Lord, The Mount of the Lord of Hosts, and The Lofty Mount of the Mountains.

[7] The word for "hills" is missing in the MS.; some other word was inserted and then erased. It occurs in the Oxford MS. (d. 35). In the letter of Aristeas (83 f.) Jerusalem is described as being situated "on the top of a mountain of considerable altitude. On the summit the Temple had been built in all its splendour."

[8] According to T.J. Joma v. 4, 42c, it was called Foundation Stone because the whole world was founded thereon; see also T.B. Joma, 54b; T.B. Synhedrin, 26b; cf. Eth. Enoch, xviii. 2; and *infra*, p. 266.

[9] The first editions read here: "beneath the Temple of God."

[10] Luria notes that according to Midrash Kônen (p. 31) the "company of Korah" are in the third department of Gehenna. Should the reading be "the company of Korah" instead of "the sons of Korah"? Cf. *J.Q.R.* v. p. 152.

[11] The Venice edition and Midrash Jonah, p. 98, read: "The fish said."

Universe![1] Thou art called "the One who kills" and "the One who makes alive," behold, my soul has reached unto death, now restore me to life. He was not answered until this word came forth from his mouth, "What I have vowed I will perform" (*ibid.* 9), namely, I vowed to draw up Leviathan and to prepare[2] it before Thee, I will perform (this) on the day of the Salvation[3] of Israel, as it is said, "But I will sacrifice unto thee with the voice of thanksgiving" (*ibid.*).[4] Forthwith the Holy One, blessed be He, hinted (to the fish) and it vomited out[5] Jonah || upon the dry land, as it is said, "And the Lord spake unto the fish, and it vomited out Jonah[6] upon the dry land" (*ibid.* 10).

The sailors saw all the signs, the miracles, and the great wonders which the Holy One, blessed be He, did unto Jonah, and they stood and they cast away[7] every one his God, as it is said, "They that regard lying vanities forsake their own shame"[8] (*ibid.* 8). They returned to Joppa and went up to Jerusalem and circumcised the flesh of their foreskins, as it is said, "And the men[9] feared the Lord exceedingly; and they offered a sacrifice unto the Lord" (*ibid.* i. 16). Did they offer sacrifice?[10] But this (sacrifice) refers to the blood of the covenant of circumcision, which is like the blood of a sacrifice.[11] And they made vows every one to bring his children and all belonging to him to the God[12] of Jonah; and they made vows and performed them,

[1] The first editions add: "Thou art called 'the One who brings up' and 'the One who brings down.' I have gone down, now bring me up."

[2] The first editions read: "to sacrifice." See Midrash Jonah, p. 99.

[3] This is the day of the Messianic judgment. For the idea of salvation in the Messianic age see Singer, pp. 49 (second paragraph), 101 (last paragraph), and 129. See also Volz, *op. cit.* pp. 226 f.

[4] This quotation is missing in the first editions.

[5] The first editions read: "it cast forth."

[6] The first editions continue the verse as in the translation; the MS. omits "upon the dry land."

[7] The first editions add: "into the sea."

[8] See Ḳimchi, *in loc.*, for the meaning of Chesed. Kimchi quotes in his commentary on Jonah ii. 9 our passage with a variant reading.

[9] The text of the Bible reads here "men," as in our MS., but the first editions read "the sailors." See Ẓohar, Ex. 231a.

[10] The first editions add: "Is it not (a fact) that they do not accept sacrifices from the nations?" See T.B. Menachoth, 73b, and cf. Paul's attitude towards the table of the idolaters of his day (see 1 Cor. x. 21).

[11] Cf. Ex. Rab. xvii. 3 and 5.

[12] The first editions read: "They vowed and performed (it) that

and concerning them it says, "Upon the proselytes, the proselytes of righteousness."[1]

each one should bring his wife and all his household to the *fear* of the God of Jonah." The "Phoboumenoi" and "Sebomenoi" correspond to these proselytes who fear God. On the subject see Schürer, II. ii. 311–319 (E.T.).

[1] This refers to the Shemoneh 'Esreh, the xiiith benediction (Singer, p. 48, last paragraph). See also T.B. Megillah, 17b, and Midrash Jonah, *loc. cit.*

This chapter should be compared with the Midrash Jonah (ed. Jellinek, and ed. Eisenstein, *Ozar Midrashim*, pp. 217b ff.). Our book was the source used by the author of the Midrash. The variant readings which a comparison of the two texts affords may be illustrated by one example: instead of "the day of the salvation of Israel," the Midrash reads, "the day of my salvation." Again, the prayer of Jonah in the Midrash is considerably longer than that of *P.R.E.*

The story of Jonah is interpreted in a fine Midrashic spirit by Zeno in his 17th tractate. Ephraim (29th chap. on the prophet Jonah) refers to Jonah's dread of being called a "lying prophet," and mentions also the dread inspired by Jonah among the terrible monsters of the deep. A very interesting point is suggested by a passage in Origen, *contra Celsum*, vii. 57, according to which Jonah was considered to be the Messiah in place of Jesus. Our book ascribes certain Messianic functions to Jonah in connection with the Leviathan and the Day of Israel's salvation. Perhaps he is a type of the "Messiah ben Joseph" who is to overcome the Anti-Christ or Satan (*i.e.* the Leviathan). The New Testament connects the story of Jonah with its Messiah; see Matt. xii. 39–41 and *ibid.* xvi. 4; cf. Luke xi. 29–32. The "Fish" as a Christian Messianic emblem may be associated with the Jonah legends.

CHAPTER XI[1]

THE WORK OF CREATION ON THE SIXTH DAY [12B. i.]

On the sixth day (God) brought forth from the earth all kinds of animals, male and female, clean and unclean. By two signs[2] are they declared to be clean: (the signs are) chewing the cud, and dividing the hoof.[3] Three[4] kinds of animals were chosen for the sacrifice of a burnt-offering, namely, the ox, the lamb, and the goat. Every kind of clean animal which is neither *Nevelah*[5] (*i.e.* which has not been slaughtered according to the rules of Shechiṭah[6]) nor Terephah[7] (*i.e.* torn) in the field[8] is permitted to be eaten, except with regard to three parts, namely, the fat, || the blood, and the sinew of the thigh,[9] as it is said, "As the green herb have I given you all" (Gen. ix. 3).[10]

[1] This is the tenth chapter in our MS.

[2] See T.B. Chullin, 59a, and *supra*, p. 60. The attention drawn to the ritual regulations of Shechiṭah and to the clean animals is what one would expect in a popular treatise for perusal in the home or Synagogue. This seems to be the tendency of much of the Pseudepigrapha, such as the Book of Jubilees or the Testaments of the Twelve Patriarchs. The Jewish law as to clean animals is explained allegorically by the Epistle of Barnabas x.

[3] See Lev. xi. 4.

[4] See Tanchuma, Shemini, § vii.; there are only these three kinds of clean animals. Cf. T.B. Chullin, 63b.

[5] This word is usually rendered "carrion."

[6] On Shechiṭah see *J.E.* xi. 253 ff.

[7] Terephah is interpreted to mean not merely the flesh of an animal torn in the field, but all animal flesh which has not been killed according to the rules of Shechiṭah, and which has become unfit for consumption according to Jewish law and custom. See Acts x. 14, for "unclean" food.

[8] The Oxford MS. (d. 35) and some editions read here "its flesh," instead of "in the field." The Prague edition reads: "it is kasher" (ritually in order and permitted). Cf. Ex. xxii. 31, on which our text is based, and see Baraitha of the 32 Middoth, ed. Reiffmann, p. 37.

[9] See Gen. xxxii. 32.

[10] According to T.B. Synhedrin, 59b (and cf. Siphra, Shemini, p. 48a), animal flesh was permitted to the "sons of Noah." Had Adam not sinned, animal flesh would have been prohibited, says the Midrash Agadah, Genesis, p. 5.

On the sixth day (God) brought forth from the earth seven clean beasts;[1] their slaughter and the method of consumption are similar[2] to the (rules observed) with a bird; and all the rest of the beasts in the field are entirely[3] unclean.

He[4] brought forth from the earth all kinds of abominations[5] and creeping things, all of them are unclean.[6] Such (creatures) which have been created from the earth, their life (or soul) and body are from the earth, and when they return they touch their dust[7] at the place whence they were created, as it is said, "Thou takest away their breath, they die, and return to their dust"[8] (Ps. civ. 29); and it is written, "And the spirit of the beast goes downward to the earth" (Eccles. iii. 21).[9]

On the sixth day He brought forth from the earth a beast (Behemoth) which lies stretched out on a thousand hills[10] and every day has its pasture on a thousand hills, and overnight (the verdure) grows of its own account as though he had not touched it, as it is said, "Surely the mountains bring him forth food" (Job xl. 20). The waters

[1] The first editions add here: "namely, the hart, the gazelle, the roebuck, the wild-goat, the pygarg, the antelope, and the chamois."[1]

[2] The text is difficult to interpret; as regards fowl, only "one sign" is essential for the ritual slaughter, whereas "two signs" are requisite in the case of the animals mentioned; see T.B. Chullin, 71a, 89b, and 92b.

[3] Lit. "all of them."

[4] The first editions read: "On the sixth day He brought forth."

[5] Perhaps the original text was "Sherazim" (reptiles), instead of "Sheḳazim" (abominations); see, however, Deut. xiv. 3. The printed texts omit "kinds of."

[6] And therefore not to be eaten.

[7] The first editions read: "when they die they return to the place whence they were created."

[8] The first editions do not give the last clause of the quotation.

[9] The distinction implied here between man and beast is in the origin of the spirit, that of man is heavenly whilst that of the beast is of the earth.

[10] Cf. Ps. l. 10 and Job xl. 15, "Behold now Behemoth, which I made"; see T.B. Baba Bathra, 74b, and Targum on Ps. l. 10. Cf. *supra*, p. 63, note 11, and see 4 Ezra (ed. Box), pp. 90 ff. The Leviathan was created, according to our author, on the fifth day, whereas the Behemoth was created on the sixth day; see Jerahmeel v. and vi.; Jalkut, Gen. § 12, and *J.E.* viii. 37 ff.; and cf. Num. Rab. xxi. 18, and Lev. Rab. xxii. 10. On "Behemoth" see Midrash Kônen, pp. 26 and 37.

---

[1] See Deut. xiv. 5. The Venice ed. (1544) adds: "and all of them (as regards) their slaughter," etc.

of the Jordan give him water to drink, for the waters of the Jordan surround all the earth,[1] half thereof (flow) above the earth and the other half below the earth,[2] as it is said, "He is confident, though Jordan swell even to his mouth" (*ibid.* 23). This (creature) is destined for the day of sacrifice, for the great banquet of the righteous,[3] as it is said, "He only that made him can make his sword[4] to approach unto him" (*ibid.* 19).

The[5] Holy One, blessed be He, spake to the Torah:[6] "Let us make || man in our image, after our likeness" (Gen. i. 26). (The Torah) spake before Him: Sovereign of all the worlds! The man[7] whom Thou wouldst[8] create will be limited in days and full of anger; and he will come into the power of sin. Unless Thou wilt be long-suffering with him, it would be well for him not to have come into the world.[9] The Holy One, blessed be He, rejoined: And is it for nought that I am called "slow to anger"[10] and "abounding in love"? He began to collect the dust of the first man from the four corners of the world;[11] red,

[1] The first editions read: "the land of Israel." Cf. Eth. Enoch xxvi. 2 f.

[2] See T.B. Baba Bathra, *loc. cit.*, and cf. Gen. Rab. v. 8, and xxiii. 7.

[3] See *supra*, p. 70. According to Midrash Agadah, Gen. p. 3, the female companion of the Leviathan is reserved for the Messianic Banquet; cf. Pal. Targ. on Gen. i. 2, and cf. T.B. Baba Bathra, 75a, Gen. Rab. vii. 4, Lekach Tob, Gen. p. 14.

[4] To slay him.

[5] The first editions read: "Forthwith the Holy One," etc.

[6] The Torah is the instrument in God's hand at the Creation; see *supra*, p. 12, and Gen. Rab. i. 1. Cf. Midrash Kônen, p. 23, based on Prov. iii. 19. The idea was used by the author of the Epistle of Barnabas v. 5, vi. 12, where God is represented as consulting the Christ. According to other traditions of the Church and Synagogue, God consulted the ministering angels at the creation of man; cf. Midrash Agadah, Gen. p. 4, and Irenæus, *adv. Hær.* i. 24.

[7] The first edition reads: "This man." The Venice edition has: "The world is Thine, this man," etc.

[8] The Venice edition adds here: "is Thine." The idea expressed by the next few words, "that man would have but few days," is to be compared with p. 125, *infra*. The sentence is based on Job xiv. 1.

[9] See Matt. xviii. 6, and Eth. Enoch xxxviii. 2.

[10] See *Rabbinic Philosophy and Ethics*, p. 212, and Test. Abraham, *A.N.C.L.* (extra vol.) p. 192, and cf. Wisdom xi. 23 f.

[11] The first editions read: "earth." The Pal. Targum on Gen. ii. 7 says: "And the Lord God created man with two inclinations; and He took dust from the place of the House of the Sanctuary and from the four quarters of the world, and mixed (the dust) with all the waters of the world, and created him red, dark red (or brown), and

black, white,[1] and "pale green,"[2] (which) refers to the body.

Why (did He gather man's dust) from the four corners of the world?[3] Thus spake the Holy One, blessed be He: If a man should come from the east to the west, or from the west to the east,[4] and his time comes to depart from the world, then the earth[5] shall not say, The dust of thy body is not mine,[6] return to the place whence thou wast created.[7] But (this circumstance) teaches thee that in every place where a man goes or comes,[8] and his end approaches when he must depart from the world, thence is the dust of his body, and there it returns to the dust, as it is said, "For dust thou art, and unto dust shalt thou return" (*ibid.* iii. 19).

The day had twelve hours;[9] in the first hour He collected

white." It is evident that the Targum has used our book in this context. See also Tanchuma, Peḳudê, § iii. On the creation of Adam see T.B. Synhedrin, 38b, Ẓohar, Gen. 35b, *ibid.* 205b, and *infra*, Chapter XII. Cf. Grünbaum, *Beiträge*, pp. 54 ff.

[1] The first editions add the following: "and yellow. 'Red,' this is the blood; 'black' refers to the entrails;[1] 'white' refers to the bones and sinews." Cf. T.B. Niddah, 31a.

[2] Jalḳuṭ, Gen. § 13, reads as our MS., "pale green." The first editions read "yellow." Might the four colours indicate the different colours of the skin of men?

[3] See Book of Adam and Eve (ed. Malan) I. xxxiv., and Slavonic Enoch xxx. 13; and cf. Tertullian, *Against the Valentinians*, xxiv., and the Book of the Bee (ed. Budge), p. 16.

[4] The first editions add: "or to any place where he may go."

[5] The first editions add: "which is in that place."

[6] The first editions add: "and I will not receive thee."

[7] According to Gen. Rab. xx. 10, and Tanna de bê Elijahu Rab. xxxi. (ed. Friedmann), p. 164, the "return" of man to the dust is held to signify the resurrection.

[8] The first editions read: "and his end comes to depart from the world, whence the dust of his body comes thence it returns, and that dust will raise its voice, as it is said," etc.

[9] Luria thinks that the order of the hours of the day whereon Adam was created is a gloss added by a copyist who knew the legends of the Talmud; cf. T.B. Synhedrin, *loc. cit.* See Aboth de R. Nathan (*a*) i. p. 3a; Pesiḳta Rabbathi, § xlvi. p. 187b, note 7; Lev. Rab. xxix. 1; Shocher Ṭob, Ps. xcii. 3; Tanchuma, Shemini, § viii. R. Bechai on Gen. ii. 7 gives parallel readings to our text. The Church literature also has many legends of the Haggadic type concerning the creation of Adam; thus the Apostolic Constitutions, vii. 34, says: "Thou hast exhibited man (Adam) as the ornament of the world, and formed him a body out of the four elements." Irenæus (*adv. Hær.* v. 23) says: "Adam sinned on the sixth day of the

---

[1] See T.B. Kerithoth, 22a; perhaps the reference is to the liver and spleen.

the dust for (the body of) Adam, in the second (hour) He formed it into a mass,[1] in the third (hour) He gave it its shape, in the fourth (hour) He endowed || it with breath,[2] in the fifth (hour) he stood on his feet,[3] in the sixth (hour) he called the (animals by their) names, in the seventh (hour) Eve was joined to him (in wedlock), in the eighth (hour) they were commanded concerning the fruits of the tree, in the ninth (hour) they went up to (their) couch as two and descended as four,[4] in the tenth (hour)[5] they transgressed His commandment, in the eleventh (hour) they were judged, in the twelfth (hour) they were driven forth, as it is said, "So he drove out the man" (*ibid.* 24).

And He formed[6] the lumps of the dust of the first man into a mass[7] in a clean place,[8] (it was) on the navel[9] of the earth. He shaped him and prepared[10] him, but breath and soul were not in him. What did the Holy One, blessed be He, do? He breathed with the breath of the soul of His mouth, and a soul was cast[11] into him, as it is said, "And he breathed into his nostrils the breath of life" (*ibid.* ii. 7).

Creation." See also Aphraates, *Homilies*, ed. Wright, p. 168; other references are given by Ginzberg, *Die Haggada bei den Kirchenvätern*, p. 50; and cf. Kohut in *Z.D.M.G.* xxv. pp. 59–94, and *J.E.* i. 174 ff.

[1] See Hippolytus (in *A.N.C.L.* vi. p. 130) for Adam legends, and cf. *Clementine Homilies*, ii.

[2] Or, "a soul was cast into him." The first editions read: "He cast a soul into him." See Jalkuṭ, Gen. § 15, and Midrash Abkhir, and cf. W. R. Harper Memorial Vols. i. p. 258.

[3] The first editions read: "He made him stand on his feet."

[4] See Jubilees iii. 34, and cf. Gen. Rab. xxii. 2 and Book of Adam and Eve (ed. Malan) I. lxxiii. Perhaps our book refers to the conception of Abel and his twin-sister. The Church Fathers deal with similar legends, see Cyril of Jerusalem, Catechism, xii. 6; cf. *Schatzhöhle*, p. 7, and the Book of the Bee, p. 24.

[5] The first editions add: "They were brought into the Garden of Eden and." This reading is contradicted by our book, see *infra*, p. 84. See also the Book of the Bee, p. 23.

[6] The story of man's creation is recapitulated here and in the next chapter. We have a collection of three variant accounts of the same legend. See Introduction.

[7] See Pal. Targ. Gen. ii. 7 quoted *supra*, p. 76, note 11; Gen. Rab. xiv. 7 and 8 on the creation of Adam. See also T. J. Sabbath ii. 4, p. 5b.

[8] Gen. Rab. xiv. 8 says: "He was created from the place of his atonement," *i.e.* the Temple.

[9] Palestine; see Ezek. xxxviii. 12 for the term "navel of the earth." See Jubilees viii. 12, 19; Eth. Enoch xxvi. i.; the Book of the Bee, p. 17; and *infra*, p. 266.

[10] *i.e.* adorned him with the faculties which distinguish man from the beast.

[11] See *supra*, note 2, on this phrase; and cf. Gen. Rab. *loc. cit.*

Adam stood and he began to gaze upwards and downwards.[1] He saw all the creatures which the Holy One, blessed be He, had created; and he[2] was wondering in his heart, and he began to praise and glorify his Creator, saying, "O Lord, how manifold are thy works!" (Ps. civ. 24).[3] He stood on his feet and was adorned with the Divine Image. His height was from east to west, as it is said, "Thou hast beset me behind and before" (*ibid.* cxxxix. 5). "Behind" refers to the west, "before" refers to the east.[4] All the creatures saw him and became afraid[5] of him, thinking that he was their Creator, and they came to prostrate || themselves before him.

Adam said to them: What (is this), ye creatures! Why are ye come to prostrate yourselves before me?[6] Come, I and you, let us go and adorn in majesty and might, and

[1] The first editions add here: "and his height was from one end of the world to the other,[1] as it is said, 'Thou hast beset me *behind* and *before*' (Ps. cxxxix. 5). 'Behind' refers to the west, 'before' refers to the east."

[2] The first editions read: "he began to glorify the Name of his Creator."

[3] This quotation from Ps. civ. is very appropriately placed in Adam's mouth, inasmuch as this psalm is a song of the Creation.

[4] This passage in this connection is not in the printed texts.

[5] See *Rabbinic Philosophy and Ethics*, p. 22, and Eccles. Rab. to Eccles. vi. 10. The word "creatures" of our text reads "ministering angels" in the Midrashim. Slav. Enoch xxxi. 3 refers to the envy of Satan "because things were subservient to Adam on earth." See also Philo, *G.T.* i. p. 57, n. 3, and Wisdom ix. 2, x. 2.

[6] Have we here a polemic against Gnostic doctrines? See Freudenthal, *Hellenistische Studien*, p. 69. The idea of the first Adam being a "lower" God is reflected in the doctrine of the "Second Adam." See 1 Cor. xv. 45–49 for the "Second Adam," and cf. *Hellenism and Christianity*, pp. 44 f.

---

[1] See T.B. Chagigah, 12a; and cf. Gen. Rab. viii. 1 and xxiv. 2. According to Ecclesiasticus xlix. 16 Adam was "above every living thing in the creation"; the Church Fathers have many legends as to the original state of Adam before he sinned; see Basil, discourse on "God not being the cause of evil," vii., where the original glory of Adam in Paradise is described; Irenæus, *adv. Hær.* i. 30. 6, refers to the legend of the immense size of Adam; according to Chrysostomus (Homilies on 1 Cor. xvii. 3) Adam was like an angel endowed with the gift of prophecy. See also Hilgenfeld, *Die Jüdische Apokalyptik*, p. 230 f. For later views of Christian scholars see Diestel, *op. cit.* pp. 488 f. On Adam's creation see also Slav. Enoch xxx. 10 ff. The Rabbis held different views on the question of the size of Adam's body; cf. T.B. Rosh Ha-Shanah, 11a; Baba Bathra, 75a. Cf. Philo, *de Mundi opific.* Mi. 32 f. and 35, C.W. i. p. 39, § 136 f., and p. 42, § 51.

acclaim as King over us the One[1] who created us. If there be no people to acclaim the king as king, the king acclaims himself.[2] If there be no people to praise the king, the king praises himself. In that hour Adam opened his mouth and all the creatures answered after him, and they adorned in majesty and might and acclaimed their Creator as King over themselves, and they said, " The Lord reigneth, he is apparelled with majesty " (*ibid.* xciii. 1).[3]

Ten kings ruled from one end of the world to the other. The first king was the Holy One, blessed be He, who rules in heaven and on earth,[4] and it was His intention to raise up kings on earth, as it is said, " And he changeth the times and the seasons; [5] he removeth kings, and setteth up kings " (Dan. ii. 21).

The second king was Nimrod, who ruled from one end of the world to the other, for all the creatures were dwelling in one place and they were afraid of the waters of the flood,[6] and Nimrod was king over them,[7] as it is said, "And the *beginning* of his kingdom was Babel"[8] (Gen. x. 10).

The third king was Joseph, who ruled from one end of the world to the other, as it is said, " And *all* the

[1] The Prague edition reads: "The Living One." The Slavonic Book of Adam and Eve (ed. Jagíc, p. 9) speaks of Adam praising God in Paradise in company with the angels.

[2] The 1st ed. reads this sentence thus: " Because the people acclaim the king and no king acclaims himself, if there be no people to acclaim him." The next sentence is omitted by the first editions; their text continues: " Adam went alone and acclaimed Him king first, and all the creatures (did likewise) after him, and he said, ' The Lord reigneth,' " etc.

[3] According to T.B. Rosh Ha-Shanah, 31a, this psalm was recited in the Temple on the sixth day of the week. This custom still obtains in the Synagogue; see Singer, p. 83.

[4] See Targumim (Rishon and Shêni) on Esth. i. 1, T.B. 'Erubin, 53a, T.B. Megillah, 11a, where Ahab, Nebuchadnezzar, and Ahasuerus only are mentioned. The text of Neh. ix. 5, 6 was probably used by the writer of our Midrash. Our book has been used by the writer of the Midrash of the Ten Kings; see Horowitz, *op. cit.* pp. 39 f.

[5] The MS. omits the rest of the quotation, which is given by the first editions.

[6] Cf. Josephus, *Ant.* i. 4. 1.

[7] See *infra*, pp. 174 f., and cf. Jalkut, Gen. § 62, and see Book of Jashar vii. 45, " And Nimrod reigned in the earth over all the sons of Noah "; and cf. Jerahmeel xxxi. 20, Pal. Targ. Gen. x. 10, and Jalkut ii. § 211. A different explanation is given by Josephus, *loc. cit.*

[8] On Nimrod see *J.E.* ix. 309 ff. and *Rabbinic Philosophy and Ethics*, pp. 44 f.

earth came || into Egypt to Joseph" (*ibid.* xli. 57). It is not written here "Egypt came,"[1] but "they came into Egypt,"[2] for they brought their tribute and their presents to Joseph to buy (corn); for forty years he was second to the king,[3] and for forty years he was king[4] alone, as it is said, "Now there arose a *new* king over Egypt" (Ex. i. 8).[5]

The fourth king was Solomon, who reigned from one end of the world to the other, as it is said, "And Solomon ruled over *all* the kingdoms" (1 Kings iv. 21); and it says, "And they brought every man his present,[6] vessels of silver, and vessels of gold, and raiment, and armour, and spices, horses, and mules, a rate year by year" (*ibid.* x. 25).

The fifth king was Ahab, king of Israel, who ruled from one end of the world to the other,[7] as it is said, "As the Lord thy God liveth, there is *no* nation or kingdom,[8] whither my lord hath not sent to seek thee" (*ibid.* xviii. 10). All the princes of the provinces[9] were controlled[10] by him; they sent and brought their tribute and their presents to Ahab. Are not all the princes of the provinces of the world two hundred and thirty-two?[11] as it is said, "Then he mustered the young men of the princes of the provinces, and they were two hundred and thirty-two" (*ibid.* xx. 15).

[1] The first editions read: "'Earth' is not written here, but 'and *all* the earth.'" Earth or land would refer to Egypt alone, *all* the earth refers to all countries.

[2] See *infra*, pp. 306 f., and cf. Gen. Rab. xc. 6. "The famine was restricted to Phœnicia, Arabia, and Palestine," says the Midrash.

[3] The first editions add: "of Egypt."

[4] See T.B. Soṭah, 11a, Book of Jashar lviii. 6; and cf. *J.E.* vii. 248 ff. for "Joseph in Rabbinical literature."

[5] The Oxford MS. (d. 35) adds "etc." The verse continues: "who knew not Joseph." Hence the inference that the new king did not know his predecessor Joseph.

[6] The rest of the verse is omitted by our MS., but it is given by the first editions. On Solomon see *J.E.* xi. 439 f.

[7] The first editions omit the words "who ruled . . . other."

[8] The first editions and our MS. do not continue the quotation, but add "etc."

[9] איפרכיא or אפרכיא (ἐπαρχία), prefecture.

[10] Or, "were conquered."

[11] The first editions read here: "Ahasuerus ruled over half the world, 116 provinces, and by the merit of Esther 11 more provinces were added to him, as it is said, 'Ahasuerus who reigned, from India unto Ethiopia, one hundred and seven and twenty provinces'"[1] (Esth. i. 1).

[1] See Esth. Rab. on Esth. i. 1 and T.B. Megillah, 11a, on the 127 provinces.

The sixth king was Nebuchadnezzar, who [1] ruled from one end of the world to the other.[2] Moreover, he ruled over the beasts of the field and the birds of heaven, and they could not open their mouth except by the permission of Nebuchadnezzar, || as it is said,[3] "And *wheresoever* the children of men dwell, the beasts of the field and the fowls of the heaven hath he given into thine hand" (Dan. ii. 38).

The seventh king was Cyrus,[4] who ruled from one end of the world to the other, as it is said, "Thus saith Cyrus king of Persia,[5] *All* the kingdoms of the earth hath the Lord, the God of heaven, given me" (2 Chron. xxxvi. 23). Ahasuerus ruled over half the world. Is not half the world but 116 provinces, as it is said, "This is Ahasuerus, who reigned from India unto Ethiopia" (Esth. i. 1).[6]

The eighth king was Alexander [7] of Macedonia, who ruled from one end of the world to the other, as it is said, "And as I was considering, behold, an he-goat came from the west [8] over the face of the *whole* earth" (Dan. viii. 5). "Over the earth" is not written here, but "over the face of the *whole* earth." [9] And not only that, but he wished to ascend to heaven in order to know what is in heaven, and to descend into the depths in order to know what is in

[1] See *supra*, p. 81, note 7.

[2] The MS. omits here the following passage, which occurs in this context in the first two editions: "as it is said, 'And wheresoever the children of men dwell'" (Dan. ii. 38). The preceding verse reads: "Thou, O king, art king of kings."

[3] The first editions vary the quotation by reading Isa. x. 14: "And there was none that moved the wing, or that opened the mouth, or chirped." This verse is applied by Isaiah to Sennacherib; see *infra*, pp. 39c ff., for a reference to Nebuchadnezzar; and cf. Dan. ii. 37, and T.B. Sabbath, 149b. The printed texts differ from the MS. here by omitting any reference to the beasts of the field.

[4] On Cyrus as king of the earth see Jeraḥmeel lxxviii. 1. See also T.B. Megillah, 12a, and T.B. Rosh Ha-Shanah, 3b.

[5] The MS. ends the quotation here; the first editions continue till "earth," adding "etc.," which also occurs in the MS.

[6] This paragraph in its context is peculiar to our MS.; see *supra*, p. 81, note 11.

[7] On Alexander the Great in Rabbinic literature see *J.E.* i. 342 f., where a good bibliography is to be found at the end of the article. See also Jeraḥmeel, Index, p. 299, *s.v.* "Alexander."

[8] The quotation in the MS. ends here; the first editions agree in this instance.

[9] The first editions add here: "that he might know what was at the ends of the earth." The phrase occurs in a modified form a few lines lower down in our MS.

the depths,[1] and not only that, but he attempted to go to the ends of the earth in order to know what was at the ends of the earth. The Holy One, blessed be He, divided his kingdom[2] among the four corners (or winds) of the heavens, as it is said, "And when he shall stand up, his kingdom shall be broken, and shall be divided towards the four winds of the heaven" (*ibid.* xi. 4).

The ninth king is King || Messiah, who, in the future, will rule from one end of the world to the other,[3] as it is said, "He shall have dominion also from sea to sea" (Ps. lxxii. 8);[4] and another Scripture text says, "And the stone that smote the image became a great mountain, and filled *the whole earth*" (Dan. ii. 35).[5]

The tenth king will restore the sovereignty to its owners.[6] He who was the first king will be the last king, as it is said, "Thus saith the Lord, the King . . . I am the first, and I am the last;[7] and beside me there is no God" (Isa. xliv. 6); and it is written, "And the Lord shall be king over *all* the earth" (Zech. xiv. 9).[8]

[1] See T.J. 'Abodah Ẓarah iii. 1, 42c.

[2] See Num. Rab. xiii. 14.

[3] Not merely over Palestine does the Messianic kingdom extend, but over the whole world. This universalism is noteworthy.

[4] This verse is not given in the first editions. The verse continues: "And from the river unto the ends of the earth."

[5] See Jalḳuṭ, *in loc.*, and Num. Rab. *loc. cit.* This verse was known to Josephus as a Messianic text; see *Ant.* x. 10. 4.

[6] The first editions read: "to its owner"; see *infra*, p. 130, and Maimonides, Hilkhoth Melakhim xi. 4.

[7] The MS. ends quotation here; the first editions continue the text.

[8] The Messianic kingdom is universal in space, but not in time; the kingdom of God which follows the kingdom of the Messiah will be eternal and universal. The first editions continue: "and the sovereignty shall return to its (rightful) heirs and then, 'The idols shall utterly pass away. And the Lord alone shall be exalted in that day' (Isa. ii. 18, 17). And He will tend His flock and cause them to lie down, as it is written, 'I myself will feed my sheep, and I will cause them to lie down' (Ezek. xxxiv. 15); and we shall see Him eye to eye, as it is written, 'For they shall see, eye to eye, when the Lord returneth to Zion'" (Isa. lii. 8).

CHAPTER XII[1]

ADAM IN PARADISE [14A. ii.]

WITH love abounding did the Holy One, blessed be He, love the first man, inasmuch as He created him in[2] a pure locality, in the place of the Temple,[3] and He brought him into His palace,[4] as it is said, "And the Lord God took the man, and put him into the garden of Eden[5] to dress it and to keep it" (Gen. ii. 15). From which place did He take him? From the place of the Temple, and He brought him into His palace, which is Eden, as it is said, "And he put him into the garden of Eden to dress it" (*ibid.*).[6] Perhaps thou wilt say:[7] To plough (the fields) and cast out[8] the stones

[1] In the MS. this is ch. xi.

[2] The first editions read: "from a pure and holy place. From which place did He take him? From the site of the Temple."

[3] Man's body is an emblem of God's sanctuary. In the preceding chapter we are told that God gathered the *dust* to form the first man from the four corners of the earth, establishing thereby the right of every human being to live and to be buried in any part of the earth. A similar idea was known to Philo, *de Mundi opific.* Mi. 35, C.W. i. p. 42, § 51. As to the Temple being the site of Adam's origin see T.J. Naẓir vii. 2, 52b, and Gen. Rab. xiv. 8, and cf. *infra*, p. 143. Eden was more than a mere garden. See T.B. Berakhoth, 34b.

[4] "Palace" recalls Dan. xi. 45.

[5] The words "to dress it and to keep it" are missing in the MS., but they are found in the 1st ed.

[6] This does not occur here in the printed texts, which continue: "What labour then was there in the midst of the garden, that (the text) should say: 'to dress it and to keep it'?" According to Jubilees iii. 15, "Adam and his wife were in the garden of Eden for seven years tilling and keeping it, and we gave him work, and we instructed him to do everything that is suitable for tillage." As we shall see, our book gives an allegorical interpretation of this "work in Eden."

[7] The first editions add here: "There was work (to be done) in the garden of Eden, namely, that he should prune the vines in the vineyards."

[8] See Isa. xxviii. 24 for phraseology.

from the ground.[1] But did not all the trees grow up of their own accord?[2]

Perhaps thou wilt say: There was some other work (to be done) in the garden of Eden, (such as) to water the garden. But did not a river flow through and issue forth from Eden, and water the garden, as it is said, || "And a river went out of Eden to water the garden" (*ibid.* 10)?

What then is the meaning of this expression: "to dress it and to keep it"? (The text) does not say "to dress it and to keep it" except (in the sense) of being occupied with the words of the Torah[3] and keeping all its commandments,[4] as it is said, "to keep the way of the tree of life" (*ibid.* iii. 24). But the "tree of life" signifies only the Torah,[5] as it is said, "It is a tree of life to them that lay hold upon it" (Prov. iii. 18).

And (Adam) was at his leisure in the garden of Eden, like one of the ministering angels.[6] The Holy One, blessed be He, said: I am alone in My world and this one (Adam) also is alone in his[7] world. There is no propagation before Me and this one (Adam) has no propagation in his life;[8] hereafter all the creatures[9] will say: Since there was no propagation in his life,[8] it is he who has created us.[10] It is

[1] The first editions add: "or again, that he should pile up the sheaves or cut (the corn)."

[2] Cf. Gen. Rab. xiii. 1.

[3] Torah means not merely the written word of God, but also its interpretation and implication.

[4] The printed texts read differently here: "to keep the way of the tree of life." See Siphrê, Deut. § 41.

[5] The Palestinian Targum renders Gen. ii. 15 as follows: "And the Lord God took the man from the mountains of worship, where he had been created, and made him dwell in the garden of Eden, to do service in the Law and to keep its commandments." A similar interpretation occurs in the Church Father Theophilus (*To Autolycus*, ii. 24) and in the Slavonic Enoch xxxi. 1: "And I made a garden in Eden in the East, and (I ordained) that he should observe the Law and keep the instruction."

[6] Man is become "like one of us," was interpreted by the Midrash, Gen. Rab. xxi. 5, and Mekhilta, Beshallach, vi. p. 33a (n. 18 for parallels) as meaning: "like one of the ministering angels." This idea of the Midrash was known to Justin Martyr, *Dial. c. Tryph.* lxii.

[7] Some texts read: "My." See Pal. Targum, Gen. ii. 18.

[8] Lit. "before him."

[9] *Supra*, p. 79, we read that the animals wished to worship Adam, thinking he was their Maker. The belief was prevalent in former days that all the animals in Paradise were endowed with speech and reasoning power. See Jubilees iii. 28 (n. 28), and Grünbaum, *op. cit.* pp. 56, 60.

[10] Our author may wish to refute the notion obtaining in some non-Jewish religions that God had physical offspring.

not good for man to be alone, as it is said, " And the Lord God said, It is not good for man to be alone; I will make him an help meet for him . . ." (Gen. ii. 18).[1]

Rabbi Jehudah said:[2] If he be worthy she shall be an help meet for him; if not, she shall be against him to fight him.[3]

When the earth heard this expression[4] thereupon it trembled and quaked, crying before its Creator: Sovereign of all worlds! I have not the power to feed the multitude[5] of mankind. The Holy One, blessed be He, replied: I and thou will (together) feed the multitude[5] of mankind. They agreed to divide (the task) between themselves: the night was for the Holy One, blessed be He, || and the day (was apportioned) to the earth.[6] What did the Holy One, blessed be He, do? He created the sleep of life,[7] so that man lies down and sleeps whilst He sustains

[1] Thereby divine attributes will not be given to him by the other creatures. They will perceive that man is not omnipotent. Our Midrash may also hint that Adam (first or Second Adam) was not the Creator. As we have pointed out, the view that the Second Adam was the Creator obtained in early Christian circles. See Gen. Rab. xii. 7.

[2] The first editions insert here: "Do not read[1] (in Gen. ii. 18) *k'negdo*, 'meet for him,' but (read) *l'negdo*, 'against him.'"

[3] Jalkut, Gen. § 23, reads: "If he be fortunate she will correspond to him (and be in harmony with him); if not, she will oppose him." According to Rashi she will be a "lash" ("Nigdo") to him; see Midrash Agadah on Gen. ii. 18.

[4] *i.e.* of man's supremacy over it. Man was to increase and multiply, to fill the earth and to *subdue* it (Gen. i. 28). The Oxford MS. (d. 35) reads: "When the earth heard the expression help-meet."

[5] Lit. sheep or herd.

[6] See Ps. xlii. 8.

[7] See Ps. iii. 5; T.B. Berakhoth, 58b; Gen. Rab. xiv. 9, and Shocher Tob, Ps. xxv. 2; and cf. *infra*, p. 253. For further references to Adam legends see *Die Sagen der Juden*, ed. Micha Josef bin Gorion, 1913 (Anhang). Two volumes of this Midrashic collection have appeared, and in the appendix the sources are given for the legends dealing with the Creation, the Patriarchs, etc. Equally interesting and valuable are the *Legends of the Jews*, by L. Ginzberg; the sources of the legends have not yet appeared in the promised final volume. Parallels to the Midrashim in Christian literature are dealt with by L. Ginzberg in his *Haggada b. d. Kirchenvätern*, i., Amsterdam, 1899. Parallels in Mohammedan literature are given by Geiger, *Was hat Mohammed*, etc., and M. Grünbaum, *op. cit.* pp. 60 ff., and in *Z.D.M.G.* xxxi. pp. 183 ff.; the monographs by Rahmer (on Jerome), Funk (on Aphraates), Gerson, and Goldfahn (on Justin Martyr) should be consulted for "Christian" Midrashic parallels.

---

[1] Jerome employs this formula of Midrashic exegesis (*e.g.* on Zech. xiv. 20).

him and heals him and (gives) him life and repose, as it is said, "I should have slept: then had I been at rest" (Job iii. 13). The Holy One, blessed be He, supports (man) with[1] the earth, giving it water; and it yields its fruit and food for all creatures—but the first[2] man's food "in toil[3] shalt thou eat of it all the days of thy life" (Gen. iii. 17).

The Holy One, blessed be He, had compassion upon the first man (Adam), and, in order that he should not feel any pain, He cast upon him the sleep of deep slumber,[4] and He made him sleep whilst He took one of his bones from his side and flesh from his heart[5] and made it into an help (meet for him) and placed her opposite to him. When he awoke from his sleep he saw her standing opposite to him.[6] And he said, "Bone of my bones and flesh of my flesh" (*ibid.* ii. 23). As long as he was alone he was called Adam (man).[7]

Rabbi Jehudah[8] said: Because of the name Adamah (ground) whence he was taken, his name was called Adam. Rabbi Joshua ben Korchah said: He was called Adam because of his flesh and blood (*dām*[9]). He said to him: Adam!

[1] The first editions read: "supports the earth."

[2] The first editions omit: "the first."

[3] Or "sorrow," see 4 Ezra vii. 12, and *Jewish Sources of the Sermon on the Mount*, p. 191.

[4] The deep sleep made Adam insensible to pain; cf. T.B. Synhedrin, 39a. Tertullian, *De Anima*, xliii., discusses the "sleep" of Adam.

[5] See Pal. Targ. Gen. ii. 21. According to the Leḳach Tob, Gen. ii. 21, Eve was made from the sixth rib. Theophilus, *op. cit.* xxviii., discusses why Eve was formed from Adam's rib.

[6] A similar expression is used by the Book of Jashar i. 4.

[7] According to the Talmud (T.B. Jebamoth, 63b) an adult male who lives without a wife is not called man ("Adam"). This designation was given when God blessed the first *pair*. This view is opposed by our author.

[8] The first editions omit till "R. Joshua ben Korchah."

[9] See 'Arukh, ed. Kohut, i. p. 34b: "The first man was called Adam because of the word for earth (Adamah), whence he was taken;" and see *ibid.* p. 307a for another version. The Church Fathers also find fanciful interpretations of the name of the first man. Augustine on the Gospel of John ix. 14 explains the four letters of Adam's name (in Greek) as referring to the East, West, North, and South. Cf. Slavonic Enoch xxx. 13, and Sibylline Oracles iii. 24–26. Augustine (*op. cit.* x. 12) gives the numerical value of Adam as 46, pointing out that the Temple had stood 46 years at the time of the death of the Founder of Christianity. The Rabbis were not the only people who had recourse to "Gemaṭria." The first editions add the following paragraph: "Immediately he embraced her and kissed her,[1] and he said: Blessed art thou of the Lord,[2] thy bone is from my bones

[1] Cf. Gen. Rab. xxiii. 5.

[2] Cf. Ruth iii. 10 for similar phraseology.

Adam! And when an help-mate had been built for him, his name was called *êsh* (fire), and she (was called) *êsh* (fire).[1]

What did the Holy One, blessed be He, do? He put His name (יה) between their (names), saying: If they go in My ways || and keep all My precepts, behold My name is given to them,[2] it will deliver them from all distress. If they do not (walk in My ways), behold I will take away My name from their (names), and they will become *êsh* (fire).[3] And fire consumes fire, as it is said, "For it is a *fire* that consumeth unto destruction" (Job xxxi. 12).[4]

The Holy One, blessed be He, made ten wedding canopies[5] for Adam in the garden of Eden. They were all (made) of precious stones, pearls, and gold. Is it not a fact that only one wedding canopy is made for every bridegroom,[6] whilst three wedding canopies are made for a king?[7] But in order to bestow special honour upon the first man, the Holy One, blessed be He, made ten (wedding canopies) in the garden of Eden, as it is said, "Wast thou in Eden the garden of God; was every precious stone[8] thy covering, the sardius, topaz, and the diamond, the beryl, the onyx, and the jasper, the sapphire, the emerald, and the carbuncle, and gold?" (Ezek. xxviii. 13).[9] Behold these are the ten canopies. The angels were playing upon timbrels and dancing with

and it is becoming for thee to be called woman (*ishah*), as it is said."

[1] The first editions read: "When an help-mate, a woman (*ishah*), had been built for him, his name was called man (*ish*), and she was called woman (*ishah*)."

[2] *Ish* (איש) and *ishah* (אשה) have the letters Yod (י) and Hêh (ה) apart from the letters אש which they have in common. See Jeraḥmeel vi. 16, and cf. Pal. Targ. Ex. xxviii. 30, on the Ineffable Name.

[3] By removing the letters Yod and Hêh from the Hebrew words *ish* and *ishah* each word spells *êsh*, fire; and see T.B. Soṭah, 17a.

[4] See 'Arukh, *s.v.* "Adam" and *s.v.* "êsh," and cf. T.B. Soṭah, 5a.

[5] The canopy used at Jewish weddings is still called Chuppah. The word may also mean Wedding Chamber. For further details, see *Jewish Encyclopædia*, *s.v.*; and cf. T.B. Baba Bathra, 75a; Gen. Rab. xviii. 1; Jalkuṭ, Gen. § 20; and Büchler in *Monatsschrift*, xlix., 1905, pp. 18 ff., and in *J.Q.R.* (New Series) iv. pp. 490 f.

[6] See Ps. xix. 5.

[7] See Cant. iii. 9–11.

[8] The rest of the verse is omitted by the MS. and the first editions, which read: "etc."

[9] On this verse see *Hellenism and Christianity*, pp. 99 f. The ten canopies are apparently indicated by the nine precious stones and gold as mentioned in the verse. Menorath Ha-Maor, § 205, states that the Messiah will have ten canopies. See also *B.H.M.* iii. p. 60.

pipes,[1] as it is said, "The workmanship [2] of thy tabrets and of thy pipes was with thee" (*ibid.*).

On the day when the first man was created, as it is said, "In the day when thou [3] wast created they were prepared" (*ibid.*), the Holy One, blessed be He, said to the ministering angels: Come, let us descend and render loving service to the first man and to his help-mate, for the world rests upon the attribute of the service of loving-kindness.[4] The Holy One, blessed be He, said: More beloved is the service of loving-kindness than the sacrifices and burnt-offerings which Israel will bring in the future upon the altar before Me, as it is said, || "For I desire love, and not sacrifice" (Hos. vi. 6).[5]

The ministering angels were going to and fro and walking before him like friends who guard the wedding canopies,[6] as it is said, "For he shall give his angels charge over thee,[7] to keep thee in all thy *ways*" (Ps. xci. 11). (The word) "*way*" here means only the way [8] of bridegrooms. The Holy One, blessed be He, was like a precentor.[9] What is the

[1] The first editions read: "like females."[1] See Jalkuṭ Makhiri, Ps. xci. p. 46a.

[2] The Hebrew here (*Melĕkhĕth*) suggests angels (*Mālākhim*). The Midrashim which deal with the "Canopies" are numerous. The subject has not been considered in all its bearings. The Jewish Messiah will be married, hence the "Canopies," for his wedding. This is probably a disguised attack on the Christian exaltation of the unmarried state, as exemplified by the Founder of the Christian Church. The discussion on the Canopies is to be found also in Lev. Rab. xx. 2; Eccles. Rab. viii. 1; Jalkuṭ, Eccles. § 764. According to Dr. Büchler (*J.Q.R.*, New Series, iv. pp. 490 f.) the word Chuppah might be rendered "bower." One also thinks of cave or cavern in this connection. According to the *Schatzhöhle*, p. 7, Adam had one cave after his expulsion from Paradise; see also Book of Adam and Eve (ed. Malan) I. v.

[3] Adam.

[4] On Gemilluth Chasadim (Service of Loving-kindness) see Paul Goodman, *Die Liebestätigkeit im Judentum*, and Bergmann, in *Soziale Ethik im Judentum*, pp. 51 ff., and see *infra*, Chapter XVI.

[5] See *infra*, p. 107.

[6] The reading in Menorath Ha-Maor, *loc. cit.*, is as follows: "And the ministering angels were going before him like friends who guard the wedding canopies, as it is said, 'For he shall give his angels charge over thee, to guard thee on all thy ways'" (Ps. xci. 11). The first editions read: "ministering angels were like groomsmen."

[7] The MS. quotes this verse up to "thee"; the entire verse is given by the first editions.

[8] See Prov. xxx. 19.

[9] Our text is preserved in Menorath Ha-Maor, *loc. cit.*, and cf. Jalkuṭ Makhiri, Ps. xcii. p. 46a. The precentor is the Chazan. The period when the Chazan became the Reader of the prayers is that

---

[1] The Hebrew in the text has the same root as the word for *female*.

custom observed by the precentor ? He stands and blesses the bride in the midst of her wedding chamber.[1] Likewise the Holy One, blessed be He, stood and blessed Adam and his help-mate, as it is said, " And God blessed them " (Gen. i. 28).[2]

of the Geonim. See Sopherim, x. 7, xi. 3, 5, and xiv. 14; Eppenstein's article in *Monatsschrift*, lii., 1908, pp. 467 ff., and *infra*, p. 109.

[1] *Or* canopy.

[2] This indicates the sacred nature of matrimony, which is aptly termed *Kiddushin* (sanctification). See Gen. Rab. xviii. 2 for the marriage of Adam and Eve.

CHAPTER XIII[1]

THE SERPENT IN PARADISE [15A. ii.]

"ENVY, cupidity, and ambition remove man (Adam) from the world."[2] The ministering angels[3] spake before the Holy One, blessed be He, saying: Sovereign of all Worlds! "What is man, that thou shouldst take note of him?" (Ps. cxliv. 3). "Man (Adam) is like unto vanity"[4] (*ibid.* 4), upon earth there is not his like.[5] (God) answered them: Just as all of you praise Me in the heights of heaven so he professes My Unity on earth,[6] nay, moreover, are you able to stand up and call the names for all the creatures which I have created? They stood up, but were unable (to give the names). Forthwith Adam stood up and called the names for all His creatures, as it is said, "And the man gave names to all cattle" (Gen. ii. 20). When the ministering angels saw this they retreated,[7] and the ministering angels said: If we do not take || counsel against this man so that he sin before his Creator, we cannot prevail against him.[8]

[1] In our MS. this is ch. xii.

[2] This is taken from Aboth iv. 28. The three sins enumerated brought about the sin and punishment of Adam and Eve. See Aboth de R. Nathan (*a*) i. and (*b*) i.; T.B. Synhedrin, 59b; and *infra*, p. 125.

[3] The parallel text preserved in the Midrash Haggadol, Gen. (ed. Schechter), c. 86, reads: "the subordinate angels became jealous of him."

[4] According to our author, if Adam had not sinned he would have lived for ever. See *Z.D.M.G.* xxxi. p. 232.

[5] See Job xli. 33 (Heb. xli. 24), and cf. *infra*, p. 265.

[6] Lit. "in the lower regions." See Jalkuṭ, Gen. § 25. According to Slavonic Enoch xxx. 2, Adam in Paradise sees the heavens open "that he should perceive the angels singing the song of triumph."

[7] Or, "they retraced their steps," or "betook themselves backward." This is missing in the first two editions. On the theme see Gen. Rab. xvii. 4.

[8] See *infra*, pp. 367 f., 436, and cf. Jeraḥmeel xxii. 1. The spirit animating the angels in desiring the fall of man is that of jealousy; this explains the "envy" quoted from Aboth iv. at the beginning of the chapter.

Sammael was the great prince in heaven;[1] the Chajjôth[2] had four wings and the Seraphim had six wings, and Sammael had twelve wings. What did Sammael do? He took his band[3] and descended[4] and saw all the creatures which the Holy One, blessed be He, had created in His world and he found among them none so skilled to do evil as the serpent, as it is said, "Now the serpent was more subtil[5] than any beast of the field" (*ibid.* iii. 1). Its appearance was something like that of the camel,[6] and he[7] mounted and rode upon it.[8] The Torah began to cry aloud, saying, Why, O Sammael! now that the world is created, is it the time[9] to rebel against the Omnipresent? Is it like a time when thou shouldst lift up thyself on high?[10] The Lord of the world "will laugh at the horse and its rider"[11] (Job xxxix. 18).

A parable, to what is the matter like?[12] To a man in

[1] At first the "great prince" was Sammael, but after his fall Michael is "the great prince"; cf. T.B. Chagigah, 12b. On Sammael and Michael see *infra*, pp. 192 f., and *J.E.* x. 665 f. (*s.v.* Samael).

[2] The Jalkut, Gen. *loc. cit.*, reads: "The Chajjôth with four wings and the Seraphim with six wings." Our text and Jalḳuṭ (*loc. cit.*) are parallel texts; the printed texts differ slightly. The first editions read: "The Chajjôth and the Seraphim with six wings." The Midrash Haggadol (Genesis), *loc. cit.*, differs in the arrangement, and omits the reference to the Chajjôth.

[3] *i.e.* troop of angels obeying him. See Geiger, *op. cit.* pp. 101 f.

[4] See *infra*, pp. 99, 193 f. The word ירד, "descended," recalls Eth. Enoch vi. 6, and Jubilees iv. 15; cf. Luke x. 18.

[5] Our MS. ends quotation here, adding "etc."

[6] The Serpent had the appearance of the camel prior to the punishment meted out to it by God. On the theme see T.B. 'Erubin, 18a; T.B. Synhedrin, 59b; Gen. Rab. xix. 1; Ẓohar, Ex. 136a; and Aboth de R. Nathan (*a*) i. p. 3a. In the Slavonic Book of Adam and Eve (ed. Jagíc, p. 26) Satan uses the Serpent to deceive Eve. See Archelaus, "Disputation with Manes," in *A.N.C.L.* xx. p. 344, for a parallel.

[7] Sammael, or Satan. See Ascension of Isaiah i. 8.

[8] The Midrash Haggadol, Gen. *loc. cit.*, adds: "and betook himself to mislead the man."

[9] The MS. reads *'ăd*, the first editions read *'ês* (time); so also Midrash Haggadol, *loc. cit.*

[10] This is quoted from Job xxxix. 18. The R.V. renders, "What time she lifteth up herself on high." The verse is intended to illustrate Sammael's sin in approaching Eve and causing Adam to rebel. According to Tertullian, *de Patient.* v., the Evil One "impatiently bore that the Lord God subjected the universal works" to man. This led on to his "envy." He deceived him because he envied him.

[11] The R.V. reads: "She scorneth the horse and his rider." The "horse" is applied in the Midrash to the Serpent and "the rider" to Sammael.

[12] The deed of Sammael is illustrated by the parable.

whom there was an evil spirit. All the deeds which he does,[1] or all the words which he utters, does he speak by his own intention? Does he not act only according to the idea of the evil spirit, which (rules) over him? So (was it with) the serpent. All the deeds which it did, and all the words which it spake, it did not speak[2] except by the intention of Sammael. Concerning him, the Scripture says, "The wicked is thrust down in his evil-doing" (Prov. xiv. 32).[3]

A parable, to what is the matter like? To a king || who married a woman and made her supreme over all that he had.[4] He said to her: All that I have shall be in thy hands, except this house,[5] which is full of scorpions. A certain old man visited her; he asks, for instance,[6] for vinegar. He said to her: Wilt thou argue that he deals kindly with thee?[7] He deals with me (thus): over all that he possesses has he made me supreme. Thus said he to her: Behold, all that I have is given into thy hands except this house,[5] which is full of scorpions. (The old man) said to her: Is not all the jewellery[8] of the king indeed in this house[5]? But[9] he wishes to marry another woman, and to give them to her. The king is the first man (Adam), the woman is Eve, and the one who asked for vinegar is the serpent;[10] and concerning them (the text) says, "There are the workers of iniquity fallen, they are thrust down, and shall not be able to rise"[11] (Ps. xxxvi. 12).

[1] The first editions add: "does he do them at his own suggestion?"

[2] The first editions read: "it neither spake nor did."

[3] Cf. the version in Jalkuṭ, Gen. *loc. cit.*

[4] The first editions add: "consisting of precious stones and pearls."

[5] The first editions read "cask" (חבית), and so throughout the parable; this is more correct than "house" (הבית) in our text.

[6] This expression is omitted in the Amsterdam edition of 1708 and in the Dyhrenfürth edition. The vinegar was used by the poor for dipping therein their bread; see Aboth de R. Nathan (*a*) xx. p. 36a.

[7] The first editions read here: "How does the king treat thee? She said to him: All that he possesses has he given to me and left in my hands except this cask."

[8] *Ḳosmin* (κόσμος), jewellery; see 'Arukh, *s.v.* קוזמי. The reading in the first editions is corrupt.

[9] The first editions read: "He spake not thus to thee save for the reason that he wishes to marry another woman."

[10] For a variant parable to illustrate the theme taken from Aboth de R. Nathan (*a*) i. p. 3b, see *Rabbinic Philosophy and Ethics*, p. 29.

[11] The printed editions omit the second half of the verse.

The serpent argued with itself, saying: If I go and speak to Adam, I know that he will not listen to me, for a man is always hard [1] (to be persuaded), as it is said, "For a man is churlish and evil in his doings" (1 Sam. xxv. 3); but behold I will speak to Eve,[2] for I know that she will listen to me; for women listen to all creatures, as it is said, "She is simple and knoweth nothing" (Prov. ix. 13). The serpent went and spake to the woman: [3] || Is it [4] (true that) you also have been commanded concerning the fruit of the tree? [5] She said (to him): Yes, as it is said, "Of the fruit of the tree which is in the midst of the garden" (Gen. iii. 3). And when the serpent heard the words of Eve, he found a way [6] through which he could enter (to approach her), so he said to her: This precept is nought else except the evil eye, for in the hour when ye eat thereof, ye will be like Him, a God. Just as [7] He creates worlds and destroys worlds,[8] so will ye be able to create worlds and to destroy worlds. Just as He slays and brings to life, so also will ye be able to kill and to bring to life, as it is said, "For God doth know that in

[1] See Gen. Rab. xvii. 8 to illustrate the notion that a man is more easily appeased than a woman. The quotation from I Sam. is not in the printed editions. The Midrash Haggadol, Gen. c. 87, reads: "for Sammael has no authority over man because he is hard."

[2] The first editions read here: "the woman whose mind is feeble." Slavonic Enoch xxxi. 6 tells us how Satanail or Satan "conceived designs against Adam; in such a manner he entered and deceived Eve. But he did not touch Adam." The "evil eye" mentioned in our text, *infra*, might be rendered "envy."

[3] For a Christian Midrash on this theme see "Fragments from the lost writings of Irenæus" in *A.N.C.L.* ix. p. 166.

[4] The first editions add the words in brackets.

[5] The text is probably corrupt here; Luria suggests that instead of the words "this tree" which occur in the printed texts we should read "this garden." This agrees with the reading preserved in the Oxford MS. (d. 35), and in Jeraḥmeel xxii. 2. According to the reading "this tree," the answer desired by the Serpent would not have been forthcoming. By asking about the "fruit of *the garden*" the Serpent was enabled to mislead Eve. The Talmud (T.B. Synhedrin, 29a) lays stress on the addition to the Divine command made by Eve when she said, "neither shall ye touch it" (Gen. iii. 3). Our MS. intends the question to be quite general: "Is it a fact that you have been commanded (not to eat) the fruit of any tree?" This agrees with the Midrash Haggadol, Gen. *loc. cit.*

[6] Lit. "opening." See Tertullian, *de Patient.*, *loc. cit.*

[7] The first editions read: "What does He do?"

[8] This idea of being able to create other worlds has a parallel in Slavonic Enoch xxxi. 3: "And the devil took thought, as if wishing *to make another world.*"

the day ye eat thereof,[1] then your eyes shall be opened" (*ibid.* 5).[2]

The serpent went and touched the tree, which commenced to cry out, saying: [3] Wicked One! do not touch me! as it is said, "Let not the foot of pride come against me, and let not the hand of the wicked drive me away. There are the workers of iniquity fallen" [4] (Ps. xxxvi. 11, 12).

The serpent went and said to the woman: Behold, I touched it, but I did not die; thou also mayest touch it, and thou wilt not die.[5] The woman went and touched the tree, and she saw the angel of death [6] coming towards her; she said: Woe is me! I shall now die, and the Holy One, blessed be He, will make another woman [7] and give her to Adam,[8] but behold I will cause || him to eat with me; if we shall die, we shall both die,[9] and if we shall live, we shall both live. And she took of the fruits of the tree, and ate thereof, and also gave (of its fruits) to her husband, so that he should eat with her, as it is said, "And she took of the fruit thereof, and did eat; and she gave also unto her husband with her" (Gen. iii. 6). When Adam had eaten of the fruit of the tree, he saw that he was naked,[10] and his eyes were opened, and his teeth were set on edge. He said to her: What is this that thou hast given me to eat, that my eyes should be opened and my teeth set on edge? [11] Just as my

[1] The MSS. end the quotation here, but add "etc."; the first editions continue the verse.

[2] Our MS. ends here the 12th chapter.

[3] See Aboth de R. Nathan (*a*) i. p. 2b, the tree cried out when Eve stared at it and (desired its fruit). See also Jeraḥmeel xxii. 3.

[4] The MSS. give only the verse from Ps. xxxvi. 11; the first two editions omit the second half of this verse and add the first half of the next verse.

[5] The Midrash Haggadol, Gen. c. 88, adds: "Forthwith the woman saw that the tree was good for food." See Aboth de R. Nathan, *loc. cit.*, and Pal. Targum, Gen. iii. 6.

[6] According to the Pal. Targum (*loc. cit.*), "and the woman beheld Sammael, the angel of death, and she was afraid."

[7] The printed editions add: "for him."

[8] See Tertullian, *de Patient.*, *loc. cit.*, where Adam is described as "not *yet* Eve's husband."

[9] See a similar Midrash in the Church Father Ephraim, Comm. in Gen. vol. i. p. 35.

[10] See *infra*, p. 98.

[11] The first editions add: "against my knowledge." See Jer. xxxi. 29, 30, and Ezek. xviii. 2. For the Rabbinic sources dealing with the Serpent, Eve, and Adam see Tosephta Sotah iv. (end); T.B. Sotah, 9a; Gen. Rab. xix. 4; Pesiḳta Rabbathi, § xv. p. 68b; Tanchuma,

teeth were set on edge, so shall the teeth of all generations be set on edge.[1]

Lekach Ṭob and Jalkut, *in loc.*; and see Midrash Agadah and Rashi on Gen. iii., and cf. Jeraḥmeel xxii.; see also *Rabbinic Philosophy and Ethics*, pp. 27 ff.; Ginzberg, *Legends of the Jews*, vol. i. pp. 71 ff.; and F. R. Tennant, *The Fall and Original Sin*, 1903, pp. 152 and 158.

[1] See the parallel version from Gen. Rab. xix. 5, translated in *Rabbinic Philosophy and Ethics*, p. 28, and cf. Aboth de R. Nathan, *loc. cit.*, Midrash Haggadol, Gen. c. 90, "*their* teeth and the teeth of all generations." According to Slavonic Enoch xxx. 16: "Therefore his *ignorance* is a woe to him that he should sin, and I appointed death on account of his sin." The expression "to set the teeth on edge" in our text means "paying the penalty." See also 4 Ezra iii. 7.

CHAPTER XIV

THE SIN OF ADAM AND EVE [16A. ii.]

TEN descents upon the earth [1] were made by the Holy One, blessed be He; they were: (1) Once in the Garden of Eden; (2) once at (the time of) the generation of the Dispersion; [2] (3) once at Sodom; [3] (4) once at the thorn-bush; [4] (5) once in Egypt; [5] (6) once at Sinai; [6] (7) once at the cleft of the rock; [7] (8) and (9) twice in the tent of Assembly; [8] (10) once in the future.[9]

Once in the Garden of Eden; whence do we know? Because it is said, "And they heard the voice of the Lord God *walking* in the garden [10] in the cool of the day" (Gen. iii. 8). And it is written,[11] "My beloved [12] *is gone down* to

[1] See Siphrê, Numbers, § 93; Mekhilta Jethro, 3, p. 64a; Aboth de R. Nathan (*a*) xxxiv. Other parallels are given by Schechter, p. 51b, note 32 of his edition of Aboth de R. Nathan. The other descents are mentioned in Chapters XXIV., XXV., XXXIX., XL., XLI., XLVI., and LIII.

[2] Cf. *infra*, pp. 176f., and Gen. Rab. xxxviii. 9.

[3] See *infra*, p. 179, and Gen. Rab. xlviii. 7; and cf. Jalkuṭ, Gen. § 27, which reads: "Once in *Egypt*, once at the thorn-bush, once at Sinai, once at the cleft of the rock." The reference to Egypt will be discussed *infra*, p. 303.

[4] See T.B. Megillah, 29a, and cf. *infra*, p. 312.

[5] This is not in the first editions. See *supra*, note 3.

[6] See Mekhilta Jethro, 9, p. 72b; and cf. *infra*, p. 318.

[7] Cf. *infra*, p. 365. The reading in the first two editions is: "*twice* at the cleft of the rock." This is probably incorrect; see *supra*, note 3, and cf. Aboth de R. Nathan, *loc. cit.*

[8] See *infra*, p. 433. Here also we should read, "Once in the tent of Assembly." Aboth de R. Nathan, *loc. cit.*, has this reading, and refers to Num. xi. 25.

[9] Aboth de R. Nathan (*loc. cit.*) refers here to Zech. xiv. 4. The ninth and tenth descents are to be in the future also: see Siphrê, *loc. cit.*; T.B. Sukkah, 5a; and Othijoth de R. 'Akiba, letter Hê (Jellinek, *B.H.M.* iii. p. 24).

[10] In the MS. the quotation ends here, the first editions continue the verse.

[11] The first editions have: "And another text says."

[12] The "beloved" is God. This verse is quoted because it contains the verb (ירד) "*to descend.*"

his garden, to the beds of spices" (Cant. vi. 2). (God) sat in judgment,[1] and He judged with judgment. He said to him (Adam): Why didst thou flee[2] before Me? He answered Him: I heard Thy voice[3] and my bones trembled,[4] as it is said, "I heard thy voice in the garden, and I was afraid, || because I was naked: and I hid myself" (Gen. iii. 10).[5]

What was the dress of the first man? A skin of nail,[6] and a cloud of glory covered him. When he ate of the fruits of the tree, the nail-skin was stripped off him,[7] and the cloud of glory departed from him, and he saw himself naked, as it is said, "And he said, Who told thee that thou wast naked?[8] Hast thou eaten of the tree, whereof I commanded thee?" (*ibid.* 11).

Adam said before the Holy One, blessed be He: Sovereign of all worlds! When I was alone, I did not sin against Thee. But the woman whom Thou hast brought to me enticed me

[1] See Gen. Rab. xx. 2 ff. for the judgment of the Serpent, Eve, and Adam. The first editions read here: "He sat in a judgment of truth, the Judge of righteousness and truth. He called to Adam and said to him." Cf. צדוק הדין (Burial Service) in Singer, pp. 318 f.

[2] For similar phraseology see Ps. cxxxix. 7. This psalm is interpreted by the Midrashim as referring to Adam; see *infra*, p. 143.

[3] The first editions read: "I heard the report of Thee." Cf. Hab. iii. 2 and Cant. Rab. iii. 6.

[4] See Job iv. 14 for a similar expression.

[5] The first editions read here: "*And I hid myself* from my deed, *and I was afraid* of my deed, for I was *bare* of (the fulfilment of) my commandment,[1] as it is said, 'For I was naked'" (Gen. iii. 10).[2]

[6] The dress of Adam and Eve was, according to the Pal. Targum, Gen. iii. 7, "onyx-coloured"; cf. Gen. Rab. xx. 12. The legend of an original skin of nail is preserved in the custom which still obtains among orthodox Jews, who gaze at their nails with the Habdalah light at the termination of the Sabbath. Dr. S. Daiches considers this custom as a relic of nail magic (see Jews' College Publications, v. pp. 31 f. n. 1). According to the Church Father Ephraim, *op. cit.* p. 139, Adam and Eve lost their angelic endowments immediately after their sin, their sight and power of discerning became limited only to matters corporeal and sensible; see the Book of Adam and Eve (ed. Malan), p. 215, for this reference. See also Odes of Solomon, pp. 66 ff. and 69, notes 1, 2.

[7] The first editions add here, "and he saw himself naked," and not after the words, "and the cloud of glory departed from him." See Pal. Targ. Gen. *loc. cit.* A similar tradition is preserved in the *Coptic Apocrypha*, ed. Budge, p. 250.

[8] The MSS. end the quotation here, the first editions continue the verse.

---

[1] Some of the old editions read: "Thy commandment"; see also Ezek. xvi. 39.

[2] "Naked," *i.e.* Adam was stripped of his dress of glory as a consequence of his disobedience.

away from Thy ways,[1] as it is said, "The woman whom thou gavest to be with me,[2] she gave me of the tree, and I did eat" (*ibid.* 12). The Holy One, blessed be He, called[3] unto Eve, and said to her: Was it not enough for thee that thou didst sin in thy own person? But (also) that thou shouldst make Adam sin? She spake before Him: Sovereign of the world! The serpent enticed my mind to sin before Thee, as it is said, "The serpent beguiled me, and I did eat" (*ibid.* 13). He brought the three[4] of them and passed sentence of judgment upon them, consisting of nine curses and death.

He cast down Sammael[5] and his troop from their holy place in heaven,[6] and cut off the feet of the serpent,[7] and decreed that it should cast its skin and suffer pain once in seven years in great pain, and cursed it || that it should drag itself with its belly (on the ground), and its food is turned in its belly into dust[8] and the gall of asps,[9] and death is in its mouth,[10] and He put hatred between it and the children of the woman,[11] so that they should bruise its

[1] The first editions read: "Thy words." See *B.H.M.* iii. pp. 60 f.

[2] The MSS. end the quotation here.

[3] The first editions add here: "He said."

[4] See Pal. Targ. Gen. iii. 16 and cf. Gen. Rab. xx. 2, 3.

[5] On the identification of Sammael with the Devil see Wisdom ii. 24, Pal. Targum on Gen. iii. 6; see also Rev. xii. 9 and xx. 2. Paul in 2 Cor. xi. 3 refers to the beguiling of Eve by the Serpent. On the speaking of the Serpent see Jubilees iii. 7 and Josephus, *Ant.* i. 1. 4. According to Slavonic Enoch xxxi. 3, "The devil took thought, as if wishing to make another world, because things were subservient to Adam on earth. . . . He became Satan *after* he left the heavens." See T.B. Sabbath, 55a, for the Haggadic account of Adam and Eve and the Serpent.

[6] "But the wicked Satan . . . *I hurled him down from heaven*, he it is who made the tree appear pleasant in your eyes," says the Book of Adam and Eve (ed. Malan) 1. i.; cf. *ibid.* xlv. The Fall of Satan is mentioned in Luke x. 18, John xii. 31, and cf. Eph. ii. 2.

[7] This Midrash was known to Josephus; see *Ant. loc. cit.* The first editions add: "And He cursed it more than all living beasts and all cattle." Two curses are set forth here; cf. T.B. Bechoroth, 8a, and see Gen. Rab. xx. 5, Tosephta Soṭah iv. 17, 18.

[8] Cf. Job xx. 14; T.B. Joma, 75a: "The serpent brought man back to dust, and therefore dust is its food."

[9] See Pal. Targum on Gen. iii. 14. "A deadly venom shall be in thy mouth, and thou shalt eat dust all the days of thy life."

[10] See Job xx. 16.

[11] The New Testament refers to this incident in 1 John iii. 8, Col. ii. 15, Heb. ii. 14 ff., Rom. xvi. 20, and see Revelation of Moses (in "Ante-Nicene Christian Library," xvi. p. 461). Ephraim, *op. cit.*, refers

head,[1] and after all these (curses comes) death.[2] He gave the woman nine curses and death: the afflictions arising from menstruation and the tokens of virginity;[3] the affliction of conception in the womb; and the affliction of child-birth; and the affliction of bringing up children; and her head is covered like a mourner,[4] and it is not shaved except on account of immorality, and her ear is pierced like (the ears of) perpetual slaves;[5] and like a hand-maid she waits upon her husband; and she is not believed in (a matter of) testimony;[6] and after all these (curses comes) death.

He extended pardon[7] to Adam (as to a part of the) nine curses and death. He curtailed his strength, and He shortened his stature[8] by reason of the impurity connected with issues and with pollution;[9] as well as the impurity arising from sexual intercourse; he was to sow wheat and to reap thistles,[10] and his food was to be the grass of the earth, like that of the beast; and (he was to earn) his bread in

to the cutting off of the Serpent's feet; see *supra*, p. 99, note 7. The first editions read: "between it and the woman."

[1] See T.J. Kiddushin iv. 11, p. 66c, and Sophrim xv. 10, for the rule, "Break the head of the best among serpents."

[2] Cf. the words of Wisdom, *loc. cit.*, "But through the devil's envy came death into the world"; see also Slavonic Enoch xxxi. 3.

[3] See T.B. 'Erubin, 100b, and Aboth de R. Nathan (*a*) i. p. 2b.

[4] For an example of this see Büchler, *The Economic Condition of Judea*, p. 53, and see T.B. Kiddushin, 72a. The New Testament also directs women to have their heads covered; see 1 Cor. xi. 5 and cf. the *Apostolic Constitutions*, i. 8. In our MS. and in the Oxford MSS. as well as in some of the old editions of our book (*e.g.* Venice, 1544) after "mourner" the words "she is not shaved except on account of immorality," occur, but later editions have deleted the passage. This phrase is of great importance in view of Dr. Büchler's interesting and learned monograph on this theme. A special note at the end of the book will recapitulate the results of Dr. Büchler's investigations, as the date of *P.R.E.* may possibly be determined by the period when the custom of cutting the hair of the immoral woman as a punishment obtained.

[5] Schwally, *Das Leben nach dem Tode*, p. 39, refers to the inference suggested by the perforation of a woman's ears; see also *Z.A.T.W.*, 1891, p. 183.

[6] Because Adam listened to Eve, and was led astray by her; see 'Arukh, ed. Kohut, v. 394b.

[7] Our MS. reads רימום (pardon). The Oxford MS. (d. 35) reads רומים (retribution), and Oxford MS. (O.A. 167) has דינו (his sentence). The printed texts omit this and read: "He drew Adam aside and decreed against him nine curses and death."

[8] See *Coptic Apocrypha*, p. 250: "his body diminished in size."

[9] See T.B. Synhedrin, 38b.

[10] See Gen. Rab. xx. 10, and Tanna de bê Elijahu Rab. xxxi. p. 164.

anxiety, and his food by the sweat (of his brow); and after all these (curses came) death.[1]

If Adam sinned, what was the sin of the earth, that it should be cursed? Because it did not speak against the (evil) deed,[2] therefore it was cursed; for in the hour when the sons of man transgress the graver sins || God sends a plague[3] to the sons of man; and in the hour when the sons of man transgress sins less vital, He smites the fruits of the earth,[4] because of (the sins of) the sons of man, as it is said. " Cursed is the ground for thy sake " (*ibid.* 17).

[1] For a Christian interpretation of the judgment, see Revelation of Moses, *loc. cit.* p. 460 f.

[2] By protesting and warning Adam; see Pal. Targum, Gen. iii. 17.

[3] See Aboth (v. end), T.B. Sabbath, 32a, and T.B. Joma, 83a. The Church Fathers have very elaborate expositions of the " Fall " and its consequences. Thus Irenæus (*adv. Hær.* iii. 3) writes: " It was for this reason, too, that immediately after Adam, as the Scripture relates, He pronounced no curse against Adam personally, but against the ground, in reference to his works; as a certain person among the ancients has observed, ' God did indeed transfer the curse to the earth, that it might not remain in man.' But man receives as a punishment of his transgression the toilsome task of tilling the earth, and to eat bread in the sweat of his face, and to return to the dust whence he was taken. Similarly also did the woman (receive) toil, and labour, and groans, and the pangs of parturition, and a state of subjection, that is, that she should serve her husband; so that they should neither perish altogether when cursed by God, nor, by remaining unreprimanded, should be led to despise God. But the curse in all its fulness fell upon the serpent which had beguiled them." For other references see Diestel, *op. cit.* (in Index), and Thalhofer, *Bibliothek der Kirchenväter* (in Index).

[4] See *Coptic Apocrypha*, p. 243: " the fruit of the earth is little because of the sins of man."

CHAPTER XV

THE TWO WAYS [17A. i.]

RABBI ELIEZER said: I heard with my ear[1] the Lord of hosts speaking. What did He speak? He said: "See, I have set before thee this day life and good, and death and evil" (Deut. xxx. 15). The Holy One, blessed be He, said: Behold, these two ways[2] have I given to Israel, one is good, the other is evil. The one which is good, is of life; and the one which is evil, is of death.[3] The good way has two byways, one of righteousness and the other of love, and Elijah,[4] be he remembered for good, is placed exactly between these two ways.[5] When a man comes to enter (one of these ways), Elijah,[6] be he remembered for good, cries aloud concerning him, saying, "Open ye

[1] See Isa. v. 9, and note the Targum thereon. R. Eliezer ben Hyrḳanos was held to be worthy of being endowed with the Holy Spirit; see T.J. Soṭah (end) and T.B. Synhedrin, 11a; Jalkut, Job, § 919.

[2] The theme of this chapter of our book is the Jewish doctrine of the Two Ways, the ways of good and evil, or of life and death. Adam did not keep the "way of life" (see *supra*, p. 85); he disobeyed God by taking of the fruit of the tree of "good and evil." The "Way of Life" in Paradise was guarded by the Cherubim, and the earthly way of "good and evil" is likewise in the charge of angels, good and evil. Slavonic Enoch xxx. 15 connects the "two ways" with Adam before his disobedience. On the "Two Ways" see *Jewish Sources of the Sermon on the Mount*, pp. 239 ff. See also Gen. Rab. xxi. 5. The Christian literature has also its doctrine of the Two Ways; see the *Apostolic Constitutions*, vii. 1; Epistle of Barnabas xviii.–xx.; Hermas, Mand. vi. 2; Pseudo-Clementine Homilies, v. 7; and for "Heaven and Hell" see the *Revelation of Peter* (ed. Robinson and James, 1892, pp. 48 ff.). See also Test. XII Pat., Asher i. 3, with Charles' note *in loc.* Some of the printed texts read "two words" instead of "two ways." The latter is, of course, the correct reading; see Jalkuṭ, Job, *loc. cit.*

[3] See T.B. Joma, 38b.

[4] On Elijah in Jewish literature see *supra*, p. 2, note 7; *J.E.* v. 122 ff.; Schechter, *Aspects of Rabbinic Theology*, p. 288.

[5] *i.e.* the ways leading to life and death.

[6] See *supra*, p. 95; T.B. Kiddushin, 70a; Ruth Rab. v. 6. On Elijah's work see Seder 'Olam Rab. xvii.

the gates, that the righteous nation which keepeth truth may enter in" (Isa. xxvi. 2). And there cometh Samuel the prophet, and he places himself between these two byways.[1] He says: On which of these (two byways) shall I go? If I go on the way of righteousness, then (the path) of || love is better than the former; if I go on the way of love, (the way) of righteousness is better: but I call heaven and earth to be my witnesses[2] that I will not give up either of them.[3]

The Holy One, blessed be He, said to him: Samuel! Thou hast placed thyself between these two good byways. By thy life! I will give to thee three good gifts. This teaches thee that everyone who doeth[4] righteousness and sheweth the service of love, shall inherit three good gifts, and they are: life, righteousness, and glory, as it is said, "He that followeth after righteousness and love, findeth life, righteousness, and glory" (Prov. xxi. 21). It is only written here (in the text): "He findeth life, righteousness, and glory."[5]

(Leading) to the way of evil, there are four[6] doors, and at each door seven angels[7] are standing—four without, and three within. The (angels) without are merciful, and those within are cruel. When a man comes to enter,[8] the merciful angels go to meet him and say to him: What hast thou to do with the fire yonder? What hast thou to do with those glowing coals?[9] Listen to us and

[1] Samuel, like Elijah, sought to reconcile God and man. On Samuel in Rabbinic literature see *J.E.* xi. 7. On the idea in our Midrash see 1 Sam. ii. 26; according to this text, Samuel grew in favour with God and man. The favour of God is the result of "righteousness," whilst the favour of man is due to "love" between man and his fellow.

[2] This expression is very common in the Tanna de bê Elijahu.

[3] The first editions add here: "but I will take them for myself." See Eccles. vii. 18.

[4] The first editions read "who desireth and doeth," instead of "doeth." Luria suggests "pursueth."

[5] This sentence is missing in the printed editions.

[6] Cf. the three sins of Israel mentioned by Amos ii. 6 and the four calls of Wisdom in Prov. i. 20 ff.

[7] The first editions read: "seven watchers, angels, are sitting," *i.e.* guardian angels.

[8] The first editions add: "the first door."

[9] The first editions read: "Why wilt thou enter into the midst of this fire? Why wilt thou enter among the uncircumcised and the glowing coals?" Luria reads "flames" instead of "uncircumcised." The picture of Gehenna in our context may be suggested by the "swords

repent.[1] If he hearken to them and repent, behold it is well, and if not, he says to them:[2] Amongst them (yonder) let my life (be). || They say to him: Thou hast entered the first door; do not enter the second door. When he comes to enter the second door, the merciful angels go to meet him and say to him: What benefit is it to thee to be erased[3] from the Torah of thy God?[4] Would it not be better to be inscribed in the Torah of thy God? Hearken unto us and repent. If he listen to them and repent, it is well; and if not, he says to them:[5] With them yonder let my life (be). They say to him: Behold thou hast entered the second door, do not enter the third door. When he is about to enter the third door the merciful angels go to meet him and say to him:[6] What benefit is to thee that they (*i.e.* the good angels) should flee from thee and call thee "Unclean"? Would it not be better that they should call thee "Pure One" and not "Unclean"? Hearken to us and repent. If he hearken unto them, behold, it is well; and if not, he says unto them: With them (yonder) let my life (be). They say to him: Behold thou hast entered the third door; do not enter the fourth door! When he is about to enter the fourth door the merciful angels go to meet him and say to him: Behold, thou hast entered these doors, and thou hast not hearkened nor returned.[7] Thus far the Holy One, blessed be He, receives

of flaming fire" in the hands of the Cherubim guarding Paradise. The "flaming fire" is outside Paradise. For the "everlasting fire" in the New Testament see Matt. xxv. 41; the old editions (*e.g.* Amsterdam) read הרים, "mountains," instead of "wicked."

[1] Or "return"; possibly the word implies "*repent and return.*"

[2] The first editions read here: "If he hearken to them it is well; and if not, verily they say to them: Amongst them (yonder) there is no life." Our MS. has undoubtedly the better reading.

[3] The first editions read: "to be removed."

[4] The first editions omit the next sentence and read instead: "that they (*i.e.* the good angels) should call thee 'Unclean,' and that they should flee from thee."

[5] See note 2 above.

[6] The first editions read, instead of our text, the following: "Why wilt thou be erased from the book of life?[1] Is it not better for thee to be inscribed (therein) rather than to be erased (therefrom)? Hearken unto us, and repent. If he listen to them, it is well; and if not, woe to him and to his head!" See Wisdom i. 13.

[7] The translation might also be, "repented." See Jalḳuṭ, Job, *loc. cit.*

---

[1] On the "Book of Life" see T.B. Rosh Ha-Shanah, 16b, and cf. Jeremias, *Babyl. im N.T.*; see also Isa. xxx. 8.

|| the penitent; thus far the Holy One, blessed be He, pardons[1] and forgives,[2] and every day He says: Return, ye children of man, as it is said:[3] "Thou turnest man to contrition"[4] (Ps. xc. 3).

The cruel angels[5] say: Since he would not hearken to the first (angels), let us cause his spirit to depart, as it is said, "Let his spirit go forth, let him return to his earth" (*ibid.* cxlvi. 4). And concerning them[6] (the Scripture) says:[7] "Upon the third and upon the fourth generation of them that hate me" (Ex. xx. 5); and another verse says: "Lo, all these things doth God work, twice, yea thrice, with a man" (Job xxxiii. 29). And thus He calls to Eliezer.[8]

The Holy One, blessed be He, said: Eliezer! Thou hast made thyself like a threefold cord,[9] as it is said, "And a threefold cord is not quickly broken" (Eccles. iv. 12). I also will apply to thee this verse: "Thou shalt be perfect with the Lord thy God" (Deut. xviii. 13). Do not read thus, but: "Thou shalt be perfect *before*[10] the Lord thy God."

[1] The first editions add "sins."

[2] See T.B. Joma, 86b, and T.B. Rosh Ha-Shanah, 16a.

[3] The first editions read, instead of our quotation, the following: "'Return, ye backsliding children' (Jer. iii. 14). If man hearken unto them, it is well; and if not, woe to him and to his destiny!"[1]

[4] Or "destruction.' See T.B. Chagigah, 16a, for an instance of repentance even after death; see also Jalkuṭ Makhiri, Ps. xci. 18, and *infra*, p. 341.

[5] See Prov. xvii. 11 and cf. Shocher Ṭob, Ps. i. 22, p. 11b, and cf. Justin Martyr, *Dialogue with Trypho*, cv., on the "evil angel taking our soul." See also Hippolytus (*Against Plato*, ed Lagarde, p. 69).

[6] The unrepentant.

[7] The printed texts omit the quotation from Ex. xx. 5 and conclude the quotation from Job xxxiii. 29 with the word "work," adding "etc."

[8] Luria thinks that probably the text originally ended with a reference to Samuel. The first editions agree with our MS. and read "to Eliezer," indicating Rabbi Eliezer ben Hyrḳanos, whose name also occurs at the beginning of the chapter.

[9] The printed texts omit the quotation from Eccles. iv. 12. Some of the texts read, "Hast thou made thyself?" etc. The threefold cord is Torah, Divine Worship, and Loving Service. R. Eliezer had acquired Torah, and devoted his life to the service of God; and by his action to his brothers he rendered loving service to them. The reference to Samuel would be just as likely.

[10] In the MS. the texts "with the Lord" are identical. This is clearly due to an error of a copyist. See Jalkut, Deut. § 919, and cf. Siphrê, Deut. § 173. I have followed the reading of the Pesikta Ẓuṭarta, p. 30b.

---

[1] מזל, planet, luck or destiny.

CHAPTER XVI

THE SERVICE OF LOVING-KINDNESS [17B. ii.]

THE world rests upon three things: upon the Torah, upon Divine Worship, and upon the service of loving-kindness.[1]

"Upon the Torah," whence do we know (this)? Because it is written, "If my covenant[2] of *day and night* stand not" (Jer. xxxiii. 25); and (another text) says, "This book of the Torah shall not depart out of thy mouth,[3] but thou shalt meditate therein *day and night*" (Josh. i. 8). Whence do we know (that the world rests) upon the service of loving-kindness? Because it is said, "For I desired love, || and not sacrifice" (Hos. vi. 6). Whence do we know (that the world rests) upon Divine Worship? Because it is written, "And the prayer of the upright is his delight"[4] (Prov. xv. 8).[5]

[1] See Aboth i. 2; Pesiḳta Rabbathi, v. p. 15b; and cf. *supra*, p. 89, and *infra*, p. 122.

[2] God's covenant is the Torah; see T.B. Sabbath, 33a; cf. T.B. Pesachim, 54a; and T.B. Nedarim, 32a. The argument by analogy afforded by comparing similar words in two different verses of Scripture is known as "Geẓerah Shavah," and is employed here. For examples see Levy, *N.H.W.* i. 320 f.; and cf. Bacher's *Terminologie*, i. *s.v.* pp. 13 ff.

[3] The rest of the verse is omitted by our MS.; it occurs in the first editions. The MS. adds the paragraph following dealing with the service of loving-kindness.

[4] Luria thinks that the text should read: "(The world rests) upon Divine Worship. What is this (Worship)? Prayer." The preceding part of the verse quoted reads: "The *sacrifice* of the wicked is an abomination to the Lord, and the prayer of the upright is his *delight*" (Prov. xv. 8). In Mal. ii. 13 "delight" is used instead of "offering." On this theme see Aboth de R. Nathan (*a*) iv. p. 9b; T.J. Megillah iii. 7. 74b; Num. Rab. xii. 12. The ethical lesson here is noteworthy: knowledge of God's Law must find expression, on the one hand, in Divine Worship, and, on the other, in the service of loving-kindness to humanity. Judaism claims to be the highest expression of religious truth, and stands or falls by the ethical teaching it enunciates.

[5] The first editions add: "What is the Divine Worship? Prayer, for thus we find in Daniel, to whom Darius said: 'Thy God whom

Whence do we learn of the service of loving-kindness for bridegrooms? We learn (this) from the Holy One, blessed be He; for He Himself bestowed loving-kindness upon Adam and his help-mate. The Holy One, blessed be He, said to the ministering angels: Come ye and let us show loving-kindness to Adam and his help-mate. The Holy One, blessed be He, descended with the ministering angels to show loving-kindness to Adam and his help-mate.[1] The Holy One, blessed be He, said: More beloved unto Me is the service of loving-kindness than sacrifices and burnt-offering which Israel, in the future, will bring on the altar before Me, as it is said, "For I *desired* love, and not sacrifice" (Hos. vi. 6).[2]

Rabbi José said: From whom do we learn of the seven days of banquet?[3] From our father Jacob.[4] For when our father Jacob married Leah, he made a banquet with rejoicing for seven days, as it is said, "Fulfil the *week*[5] of this one" (Gen. xxix. 27).[6]

thou *servest* continually, he will deliver thee' (Dan. vi. 16). Was there any Divine Worship in Babylon?[1] But this (refers to) Prayer."

[1] In the Garden of Eden; see *supra*, pp. 88 ff.

[2] See *supra*, pp. 76, 84, 89, for the idea that the world rests on love. Here the stress is on "*I desired*," since God's desire or will is the cause of the world's existence. The bridegroom is especially mentioned, because the study of the Torah is to be set aside in order to render the service of loving-kindness to the bride and bridegroom. The Jewish teachers did not encourage celibacy; neither was the cult of virginity considered a desirable element in religion, as was the case in the Christian Church. It is possible that the emphasis laid on the Divine participation in Adam's nuptials was intended to counteract the attitude of the Church towards marriage; see 1 Cor. vii. 8; Matt. xix. 10, 12. This section in our book should be compared with the latter part of Chapter XII.; see also Pesiḳta de R. Kahana, p. 172b (end).

[3] At a wedding. The marriage feast is mentioned in the parables of the N.T.; see Matt. xxii. 2 ff.

[4] See Nachmanides on Gen. xxix. 27; and cf. T.J. Kethuboth i. 1, p. 25a, and Jalkuṭ, Judges, § 70.

[5] See Pal. Targum, *in loc.*

[6] The first editions add: "And all the men of the place were gathered together to render loving service to Jacob, as it is said: 'And Laban gathered together all the men of the place, and made a feast' (Gen. xxix. 22). The Holy One, blessed be He, said to them: Ye have shown loving-kindness to Jacob, My servant. I will deal kindly and give you your reward in this world,[2] because there is no reward for evil-doers in the world to come, as it is said, 'Because by him the Lord

---

[1] In Babylon and elsewhere outside Palestine the sacrificial cult was replaced by prayer; see Siphrê, Deut. § 41, p. 80a; and cf. Esther Rab. viii. 7.

[2] See T.B. Kiddushin, 40b, and T.B. 'Erubin, 22a.

Rabbi Simeon[1] said: Our father Abraham wrote (in his will and bequeathed) all that he had as an inheritance[2] to Isaac, as it is said, "And Abraham gave all that he had unto Isaac" (*ibid.* xxv. 5). He took the document and gave it into the hands of Eliezer, his servant, (who) said, Since the document is in my hand all his money is in my hand,[3] so that he might go and be recommended[4] (thereby) in his[5] father's house and with his family.

From Kirjath ‖ Arba unto Haran was a journey of seventeen days; and in three hours[6] the servant came to Haran. He was astonished in his mind[7] and he said: This day I went forth, and this day I arrived, as it is said, "And I came *this day* unto the fountain" (*ibid.* xxiv. 42).

Rabbi Abbahu said: The Holy One, blessed be He, wished to show loving-kindness to Isaac, and he sent an angel[8] before Eliezer; and the way was shortened for him, so that the servant came to Haran in three hours.

And everything[9] is revealed before the Holy One, blessed be He. A daughter of kings,[10] who in all her life had never gone forth to draw water, went out to draw water in that hour. And the girl, who did not know who the man[11] was, accepted (the proposal) to be married to Isaac. Why?

had given victory unto Syria' (2 Kings v. 1), and he[1] received his reward."[2]

[1] The first editions read: "Shemajah."

[2] See *infra*, p. 215; and cf. T.B. Baba Bathra, 130a. Isaac was destined to be Abraham's heir according to God's promise; see Gen. xv. 4. The first editions omit the quotation, Gen. xxv. 5.

[3] The words of Eliezer are not in the first editions.

[4] By the will of Abraham everything in his possession passed to Isaac. This circumstance would be appreciated by the family of Rebecca. See Gen. Rab. lix. 10.

[5] Abraham's.

[6] The "shortening of the way" occurs also in the Gospel of Pseudo-Matthew xxii. (*A.N.C.L.* xvi. p. 38), and see *A.R.W.* xvi. p. 169.

[7] Lit. "heart."

[8] See Gen. xxiv. 7, and cf. Gen. Rab. *loc. cit.*

[9] Cf. Luria's reading based on Jalkuṭ Makhiri, Ps. lxii. 5.

[10] See Midrash Haggadol, Gen. c. 367. For Bethuel as king see Jalkuṭ, Gen. § 109, and Sopherim xxi. (ed. Müller) p. 304, n. 46.

[11] The reading in the Jalkuṭ, *loc. cit.*, is: "And the girl knew not man." This reading is probably due to Gen. xxiv. 16. Clement of Alexandria gives a parallel Haggadic interpretation in his *Strom.* iv. 25.

---

[1] Laban.

[2] By the victory of Aram, the service of loving-kindness rendered to Jacob by Laban was requited to the descendants of Laban the Aramean. See *infra*, p. 112.

Because she had been destined[1] for him from his mother's womb,[2] as it is said, "In the balances they will go up, they are together lighter than vanity" [3] (Ps. lxii. 9).

Laban and Bethuel answered: Since (this) word has come forth from the mouth of the Almighty, we cannot prevent it, as it is said, "Then Laban and Bethuel answered and said, The thing proceedeth from the Lord:[4] we cannot speak unto thee bad or good" (Gen. xxiv. 50). "Behold, Rebecca is before thee; take her and go" (*ibid.* 51).

The servant arose early in the morning and saw the angel standing and waiting for him in the street. He said to them:[5] "Do not hinder me,[6] for the Lord hath prospered my way" (*ibid.* 56). For behold, the man who came with me yesterday, he has prospered my way; behold, he is standing || and waiting for me in the street,[7] as it is said, "And he said to them, Do not hinder me, for the Lord hath prospered my way." They ate and drank at Rebecca's (bridal) banquet.[8] Like a precentor, who is standing and blessing the bride in her bridal canopy,[9] so they stood and blessed Rebecca their sister (wedded) to Isaac, as it is said, "And they blessed Rebecca, and said unto her, Our sister . . ." (*ibid.* 60).[10]

At six hours of the day[11] the servant went forth from Haran, and he took Rebecca and Deborah her nurse and made them ride upon the camels. So that the servant should not be alone with the maiden (Rebecca) by night,

[1] See Targum Onḳelos to Gen. xxiv. 14.

[2] *i.e.* from his birth. The first editions read: "from her mother's womb."

[3] Cf. Lev. Rab. xxix. 8, Gen. Rab. lix. 9, T.J. Bezah v. 2, 63a.

[4] The MS., the Midrash Haggadol, Gen. c. 368, and the first editions end the quotation here, and add: "etc."

[5] Eliezer is speaking to Laban and his friends.

[6] The MS. ends the quotation here; the first editions continue the verse, and then the printed texts read: "Behold he is in the street, waiting for me. They ate and drank at Rebecca's banquet, as it is said."

[7] The Midrash Haggadol, Gen. c. 370, refers here to the "angel" who accompanied Eliezer.

[8] The first editions add parts of verses 54 and 56 of Gen. xxiv.

[9] See Midrash Haggadol, Gen. *loc. cit.*; and cf. *supra*, pp. 89 f., and see Kallah i., and Tosaphoth, Kethuboth, 7b, *s.v.* שנאמר.

[10] This was a marriage by proxy. The Rabbis differ as to whether the nuptial benedictions can be said only in the presence of the bride and bridegroom; see R. Nissim on T.B. Sukkah, 25b, and RIṬBA on Kethuboth, 8a.

[11] *i.e.* at noon, twelve o'clock. See Midrash Haggadol, Gen. c. 371, for a parallel text.

the earth was contracted[1] before him, and in three hours the servant came to Hebron at the time of the prayer of the afternoon-evening.[2] And Isaac had gone forth to say the afternoon-evening prayer, as it is said, "And Isaac went forth to *meditate* in the field towards even" (*ibid.* 63).[3]

Rabbi Simeon[4] said: Abraham spake to Isaac his son (saying), This servant[5] is suspected of all the transgressions of the Torah, and deceit is in this servant,[6] as it is said, "He is a Canaanite,[7] the balances of deceit are in his hand; he loveth to defraud" (Hos. xii. 7). See, lest he has defiled her,[8] therefore bring the girl into the tent and examine her tactually;[9] || and if she be undefiled, behold, she is destined

[1] The Pal. Targum on Gen. xxiv. 61 states: "And as the way was shortened for him in his journey to Paddan-Aram, so was it shortened for him on his return, so that in one day he went and in one day he returned."

[2] *i.e.* at 3 p.m. The MS. reads: "the afternoon of the evening." The first editions read "afternoon." Midrash Haggadol, *loc. cit.*, has "evening." The word "Minchah" is used to designate the "afternoon prayer" or the "afternoon offering"; see Jastrow, *T.D.* 779a.

[3] The first editions add: "*Meditation* (Sichah) is nought else save prayer,[1] as it is said, 'A *prayer* of the afflicted, when he is overwhelmed and poureth out his *complaint* (Siach) before the Lord'" (Ps. cii. 1). See *Rabbinic Philosophy and Ethics*, p. 84. Gen. Rab. lxviii. 9 quotes here Ps. cxlii. 2, instead of Ps. cii. 1 as above.

[4] The first editions read: "Ishmael."

[5] The Prague edition reads: "O my son! this servant," etc.

[6] The first editions read: "This servant is suspected of transgressions, and deceit is in his hand." עבירה (transgression) often means "immorality."

[7] Servants or slaves were called "Canaanites" in consequence of Noah's curse upon his son Ham, whose son was Canaan; cf. T.B. Baba Bathra, 92b.

[8] "Zinôr," euphem. for vagina; see 2 Sam. v. 8.

[9] For a parallel see the legends of the Virgin Mary and Salome in "Ante-Nicene Christian Library," xvi. p. 12 (The Protevangelium of James); and cf. same story in same volume, p. 32, The Gospel of Pseudo-Matthew, and see Hennecke, *Apokryphen d. N.T.*, p. 61; see also Tertullian, "On the Veiling of Virgins," xi. R. Simeon's inference is based on the view that obtained in ancient times that slaves could be reasonably suspected of loose conduct; see T.B. Berakhoth, 45b; T.B. Pesachim, 91a and 113b. Clement of Alexandria, to quote but one of the Church Fathers, held a similar opinion of the slaves of his day; see *The Instructor*, iii. 4. The Midrash in our text also occurs in Jalkuṭ on Gen., § 109, Midrash Abkhir, and in the Midrash Agadah, Gen. p. 60. See also Rokeach, pp. 54a, b (1st ed.). According to the Book of Jashar (xxiv. 40) Rebecca was ten years old when wedded to

[1] Jerome, *in loc.*, knew this Haggadic interpretation, which also occurs in Onkelos and Pal. Targum, *in loc.* See Gen. Rab. lx. 14; T.B. Berakhoth, 26b; cf. Rahmer, *Die Hebräischen Traditionen in den Werken des Hieronymus* (1861), p. 38.

for thee from her mother's womb.[1] He brought her into the tent and examined her tactually, and he showed the result to Abraham his father, and afterwards he took her to be his wife, as it is said, "And Isaac brought her into the tent of Sarah his mother . . . And Isaac was comforted after his mother's death" (Gen. xxiv. 67); [2] for the deeds of Rebecca were like unto those of Sarah.[3] Hence the Israelites have the custom of producing the tokens of the damsel's virginity,[4] as it is said, "Then shall the father of the damsel, and her mother, take and bring forth the tokens of the damsel's virginity" (Deut. xxii. 15).[5]

The steward of Abraham's household[6] was his servant Eliezer, and whence was his servant? When (Abraham) went forth from Ur of the Chaldees all the magnates of the kingdom[7] came to give him gifts; and Nimrod[8] took his first-born (son)[9] Eliezer and gave him to (Abraham) as a perpetual slave.

When (Eliezer had thus) dealt kindly with Isaac, he set him free, and the Holy One, blessed be He, gave him his reward in this world, so that there should not be a reward

Isaac. Another opinion is to be found in Sopherim xxi. 9, and in Seder 'Olam Rab. i. p. 4a.

[1] The first editions read: "She is thine by the word of the Almighty." See Midrash Haggadol, c. 373.

[2] The last clause of the quotation is not in the first editions.

[3] The first editions add: "she was found to be as perfect as Sarah his mother.[1] 'The king's daughter *within* is all glorious' (Ps. xlv. 13); 'And Isaac was comforted after his mother's death'" (Gen. xxiv. 67).

[4] The first editions read: "custom of tactual examination so that they should not be in doubt, as it is said, 'Then shall the father of the damsel, and her mother, take'" (Deut. xxii. 15). On the custom see Müller's *Chiluf Minhagim*, p. 37, where it is pointed out that it is a Palestinian custom. This might point to a Palestinian as the author of *P.R.E.*, or to Palestine as its home.

[5] See the rest of the verse.

[6] Lit. "The steward of his house (was) the servant of Abraham, for Eliezer was his servant." Our translation agrees with the text of the first two editions.

[7] The first editions read: "All the magnates of the generation arose and gave him gifts."

[8] On Nimrod see *Rabbinic Philosophy and Ethics*, pp. 44 f. and 51; *J.E.* ix. 309; Ginzberg, *Legends of the Jews*, i. pp. 177; cf. Augustine, *de Civ. Dei*, xvi. 11, 3. See also Jeraḥmeel, *s.v.* in Index, for references. The first editions add: "arose and wrote a document transferring his servant Eliezer to Abraham."

[9] The rest of the sentence is wanting in the first editions.

---

[1] This is like the reading in the Targumim, Gen. *in loc.*

for the wicked in the world to come;[1] and He raised him to kingship, and he is Og, king of Bashan.[2]

Rabbi José[3] said: From whom do we learn (that there should be) seven days of (the wedding) banquet?[4] From our father Jacob, who || made a banquet with rejoicing for seven days, and he took Leah (as his wife). Again he kept another seven days of banquet and rejoicing, and took Rachel (as his wife), as it is said, "And Laban gathered together all the men of the place, and made a feast" (Gen. xxix. 22). The Holy One, blessed be He, said to them: Ye have shown loving-kindness to Jacob, My servant. I will give a reward to your children, so that there be no reward for the wicked in the world to come: "Because by him the Lord *had given* victory unto Syria" (2 Kings v. 1). From whom do we learn (that there should be) seven days of banquet? From Samson the Nazirite of God, for when he went down to the land of the Philistines, he took a wife and kept seven days of banquet and rejoicing, as it is said, "And it came to pass, when they saw him,[5] that they brought thirty companions to be with him" (Judg. xiv. 11). What were they doing with him? They were eating and drinking and rejoicing,[6] as it is said, "And Samson said unto them, Let me now put forth a riddle unto you" (*ibid.* 12); and another text says, "They could not declare the riddle in three days" (*ibid.* 14).[7]

The bridegroom is like a king. Just as a king is praised by everybody,[8] so is the bridegroom praised by everybody (during) the seven days of the feast. Just as a king is

[1] Eliezer, however, inherited the future world according to the tradition of some Rabbis; see Derekh Erez Ẓuṭṭa, i. (end), and Midrash Agadah, Gen. xxiv. p. 60.

[2] See *J.E.* v. 112, Pal. Targum on Gen. xiv. 13, *infra*, p. 167; and cf. Jalkuṭ on Num. § 765, Gen. Rab. lx. 2, Deut. Rab. i. 25, T.B. Baba Bathra, 58a, T.B. Joma, 28b, and Sopherim xxiv. 9.

[3] The first editions read: "Rabbi"; *i.e.* Jehudah I (*c.* 200 C.E.); see, however, *supra* in this chapter, p. 107, for a similar text. The whole of this section till "Syria (2 Kings v. 1)" is wanting in the first two editions. See *supra*, p. 107, note 6.

[4] The custom is clearly indicated in the text Judg. xiv. 10 and 12; cf. Matt. ix. 15, and *supra*, p. 107.

[5] The first editions end the quotation here.

[6] The first editions read differently: "What is the meaning of ('when they saw) *him*'? They were eating and drinking *with him*, as it is said," etc.

[7] See Jalkuṭ, *in loc.*, and Menorath Ha-Maor, § 173.

[8] See T.B. Kethuboth, 17a; and cf. Singer, p. 299: "The jubilant voice of bridegrooms from their canopies," and Jer. xxxiii. 11.

dressed in garments of glory,[1] so the bridegroom is dressed in garments of glory.[2] Just as a king is rejoicing, with feasts in his presence, all his days, so || the bridegroom is rejoicing and has feasts before him all the seven days of the banquet. Just as the king does not go into the market-place alone, likewise the bridegroom does not go into the market-place alone.[3] Just as the face of a king is shining like the light of a sun,[4] so the face of the bridegroom is shining like the light of a sun, as it is said, " And he [5] is as a bridegroom coming out of his chamber,[6] and rejoicing to run his course " (Ps. xix. 5).

[1] Cf. Isa. lxi. 10.
[2] The first editions add : " all the seven days of the banquet."
[3] See Rashi on T.B. Menachoth, 98a, catchword ויריק. The mourners likewise are not permitted to go out alone. The order of the narrative here is different in the printed texts.
[4] Cf. Prov. xvi. 15.
[5] *i.e.* the sun.
[6] The MS. ends the quotation here ; the first editions add " etc."

CHAPTER XVII

LOVING SERVICE TO MOURNERS [19A. ii.]

CONCERNING the one who tenders the service of loving-kindness to mourners.[1] Whence do we learn of the service of loving-kindness to mourners?[2] From the Omnipresent, who alone showed loving-kindness to Moses, His servant, and buried him[3] with His own hand. If this story had not been written (in the Torah) it would be impossible to say it, as it is said, "And he buried him in the valley in the land of Moab" (Deut. xxxiv. 6).[4]

Rabban Gamaliel,[5] the son of R. Jehudah, said: Not to Moses alone did He show loving-kindness, but also to Aaron. For when they[6] went up Mount Hor all the tribes of Israel were contending and saying, Moses and Eleazar have left Aaron on Mount Hor and have gone down (by themselves).[7] They did not believe that he was dead. To show loving-kindness to him, what did the Holy One, blessed be He, do? He took Aaron's coffin and brought it above the camp of Israel, and all Israel saw

[1] This sentence is missing in the printed editions.

[2] On mourning customs see Bender's article in *J.Q.R.* vi. pp. 317 ff. and 664 ff., also article in *J.E.* ix. 101 ff.

[3] On the death of Moses see *Rabbinic Philosophy and Ethics*, pp. 270–272. The service of loving-kindness to mourners is not proved from the burial of Moses. See T.B. Soṭah, 14a, where the custom is inferred from the case of Abraham; cf. T.B. Synhedrin, 46a.

[4] See T.B. Soṭah, 13b, and Siphrê, Deut. § 357.

[5] On R. Gamaliel see *J.E.* v. 560 ff. On the theme in our text see Jalḳuṭ, Num. § 787, and cf. Num. Rab. xix. 20.

[6] Moses, Aaron, and Eleazar. The Gaster MS. 9 begins with the words "were contending," and continues to the end of the book as in the printed editions. The text, apart from the inserted and older MS. section, follows the Venice edition very closely.

[7] For their own advantage and glory; see *Rabbinic Philosophy and Ethics* on the death of Aaron, pp. 235–238.

Aaron's coffin flying and moving in the air.[1] They then believed that he was dead, and they showed loving-kindness to him, as it is said : || " And *all* the congregation *saw* that Aaron was dead " (Num. xx. 29). Only the men [2] showed loving-kindness to Moses, as it is said, " And the *sons* of Israel wept for Moses " (Deut. xxxiv. 8). The men and the women and the children [3] showed loving-kindness to Aaron.

Why (was this) ? Because he loved peace and pursued peace,[4] and passed daily through the entire camp of Israel and promoted peace between a man and his wife, and between a man and his neighbour ; therefore *all* Israel showed loving-kindness to him, as it is said, " And when *all* the congregation saw that Aaron was dead,[5] they wept for Aaron thirty days, even *all* the house of Israel " (Num. xx. 29).[6]

Rabbi José said : From whom do we learn of the seven days of mourning ? [7] From Jacob, our father, for thus did his son Joseph unto him,[8] as it is said, " And he made a mourning for his father seven days " (Gen. l. 10).[9]

[1] See *Rabbinic Philosophy and Ethics*, p. 228 ; and for the loving-kindness see *ibid.* p. 240. A similar legend as to Mohammed's coffin occurs in Arabian literature.

[2] Not " all the congregation," as at the death of Aaron.

[3] The first editions omit " and the children."

[4] See Aboth de R. Nathan (*a*) xii. pp. 24b ff.

[5] The first editions insert the quotation, " they wept for Aaron," etc., before the paragraph beginning, " Why (was this) ? " The MS. as well as the first editions do not quote the first part of the verse (Num. xx. 29).

[6] The first editions add the following : " This verse [1] is not in its right place, for at 'Moserah there Aaron died, and there he was buried' (Deut. x. 6). And the text points to this (place) as though he died there and was buried there." [2]

[7] See Gen. Rab. c. 7, and T.B. Mo'ed Kaṭan, 20a ; Tanchuma Vajechi, § xvii. Cf. T.J. Soṭah i. 10, 17c ; Jalkuṭ i. § 161.

[8] The first editions read : " for Joseph kept for him seven days of mourning."

[9] The first editions add the following : " And all the magnates of the kingdom [3] went up with him, as it is said : ' And there went up with him both chariots and horsemen ' (Gen. l. 9).[4] The Holy One,

---

[1] The weeping was at Moserah ; see Seder 'Olam Rab. ix., T.J. Joma i. 1, p. 38b, T.J. Soṭah i. 10, p. 17c, and Pal. Targum on Deut. x. 6, and cf. Rashi on Num. xxvi. 13.

[2] See Num. xxxiii. 38.

[3] The Amsterdam edition reads : " the kingdoms."

[4] The rest of the verse should be considered, " and it was a very great company " (Gen. l. 9).

Whence do we learn (the duty of) showing loving-kindness to mourners? From Jezebel, the daughter of Ethbaal.[1] The palace of Jezebel, daughter of Ethbaal, was near the market-place.[2] When any corpse was carried through the market-place, she would go forth from her palace, and she clapped [3] with the palms of her hands and praised with her mouth, and she followed the corpse [4] ten steps. Concerning her, Elijah, be he remembered for good,[5] prophesied (and said): "In the portion of Jezreel shall the dogs eat the flesh of Jezebel" (2 Kings ix. 36). But over the limbs which were (employed in) showing loving-kindness, the dogs had no power, as it is said, "And they went || to bury her: but they found no more of her than the skull, and the feet, and the palms of her hands" (*ibid.* 35).[6]

blessed be He, said to them: Ye have shown loving-kindness to Jacob, My servant,[1] and I will also give you and your children a good reward in this world. When the Egyptians died in the (Reed) Sea, they were not drowned [2] in the sea, but they were worthy to be buried,[3] as it is said: 'Thou stretchedst out thy right hand, the earth *swallowed* them'" (Ex. xv. 12).[4]

[1] See 1 Kings xvi. 31.

[2] Or "street." The basis of this Haggadah is to be sought in 2 Kings ix. 35. The palace was near the city gate which is generally near the market-place or the "High Street." The first editions add here: "When any bridegroom happened to pass (her palace) she would go forth from her palace, and she clapped her hands and praised with her mouth, and she would go ten steps."

[3] The first editions read: "And she made a noise by rubbing her hands, and she bewailed with her mouth." The reading in our MS. seems to be drawn from the account describing Jezebel's conduct when she saw bridegrooms.

[4] The usual distance was four cubits. See Ṭur, Joreh Di ah, § 361; Maimonides, Hilkhoth Abel, xiv.; and see also T.B. Soṭah, 35b and 46b.

[5] See *supra*, p. 2, note 8.

[6] The quotation in the MS. is abbreviated thus: "And they went to bury her, but they found no more of her than the palms," etc. See Rashi and Ḳimchi on 2 Kings ix. 36. On the theme of our text see Jalḳuṭ, 2 Kings ix. (§ 232); Menorath Ha-Maor, § 216; Kad Ha-Ḳemach, *s.v.* אבל. Ṭur, Eben Ha-'Ezer, 65, quotes the Midrash, as though the text were "bridegroom and bride," and not merely "bridegroom."

---

[1] See *infra*, p. 309.

[2] See T.B. Pesachim, 117a, and cf. *infra*, p. 332.

[3] The bodies of drowned men are liable to be thrown ashore; they would lie exposed and remain unburied. God, however, had mercy on the doomed Egyptians and bade the sea cast up the drowned, whereupon the earth was constrained to receive the dead, and thus they were buried. The idea contained in this Midrash is the belief of the Jew in the dignity of man, created in the image of God.

[4] See *Rabbinic Philosophy and Ethics*, p. 169, and cf. *infra*, pp. 334 f.

Whence do we learn (the duty of) showing loving-kindness to mourners? From the men of Jabesh-Gilead. For when Saul and his sons were slain, the men of Jabesh Gilead said: Are we not bound to show loving-kindness to the man who delivered us from the disgrace of the sons of Ammon?[1] All their mighty men arose and went all night to the walls of Beth-Shan,[2] and they took the body of Saul and the bodies of his sons from the walls of Beth-Shan, as it is said, "All the valiant men arose, and took away the body of Saul" (1 Chron. x. 12).

The mourners are comforted with bread and wine,[3] as it is said, "Give strong drink unto him that is ready to perish, and wine unto the bitter in soul" (Prov. xxxi. 6).[4]

The men of Jabesh-Gilead showed (loving-kindness [5]) to Saul and his sons.[6] (God said,) I will also give you and your sons your reward in the future; for when the Holy One, blessed be He, in the future will gather Israel from the four corners of the world, the first whom He will gather, will be the half-tribe of Manasseh,[7] as it is said, "Gilead is mine, and

[1] Cf. 1 Sam. xi. and see Pseudo-Rashi on 1 Chron. x. 12. Gilead was nigh to Benjamin, Saul's tribe; see Num. Rab. xiv. i.

[2] *i.e.* they came to Beth-Shan at night. Beth-Shan is three hours' journey from Jabesh-Gilead. The first editions omit the next clause, and continue: "as it is said."

[3] See Semachoth xii. The subject has been dealt with by Perles in his *Leichenfeierlichkeiten im Nachbiblischen Judentum.* See *J.E.* v. 529 f. and *ibid.* ix. 101 f.

[4] The first editions omit the first half of the verse. See T.B. 'Erubin, 65a: "wine was only created in order to comfort the mourners." "Bread" is mentioned in Jer. xvi. 7, Ezek. xxiv. 17, 22, and Hos. ix. 4, in connection with mourning.

[5] The MS. omits "loving-kindness." It occurs in the first editions. Saul had rescued the men of Jabesh-Gilead from the attack of the children of Ammon (see also Josh. ii. 12 for the term "*dealing kindly*"). The context refers to 2 Sam. ii. 5. Loving-kindness is that extra service of love which is more than one is in duty bound to do to one's fellow. The latter sums up one's obligation to any and every human being, namely, to deal justly and truly with all men, and not to hurt anyone. Loving service goes beyond this. See *Jewish Sources of the Sermon on the Mount*, pp. 97, 104 f.

[6] The first editions and Jalkut Makhiri, Pss., p. 154b, add: "by fasting, weeping, and lamentation,[1] as it is said: 'And they *fasted*[2] seven days' (1 Sam. xxxi. 13). The Holy One, blessed be He, said to them: In the future."

[7] In the land of Gilead; see Siphrê, Deut. § 355.

---

[1] The mourning consisted of the three phases enumerated. See 2 Sam. i. 11, 12 and Esth. iv. 1–3.

[2] Fasting was not the usual custom. The rule to fast is limited now to the anniversary of the day of death of one's father or mother.

Manasseh is mine" (Ps. lx. 7). Afterwards (will He gather in) Ephraim,[1] as it is said, "Ephraim is the defence of mine head" (*ibid.*). Afterwards Judah (will be gathered in), as it is said, "Judah is my sceptre" (*ibid.*).

"Gilead is mine," refers to Ahab, king of Israel, who died in Ramoth-Gilead;[2] "and Manasseh is mine," is to be taken literally; "Ephraim is the defence of mine head," refers to Jeroboam;[3] "Judah || is my sceptre," points to Ahithophel;[4] "Moab is my *washpot*" (*ibid.* 8), means Gehazi;[5] "upon Edom will I cast my shoe" (*ibid.*), refers to Doeg;[6] "Philistia, shout thou because of me" (*ibid.*). The Holy One, blessed be He, said:[7] It is for Me to search for merit on their behalf,[8] and to make them friendly towards one another.[9]

Rabbi Phineas said: Thirty years[10] after Saul and his sons had been killed, a famine lasting three years arose in the days of David, year after year,[11] as it is said, "And there was a famine in the days of David three years, year after year" (2 Sam. xxi. 1). Why was it year after year? In the first year all Israel went up to (celebrate the great) festivals. David said to them: Go and look if perchance there be among you some who worship idols, for because of the sin of idolatry rain is withheld, as it is said, "Take heed to yourselves, lest your heart be deceived,[12] and ye turn aside, and

[1] See *infra*, p. 141. The children of Joseph will be the first to be redeemed in the future, says the Abkath Rochel, ii. We are now in the field of Messianic Eschatology.

[2] See 1 Kings xxii. 29 ff.

[3] He was an Ephraimite; see 1 Kings xi. 26. The first editions add: "the son of Nebat."

[4] He was of the tribe of Judah; see 2 Sam. xvii. 15 for the story of Ahithophel.

[5] Gehazi inherited the leprosy of Naaman; the "washpot" receives the dirt of the one who washes therein. On Gehazi see *J.E.* v. 580 and 582, and see Num. Rab. xiv. 1.

[6] The first editions add: "the Edomite."

[7] The first editions add: "to them."

[8] The reading of the Amsterdam edition is: "It is for Me to search for their merit."

[9] See T.J. Synhedrin x. 2, 29b and Num. Rab., *loc. cit.*

[10] Jalkuṭ to 2 Sam. xxi. § 154 reads like our MS., "After thirty years"; see Rashi on T.B. Jebamoth, 79a. The first editions read: "In the year after Saul and his sons had been killed."

[11] See T.J. Kiddushin, iv. 1, 65b, c, which is the source of our text; see also T.J. Ta'anith, iii. 3, 66c, and Num. Rab. viii. 4, and Midrash Samuel xxviii. 5; cf. T.B. Jebamoth, 78b.

[12] The MS. and the first editions end the quotation here.

serve other gods, and worship them" (Deut. xi. 16). What is written after this? "And the anger of the Lord will be kindled against you, and he will shut up the heaven, that there be no rain" (*ibid.* 17).[1] They went forth and investigated, but did not find (any idolatry).

In the second year[2] all Israel went up (to celebrate) the festivals. David said to them: Go forth and see if there be among you people who lead immoral lives, because owing to the sin of immorality the heavens[3] are closed, as it is said, "And thou hast polluted the land with thy whoredoms"[4] (Jer. iii. 2). What is written after this in this context? "Therefore the showers have been withholden, and there hath been no latter rain" (*ibid.* 3). They investigated, but they did not find (any immoral people).

In the third || year all Israel went up (to celebrate) the festivals. David said to them: Go forth and see if there be among you people who shed blood, because on account of the sin of those who murder[5] the rain is withheld, as it is said, "So ye shall not pollute the land[6] wherein ye are; for blood, it polluteth the land" (Num. xxxv. 33). They went forth and investigated, but they did not find (any murderer). David said to them: Henceforth the matter only depends upon me.

David arose and prayed before the Holy One, blessed be He. And He answered him: It is for Saul;[7] was not Saul one who was anointed with the oil of consecration? and was it not Saul in whose days there was no idolatry in Israel? and was it not Saul who secured his portion[8] with

[1] The first editions omit from "What is written" to the end of the quotation.

[2] Of the famine.

[3] The first editions read: "the rain is withheld."

[4] The first editions continue: "and with thy wickedness."

[5] The first editions read: "the shedding of blood." Other reasons for the famine are suggested in T.B. Jebamoth, *loc. cit.*; Jalkuṭ, Num. § 771; Midrash Samuel, *in loc.*; and cf. T.J. Ḳiddushin, *loc. cit.*

[6] The MS. and the first editions end the quotation here; the MS. adds "etc." Cf. Isa. xxiv. 5.

[7] See Num. Rab., *loc. cit.*, and Jalkuṭ, 2 Samuel (§ 154). The first editions read: "David said, Sovereign of the World! I am not Saul, for in my days idolatry has not been done in Israel, and I am not Saul who was anointed with the oil of consecration, and I am not Saul who quarrelled with Samuel the prophet." This agrees with MS. Gaster.

[8] See *infra*, p. 246, and cf. T.B. Berakhoth, 12b, and Kaphtor Va-Pherach vii. (ed. Edelmann), p. 21a.

Samuel the prophet? Yet ye are in the land (of Israel) and he is (buried) outside the land (of Israel).

David forthwith arose and gathered together all the elders of Israel and the nobles, and they crossed the Jordan. They came to Jabesh-Gilead and they found the bones of Saul and Jonathan his son. No worm[1] had been able to touch[2] them, as it is said, "He keepeth all his bones,[3] not one of them is broken" (Ps. xxxiv. 20). They took the bones of Saul and Jonathan his son, and placed them in a coffin, and they crossed the Jordan, as it is said, "And they buried the bones of Saul and Jonathan his son . . . and they performed[4] all that the king commanded" (2 Sam. xxi. 14). The king commanded that they should bring the coffin of Saul in all the borders of each tribe. And it came to pass that the tribe || wherein they brought the coffin of Saul, the people (there) with their wives and their sons and their daughters came forth and displayed loving-kindness to Saul and to his sons, so that all Israel should discharge their obligation of showing loving-kindness. And thus (did they do) until it came to the border of his possession to the border of Jerusalem,[5] in the land of Benjamin[6] in Jerusalem, as it is said, "And they buried the bones of Saul and Jonathan his son in the country of Benjamin" (*ibid.*),[7] in the vicinity of Jerusalem. When the Holy One, blessed be He, saw that all Israel had displayed loving-kindness (to him[8]), He was forthwith full of compassion, and He sent rain upon the land, as it is said, "And after that God was intreated for the land" (*ibid.*).

[1] Worms destroy bones as well as flesh. Luria prefers to read רקבה, "decay," and not "worm."

[2] Lit. "to rule over them."

[3] In spite of the prolonged transportation, the bones were not broken.

[4] The printed text and MS. Gaster add, "to them"; this is not in the Bible text.

[5] Luria reads: "the border of his inheritance, to the land of Benjamin"; see Num. Rab., *loc. cit.* The first editions read: "until it came to the border of Israel and to the land of Benjamin, as it is said, 'And they buried him in the border of his inheritance'" (Josh. xxiv. 30).

[6] The text in the printed editions differs here from our reading.

[7] The quotation continues: "In Zela, in the sepulchre of Kish his father" (2 Sam. xxi. 14).

[8] Saul.

Rabbi Nathaniel said: Three hundred years[1] before the birth of Josiah, was his name mentioned,[2] as it is said, "Behold, a child shall be born unto the house of David, Josiah by name" (1 Kings xiii. 2); "And he was eight years old when he began to reign" (2 Kings xxii. 1). What is the disposition of a lad of eight years of age?[3] He despised[4] the idols and broke in pieces the pillars, and smashed the images[5] and cut down the groves.[6] His merit was great[7] before the[8] Throne of Glory. Because of the evil which Israel did in secret[9] the righteous one[10] was gathered (to his fathers), as it is said, "For the righteous is taken away because of the evil" (Isa. lvii. 1).[11] || All[12] Judah gathered together also with Jeremiah the prophet to show loving-kindness to Josiah, as it is said, "And Jeremiah lamented for Josiah,[13] and all *the singing men* and *the singing women* spake of Josiah" (2 Chron. xxxv. 25). Rabbi Meir said: "The singing men" refer to the Levites, who stood upon the platform[14] singing; "and the singing women" refer to their wives. Rabbi Simeon said: These terms do not refer merely to the Levites and their wives; but to the skilled women, as it is said, "Thus saith the Lord

[1] Between the accession of Jeroboam and Josiah there elapsed 320 years. Josiah was eight years old when he ascended the throne, so that 312 years elapsed from the accession of Jeroboam to the *birth* of Josiah. In round numbers this is 300 years, see *infra*, p. 233.

[2] See *infra*, p. 233.

[3] This refers to 2 Chron. xxxiv. 3; see Targum on this text and also Pseudo-Rashi thereto.

[4] This is based on Isa. vii. 16.

[5] See 2 Chron. xxxiv. 4, 7.

[6] See 2 Kings xxiii. 14.

[7] Lit. shining or illustrious. See T.B. Mo'ed Ḳaṭan, 25b, where Amos viii. 8 is applied to Josiah.

[8] The first editions read: "before the Holy One, blessed be He, and the Throne of Glory."

[9] Idolatry was again rife in the homes of the Hebrew people; see Lam. Rab. i. (53) and T.B. Ta'anith, 22b.

[10] Josiah.

[11] This quotation is missing in the printed editions. The R.V. renders somewhat differently.

[12] The first editions read: "All the men of Judah and Jerusalem."

[13] The MS. and the first editions end the quotation here, the printed texts add "etc." The context justifies the insertion of the entire verse.

[14] The first editions read: "their platform." On the meaning of "Dukhan" see Levy, *N.H.W.B.* i. 382a.

of hosts,[1] Consider ye, and call for the mourning women,[2] that they may come; and send for the *cunning* women, that they may come: and let them make haste, and take up a wailing for us" (Jer. ix. 17, 18). Hence the wise men instituted (the rule) that this should be done[3] to all the *wise* men of Israel and to their great[4] men, as it is said, "And they made them an ordinance in Israel" (2 Chron. xxxv. 25).

Solomon saw that the observance[5] of loving-kindness was great before the Holy One, blessed be He. When he built the Temple he erected two gates, one for the bridegrooms, and the other for the mourners and the excommunicated. On Sabbaths the Israelites went and sat between those two gates; and they knew that anyone who entered through the gate of the bridegrooms[6] was a bridegroom, and they said to him, May He who dwells in this house cause thee to rejoice with sons and daughters. If one entered through the gate of the mourners with his upper lip covered, then they knew that he was a mourner, and they would say to him, May He who dwells || in this house comfort thee. If one entered through the gate of the mourners without[7] having his upper lip covered, then they knew that he was excommunicated, and they would say to him, May He who dwells in this house[8] put into thy heart (the desire) to listen to[9] the words of thy associates, and may He put into the hearts of thy associates that they may draw thee near (to themselves), so that all Israel may discharge their duty by rendering the service of loving-kindness.

[1] The MS. reads "the Lord." The first editions read according to the Massoretic text.

[2] The MS. ends verse 17 here and continues verse 18. The first editions end the quotation at the words, "that they may come."

[3] The first editions read: "Thus all Israel took upon themselves to show loving-kindness."

[4] This agrees with Luria's emendation.

[5] The first editions read: "the attribute."

[6] See Sopherim xix. 12 (ed. Müller, pp. 278 f.) for historical material. On the "gates" see Middoth ii. 2, and Tamid, 27a, and Kaphtor Va-Pherach vi. p. 16b. Dr. Büchler has written on the subject of the gates of the Temple; see *J.Q.R.* x. 678 and xi. pp. 46 ff.

[7] The 1st ed. omits the negative.

[8] The first editions read: "comfort thee." Nachmanides, in his *Torath Ha-Adam* (ed. Venice), p. 7, omits these words.

[9] The first editions omit "the words of." Nachmanides, *op. cit.*, agrees with our MS.

When the Temple was destroyed, the sages[1] instituted (the rule) that the bridegrooms and mourners should go to the synagogues and to the houses of study. The men of the place see the bridegroom and rejoice with him; and they see the mourner and sit with him upon the earth, so that[2] all the Israelites may discharge their duty in the service of loving-kindness. With reference to them he[3] says: Blessed art Thou,[4] who giveth a good reward to those who show loving-kindness.[5]

[1] Nachmanides (*ibid.*) reads: "the sages"; see Semachoth vi. and Middoth (ii. 12). Sopherim, *loc. cit.*, quotes this rule in the name of R. Eliezer ben Hyrḳanos, clearly showing that the compiler of Sopherim used our book and regarded it as the work of R. Eliezer b. Hyrḳanos. The rule is a Palestinian custom; see Brüll, *Jahrbücher*, i. p. 30.

[2] Nachmanides (*ibid.*) omits "and they sit," and reads: "all the Israelites."

[3] See for a similar expression, *supra*, p. 73. It might be that "he" refers to the one who receives the service of loving-kindness. Perhaps it merely refers to any Israelite who has to say the benediction. Or, we might render: "it says."

[4] The first editions add: "O Lord."

[5] See T.B. Kethuboth, 8b. The form of the benediction has its parallel in the Daily Morning Service; see Singer, p. 7.

CHAPTER XVIII[1]

THE CREATION ON THE EVE OF THE SABBATH [21A. i.]

TEN things were created (on the eve of the Sabbath) in the twilight (namely):[2] the mouth of the earth;[3] the mouth of the well;[4] the mouth of the ass;[5] the rainbow;[6] the Manna;[7] the Shamir;[8] the shape of the alphabet;[9] the writing[10] and the tables (of the law);[11] and the ram of

[1] In the printed text and MS. Gaster this is ch. xix.

[2] The words in brackets are missing in the MS. but they occur in the first editions and in MS. Gaster.

[3] See Num. xvi. 32. For the subject-matter of this paragraph see Aboth v. 9, with the excellent observations of Taylor in his 2nd edition of *Aboth*, pp. 83 ff. Our text agrees to a large extent with this Mishnah, but differs from the version in T.B. Pesachim, 54a; Siphrê, Deut. § 355, Pal. Targum, Num. xxii. 28, Mekhilta, p. 51a, and *supra*, p. 14. Eight things enumerated in our context were said (*supra*, p. 14, note 1) to have been created on the second day. This statement is wanting in our MS.; it was inserted for the first time in the second edition of *P.R.E.* For the ten things see *Rabbinic Philosophy and Ethics*, pp. 24 f. See also Leḳach Ṭob, Gen. ii. 3, p. 9a.

[4] In T.B. Pesachim and Siphrê, *loc. cit.*, the "well" only is mentioned. The "*mouth* of the well" is mentioned in our text and in Aboth v. 9; this may refer to the well of Hagar or Jacob, or the reference might be to Num. xxi. 16. See *infra*, pp. 268, 323.

[5] See Num. xxii. 28.

[6] See Gen. ix. 13 and *J.E.* x. 312.

[7] See Ex. xvi. 15, and Pal. Targ. to Ex. xvi. 4, 15; and cf. *J.E.* viii. 293. The Oxford MS. and MS. Gaster and the first editions add: "the Rod." See *infra*, pp. 312 f., and cf. Ex. iv. 17.

[8] See 1 Kings vi. 7 for the information that no tool was used in the Temple. How then were the stones cut? The legend says, "By the worm called Shamir"; see T.B. Giṭṭin, 68a. On the Shamir see *J.E.* xi. 229 f. and T.J. Soṭah ix. 13, 24b, and T.B. Soṭah 48b. For the references to the "Ten Marvels" created on the eve of the first Friday, see Siphrê, Deut., *loc. cit.*

[9] See *supra*, p. 14, note 6.

[10] Interesting material on the Hebrew alphabet is contained in the Othijoth de R. 'Aḳiba.

[11] On the "tables of the Law" in Rabbinical literature see *J.E.* xi. 662 ff. The "tables" are not mentioned *supra*, p. 14, note 1; see, however, p. 15.

Abraham.[1] (Some sages say: the destroying spirits[2] also, and the sepulchre of Moses,[3] and the ram of Isaac; and other sages say: the tongs also.[4])

At the seventh hour (of the day[5] on Friday[6]), the first man entered the garden of Eden, and the ministering || angels were praising before him,[7] and dancing before him, and escorting him[8] into the garden of Eden; and at twilight at the eve of Sabbath,[9] he was driven forth, and he went out. The ministering angels were crying aloud concerning him, saying to him: "Man[10] in glory tarrieth not overnight,[11] when he is like the beasts that pass away"[12] (Ps. xlix. 12).

"Like a beast that passes away" is not written here, but "like the beasts that pass away," (so) were they both.[13] The Sabbath day arrived and became an advocate[14] for the first man, and it spake before Him: Sovereign of all worlds!

[1] See *infra*, pp. 228 ff. The Oxford MS. and MS. Gaster omit this. The next section in brackets is wanting in our MS.; it occurs in the Oxford MS. (O.A. 167), MS. Gaster, and in almost the same reading in the first editions.

[2] See *supra*, p. 14, note 8; and see Gen. Rab. vii. 4; and cf. *J.E.* iv. 514 ff.

[3] See Deut. xxxiv. 6.

[4] See Taylor, *Aboth*, p. 86, note 22, and Hoffmann, *Mishnajoth*, p. 352, note 37.

[5] *i.e.* 1 o'clock p.m.; see Shocher Ṭob, Ps. xcii. 3, p. 202a. This contradicts the statement in Chapter XI.; see *supra*, p. 78.

[6] "Of the day on Friday" is missing in our MS., but it occurs in the 2nd ed., and in the MS. Gaster. This was the day of his creation. The text is lit. "eve of the Sabbath."

[7] See *supra*, p. 89; and cf. Slav. Enoch xxxi., where Adam perceives "the angels singing the song of triumph." Cf. Koran, ed. Rodwell, 1911, p. 341.

[8] So also in Jubilees iii. 9.

[9] Friday afternoon between sunset and night; see also Slav. Enoch xxxii. 2, which implies that the expulsion of Adam was followed by the Sabbath. See *supra*, p. 78.

[10] The Hebrew word is also "Adam."

[11] For he did not tarry overnight in his glory in Paradise; see T.B. Synhedrin 38b.

[12] *i.e.* when they were driven forth out of Paradise; see *infra*, p. 143. This Psalm (xlix.) is applied to Adam by our book and by many Midrashim, see Shocher Ṭob, Ps. xcii. 3, p. 202b.

[13] The point here is the change from the singular to the plural: "they were like"; see Gen. Rab. xxi. 7. They (*i.e.* Adam and Eve) became like the beasts when they were expelled from Eden; they had to die like the beasts. Perhaps the meaning of the Midrash would be better understood by translating verse 12 of Ps. xlix. thus: "Adam did not tarry overnight in glory, he was to be likened to the beasts; yea, they (Adam and Eve) were to be (thus) compared."

[14] See *Rabbinic Philosophy and Ethics*, p. 74. Cf. *infra*, pp. 143 f.

No murderer[1] has been slain in the world during the six days of creation, and wilt Thou commence (to do this) with me?[2] Is this its sanctity, and is this its blessing? as it is said, " And God blessed the seventh day, and hallowed it" (Gen. ii. 3). By the merit of the Sabbath day Adam was saved from the judgment of Gehinnom.[3] When Adam perceived the power of the Sabbath, he said: Not for nought did the Holy One, blessed be He, bless and hallow[4] the Sabbath day. He began to observe (the Sabbath)[5] and to utter a psalm for the Sabbath day, and he said: " A psalm, a song for the Sabbath day" (Ps. xcii. 1).[6] Rabbi Simeon[7] said: The first man said this psalm, and it was forgotten throughout all the generations until Moses[8] came and renewed it || according to his name,[9] "A psalm, a song for the Sabbath day" (*ibid.*), for the day which is entirely Sabbath and rest in the life of eternity.[10]

" It is good to confess[11] to the Lord" (*ibid.*). The first man said: Let all the generations learn from me,[12] that whosoever sings and utters psalms to the name of the Most High, and confesses his transgressions in the court of justice[13] and abandons (them), will be delivered from the judgment

[1] Perhaps the text should read: "No man has been slain." In Shocher Ṭob, *loc. cit.*, the reading is: " No man has been punished."

[2] On the Sabbath.

[3] See T.B. Sabbath, 118a. No mourning is permitted on the Sabbath, for the dead are not in the power of Gehenna on that day. For parallel Christian legends see Wisdom, ed. Deane, p. 163.

[4] By showing Divine love and mercy to Adam, the sanctity and the blessing of the Sabbath were realized by him.

[5] The first editions read: " to sing."

[6] According to Shocher Ṭob, *loc. cit.*, Adam wished to sing hymns to the Sabbath day: but the latter declined the honour, and told Adam to join in singing praises to God.

[7] The first editions read: " Ishmael."

[8] See Gen. Rab. xxii. 13, and Ḳimchi, Preface to *Commentary on Psalms*.

[9] The first editions omit: " according to his name." See T.B. Baba Bathra, 14b, for the Mosaic Psalms.

[10] This is missing in Shocher Ṭob, *loc. cit.*, and Jalḳuṭ, Ps. xcii. § 843. It probably owes its place in our text to a marginal gloss by some scribe of our book, being based on the Mishnah Tamid (end). See Senior Sachs' remarks on this passage in *Ha-Techiyah*, i. p. 20 (notes).

[11] R.V. " to give thanks."

[12] See *infra*, p. 147. The next clause occurs in our MS. and in the Oxford MS. only.

[13] The MS. uses here an abbreviation, בבד (Bbd). It does not occur in any of the printed texts. The Oxford MS. reads: "at the judgment."

of Gehinnom,[1] as it is said, " It is good to confess to the Lord " (*ibid.*).

" To declare thy loving-kindness in the *morning* " (*ibid.* 2). Adam said: (This refers to) all who enter this world [2] which is like unto the night; [3] and to all who come into the world to come, which is like unto the morning.[4] They shall declare the faithfulness and love of the Holy One, blessed be He, which He has shown to me,[5] (for He has) delivered me from the judgment of Gehinnom, as it is said, " To declare thy loving-kindness in the morning, and thy faithfulness every night " (*ibid.*).

" Upon a ten-stringed instrument and upon the psaltery " (*ibid.* 3). All testimonies reliable to Israel are (celebrated) with ten (males). The harp upon which David played had ten strings.[6] The testimony for the dead is through ten (males).[7] The testimony for the (public) benediction of (God's) Name is through ten (males).[8] The testimony of the covenant of circumcision is through ten (males).[9] The testimony for Chalizah [10] is through ten (males),[11] as it

[1] Cf. Prov. xxviii. 13. See also Wisdom, x. 1, 2.

[2] The first editions read: " the world to come which is like unto the morning. 'And thy faithfulness every *night*' (Ps. xcii. 2) (refers) to all who come into this world, which is like unto the *night*."

[3] In Aboth de R. Nathan (*a*) i. p. 4a this is derived from Isa. xxi. 11: " Watchman, what of the night? "

[4] Cf. the term " Dayspring " applied to the Christian Messiah; see *Hellenism and Christianity*, p. 119. Aboth de R. Nathan, *loc. cit.*, derives the lesson of our Haggadah from Lam. iii. 23.

[5] In this world by prolonging my life.

[6] Luria thinks the reading should be " Nimin " and not " Nebalim "; see Targum, *in loc.*, and cf. *infra*, p. 229.

[7] To enable the benediction for the mourners to be recited, ten adult males are required to form a quorum, see T.B. Kethuboth, 8b, and Sopherim x. 8, xix. 12. See T.B. Megillah, 23b; Nachmanides, *Torath Ha-Adam*, pp. 49 ff., and Shocher Ṭob, *loc. cit.*, p. 203b, note 61, and Joreh Di'ah, 361. On the Minyan (or ten adult males) see *J.E.* viii. 603, and Elbogen, *Der Jüdische Gottesdienst in seiner geschichtlichen Entwicklung*, p. 493.

[8] This refers to the " Bar'khu "; see Singer, pp. 37, 96.

[9] See Ṭur, Joreh Di'ah, 265, quoting Zemach Gaon, who holds that if the rite can be performed in the presence of ten males it should be done, but it may be done even if ten be not present. See also Shocher Ṭob, Ps. xcii. 7, p. 203b, note 62; and Jalkuṭ to Ps. xcii. § 843. Our text is referred to by Maharil in his Laws on the rite of Circumcision; see also Piskê Rikanati, 593.

[10] The ceremony of untying and taking off the shoe of a brother-in-law by the childless sister-in-law who has become a widow, see Deut. xxv. 5–11, and cf. T.B. Jebamoth, 101a, and Eben Ha-'Ezer, § 169, 13, and Shocher Ṭob, *loc. cit.*, p. 204a, note 64.

[11] The first editions add here: " The testimony for the benediction

is said, "And he [1] took ten men of the elders of the city" (Ruth iv. 2).[2]

The Holy One, blessed be He, said: I desire of Israel the meditation of their mouths like [3] the psaltery and an instrument of ten strings,[4] as it is said, "With [5] the meditation of || the harp" (Ps. xcii. 3).

"For thou, O Lord, hast made me glad through thy work" (*ibid.* 4). Adam said: The Holy One, blessed be He, had made me glad and brought me into the garden of Eden, and showed me the place of the abode of the righteous in the garden of Eden,[6] and He showed me the four kingdoms,[7] their rule and their destruction;[8] and He showed me David,[9] the son of Jesse, and his dominion in the future that is to come.[10] I took from my years seventy years [11] and added them to his days,[12] as it is said, "Thou wilt add days to the

of marriage is through ten (males)." See T.B. Kethuboth, 8b, for the custom.

[1] The MS. and the first editions read "Boaz," which is not in accordance with the Hebrew text.

[2] See Shocher Ṭob, *loc. cit.*, for the entire passage; and cf. T.B. Kethuboth, 7a.

[3] The printed text reads "with," Luria suggests "like"; see Jalḳuṭ, Ps., *loc. cit.*, and Shocher Ṭob, *in loc.*, p. 204a.

[4] The first editions read: "psaltery and harp."

[5] "With" (עלי) is probably to be explained according to the Midrash as though it meant "it is for Me"; *i.e.* My lot is to hear their psalms.

[6] Slav. Enoch viii. 1 ff.–ix. 1 describes the heavenly garden of Eden: "This place is prepared for the righteous." See Introduction.

[7] Luria adds in his text: "namely, Babylon, Media, Macedonia, and Syria." The last name should probably be *Edom* (*i.e.* Rome).

[8] The first editions read: "ruling and destroying." The Shocher Ṭob (*in loc.*), p. 204b, agreeing with our MS., reads: "And He led me into the garden of Eden and showed me the place of the abode of the righteous, and He showed me the four kingdoms." The printed editions omit the passage referring to the abode of the righteous.

[9] *i.e.* the Messiah.

[10] The Messianic kingdom. This is to be followed by the "Future World." The two periods, in contradistinction to the present age, are often spoken of as "the future that is to come."

[11] This Haggadic fancy, which occurs in Jubilees iv. 30, was known to Justin Martyr, *Dial. c. Tryph.* lxxxi.: "For according to the days of the tree of life . . . we believe a thousand years to be figuratively expressed. For as it was said to Adam, 'In the day that he should eat of the tree, he should surely die' (Gen. ii. 17), so we know he did not live a thousand years. *We* believe also this expression, 'The day of the Lord is a thousand years' (Ps. xc. 4; 2 Pet. iii. 8) relates to this." See also Epistle of Barnabas xv. The origin of the legend is to be traced to the verse quoted (Ps. lxi. 6) and the psalmist's interpretation of man's life which is said to consist of seventy years; see Ps. xc. 10; see also Gen. Rab. xix. 8, and Num. Rab. xiv. 12.

[12] *i.e.* David's life, which lasted seventy years.

days of the king;[1] his years shall be as many generations" (*ibid.* lxi. 6). The Holy One, blessed be He, said to him: Thou wilt add days to the days of (the king Messiah); I also will add to his years in the future which is to come, as though they were many generations, as it is said, "His years shall be as many generations" (*ibid.*).[2] I have given to God praise, and song (lauding) His works, as it is said, "I will sing of the works of thy hands" (*ibid.* xcii. 4).

"How great are thy works, O Lord!" (*ibid.* 5). Adam began to glorify and to praise the Name of the Most High, as it is said, "How great are thy works, O Lord!" (*ibid.*) but Thy thoughts are very deep,[3] like the great deep[4] exceedingly (deep), as it is said, "Thy thoughts are very deep" (*ibid.*). "A brutish man knoweth not" (*ibid.* 6). Every man of Israel[5] who is brutish (in knowledge) and has not learnt understanding, let the wise men of Israel teach him the ways of the Torah,[6] as it is said, "Consider, ye brutish among the people" (*ibid.* xciv. 8).[7] But a man who is an expert among the nations of the world[8] is still foolish. Why? For he knoweth not the words of the Torah, as it is said, "Neither doth a fool || understand *this*"[9] (*ibid.* xcii. 6).

"When the wicked spring up as the grass" (*ibid.* 7). True[10] (it is) that Thou, O Lord, beholdest the wicked, that they are as numerous[11] as the grass to cover the face of all the earth,[12] and all the worshippers of idols flourish,[13] (Thou

[1] In the MS. the quotation ends here; the first editions continue the verse.

[2] This entire sentence is missing in the printed texts.

[3] The first editions read: "to the depth of Thy thoughts (is similar to) the deep (which is) exceedingly deep."

[4] The deep (Tehom) was held to be unsearchable. See Job xxxviii. 16: "Hast thou walked in the recesses of the deep?" Cf. T.B. Pesachim, 54b.

[5] The first editions read here: "A man who is brutish among Israel."

[6] The first editions read: "teach him understanding."

[7] This is Israel; see Jalḳuṭ, Ps. § 843.

[8] The first edition reads: "Expert in faith." The Venice edition has the same reading as our MS. Paul held the wisdom of the world to be foolishness before God; see 1 Cor. iii. 19.

[9] "This" (*zôth*) is interpreted to mean the Torah; see T.B. 'Abodah Ẓarah, 2b.

[10] The first editions read: "At the time when Thou seest."

[11] The 1st ed. reads: "who are seen."

[12] Cf. Isa. xxvii. 6.

[13] The 1st ed. omits from this word till "And he did not say, Hallelujah."

9

knowest) that they and their works are an evil iniquity[1] for the days of the Messiah.[2] The Holy One, blessed be He, has only multiplied them in order to destroy them from this world[3] and from the world to come, as it is said, "To have them destroyed for ever and ever. And thou, O Lord, art on high for evermore" (*ibid.* 7, 8). David saw that the wicked increased like grass, (so as) to cover the face of all the earth, and that all the worshippers of idols flourished, and that they and their works were iniquity, and he did not say "Hallelujah" ("praise ye the Lord") until he perceived that in the future they would be destroyed from[4] this world and from the world to come; and he said "Hallelujah," as it is said, "Sinners shall be consumed out of the earth,[5] and the wicked shall be no more. Bless the Lord, O my soul. *Praise ye the Lord*" (*ibid.* civ. 35).[6] (Then will He be) King exalted[7] in the heights and in the depths, as it is said, "And thou, O Lord, art on high for evermore" (*ibid.* xcii. 8).

"For, lo, thine enemies, O Lord" (*ibid.* 9); Israel said: Sovereign of all worlds! Thou hast placed all our enemies over us[8] (to afflict us with) a heavy yoke on our backs, but we know that they are doomed to destruction, as it is said, "O Lord, for, lo, thine enemies shall perish"[9] (*ibid.*). And all || idolaters, for they and their works are iniquity, shall] be scattered like chaff[10] before the wind.[11]

[1] The reading of Shocher Ṭob (*in loc.*) is: "an iniquity hidden."

[2] The Venice edition adds: "And the wicked, who are as numerous as grass."

[3] In the days of the Messiah. According to the Christian doctrine of election, very many of the sons of men will be doomed to enter Hell and to remain there for all eternity. See Matt. vii. 13, xxiii. 33, and Mark ix. 48.

[4] The printed texts omit from "from this world" to "Hallelujah."

[5] The printed texts omit the rest of the verse.

[6] See T.B. Berakhoth, 10a. Note the interpretation given by Beruria, the wife of Rabbi Meir: "Let *sins* be consumed out of the earth, and then there will be no more wicked people." The first edition omits the next sentence in our text. The Venice edition reads: "Then the Holy One, blessed be He, (will be) King, exalted."

[7] MS. reads "Marom," exalted; the Venice edition reads "Masor," which is an error. See Jalḳuṭ on Ps. xcii. 8, § 843.

[8] In Egypt and Babylon.

[9] See *infra*, p. 383.

[10] Cf. Dan. ii. 35.

[11] The first editions add: "As it is said, 'All the workers of iniquity shall be scattered'" (Ps. xcii. 9).

"But my horn hast thou exalted like that of the reêm"[1] (*ibid.* 10). Just as the horns of the reêm[2] are taller than those of all beasts and animals,[3] and it gores to its right and to its left, likewise (is it with) Menachem, son of 'Ammiel, son of Joseph,[4] his horns are taller than those of all kings,[5] and he will gore in the future towards the four corners of the heavens, and concerning him Moses said this verse, "His firstling bullock, majesty is his, and his horns are the horns of the reêm: with them he shall gore[6] the peoples all of them, even the ends of the earth" (Deut. xxxiii. 17). All[7] the kings will rise up against him to slay him, as it is said, "The kings of the earth set themselves, and the rulers (take counsel together)" (Ps. ii. 2). And Israel who (will be) in the Land (of Palestine) (will experience) great trouble,[8] but in their troubles they (will be) like a green olive,[9] as it is said, "I am anointed with fresh oil" (*ibid.* xcii. 10).[10]

[1] Or "wild-ox." On the reêm see Delitzsch, *Babel and Bible* (E.T.), p. 164, where the reêm is shown in a beautiful illustration.

[2] Lit. "this reêm."

[3] See Shocher Ṭob, p. 204a. The Venice edition reads: "of all animals." This is wanting in the 1st ed.

[4] "Son of Joseph" probably means "of the tribe of Joseph." The reference to the reêm is suggested by the Blessing of the tribe in Deut. xxxiii. 17. According to the Ẓohar (Num. p. 173b), Messiah ben David is Menachem; this is also the view of the Book of Zerubbabel (ed. Jellinek, *B.H.M.* i. 59). Cf. Abḳath Rochel ii.; T.B. Synhedrin, 98b; *J.E.* viii. 511 f.; and *R.É.J.* lxviii. pp. 135, 150. 'Ammiel appears to be another form of "Emanuel."

[5] The Venice edition reads: "all animals." The 1st ed. omits the name of "Menachem, son of 'Ammiel, son of Joseph," and reads instead: "the son of David."

[6] The MS. ends quotation here, adding "etc." The printed texts conclude the quotation with "reêm."

[7] This paragraph occurs in the first editions, but in the Venice edition it is inserted after the following passage, which is wanting in our MS. and in the 1st ed.: "With him are the ten thousands of Ephraim, and the thousands of Manasseh,[1] as it is said, 'And they are the ten thousands of Ephraim, and they are the thousands of Manasseh'" (Deut. xxxiii. 17).

[8] See Pesiḳta Ẓuṭarta, Balaḳ, p. 129b.

[9] The MS. adds: "I am afflicted"; it is missing in the printed texts.

[10] See Shocher Ṭob, *in loc.* The Midrash interprets "I am anointed" as though it were connected with the root "Balah," "to afflict," cf. 1 Chron. xvii. 9, and not from "Balal." In the time of trouble Israel trusts in God and shall be like a green olive tree full of sap; cf. Ps. lii. 8; T.B. Berakhoth, 35a, and Jalḳuṭ, Ps. § 845. Perhaps

[1] These tribes are to come with the Messiah ben Joseph to oppose Gog and Magog; see *supra*, pp. 117 f., and Abḳath Rochel ii.

"Mine eyes have looked on mine enemies" (*ibid.* 11). The Israelites in the Land (of Israel[1]) behold the downfall of their enemies, as it is said, "Mine eyes have looked on mine enemies" (*ibid.*). And[2] such who in the future will come against them (Israel), their ears shall hear of their destruction, as it is said, "Mine ears have heard concerning the evil-doers that rise up against me" (*ibid.*).

"The righteous shall flourish like the palm tree" (*ibid.* 12). Just as this palm tree is beautiful in all its appearance,[3] and all its fruits are sweet and good,[4] likewise the son of David[5] is beautiful in his appearance[6] and in his glory, and all his deeds || are good and sweet before the Holy One, blessed be He, as it is said, "The righteous shall flourish like the palm tree: he shall grow like a cedar in Lebanon" (*ibid.*). Just as this cedar has very many roots beneath the earth, and even if the four winds[7] of the world came[8] against it, they could not move it from its place,[9] as it is said, "He shall grow like a cedar in Lebanon. They that are planted in the house of the Lord" (*ibid.* 12, 13). In the future when the Holy One, blessed be He, will gather Israel from the four corners of the world,[10] just like this gardener who transplants[11] his fir trees from one garden-bed to another garden-bed, likewise in the future will the Holy One, blessed

our text should be rendered: "But their trouble, being like a green olive tree, made one distressed"; or: "But (in) their trouble am I anointed as with (the oil of) a green olive tree."

1 After the great trouble and misfortunes endured by Israel the Messianic redemption will take place, and the enemies will be finally judged. See Jalkuṭ, *loc. cit.*

2 This paragraph does not occur in the printed editions.

3 On the palm tree see Shocher Ṭob, Ps. xcii. 11, with notes 87 ff.

4 See T.B. Kethuboth, 10b. The palm branch forms a striking element in the public entry into Jerusalem by the Founder of Christianity; see John xii. 13.

5 This is the Messiah.

6 See Ps. xxi. 5; and cf. Shocher Tob on Ps. xcii. 11.

7 *i.e.* the winds from all four quarters of the world. Cf. Matt. vii. 24, 25, and Wisdom, iv. 4.

8 The first editions add: "to blow."

9 The 1st ed. agrees here with our MS. The Venice edition adds: "Likewise (will it be) with the son of David, whose might and deeds are manifold before the Holy One, blessed be He. Even if all the nations come against him they will not move him from his place."[1]

10 So Isaiah (xi. 12) prophesies.

11 To improve them.

---

1 It will be otherwise with the Messiah ben Joseph, who will be slain in the conflict with Gog and Magog; see Abkath Rochel, *loc. cit.*

be He, gather them[1] from an impure land and (plant them) in a pure land,[2] as it is said, " They that are planted in the house of the Lord " (*ibid.*). Like this grass, they shall blossom and sprout forth in the Temple, as it is said, " In the courts of our God they shall flourish " (*ibid.*).

" They shall still bring forth fruit in old age " (*ibid.* 14). Just as this[3] old age is glory and honour to old men,[4] so shall they be in glory and honour[5] before the Holy One, blessed be He, as it is said, " They shall be full of sap and green "[6] (*ibid.*). These are the mighty heroes by reason of their good deeds, as it is said, " They shall be full of sap and green, to declare that the Lord is upright " (*ibid.* 14, 15). Why all these (statements)?[7] To declare, and to proclaim clearly the works of the Holy One, blessed be He, for He is righteous and upright, and that there is no unrighteousness (in Him), as it is said,[8] " And there is no unrighteousness in him " (*ibid.* 15).[9]

[1] " An unclean land " is expressed by " outside the Land " (of Palestine) in the Amsterdam ed. Any land outside the " Holy " Land is held to be unclean in the sense that the Biblical Laws of purity are not observed therein, such laws being only intended for Palestine; see Lev. xviii. 25.

[2] See *supra*, p. 84. Just as Jews consider the soil of Palestine to be " terra sancta," so the English Church has a preference for the water of the river Jordan in administering the rite of baptism; this, at least, was the case at the baptism of the late King Edward VII.

[3] Luria omits the word " this."

[4] See Prov. xx. 29.

[5] Cf. Jalkuṭ, *loc. cit.*

[6] The next words until " To declare " are missing in the first editions.

[7] As to the prosperity of the wicked. The Venice edition reads: " To declare, to praise," etc.

[8] The first editions add: " He is my rock."

[9] On God's justice see Siphrê, Deut. § 307.

CHAPTER XIX[1]

THE SABBATH [22B. ii.]

The School of Shammai said: The heavens[2] were created first, and the earth afterwards, as it is said,[3] "In the beginning God created *the heavens* and the earth" (Gen. i. 1). The School of Hillel said: The earth was created first, and the heavens afterwards, as it is said, "Of old hast thou laid the foundation of the *earth*; and the heavens are the work of thy hands" (Ps. cii. 25).[4] The School of Shammai said: The heavens were created first, and the earth afterwards, as it is said,[5] "These are the generations of the *heavens* and of the earth" (Gen. ii. 4). The School of Hillel said: The earth was created first, and the heavens afterwards, as it is said, "In the day that the Lord God made *earth* and heaven" (*ibid.*). The School of Shammai said: The heavens were created first, because it is said, "And the *heavens* and the earth were finished" (*ibid.* 1). The School of Hillel

[1] This is ch. xviii. in the printed editions.

[2] The history of the creation of man is associated by the Rabbis with the fundamental law of Jewish ethics, the rule of loving-kindness. To quote their dictum, "The Torah begins and ends with the service of loving-kindness" (T.B. Soṭah, 14a). The preceding chapters xvi. and xvii. dealt with the service of loving-kindness, and the story of the Creation is now resumed.

[3] The controversy was evoked by the precedence given to heaven or earth in the texts of Scripture quoted by the different teachers; see *Rabbinic Philosophy and Ethics*, pp. 6 f.

[4] See T.B. Chagigah, 12a; T.J. Chagigah ii. 1, 77c, d; Gen. Rab. i. 15; Lev. Rab. xxxvi. 1; Midrash on Samuel v. (where the School of Shammai is represented as expressing the opinions which are elsewhere attributed to the School of Hillel); and cf. Sepher Ha-Bahir, § 17, and Bacher, T. i. 14.

[5] The first editions quote here Isa. xlviii. 13: "Yea, mine hand hath laid the foundation of the earth." The earth is mentioned *first* in this verse, and therefore the opinion of the School of Hillel is thereby substantiated. The "School of Hillel" is the correct reading, as in our MS. The following passage until "Yea, mine hand" is omitted in the printed texts.

said: The earth was created first, and the heavens afterwards, as it is said, "Yea, mine hand hath laid the foundation of the earth, and my right hand hath spread out the heavens" (Isa. xlviii. 13). The School of Shammai said: The heavens were created first, and the earth afterwards, because it is said, "Thus saith the Lord, The *heaven* is my throne, and the earth is my footstool" (*ibid.* lxvi. 1). Contention arose between them (*i.e.* the Schools[1]) on this question, until the Holy Spirit[2] rested between them, and they both agreed that both (heavens and earth) were created in one hour and at one moment.[3]

What did the Holy One, blessed be He, do? He put forth His right hand and stretched forth the heavens, and He put forth His left hand and founded the earth, as it is said, "Yea, mine *hand* || hath laid the foundation of the earth, and my *right hand* hath spread out the heavens:[4] when I called unto them, they stood up *together*" (*ibid.* xlviii. 13). Both of them were created simultaneously, as it is said, "And the *heavens* and the *earth* were finished, and all their host" (Gen. ii. 1).[5] And, indeed, were the heavens and the earth completed (so as not to require God's providence) for their continued existence and maintenance? Has it not been written concerning them, "Thus saith the Lord, The heaven is my throne, and the earth is my footstool" (Isa. lxvi. 1)?[6] But they were finished with reference to the original deed (of creation) and with reference to the work (of being created) and being called into existence. Therefore it is said, "And the heavens and the earth *were finished*" (Gen. ii. 1).

Israel spake before the Holy One, blessed be He: Sovereign of the worlds! Thou didst complete the heavens and the earth with reference to being made, created, and called into existence;[7] let not Thy mercy and loving-kindness be

[1] Lit. them.

[2] The first editions read "Shekhinah."

[3] The Ẓohar, Gen. 17b, has this idea; cf. *ibid.* 29b. The basis for this third view is afforded by the text Isa. xlviii. 13: "When I called unto them, they stood up together." The Targum renders this text thus: "Yea, with my word I completed the earth, and with my power I expanded the heavens; I called to them, they stood together."

[4] The MS. and the printed texts end the quotation here.

[5] See Mekhilta, p. 1a.

[6] The first editions do not quote this verse, but "Do not I fill heaven and earth?" (Jer. xxiii. 24) instead.

[7] The first editions add: "in the six days of Creation."

withheld,[1] for if Thou withholdest Thy mercy and loving-kindness we are unable to exist,[2] because the world rests upon Thy mercy and loving-kindness,[3] as it is said, "For the mountains shall depart,[4] and the hills be removed; but my kindness shall not depart from thee . . . saith the Lord that hath mercy on thee" (Isa. liv. 10);[5] and it says (elsewhere), "Remember, O Lord, thy tender mercies and thy loving-kindnesses; for they have been ever of old" (Ps. xxv. 6).[6]

"And on the seventh day God finished[7] his work" (Gen. ii. 2). The Holy One, blessed be He, created seven dedications,[8] six of them He dedicated, and one is reserved for the (future) generations. He created the first day and finished all His work and dedicated it,[9] as it is said, "And it was evening, and it was morning, one day" (*ibid.* i. 5). He created the second day and finished all His

[1] "From us" should probably be added to the text; cf. Ps. xl. 11.

[2] Man sins, and therefore needs God's grace and mercy. This idea is well expressed by the teaching of 4 Ezra vii. 135–137. The Bible text, "Remember, O Lord, thy tender mercies and thy loving-kindnesses, for they have been *ever of old*" (Ps. xxv. 6), is a parallel to our passage; cf. Targum of this verse, which renders the last words, "for they have been from eternity." Cf. Gen. Rab. xxii. 1, Jalkuṭ, Ps. § 702, and Shocher Ṭob to Ps. xxv. 8, p. 107a, where the question is discussed, How would mankind have arisen if God had dealt with Adam with strict justice? The grace of God was granted to Adam so as to enable mankind to arise and flourish on earth before the doom of death overtook him. There may be an attempt here to counteract the un-Jewish doctrines of the Pauline school, which taught that, owing to Adam's sin, God's grace was withdrawn, and only through the advent of a Second Adam (or Christ) could this Divine grace be restored to the world. The theologians who suggest that Judaism has something to learn from the Pauline doctrine of grace must be unaware of the Jewish teaching on this theme.

[3] This idea has already been mentioned in our book. See *supra*, pp. 76, 84, 106.

[4] The quotation ends here in the first editions, which add "etc."; in the MS. the quotation ends with the words, "be removed."

[5] God's love and mercy *cannot* cease, they are eternal attributes.

[6] This quotation is wanting in the printed texts; it concludes in the MS. with the words, "loving-kindnesses." The point in the quotation lies in the words "ever of old," which might be rendered "eternal" or "from everlasting."

[7] "His work" is not in the MS., but is covered by "etc." of the printed editions. See Pesiḳta Rabbathi, p. 187b; Jalkuṭ, Gen. § 16.

[8] The six days of Creation were complete, and each day's work had its dedication. This did not apply to the seventh day; see T.B. Sabbath, 11b; T.B. Berakhoth, 58b. The Sabbath will only receive its completion in the future world; see T.B. Rosh Ha-Shanah, 31a.

[9] The reading has its parallel in Menorath Ha-Maor, § 159 (end).

work and dedicated it, as it is said, || "And it was evening, and it was morning, a second day" (*ibid.* 8); and so through the six days of creation. He created the seventh day, (but) not for work, because it is not said in connection therewith, "And it was evening and it was morning." Why? For it is reserved for the generations (to come), as it is said, "And there shall be one day which is known unto the Lord; not *day*, and not *night*" (Zech. xiv. 7).[1]

A parable: To what is this matter to be compared? To a man who had precious utensils.[2] And he did not desire to give them as an inheritance except to his son;[3] likewise with the Holy One, blessed be He. The day of blessing and holiness[4] which was before Him, He did not desire to give it as an inheritance except to Israel.[5] Know that it is so! Come and see! for when the Israelites went forth from Egypt,[6] whilst yet the Torah had not been given to them, He gave them the Sabbath as an inheritance. Israel kept two Sabbaths[7] whilst as yet the Torah had not been given to them, as it is said, "And thou madest known unto them thy holy Sabbath"[8] (Neh. ix. 14). And afterwards He gave them the Torah, as it is said, "And commandedst them commandments, and statutes, and *Torah* by the hand of Moses, thy servant" (*ibid.*).[9]

The Holy One, blessed be He, observed and sanctified the

[1] This is the Sabbath day, concerning which "day and night" are not mentioned in the Creation story. See *infra*, p. 143.

[2] Cf. Aboth iii. 23 with reference to the Torah.

[3] Cf. Mal. iii. 17. The first editions add: "who serves him." God and His children are referred to by the parable. Every nation is a child of God, Israel is the son who serves Him. See *infra*, p. 319, and Shocher Ṭob, Ps. xcii. p. 201b, where this Haggadah is used, and as a parallel see Jubilees ii. 20.

[4] In Menorath Ha-Maor, *loc. cit.*, "blessing and holiness" occur instead of "rest and holiness," of the first editions, based on the words of the Scripture, "He blessed and hallowed" (cf. Ex. xx. 11).

[5] Cf. Jubilees ii. 18 f.

[6] According to the Midrash (cf. Book of Jashar lxx. 47), the Sabbath had been given to Israel in Egypt, but not by God. See T.B. Ḳiddushin, 41b.

[7] See Tosaphoth in T.B. Sabbath, 87b, catchword "Just as."

[8] In the MS. the quotation ends here, in the first editions it is continued without any interruption.

[9] This text mentions the Sabbath before the "Commandments, statutes, and Torah." The Sabbath law is mentioned in Exodus xvi. 23, in connection with the Manna prior to the revelation at Sinai.

Sabbath,[1] and Israel is obliged[2] only to observe and sanctify the Sabbath. Know that it is so! Come and see! for when He gave them the Manna, He gave it to them in the wilderness during forty years on the six days of creation,[3] but on the Sabbath He did not give (it) || to them. Wilt thou say that He did not have power enough to give it to them every day?[4] But (the fact was) the Sabbath was before Him; therefore He gave to them bread for two days on the Friday, as it is said, "See, for that the Lord hath given you the Sabbath,[5] therefore he giveth you on the sixth day the bread of two days" (Ex. xvi. 29). When the people[6] saw that Sabbath (was observed) before Him, they also rested, as it is said, "So the people rested on the seventh day" (*ibid.* 30).

"And God blessed the seventh day,[7] and hallowed it" (Gen. ii. 3). The Holy One, blessed be He, blessed and hallowed the Sabbath day, and Israel is bound only to *keep* and to hallow the Sabbath day.[8] Hence they[9] said: Whosoever says the benediction and sanctification over the wine on the eves of Sabbath,[10] his days[11] will be increased in this world, and[12] in the world to come, as it is said, "For by me thy days shall be multiplied" (Prov. ix. 11) in this world; "and the years of thy life shall be increased" (*ibid.*) in the world to come.

"Ye shall keep the Sabbath,[13] for it is holy unto you"

1 See Jubilees ii. 18.
2 See Shochar Ṭob, Ps. xcii. p. 201b.
3 Sunday to Friday, the days of work.
4 See Menorath Ha-Maor, *loc. cit.*, which reads, "Lest thou shouldst say that He had no power to give, He continued to give it (*after* the Sabbath)." Another reading is given in Shocher Ṭob, Ps. xcii., *loc. cit.*
5 In the MS. the quotation ends here, but "etc." is added; in the first editions the verse is continued.
6 The first editions read "Israel."
7 In the MS. the quotation ends here, but "etc." is added; the first editions continue the quotation as in our version.
8 See Gen. Rab. xi. 2, and Mekhilta, p. 50b; and see *supra*, p. 137, and *infra*, p. 141.
9 The Sages.
10 Friday evenings. See Jubilees ii. 21.
11 The first editions add: "and years."
12 Variant readings are given in Menorath Ha-Maor, *loc. cit.*, and Roḳeach, 52. The first editions add here: "And years of life will be given to him." As we shall see, the phraseology of this reading is borrowed from Prov. ix. 11, according to the interpretation given in T.B. Synhedrin, 38a, and Lev. Rab. xi. 1.
13 In the MS. the quotation ends here, but the first editions continue the verse.

(Ex. xxxi. 14). What is the keeping of the Sabbath? Neither to do any work thereon,[1] nor to kindle fire thereon, neither to take forth nor to bring in beyond the Techum (limit)[2] of the Sabbath even one foot,[3] nor to fetch in his hand something[4] which is not his food nor the food for his cattle.[5] This is the keeping of the Sabbath,[6] as it is said, "Wherefore the children of Israel shall keep the Sabbath" (*ibid.* 16).

"It[7] is a sign between me and the children of Israel[8] for ever" (*ibid.* 17). The Holy One, blessed be He, said: This (Sabbath) have I given to Israel[9] as a sign between Me || and them; for in the six days of creation I fashioned all the world, and on the Sabbath I rested, therefore have I given to Israel the six days of work, and on the Sabbath, a day[10] (for) blessing and sanctification,[11] for Me and for them; therefore it is said, "Between me and the children of Israel it is a sign for ever" (*ibid.*).[12]

[1] The first editions reverse the order of the clauses, "Not to kindle fire thereon, nor to do any work thereon." The order in our MS. is based on the sequence of the texts dealing with the Sabbath commandments in Ex. xxxi. 14. To kindle fire is prohibited in Ex. xxxv. 3, and in the *previous* verse the prohibition to work is set forth; see Luria's commentary, *in loc.*, where the reading of our MS. had been anticipated.

[2] The 2000 spaces or ells from the town, called a Sabbath-journey; see Acts i. 12, Jubilees l. 8, and Zadokite Documents xiii. 7. See Tosephta Soṭah v. 13, p. 303, for a discussion as to whether the Techum principle is contained in the Torah, and cf. *J.E.* x. 592.

[3] See T.B. 'Erubin, 52b.

[4] Anything not permitted to be used on the Sabbath is called "Muḳzeh."

[5] The first editions read after the word "something": "and carry it four *spaces* in a public thoroughfare, and to bring it from one *allotment* to another." See *J.E.* x. 582 on the "four ells" or *spaces*. "Reshuth," territory, domain, *allotment*, one's area or court. See Baba Ḳamma iii. 1 for the different terms in connection with Reshuth; see also T.B. Sabbath, 6a, and cf. Jubilees ii. 29 and l. 8, Zadokite Documents xiii. 16. The first editions omit the words: "which is not his food, nor the food for his cattle."

[6] Trafficking on the Sabbath was a cause of reproach on the part of Jeremiah (xvii. 20 ff.) and Nehemiah (xiii. 17 ff.). The rest of this sentence is wanting in the first editions.

[7] The Sabbath.

[8] The quotation is concluded here in the MS.; the first editions continue as in our version.

[9] "It is a sign" is added here by Shocher Ṭob, Ps. xcii., *loc. cit.*

[10] The first editions read: "and the seventh day (for) blessing," etc.

[11] The first editions add: "and rest." Scripture speaks of God blessing and sanctifying the seventh day (Gen. ii. 3), and resting on the Sabbath (Ex. xx. 11), "Wherefore the Lord blessed the Sabbath day and hallowed it" (*ibid.*). See *supra*, p. 137, note 4.

[12] The first editions omit: "it is a sign for ever."

The Holy One, blessed be He, created seven[1] firmaments, and He selected from them all 'Araboth[2] only for the place of the throne of glory of His kingdom, as it is said, "Cast up a highway for him that rideth on the 'Araboth,[3] with Jah, his name" (Ps. lxviii. 4). The Holy One, blessed be He, created seven lands,[4] and He chose from all of them the land of Israel only, as it is said, "A land . . . the eyes of the Lord thy God are always upon it, from the beginning of the year even unto the end of the year" (Deut. xi. 12).[5] Another verse says, "I said, I shall not see the Lord, even the Lord in the land of the living" (Isa. xxxviii. 11).[6] The Holy One, blessed be He, created seven deserts, and of them all He chose the *desert* of Sinai[7] only to give therein the Torah, as it is said, "The *mountain* which God hath desired for his abode" (Ps. lxviii. 16).

The Holy One, blessed be He, created seven seas,[8] and of

[1] The Sepher Jezirah iv. emphasizes the superior nature of the seventh kind of the various works of Creation; see also Lev. Rab. xxix. 11; Num. Rab. iii. 8; Jalḳuṭ, Psalms (Ps. cxxxix.), § 888.

[2] See T.B. Chagigah, 12b. 'Araboth is the seventh heaven. See also Hekhaloth iv. and also Maimonides, *Guide*, i. 70, who quotes our text. The New Testament speaks of the "third heaven" (2 Cor. xii. 2). See the *Apocalypse of Peter* on this theme. On the seven heavens see Slavonic Enoch, pp. xxx ff.

[3] R.V. has "deserts." The quotation ends here in our MS., the printed texts continue the same.

[4] They are enumerated in Lev. Rab., *loc. cit.*, cf. Aboth de R. Nathan (a) xxxvii. p. 55b (n. 10); see also Midrash, Proverbs viii., where ten lands are mentioned. Israel passed through seven lands after leaving Egypt to enter the Holy Land. The lands are: Edom, Ammon, Moab, Midian, the land of the Amorites, Bashan, and the Holy Land, which is the seventh land. See also Siphrê, Deut. § 40, and *infra*, p. 167.

[5] See also Mal. iii. 12, and for the reading of the text see Kaphtor Va-Pherach x. The latter part of the quotation is wanting in the first editions. The first editions add the following: "The Holy One, blessed be He, created seven mountains,[1] and he chose only Mount Sinai from all of them, as it is said, 'Why look ye askance, ye high mountains, at *the mountain*[2] *which God hath desired for his abode*?'" (Ps. lxviii. 16).

[6] This quotation is missing in the printed texts of our book.

[7] The first editions read "Kadesh." The order of the paragraphs here in the MS. does not agree with that of the printed editions. In Jalḳuṭ, Ps. lxviii. § 796, the wilderness of Sinai is the "chosen" one; this is another name of the wilderness of Kadesh. See T.B. Sabbath, 89a.

[8] See T.B. Baba Bathra, 74b, and Shocher Ṭob, Ps. xxiv. 6, p. 103a, notes 23 and 24, which refer to the seven seas in Palestine.

---

[1] See T.B. Megillah, 29a, and *infra*, p. 318. See also Eth. Enoch xxxii. 1.

[2] This is interpreted as Sinai; see Shocher Ṭob, *in loc.* p. 159b.

them all He chose the Sea of Kinnereth[1] only, and gave it as an inheritance to the tribe of Naphtali,[2] as it is said, "O Naphtali, *satisfied with favour*,[3] and full with the blessing of the Lord:[4] possess thou the *sea* and the south" (Deut. xxxiii. 23). What is the "blessing of the Lord"? (It means) that He blessed him and gave him as an inheritance the sea and the south, as it is said, "Possess thou the sea and the south" (*ibid.*).[5]

The Holy One, blessed be He, created seven æons, || and of them all He chose the seventh æon[6] only; the six æons are for the going in and coming out (of God's creatures) for war and peace. The seventh æon is entirely Sabbath and rest in the life everlasting.[7] Seven lamps were made for the sanctuary, and the lamp of Sabbath was illuminating opposite the other six (lamps), as it is said, "In front of the lampstand the seven lamps shall give light" (Num. viii. 2).[8] The Holy One, blessed be He, created seven days, and of them all He chose the seventh day only, as it is said, "And God *blessed* the seventh day, and hallowed it" (Gen. ii. 3).[9]

Everyone[10] who keeps the Sabbath, happy is he in this world and happy will he be in the world to come,[11] as it is said, "Happy is the *man* that doeth this, and the *son of man* that holdeth fast by it: who keepeth the Sabbath from

[1] *i.e.* the Lake or Sea of Gennesareth.

[2] The pre-eminence of Naphtali was due to the fact that the east side of his territory touched the Sea of Gennesareth and the west side was on the Mediterranean.

[3] *i.e.* God's favour; see Shocher Ṭob, Ps. lxviii. p. 160b.

[4] The quotation ends here in our MS., in the first editions the verse is continued.

[5] This sentence is not in the printed editions.

[6] The æon was a period of 1000 years. On the Millennium see Slav. Enoch xxxii. 2–xxxiii. 2, where the *eighth* day is the day of rest.

[7] See *supra*, p. 126, note 10, and cf. Tanna de bê Elijahu Rab. ii. p. 6, and Jalkuṭ, Ps. cxxxix. § 888.

[8] This sentence is not in the printed editions.

[9] The printed editions add here: "The Holy One, blessed be He, created seven years, and of them all He chose the year of release only. The year of release is every seventh year." See Jalkuṭ, Ps. cxxxix. § 888, and Lev. Rab., *loc. cit.*

[10] According to T.B. Sabbath, 118b, even idolaters will be forgiven; see *infra*, p. 146. The first editions read: "Everyone who keeps the Sabbath in this world, the Holy One, blessed be He, will forgive all his sins."

[11] Cf. Jubilees ii. 2. 8: "Everyone who observes it and keeps Sabbath thereon from all his work will be holy and blessed throughout all days."

profaning it" (Isa. lvi. 2). Do not read "(He who keepeth the Sabbath) *from profaning*[1] *it*," but read "He who keepeth the Sabbath *is pardoned*"[2] concerning all his transgression.[3]

[1] *Mechallelô* (from profaning it).

[2] *Machul lô* (it is forgiven him). This is a play on the word of the text of Isa. lvi. 2. See Tanna de bê Elijahu Rab. xxvi. p. 134.

[3] The printed texts read: "to teach (us) that all his transgressions are forgiven him." The section on the Sabbath in Jubilees ii. 17 ff. and l. 6 ff. should be compared with the regulations as to the Sabbath in our book. There are some striking resemblances as well as considerable points of dissimilarity. Jubilees (ii. 23, 24) connects the Sabbath with Jacob. Our book refers this institution to Adam; see previous chapter, and Introduction.

CHAPTER XX

ADAM'S PENITENCE [24A. i.]

"So he *drove out* the man" (Gen. iii. 24). *Driving out* (*i.e.*) and he went forth outside the garden of Eden (and he abode)[1] on Mount Moriah, for the gate of the garden of Eden is nigh unto Mount Moriah.[2] Thence He took him and thither He made him return to the place whence he was taken, as it is said, "To till the ground from whence he was taken" (*ibid.* 23).[3]

Rabbi Jehudah said: The Holy One, blessed be He, kept the Sabbath[4] first in the heavenly regions, and Adam kept the || Sabbath first in the lower regions. The Sabbath day protected him from all evil, and comforted[5] him on

[1] The MS. does not read: "and he abode." This is the reading of the first editions. Jalkuṭ, Gen. § 34 (end), adds: "outside the garden of Eden." The new abode of Adam was near the garden of Eden. The Midrash appears to understand, Gen. iii. 24, thus: "So he drove out the man and he dwelt at the east of the garden of Eden." This Haggadic interpretation already appears in the LXX.

[2] See T.B. 'Erubin, 19a. Beth-Shan is described as the door to Palestine; see *J.Q.R.* v. p. 148, where Origen's Midrash about the garden of Eden being the centre of the world is quoted. As to where the garden of Eden was believed to be, see Delitzsch, *Wo lag das Paradies*, pp. 45 ff.

[3] Instead of this quotation the first editions cite Gen. ii. 15: "And the Lord God took the man," and then they add: "From what place did He take him? From the place of the Temple, as it is said: 'To till the ground from whence he was taken'" (Gen. iii. 23).[1]

[4] "In the heavens" is also added by Shocher Ṭob, p. 203a, but it is wanting in the first editions of our book; see *supra*, pp. 125 f. The idea of Sabbath being observed in heaven occurs in Jubilees ii. 18; see previous chapter in our book, p. 138.

[5] See *supra*, pp. 125 f.

---

[1] Shocher Ṭob, Ps. xcii. p. 203a, reads: "From the place of the Sanctuary and thence He restored him to the place whence he was taken, as it is said, 'To till the ground from whence he was taken'" (Gen. iii. 23). See also Pal. Targ. Gen. ii. 7, and *supra*, p. 84.

account of all the doubts of his heart, as it is said, "In the multitude of my doubts within me, thy comforts delight my soul" (Ps. xciv. 19).

Rabbi Joshua ben Ḳorchah said: From the tree under which they hid themselves,[1] they took leaves and sewed (them), as it is said, "And they sewed fig leaves together,[2] and made themselves aprons" (Gen. iii. 7). Rabbi Eliezer said: From the skin [3] which the serpent sloughed off, the Holy One, blessed be He, took [4] and made coats of glory [5] for Adam and his wife, as it is said, "And the Lord God made for Adam and for his wife coats of skin, and clothed them" (*ibid.* 21).

At twilight on Saturday [6] (evening), Adam was [7] meditating in his heart and saying: [8] Perhaps the serpent, which deceived me, will come in the evening,[9] and he will bruise me in the heel. A pillar of fire was sent to him to give illumination about him and to guard him from all evil.[10] Adam saw the pillar of fire and rejoiced in his heart,[11] and he put forth his hands [12] to the light of the fire, and said: Blessed art Thou, O Lord our God, King of the universe, who creates the flames of fire.[13] And when he removed

[1] See the Book of Adam and Eve (ed. Malan) I. xxxvi.

[2] The MSS. and the first editions conclude the quotation here.

[3] So also according to Pal. Targ. Gen. iii. 21; and cf. *supra*, p. 99.

[4] The first editions omit "took."

[5] In the Torah scroll of Rabbi Meir the reading was "coats of light"; see Gen. Rab. xx. 12 and Epstein in *Monatsschrift*, 1884, pp. 343 ff. Cf. *supra*, p. 98, for the skin of nail, as the covering of glory of the first man.

[6] Luria holds that this section is out of place. It should be inserted in the previous chapter at the point where the Blessing of the Sabbath occurs. See T.J. Berakhoth viii. 6, 12b, on the day of 36 hours, during which the light of the first Sabbath lasted; and cf. Shocher Ṭob, p. 202b.

[7] The first editions read: "sitting and meditating."

[8] The first editions read: "Woe is me, perhaps the serpent which deceived me on the eve of the Sabbath will come and bruise me in the heel."

[9] Oxford MS. (e. 76) reads: "deceived me on the eve (before) the termination of the Sabbath" will come.

[10] See Book of Adam and Eve (ed. Malan) I. xxix., and T.B. 'Abodah Ẓarah, 8a.

[11] The first editions add: "and he said: Now I know that the Omnipresent is with me."

[12] Oxford MS. (e. 16) reads: "hand."

[13] See Singer, p. 216; and see T.B. Berakhoth, 52b; T.B. Pesachim, 53b; T.J. Berakhoth viii. 7, 12c; Gen. Rab. xii. 6; and cf. Shocher Ṭob, p. 203a.

his hands [1] from the light of the fire,[2] he said: Now I know that the holy day has been separated from the work day here below (on earth), for fire may not be kindled on the Sabbath day; and in that hour he said: Blessed art Thou, O Lord our God, King of the universe, who divides || the holy from the profane,[3] the light from the darkness.

Rabbi Mana said: How must [4] a man say the Habdalah blessing? (He does this) over the cup of wine, with the light of fire,[5] and he says: Blessed art Thou, O Lord our God, King of the universe, who creates the various flames of fire; and when he removes his hand from the fire (flame) he says: Blessed art Thou, O Lord, who divides the holy from the profane.

If he have no wine he puts forth his hands [6] towards the light of the lamp and looks at his nails,[7] which are whiter than his body, and he says: Blessed art Thou, O Lord our God, King of the universe, who creates various flames of fire; and when he has removed his hands [8] from the fire, he says:

[1] Oxford MS. (e. 16) reads: "hand."

[2] Oxford MS. (e. 16) and the first editions read: "from the fire"; has our MS. an incorrect reading here?

[3] See *supra*, pp. 126, 138; and cf. Sepher Ha-Manhig, Hilkhoth Shabbath, § 67. The next words are not in the first editions.

[4] Lit. "is he obliged." Siddur Rab 'Amram, 59b, reads: "How is a man obliged (to perform Habdalah) with the cup of wine? He brings his hand near to the light of the fire." See also *Ravia*, ed. Aptowitzer, p. 131, and *Or Zaru'a*, ii. 24d, § 93. Both hands are to be stretched forth to the light according to our author and the authorities quoted (see Sha'arê Teshubah, § 102, and Shibbolê Ha-Leḳeṭ (52b), § 130). See Siddur R. 'Amram, 59a, for the expression to "look at the palms"; cf. Ha-Manhig, § 65, p. 34a. This was the custom of R. Naṭronai. The Mishnah Berakhoth viii. 6 deals with the necessity of *enjoying* the light in order to say the blessing over same; see T.B. Berakhoth, 53b. According to our book the custom of looking at the nails is only to be observed when there is no wine. The Pirḳê de R. Eliezer seems to have the same custom here and in reference to rinsing the cup mentioned *infra*, p. 146, note 7, as obtained in Sura, and these customs were known to R. Naṭronai.

[5] The light will enable him to see the wine in the cup, and then he need not look at his nails, nor put forth his hands to the light; for he has already derived some benefit from the light. If he have no wine, he looks at his nails. On the customs of the Habdalah see T.B. Berakhoth, 33b and 52b, and T.B. Sabbath, 150b, and *J.E.* vi. pp. 118 ff.

[6] This is according to the reading in our MS. The plural occurs also in Oxford MS. (e. 76) and the second edition.

[7] See Sepher Ha-Orah, i. pp. 57 f., notes 13 and 14, and Machzor Vitry, 117 f.

[8] The 2nd ed. reads: "hand." This section is wanting in the 1st ed.

Blessed art Thou, O Lord, who divides the holy from the profane.

If he be on a journey,[1] he puts forth his hand[2] to the light of the stars, which are also fire,[3] and says: Blessed art Thou, O Lord our God, King of the universe, who creates the various flames of fire. If the heavens be darkened,[4] he lifts up a stone outside,[5] and says: [6] Blessed art Thou, O Lord our God, who creates the various flames of fire.[7]

Rabbi Zadok said: Whosoever does not make Habdalah[8] at the termination of Sabbaths, or does not listen to those who perform the ceremony of Habdalah, will never see a sign[9] of blessing.[10] Everyone who makes Habdalah at the termination of Sabbaths, or whosoever hears those who perform the Habdalah, the Holy One, blessed be He, calls

[1] The first editions read: "If he have no fire."

[2] Oxford MS. (e. 76) reads: "hands."

[3] The first editions add: "and he looks at his nails which are whiter than his body."

[4] Oxford MS. (e. 76) reads: "darkened with clouds."

[5] Oxford MS. (e. 76) and the first editions read: "from the earth," and he obtains a spark by striking the two stones together.

[6] See Friedländer, *The Jewish Religion*, pp. 254, 340, and 343, for the rules of the rite. The 1st ed. reads: "and he performs the Habdalah." This is also the reading of the Venice edition, which adds: "and he says: Blessed (is He) who separates the holy from the profane."

[7] The ritual here set forth is not on all fours with the rules prescribed by the Shulchan 'Arukh. Spices are not mentioned at all. We should not say the benediction over the light when the light of the stars is the only light available; see T.B. Berakhoth, 52b, and Ṭur, Orach Chayyim, 296 and 297. The following section occurs in the MS. Gaster and in the 2nd ed.: "Rabbi Eliezer said: After a man has drunk the (contents) of the cup of Habdalah, it is a religious privilege and duty to put a little water in the cup (of wine used at the Habdalah), and to drink in order to show that the precepts are beloved,[1] and what remains of the water in the cup should be put over his eyes. Why? Because the Wise Men have said: The (observance of the) 'remnants' left over in connection with a religious act keeps back punishments."

[8] The Oxford MS. (e. 76) and the first editions add: "over wine."

[9] See *supra*, p. 138. On the Habdalah see Elbogen, *op. cit.* pp. 120, 532.

[10] See T.B. 'Erubin, 65a, T.B. Shebu'oth, 18b, and Jalkuṭ, Gen. § 34, and cf. Siddur Rab 'Amram, § 40, p. 60a, b. A variant reading is to be found in Ṭur, Orach Chayyim, 299.

---

[1] A similar custom still obtains in the Church of England. After the rite of Communion has been done, the officiating minister pours water into the chalice, and then drinks the water to prevent the waste of any drops of the consecrated wine. The custom mentioned by our text is referred to by the Geonim; see Siddur Rab 'Amram, pp. 59a ff., on the Habdalah.

him holy to be His holy treasure, and delivers him from the affliction of the peoples, as it is said, "And ye shall be holy unto me: for I the Lord am holy" (Lev. xx. 26).[1] ||

On the first day of the week[2] he[3] went into the waters of the upper Gihon[4] until the waters reached up to his neck, and he fasted seven weeks of days,[5] until his body became like a species of seaweed.[6] Adam said before the Holy One, blessed be He: Sovereign of all worlds! Remove, I pray Thee, my sins from me and accept my repentance, and all the generations will learn that repentance is a reality.[7] What did the Holy One, blessed be He, do? He put forth His right hand,[8] and accepted his repentance,[9] and took away from him his sin, as it is said, "I acknowledge my sin unto thee, and mine iniquity have I not hid:[10] I said, I will confess my transgressions unto the Lord; and thou forgavest the iniquity of my sin. Selah" (Ps. xxxii. 5). Selah[11] in this world and Selah in the world to come. Adam returned[12] and meditated in his heart, and said: I

[1] In the first editions the latter part of this paragraph reads: "Everyone who listens to those who perform the Habdalah or whosoever makes the Habdalah over the wine, the Holy One, blessed be He, acquires him as a treasure, as it is said: 'I have separated you from the peoples, that ye should be mine'" (Lev. xx. 26). The Venice edition adds: "And ye shall be a peculiar treasure unto me" (Ex. xix. 5). This last reading agrees with Oxford MS. (e. 76), which omits the quotation from Lev. (xx. 26).

[2] Sunday. On the incident see Israel Lévi's article in *R.É.J.* xviii. pp. 86 ff., where it is suggested that our author has used the Arabic, Ethiopic, or the Latin version of the Book of Adam and Eve xxxii.–xxxiv.

[3] The first editions read: "Adam." See Introduction, p. xlvii.

[4] *i.e.* the pool of Siloam; cf. 2 Chron. xxxii. 30. See Coptic Apocrypha, p. 245, and cf. Ginzberg, *Die Haggada, etc.*, p. 52.

[5] *i.e.* forty-nine days. According to T.B. 'Erubin, 18b, Adam fasted 130 years; see also Ẓohar, Gen. 55a, and T.B. 'Abodah Ẓarah, 8a.

[6] The first editions read: "like a sieve." Our MS. agrees here with the Oxford MS. (e. 76); see Jalḳuṭ, Gen., *loc. cit.*

[7] The first editions add: "and that Thou dost accept the repentance of the penitent."

[8] This expression is peculiar to our book; it occurs several times, cf. the legend in the Book of Adam and Eve, in *A. and P.* ii. p. 135.

[9] On Adam's repentance see Tertullian, *Against Marcion*, ii. 25.

[10] The quotation ends here in the MSS. and in the first editions.

[11] The last word of the previous verse is *Selah*, and the verse quoted concludes with *Selah*. The word is used in the sense of "so be it," or perhaps it suggests "pardon" (*Selach*).

[12] The Oxford MSS. and the printed texts read: "sat."

know that death will remove me [1] (to) "the house appointed for all living" (Job xxx. 23). Adam said: Whilst I am yet alive [2] I will [3] build for myself a mausoleum to rest therein.[4] He planned [5] and built for himself a mausoleum to rest therein beyond [6] Mount Moriah. Adam said: If in the case of the tables (of stone), just because in the future they will be written by the finger (of God), the waters of the Jordan are destined to flee before them; [7] how much more so will this be the case with my body which His two hands [8] kneaded, and because He breathed into my nostrils the breath of the spirit of His mouth? After my death they will come and take my bones, and they will make them into an image for idolatry; [9] but verily I will put || my coffin deep down beneath the cave and within the cave.[10] Therefore it is called the Cave of Machpelah, which is a double cave.[11] There Adam was put and his help-meet,[12] Abraham and his help-meet, Isaac and his help-meet, Jacob and his help-meet. Therefore it is called "the city of four"

1 The first editions read: "he said: For I have said, 'thou wilt bring me to death and to the house,' etc." The text of Job xxx. 23 reads: "For I know thou wilt bring," etc. The Oxford MS. (e. 76) reads: "I know that thou wilt bring me to death," etc.

2 The first editions read: "yet in the world."

3 See the Book of Adam and Eve (ed. Malan) II. ix. for the death and burial of Adam.

4 The first editions add here: "beyond Mount Moriah."

5 The first editions read: "He dug out"; so also in Oxford MSS.

6 Luria reads: "he went beyond Mount Moriah and dug," etc.; see Ẓohar, Gen. 57b, and *infra*, p. 275.

7 In the days of Joshua.

8 See *supra*, pp. 76 f.; and cf. T.B. Kethuboth, 5a, and Aboth de R. Nathan (*a*) i. p. 4b. This legend was known to the Church Fathers; see Theophilus, *To Autolycus*, ii. 18.

9 Here Adam seems to exercise prophetic powers. This agrees with the legend in the *Recognitions of Clement*, i. 47. Is our author attacking the worship of relics?

10 Owing to the power inherent in his divinely shaped and fashioned body, the waters of the Flood would have no power to destroy his remains; see T.B. Baba Bathra, 58a, Gen. Rab. xxviii. 3. The Book of Jashar iii. 14 refers to the burial of Adam in the "cave." In the Book of Jubilees viii. 19 the Garden of Eden is facing Mount Zion, *i.e.* Mount Moriah. The three things, according to Jubilees vii. 20, which brought the Flood were, "fornication, uncleanness, and all iniquity." Cf. T.B. Synhedrin, 74a, for the three cardinal sins, idolatry, immorality, and murder. For a parallel text with slight variations see Midrash Haggadol, c. 122.

11 See T.B. 'Erubin, 53a, and Jalḳuṭ, Gen., *loc. cit.* The legend of the *double* cave was known to Jerome; see Rahmer, *op. cit.* p. 36.

12 On the order of the burials see T.J. Ta'anith iv. 2, 68a; Ẓohar, Num. 164a.

(Kirjath Arba'); for four pairs (were buried there),[1] and concerning them the verse says, "He entereth into peace; they rest in their beds,[2] each one that walketh in his uprightness" (Isa. lvii. 2).[3]

[1] These words in brackets occur in the Oxford MS. (e. 76). Hippolytus (*A.N.C.L.* vi. p. 491) mentions eight people buried in the cave. This is another form of the legend of the "four pairs" mentioned in our text.

[2] In the MS. and the Midrash Haggadol, *loc. cit.*, the quotation ends here; in the first editions it is continued.

[3] See T.B. Kethuboth, 104a. In the first editions instead of helpmeet the names are given, namely, Eve, Sarah, Rebecca, and Leah.

CHAPTER XXI

CAIN AND ABEL [25A. i.]

"BUT[1] of the fruit of the tree which is in the midst of the garden" (Gen. iii. 3). It was taught in a Baraitha,[2] Rabbi Ẓeʿera said: "Of the fruit of the tree"—here "tree" only means man, who is compared to the tree, as it is said, "For man is the *tree* of the field" (Deut. xx. 19). "Which is in the midst of the garden"—"in the midst of the garden" is here merely an euphemism.[3] "Which is in the midst of the garden"—for "garden" means here merely woman, who is compared to a garden, as it is said, "A garden shut up is my sister, a bride" (Cant. iv. 12). Just as with this garden whatever is sown therein, it produces and brings forth, so (with) this woman, what seed she receives, she conceives and bears[4] through sexual intercourse.

(Sammael) riding on the serpent came to her, and she conceived;[5] afterwards Adam came to her, and she conceived

[1] The first editions begin the chapter with the expression: "It is written." Our MS. agrees with the Oxford MSS. here.

[2] "A tannaite tradition not incorporated in the Mishnah," see *J.E.* ii. 513. The use of the term תני (it was taught in a Baraitha) in connection with a statement by Rabbi Ẓeʿera (4th cent. C.E.) is incongruous.

[3] The first editions read here: "Just as 'in the *middle* of the body' (has its implication, likewise), 'in the midst of the garden' refers to that which is in the middle of the woman, because 'garden' means woman," etc.

[4] The first editions read "from her husband." This allegorical interpretation of the Paradise narrative is exceptionally bold. The Ẓohar, Gen. 35b, offers a parallel, having used our book as its original; see also Nachmanides, Torath Ha-Adam, 102b. The texts (Isa. lxi. 3, lx. 21, and xvii. 11) quoted by the Ẓohar *in loc. cit.* afford the scriptural basis for the interpretation in question.

[5] The first editions add "Cain." See Jalḳuṭ, Gen. § 29 and § 35, and Ẓohar, *loc. cit.*, for the reading: "Satan riding on the serpent." See Pal. Targ. Gen. iv. 1, which has used our author. This Haggadah occurs also in the Church Father Ephraim (in Gen. vol. i. p. 35); he says that the

Abel,[1] as it is said, " And Adam knew Eve his wife " (Gen. iv. 1). What is the meaning of " knew " ? (He knew) that she had conceived.[2] And she saw his [3] likeness that it was not of the earthly beings, but of the heavenly beings, and she prophesied [4] || and said : " I have gotten a man with the Lord " (ibid.).[5]

serpent was made to crawl on its belly "for having increased the pangs of child-bearing, through the seduction of Eve " ; see also Slavonic Enoch xxxi. 6. The legend was most probably known to Paul, who refers to the " serpent " as having " beguiled Eve in his craftiness " ; see 2 Cor. xi. 2, 3, and cf. 1 Tim. ii. 14, 15 ; and Protevangelium of James, 13 (A.N.C.L. xvi. p. 8), and cf. 4 Macc. xviii. 8.

[1] This agrees with Luria's emendation, based on the Jalḳuṭ, Gen. § 35, and Ẓohar, loc. cit. ; see supra, p. 78.

[2] Some of the Haggadic details of this chapter appear in Josephus, Ant. i. 1. 4. For the reading of the text here see Jalḳuṭ, loc. cit.

[3] Cain's. The Pal. Targum, Gen. iv. 1, reads : " And Adam knew Eve his wife, who was pregnant by the angel Sammael, and she conceived and bare Cain ; and he was like the heavenly beings, and not like the earthly beings, and she said, I have acquired a man, the angel of the Lord." Cf. infra, pp. 158 f., and see Ẓohar, in loc., and Jalḳuṭ, Gen. § 35. See also Vita Adæ et Evæ xxi. 3, in A. and P. ii. p. 138.

[4] The Jalḳuṭ, loc. cit., reads : " she understood."

[5] The Oxford MS. (e. 76) and the first editions insert here the following : " Rabbi Ishmael said : From Seth [1] arose and were descended all the generations of the righteous, and from Cain arose and were descended all the generations of the wicked, who rebelled and sinned against Heaven, and said, We do not need the drops of Thy rains, as it is said, ' Yet they said unto God, Depart from us ' " (Job xxi. 14).[2]

[1] Read Meshêth, " from Seth," instead of Meshom, " thence." See next chapter for a repetition of this section. The Midrashic interpretation seems to have been known to Philo, who speaks of Cain as the type " of folly and impiety" (De Cherub. xx.). See Heb. xi. 4 ; 1 John iii. 12 ; Jude 11. On the Cainites see Epiphanius, adv. Hær. i. 3. 38, i. 7. 5 ; and Irenæus, adv. Hær. i. xxxi. 1. In Ecclus. xlix. 16, Seth is compared with Shem as " glorified among men." Josephus, Ant. i. 2. 1 ff., described Abel as " a lover of righteousness " . . . " but Cain was not only very wicked . . . and it came to pass that the posterity of Cain became exceeding wicked. . . . Seth became a virtuous man, and as he was himself of an excellent character so did he leave behind him (children) who imitated his virtues. All these proved to be of good dispositions." Cain is " a son of wrath," according to the Apoc. Mosis 3. See also the Book of Adam and Eve (ed. Malan) i. lxxix. and the Book of Jubilees iv. 11 ff., xix. 24, on this subject. The Gnostics taught that " Cain derived his being from the Power above," says Irenæus, adv. Hær., loc. cit. According to the Gnostics, Eve had several sons, who were declared to be angels ; see Irenæus, op. cit. i. xxx. 7. On Sammael or Michael, as the name of the serpent, see Irenæus, loc. cit. 9. There are several points of contact in this chapter, as well as in the preceding chapter, with the doctrines of the Gnostics as set forth in the writings of Irenæus. See also Grünbaum, op. cit. pp. 73 ff.

[2] The Book of Job was frequently used by the Haggadists in their Midrashim on the Book of Genesis.

Rabbi Miasha[1] said: Cain was born, and his wife,[2] his twin-sister,[3] with him.[4] Rabbi Simeon[5] said to him: Has it not already been said, "And if a man shall take his sister, his father's daughter, or his mother's daughter, and see her nakedness, and she see his nakedness; it is a shameful thing"?[6] (Lev. xx. 17). From these words know that there were no other women whom they could marry, and these were permitted to them, as it is said, "For I have said, The world shall be built up by love"[7] (Ps. lxxxix. 2). With love was the world built up before the Torah had been given.[8] Rabbi Joseph[9] said: Cain and Abel were twins,[10] as it is said, "And she conceived, and bare (with) Cain" (Gen. iv. 1). At that hour she had an additional capacity for child-bearing (as it is said), "And she *continued* to bear his brother Abel" (*ibid.* 2).[11]

[1] Oxford MS. (e. 76) reads "Meir" (2nd cent. C.E.). Miasha lived in the 4th cent. C.E.

[2] "His wife" does not occur in the first editions.

[3] According to the Book of Adam and Eve (ed. Malan) I. lxxiv., Luluwa was the twin-sister of Cain; see *Schatzhöhle*, p. 34, and also the Book of Jashar i. 12. Other references are given by Ginzberg, *op. cit.* pp. 60 f.

[4] The Oxford MS. (e. 76) and the printed editions add: "Abel was born, and with him his twin-sister." Her name was Aklima (Book of Adam and Eve (ed. Malan) I. lxxv). The first edition differs slightly in the order of the words here.

[5] According to the first editions the name is "Ishmael," who lived *c.* 90–135 C.E., and was a contemporary of R. 'Aḳiba, the teacher of R. Meir. R. Simeon (? son of Jochai) was also a disciple of R. 'Aḳiba.

[6] חסד, love, permissible or shameful; see Jalḳuṭ, Ps. lxxxix. § 839. Our MS. does not give the last few words of the quotation. In the first editions the quotation ends with the words: "his father's daughter." In the Oxford MS. (e. 76) the quotation ends with the words: "mother's daughter."

[7] The R.V. renders the passage: "Mercy shall be built up for ever."

[8] R. Ishmael seems to imply that, prior to the giving of the Law (Torah), the world's law was based on the impulses of nature and therefore immoral. See the Book of Adam and Eve (ed. Malan) II. vii., as to the marriage of Adam's son Seth. Epiphanius, *op. cit.* xxxix. 5, refers to this subject.

[9] The Oxford MS. (e. 76) agrees with our MS., but the first editions read "José"—R. José bar Chalaphta was a pupil of R. 'Akiba.

[10] See T.B. Synhedrin, 38b; Aboth d. R. Nathan (*a*) i.; Gen. Rab. xxii. 2. According to the Book of Jashar, *loc. cit.*, "Eve bore two sons and three daughters." According to this book the union of Adam and Eve was consummated *after* the expulsion from Paradise; see also Jalḳuṭ, Gen. § 15 and § 35, and T.B. Jebamoth, 62a. Josephus says: "Adam and Eve had two sons . . . they had also daughters" (*Ant.* i. 2. 1).

[11] Our MS. agrees with Oxford MS. (e. 76), and partially with the Oxford MS. (OA. 167). The first editions read: "At that hour she

Now Cain was a man who loved the ground in order to sow seed; and Abel was a man who loved to tend the sheep; the one gave of his produce as food for the other, and the latter gave of his produce as food for his (brother). The evening of the festival of Passover[1] arrived. Adam called his sons and said to them: In this (night) in the future Israel will bring Paschal offerings, bring ye also (offerings) before your Creator.

(Cain) brought the remnants of his meal of roasted grain, (and) the seed of flax,[2] and Abel brought of the firstlings of his sheep, and of their fat, he-lambs, which had not been shorn of their wool.[3] The offering of || Cain was precluded,[4]

was debarred from bearing," as it is said, "And she *ceased* to bear." Here "Asaph" = to cease. Our text agrees with Pal. Targ. Gen. iv. 2. See Gen. Rab. xxii. 3, and cf. the Book of Adam and Eve (ed. Malan) I. lxxv.

[1] Our book lays stress on the Passover in contradistinction to Jubilees, which exalts Pentecost and Tabernacles. Luria argues that as there was a tradition that the world was created on the 1st of Nisan, Adam was therefore created on the 6th, and "at the end of days" (Gen. iv. 3) means one week, and these numbers equal thirteen, and after this day is the 14th, which is the eve of Passover. The offering was brought on the 14th, and eaten that day at even, which is the beginning of the 15th. On the other hand, according to our book, *supra*, p. 52, the creation began on the 25th of Ellul, and Adam was fashioned on the 1st of Tishri; "at the end of days" would be interpreted as the change in the seasons from autumn to spring, when the first-fruits would be brought. Cf. *infra*, p. 236. Our text is reproduced by Pal. Targ. Gen. iv. 3, and Midrash Agadah (ed. Buber), Gen. p. 10, and see *ibid.* note 6.

According to Dr. Büchler (*J.Q.R.* v. 442), in the first year of the triennial cycle of reading the Torah, a Palestinian custom, on the first day of Passover, Gen. iii. 22–iv. 26 was read. Now, the story of the offering of Cain and Abel occurs in Gen. iv. 3 ff., and would fall in the Passover week. This explains our text, "the night of the festival of Passover arrived." See *J.E.* xii. p. 256a, line 6; Gen. iii., which is quoted there, should probably be Gen. iv.

Chrysostomus (about 175 C.E.) declared that it was customary to begin reading from Genesis during Lent, *i.e.* Nisan. This shows that the Early Church followed the old Jewish custom of commencing the reading of the Torah in Nisan, the beginning of the Jewish ecclesiastical new year; see *J.E. ibid.* p. 257b. For a parallel reading, with slight variants, see Midrash Haggadol, c. 106 f.

[2] In Tanchuma, Bereshith, § IX., we read: "Some sages say, The remnants of his meal; other sages say, The seed of flax." See 'Arukh (ed. Kohut) iv. p. 229b; and cf. Zohar, Lev. 87a, where flax is mentioned as the offering of Cain.

[3] The offering was the first-fruit of the animal and the first shearing of the wool.

[4] This is also the reading of Oxford MS. (e. 76). The Oxford MS. (O.A. 167) and the first editions read "was abhorred"; cf. Prov. xxviii. 9.

and the offering of Abel was acceptable, as it is said, "And the Lord had respect unto Abel and to his offering" (*ibid.* 4).

Rabbi Joshua ben Ḳorchah said: The Holy One, blessed be He, said: Heaven forbid! Never let the offerings[1] of Cain and Abel be mixed up (with one another), even in the weaving of a garment, as it is said, "Thou shalt not wear a mingled stuff, *wool* and *linen* together" (Deut. xxii. 11). And even if it be combined[2] let it not come upon thee, as it is said, "Neither shall there come upon thee a garment of two kinds of stuff mingled together" (Lev. xix. 19).

Rabbi Zadok said: A great hatred[3] entered Cain's heart against his brother Abel, because his offering had been accepted.[4] Not only (on this account), but also because Abel's twin-sister was the most beautiful of women, and he desired her in his heart. Moreover he said: I will slay Abel my brother, and I will take his twin-sister[5] from him, as it is said, "And it came to pass when they were in the *field*" (Gen. iv. 8).

"In the field" means woman, who is compared to a field.[6] He took the stone and embedded it in the forehead[7]

[1] Wool from Abel's sheep and flax from Cain's offering. The two combined would come under the prohibition of Sha'aṭneẓ (cf. Deut. xxii. 11). Perhaps the prohibition of Kilayim (Lev. xix. 19) is also intended. This reference to Adam in connection with Sha'atnez is probably intentional, and is our author's imitation of Jubilees, which also connects various laws with the Patriarchs. See Tanchuma, Bereshith, *loc. cit.*, for a variant reading, and cf. 'Arukh, *loc. cit., s.v. Kilayim,* and see Maimonides, *Guide*, iii. 37, and *J.E.* xi. 212 f.

[2] The 1st ed. reads "embroidered." This agrees with the Oxford MSS. The 2nd ed. reads "decomposed."

[3] The Book of Jashar i. 16 says: "And Cain was jealous of his brother on this account." Josephus, *Ant., loc. cit.*, also agrees with this view. The first editions read: "*Envy* and a great *hatred*." The Oxford MS. (e. 76) reads: "Envy and hatred." Test. XII Pat., Benj. vii. 5: "Because forever those who are like unto Cain in *envy* and *hatred* of brethren, shall be punished with the same judgment."

[4] This agrees with Jubilees iv. 2; see also Irenæus, *adv. Hær.* iv. 3 (*A.N.C.L.* v. p. 433).

[5] In Jubilees iv. 1 the wife of Cain is 'Avan, who was born after Abel. See Book of Adam and Eve (ed. Malan) I. lxxviii.

[6] The Oxford MS. (e. 76) adds: "as it is said: 'But if a man find the damsel that is betrothed in the *field*'" (Deut. xxii. 25). The first editions read: "as it is said: 'For man is the tree of the field'" (Deut. xx. 19). Man is the *tree*, woman is the *field*. This fine figure has a parallel in Euripides, Orestes, 552 ff. Compare our expression, "*Mother* Earth."

[7] The Book of Adam and Eve (ed. Malan) I. lxxix. states: "And Cain . . . took a large stone and smote his brother with it upon his head." See Pal. Targum, Gen. iv. 8, which reproduces our text: "he embedded a

of Abel, and slew him, as it is said, "And Cain rose up against Abel his brother, and slew him" (*ibid.*).

Rabbi Jochanan said: Cain did not know that the secrets are revealed before the Holy One, blessed be He.[1] He took the corpse of his brother Abel and hid it in the field.[2] The Holy One, blessed be He, said to him: "Where is Abel thy brother?" (*ibid.* 9). He replied to Him: Sovereign of the world! A keeper of vineyard and field hast Thou made me.[3] A keeper of my brother Thou hast not made me; as it is said, "Am I my brother's keeper?" (*ibid.*). The Holy One, blessed be He, said to him: || "Hast thou killed, and also taken possession?"[4] (1 Kings xxi. 19). "The voice of thy brother's blood crieth unto me from the ground" (Gen. iv. 10). When Cain heard this word[5] he was confused. And He cursed him, that he became[6] a wanderer on the earth because of the shedding of the blood,[7] and because of the evil death.

Cain spake before the Holy One, blessed be He: Sovereign of all the worlds! "My sin is too great to be borne" (*ibid.* 13), for it has no atonement.[8] This utterance was

stone in his forehead and slew him." The Book of Jashar i. 25 speaks of "the iron part of the ploughing instrument with which he suddenly smote his brother." See also Book of the Bee, p. 26.

[1] Jubilees (iv. 6) states, in connection with Cain's crime, that "we announce when we come before the Lord our God, all the sin which is committed in heaven and on earth, and in light and in darkness, and everywhere. The 1st eds., Oxford MS. (e. 76) and Gaster MS. add: "What did he do?"

[2] The Oxford MS. (e. 76) reads: "he dug in the earth and hid (or buried) it." The first editions have almost the same reading. According to our book there was apparently no actual burial by Cain, this was done by Adam and Eve; see *infra* in this chapter. See Tanchuma, *loc. cit.*, and Jalkuṭ, Gen. § 38. Our Midrash was known to Jerome, *Ep. ad Dam.* 125. See Book of Adam and Eve (ed. Malan), *loc. cit.* According to the Book of Jashar, *loc. cit.*, "Cain rose up and dug a hole in the field, wherein he put the body of his brother, and he turned the dust over him." Ginzberg, *op. cit.* p. 66, note 2, deals with this theme; see also Grünbaum, *op. cit.* pp. 83 f.

[3] Abel's flocks would not be in the fields or vineyards of Cain, and therefore, in the ordinary course of events, he would not have known the whereabouts of his brother.

[4] "Hast thou taken possession" of thy brother? (*i.e.* his wife and his flock). The later editions read: "I have also heard."

[5] See T.B. Synhedrin, 37a, b.

[6] The first editions read: "that he should be."

[7] Almost a literal quotation from Jubilees iv. 4, surely this must be something more than a mere coincidence.

[8] Luria suggests that the last words might be read as a question: "Is there no atonement for it?"

reckoned to him as repentance,[1] as it is said, "And Cain said unto the Lord, My sin is too great to be borne" (*ibid.*); further, Cain said before the Holy One, blessed be He: Now will a certain righteous one[2] arise on the earth and mention Thy great Name against me and slay me.[3] What did the Holy One, blessed be He, do? He took one letter from the twenty-two letters,[4] and put (it) upon Cain's arm[5] that he should not be killed, as it is said, "And the Lord appointed a sign for Cain" (*ibid.* 15). The dog[6] which was guarding Abel's flock also guarded[7] his corpse[8] from all the beasts of the field and all the fowl of the heavens.[9] Adam and his helpmate were sitting and weeping and mourning[10] for him, and they did not know what to do (with Abel), for they were unaccustomed to burial. A raven[11] (came), one of its fellow birds was dead (at its side). (The raven) said: I will teach this man what to do. It took its fellow and dug in the earth, hid it and buried it before them. Adam said: Like this raven will I act. He took || the corpse of Abel and dug in the earth and buried it. The Holy One, blessed be He, gave a good reward to the ravens in this world. What reward did He give them? When they bear their young and see that they are white[12] they fly from them, thinking that they are the offspring of a serpent, and the Holy One, blessed be He, gives them their sustenance[13] without lack, as it is said, "Who provideth

[1] Cf. T.B. Synhedrin, 101b, and Lev. Rab. x. 5.

[2] See Jalkuṭ, Gen., *loc. cit.*, and Jalkuṭ Makhiri, Ps. cxlvii. pp. 143a, b.

[3] By mentioning God's name, see *J.Q.R.* v. p. 409, and cf. *infra*, p. 379.

[4] The first editions add: "which are in the Torah and wrote (it)." See Ẓohar, Gen. 36b. Most of this chapter has close parallels in the Ẓohar. See also Pal. Targum, *in loc.*

[5] In Pal. Targum, *in loc.*, "Upon the face of Cain" is the reading. The sign of the Tephillin is placed on the *forehead* and on the left *arm*. See also Ezek. ix. 4, 6, and Othijoth de R. 'Aḳiba, ch. i. Cf. Rashi on Gen. iv. 15, and Midrash Agadah, Gen. p. 12.

[6] See Job xxx. 1. A parallel text occurs in Midrash Haggadol, c. 116f.

[7] This contradicts the earlier story of Abel being buried by Cain.

[8] Jubilees iv. 7 says: "Adam and his wife mourned for Abel."

[9] See Book of Adam and Eve (ed. Malan) II. i.

[10] For the phraseology see Neh. i. 4. The legend occurs also in the Koran, Sura v.

[11] Tanchuma, *loc. cit.*, reads: "Two clean birds"; cf. Gen. Rab. xxii. 8. See Midrash Haggadol, c. 116.

[12] See Jalkuṭ to Job, § 925; cf. T.B. Kethuboth, 49b.

[13] See Tanchuma, 'Eḳeb, § ii. In the first editions the quotation from Job is not given.

for the raven his food, when his young ones cry unto God, and wander for lack of meat" (Job xxxviii. 41). Moreover, that rain should be given [1] upon the earth (for their sakes), and the Holy One, blessed be He, answers them, as it is said, "He giveth to the beast his food, and to the young ravens which cry" (Ps. cxlvii. 9).[2]

[1] The first editions read: "they cry that rain should be given."

[2] The previous verse of the Psalm speaks of rain. See also Jalkuṭ Makhiri, *in loc.*, p. 143b. The Midrash Haggadol, c. 117, gives this verse as Ps. cxliv. 9. This is a printer's error for Ps. cxlvii. 9. It adds Job xxxviii. 41.

CHAPTER XXII

THE FALL OF THE ANGELS [26A. i.]

"AND [1] Adam lived an hundred and thirty years, and he begat in his own likeness after his image" (Gen. v. 3). Hence thou mayest learn that Cain was not of Adam's seed,[2] nor after his likeness, nor after his image.[3] (Adam did not beget in his own image) [4] until Seth was born, who was [5] after his father Adam's likeness and image,[6] as it is said, "And he begat in his own likeness, after his image" (*ibid.*).

Rabbi Simeon [7] said: From Seth arose and were descended [8] all the generations of the righteous.[9] From

[1] The first editions read: "It is written: 'And Adam,'" etc.

[2] See *supra*, pp. 150 f., for the statement that Cain was the offspring of Eve and Sammael. The Scripture text seems to have afforded ground for the distinction which the Rabbis and others drew between Cain and Seth: "And Adam knew Eve his wife, and she conceived and bare Cain, and *she* said, I have acquired a man (child) from the Lord" (Gen. iv. 1). Concerning Abel the Bible states, "And she continued to bare his brother Abel" (*ibid.* 2), without adding any further qualification as in the case of Cain. With reference to Seth the text says, "And Adam lived an hundred and thirty years, and he begat in *his own likeness* after *his image*, and *he* called his name Seth" (*ibid.* v. 3). The fifth chapter of Genesis begins afresh the history of Adam's offspring, but omits all reference to Cain, whose descendants are mentioned in ch. iv. The Pal. Targum to Gen. v. 3 adds: "but before Eve had borne Cain, who was not like to him" (*i.e.* Adam).

[3] The words "likeness and image" are not mentioned in the story of Cain's birth. The first editions add: "neither did his deeds resemble those of Abel his brother." Cain inherited the nature of Sammael, the angel of Death, and became a murderer.

[4] The words in brackets are not in the text.

[5] The first editions add: "of his seed."

[6] The first editions add: "and his deeds were similar to those of Abel his brother."

[7] The first editions read: "Ishmael." Our MS. agrees with the Midrash Haggadol, c. 117, and the Oxford MS. (O.A. 167). Dr. Büchler observes: "Also in the text of the Talmud Ishmael and Simeon are very frequently interchanged."

[8] The first editions add: "all the creatures."

[9] See *supra*, p. 151, note 5, for this paragraph. There is probably some confusion in the texts here. "The generations of the righteous" are

Cain arose and were descended all the generations of the wicked, who rebel [1] and sin, who rebelled against their Rock,[2] and they said: We do not need the drops of Thy rain,[3] neither to walk in Thy ways, as it is said, "Yet they said unto God, Depart from us" (Job xxi. 14).

Rabbi Meir said: || The generations of Cain went about stark naked,[4] men and women, just like the beasts,[5] and they defiled themselves with all kinds of immorality, a man with his mother or his daughter, or the wife of his brother,[6] or the wife of his neighbour, in public [7] and in the streets, with evil inclination which is in the thought of their heart,[8] as it is said, "And the Lord

the offspring of Seth mentioned in Gen. v.; and "the generations of the wicked" are the offspring of Cain enumerated in Gen. iv. See Ẓohar, Gen. 35b, and Gen. Rab. xxiii. 1. Pal. Targum to Gen., *loc. cit.*, adds: "And Cain was cast out; neither is his seed enumerated in the 'Book of the generations of Adam.'"

[1] The expression is based on Ezek. xx. 38.

[2] Cf. *infra*, p. 341. The expression is often used to denote God as Creator. The first editions read: "The Omnipresent." The Oxford MS. (O.A. 167) and the Midrash Haggadol, *loc. cit.*, read: "their Creator."

[3] Cf. Job xxiv. 13. The Midrash applies this chapter of Job to the generation of the Flood. See Gen. Rab. xxxi. 2.

[4] Pal. Targum on Gen. vi. 2 says: "And the sons of the great saw that the daughters of men were beautiful . . . walking with naked flesh"; cf. Job xxiv. 10, and Grünbaum, *op. cit.* pp. 75 ff.

[5] See Jubilees iii. 30, 31 and cf. *ibid.* vii. 16, for a strong protest against nudity. See also Jalkuṭ, Deut. § 945; and cf. Brüll, *Trachten der Juden*, pp. 4 ff. The fact that our book protests so strongly against the immodest vogue which probably obtained at the period and in the place where the author lived might point to the "origin" of our book, if we could only locate the fact referred to. One is apt to think of the vagaries of certain classes of recluses who belonged to the Christian Church and led solitary lives in the deserts of Egypt. Thus, in the *Paradise of the Holy Fathers* (ed. Budge, vol. i. p. 242), we read of the Abba Bessarion, who "wandered hither and thither like one possessed; in the season of frost he went naked." In the Jalkuṭ quoted above, the passage states (on the text, Deut. xxxii. 21, "They have moved me to jealousy with that which is *not God*"): "this refers to those who come from Barbary (or Mauretania) who walk naked in the street." See also Siphrê, Deut. § 320. Have we an echo of the warnings against incest referred to in Jubilees xxxiii. 10 ff.? and cf. *ibid.* xli. 25–26. See also *Schatzhöhle*, pp. 14 f.

[6] For Rabbinic references to the subject see T.B. Synhedrin, 58a; and cf. T.B. Jebamoth, 63b. See also T.J. Jebamoth xi. 1. 11d, Gen. Rab. xviii. 5, and Siphra, Ḳedoshim x. 11.

[7] See Ẓohar, Gen. 60b. The first editions omit: "or the wife of his neighbour"; they read: "in secret and in public with evil inclination," etc.

[8] Cf. Gen. vi. 5.

saw that the wickedness of man was great [1] in the earth" (Gen. vi. 5).

Rabbi said: The angels who fell [2] from their holy place in heaven saw the daughters of the generations of Cain [3] walking about naked, with their eyes painted [4] like harlots, and they went astray after them,[5] and took wives from amongst them, as it is said, "And the sons of Elohim [6] saw the daughters of men that they were fair; and they took them wives of all that they chose" [7] (*ibid.* 2).

Rabbi Joshua [8] said: The angels are flaming fire, as it is said, "His servants are a flaming fire" (Ps. civ. 4), and fire came with the coition of flesh and blood, but did not burn the body; [9] but when they fell from heaven, from their holy place, their strength and stature (became) like that of the sons of men, and their frame was (made of) clods of dust, as it is said, "My flesh is clothed with worms and clods of dust" (Job vii. 5).

Rabbi Zadok said: From them were born the giants

[1] The quotation ends here. The first editions continue as in our version. "Rabbi" mentioned in the next paragraph is R. Jehudah, the Prince.

[2] These "fallen angels" were called Nephilim (the fallen ones). "Giants" is the usual rendering of this term. On the angels, cf. *supra*, pp. 46, 99; and *infra*, pp. 193 f. These angels who fell from heaven are not mentioned by name in our book, but they are named Shemchazai and Uzziel in Pal. Targum to Gen. vi. 4, and also in the Azazel Midrash in Jellinek's *B.H.M.* iv. pp. 127 f.; see Jeraḥmeel, pp. 52 ff., also Deut. Rab. xi. 9, and Zohar, Gen. 46b, 47a. The source of the legend is the Book of Enoch; see Introduction. On the names of the angels, see Brüll, *Jahrbücher für Jüd. Gesch.* i. 147 f., where the reference to our text must be corrected.

[3] See Nachmanides (in Gen. *in loc.*), who quotes our text.

[4] See Pal. Targum, Gen. vi. 2; and cf. Gen. Rab. xxvi. 7, and Jalkuṭ, Gen. § 44, quoting Midrash Abkhir.

[5] See Pal. Targum *in loc.*; and cf. Tanna de bê Elijahu Rab. xxxi. p. 158.

[6] The R.V. renders, "the sons of God." The Targum gives "the sons of the nobles" (or the "mighty") in the sense of "angels." Our MS. quotes the second half of this verse only, the first editions quote the first half of the verse.

[7] The Pal. Targum renders: "And they took to themselves wives of all who pleased them."

[8] The first editions add: "ben Korchah."

[9] Cf. Paul's expression, "burned in their lust one toward another" (Rom. i. 27). On the "sin of the angels," see the Book of Adam and Eve (ed. Malan) III. iv., which gives a very interesting version, denying the possibility of "angels . . . committing sin with human beings"; and see *Recognitions of Clement*, iv. 26, and Methodius, *Discourse on the Resurrection*, vii.

(Anakim),[1] who walked with pride in their heart,[2] and who stretched forth their hand to all (kinds of) robbery and violence, and shedding of blood,[3] as it is said, " And there we saw the Nephilim,[4] the sons of Anak " (Num. xiii. 33); and it says, " The Nephilim were on the earth in those days " (Gen. vi. 4).

Rabbi Joshua [5] said : || The Israelites are called " Sons of God," [6] as it is said, " Ye are the sons of the Lord your God " (Deut. xiv. 1). The angels are called " Sons of God," as it is said, " When the morning stars sang together, and all the sons of God shouted for joy " (Job xxxviii. 7); [7] and whilst they were still in their holy place in heaven, these were called " Sons of God," as it is said, " And also after that, when [8] the sons of God came in unto the daughters of men, and they bare children to them; the same became the mighty men, which were of old, men of renown " (Gen. vi. 4).[9]

Rabbi Levi said: They bare their sons and increased and multiplied [10] like a great reptile, six children at each birth.[11] In that very hour they [12] stood on their feet, and spoke the holy language, and danced before them like sheep, as it is said, " They cast their young like sheep, and their children danced " (Job xxi. 11).

Noah [13] said to them: Turn from your ways and evil

[1] On the Anakim "giants" see T.B. Soṭah, 34b, and Gen. Rab., *loc. cit.*

[2] The first editions read : " with high stature." Cf. Wisdom xiv. 6.

[3] Cf. Job xxiv. 14.

[4] See *supra*, p. 160, note 2.

[5] First editions add : " ben Ḳorchaḥ."

[6] On "Sons of God" in Gen. vi. 2 see LXX, Aquila, and Pesh.; and Philo, *de Gigant.* 2, i. M. 1. 263, C.W. ii. 6 ff. p. 44, and other references given by Charles on Jubilees v. 1. See also Wisdom ii. 13, 15.

[7] See Jubilees v. 1. The LXX version of Job xxxviii. 7 is interesting as a parallel to our author's interpretation of the " sons of God." " When the stars were made, all my *angels* praised me with a loud voice." See also the Targum to Job *in loc.*

[8] The MS. and the first editions give only part of the verse.

[9] The angels whilst in heaven were the sons of " Elohim "; when they fell and sinned they lost their right to this designation. Men may rise by virtue and holiness and become worthy of being called " the sons of Elohim."

[10] See Gen. Rab. xxxvi. 1 and Lev. Rab. v. 1. Luria holds that this dictum of R. Levi has been interpolated here from Gen. Rab. *loc. cit.*

[11] See *infra*, p. 174; and cf. T.B. Berakhoth, 6a.

[12] The offspring.

[13] The Book of Adam and Eve (ed. Malan), *loc. cit.*, offers a close parallel: " But Noah preached repeatedly to the children of Cain, saying,

deeds, so that He bring not upon you the waters of the Flood, and destroy all the seed of the children of men.[1] They said to him: Behold, we will restrain ourselves from multiplying and increasing, so as not to produce the offspring of the children of men. What did they do? When they came to their wives they spilled the issue of their seed upon the earth[2] so as not to produce offspring of the children of men, as it is said, "And God saw the earth, and behold it was spilled" (Gen. vi. 12). They said: If He bring from heaven the waters of the Flood upon us, behold, we are of high stature, and the waters will not reach || up to our necks;[3] and if He bring the waters of the depths against us, behold, the soles of our feet can close up all the depths. What did they do? They put forth the soles of their feet, and closed up all the depths.[4] What did the Holy One, blessed be He, do? He heated the waters of the deep, and they arose and burnt their flesh, and peeled off their skin from them, as it is said, "What time they wax warm, they vanish; when it is hot, they are consumed out of their place" (Job vi. 17). Do not read thus ("When it is hot," בְּחֻמּוֹ), but (read) "in his hot waters" (בחמימיו).[5]

'The flood will come and destroy you, if we do not repent.' But they would not hearken to him; they only laughed at him." See also Gen. Rab. xxx. 7, Tanna de bê Elijahu Rab. xv. p. 74, the Book of Jashar v. 22 ff., Midrash Agadah, Gen. p. 18, and T.B. Synhedrin, 108b. See also Ephraim, on the Repentance of Nineveh (E.T. p. 34), for the refusal of the people to repent at the bidding of Noah. The Church Fathers speak of Noah as a preacher. See Methodius, *Banquet of Ten Virgins*, x. 3, and cf. Hippolytus, *A.N.C.L.* vi. pp. 492 f.

[1] See *Rabbinic Philosophy and Ethics*, pp. 39 f., and Wisdom x. 4.

[2] The Oxford MS. (O.A. 167) reads: "And the Holy One, blessed be He, saw that they had corrupted their way." See R.V. Gen. vi. 12.

[3] "Water up to the neck" is an expression of extreme peril; cf. Isa. viii. 8, xxx. 28; Ps. lxix. 2.

[4] See Pal. Targum on Gen. vii. 10, T.B. Synhedrin, *loc. cit.*, and *infra*, p. 167.

[5] The Hebrew could be interpreted as meaning "anger." The later editions add: "The Parashah (Portion) of Bereshith (Gen. i. 1–vi. 8) is completed." These words are highly significant. They seem to indicate that our book was intended originally to be a Midrash on the Torah, and as it is now preserved it is but a fragment of what it might have been. The "Portion" of Genesis is not to be identified with the "Book" of Genesis. The question of the triennial cycle of reading the Torah must also be borne in mind in dealing with our book. The narrative dealing with the Adam legends recurs three times: (1) Chapters III.–V., (2) Chapters XI.–XIV., and (3) Chapters XVIII.–XXII. Thus far in the first twenty-two chapters of the book we have only covered the first six chapters of Genesis. The first two

chapters were biographical, and apart from them, the actual Midrash of twenty chapters may be subdivided as follows:

III.–V. Creation.
VI.–VIII. Astronomy.
IX. Ritual.
X. Jonah.
XI. Creation Story resumed.
XII.–XIV. Adam and Eve and Sammael.
XV. Ethical matter.
XVI. Abraham, Isaac, Eliezer, and Rebecca, and Wedding Customs.
XVII. Mourning Rites.
XVIII. Adam.
XIX.–XX. Sabbath.
XXI.–XXII. Cain, Abel, and the Fall of the Angels.

Chapters XVI. and XVII. seem out of place in this scheme.

A considerable portion of this chapter and the one following occurs in the Midrash Haggadol. Several parallels are to be found in Leḳach Tob, Midrash Agadah, and Aggadath Bereshith.

CHAPTER XXIII

THE ARK AND THE FLOOD [26B. ii.]

"*And this* is how thou shalt make the ark "[1] (Gen. vi. 15). R. Shemiah taught: The Holy One, blessed be He, showed Noah with a finger[2] and said to him, Like this and that shalt thou do to the ark. One hundred and fifty rooms[3] were along the length at the left[4] side of the ark, thirty-three[5] rooms across the width in the side within,[6] and thirty-three rooms in the side across the width on the outside;[7] and ten compartments in the centre, which were for the storerooms for the food.[8] And there were five protected cisterns[9] on the right side of the ark, and fifty[10] protected cisterns on the left side of the ark, and the openings for the water pipes opened and closed, and so was it in the lowest

[1] The Scripture text reads "it," referring to the ark. See *J.E. s.v.* Noah, Ark, Deluge; the Pal. Targum has undoubtedly used our Midrash in the paraphrase of the Noah narrative (Gen. vi.–vii.). The subject has been dealt with by Grünbaum, *op. cit.* pp. 79 ff., and by Ginzberg, *op. cit.* pp. 39 ff., 79 ff., 87.

[2] See *infra*, pp. 382 f., and T.B. Menachoth, 29a, Mekhilta, p. 2b, Tosaphoth to T.B Chullin, 42a, and Midrash Haggadol, c. 148.

[3] Lit. "nests" or "cells"; see Pal. Targum, Gen. vi. 15, and Book of Adam and Eve (ed. Malan) III. ii., for a parallel tradition.

[4] The first editions read: "right side of the ark, and one hundred and fifty along the left side." MS. Gaster reads: "One hundred rooms along the right side," etc.

[5] Pal. Targum, *loc. cit.*, has: "thirty-six in the middle." Ginsburger, *Pseudo-Jonathan, in loc.*, reads: "thirty-three."

[6] Where the entrance was, *i.e.* on the east of the ark.

[7] Luria suggests that "within" may refer to the east, and "the outside" to the west.

[8] See Book of Adam and Eve (ed. Malan), *loc. cit.*, for a parallel, and cf. Hippolytus, *A.N.C.L.* vi. p. 491.

[9] אפטמיות = אֲפּוּטְנִיּוֹת (*puteana*), enclosures surrounding a well; see Book of Adam and Eve, *loc. cit.*: "line the well with lead." This word occurs in the Pal. Targum, *loc. cit.*

[10] The printed editions read: "five."

division;[1] and so || on the second floor, and so on the third floor.[2]

The dwelling-place of all the cattle and animals [3] was in the lowest compartment, the dwelling-place for all fowl was in the second compartment, and the dwelling-place for the reptiles [4] and the human beings was in the third compartment.[5] Hence thou mayest learn [6] that there were 366 kinds of cattle on the earth, and 366 kinds of fowl on the earth, and 366 kinds of reptiles on the earth, for thus was (the number) in the lowest compartment,[7] so in the second compartment, and so in the third floor, as it is said, "With lower, second, and third stories shalt thou make it" (*ibid.* 16).

Rabbi Tachanah [8] said: Noah made the ark during fifty-two years,[9] so that they should repent of their ways.[10] But they did not repent. Whilst yet the Flood had not come, the unclean (animals) were more numerous than the clean (animals). But when the waters of the Flood came, and

[1] *i.e.* the hold.

[2] Cf. Book of Adam and Eve (ed. Malan), *loc. cit.*

[3] See T.B. Synhedrin, 108b. A parallel to our Midrash is to be found in Hippolytus in *A.N.C.L.* vi., *loc. cit.*, and see German edition (Achelis), p. 88. Schatzhöhle, p. 17, has also a parallel.

[4] The first editions add: "and creeping things."

[5] Cf. Book of Adam and Eve, *loc. cit.*

[6] Cf. Luria's reading, which agrees with the tradition preserved in Midrash Kônen, *B.H.M.* ii. 36; cf. Leḳach Ṭob, Gen. p. 39. According to Luria the text should be: "Hence thou mayest learn, that all the kinds of fowl on the earth equal 365; and likewise with the kinds of reptiles on the earth, and so with the kinds of cattle and animals on the earth." The first editions read: "32 kinds of fowl on the earth, 365 kinds of reptiles on the earth."

[7] 366 rooms. This number is found thus:

150	on the right.
150	on the left.
33	"within."
33	"without."
366	

Does this number refer to the 366 days of our author's solar year? Noah was in the ark one solar year.

[8] The first editions read: "Tanchuma."

[9] According to the Book of Jashar v. 34 Noah took five years to build the ark; see *A.N.C.L.* xviii. p. 344.

[10] The first editions add: "and evil deeds," but omit: "But they did not repent." See the Book of Adam and Eve, *loc. cit.* The same tradition occurs in the writings of several of the Church Fathers: Theophilus of Antioch (*To Autolycus*, iii. 19), Ephraim of Syria (on Jonah, 13); Revelation of Paul, *A.N.C.L.* xvi. p. 491; and Book of the Bee, p. 31; see also *supra*, pp. 161 f.

the Holy One, blessed be He, wished to increase the clean and to diminish the unclean (animals), He called to Noah and said to him: Take to thee into the ark of all clean beasts seven and seven,[1] the male and his female; and of the unclean beasts two and two, the male and his female, as it is said, "Of every || clean beast thou shalt take to thee [2] seven and seven, the male and his female; and of the beasts that are not clean two, the male and his female" (*ibid.* vii. 2).

Noah said to the Holy One, blessed be He: Sovereign of all the world! Have I then the strength to collect them unto me to the ark? The angels appointed over each kind went down and gathered them,[3] and with them all their food unto him to the ark. They came to him of their own accord,[4] as it is said, "And *they* came unto Noah into the ark" (*ibid.* 9); they came by themselves. "And they brought (them) to Noah" is not written here, but, "And they *came* unto Noah into the ark." [5]

Rabbi Mana said: When all the creatures had entered (the ark), the Holy One, blessed be He, closed and sealed [6] with His hand the gate [7] of the ark, as it is said, "And the Lord shut him in" (*ibid.* 16).

Rabbi Meir said: One pearl was suspended in the ark, and shed light upon all the creatures in the ark, like a lamp which gives light [8] inside [9] the house, and like the sun

[1] The first editions end the paragraph here.

[2] The quotation ends here in the MS., which adds "etc."

[3] The Book of Adam and Eve (ed. Malan) III. viii. says: "My power shall go with it (the trumpet blast) to make it come into the ears of the beasts and the birds. . . . I will command my angel to blow the horn from heaven, and all these animals shall be gathered unto thee." Cf. Pal. Targum on Gen. vi. 20: "they shall enter to thee by the hand of the angel, who will take and cause them to enter to thee."

[4] This is not in the printed texts. For a similar legend see Gen. Rab. xxxii. 4 and 5, and cf. Ephraim, Sermon on Repentance i. 3.

[5] This sentence is not in the printed texts. In the previous sentence the first editions read: "'And Noah brought' is not written in the Scripture, but 'And they came unto Noah.'"

[6] The same expression occurs in the Book of Adam and Eve (ed. Malan) III. ix.

[7] Or, "door."

[8] See Pal. Targum, *in loc.*; T.B. Synhedrin, *loc. cit.*; Jalkuṭ, Gen., *in loc.*; Gen. Rab. xxxi. 11, which has a different version as compared with the Talmudic version of the legend. According to the Midrash it is Rabbi Levi who gives the tradition. Cf. Lekach Tob, *in loc.*, and *supra*, p. 21.

[9] The first editions read: "by its power, as it is said: 'A light shalt thou make,'" etc.

yonder which shines in his might, as it is said, "A light shalt thou make to the ark" (*ibid.* vi. 16).

Rabbi Zadok said: On the 10th of Marcheshvan all the creatures entered the ark; on the 17th of the same[1] (month) the waters of the Flood descended from heaven upon the earth, for they were the waters (endowed with the) male (principle). And there came up the waters of the depths, for they are the waters (endowed) with the female (principle),[2] and they were joined with one another, and they prevailed so as to destroy || the world,[3] as it is said, "And the waters prevailed exceedingly upon the earth" (*ibid.* vii. 19).

And all living things which were upon the face of the earth decayed,[4] as it is said, "And every living thing was destroyed which was upon the face of the ground" (*ibid.* 23), except Noah and those who were with him in the ark, as it is said, "And Noah only was left, and they that were with him in the ark" (*ibid.*), except Og,[5] king of Bashan, who sat down on a piece of wood under the gutter[6] of the ark. He swore to Noah and to his sons that he would be their servant for ever.[7] What did Noah do? He bored an aperture in the ark, and he put (through it) his food daily for him, and he also was left, as it is said, "For only Og, king of Bashan, remained of the remnant of the giants" (Deut. iii. 11).

(The Flood was universal) except in the land of Israel,[8] upon which the water of the Flood did not descend from

[1] See Pal. Targum, Gen. vii. 11; and compare our text with the Scripture text. See also T.B. Rosh Ha-Shanah, 11b; Seder 'Olam Rab. iv. p. 10a, note 17. Rabbi Eliezer held the view that the world was created in Ellul and Adam in Tishri.

[2] See *supra*, p. 30; T.J. Berakhoth ix. 3. 14a, and Eth Enoch liv. 8 The rain from heaven is the male principle.

[3] The living creatures in the world.

[4] The first editions read: "were destroyed."

[5] See T.B. Niddah, 61a, and *Rabbinic Philosophy and Ethics*, p. 267. The Midrashic interpretation of the word "Rephaim" (Deut. iii. 11) gave rise to this legend. See Job xxvi. 5, *supra*, p. 112, and *infra*, p. 253. The legend which connects Og with the "Paliṭ" is ignored by our book, which identifies Og with Eliezer, the servant of Abraham. The "Paliṭ" is identified with Michael, see *infra*, pp. 193 f.; and cf. *J.E.* ix. 388, and Grünbaum, *op. cit.* p. 80.

[6] The first editions read: "On a rung of (one of) the ladders."

[7] See *supra*, p. 112.

[8] See T.B. Ẓebachim, 113a; Nachmanides in his commentary on Gen., *in loc.*, and 3 Baruch iv. 10.

heaven, but the waters were gathered together from all lands, and they entered therein, as it is said, "Son of man, say unto her, Thou art a land that is not cleansed, nor rained upon, in the day of indignation"[1] (Ezek. xxii. 24). He[2] sent forth the raven to ascertain what was (the state of) the world. It went and found a carcase of a man cast upon the summit of a mountain,[3] and it settled thereon for its food,[4] and it did not return with its message to its sender, as it is said, "And he sent forth the raven" (Gen. viii. 7). He sent forth the dove to see what was (the state of) the world, and she brought back her message to her sender, as it is said, "And the dove came in to him at eventide,[5] and, lo, in her mouth an olive leaf pluckt off"[6] (*ibid.* 11). And why in her mouth was an olive leaf pluckt off? || The dove spake before the Holy One, blessed be He, saying: Sovereign of all worlds! Let my food be bitter like this olive, and let it be entrusted[7] to Thy hand, and let it not be sweet (even) as honey, and given by the hand of flesh and blood.[8] Hence they[9] said: He who sends a message by the hand of an unclean (messenger)[10] is (like) sending by the hand of a fool, and he who sends a message by the hands of a clean (messenger) is like sending by the hand of a messenger faithful to his senders.[11]

Rabbi Zadok said: For twelve[12] months all the creatures

[1] The land in the text is interpreted by the Midrash as referring to the Holy Land at the time of the Flood.

[2] *i.e.* Noah. The first editions read: "Noah."

[3] Lit. "upon the tops of the mountains."

[4] Cf. the interpretation of Job xxiv. 20, in Gen. Rab. xxxiii.

[5] The MS. ends the quotation at "eventide." The first editions continue the verse. Pal. Targum, Gen. viii. 11, reads: "And the dove came to him at the evening time, and behold, a leaf of olive gathered, broken off, she brought in her mouth, and which she had taken from the mount of Olives." Palestine had escaped the deluge. See Seder 'Olam Rab. iv. p. 10b, note 27, and Tosaphoth to 'Erubin 18b.

[6] Cf. the R.V.

[7] The first editions read: "and given by Thy hand."

[8] Cf. Gen. Rab. xxxiii. 6; T.B. Synhedrin, 108b; and *Rabbinic Philosophy and Ethics*, p. 41. See also Revelation of Paul, *loc. cit.*

[9] The sages of Israel.

[10] Later editions read: "evil." The raven was "unclean," whilst the dove was a "clean" bird; see *Rabbinic Philosophy and Ethics*, pp. 40 f.

[11] Cf. Prov. xxv. 13 for a similar expression; see Jalkut, Gen. § 58; Aboth de R. Nathan (*a*) xxxiv. p. 51b.

[12] See Mishnah 'Edujoth ii.; and Seder 'Olam Rab. iv. p. 9b. The Flood began on the 17th of Marcheshvan, and on the 27th of this month, a

were in the ark; and Noah stood and prayed before the Holy One, blessed be He, saying before Him:[1] Sovereign of all worlds! Bring me forth from this prison, for my soul is faint, because of the stench[2] of lions.[3] Through me will all the righteous crown Thee with a crown of sovereignty,[4] because Thou hast brought me forth from this prison, as it is said, "Bring my soul out of prison,[5] that I may give thanks unto thy name: for the righteous shall crown me, when thou wilt have dealt bountifully with me" (Ps. cxlii. 7).[6]

Rabbi Levitas, a man of Jamnia, said: He separated the males from the females of all which came to the ark[7] when they came into the ark, as it is said, "And Noah went in, and his sons, and his wife, and his sons' wives" (Gen. vii. 7). Verily the males were on one side.[8] When they went forth from the ark, He caused the males to be joined with the females, as it is said, "Go forth of the ark, thou, and thy wife,[9] and thy sons, and thy sons' wives with thee" (*ibid.* viii. 16). Verily a man with his wife (went forth), "Thy sons, and thy sons' wives with thee"[10] (*ibid.*) || He blessed them, that they might increase and multiply on the earth, as it is said, "And God blessed Noah and his sons,[11]

year later, Noah was released. This period lasted one year and eleven days, *i.e.* one lunar year plus eleven days, which is the duration of a solar year.

[1] See the fine prayer in the Book of Jashar vi. 31, which has used our *P.R.E.* See Tanchuma, Noah § ix. The basis of the prayer here is probably Isa. xlix. 9.

[2] Luria suggests that the text should read: "the dread."

[3] The first editions add: "bears and leopards."

[4] The story of Noah forms part of the "Zichronoth" in the Synagogue liturgy for the New Year. For another explanation see Tanchuma, Gen., *loc. cit.* See Introduction.

[5] In the MS. the quotation ends here; the first editions continue the verse.

[6] See the Book of Jashar vi. 36.

[7] The first editions omit: "when they came into the ark." See the Book of Adam and Eve (ed. Malan) III. vii. f.; T.J. Ta'anith i. 6. 64d; T.B. Synhedrin, *loc. cit.*; Gen. Rab. xxxi. 12. The Church has in some quarters to this day retained the custom of separating the sexes at Divine worship. For other references see Ginzberg, *op. cit.* p. 82, who quotes Origen and Ephraim.

[8] The first editions add: "And the females were on the other side." The legend occurs also in Hippolytus (ed. Achelis), G.T., *loc. cit.*

[9] The MSS. end the quotation here: the first editions continue the verse.

[10] Cf. Luria's reading.

[11] The MS. ends the quotation here; the first editions continue the verse till the word "multiply."

and said unto them, Be fruitful, and multiply, and replenish the earth" (*ibid.* ix. 1). The sons of Noah were fruitful and multiplied, and they begat sons with their twins with them.[1]

Noah found a vine which was lying there,[2] which had come out of the garden of Eden.[3] It had its clusters with it, and he took of its fruit and ate, and rejoiced in his heart,[4] as it is said, "My wine, which cheereth God and man" (Judg. ix. 13). He planted a vineyard with it. On the selfsame day it produced and became ripe [5] with its fruits, as it is said, "In the day of thy planting thou dost make it grow,[6] and in the morning thou makest thy seed to blossom" (Isa. xvii. 11).[7] He drank wine thereof, and he became exposed in the midst of the tent, as it is said, "And he drank of the wine, and was drunken; and he was uncovered within his tent" (Gen. ix. 21).[8] Canaan entered and saw the nakedness of Noah, and he bound a thread (where the mark of) the Covenant [9] was, and emasculated him. He went forth and told his brethren. Ham entered and saw his nakedness. He did not take to heart the duty of honouring (one's father [10]). But he [11] told his two brothers in the market,[12] making sport [13] of his father. His two

[1] This sentence does not occur in the printed editions. See Midrash Haggadol, c. 165.

[2] The first editions read: "which had been cast forth."

[3] Pal. Targum, Gen. ix. 20, reads: "And he found a vine which the river had brought away from the garden of Eden." Apparently our Midrash wishes to connect the folly of Noah with the sin of Adam; see Siphrê, Deut. § 323. Cf. T.B. Synhedrin, 70a, Gen. Rab. xxxvi. 3, and Zohar, Gen. 73a. See 3 Baruch iv. 10 ff.

[4] The first editions read: "and he desired them in his heart." The quotation which follows in our text is omitted by the printed editions.

[5] The 1st ed. and several later editions read: "its fruits ripened."

[6] The quotation ends here in the MS. and first editions.

[7] Note the preceding verse in Isaiah. See *Rabbinic Philosophy and Ethics*, p. 43.

[8] The quotation does not occur in the printed editions of our book.

[9] *i.e.* Circumcision. The legend that Noah was an eunuch occurs also in Theophilus of Antioch (*To Autolycus*, iii. 19). See also Zohar, Gen. 73b, and Grünbaum, *op. cit.* p. 86.

[10] Our MS. reads: "the duty (or precept) of 'Honour'" (Ex. xx. 12). Some editions (Amsterdam) add: "and mother." See Book of Adam and Eve (ed. Malan) III. xiii. According to Luria the text should continue: "therefore was he cursed by being called a slave"; see Tanchuma, ed. Buber, Gen. 24b.

[11] The first editions read: "He went forth and told."

[12] So also the Targumim, *in loc.* Perhaps the translation should be "outside."

[13] See Justin Martyr, *Dial. c. Tryph.* cxxxix.; "who *mocked* at his father's nakedness."

brothers rebuked him. What did they do? They took the curtain of the east [1] with them, and they went backwards and covered [2] the nakedness of their father, as it is said, "And Shem and Japheth took a garment,[3] and laid it upon both their shoulders, and went backward, and covered the nakedness of their father; and their faces were backward, and they saw not their father's nakedness" (*ibid.* 23).

Noah awoke from his wine, and he knew what the younger son of Ham had done unto him, and he cursed him,[4] as it is said, "And he said, Cursed be Canaan" (*ibid.* 25). Noah sat and mused in his heart, saying: The Holy One, blessed be He, delivered me || from the waters of the Flood, and brought me forth from that prison, and am I not obliged to bring before Thee a sacrifice and burnt offerings? [5] What did Noah do? He took from the clean [6] animals an ox and a sheep,[7] and from all the clean birds, a turtle-dove and pigeons; and he built up the first altar upon which Cain and Abel [8] had brought offerings, and he brought four burnt offerings, as it is said, "And Noah builded an altar unto the Lord; and took of every [9] clean beast, and of every clean fowl, and he offered burnt offerings on the altar" (*ibid.* viii. 20). It is written here only, "and he offered burnt offerings on the altar," and the sweet savour ascended before the Holy One, blessed be He, and [10] it was pleasing to Him, as it is said, "And the Lord smelled the sweet savour" (*ibid.* 21). What did the Holy One,

[1] Or "veil of the east," the veil or curtain used to shield one from the heat and glare of the sun. The 2nd ed. reads: "the cover."

[2] See Midrash Agadah, Gen. p. 23, note 16.

[3] The quotation ends here in the MS. and first editions.

[4] See Gen. Rab., *loc. cit.*, and Justin Martyr, *Dial. c. Tryph.*, *loc. cit.*; for other references to Church Fathers see Ginzberg, *op. cit.* p. 86.

[5] See Zohar, Gen. 70a. There is considerable agreement between the Zohar and *P.R.E.* in this and the next chapter.

[6] See Book of Adam and Eve (ed. Malan) III. xi.

[7] The first editions add: "and a goat."

[8] Pal. Targum, Gen. viii. 20, reads: "And Noah built an altar before the Lord; that altar which Adam had built at the time when he was cast forth from the garden of Eden, and had offered an offering upon it; and upon it had Cain and Abel offered their offerings." Cf. also T.B. Zebachim, 115b, and Gen. Rab. xxxiv. 9.

[9] The quotation ends here in the MS.

[10] The first editions add: "as it is said, 'and he offered burnt offerings on the altar'" (Gen. viii. 20).

blessed be He, do? He put forth His right hand, and swore to Noah[1] that He would not[2] bring the waters of the Flood upon the earth, as it is said, "For this is as the waters of Noah unto me; for as I have sworn[3] that the waters of Noah should no more go over the earth" (Isa. liv. 9). And He gave a sign in the rainbow as a sign of the covenant of the oath between Himself and the people, as it is said, "I do set my bow in the cloud,[4] and it shall be for a token of a covenant" (Gen. ix. 13).

And thus our sages instituted[5] that they should (mention)[6] the oath to Noah every day, as it is said, "That your days may be multiplied, and the days of your children, upon the land[7] which the Lord sware unto your fathers to give them, as the days of the heavens above the earth" (Deut. xi. 21).

Noah brought his sons and his grandsons, and he blessed them with their (several) settlements,[8] and he gave them as an inheritance all the earth.[9] He especially blessed[10] Shem and his sons, (making them) dark but comely,[11] and he gave them the habitable earth.[12] He blessed Ham and

[1] See *infra*, pp. 335, 347; and cf. Tanchuma, Noah § xi.

[2] The first editions add here: "again."

[3] The quotation ends here in the MS. and the first editions, which add: "etc."

[4] In the MS. the quotation ends here; it is continued in the first editions.

[5] See T.B. Berakhoth, 13a, for the daily recital of the story of the Exodus. The Scripture passage quoted occurs in the second section of the "Shema'"; see Singer, p. 41. The ritual question involved here is interesting, because the actual narrative of the oath to Noah is not recited daily. The verse quoted as a reason for this institution continues, after the word "land," thus: "which the Lord *sware* unto your fathers to give them." This was not the oath to Noah. See Eth. Enoch lv. 2.

[6] The MS. omits "mention"; it occurs in the first editions.

[7] The first editions end the quotation here; in the MS. the last word quoted is "children." In the printed texts this quotation is the conclusion of the chapter. Our MS. continues with a section which forms part of chapter xxiv. in the printed editions.

[8] The first editions read: "gifts."

[9] The division of the earth among the sons of Noah is also mentioned by Jubilees viii. 10, and was known to the Church Father, Epiphanius (G.T. pp. 217 ff.).

[10] The verb is repeated.

[11] Cf. Cant. i. 5; but they were not "black"; the Oxford MS. (O.A. 167) reads: "white and comely."

[12] Not the sea which was the lot of the sons of Ham, nor the deserts which fell to the sons of Japheth. Shem has his tents and fixed abode in the habitable lands of the earth.

his sons, (making them) dark || like the raven,[1] and he gave them as an inheritance the coast of the sea.[2] He blessed Japheth and his sons, (making) them entirely white,[3] and he gave them for an inheritance the desert and its fields;[4] these (are the inheritances with) which he endowed them.[5]

[1] Luria reads, as an emendation, "black and uncomely"; cf. Gen. Rab. xxxvi. 7. If our MS. text be accepted, a parallel may be found in Cant. v. 11.

[2] *e.g.* the Egyptians on the seacoast, or the Sidonians on the Phœnician coast; cf. Jer. xlvii. 7.

[3] The first editions add: "and beautiful." Japheth as a word signifies "beauty." The sons of Japheth were the migratory tribes from the north, *e.g.* the Goths who settled in Europe. See Eth. Enoch lxxxviii. 9.

[4] The first editions read: "desert and fields."

[5] *i.e.* the children of Noah. The words in brackets occur in the first editions. See Introduction, pp. xxiv. f., and li.

CHAPTER XXIV

NIMROD AND THE TOWER OF BABEL [28B. i.]

RABBI ELIEZER [1] said: They begat their sons and increased and multiplied like a great reptile, six at each birth,[2] and they were all one people, and one heart, and one language, as it is said, "And the whole earth was of one language and of one speech" (Gen. xi. 1).[3] They despised the pleasant land,[4] as it is said, "And it came to pass, as they journeyed [5] in the east" (*ibid.* 2). They went to the land of Shinar, and found there a large stone,[6] very extensive, and the whole plain, and they dwelt there, as it is said, "And they found a plain in the land of Shinar, and they dwelt there" (*ibid.*).

Rabbi 'Aḳiba said: They cast off the Kingdom of Heaven [7] from themselves, and appointed Nimrod king over themselves; a slave son of a slave. Are not all the sons of Ham slaves? [8] And woe to the land when a slave rules,[9] as it is said, "For a servant, when he is king" [10] (Prov. xxx. 22).

Rabbi Chakhinai [11] said: Nimrod was a mighty hero,

[1] The first editions read "Ilai."

[2] We have had this expression *supra*, p. 161. It is an "Oriental" exaggeration, signifying the prolific nature of the people.

[3] See Pal. Targum, *in loc.*

[4] Palestine; cf. Ps. cvi. 24, and Ẓohar, Gen. 75b.

[5] "In the east" might also be rendered "in the commencement," or "at first"; see Ẓohar, Gen. 74b.

[6] The first editions read: "a large and extensive land, entirely a plain."

[7] See T.B. 'Erubin, 53a; cf. Pal. Targum to Gen. x. 8 on Nimrod; see also the Book of Jashar vii. 46 ff., and Jeraḥmeel lvii. 14. Augustine rendered Gen. x. 9, "Nimrod was a hunter against God" (*de Civ. Dei*, xvi. 4).

[8] The Venice edition reads: "are slaves."

[9] The phraseology is based on Eccles. x. 16.

[10] The previous verse says, "The earth trembles." Nimrod caused the people to tremble, as a result of discarding the Kingdom of Heaven.

[11] The first editions read "Chanina."

as it is said, "And Cush begat Nimrod, who began to be a mighty one in the earth" (Gen. x. 8). Rabbi Jehudah said:[1] The coats[2] which the Holy One, blessed be He, made for Adam and his wife, were with Noah[3] in the ark, and when they went forth from the ark, || Ham, the son of Noah, brought them forth with him, and gave them as an inheritance to Nimrod.[4] When he put them on, all beasts, animals, and birds, when they saw the coats,[5] came and prostrated themselves before him.[6] The sons of men[7] thought that this (was due) to the power of his might; therefore they made him king over themselves, as it is said, "Wherefore it is said, Like Nimrod, a mighty hunter before the Lord" (*ibid.* 9).[8]

Nimrod said to his people:[9] Come, let us build a great city for ourselves, and let us dwell therein, lest we be scattered upon the face of all the earth, as the first people[10] (were). Let us build a great tower in its midst, ascending to heaven,[11] for the power of the Holy One, blessed be He, is only in the water,[12] and let us make us a great name on the earth, as it is said, "And let us make us a name" (*ibid.* xi. 4).

[1] See *Rabbinic Philosophy and Ethics*, pp. 44 f. On the garments of Adam and Eve see the Book of Jashar, vii. 24 ff.; Gen. Rab. xx. 12 and lxv. 16; Pal. Targ. Gen. xxv. 27, xxvii. 15.

[2] The first editions read "coat." See Book of the Bee, p. 35.

[3] The first editions read "them." See Hippolytus, *A.N.C.L.* vi. p. 492.

[4] The *Recognitions of Clement*, iv. 27, speak of Ham as the first magician and refer to Nimrod as follows: "the magic art having been handed down to him as by a flash" (*ibid.* 29).

[5] The MS. reads: "the writing" (הכתב).

[6] See Rashi on T.B. Pesachim, 54b, and the Book of Jashar, *loc. cit.*

[7] The first editions read "they," *i.e.* his fellow-countrymen; see Jalkut, Gen. § 62. See *J.E.* ix. 309.

[8] The next verse says, "The beginning of his *kingdom*." See Josephus, *Ant.* i. 4. 2; T.B. Pesachim, 94b; and cf. Pal. Targum, *in loc.*, and the Book of the Bee, p. 37.

[9] See T.B. Chullin, 89a; Gen. Rab. xxvi. 4; and cf. Leḳach Ṭob, Gen. p. 27a.

[10] At the Flood. According to Jubilees vii. 20, Noah enjoined upon his sons commandments "to cover the shame of their flesh, and to bless their Creator, and honour father and mother, and love their neighbour, and guard their souls from fornication and uncleanness and all iniquity. For owing to these three things came the flood upon the earth."

[11] See T.B. Synhedrin, 109a, and Othijoth de R. 'Aḳiba, letter Resh. *B.H.M.* iii. pp. 46 f.

[12] Luria thinks that the correct reading should be "in heaven," and not "in the water."

Rabbi Phineas said: There were no stones there wherewith to build the city and the tower. What did they do? They baked bricks and burnt them like a builder[1] (would do), until they built it seven[2] mils[3] high, and it had ascents on its east and west. (The labourers) who took up the bricks went up on the eastern (ascent), and those who descended went down on the western (descent). If a man fell and died they paid no heed to him, but if a brick fell they || sat down and wept, and said: Woe is us! when will another one come in its stead?[4]

And Abraham,[5] son of Terah,[6] passed by, and saw them building the city and the tower, and he cursed them in the name of his God,[7] as it is said, "Swallow up, O Lord, divide their language" (Ps. lv. 9). But they rejected his words,[8] like a stone cast upon the ground. Is it not a fact that every choice and good[9] stone is only put at the corner of a building? and with reference to this, the text says, "The stone which the builders rejected is become the head of the corner" (*ibid.* cxviii. 22).

Rabbi Simeon said: The Holy One, blessed be He, called to the seventy[10] angels, who surround the throne of His glory, and He said to them: Come, let us descend and let us confuse the seventy nations and the seventy languages.[11]

Whence (do we know) that the Holy One, blessed be

[1] Or "stone mason."

[2] The first editions read "seventy." See Book of the Bee, p. 41.

[3] "Mil" (mille) =2000 cubits. According to the Jalkut, Gen. *in loc.*, the height was seven miles; see also Jalkut Makhiri, Ps. lv. p. 145b. The MS. adds "of property."

[4] This indifference to the value of human life reappears in the story of the Egyptian bondage; see *infra*, p. 386. See also *Rabbinic Philosophy and Ethics*, p. 46, and cf. 3 Baruch iii. 5.

[5] In the first editions the name is "Abram." See Wisdom x. 5.

[6] Terah was one of those who assisted in the building of the Tower of Babel, according to the Zohar, Lev. 111b.

[7] The expression is borrowed from 2 Kings ii. 24. See Seder 'Olam Rab. i. p. 3a.

[8] Abraham uttered his reproof in vain. See Jalḳuṭ, Pss. § 703.

[9] See 1 Sam. ix. 2 for this phrase.

[10] The seventy nations with Israel form the human family. Israel has no guardian angel; God is the Guardian of Israel. See LXX, Deut. xxxii. 8, for the earliest form of this Midrash. Augustine, *de Civ. Dei*, xvi. 5, offers a parallel to this Haggadah. See also Hippolytus (ed. Achelis), ii. p. 243; Clement of Alexandria, *Strom.* vi. 17; and *Recognitions of Clement*, ii. 42.

[11] The first editions read: "Come, let us confuse their speech."

He, spake[1] to them? Because it is said, "Go to, let *us* go down" (Gen. xi. 7). "I will go down" is not written, but "Go to, let *us* go down."[2] And they cast lots among them. Because it is said, "When the Most High gave to the nations their inheritance" (Deut. xxxii. 8). The lot of the Holy One, blessed be He, fell upon Abraham and upon his seed,[3] as it is said, "For the Lord's portion is his people; Jacob is the *lot* of his inheritance" (*ibid.* 9).

The Holy One, blessed be He, said: The portion and lot which have fallen to Me,[4] My soul liveth thereby,[5] as it is said, "The lots have fallen unto me in pleasures; yea, I have a goodly heritage" (Ps. xvi. 6). The Holy One, blessed be He, descended with the seventy angels, who surround || the throne of His glory, and they confused their speech into seventy[6] nations and seventy languages. Whence do we know that the Holy One, blessed be He, descended? Because it is said, "And the Lord God *came down* to see the city and the tower" (Gen. xi. 5). This was the second descent.[7]

And they wished to speak one to another in the language[8] of his fellow-countryman, but one did not understand the language of his fellow. What did they do? Every one took his sword, and they fought one another to destroy (each other), and half the world fell there by the sword, and thence the Lord scattered them upon the face of all the earth, as it is said, "So the Lord scattered them abroad on that account, upon the face of all the earth" (*ibid.* 8).

Rabbi Meir said: Esau, the brother of Jacob, saw the

[1] Luria reads, "He called." The first editions read: "descended unto them."

[2] See Jalkuṭ Makhiri, Pss., *loc. cit.*, and cf. Gen. Rab. xxxviii. 10.

[3] Some editions read: "and upon his house."

[4] See Jalkuṭ, Psalms, § 667.

[5] The first editions read: "My soul delighteth in him."

[6] Some editions read, "seventy languages." The first editions add: "Each nation had its own writing and its own language, and He appointed an angel over each people. And Israel fell unto His lot and portion, and concerning this it is said, 'For the Lord's portion is his people'" (Deut. xxxii. 9). Each nation had not only its own language but also its peculiar style of writing.

[7] See *supra*, p. 97.

[8] The first editions read, "in the holy language." See *supra*, p. 161. The original language was Hebrew. See for a parallel legend, *Recognitions of Clement*, i. 30, and the Book of the Bee, p. 42.

coats [1] of Nimrod, and in his heart he coveted them,[2] and he slew him,[3] and took them from him.[4] Whence (do we know) that they were desirable in his sight? Because it is said, "And Rebecca took the *precious* raiment of Esau, her elder son" (*ibid.* xxvii. 15). When he put them on he also became, by means of them, a mighty [5] hero, as it is said, "And Esau was a cunning hunter" (*ibid.* xxv. 27). And when Jacob went forth [6] from the presence of Isaac, his father, he said: Esau, the wicked one, is not worthy to wear these coats. What did he do? He dug in the earth and hid them there, as it is said, "A noose [7] is hid for him in the earth" (Job xviii. 10).

[1] The first editions add: "which the Holy One, blessed be He, made for Adam and Eve."

[2] The Venice edition reads, as in our text, "them"; but the Prague edition reads "it" (*i.e.* one garment).

[3] See the Book of Jashar vii. 24, and Pal. Targum, Gen. xxv. 27 f. The wonderful garments of Adam and Eve have a parallel in the seamless tunic of the Founder of Christianity, see *A.N.C.L.* xvi. pp. 235 f.

[4] See Midrash Agadah, Gen. xxvii. 13; Leḳach Ṭob, Gen. p. 66b and 67a; Jalḳuṭ, Gen. § 115; cf. Rashi on T.B. Pesachim, 54b, and Tanchuma, Toledoth, § xii.

[5] The sentence is wanting in the Oxford MS. (O.A. 167).

[6] After receiving the blessing from Isaac.

[7] The rest of the verse says, "and a trap for him in the way." The garments enabled the wearer to catch the animals. See Pal. Targum, Gen. xxvii. 15; and Jalḳuṭ, Gen. § 115.

CHAPTER XXV

THE SIN OF SODOM [29A. ii.]

THE third descent [1] which He descended [2] || was at Sodom, as it is said, "I will go down now and see" (Gen. xviii. 21). The Holy One, blessed be He, said: Shall I not [3] tell My friend Abraham an important matter which I will do in My world in the future, as it is said, "And the Lord said, Shall I hide from Abraham that which I do?" (*ibid.* 17). Rabbi Chanina, son of Dosa,[4] said: The Holy One, blessed be He, was revealed, and three angels [5] (appeared) unto our father Abraham, as it is said, "And he lifted up his eyes and looked, and, lo, three men" (*ibid.* 2). He [6] began to inform him about the conception [7] of the womb by Sarah his wife, as it is said, "I will certainly return unto thee when the season cometh round" (*ibid.* 10). Afterwards He [8] told (him) about the doom [9] of Sodom,[10] as it is said, "And the Lord said, Because the cry of Sodom and Gomorrah is great" (*ibid.* 20).

[1] See preceding chapter. On the ten descents see Ẓohar, Gen. 75a; Aboth de Rabbi Nathan (*a*) xxxiv.; Gen. Rab. xxxviii. 9 and xlix. 6; and Jalḳuṭ, Gen. § 27 and § 83, and *supra*, p. 97, note 1.

[2] The first editions read: "which the Holy One, blessed be He, descended."

[3] The first editions read: "I will tell."

[4] The first editions read here "Chaninah."

[5] According to our book, God with three angels appeared to Abraham at Mamre; see Rashbam, Ibn Ezra, and Nachmanides, *in loc.* (Gen. xviii.). According to Midrash Agadah, Gen. (p. 39), the three angels were Michael, Gabriel, and Raphael. See also T.B. Joma, 37a, and Leḳach Ṭob, Gen. p. 41b.

[6] The first editions read: "One" (angel).

[7] On the angelic message to Abraham see T.B. Baba Mezi'a, 86b; Pal. Targum to Gen. xviii. 2; Gen. Rab. xlviii. 16 and l. 2; Ẓohar, Gen. 99a.

[8] Instead of "Afterwards," the first editions read: "Another" (angel).

[9] Lit. the work, or affair, or business.

[10] The first editions add: "and Gomorrah."

Hence thou mayest learn:[1] Everyone, who wishes to tell his companion a matter which is a disgrace to him, begins with a good word[2] and concludes with the evil matter which is unpleasant to him. Whence do we learn this? From the Holy One, blessed be He, for when He was revealed to our father Abraham, He began to announce to him (the good news) concerning the conception by Sarah his wife. Afterwards He told him about the fate of Sodom, as it is said, "And the Lord said, Because the cry of Sodom and Gomorrah is great" (*ibid.*).[3] (Abraham) began to ask for compassion before Him on behalf of Lot, the son of his brother. He spake before Him: Sovereign of all worlds! Like the death of the wicked shall the death of the || righteous be? (As it is said),[4] "Wilt thou consume the righteous[5] with the wicked?" (*ibid.* 23). The Holy One, blessed be He, answered him: Abraham![6] By the merit of the righteous[7] (one) will I forgive Sodom.[8] "If I find in Sodom fifty righteous" (*ibid.* 26), then will I forgive it all its[9] sins.

Hence they[10] said: If there be fifty righteous in the world, the world exists through their righteousness. (Abraham) arose and began to beseech (God), and made supplication before Him until he brought (the number down to) ten. Hence (the sages said):[11] (When there are) ten people in a place, the place is delivered by their righteousness, as it is said, "And he said, I will not destroy it for the sake of the ten" (*ibid.* 32).[12]

[1] The first editions read: "they said," *i.e.* the sages.

[2] This rule still obtains in connection with the public recital of the Torah; see Orach Chayyim, 138.

[3] The first editions omit the repetition of the quotation here.

[4] "As it is said" is omitted in the MS.

[5] "The righteous" in the Hebrew is in the singular number; this fact might suggest the idea that Abraham was referring to Lot.

[6] The first editions add: "By thy life!"

[7] The first editions read: "By the merit of fifty righteous (people)."

[8] The first editions read: "as it is said."

[9] The first editions read: "their."

[10] The sages.

[11] The first editions read: "Hence the sages said: If there be ten righteous people in a place, by their merit the place is delivered."

[12] See Gen. Rab. xlix. 13; Shocher Tob, Ps. v. p. 26b; and Ẓohar, Gen. 105b. Jer. v. 1 is the Biblical authority for the doctrine that the merit of the individual procures Divine forgiveness; cf. Ezek. xiv.

Rabbi Ẓeera said: The men of Sodom were the wealthy men of prosperity,[1] on account of the good and fruitful land[2] whereon they dwelt. For every need which the world requires, they obtained therefrom. They procured gold therefrom, as it is said, "And it had dust of gold" (Job xxviii. 6). What[3] is the meaning (of the text), "And it had dust of gold"? At the hour when one of them wished to buy a vegetable, he would say to his servant, Go and purchase for me (for the value of) an assar.[4] He went and bought (it), and found beneath it heaps of gold;[5] thus it is written, "And it had dust of gold"[6] (*ibid.*). They obtained silver therefrom, as it is said, "Surely there is a mine for silver" (*ibid.* 1). They procured precious stones and pearls thence, as it is said, || "The stones thereof are the place of sapphires" (*ibid.* 6). They obtained bread therefrom, as it is said, "As for the earth, out of it cometh bread" (*ibid.* 5). But they did not trust in the shadow of their Creator, but (they trusted) in the multitude of their wealth,[7] for wealth thrusts aside its owners from the fear of Heaven,[8] as it is said, "They that trust in their wealth" (Ps. xlix. 6).[9]

Rabbi Nathaniel[10] said: The men of Sodom had no consideration for the honour of their Owner by (not) distributing

19. The inference as to the salvation of the *world* by the merit of fifty righteous people is derived from God's words in Gen. xviii. 26: "And I will spare for their sake *all* the place" (*i.e.* every place). Abraham had spoken merely of "the place."

1 The first editions read: "the wealthy men of the world."

2 Sodom was situated at the right of Jerusalem; see Ezek. xvi. 46. The phraseology in our text is borrowed from Num. xiii. 19, 20.

3 The first editions omit this sentence.

4 Assar = Assarius = $\frac{1}{24}$ of a silver Denar. On this point see Krauss, *T.A.* ii. p. 407. The first editions add: "(some) vegetables."

5 Lit. "full of gold." The first editions read: "gold." See T.B. Synhedrin, 109a; Siphrê, Deut. § 43; and Tosephta Soṭah iii. p. 296.

6 See Lev. Rab. v. 2; and Jalkuṭ, Job, § 915. The idea of the Haggadah seems to be as follows: When the vegetable was bought at the cost of an Assar, the dust of the earth which was clinging to the vegetable was so valuable (owing to the gold which it contained) that the purchaser received back more than he had paid.

7 See Ps. lii. 9; the Midrashim refer this passage to the story of Sodom.

8 The first editions read: "thrusts aside from its owners the fear of Heaven."

9 See Prov. xxx. 8.

10 The first editions read: "Joshua, son of Ḳorchah."

food to the wayfarer and the stranger,[1] but they (even) fenced in [2] all the trees on top above their fruit so that they should not be seized;[3] (not) even by the bird of heaven, as it is said, "That path no bird of prey knoweth" (Job xxviii. 7).

Rabbi Joshua, son of Ḳorchah,[4] said: They appointed over themselves judges who were lying judges, and they oppressed every wayfarer [1] and stranger who entered Sodom by their perverse judgment, and they sent them forth naked, as it is said, "They have oppressed the stranger without judgment" (Ezek. xxii. 29).[5]

They were dwelling in security without care and at ease, without the fear of war from all their surroundings, as it is said, "Their houses are safe from fear" (Job xxi. 9).[6] They were sated with all the produce of the earth, but they did not strengthen with the loaf of bread either the hand of the needy or of the poor,[7] as it is said, "Behold, this was the iniquity of thy sister Sodom; pride, fulness of bread,[8] and prosperous ease was in her and in her daughters; neither did she strengthen the hand of the poor and needy" (Ezek. xvi. 49).[9] ||

Rabbi Jehudah said: They made a proclamation in Sodom (saying): Everyone who strengthens the hand of the poor or the needy with a loaf of bread shall be burnt

[1] The first editions read: "the native and the stranger"; see Job xxviii. 4. They caused human intercourse with the outside world to cease. To honour God is to be merciful; see Prov. iii. 3 and xiv. 31; T.B. Sabbath, 127a. The men of Sodom did not suffer the birds to praise God by singing on the trees in their land. The Book of Jashar (xix. 7) says: "And when men heard all these things that the people of the cities of Sodom did, they refrained from coming there." For further stories of cruelty see Pal. Targum on Gen. xviii.; and cf. *Rabbinic Philosophy and Ethics*, pp. 60 ff.

[2] The first editions read: "they cut off."

[3] The first editions read: "so that there should not be any benefit from them."

[4] The first editions read "Nathaniel."

[5] See the Book of Jashar xix. 3 ff.; T.B. Synhedrin, 109a.

[6] The first editions omit this quotation.

[7] The Book of Jashar (xix. 44) reads: "For they (the men of Sodom) had abundance of food and had tranquillity amongst them, still they would not sustain the poor and needy."

[8] In the MS. the quotation ends here, "etc." being added.

[9] Their prosperity led to their rebellion against God; cf. Hos. xiii. 6. In the Book of Jashar, chapter xix., we have two stories on the theme of this paragraph; they are probably variants of one tradition.

by fire. Peleṭith,[1] daughter of Lot, was wedded to one of the magnates of Sodom. She saw a certain very [2] poor man in the street of the city, and her soul was grieved on his account, as it is said, "Was not my soul grieved for the needy?" (Job xxx. 25).[3] What did she do? Every day when she went out to draw water she put in her bucket all sorts of provisions from her home, and she fed that poor man. The men of Sodom said: How does this poor man live? When they ascertained the facts, they brought her forth to be burnt with fire. She said: Sovereign of all worlds! Maintain my right and my cause [4] (at the hands of) the men of Sodom. And her cry ascended before the Throne of Glory. In that hour the Holy One, blessed be He, said: "I will now descend, and I will see" (Gen. xviii. 21) [5] whether the men of Sodom have done according to the cry [6] of this young woman, I will turn her foundations upwards,[7] and the surface thereof shall be turned downwards, as it is said, "I will now descend, and I will see whether they have done altogether according to her cry, which is come unto me" (*ibid.*). "According to *their* cry" is not written here (in the text), only "According to her cry."

And thus the text says,[8] "He who walketh with wise

[1] See T.B. Synhedrin, 109b. The name Peleṭith is given by the Pal. Targum on Gen. xviii. 21, Book of Jashar xix. 24; cf. Gen. Rab. xlix. 6; Jalḳuṭ, Gen. § 83; and *Rabbinic Philosophy and Ethics*, p. 63. In the Midrash Agadah (Genesis), p. 42, the name of Lot's daughter is Kalah. The Oxford MS. (O.A. 167) reads "Palṭia."

[2] Lit. "broken," "afflicted," or "humiliated." See *J.E.* xi. 424.

[3] This quotation is not in the printed texts of *P.R.E.*

[4] Ps. ix. 4 may have suggested the phrase of our text. Luria observes that this Psalm might well apply to the story of Sodom.

[5] The first editions continue the verse: "whether according to her cry which is come unto me." The word in the Hebrew text which the R.V. renders "according to the cry of it" is rendered by the Midrash literally "according to her cry."

[6] Pal. Targum, Gen. xviii. 20 f., reads: "And the Lord said to the ministering angels, The cry of Sodom and Gomorrah, because they oppress the poor, and decree that whosoever giveth bread to the needy shall be burnt with fire, is therefore great; and their guilt is exceedingly heavy. I will now appear, and see whether, as the cry of the *damsel* Peleṭith, which ascendeth before Me, they have completed their sins."

[7] See Job xxviii. 5. This chapter is applied by our author to the story of Sodom. See also Lev. Rab. v. 2; and Midrash Haggadol, c. 282, note 98.

[8] Luria reads: "Behold (the text) says." The reading, if rendered literally, is: "And thus it (or he) says."

men shall be wise: but the companion of fools shall be broken" (Prov. xiii. 20). ‖ "He who walketh with wise men shall be wise." To what is this like? To one who enters a perfumer's shop, although he neither takes anything nor gives anything,[1] nevertheless he absorbs a good scent, and goes away (therewith). Likewise everyone who walks with the righteous acquires some of their good ways and deeds. Therefore it is said, "He who walketh with wise men shall be wise." "But the companion of fools shall be broken" (*ibid.*). To what is this comparable? To a man who enters a tannery, although he neither takes or gives anything,[1] nevertheless he has absorbed a foul odour.[2] Likewise he who walks with the wicked acquires some of their evil ways and deeds, that is according to what is written,[3] "But the companion of fools shall be broken" (*ibid.*).

Another explanation:[4] "He who walketh with wise men shall be wise" (*ibid.*). This refers to Lot,[5] who walked with our father Abraham, and learned of his good deeds and ways. They[6] said: What did our father Abraham do? He made for himself a house opposite to Haran,[7] and he received everyone who entered into or went out from Haran, and he gave him to eat and to drink. He said to them: Say ye, The God of Abraham is the only one in the universe.[8] ‖ When Lot came to Sodom he did likewise. When they made proclamation in Sodom: All who strengthen the hand of the poor or needy with a loaf of bread shall be burnt by fire,[9] he was afraid of the men of the city, (and did not venture) to do so by day, but he did it by night, as it is said, "And the two angels came to Sodom at even; and Lot sat in the gate of Sodom" (Gen.

[1] Or, "he neither sells nor buys."
[2] The first editions add: "and he brings it away with himself."
[3] The first editions read: "as it is said."
[4] This is missing in the first edition.
[5] See Jalḳuṭ, Deut. § 824; Midrash, Prov. (ed. Buber), ch. xiii. p. 36b; and Jalḳuṭ, Prov. xiii. § 950.
[6] The sages.
[7] Cf. Gen. xii. 4 f. Luria suggests that the reading should be "Sodom." See Agadath Bereshith, 25; Gen. Rab. lii. 1 and liv. 6; Jalḳuṭ, Gen. § 84, reads: "outside Haran."
[8] The first editions read: "He said to him: There is one God in the Universe."
[9] See Pal. Targum, quoted *supra*, p. 183, note 6.

xix. 1). Why did Lot sit in the gate of Sodom?[1] Because he was afraid of the men of the city, (and did not venture) to act (charitably) by day, but he did so by night. He saw the two angels walking in the street of the city, and he thought that they were wayfarers in the land, and he ran to meet them. He said to them: Come and lodge ye overnight in my house, eat and drink, and ye shall go your way in peace. But the men would not accept this for themselves, and he took them by the hand against their will, and brought them inside his house, as it is said, "And he urged them greatly" (*ibid.* 3).

A certain young man of the people of that city saw them, and he ran and told all the men of that city, and they all gathered together at the door of the house to do according to their wont, even deeds of sodomy,[2] as it is said, "And they called unto Lot, and said unto him, || Where[3] are the men who came to thee to-night? bring them forth unto us that we may know[4] them" (*ibid.* 5). What did Lot do? Just as Moses gave his life for the people,[5] so Lot[6] gave up his two daughters instead of the two angels, as it is said, "Behold, now, I have two daughters" (*ibid.* 8). But the men[7] would not agree (and did not accept them). What did the angels do to them? They smote them with blindness until the dawn of the (next) morning. All were treated with (measure for) measure.[8] Just as he had taken

[1] The first editions read: "For on that day they had appointed him (judge) over themselves. (Lot) overtook them (the angels) and said to them," etc. Cf. Esth. v. 13, for Mordecai who sits in the "king's *gate*," *i.e.* as a judge; cf. Sublime Porte for the use of "gate" as a court of government or law.[1] The MS. seems to have a mistake here; it merely repeats what was stated a few lines previously, without explaining why Lot sat in the gate of Sodom. See Pal. Targum, *in loc.*

[2] The first editions omit "deeds of sodomy." A parallel occurs in Clement of Alexandria, *Pæd.* iii. 8.

[3] The MS. does not give this part of the verse.

[4] "Know" in the sense of punishing offenders, cf. Judg. viii. 16; see Parchon's Heb. Lexicon, *s.v.* ידע; or perhaps it is used here in the sense of carnal knowledge.

[5] The first editions read "Israel." See Mekhilta, p. 34b.

[6] The first editions read: "So Lot gave his life for them." By going out to reason with the men of Sodom, who threatened to deal with him according to their wont.

[7] Of Sodom.

[8] See Pal. Targum, Gen. xix. 24: "And the word of the Lord had caused showers of favour to descend upon Sodom and Gomorrah that they might repent, but they did not."

---

[1] Dr. Büchler notes as a parallel the expression דיינא דבבא of the court of the Exilarch of Babylon.

them by the hand without their will and taken them into his house, so they took hold of his hand,[1] and the hand of his wife, and the hand of his two daughters, and took them outside the city, as it is said, " But he lingered ; and the men laid hold upon his hand " (*ibid.* 16). And they [2] said to them : [3] Do not look behind you, for verily the Shekhinah of the Holy One, blessed be He, has descended in order to rain upon Sodom and upon Gomorrah brimstone and fire.[4] The pity of 'Edith [5] the wife of Lot was stirred for her daughters, who were married in Sodom,[6] and she looked back behind her to see if they were coming after her or not. And she saw behind [7] the Shekhinah, and she became a pillar of salt, as it is said, " And his wife looked back from behind him, and she became a pillar of salt " (*ibid.* 26).[8]

[1] Cf. Gen. xix. 16 ff. Some of the later editions omit the words " the hand of his wife." See Midrash Haggadol, c. 291 f.

[2] The angels.

[3] Lot and his family. The text in Gen. (xix. 17) says, " Do not look behind *thee* " ; note that the singular number is employed.

[4] Pal. Targum, Gen. xix. 24, reads : " There are now sent down upon them sulphur and fire from before the word of the Lord from Heaven." See Zohar, Gen. 107b f.

[5] The MS. reads either " 'Erith " or " 'Edith." Midrash Haggadol, c. 293, has "'Edith." In Jalkuṭ, *in loc.*, "'Erith " is the reading. *'Edith* points to "'Ed," witness, for such was the pillar of salt. " Ado " is the reading in the Book of Jashar (xix. 52). Pal. Targum, *loc. cit.* 26, reads : " And his wife looked after the angel to know what would be the end of her father's house, for she was of the daughters of the men of Sodom, and because she sinned by salt she was manifestly punished ; behold, she was made a statue of salt." The Second Version adds : " until the time of the resurrection shall come when the dead shall arise."

[6] See Midrash Haggadol, *loc. cit.*

[7] The first editions read : " behind her."

[8] The first editions add the following : " And she stands even now. All day the oxen lick it and it decreases up to her feet, and in the morning (the pillar of salt) grows afresh, as it is said : 'And his wife looked back from behind him, and she became a pillar of salt' " (Gen. xix. 26). In the days of Maimonides all trace of the pillar had been lost. The Book of Jashar (xix. 54) reads : " And the oxen which stood in that place daily licked up the salt to the extremities of their feet, and in the morning it would spring forth afresh and they again licked it up, unto this day." For a parallel Christian Midrash, see " A Strain of Sodom " in *A.N.C.L.* xviii. p. 230. See Jalkuṭ, Esth. § 1055 ; Jalkuṭ, Exodus, § 256. See Koran (ed. Rodwell), lxxxvii. p. 301, and Josephus, *Ant.* i. 11. 4, for references to Sodom. On Lot's wife, see Wisdom x. 7 ; Cyril of Jerusalem ; Mystagogue's Catechism viii. ; Augustine, *de Civ. Dei*, x. 8. On the Flight from Sodom, see Ambrose, *Flight from the World*, 54 ; Gregory the Great, *Pastoral Rule*, iii. 27. On Lot's hospitality, see Chrysostomus, Hom. xxxiii. 2 ; cf. Heb. xiii. 2. See also Grünbaum, *op. cit.* pp. 132 ff., and Ginzberg, *op. cit.* pp. 108 ff.

CHAPTER XXVI

THE TRIALS OF ABRAHAM [31A. ii.]

OUR father Abraham was tried with ten trials,[1] || and he stood firm in them all.[2] The first trial [3] was when our father Abraham was born; all the magnates of the kingdom [4] and the magicians sought to kill him, and he was hidden under the earth [5] for thirteen years without seeing sun or moon. After thirteen years [6] he went forth from beneath

[1] See Jubilees xvii. 17 and xix. 8. Parallels to our text are to be found in Aboth v. 3 (with a variant reading); Aboth de R. Nathan (*a*) xxxiii. and (*b*) xxxvi.; Jalkut, Gen. § 68; Book of Jashar xii. ff.; Shocher Tob, Ps. xviii. p. 77a; Midrash Agadah (Genesis), p. 26; and cf. Liturgy for the Second Day of the New Year, the Piyyut: "Thy Word is pure"; and see *Rabbinic Philosophy and Ethics*, p. 75, and cf. Grünbaum, *op. cit.* pp. 99 f.

[2] The first editions insert here the following: "and it was foreseen by him that in the future his children would tempt the Holy One, blessed be He, with ten trials, and He anticipated the cure for their wound,[1] and He tried him with ten trials."[2]

[3] The Aboth de R. Nathan, *loc. cit.*, does not enumerate this nor the second trial. On the order of the trials, see Hoffmann, *Mishnajoth*, p. 352.

[4] See *Rabbinic Philosophy and Ethics*, pp. 49 f., and Jalkut, Gen. *loc. cit.*, which reads as our MS.; and see the Book of Jashar (viii. 15 ff.), and Jeraḥmeel xxxiv. The first editions omit: "and the magicians." Instead of "the kingdom" later editions read "Nimrod." The magicians were led to persecute Abram by observing his star at his birth; see *infra*, pp. 377 f.; and cf. Beer, *Das Leben Abrahams*, pp. 98 f. The birth stories of Abraham, Moses (cf. Josephus, *Ant.* ii. 9. 2, and T.B. Sotah, 12a), and Jesus have much in common except the "Virgin Birth," which is peculiar to the narrative concerning the birth of the founder of Christianity.

[5] Lit. "in a house of the earth," *i.e.* a cave. Cf. Isa. xli. 2 and the Book of Jashar viii. 35.

[6] The Midrashim differ on this point; see Gen. Rab. xxxviii. 12, xcv. 3; Cant. Rab. on Cant. ii. 5. See the Book of Jashar ix. 4; and R. Bechai on Gen., *in loc.* See also T.B. Nedarim, 32a; Est. Rab. ii. 5; and generally for the legends of Abraham, see Ginzberg, *The*

---

[1] See T.B. Megillah, 13b.

[2] In Aboth de R. Nathan, *loc. cit.*, the ten plagues in Egypt are referred to as a parallel to the ten trials. See also Jalkut, Ps. § 777.

the earth, speaking the holy language;[1] and he despised idols[2] and held in abomination the graven images, and he trusted in the shadow of his Creator, and said:[3] "Blessed is the man who trusts in thee" (Ps. lxxxiv. 12).

The second trial was when he was put into prison for ten years—three years in Kuthi,[4] seven years in Budri.[5] After[6] ten years they sent and brought him forth and cast him into the furnace of fire,[7] and the King of Glory[8] put forth His right hand[9] and delivered him from the furnace of fire, as it is said, "And he said to him, I am the Lord who brought thee out of the furnace[10] of the Chaldees" (Gen. xv. 7). Another verse (says), "Thou art the Lord the God, who didst choose Abram, and broughtest him forth out of the furnace of the Chaldees" (Neh. ix. 7).[11]

The third trial was his migration[12] from his father's house[13] and from the land of his birth; and He brought him to

Legends of the Jews, i. pp. 185 ff., and Gorion's *Die Sagen der Juden*, ii. pp. 26 ff. For further references see Beer, *op. cit.* pp. 102 f. Our book relates that Abraham was in his fourteenth year when he abandoned idol worship. This agrees with Jubilees xi. 16, which also speaks of his learning writing. Our author varies this by referring to his knowledge of the Holy language. Jubilees xii. 25, 26, however, refers to Abraham's ability to speak Hebrew.

1 See Gen. Rab. xlii. 8.

2 The first editions read: "groves."

3 The first editions add: "O Lord of Hosts." This is part of the verse quoted. See the Gospel of Pseudo-Matthew vi. (*A.N.C.L.* xvi. p. 23) for a parallel Christian Midrash.

4 The first editions read Kutha, which is identified by the Talmud (B. Baba Bathra, 91a) with the Casdim; see also Josephus, *Ant.* i. 6. 5 and i. 7. 1.

5 Cf. T.B. Baba Bathra, *loc. cit.* and Jalkut, Gen. § 77. The first editions read Ḳardi; for the variant spellings see Jastrow, *T.D.* 1412a. Probably our MS. should read Kudri. See also Hippolytus (ed. Achelis), p. 90.

6 In the first editions the reading is: "Some say three years in Kardi and seven years in Kutha."

7 See *Rabbinic Philosophy and Ethics*, pp. 52 ff., and cf. Pal. Targum, Gen. xi. 28. See also *infra*, p. 420.

8 See T.B. Pesachim, 118a, and Cant. Rab. on Cant. i. 1.

9 See Gen. Rab. xliv. 4.

10 אור (Ur), "furnace." Cf. Isa. xliv. 16 and Grünbaum, *op. cit.* pp. 90 ff., and see Introduction, p. li.

11 This quotation is omitted by the printed texts. It forms part of the morning liturgy; see Singer, p. 34.

12 See Jubilees xvii. 17. This trial is the first according to the Midrash Haggadol, Gen. c. 201.

13 From Ur of the Chaldees, his country. This agrees with Ibn Ezra's interpretation of the text, Gen. xii. 1.

Haran,[1] and there his father Terah died,[2] and Athrai [3] his mother.[4] Migration is harder for man than for any other creature.[5] Whence do we know of his migration? Because it is said, "Now the Lord said || unto Abram, Get thee out" (Gen. xii. 1).[6]

The fourth trial (was the famine). From the day when the heavens and the earth were created, the Holy One, blessed be He, had not brought into the world a famine but only in the days of Abraham,[7] and not in any of the lands but only in the land of Canaan,[8] in order to try him and to bring him down into Egypt, as it is said, "And there was a famine in the land, and Abram went down into Egypt" (*ibid.* 10).

The fifth trial was when Sarah his wife was taken to Pharaoh to be (his) wife. And is there any man, who seeing his wife taken away to another man, would not rend his garments? But (he trusted in the Holy One, blessed be He,) that he would not approach her.[9] Whence do we know that Sarah was taken to Pharaoh to be his wife? Because it is said, "And the princes of Pharaoh saw her" (*ibid.* 15).[10]

Rabbi Joshua, son of Ḳorchah,[11] said: In that night when our mother Sarah was taken, it was Passover night,[12] and

[1] Luria thinks that the text should continue: "as it is said: 'Get thee out of thy land and from thy birthplace'" (Gen. xii. 1).

[2] See Seder 'Olam Rab. i. p. 2b, note 22, and p. 3a, note 24.

[3] The 2nd ed. reads Amathlai; see T.B. Baba Bathra, 91a, and Beer, *op. cit.* pp. 96 f.

[4] See T.B. Baba Bathra, *loc. cit.*

[5] Cf. T.B. Kethuboth, 28a, based on Isa. xxii. 17; see also T.B. Synhedrin, 26a, and Jalkut on Isa. § 280. Perhaps the last words of the sentence in our text should read: "than anything else." The reading in the Midrash Haggadol, Gen., *loc. cit.*, is: "which was the hardest of all" (the trials).

[6] The first editions continue the quotation.

[7] This does not agree with Gen. Rab. xxv. 3, according to which there were two famines prior to the days of Abraham.

[8] See Rashi, Gen. xii. 10.

[9] The words in brackets are missing in our MS.; they are based on Luria's emendation. The first editions read: "But in accordance with her counsel he did not approach her."

[10] The printed texts omit the question and answer. The rest of the quotation reads: "And they praised her to Pharaoh: and the woman *was taken* into Pharaoh's house."

[11] The first editions read: "Rabbi Ṭarphon." This agrees with the reading preserved in the Midrash Haggadol, Gen. c. 208 f.

[12] See *supra*, p. 153, for a similar expression in connection with the offering of Cain and Abel; cf. Zohar, Gen. 21b, 22a.

the Holy One, blessed be He, brought upon Pharaoh and upon his house great plagues,[1] to make known[2] that thus in the future would He smite the people of his land,[3] as it is said, "And the Lord plagued Pharaoh and his house with great *plagues*" (*ibid.* 17). Concerning the Egyptians it is written, "Yet one *plague* more will I bring upon Pharaoh, and upon Egypt" (Ex. xi. 1). Was this a plague? Was it not (the slaying of) the first-born of the Egyptians? But the slaying is compared with the plagues, therefore it is said, "And the Lord *plagued* || Pharaoh" (Gen. xii. 17).[4]

Rabbi Joshua ben Ḳorchah said: Because of his love for her, (Pharaoh)[5] wrote in her marriage document (giving her) all his wealth,[6] whether in silver, or in gold, or in man-servants, or land,[7] and he wrote (giving) her the land of Goshen for a possession. Therefore the children of Israel dwelt in the land of Goshen, in the land of their mother Sarah.[8] He (also) wrote (giving) her Hagar, his daughter[9] from a concubine, as her handmaid. And whence do we know that Hagar was the daughter of Pharaoh?[10] Because it is said, "Now Sarai Abram's wife bare him no children; and she had an handmaid, an Egyptian, whose name was Hagar" (*ibid.* xvi. 1). Pharaoh rose up early in the morning confused[11] because he had not approached her,[12] and he sent and called Abraham, and said to him: Behold, Sarai thy wife is before thee, and all the deeds of her marriage contract are with her, take (her)

[1] Cf. Jalḳuṭ, Gen. § 68.

[2] The Venice edition reads: "to make known to him."

[3] The first editions read: "the Egyptians with great plagues."

[4] This entire section from "Concerning" is omitted in the printed texts. On the subject-matter see Midrash Agadah (Gen.), p. 47.

[5] "Pharaoh" is missing in the MS.; it occurs in the first editions.

[6] Lit. "his Mammon." On this term see *Jewish Sources of the Sermon on the Mount*, p. 169.

[7] Jalḳuṭ, *loc. cit.*, adds: "maid-servants."

[8] The first editions read: "which belonged to our mother Sarah." Have we an apology on behalf of Jews, who in the days of our author were living in Egypt, claiming to be in their *own* land?

[9] See Pal. Targum, Gen. xvi. 1, and Gen. Rab. xlv. 1., and the Book of the Bee, p. 42.

[10] The first editions read: "Hagar the Egyptian was an handmaid?" See Midrash Haggadol, Gen. c. 208, and c. 241.

[11] The first editions add: "and agitated."

[12] The first editions read: "Sarah." The various incidents are based on the story of Abimelech's conduct in a similar instance.

and go, do not tarry in this land, as it is said, "Now therefore behold thy wife, take her, and go" (*ibid.* xii. 19).[1] "And Pharaoh gave men charge concerning him,[2] and they sent him forth" (*ibid.* 20). And he had Abraham led so as to come[3] to the land of Canaan. He sojourned in the land of the Philistines[4] in order to be refreshed there. And he went away. And everything is foreseen by the Holy One, blessed be He, and Abimelech[5] sent and took Sarah, thinking to raise up children from her, as it is said, "And Abimelech . . . sent, and took Sarah" (*ibid.* xx. 2).

And Abimelech became impotent, and all the women of his house became barren,[6] even || to the smallest insect (which also became) barren, as it is said, "For the Lord had fast closed up all the wombs of the house of Abimelech" (*ibid.* 18). And the angel Michael descended and drew his sword against him.[7] Abimelech said to him: Is this a true judgment and a true sentence to slay me as long as I had no knowledge?[8] "Wilt thou slay even a righteous nation?" (*ibid.* 4).[9] He said unto him:[10] "Restore the

[1] The first editions add: "And it is written after this (text)."

[2] The quotation ends here. See Pal. Targum, *in loc.* The first editions add: "Whatever he gave to Sarah, Abimelech gave to Abram, as it is said, 'And Abimelech took sheep and oxen, and menservants and womenservants'" (Gen. xx. 14).

[3] The first editions read: "And he had Abram led (so as) to come in the land of Canaan as far as the land of the Philistines."

[4] Luria thinks that the reading of our text was originally thus: "Let us pass over the narrative of Abraham, from his entrance into Egypt till he came to the land of the Philistines; all this story will be narrated farther on in this book." Our MS. preserves apparently a better reading.

[5] Luria holds that the text should read: "As far as the land of the Philistines, and (here) Abimelech sent and took Sarah, thinking that he would be enabled to acquire children from her; but everything is revealed before the Holy One, blessed be He, Michael descended," etc. Our MS. seems to have preserved the true text.

[6] See T.B. Baba Ḳamma, 92a. The MS. adds: "and even Michael (came before) Abimelech." The words are out of place, and are wanting in the Oxford MS.

[7] The first editions add: "to slay him." For the narrative see Pesiḳta Rabbathi, p. 176b; and cf. Liturgy for the Second Day of the New Year (ed. Heidenheim), p. 33a, where the ten trials are enumerated; and cf. T.B. Baba Ḳamma, *loc. cit.*, and *R.É.J.*, lxviii. p. 147.

[8] The first editions read: "to slay me for a matter which I did not know, as it is said."

[9] The first editions add: "Verily he said unto me: 'She is my sister'" (Gen. xx. 2).

[10] Abimelech.

man's wife, for he is a prophet" (*ibid.* 7).[1] "And he shall pray for thee, and thou shalt live" (*ibid.*).

Rabbi Joshua, son of Korchah, (rehearsed) before Rabbi Ṭarphon (saying): Whatever Pharaoh gave, he gave to Sarah; whatever Abimelech gave, he gave to Abraham; as it is said, "And Abimelech took sheep and oxen" (*ibid.* 14).[2] Abraham arose and prayed before the Holy One, blessed be He, and said before Him: Sovereign of all the worlds! Thou hast created the whole world to increase and multiply, and let Abimelech and all the females of his household increase and multiply. The Holy One, blessed be He, was entreated of him, as it is said, "And Abraham prayed[3] unto God: and God healed Abimelech, and his wife, and his maidservants;[4] and they bare children" (*ibid.* 17).

[1] The first editions add here: "From thee one may learn, if a man come to a town, let people ask him concerning his requirements of food, but let them not inquire after his wife." See T.B. Maccoth, 9b, and T.B. Baba Ḳamma, 92b.

[2] The text continues: "and gave them unto Abraham." The entire sentence is wanting in the first editions. The section seems out of place here.

[3] The quotation ends here in the MS.; it is continued in the first editions.

[4] The first editions read: "his household." The legend of Abram in the furnace was known to Augustine, *de Civ. Dei*, xvi. 15. The incident with Sarah and Abimelech is discussed by Chrysostomus, *To Olympias*, iii. 3; Theodoret, *On Divine Providence*, x. Augustine, *de Civ. Dei*, xvi. 19, defends Abraham's conduct and praises him in this connection.

CHAPTER XXVII

THE TRIALS OF ABRAHAM (*continued*) [32A. i.]

THE sixth trial[1] was (when) all the kings[2] came against him[3] to slay him.[4] They said: Let us first begin with the house[5] of his brother, and afterwards let us begin with him.[6] On account of Lot they took all (the wealth of)[7] Sodom and Gomorrah,[8] as it is said, "And they took all the goods of Sodom and Gomorrah" ‖ (Gen. xiv. 11). Afterwards they took Lot captive, and all his wealth, as it is said, "And they took Lot . . . and[9] his goods" (*ibid.* 12).

Michael came and told Abraham, as it is said, "And there came *one who had escaped*, and told Abram[10] the Hebrew" (*ibid.* 13). He[11] is the prince of the world, he was the one who told, as it is said, "Curse not the king, no, not in thy thought; . . . *he who hath wings* shall tell the matter" (Eccles. x. 20). Why was his name called "Palit" ("One who had escaped")? Because in the hour when the Holy One, blessed be He, caused Sammael and

[1] According to Midrash Agadah, Gen. p. 26, this incident is not enumerated among the ten trials of Abraham. A good deal of the material of this chapter is preserved in Midrash Haggadol, Gen. c. 214 ff.; especially cols. 217 and 218.

[2] Amraphel and his allies mentioned in Gen. xiv. 1. Amraphel is identified with Nimrod in T.B. 'Erubin, 53a. See Gen. Rab. xlii. 4.

[3] See Jalkut, Gen. § 68, which has used *P.R.E.*

[4] See T.B. Synhedrin, 95b.

[5] The first editions read: "with the son of his brother." The reference is to Lot.

[6] See Lekach Tob and Agadath Bereshith on Gen. xiv. 11.

[7] Our MS. omits "the wealth of"; it occurs in the first editions; see also for similar text, Midrash Haggadol, Gen. c. 216.

[8] See Gen. Rab. xlii. 7.

[9] The MS. reads: "and all his goods"; the word "all" is not in the actual quotation.

[10] See *Rabbinic Philosophy and Ethics*, p. 182.

[11] *i.e.* Michael. See Midrash Haggadol, Gen., *loc. cit.*, which has a better text: "for he discloses all the secrets of the world."

his band to descend from heaven from their holy place,[1] he caught hold of *the wings* of Michael to make him fall[2] with himself, and the Holy One, blessed be He, saved[3] him from his power;[4] therefore was his name called "The one who had escaped."[5] Concerning him Ezekiel said, "One who had escaped[6] out of Jerusalem came to me, saying, The city is smitten" (Ezek. xxxiii. 21).

Abraham rose up early in the morning, and he took his three disciples, Aner, Eshcol, and Mamre, with him, and Eliezer[7] his servant with him (also), and he pursued after them as far as Dan, which is Pameas,[8] as it is said, "And he pursued as far as Dan" (Gen. xiv. 14). And there the righteous man[9] was hindered, for there it was told him: Abraham, know thou that in the future[10] thy children's children will serve idols in this place; therefore was he hindered there. Whence do we know that Israel served idols there? Because it is said, "And he made two calves of gold . . . and he set the || one[11] in Bethel, and the other put he in Dan" (1 Kings xii. 28, 29). There he left his three disciples,[12] and he took his servant Eliezer. The numerical value of the letters of his name equals 318.[13] He pursued

[1] See *supra*, pp. 46, 92, 99.

[2] "With him" is added by the 'Arukh, ed. Kohut, vi. p. 340b.

[3] פלט, hence פלים (Paliṭ).

[4] Lit. "hand." See Assumption of Moses x. 1, 2 for the final conflict between Michael and Satan. Cf. Jude 9.

[5] Paliṭ. The title of Michael as PALIṬ (פלים) may possibly be due to an abbreviated form of his other title of PRAḲLIṬ (פרקלים); see *Rabbinic Philosophy and Ethics*, p. 74.

[6] See Pal. Targum, Gen. xiv. 13.

[7] The first editions read: "three disciples and Eliezer his servant."

[8] See T.B. Megillah, 6a, Bechoroth, 55a, and 'Arukh, ed. Kohut, vi. p. 369b; and cf. Targum to Cant. v. 4.

[9] Abraham.

[10] See T.B. Synhedrin, 96a; and Pal. Targum, Gen. xiv. 14.

[11] The calf of gold.

[12] See T.B. Nedarim, 32a; Gen. Rab. xliii. 2; Agadath Bereshith, 13; and cf. Tanchuma, Lekh Lekha, § ix. The first editions add: "and their wives with them."

[13] This Haggadah was known to Clement of Alexandria, whose book *The Miscellanies*, vi. 11, states: "As then in astronomy we have Abraham as an instance, so also in arithmetic we have the same Abraham. For, hearing that Lot was taken captive, and having numbered his own servants born in his house, 318, he defeats a very great number of the enemy." See also the Epistle of Barnabas ix., where the "318" is interpreted as a Christian Midrash. See Siegfried, *Philo von Alexandria*, p. 330, and Güdemann, *Religionsgeschichtliche Studien*, pp. 119–121. Other Rabbinic parallels are Pal. Targum, Gen., *loc. cit.*, and Pesiḳta Rabbathi, § xviii. p. 91b. The first editions add

them as far as the left of Damascus,[1] as it is said, "And he pursued them unto Hobah" (Gen. xiv. 15).

Samuel the Younger said: There the night was divided for him; (the night) when the children of Israel went forth out of Egypt,[2] that was the night in which Abraham smote the kings and their camps with them, as it is said, "And he divided himself against them by night, he and his servants" (*ibid.*).[3]

Hillel the Elder said: Abraham took all the wealth of Sodom and Gomorrah and all the wealth of Lot, the son of his brother, and he returned in peace,[4] and not even one of his men failed [5] him, as it is said, "And he brought back *all* [6] the goods, and also his brother Lot" (*ibid.* 16).[7]

Rabbi Joshua [8] said: Abraham was the first to begin to give a tithe. He took all the tithe of the kings and all the tithe of the wealth of Lot, the son of his brother, and gave (it) to Shem,[9] the son of Noah, as it is said, "And he gave him a tenth of all" (*ibid.* 20).

after 318: "He led forth his trained men, born in his house" (Gen. xiv. 14). There are also variations in the next quotation, according to our MS. and the first editions respectively.

[1] See Gen. xiv. 15.

[2] The first editions read: "That is the night which was from of old, that is the night in which He smote the first-born of the Egyptians." This night was destined from the beginning, prepared for the victories of Abraham and his seed, see Mekhilta, p. 13a; Gen. Rab. xliii. 3; and cf. *infra*, pp. 201, 402. The night itself was divided, one-half being spent in the days of Abraham in gaining victory, and the other half of the night was destined to be reserved for the victory of God over Egypt at the Exodus. See Wisdom xviii. 6.

[3] The first editions add: "And concerning this (night) it is said: 'And it came to pass at midnight'" (Ex. xii. 29). See Pal. Targum, Gen. xiv. 15.

[4] This is based on the Haggadic interpretation of Isa. xli. 3. See Pal. Targum, Gen. xiv. 16, and cf. T.B. Synhedrin, 108b; Ẓohar, Gen. 26a, and Gen. Rab., *loc. cit.*

[5] For the word in the text see 2 Sam. xvii. 22. Luria interprets: "nothing of the wealth was missing."

[6] Our MS. omits "all."

[7] The first editions add here: "Abraham was afraid, and said: Perchance I have slain all these troops (or, multitude), and no righteous person can be found among them. The Holy One, blessed be He, said to him: 'Fear not, Abram' (Gen. xv. 1). With reference to this it is said: 'He pursueth them and passeth on safely, even by a way that he had not gone with his feet' (Isa. xli. 3). It has not come on thy foot to soil thee in this matter." See Shocher Ṭob, p. 233b.

[8] The first editions add: "son of Ḳorchah."

[9] He was the chief priest then; see *supra*, pp. 53 f., and cf. *J.E.* xi. 261 f. As we have seen, *P.R.E.* identifies Shem with Melchizedek; see Jubilees xiii. 25, especially Charles' note on pp. 100 f.

Shem, the son of Noah, came forth to meet him,[1] and when he saw all the deeds which he had done and all the wealth which he had brought back, || he wondered in his heart. He began to praise, to glorify, and to laud the name of the Most High, saying: "And blessed be God the Most High, who hath delivered thine enemies into thy hand" (*ibid.*). Abraham arose and prayed before the Holy One, blessed be He, saying: Sovereign of all worlds! Not by the power of my hand, nor by the power of my right hand have I done all these things, but by the power of Thy right hand with which Thou dost shield me in this world and in the world to come, as it is said, "But thou, O Lord, art a shield about me" (Ps. iii. 3) in this world; "my glory, and the lifter up of mine head" (*ibid.*)[2] in the world to come.[3] The angels answered and said: Blessed art Thou, O Lord, the shield of Abraham.[4]

[1] With bread and wine; see Gen. xiv. 18.

[2] The first editions read: "'But thou, O Lord, art a shield about me; my glory, and the lifter up of mine head' (Ps. iii. 3) in the world to come."

[3] See next chapter. According to the Midrash, Ps. cx. refers to Abraham; see Shocher Ṭob, pp. 233a, b.

[4] See Singer, p. 44. These angelic words form the end of the first benediction of the Shemoneh 'Esreh. Other chapters of *P.R.E.* terminate with the last words of other benedictions of this Prayer. This fact is not mentioned in the annotated edition of Singer's Prayer Book. From this aspect our book forms a Midrash on the Shemoneh Esreh. See Roḳeach, 322, and Gen. Rab. xliv. 4. See also Sirach (li. x.*) in *A. and P.* i. p. 515. The last chapter of our book probably ended with the words printed in the "contents of the chapters" in the Venice edition (1544) and in later editions thus: "Blessed art Thou, O Lord, who healest the sick of Thy people Israel." This is the eighth benediction of the Shemoneh 'Esreh. See Singer, p. 47.

CHAPTER XXVIII

THE TRIALS OF ABRAHAM (*continued*)

The Vision between the Pieces [32B. ii.]

THE seventh trial (was as follows): "After these things the word of the Lord came unto Abram in a vision, saying" (Gen. xv. 1). To all the prophets He was revealed in a vision,[1] but to Abraham He was revealed [2] in a revelation and in a vision. Whence do we know of the revelation? Because it is said, "And the Lord *appeared* unto him by the oaks of Mamre" (*ibid.* xviii. 1). Whence do we know of the vision? Because it is said, "After these things the word of the Lord came unto Abram in a *vision*" (*ibid.* xv. 1). He said to him: Abraham! Do not fear, for My right hand is shielding thee in every place where thou goest; [3] it is like a shield [4] against misfortunes, and it gives thee a good reward, (even) to thee and to thy children, || in this world and in the world to come, as it is said, "Thy *exceeding great* reward" (*ibid.*).[5]

[1] The first editions add: "he appeared in a vision of the night." Instead of reading "of the night," Luria holds that the reading should be, "or in a revelation." This passage was possibly the authority used by Maimonides in dealing with the subject of prophecy; see his Hilkhoth Jesodê Ha-Torah vi. 2 and 6. For Luria's suggested reading see Lev. Rab. i. 4. On "vision and revelation" see Gen. Rab. xliv. 6.

[2] The first editions read: "but to Abraham in a vision and in a revelation. Whence do we know of the vision? Because it is said: 'In a vision saying, Fear not, Abram, I am thy shield' (Gen. xv. 1) in this world; 'thy exceeding great reward' (*ibid.*) in the world to come." See Pal. Targum, *in loc.*, and Gen. Rab., *loc. cit.*

[3] Cf. Isa. xli. 10, 13.

[4] Cf. Aboth iv. 15.

[5] The Midrashim and Pal. Targum (Gen. xv. 1) interpret the fear of Abraham as implying that his victory was his entire recompense for his life's devotion to the cause of God. This would be covered by the word of the text, "Thy reward"; "exceeding great" would imply the reward in the future life.

Rabbi[1] said: The Holy One, blessed be He, brought Abraham outside (his house) on the night of Passover,[2] and He said to him: Abraham! Hast thou the ability to count all the host of heaven? He said before Him: Sovereign of all worlds! Is there then a limit to Thy troops[3] (of angels)? He said to him: Likewise thy seed shall not be counted owing to their great number, as it is said, "And he said unto him, So shall thy seed be" (*ibid.* 5).[4]

Rabbi Eliezer[5] said: The Holy One, blessed be He, showed to our father Abraham (at the covenant) between the pieces[6] the four kingdoms, their dominion and their downfall, as it is said, "And he said unto him, Take me an heifer of three years old, and a she-goat of three years old" (*ibid.* 9). "An heifer of three years old" (*ibid.*) refers to the kingdom of Edom,[7] which is like the heifer of a sheep. "And a she-goat of three years old" (*ibid.*) refers to the kingdom of Greece,[8] as it is said, "And the he-goat magnified himself exceedingly" (Dan. viii. 8). "And a ram of three years old" (Gen. xv. 9); this is the kingdom of Media and Persia, as it is said, "And the ram which thou sawest that had the two horns, they are the kings of Media and Persia" (Dan. viii. 20). "And a turtle-dove"

[1] *i.e.* Jehudah the Prince. The first editions read: "Rabbi Jehudah."

[2] The attack of Amraphel was also on the Passover night; see Pal. Targum, Gen. xiv. 13, and cf. Passover Haggadah *Oẓ Rob Nissim* and the poem *Omez Geburathekha*. The chief references for these traditions are: Mekhilta, Bo, p. 5a; Pal. Targum on Ex. xii. 42, translated in *Rabbinic Philosophy and Ethics*, pp. 164 f. See also Seder 'Olam Rab. v. 1. p. 11b. Is there perhaps a reference here to the triennial reading of the Law, this section in Genesis being read on Passover?

[3] This is based on Job xxv. 3; see T.B. Chagigah, 13b, and Siphrê, Numb. § 42.

[4] The rest of this chapter is missing in Luria's edition. It is to be found in the old editions, *e.g.* Venice, Prague, Amsterdam. There is no reason to dispute its authenticity. The Censor is probably responsible for Luria's omission. His book was printed in Warsaw.

[5] The first editions read "'Aḳiba."

[6] See Gen. xv. 9 ff. For a Christian Midrash on this theme see Methodius, *Banquet of the Ten Virgins*, v. 2.

[7] The Roman Empire is referred to under this designation. Some of the old editions read, "Seir." "Edom" is the usual term for the Roman Empire. MS. Gaster adds: "This is the fourth Kingdom."

[8] On the kingdoms, Greece and Rome, see 4 Ezra v. 3; Rev. xvii.; Lactantius, *Divine Institutes*, vii. 15. "In the Johannine Apocalypse," says Bousset, *Antichrist*, E.T., p. 126, "the Roman Empire is plainly enough indicated as the last anti-Christian power."

(Gen. xv. 9); this refers to the sons of Ishmael.[1] This expression is not to be understood in the literal meaning of Tôr (turtle-dove), but in the Aramaic language, in which Tôr means *Ox*, for when the male ox is harnessed to the female, they will open and break all the valleys,[2] even as it says (about) "the fourth beast" (Dan. vii. 19).[3] "And a young pigeon" (Gen. xv. 9); this refers to the Israelites, who are compared || to a young pigeon, as it is said, "O my dove, thou art in the clefts of the rock" (Cant. ii. 14). For thy voice is pleasant in prayer, and thy appearance is beautiful in good deeds. "And a young pigeon" (Gen. xv. 9); this refers to the Israelites, who are compared to a young pigeon: "My dove, my perfect (one), is (but) one" (Cant. vi. 9).[4]

Rabbi Acha ben Jacob said: This expression, "three years old" (Gen. xv. 9), is said only with reference to the mighty in power, as it is said, "And a threefold cord is not quickly broken" (Eccles. iv. 12).[5]

Rabbi Mesharshyah[6] said: (Three years old) refers to a threefold (dominion) which they would exercise three times in the future in the land of Israel. At the first time each one would rule by himself; at the second time two together (would rule); on the third occasion (all) altogether to fight against the house of David,[7] as it is said, "The

[1] The Mohammedan Empire. Is this an indication of the date of our book? It fixes a limit, in the sense that it must have been written after the rise of the Mohammedan Empire. We shall have ground for asserting that the beginning of the ninth century is probably the earliest date of the final redaction of our book.

[2] See Gen. Rab. lxxvi. 6. The first editions read: "they will open and break the (clods of) all the valleys. For phraseology cf. Isa. xxviii. 24: "to open and break the clods" of the ground. The next words about the fourth beast are not in the printed editions.

[3] The entire passage in the first editions reads thus: "This (expression) Tôr (turtle dove) is not said here in the language of the Torah (*i.e.* Hebrew), but in the Aramaic language. Tôr is the ox, and when the male ox is harnessed to the female they will open and break (the ground of) all the valleys."

[4] The Oxford MS. (O.A. 167) reads: "Another explanation. 'A young pigeon' refers to Israel, as it is said, 'My *dove*, my perfect (one), is (but) one'" (Cant. vi. 9).

[5] The Oxford MS. (O.A. 167) reads: "Rabbi Acha ben Jacob said: What is the meaning of this expression, 'three years old'? It refers to the mighty in power, (who are) like a threefold cord, as it is said," etc. On R. Acha ben Jacob, see *J.E.* i. p. 278.

[6] There were several teachers so named; *J.E.* viii. 502b gives one only.

[7] Messianic wars are referred to here. The first editions read: "to fight against the Son of David."

kings of the earth set themselves,[1] and the rulers take counsel together, against the Lord, and against his *anointed* " (Ps. ii. 2).

Rabbi Joshua said : Abraham took his sword and divided them, each one into two parts, as it is said, " And he took him all these, and he divided them in the midst " (Gen. xv. 10). Were it not for the fact that he divided them, the world would not have been able to exist, but because he divided them, he weakened their strength, and he brought each part against its corresponding part, as it is said, " And he laid each half over against the other " (*ibid.*). And the young pigeon he left alive, as it is said, " But the bird he divided not " (*ibid.*). Hence thou mayest learn that there was not any other bird there except a young pigeon.[2] The bird of prey came down upon them ‖ to scatter them and to destroy them.[3] " The bird of prey " is nought else but David, the son of Jesse,[4] who is compared to a " speckled bird of prey," as it is said, " *Is mine heritage* unto me as a speckled *bird of prey* ? " (Jer. xii. 9).

When the sun was about to rise in the east, Abraham sat down and waved his scarf over them, so that the bird of prey should not prevail over them until the raven came.[5]

Rabbi Elaẓar ben 'Aẓariah said : From this incident thou mayest learn that the rule of these four kingdoms will only last one day[6] according to the day of the Holy One, blessed be He. Rabbi Elaẓar ben 'Arakh said unto him : Verily it is so, according to thy word, as it is said, " He hath made me desolate and faint *all the day* " (Lam. i. 13), except for

[1] The quotation ends here in the MS.
[2] The first editions read : " Hence thou mayest learn that the word Zippòr in the Torah means only a young pigeon."
[3] Pal. Targ. Gen. xv. 11 reads : " And there came down people who were like unto an unclean bird, to steal away the sacrifices of Israel ; but the merit of Abram was a shield over them."
[4] The first editions read : " is nought else but the Son of David." See Hastings' *D.B.* iv. p. 610a, on " the speckled bird." This passage, in its Messianic interpretation, has escaped the notice of Schöttgen.
[5] The first editions read : " until evening set in." This seems a better reading. Cf. Jubilees xi. 11.
[6] The one day of God is 1000 years, see *supra*, p. 128. Do the four kingdoms referred to by Daniel begin with the Greek persecutions under Antiochus Epiphanes, 168 B.C.E., so that the end of these hostile kingdoms was to be expected about 1000 years later, *i.e.* about 832 C.E. ? If so, this is another indication as to the date of our book. It would not be later than this date (832 C.E.). Accordingly, we may fix the date of its final redaction in the early years of the ninth century.

two-thirds of an hour (of God). Know that it is so. Come and see, for when the sun turns to set in the west, (during) two hours [1] its power is weakened,[2] and it has no light, likewise whilst the evening has not yet come, the light of Israel shall arise,[3] as it is said, "And it shall come to pass, that at *evening time* there shall be *light*" (Zech. xiv. 7).

Abraham arose and prayed before the Holy One, blessed be He, that his children should not be enslaved by these four kingdoms. A deep sleep fell upon him, and he slept, as it is said, "A deep sleep fell upon Abram" (Gen. xv. 12). Does then a man lie down and sleep, and yet be able to pray? But this teaches thee that Abraham was lying down and sleeping because of the intensity of his prayer that his children might enslave || these four kingdoms,[4] as it is said, "And, lo, an horror of great darkness fell upon him" (*ibid.*).[5] "Horror" refers to the kingdom of Edom, as it is written, "And behold a fourth beast, *terrible* and powerful, and strong exceedingly" (Dan. vii. 7). "Darkness" is the kingdom [6] of those who *darken* the eyes of Israel (by preventing the observance of) all the precepts which are in the Torah. "Great" (Gen. xv. 12) refers to the kingdom of Media and Persia, which was *great* (enough to be able to afford) to sell Israel for nought.[7] "Fell" (*ibid.*) refers to the kingdom of Babylon, because in their hand *fell* the crown [8] of Israel, as it is said, "Babylon is fallen, is fallen" (Isa. xxi. 9). "*Upon him*" (Gen. xv. 12) refers to the

[1] The first editions read: "two-thirds of an hour."

[2] The 1st ed. reads: "remain over." The Venice edition omits this and reads instead: "it is dark and it has no light." The words "it is dark" is an error, and should be "its strength fails."

[3] The first editions read: "the Son of David will cause the light of Israel to arise." Cf. the use of "Zemach" (Dayspring) as a Messianic title in *Hellenism and Christianity*, pp. 119 f.

[4] The first editions read here: "that his children might escape these four kingdoms." In the preceding words the first editions read: "and sleeping and he prayed" that his children, etc.

[5] Cf. Pal. Targ., *in loc.*, for a different reading; see also Gen. Rab. xliv. 18; Ex. Rab. li. 7; Pesiḳta de R. Kahana, 42b.

[6] The first editions read: "the kingdom of Greece." See also Shocher Ṭob, Ps. lii. 8, pp. 143b f.; and Lev. Rab. xiii. 5. The idea in our context has a parallel in Wisdom xviii. 4.

[7] See Esth. iii. 11: "And the king said to Haman: The silver is given to thee, the people also, to do with them as it seemeth good to thee."

[8] *i.e.* the Temple of God at Jerusalem. In the printed editions the quotation from Isa. xxi. 9 is missing.

Ishmaelites, *upon whom* the Son of David will flourish,[1] as it is said, "His enemies will I clothe with shame:[2] but *upon him* shall his crown flourish" (Ps. cxxxii. 18).

Rabbi Ẓe'era[3] said: These kingdoms were created only as fuel for Gehinnom, as it is said, "Behold, a smoking furnace,[4] and a flaming torch that passed" (Gen. xv. 17). Here the word "furnace"[5] signifies only Gehinnom, which is compared to a furnace, as it is said, "Saith the Lord, whose *fire* is in Zion, and his *furnace* in Jerusalem" (Isa. xxxi. 9).

[1] Or it might mean "arise"; cf. *supra*, p. 201, note 3.

[2] In the MS. the quotation ends here, "etc." being added; in the first editions the verse is continued.

[3] The printed editions read "'Azariah."

[4] Pal. Targ., *in loc.*, renders: "And lo, Abram saw Gehinnom bringing up flaming coals and burning flakes of fire, wherein the wicked are to be judged." See Jer. Targum, *in loc.*, and cf. also Gen. Rab. xliv. 21; Apoc. Baruch iv. 4: and 4 Ezra iii. 14 (ed. Box), p. 12, note a.

[5] The first editions read: "'Furnace' and 'torch' refer only to Gehinnom, as it is said," etc. The readings preserved in the Jalkuṭ, Gen. § 77, and the Midrash Haggadol, c. 234, should be compared with our text. Beer's *Leben Abraham's* should also be consulted for further references to the Midrashic sources.

CHAPTER XXIX

THE TRIALS OF ABRAHAM (*continued*)

The Covenant of Circumcision [33B. ii.]

THE eighth trial (was as follows): " And when Abram was ninety-nine years old " (Gen. xvii. 1),[1] the Holy One, blessed be He, said to him: Until now thou hast not been perfect before Me; but circumcise the flesh of thy foreskin, and " walk before me, and be thou perfect "[2] (*ibid.*). Moreover, the foreskin is a reproach, as it is said, " For that is a reproach unto us " (*ibid.* xxxiv. 14), because the foreskin is more unclean than all unclean things, as it is said, " For henceforth there shall no more || come into thee the uncircumcised and the unclean " (Isa. lii. 1). For the foreskin is a blemish above all blemishes. Circumcise the flesh of thy foreskin and be perfect.

Rabban Gamaliel said: Abraham sent and called for Shem,[3] the son of Noah, and he circumcised the flesh of the foreskin of our father Abraham,[4] and the flesh of the foreskin of Ishmael his son, as it is said, " In the selfsame day was Abraham circumcised, and Ishmael his son "[5] (Gen. xvii. 26). " In the selfsame day " (means) in the might of the sun at midday.[6] Not only that, but (it indicates) the

[1] The first editions add: " the Holy One, blessed be He, said to him, ' Walk before me, and be thou perfect ' " (Gen. xvii. 1).

[2] See Midrash Agadah, Gen. xvii. 21, p. 36.

[3] On Abraham's circumcision see Gen. Rab. xlvi. 4 and xlvii. 8. Shem was born circumcised; see Jalkuṭ, Gen. § 80; *J.E.* xi. 261; Hippolytus (ed. Achelis), p. 91; and Jerome, Ep. cxxvi. quoted by Rahmer, *op. cit.* p. 72.

[4] See Agadath Bereshith, p. 35, and Tanchuma Vayêra, § ii.

[5] Luria thinks that the rest of the verse, " And also all those born in his house," etc., is missing in our text.

[6] And then it is at its zenith. See Gen. Rab. xlvii. 9; Rashi on Gen., *in loc.*; and Leḳach Ṭob, *in loc.*

tenth day of the month,[1] the Day of Atonement. It is written in connection with the Day of Atonement, "Ye shall do no manner of work on that *selfsame day*, for it is a day of atonement" (Lev. xxiii. 28); and in the present instance the text says, "In the *selfsame day* was Abraham circumcised" (Gen. xvii. 26). Know then that on the Day of Atonement Abraham our father was circumcised.[2] Every year the Holy One, blessed be He, sees the blood of our father Abraham's circumcision, and He forgives all the sins of Israel, as it is said, "*For on this day*[3] shall atonement be made for you, to cleanse you" (Lev. xvi. 30). In that place where Abraham was circumcised and his blood remained, there the altar was built,[4] and therefore, "And all the blood thereof shall he pour out at the base of the altar" (*ibid.* iv. 30). (It says also),[5] "I said unto thee, In thy blood, live;[6] yea, I said unto thee, In thy blood, live" (Ezek. xvi. 6).

Rabbi Chanina ben Dosa said: All who are circumcised have (excessive) pain on the third day, as it is said, "And it came to pass on the third day, when they were sore" (Gen. xxxiv. 25).[7] They may wash || the child on the third day,[8] when it happens to fall on the Sabbath, and all things necessary for a circumcision[9] are permitted to be done on the Sabbath.[10]

[1] Tishri, the 7th month.

[2] This is mentioned by Tosaphoth to T.B. Rosh Ha-Shanah, 11a, catchword "But." The story is given by R. Bechai, Comm. on Gen., *in loc.*, with a different reading; see also Midrash Agadah, Gen. xvii. 21. According to T.B. Baba Mezi'a, 86b, the circumcision of Abraham took place on Passover. Jubilees xxxiv. 18 speaks of the institution of the Day of Atonement in connection with Joseph. Our author, in his opposition to Jubilees, connects the Day of Atonement with the life of Abraham. Such variant traditions are common to all histories; cf. Usener, "Weihnachsfest," for the different dates observed by the Church to celebrate the birthday of the Founder of the Christian faith.

[3] *i.e.* the event that marked this day, namely, the circumcision of the Founder of the Hebrew religion. The circumcision of the Founder of the Christian Church is now observed annually on 1st January.

[4] Mount Moriah. Cf. the legends of Golgotha and Akeldama, see Jerome, Com. in Eph. v. 14.

[5] The last two sentences of this paragraph are wanting in the Oxford MS.

[6] The MS. omits here the second half of the verse; it occurs in the first editions.

[7] The first editions add: "Accordingly the sages have taught."

[8] After birth. This is a Mishnah in T.B. Sabbath xix. 3. 134b, and cf. Jalkut, Gen. § 135.

[9] See T.B. Sabbath, 132a.

[10] See T.B. Sabbath, 128b and 133a.

Every uncircumcised (man) shall not eat (of the Paschal offering), and shall not touch the sanctuary. He who separates himself from circumcision is like one separated from the Holy One, blessed be He.

Rabban Gamaliel,[1] the son of Rabbi Jehudah the Prince, said: When our father Abraham was circumcised, on the third day he was very sore,[2] in order to test him.[3] What did the Holy One, blessed be He, do? He pierced one hole in the midst of Gehinnom, and He made the day hot, like the day of the wicked.[4] He[5] went forth, and sat down at the entrance of the tent in the cool of the day, as it is said, "And he sat at the tent door (in the heat of the day)" (*ibid.* xviii. 1). The Holy One, blessed be He, said to the ministering angels: Come ye, let us descend and visit the sick, for the virtue of visiting the sick is great before Me.[6] The Holy One, blessed be He, and the angels descended to visit our father Abraham, as it is said, "And the Lord appeared unto him" (*ibid.*). The Holy One, blessed be He, said to the ministering angels: Come ye and see ye[7] the power of circumcision.[8] Before Abraham was circumcised he fell[9] on his face (before Me), and afterwards I spake with him, as it is said, "And Abraham fell upon his face" (*ibid.* xvii. 17). Now that he is circumcised he sits and I stand. Whence do we know that the Holy One, blessed be He, was standing? Because it is said, "And he looked, and, lo, three men *stood* over against him" (*ibid.* xviii. 2).

[1] This is Gamaliel II., to be distinguished from his grandfather Gamaliel I. mentioned previously.

[2] The pain on the third day was made exceptionally severe in order to test Abraham. This was the eighth trial according to our Book.

[3] See Agadath Bereshith, pp. 37 ff., and Jalkut, Gen. § 82, which reads: "What did He do to try him? He pierced an aperture in Gehinnom."

[4] See T.B. Baba Mezi'a, 86b, and see *infra*, p. 416, and cf. 'Arukh, ed. Kohut, v. 390, *s.v.* נרתק, and *ibid.* p. 20, *s.v.* להט. There is no eternal Gehenna in the future life, only a day of heat; see T.B. Nedarim, 8b.

[5] *i.e.* Abraham.

[6] Cf. *supra*, pp. 89, 107.

[7] This expression is a characteristic of our author.

[8] On Circumcision see *J.E.* iv. 92 ff., and on "'Orlah" see *ibid.* ix. 435.

[9] Pal. Targum, Gen. xvii. 17, reads: "And because Abraham was not circumcised he was not able to stand, but he bowed himself upon his face." Balaam also fell down when receiving the Divine oracles.

Rabbi Ẓe'era || said: There are five [1] kinds of 'Orlah (things uncircumcised) in the world: four with reference to man, and one concerning trees. Whence do we know this concerning the four (terms) applying to man? (Namely,) the uncircumcision of the ear, the uncircumcision of the lips, the uncircumcision of the heart, and the uncircumcision of the flesh. Whence do we know of the uncircumcision of the ear? Because it is said, "Behold, their ear is uncircumcised" (Jer. vi. 10). Whence do we know of the uncircumcision of the lips? Because it is said, "For I am of uncircumcised lips" (Ex. vi. 12). Whence do we know of the uncircumcision of the heart? Because it is said, "Circumcise the foreskin of your heart" (Deut. x. 16); and (the text) says, "For all the nations are uncircumcised, and all the house of Israel are uncircumcised in heart" (Jer. ix. 26). Whence do we know of the uncircumcision of the flesh? Because it is said, "And the uncircumcised male who is not circumcised in the flesh of his foreskin" (Gen. xvii. 14). And "all the nations are uncircumcised" in all the four cases, and "all the house of Israel are uncircumcised in heart." The uncircumcision of the heart does not suffer Israel to do the will of their Creator. And in the future the Holy One, blessed be He, will take away from Israel the uncircumcision of the heart, and they will not harden their stubborn (heart) any more before their Creator, as it is said, "And I will take away the stony heart [2] out of your flesh, and I will give you an heart of flesh" (Ezek. xxxvi. 26); and it is said, "And ye shall be circumcised in the flesh of your foreskin" [3] (Gen. xvii. 11). Whence do we know concerning the one ('Orlah) for trees? [4] Because it is said, "And when ye shall come into the land, and shall have planted all manner of trees for food, then ye shall

[1] See Gen. Rab. xlvi. 5. The tractate of 'Orlah in the Mishnah, Tosephta, and Jerushalmi deals with the "uncircumcision" of trees based on Lev. xix. 23–25.

[2] In the MS. the quotation ends here; in the first editions it is continued as in our version. The MS. adds "etc."

[3] The first editions read: "And ye shall circumcise the foreskin of your flesh," which is not an actual quotation, but a combination of Gen. xvii. 11 and Deut. x. 16. The MS. originally read: "the foreskin of your heart," which has been deleted.

[4] In addition to the Mishnah and Tosephta on "'Orlah" see Maimonides, Ma'akhaloth 'Asuroth, x. 9 ff. According to T.B. Ḳiddushin, 37a, the law of 'Orlah is limited to Palestine.

count the fruit thereof as their uncircumcision:[1] three years shall they be as uncircumcised unto you" (Lev. xix. 23).

Rabbi Ẓe'era[2] taught: The tree ‖ which is mentioned here is none other than the vine tree.[3] If they do not cut off from the tree the fruit of the first three years, all the fruit which it yields will be gleanings fit to be pluckt off, and not good; and its wine will be disqualified for the altar; but if they cut off from the tree the fruit of the first three years, all the fruit which it yields will be good for the sight, and their wine will be selected to be brought upon the altar. So with our father Abraham; before he was circumcised, the fruit which he produced was not good [in its effects,[4] and was disqualified from the altar; but when he had been circumcised, the fruit which he produced was good in its effects,[5] and his wine][6] was chosen to be put upon the altar like wine for a libation, as it is said, "And wine for the drink offering" (Num. xv. 5).

Rabbi[7] said: Abraham did not delay aught[8] with reference to all (things) which He commanded him, as it is said, "And he that is eight days old shall be circumcised" (Gen. xvii. 12); and when Isaac was born, (and when) he was eight days old (Abraham) brought him to be circumcised, as it is said, "And Abraham circumcised his son Isaac when he was eight days old" (*ibid.* xxi. 4). Hence thou mayest learn that everyone who brings his son for circumcision is as though (he were) a high priest bringing his meal offering and his drink offering upon the top of the altar.[9] Hence

[1] In the MS. the quotation ends here.

[2] The first editions read "Ẓeriḳa." On "Ẓe'era" see *J.E.* xii. 651 f., and on "Ẓeriḳa" see *ibid.* 662.

[3] See Joreh Di'ah, 294. For a similar law see Jubilees vii. 1 and 35–38. *All* trees bearing fruit fit to be eaten were subject to this law; cf. Ezek. xvii. 5 ff. It is very remarkable that our author restricts the law of 'Orlah to the vine, which the Rabbis included among the fruit-bearing trees; see Siphra, 90a.

[4] With reference to Ishmael. See Jalḳuṭ, Gen. § 81.

[5] With reference to Isaac.

[6] This portion in square brackets is missing in the MS., but undoubtedly it must be supplied; it occurs in the first editions.

[7] The first editions read: "Rabbi Ishmael." This section occurs in a later part of the chapter in the printed texts.

[8] See T.B. Pesachim, 4a.

[9] This sentence is not in the printed texts. The first editions read: "And he brought him (as) a meal offering upon the top of the altar, and he made festivities and a banquet." See Shocher Ṭob, Ps. cxii. p. 234b. This Midrash has used our book. Some of the printed texts

the sages said: A man is bound to make festivities and a banquet on that day when he has the merit of having his son[1] circumcised, like Abraham our father, who circumcised his son, as it is said, "And Abraham circumcised || his son Isaac"[2] (*ibid.*).

Rabbi Jochanan said: All heathens who come to Israel are circumcised by their own freewill and with their consent, and in the fear of Heaven are they circumcised. We do not believe a proselyte until seven generations (have passed), so that the waters should not return to their source.[3] But slaves are circumcised both by their freewill and with their consent as well as without their consent, and no confidence is placed in slaves. Likewise with all the slaves who were circumcised with our father Abraham, they did not remain true (converts) in Israel, neither they nor their seed, because it is said, "All the men of his house, those born in the house,[4] and those bought with money of the stranger, were circumcised with him" (*ibid.* xvii. 27). Why did he circumcise them? Because of purity, so that they should not defile their masters with their food and with their drink, for whosoever eateth with an uncircumcised person is as though he were eating flesh of abomination.[5] All who bathe with the uncircumcised are as though they bathed with carrion,[6] and all who touch an uncircumcised person are as though they touched the dead, for in their lifetime they are like (the) dead;[7] and in their death they

read: "he presented him like an offering" (by circumcision). See Jalkut, Gen., *loc. cit.*, and Tania Rabbathi, 96 (ed. Warsaw), p. 101b.

[1] See Tosaphoth on Sabbath, 130a; Joreh Di'ah, 265.

[2] The first editions do not use this quotation, but "And Abraham made a great feast on the day that Isaac was weaned" (Gen. xxi. 8). This was not the day of circumcision. But just as Abraham made a feast at the weaning of his son, it was inferred that he had also made a feast at the circumcision.

[3] To test whether they might revert to their former idolatry. Cf. T.B. Synhedrin, 94a, and Midrash Haggadol, c. 257.

[4] The quotation ends here in the MS.

[5] The first editions read: "as though he were eating with a dog. Just as the dog is not circumcised so the uncircumcised person is not circumcised." For parallel N.T. teaching see Phil. iii. 2 and Eph. ii. 11.

[6] The first editions read: "a leper." See Maimonides, *On Idolatry*, vii. 18.

[7] Cf. Matt. viii. 22, where the Jews are referred to as "the dead." The heathens or Gentiles were, according to the N.T., believed to be under the control of Satan (see 2 Cor. vi. 15-18; and cf. 1 Cor. x. 19 and xii. 2) and therefore children of death (see Heb. ii. 14 f.), whereas the

are like the carrion of the beast,[1] and their prayer does not come before the Holy One, blessed be He, as it is said, "The dead praise not the Lord" (Ps. cxv. 17). But Israel who are circumcised, their prayer comes before the Holy One, blessed be He, || like a sweet savour, as it is said, "But *we will bless* the Lord[2] from this time forth and for evermore. Praise ye the Lord" (*ibid.* 18).

Rabbi said: Isaac circumcised Jacob, and Esau;[3] and Esau despised the covenant of circumcision just as he despised the birthright, as it is said, "So Esau despised his birthright" (Gen. xxv. 34). Jacob clung to the covenant of circumcision, and circumcised his sons and his grandsons. Whence (do we know) that the sons of Jacob were circumcised? Because it is said, "Only on this condition will the men consent unto us to dwell[4] with us . . . if every male among us be circumcised, as they are circumcised." (*ibid.* xxxiv. 22). Another text says, "Only on this condition will we consent unto you: if ye will be as we be" (*ibid.* 15).[5] Hence thou canst learn that the sons of Jacob were circumcised. The sons of Jacob circumcised their sons and their grandsons. They gave it to them as an inheritance for an everlasting statute, until Pharaoh the Wicked arose[6] and decreed harsh laws concerning them,

believers or Christians are the only ones who really live (cf. Rom. v. 12–21, *ibid.* i. 16–32, *ibid.* vi. 13, and *ibid.* viii. 6–10). The Ephesians, formerly "Gentiles in the flesh who are called Uncircumcision" (Eph. ii. 11), are addressed thus: "You who were *dead* in trespass and sins" (*ibid.* 1).

[1] The first editions read: "of the field." A parallel to the teaching of this section is to be found in the doctrine so strongly emphasized by Paul that the Christians should not partake of "the things which the Gentiles sacrifice" (1 Cor. x. 20). Jesus also said, "Give not that which is holy unto the *dogs*, neither cast your pearls before the swine, lest haply they trample them under their feet, and turn and rend you" (Matt. vii. 6). On "Dog" as applied to non-Christians in the New Testament and Christian literature, see *Jewish Sources of the Sermon on the Mount*, pp. 219 ff. See also Jubilees xv. 26. The Church Councils prohibited Christians eating with the Jews, see *Apostolic Constitutions*, ii. 62 and viii. 47.

[2] The quotation ends here in the MS., it is continued in the first editions.

[3] Jubilees xv. 30 says of Esau: "the Lord did not cause him to approach him." See Jalkuṭ, Gen. § 116.

[4] In the MS the quotation ends here.

[5] This quotation is not in the printed texts. The verse continues: "that every male of you be circumcised."

[6] See Eccles. Rab. on Eccles. ix. 12; Ruth Rab. Proem. 6. According to Num. Rab. xv. 12, only the tribe of Levi kept the rite of circum-

and withheld from them the covenant of circumcision. And on the day when the children of Israel went forth from Egypt all the people were circumcised, both young and old, as it is said, " For all the people that came out were circumcised " (Josh. v. 5).

The Israelites took the blood of the covenant of circumcision,[1] and they put (it) [2] upon the lintel of their houses, and when the Holy One, blessed be He, passed over to plague the Egyptians, He saw the blood of the covenant of circumcision upon the lintel of their houses and the blood of the Paschal lamb, He was filled || with compassion [3] on Israel, as it is said, " And when I passed by thee, and saw thee weltering in thy (twofold) blood,[4] I said unto thee, In thy (twofold) blood, live; yea, I said unto thee, In thy (twofold) blood, live " (Ezek. xvi. 6). " In thy blood " is not written here, but in " thy (twofold) blood," with twofold blood, the blood of the covenant of circumcision and the blood of the Paschal lamb; therefore it is said, " I said unto thee, In thy (twofold) blood, live; yea, I said unto thee, In thy (twofold) blood, live " (*ibid.*).

Rabbi Eliezer said: Why [5] did the text say twice, " I said unto thee, In thy blood, live; yea, I said unto thee, In thy blood, live "? But the Holy One, blessed be He, said: By the merit of the blood of the covenant of circumcision and the blood of the Paschal lamb ye shall be redeemed from Egypt, and by the merit of the covenant of circumcision and by the merit of the covenant of the Passover in the future ye shall be redeemed at the end of the fourth kingdom; [6] therefore it is said, " I said unto thee, In

cision in Egypt; the other tribes refused to obey in this matter. See Ex. Rab. i. 20, and xix. 5; Tanna de bê Elijahu Rab. xxiii. p. 123; and Siphrê, Num. § 67.

[1] The first editions add: " and the blood of the Paschal lamb." See Pal. Targum on Ex. xii. 13, which reads, " And the blood of the Paschal offering and the rite of circumcision shall be a guarantee to you, to become a sign upon the houses where ye dwell "; see also Mekhilta (on Ex. xii. 6) p. 5a, Ẓohar, Lev. 95a, and Num. Rab. xiv. 12.

[2] The first editions read " them," *i.e.* the blood of the circumcision as well as the blood of the Paschal lamb.

[3] The root " Pasach " (פסח) means to spare, hence to be compassionate.

[4] The quotation ends here in the MS.; in the first editions it is continued.

[5] Lit. " For what purpose did the text see to say."

[6] At the Messianic redemption.

thy blood, live; yea, I said unto thee, In thy blood, live" (*ibid.*).[1]

There are three afflictions,[2] (namely,) the affliction of the fast, the affliction of the prison, and the affliction of the road.[3] Whence do we know of the affliction of the fast? (Because it is said,)[4] "I *afflicted* my soul with *fasting*" (Ps. xxxv. 13). Whence do we know of the affliction of the prison? (Because it is said,)[4] "They *hurt* his feet with *fetters*" (*ibid.* cv. 18). Whence do we know of the affliction of the road? (Because it is said,)[4] "He weakened my strength *in the way*" (*ibid.* cii. 23). On account of the affliction of the road, (the children of Israel)[4] did not circumcise, and when they went forth from Egypt all the people were circumcised, both young and old, as it is said, "For all the people that came out were circumcised" || (Josh. v. 5).[5]

Rabbi Ishmael said: Did the uncircumcised[6] hear the voice of the Holy One, blessed be He, on Mount Sinai, saying, "I am the Lord thy God" (Ex. xx. 2)?[7] They were circumcised, but not according to its regulation.[8] They had cut off the foreskin, but they had not uncovered the corona. Everyone who has been circumcised, but has not had the corona uncovered, is as though he had not been circumcised, therefore the text says, "Israel was not circumcised of old."[9]

When they came to the land (of Canaan),[10] the Holy One, blessed be He, said to Joshua: Joshua! Dost thou not know that the Israelites are not circumcised according to the proper regulation? He again circumcised them a second time, as

[1] See Targum on Ezek. xvi. 6; and cf. *infra*, pp. 383 ff.
[2] See T.B. Nedarim, 31b, 32a; T.B. Giṭṭin, 70a; Shocher Ṭob, Ps. xxxi. p. 121a; Lam. Rab. i. 50; T.B. Jebamoth, 71b, on the danger of circumcision when one travels.
[3] Or, journey.
[4] This is omitted by the MS., but it occurs in the first editions.
[5] The printed editions quote Josh. v. 7.
[6] *i.e.* the Israelites.
[7] See Num. Rab. xi. 3, Cant. Rab. i. 12, and Shocher Ṭob, Pss. p. 39a; and cf. T.B. Jebamoth, 72a. The first editions add: "And did He give them the Torah? But, Heaven forbid! They were circumcised, but they did not have the corona uncovered."
[8] This refers to (פריעה) "P'ri'ah" (having the corona uncovered).
[9] This is not a Biblical quotation. Should Josh. v. 5 be quoted?
[10] The first editions read: "When the Israelites came to the land of Israel."

it is said, " The Lord said unto Joshua, Make thee knives of flint,[1] and circumcise again the children of Israel a second time " (Josh. v. 2). " And Joshua made him knives of flint " (*ibid.* 3), and he gathered all the foreskins until he made them (as high) as a hill, as it is said, " And he circumcised the children of Israel at the *hill* of the foreskins " (*ibid.*). The Israelites took the foreskin and the blood [2] and covered them with the dust [3] of the wilderness. When Balaam [4] came, he saw all the wilderness filled with the foreskins of the Israelites, he said: Who will be able to arise by the merit of the blood of the covenant of this circumcision, which is covered by the dust? as it is said, " Who can count the dust of Jacob? " (Num. xxiii. 10).

Hence || the sages instituted that they should cover the foreskin and the blood with the dust of the earth,[5] because they [6] are compared to the dust of the earth, as it is said, " And thy seed shall be as the dust of the earth " (Gen. xxviii. 14). Thus the Israelites were wont to circumcise until they were divided into two kingdoms. The kingdom of Ephraim cast off from themselves the covenant of circumcision.[7] Elijah, may he be remembered for good, arose and was zealous with a mighty passion, and he adjured the heavens to send down neither dew nor rain upon the earth. Jezebel heard (thereof), and sought to slay him. Elijah arose and prayed before the Holy One, blessed be He.

The Holy One, blessed be He, said to him: " Art thou better than thy fathers? " [8] Esau sought to slay Jacob,

[1] The quotation ends here in the MS.; in the first editions the latter part of the verse only is given.

[2] The law of the covering of the blood is ascribed by Jubilees vii. 30 to Noah, who tells his sons: " and work ye a good work to your souls by covering that which has been shed on the face of the earth "; see also *ibid.* 31, 33. In opposition to Jubilees, our author transfers the precept to Abraham.

[3] The Babylonian Jews appear to have used water to cover the blood at the circumcision, whereas the Palestinian Jews used earth to cover the blood and the foreskin after the circumcision. See Sha'arê Zedeḳ v. 10; Ṭur Joreh Di'ah, 265; Ẓohar, Gen. 95a. Cf. Menorath Ha-Maor § lxxx.

[4] The Venice edition adds here: "the magician." See Jalḳuṭ, Gen. § 71.

[5] See previous note 3; and see Chiluf Minhagim, ed. Müller, pp. 18 f., and see also the Haggadic Commentary Sekhel Tob i. p. 19.

[6] The Israelites.

[7] Jubilees xv. 33 refers to the neglect of circumcision by the children of Israel.

[8] Cf. 1 Kings xix. 4.

but he fled before him,[1] as it is said, "And Jacob fled into the field of Aram "[2] (Hos. xii. 12). Pharaoh sought to slay Moses, who fled before him and he was saved, as it is said, "Now when Pharaoh heard this thing,[3] he sought to slay Moses. And Moses fled from the face of Pharaoh" (Ex. ii. 15). Saul sought to slay David, who fled before him and was saved, as it is said, "If thou save not thy life to-night, to-morrow thou shalt be slain" (1 Sam. xix. 11).[4] Another text says, "And David fled and escaped" (*ibid.* 18). Learn that everyone, who flees, is saved. Elijah, may he be remembered for good, arose and fled from the land of Israel,[5] || and he betook himself to Mount Horeb, as it is said, "And he arose, and did eat and drink" (1 Kings xix. 8). There the Holy One, blessed be He, was revealed unto him, and He said to him: "What doest thou here, Elijah?" (*ibid.* 9). He answered Him, saying: "I have been very zealous" (*ibid.* 10). (The Holy One, blessed be)[6] He, said to him: Thou art always zealous![7] Thou wast zealous in Shittim[8] on account of the immorality. Because it is said, "Phineas,[9] the son of Eleazar, the son of Aaron the priest,[10] turned my wrath away from the children of Israel, in that he was zealous with my zeal among them" (Num. xxv. 11). Here also art thou zealous. By thy life! They[11] shall not observe the

[1] The first editions add: "and he was saved."

[2] See Jalḳuṭ, Ex. § 168, and Menorath Ha-Maor § lxxx. Eventually Jacob escaped from Laban, as well as from Esau. The first editions read: "Esau attempted to slay Jacob, as it is said, 'The days of mourning for my father are at hand; then will I slay my brother Jacob'" (Gen. xxvii. 41).

[3] In the MS. the quotation ends here; the first editions quote the latter part of the verse.

[4] The first editions quote (1 Sam. xix. 11) only.

[5] To Horeb, which was outside Palestine.

[6] This is missing in the MS., but it occurs in the first editions.

[7] See Cant. Rab. i. 6; Tanna de bê Elijahu Ẓuṭṭa (viii.), p. 187; Jalḳuṭ to 1 Kings § 217; Agadath Shir Ha-Shirim, p. 45, quoted by Schechter in his *Aspects of Rabbinic Theology*, p. 205; see also *ibid.*, p. 52, on Elijah's zeal.

[8] See *infra*, p. 370, and Jalḳuṭ, Gen. § 71.

[9] Phineas is identified with Elijah. Just as we find in the New Testament that John the Baptist was held to be Elijah, see Matt. xi. 14. According to some Jewish authorities Elijah was a priest, see Tanna de bê Elijahu Rab. xviii. pp. 97 f. This legend occurs also in the Book of the Bee (ed. Budge), p. 70.

[10] In the MS. the quotation ends here.

[11] The first editions and Jalḳuṭ, *loc. cit.*, read "Israel."

covenant of circumcision until thou seest it (done) with thine eyes.

Hence the sages [1] instituted (the custom) that people should have a seat of honour for the Messenger of the Covenant; for Elijah, may he be remembered for good, is called the Messenger of the Covenant, as it is said, "And the messenger of the covenant, whom ye delight in, behold, he cometh" (Mal. iii. 1).[2]

[1] See Ṭur, Joreh Di'ah, 265; Tania Rabbathi, 96, p. 101a, and Halakhoth Gedoloth quoted by Schorr in החלוץ, v. 38.[1]

[2] The chair for Elijah is to this day a feature at every circumcision. The MS. Gaster and the first editions add: "O God of Israel! Hasten and bring the Messiah in our lifetime to comfort us, and may he restore [2] our hearts, as it is said: 'And he shall restore [3] the heart of the fathers to the children, and the heart of the children to the fathers'" (Mal. iv. 6).[4] According to this reading the chapter closes with a rhyme. Luria argues that as the verse quoted from Malachi speaks of Elijah, the reading might originally have been "Elijah" in place of the word "Messiah," or perhaps both words were in the context. See *infra*, p. 344. The Oxford MS. reads the entire verse Mal. iii. 1.

---

[1] Dr. Büchler observes: "The earliest reference known besides this, is R. Jacob b. Nissim of Kairwân about 970 C.E. אורחות חיים (ed. Schlesinger) 12; see also Güdemann, *Erziehungswesen in Italien*, p. 28, n. 4; Zunz, *Zur Gesch.*, pp. 485, 590 ff.; and Lewysohn, מקורי מנהגים 93.

[2] Lit. "renew."

[3] The R.V. renders "turn."

[4] This is not the mission of the Messiah, but of Elijah, the great Reconciler.

CHAPTER XXX

THE TRIALS OF ABRAHAM (*continued*)

Abraham and Ishmael [36A. ii.]

THE ninth trial (was as follows): Ishmael was born with (the prophecy of the) bow,[1] and he grew up with the bow,[2] as it is said, "And God was with the lad, and he grew . . .[3] and he became an archer" (Gen. xxi. 20). He took bow and arrows and began to shoot at the birds.[4] He saw Isaac sitting by himself, and he shot an arrow[5] at him to slay him.[6] Sarah saw (this), and told Abraham. She said to him: Thus and thus has Ishmael done to Isaac, but (now) arise and write (a will in favour) of Isaac, (giving him) all that the Holy One has sworn to give || to thee and to thy seed.[7] The son of this handmaid shall not inherit with my son, with Isaac, as it is said, "And she said unto Abraham, Cast out this bondwoman and her son" (*ibid.* 10).

Ben Tema[8] said: Sarah said to Abraham, Write[9] a bill of

[1] Perhaps the version should be, "Ishmael was born under (the constellation) Sagittarius." The word "Ḳêshêth" sometimes means this constellation, or it might indicate "harshness."

[2] Jalkuṭ, Gen. § 94 reads: "Ishmael was born and grew up with the bow." Cf. Isa. xxi. 15.

[3] The quotation ends here in the MS.; the first editions quote the latter part of the verse only.

[4] See Tosephta Soṭah vi. p. 308; Jalkuṭ, *loc. cit.*, and Gen. Rab. liii. 15. The MS. reads "Pugoth." This agrees with the Oxford MS. "Puga" is identified with "Suga," the name of a bird. See T.B. Baba Bathra, 90b.

[5] MS. O.A. 167 reads: "the arrows." See Gen. Rab. liii. 11.

[6] See Leḳach Ṭob, Gen. p. 47, note 20, for other parallels.

[7] Cf. Gen. xv. 5 and xvii. 7. The first editions add: "By thy life." Luria would read: "In thy life time" and connects it with the preceding sentence: "Write in thy life time."

[8] This is missing in the printed editions and in Jalkuṭ, Gen., *loc. cit.*, but it occurs in MS. O.A. 167. Ben Tema was an Amora.

[9] MS. O.A. 167 reads: "Arise and write."

divorce,[1] and send away this handmaid and her son from me and from Isaac my son, in this world and from the world to come. More than all the misfortunes which overtook Abraham, this matter was exceedingly evil in his eyes, as it is said, "And the thing was very grievous in Abraham's sight on account of his son" (*ibid.* 11).[2]

Rabbi Jehudah[3] said: In that night the Holy One, blessed be He, was revealed unto him. He said to him: Abraham! Dost thou not know that Sarah was appointed to thee for a wife[4] from her mother's womb? She is thy companion, and the wife of thy covenant;[5] Sarah is not called thy handmaid, but thy wife;[6] neither is Hagar called thy wife, but thy handmaid; and all that Sarah has spoken[7] she has uttered truthfully. Let it not be grievous in thine eyes, as it is said, "And God said unto Abraham, Let it not be grievous in thy sight" (*ibid.* 12).

Abraham rose up early,[8] and wrote a bill of divorce, and gave it to Hagar, and he sent her and her son away from himself, and from Isaac his son, from this world and from the world to come, as it is said, "And Abraham rose up early in the morning, and took[9] bread and a bottle of water" (*ibid.* 14). He sent her away || with a bill of divorcement, and he took the veil,[10] and he bound it around her waist, so that it should drag behind her to disclose (the fact) that she was a bondwoman.[11] Not only this, but also because

[1] See Pal. Targum, Gen. xxi. 10.

[2] The Pal. Targum, Gen., *loc. cit.*, explains that this was due to the evil deeds of Ishmael in the future. The inference in our Midrash is derived from the quotation, and it was only in this instance that Scripture refers to the sorrow of Abraham. See Midrash Haggadol, c. 308.

[3] MS. O.A. 167 adds: "the Prince."

[4] The Venice edition adds: "from her birth."

[5] *i.e.* the first wife. See Mal. ii. 14; and Targum, *in loc.*, and cf. Rashi on Mal. ii. 14.

[6] MS. O.A. 167 adds: "as it is said: 'And God said, But Sarah thy wife'" (Gen. xvii. 19). This verse is also given by the first editions.

[7] MS. O.A. 167 adds: "to thee."

[8] MS. O.A. 167 adds: "in the morning." See Midrash Haggadol, c. 309.

[9] In the MS. the quotation ends here, but "etc." is added. The first editions and MS. O.A. 167 continue the verse. Luria adds: "And the child."

[10] See Jalkuṭ, Gen. § 95, according to Jastrow, *T.D.* 1452b, for a variant reading. Cf. Gen. Rab. liii. 13. The Venice edition reads "water-barrel"; cf. Siphrê, Num. § 115, and Jalkuṭ, Num. § 750, which reads "water-barrel." Our MS. agrees with the text in the 1st ed.

[11] See T.B. Baba Mezi'a, 87a.

Abraham desired to see Ishmael, his son, and to see the way whereon they went.

By the merit of our father Abraham the water did not fail in the bottle, but when she reached the entrance to the wilderness, she began to go astray after the idolatry of her father's house; [1] and forthwith the water in the bottle was spent, as it is said, "And she departed and wandered" (*ibid.*). Ishmael was seventeen [2] years old (when) he went forth from the house of Abraham, and Isaac was forty [3] years old. By the merit of our father Abraham the water did not fail in the bottle, but when she reached the entrance to the wilderness, she began to go astray after the idolatry of her father's house; the water in the bottle was spent,[4] and the soul of Ishmael was faint with thirst.

"And she departed and wandered" (*ibid.*). The meaning of "and she wandered" is merely idolatry, because it is written, concerning (this root),[5] "They are vanity, a work of delusion" [6] (Jer. x. 15).[7] He went and cast himself beneath the thorns of the wilderness,[8] so that the moisture might be upon him, and he said: O God of my father Abraham! [9] Thine are the issues of death; take away from me

[1] The first editions read: "the house of Pharaoh her father"; according to Rabbinic legend Hagar was the daughter of Pharaoh. See *supra*, p. 190, Gen. Rab. xlv. 2, and the Book of Jashar xv. 31.

[2] The Venice edition gives twenty-seven years for Ishmael's age.

[3] The first editions read: "ten years." The "forty years" may refer to Isaac's age when he married Rebecca and left his father's house to dwell in Sarah's tent. It seems very probable that the MS. reading is based on a copy which read "four" years. This was altered by the writer of our MS. into "forty." Ishmael was thirteen years older than Isaac, and as the former was seventeen years old when he left Abraham's house Isaac must have been four years old. See *infra*, p. 225. See Gen. Rab. liii. 13, according to which Ishmael was twenty-seven years old; see also the Book of Jashar xxi. 14, Jalḳuṭ, Gen., *loc. cit.*, and Midrash Haggadol, *loc. cit.*

[4] The whole of this sentence thus far is an exact repetition of a few lines above. See also Midrash Haggadol, *loc. cit.*, for the same circumstance.

[5] Cf. Isa. xix. 13.

[6] The root of this word (תעתע) is connected apparently with the Hebrew "to err" or "to wander" (תעה); see Ẓohar, Gen 118b.

[7] The previous verse refers to the images.

[8] Cf. Jalḳuṭ, Gen., *loc. cit.* The phraseology is based on Job xxx. 7. This chapter is applied to Ishmael by the Midrash. The next few words (up to "upon him") are wanting in the printed texts.

[9] Cf. the version of the prayer in Jalkut, Gen., *loc. cit.* The printed editions of our book differ here from our MS. The first editions read thus: "Sovereign of the Worlds! If it be Thy pleasure to give me water to drink, give me to drink and let not my soul depart because of

my soul, for I would not die of thirst. And He was entreated of him, as it is said, " For God hath heard the || voice of the lad where he is" (Gen. xxi. 17). The well[1] which was created at twilight[2] was opened for them there, and they went and drank and filled the bottle with water, as it is said, " And God opened her eyes, and she saw a well of water" (*ibid.* 19). And there[3] they left the well,[4] and thence they started on their way,[5] and went through all the wilderness until they came to the wilderness of Paran, and they found there streams of water, and they dwelt there, as it is said, " And he dwelt in the wilderness of Paran" (*ibid.* 21). Ishmael sent for a wife from among the daughters[6] of Moab, and 'Ayeshah[7] was her name. After three years[8] Abraham went to see Ishmael his son, having sworn to Sarah that he would not descend from the camel in the place where Ishmael dwelt. He arrived there at midday and found there the wife of Ishmael. He said[9] to her: Where is Ishmael? She said to him: He has gone with his mother to fetch the fruit of the palms[10] from the wilderness. He said to her: Give me a little bread and a little water,[11] for my soul is faint after the journey in the desert. She said to him: I have neither bread nor water. He said to her: When Ishmael comes (home) tell him this || story, and say to him: A certain old man came from the land of Canaan to see thee, and he said, Exchange[12] the

thirst; for death by thirst is unnatural, and it is harder than all other (kinds of) death. The Holy One, blessed be He, heard his prayer."

[1] See *infra*, p. 263.

[2] Of the eve of the first Sabbath in the week of Creation. See *supra*, p. 124.

[3] In the wilderness of Beer-Sheba.

[4] See *infra*, pp. 268, 323.

[5] Lit. " they lifted up their feet."

[6] The first editions read: " fords." The reading in our MS. is the correct text.

[7] In later editions other readings of this name are found, namely, "'Essah" and "'Ephah." See Grünbaum, *op. cit.* p. 125.

[8] Cf. the narrative in the Book of Jashar xxi. 22 ff.; Jalkuṭ, Gen., *loc. cit.*, and Midrash Haggadol, c. 310.

[9] The scribe has made a little mistake here by writing " She said."

[10] Luria objects to the text, and prefers to read, " fruit of the broom-tree"; cf. Job xxx. 4. See Jalkuṭ, *loc. cit.*; T.B. Baba Bathra, 75b; perhaps the text should read: " fruit and broom-trees."

[11] The first editions read: " a little bread and dainties." The Prague edition reads: " a little water and bread and dainties."

[12] The first editions read: " That the door-sill of the house is not good." See the Book of Jashar xxi. 31, and Jalkuṭ, *loc. cit.*

threshold of thy house, for it is not good for thee. When Ishmael came (home) his wife told him the story. A son of a wise man is like half a wise man. Ishmael understood. His mother sent and took for him a wife from her father's house,[1] and her name was Fatimah.[2]

Again after three years Abraham went to see his son Ishmael, having sworn to Sarah as on the first occasion that he would not descend from the camel in the place where Ishmael dwelt. He came there at midday, and found there Ishmael's wife. He said to her: Where is Ishmael? She replied to him: He has gone with his mother to feed the camels in the desert. He said to her: Give me a little bread and water, for my soul is faint after the journey [3] of the desert. She fetched it and gave it to him. Abraham arose and prayed before the Holy One, blessed be He, for his son, and (thereupon) Ishmael's house was filled with all good things of the various blessings.[4] When Ishmael came (home) his wife told him what had happened, and Ishmael knew that his father's love was still extended to him, as it is said, || "Like as a father pitieth his sons" (Ps. ciii. 13). After the death of Sarah, Abraham again took (Hagar) his divorced (wife), as it is said, "And Abraham again [5] took a wife, and her name was Keturah" (Gen. xxv. 1). Why does it say "And he *again*"? Because on the first occasion she was his wife, and he *again* betook himself to her. Her name was Keturah, because she was perfumed with all kinds of scents.[6]

Another explanation of Keturah (is): because her

[1] From Pharaoh's house. See *supra*, p. 190, and cf. the Book of Jashar xxi. 17.

[2] See Pal. Targum, Gen. xxi. 21, and Jalkuṭ, *loc. cit.* These names Fatimah and 'Ayeshah point to Arabian influence, and give us another *terminus a quo* to fix the date and locality of its redaction. 'Ephah, mentioned above (p. 218, note 7), occurs as a woman's name in I Chron. ii. 46.

[3] For this legend, see *Rabbinic Philosophy and Ethics*, pp. 66 f. with notes.

[4] Jalkuṭ, *loc. cit.*, reads "food and blessing." See *infra*, p. 328, and cf. Midrash Haggadol, c. 311.

[5] In our MS. the quotation ends here; it is continued in the first editions as in our version. See Pal. Targum, Gen. xxv. 1, and Midrash Haggadol, c. 375, note 8, where the parallel passages are given.

[6] The Ishmaelites in the wilderness were the buyers and sellers of precious spices. Cf. Cant. iii. 6, and Ezek. xxvii. 21.

actions were beautiful like *incense*,[1] and she bare him six sons,[2] and they were all called according to the name of Ishmael,[3] as it is said, "And she bare him Zimran" (*ibid.* 2).

Like a woman sent away from her husband, so likewise Abraham arose and sent them away from Isaac his son, from this world and from the world to come, as it is said, "But unto the sons of the concubines, which Abraham had,[4] Abraham gave gifts, and he sent them [5] away from Isaac his son" (*ibid.* 6), by a deed of divorcement.

Corresponding to the name of Ishmael's son [6] Kedar, the *sons of Kedar* were so called, as it is said, "Of Kedar, and of the kingdoms of Hazor" (Jer. xlix. 28). Corresponding to the name of Ishmael's son "Kedemah" [7] (Gen. xxv. 15), the "sons of Kedem" were so called.[8] Because they dwelt in the territory belonging to Cain, his children were called "sons of Cain," as it is said, "Now Heber the Kenite had separated himself from Cain" (Judg. iv. 11). Were not all the sons of Cain cut off [9] by the waters of the Flood? But because they dwelt in the territory of the children of Cain, his children were called "sons of Cain," as it is said, "Nevertheless || Cain shall be wasted,[10] as long as Asshur shall dwell in thy place" (Num. xxiv. 22). "Nevertheless Cain shall be wasted away" by fire, through the seed

[1] The Hebrew for "incense" (Ketoreth) suggests a connection with the name Keturah.

[2] The first editions read here (instead of our context) the following: "Zimran, and Jokshan, and Medan and Midian, and Ishbak and Shuah."

[3] The meaning is not quite evident; does it mean that the six names have some part of their spelling in common with the various letters of the name Ishmael? This is the case with the initial letter of five names, but Zimran is the exception.

[4] In the MS. the quotation ends here; it is continued in the first editions.

[5] The MS. reads: "'and he sent them away' by a deed of divorcement."

[6] The first editions read "sons." The descendants of Ishmael intermarried with the children of Keturah.

[7] In the MS. the word has been partly erased, only the letters קד are legible.

[8] The first editions add: "as it is said: 'The children of Ḳedem'" (Jer. xlix. 28).

[9] Cf. Rabbi Bechai's commentary on Num. xxiv. 22, which reads: "Were not all the sons of Cain cut off?" according to our text. The later editions read: "separated at the generation of the flood."

[10] In the MS. the quotation ends here. Our translation of the Scripture text differs from the usual version.

of Ishmael, the latter shall cause the kingdom of Assyria to cease.[1]

Balaam said: Of the seventy nations that the Holy One, blessed be He, created in His world, He did not put His name on any one of them except on Isra*el*;[2] and since the Holy One, blessed be He, made the name of Ishma*el* similar to the name of Isra*el*, woe to him who shall live in his days, as it is said, "Alas, who shall live when God establisheth him?"[3] (*ibid.* 23).

Rabbi Ishmael said: In the future the children of Ishmael will do fifteen things in the land (of Israel) in the latter days, and they are: They will measure the land with ropes;[4] they will change a cemetery into a resting-place for sheep (and) a dunghill; they will measure with them and from them upon the tops of the mountains; falsehood will multiply and truth will be hidden; the statutes will be removed far from Israel; sins will be multiplied in Israel; worm-crimson will be in the wool, and he will cover[5] with insects paper and pen; he will hew down the rock of the kingdom,[6] and they will rebuild the desolated cities and sweep the ways; and they will plant gardens and parks, and fence in the broken walls of the Temple; and they will build a building in the Holy Place; and two brothers will arise over them,[7] princes at the end;

[1] The reference may be to the Moslem possession of Bagdad in Babylon. See *infra*, p. 350; and also Rashbam, *in loc.* (Num. xxiv. 22).

[2] Some of the later editions add here: "And Ishma*el*, as it is said: 'And thou shalt call his name Ishmael'" (Gen. xvi. 11).

[3] By giving him the name of *El*. "Alas, who shall live when he is appointed (with the name) *El*," may be the meaning read into the verse in question, or probably there is a play on the name Ishmael and the last two words Missumô el. The usual rendering is, "Alas, who shall live when God *doeth this*." See Midrash Haggadol, c. 383.

[4] To obtain exact dimension: cf. T.B. Baba Bathra, 103b.

[5] The root קמל means to be decayed. See Isa. xxxiii. 9: "Lebanon mouldereth"; or should we render "The paper will be decayed with the pen"? Literature will then perish. Krauss, *Studien zur Byzantisch-Jüdischen Geschichte*, p. 145, renders the preceding clause: "purple will be exceedingly dear."

[6] The tombs of the Kings of Judah. Krauss, *op. cit.*, renders here: "the coinage will be withdrawn from circulation."

[7] Or, "against them," *i.e.* the two Caliphs, Mohammed Alemin and Abdallah Almamum (809–813 C.E.). See Graetz, *Geschichte*, v. pp. 197 f., and his article in Frankel's *Monatsschrift*, 1859, p. 112. This gives us again a date for determining the period when our book was finally edited. Krauss, *op. cit.*, points out that the reference in the preceding clause is to the Mosque of Omar, the foundation of which

and in their days the Branch, the Son of David, will arise, as it is said, || "And in the days of those kings shall the God of heaven set up a kingdom, which shall never be destroyed" (Dan. ii. 44).

Rabbi Ishmael also said: Three wars of trouble[1] will the sons of Ishmael in the future wage on the earth in the latter days, as it is said, "For they fled away from the swords" (Isa. xxi. 15). "Swords" signify only wars, one in the forest of Arabia, as it is said, "From the drawn sword" (*ibid.*); another on the sea, as it is said, "From the bent bow" (*ibid.*); and one in the great city which is in Rome,[2] which will be more grievous than the other two, as it is said, "And from the grievousness of the war" (*ibid.*). From there the Son of David shall flourish and see the destruction of[3] *these and these*, and thence will He come to the land of Israel, as it is said, "Who is this that cometh from Edom,[4] with crimsoned garments from Bozrah? this that is glorious in his apparel, marching in the greatness of his strength? I that speak in righteousness, mighty to save" (*ibid.* lxiii. 1).

was laid by the Caliph Omar after his conquest of Jerusalem in 636 C.E. In the next line we have the expression, "the Branch, the son of David," cf. *supra*, p. 201, note 3, and see also the Shemoneh 'Esreh, p. 49 (Singer).

[1] Or, "commotion."

[2] The later editions read here "Aram," owing to the Censor.

[3] The Prague edition reads: "the idolaters." See also Graetz, *Geschichte*, v. pp. 441 ff., especially p. 446, on the connection between our book and the *Secrets of R. Simeon ben Jochai*. The latter work, according to Graetz, was the source used by our author. The theory of Graetz was controverted by Steinschneider in *Z.D.M.G.* xxviii. pp. 645 f. The *Secrets* are printed in Jellinek's *B.H.M.* iii. p. 78. A very interesting parallel to the latter part of this chapter of *P.R.E.* is to be found in the Book of the Bee, liii. (pp. 124 ff.).

[4] In the MS. the quotation ends here; it is continued in the first editions.

CHAPTER XXXI

THE BINDING OF ISAAC ON THE ALTAR [38A. i.]

THE tenth trial was (as follows): "And it came to pass after these things, that God did prove Abraham" (Gen. xxii. 1). He tried Abraham each time [1] in order to know his heart, whether he would be able to persevere and keep all the commandments of the Torah [2] or not, and whilst as yet the Torah had not been given, Abraham kept all the precepts [3] of the Torah, as it is said, "Because that Abraham obeyed my voice,[4] and kept my charge, my commandments, my statutes, and my Torah" (*ibid.* xxvi. 5).[5] And Ishmael went repeatedly from the wilderness to see || his father Abraham.[6]

Rabbi Jehudah said: In that night was the Holy One, blessed be He, revealed unto him, and He said unto him: Abraham! "Take now thy son,[7] thine only son, whom thou

[1] See Gen. Rab. lv. 1, and Cant. Rab. i. 9.

[2] The next words, up to "as it is said," are not in the printed editions.

[3] According to the Book of Jubilees, Abraham not only enacted the *laws of tithes* (xiii. 25–29), but he also celebrated the feast of first-fruits of the grain harvest on the 15th of Sivan (xv. 1, 2), and the feast of Tabernacles (xvi. 20–31); he ordained peace-offerings and the regulations as to the use of salt and wood for the offerings, washings before sacrifices, *and the duty of covering blood* (xxi. 7–17), and prohibited intermarrying with the Canaanites (xxii. 20, xxv. 5), and adultery (xxxix. 6). On this theme see Apoc. Baruch lvii. 2, and cf. Ecclus. xliv. 20.

[4] In the MS. the quotation ends here, but it is continued in the first editions.

[5] See T.B. Joma, 28a f.

[6] As Abraham had visited Ishmael, the latter knew that his father would receive him. See Pal. Targum, Gen. xxii. 1, and Gen. Rab. lv. 4, for the story of the dispute between Isaac and Ishmael, and for the account of the readiness of the former to offer up his life to the service of God.

[7] In our MS. the quotation ends here, but it is continued in the first editions.

lovest, even Isaac" (*ibid.* xxii. 2). And Abraham, having pity upon Isaac,[1] said before Him: Sovereign of all worlds! Concerning which son[2] dost Thou decree upon me? Is it concerning the son lacking circumcision,[3] or the son born for circumcision? He answered him: "Thine only son." He rejoined: This one is the only son of *his* mother, and the other son is the only son of *his* mother. He said to him: "The one, whom thou lovest." He said to Him: Both of them do I love.[4] He said to him: "Even Isaac."

"And offer him there for a burnt offering"[5] (*ibid.*). He spake to Him: Sovereign of all worlds! On which mountain hast Thou told me (to offer him)? (God) answered him: In every place where thou dost see My glory abiding and waiting for thee there, and saying,[6] This is Mount Moriah;[7] as it is said, "Upon one of the mountains which *I will tell thee* of" (*ibid.*).[8]

Abraham rose up early in the morning, and he took with him Ishmael, and Eliezer, and Isaac his son, and he saddled the ass. Upon this ass did Abraham ride. This was the ass, the offspring of that ass which was created during the twilight,[9] as it is said, "And Abraham rose early in the morning, and saddled his ass" (*ibid.* 3).[10] The same ass was also ridden upon by Moses when he came to Egypt, as it is said, "And Moses took his wife and his sons, and set them upon *the* ass" (Ex. iv. 20). This || same ass will be ridden

[1] Luria thinks that the reading should be: "The Holy One, blessed be He, had pity upon Isaac" (and ordered that Ishmael should be offered as an atonement for his past evil life). See Jalkut, Gen. § 96, Midrash Haggadol, c. 317, and cf. Wisdom x. 5.

[2] See *Rabbinic Philosophy and Ethics*, p. 69, and cf. the Liturgy for the second day of the New Year, ed. Heidenheim, pp. 34b ff.

[3] Ishmael had been born thirteen years before God commanded the rite of circumcision, and when he was born his father was uncircumcised, but when Isaac was born Abraham was circumcised. On the theme of the "'Aḳedah" see Gen. Rab. lv. 1 f.

[4] See T.B. Synhedrin, 89b; Gen. Rab. xxxix. 12.

[5] See the rest of this quotation.

[6] The first editions add "to thee"; see Jalḳuṭ, Gen., *loc. cit.*

[7] The 1st ed. reads here: "the altar."

[8] The first editions add: "'Which I have told thee of,' is not written here, but, 'which I will tell thee of.'" God would indicate to Abraham the place in His own good time; cf. Gen. Rab. lv. 8.

[9] Preceding the first Sabbath in the week of creation. See Aboth v. 9; Jalḳuṭ, Gen. § 98; Jalkut on Zech. ix. 9 (ed. King, p. 48); and cf. *supra*, p. 124.

[10] This quotation should probably belong to the previous sentence, and follow the word "ass."

upon in the future by the Son of David,[1] as it is said, "Rejoice greatly, O daughter of Zion; shout, O daughter of Jerusalem: behold, thy king cometh unto thee: he is just, and saved;[2] lowly, and riding upon an *ass*, even upon a colt, the foal of an ass"[3] (Zech. ix. 9).

Isaac was thirty-seven years old[4] when he went to Mount Moriah, and Ishmael was fifty years old. Contention arose between Eliezer and Ishmael. Ishmael said to Eliezer: Now that Abraham will offer Isaac his son for a burnt offering, kindled upon the altar,[5] and I am his first-born son, I will inherit (the possessions of) Abraham. Eliezer replied to him, saying: He has already driven thee out like a woman divorced from her husband, and he has sent thee[6] away to the wilderness, but I am his servant, serving him by day and by night, and I shall be the heir of Abraham. The Holy Spirit answered them, saying to them: Neither this one nor that one shall inherit.[7]

On the third day they reached Zophim,[8] and when they reached Zophim they saw the glory of the Shekhinah[9]

[1] The Messiah; see *Rabbinic Philosophy and Ethics*, p. 71, note 2, and *Jewish Sources of the Sermon on the Mount*, p. 143, for the strange interpretation given to this Messianic function by Matthew (xxi. 7), and cf. Justin Martyr, *Dial. c. Tryph.* liii.

[2] In the MS. this first part of the verse is not quoted.

[3] Later Rabbinic interpretation applied this verse sometimes to the Messiah ben Joseph. See Ibn Ezra, *in loc.*

[4] See Tanna de bê Elijahu Rab. xxv. p. 138, and cf. Seder 'Olam Rab. i.; Tosaphoth to T.B. Jebamoth, 61b; Ex. Rab. i. 1, and the previous chapter in our book.

[5] The wording here is based on Lev. vi. 13.

[6] See Jalkuṭ, *loc. cit.*

[7] See Gen. Rab. lvi. 1; Midrash Haggadol, col. 320; Tanchuma, *in loc.* For the story see also the Book of Jashar xxiii. 22 ff., Pal. Targum, and the second version to Gen. xxii. The Church Fathers deal with the theme in their usual style. See Ephraim of Syria on Jonah, 6; Ambrose *On Faith in Immortality*, G.T. i. pp. 404 f.; Zeno of Verona *On Patience*, 5.

[8] *i.e.* Mount Moriah, on which the Temple was built; see 2 Chron. iii. 1. See Rashi on T.B. Pesachim, 49a; 'Arukh, ed. Kohut, vii. 33a; and cf. T.B. Berakhoth, 61b. The word צופים means "watch-towers." The Midrash Haggadol, *loc. cit.*, reads "Zuphith." Jubilees (xviii. 13) agrees with our book in identifying the mount with Mount Zion. See also Book of the Bee, xxv. p. 43.

[9] This passage is of considerable interest. We are in the domain of Philonic interpretation of the Bible. Thus Clement of Alexandria, under the influence of Philo's allegorical interpretation, says on the text, Gen. xxii. 3, 4: "Abraham, when he came to the place which God told him of on the third day, looking up, saw the place afar off. For the first day is that which is constituted by the sight of good things;

resting upon the top of the mountain, as it is said, "On the third day Abraham lifted up his eyes, and saw *the place* afar off" (Gen. xxii. 4). What did he see? (He saw) a pillar of fire standing from the earth to the heavens.[1] Abraham understood that the lad had been accepted for the perfect burnt offering. He said to Ishmael and Eliezer: Do ye see anything upon one of those mountains? || They said to him: No. He considered them (as dull) as an ass. He told them: Since ye do not see anything, "Abide ye here with the ass" (*ibid.* 5),[2] with such who are similar to the ass.[3]

He took the wood and placed it upon the back of his son Isaac, and he took the fire and the knife in his hand, and they went both of them together.[4] Isaac said to his father: O my father! Behold the fire and the wood, where is the lamb for the burnt offering? He replied to him: My son! Thou art the lamb for the burnt offering, as it is said, "And Abraham said, God will provide[5] for himself the lamb" (*ibid.* 8).

Rabbi Simeon[6] said: The Holy One, blessed be He,

and the second is the soul's best desire; on the third, the mind perceives spiritual things" (*Strom.* v. 11).

Our book identifies the place (מקום) with the Shekhinah, just as Philo does (*De Somniis*, i. M. i. 638, C.W. iii. p. 213); see Gen. Rab. lvi. 1 f.; and cf. the valuable note in Weinstein's *Zur Genesis der Agada*, p. 88. The representation of the Shekhinah as a "Pillar of Fire" corresponds with Philo's identification of the Logos with the "Pillar of Cloud," which at night became the "Pillar of Fire" in the wilderness, leading God's people to the Holy Land; see *Hellenism and Christianity*, p. 25, note. According to Jubilees xviii. 4: "And he came to a *well of water* and he said to his young men, 'Abide ye here with the ass.'" Does our author intentionally vary this by substituting the "cloud" for the well?

[1] The first editions add here: "He said to his son Isaac: My son! dost thou see anything upon one of these mountains? He said to him: Yes. (Abraham) said to him: What dost thou see? He replied: I see a pillar of fire standing from the earth up to the heavens." See, for further references to the vision of Isaac and Abraham, Gen. Rab. lvi. 1, Pal. Targum, Gen. xxii. 4, and Tanchuma, Vayêra, § xxiii., which refers to "a cloud enwrapt on the mountain." See also Jalkuṭ, Gen. § 99, and the Book of Jashar xxiii., which has used our book.

[2] See T.B. Jebamoth, 62a; Gen. Rab. lvi. 2; Eccles. Rab. on Eccles. ix. 7; T.B. Ḳiddushin, 68a; and Midrash Haggadol, c. 320.

[3] The first editions add: "Just as the ass does not see anything, likewise do ye not see anything, as it is said: 'And Abraham said to his young men: Abide ye here with the ass'" (Gen. xxii. 5).

[4] Cf. Gen. xxii. 6.

[5] The word might be rendered: "accept." The verse might be translated thus: "God will accept for Himself the lamb, *i.e.* my son."

[6] The first editions read: "Ishmael."

pointed out[1] the altar with a finger to Abraham our father, and said to him: This is the altar. That was the altar[2] whereon Cain and Abel sacrificed; it was the same altar whereon Noah[3] and his sons sacrificed, as it is said,[4] "And Abraham built *the* altar there" (*ibid.* 9). "And Abraham built an altar there" is not written here, but "And Abraham built *the* altar there." That was the altar whereon the first ones (of old) had sacrificed.[5]

Isaac said to his father Abraham: O my father! Bind for me my two hands, and my two feet, so that I do not curse[6] thee; for instance, a word may issue from the mouth because of the violence and dread of death, and I shall be found to have slighted || the precept, "Honour thy father" (Ex. xx. 12).[7] He bound his two hands and his two feet, and bound him upon the top of the altar, and he strengthened his two arms and his two knees[8] upon him, and put the fire and wood in order, and he stretched forth his hand and took the knife. Like a high priest[9] he brought near his meal offering, and his drink offering;[10] and the Holy One, blessed be He, was sitting and beholding the father binding with all (his) heart and the son bound with all (his) heart. And the ministering angels[11] cried aloud and wept, as it is said, "Behold, the

[1] The Venice edition adds: "with the finger"; see *infra*, pp. 382 f.

[2] See *supra*, pp. 153, 171; see also Aboth de Rabbi Nathan (*a*) i. p. 4a; Jalḳuṭ, Gen. § 101, for a parallel text. The first editions add: "whereon the first man brought (his offering)."

[3] See *supra*, p. 171, note 8, and cf. Midrash Haggadol, c. 321.

[4] The first editions quote Gen. viii. 20 also.

[5] Luria suggests a variant reading, based on Jalḳuṭ Makhiri, Ps. xxxvi. 5. "As it is said: 'And Noah built an altar to the Lord.' 'Abraham built there an altar' is not written here, but 'and he built *the* altar.'" The reading in Jalḳuṭ, Gen., *loc. cit.*, is similar; see also Pal. Targum, Gen. xxii. 9.

[6] The Venice edition reads: "on account of reflex movement." Read פשימותא, see Pesiḳta Rabbathi xl. (p. 170b), Tanna de bê Elijahu Rab. xxvii. p. 138; and Tanna de bê Elijahu Ẓuṭṭa ii. p. 174; and cf. Agadath Bereshith xxxi. p. 62, and Grünbaum, *op. cit.* p. 112.

[7] See Pal. Targum, Gen. xxii. 10, and Jalḳuṭ, Gen., *loc. cit.*

[8] See Shocher Ṭob, Ps. xx. 8, p. 176.

[9] See Lev. Rab. xxix. 9 f., which implies that the 'Aḳedah (Binding of Isaac) was on the Day of Atonement, so that the service of Abraham on that occasion might be considered as resembling that of the High Priest.

[10] The meal offering and the drink offering accompanied the "burnt offering" in the Tabernacle and Temple.

[11] Jubilees xviii. 9 reads: "And I (the angel) stood before Him, and before the prince of the Mastêmâ, and the Lord said, Bid him not to lay his hand on the lad."

Erelim[1] cry[2] without; the angels of peace weep bitterly" (Isa. xxxiii. 7). The ministering angels said before the Holy One, blessed be He: Sovereign of all the worlds! Thou art called merciful and compassionate, whose mercy is upon all His works;[3] have mercy upon Isaac, for he is a human being, and the son of a human being, and is bound before Thee like an animal. "O Lord, Thou preservest man and beast"; as it is said, "Thy righteousness is like the mighty mountains;[2] thy judgments are like a great deep: O Lord, thou preservest man and beast" (Ps. xxxvi. 6).

Rabbi Jehudah said: When the blade[4] touched his neck, the soul of Isaac fled and departed, (but) when he heard His voice from between the two Cherubim,[5] saying (to Abraham), "Lay not thine hand upon the lad" (Gen. xxii. 12), his soul returned to his body, and (Abraham) set him free, and Isaac stood upon his feet. And Isaac knew[6] that in this manner the dead in the future will be quickened. He opened (his mouth), and said: Blessed art thou, O Lord, who quickeneth the dead.[7] ||

Rabbi Zechariah said: That ram, which was created at the twilight,[8] ran and came to be offered up instead of Isaac, but Sammael[9] was standing by, and distracting it, in order to annul the offering of our father Abraham. And it was caught by its two horns in the trees, as it is said, "And Abraham lifted up his eyes, and looked, and behold,

[1] *i.e.* angels; see Kimchi's *Book of Roots*, *s.v.* ארה. Cf. T.B. Chagigah, 5b; *Rabbinic Philosophy and Ethics*, p. 73, note 1; and cf. Gen. Rab. lvi. 5, and Midrash Haggadol, c. 322.

[2] The quotation ends here in our MS.

[3] Cf. Ps. cxlv. 9.

[4] Lit. "sword." See Midrash Haggadol, c. 323.

[5] See *supra*, p. 24. Cf. Heb. xi. 19.

[6] The first editions add: "of the resurrection of the dead from the Torah." The connection with the word Torah is not quite clear, and the word should be probably deleted. See Roḳeach, 322, and cf. Brode's comment, *in loc.* The Jalḳuṭ, Gen., *loc. cit.*, reads: "He knew that in the future He would revive the dead."

[7] This is the second benediction of the Shemoneh 'Esreh; see Singer, p. 45. The benediction is appropriately placed in Isaac's mouth, for he had also been bound unto death and then set free. The benediction speaks of the loosening of the bound, as well as of the resurrection.

[8] Of the eve of the first Sabbath; see *supra*, p. 125.

[9] See Jubilees xviii. 12: "And the prince of the Mastêmâ was put to shame. And Abraham lifted up his eyes and looked, and behold, a *single* ram caught and it came (?)." The word translated "and distracting it" is Masṭenô; it reminds one of Mastêmâ of Jubilees. See also Midrash Haggadol, c. 324.

behind him a ram caught in the thicket by its horns" (*ibid.* 13). What did that ram do? It put forth its leg and took hold of the coat of our father Abraham, and Abraham looked, saw the ram, and he went and set it free. He offered it up instead of Isaac his son, as it is said, "And Abraham went and took the ram,[1] and offered it up for a burnt offering in the stead of his son" (*ibid.*).

Rabbi Berachiah said: The sweet savour (of the ram) ascended before the Holy One, blessed be He, as though it were the sweet savour of Isaac,[2] and He swore that He would bless him[3] in this world and in the world to come, as it is said, "By myself have I sworn, saith the Lord, because thou hast done this thing"; and it says, "That in blessing I will bless thee, and in multiplying I will multiply thy seed, as the stars of the heaven" (*ibid.* 16, 17). "That in blessing" (refers) to this world; "I will bless thee," in the world to come; and "I will greatly multiply thy seed," in the future that is to come.

Rabbi Chanina ben Dosa said:[4] From that ram, which was created at the twilight, nothing came forth which was useless.[5] The ashes of the ram[6] were || the base[7] which was upon the top of the inner altar.[8] The sinews of the ram were the strings[9] of the harp whereon David played. The ram's skin[10] was the girdle (around) the loins of Elijah, may he be remembered for good, as it is said, "And they answered him, He was an hairy man, and girt with

[1] The quotation ends here in our MSS.

[2] See Ẓohar, Gen. 120b.

[3] See Jalḳuṭ, *loc. cit.*, and Apoc. Baruch, *loc. cit.*

[4] See Jalḳuṭ, Isa. § 436, and Midrash Haggadol, c. 325.

[5] See Mishnah, Ẓebachim ix. 5, as to the parts of a burnt offering which were not offered on the altar.

[6] See *supra*, p. 204, and cf. T.B. Ẓebachim, 62a.

[7] Or, foundation. Does the text here refer to the horns of the altar? or should the text read, "the foundation whereon (stood) the inner altar"? See Midrash Haggadol, *loc. cit.*

[8] The first editions add here: "as it is said: 'And Aaron shall make atonement upon the horns of it once in the year'" (Ex. xxx. 10).

[9] Read Nimin instead of Nebalim, and see *supra*, p. 127. The first editions read: "The sinews of the ram were ten, corresponding to the ten strings of the harp," etc. According to one tradition the harp of David had only eight strings, and it is the harp of the Messiah which is to have ten strings. See Josephus, *Ant.* vii. 12. 3, and cf. Pesiḳta Rabbathi, pp. 98b f.

[10] The inference here is drawn from the word "'Ôr" (עור), leather.

a girdle of leather about his loins" (2 Kings i. 8).[1] The horn[2] of the ram of the left side[3] (was the one) wherein He blew upon Mount Sinai, as it is said, "And it shall come to pass, that when the ram's horn soundeth long"[4] (Josh. vi. 5). (The horn) of the right side, which is larger than that of the left, is destined in the future to be sounded in the world that is to come,[5] as it is said, "And it shall come to pass in that day, that a great trumpet shall be blown" (Isa. xxvii. 13);[6] and it is said, "And the Lord shall be king over all the earth" (Zech. xiv. 9).

Rabbi Isaac said: Nothing has been created except by the merit of worship. Abraham returned from Mount Moriah only through the merit of worship, as it is said, "We will *worship*, and come again to you" (Gen. xxii. 5).[7] The Temple was fashioned only through the merit of worship, as it is said, "Exalt ye the Lord our God, and *worship*" (Ps. xcix. 5).[8]

[1] The first editions have a corrupt quotation based on 2 Kings i., verses 6 and 8. The MS. only quotes the few words: "He was an hairy man," etc.

[2] See Othijoth de Rabbi 'Aḳiba, letter Ṭ; ed. Jellinek, *B.H.M.* iii. p. 31; and Roḳeach, 203. The first editions read: "the two horns."

[3] The first editions read here: "Wherein the Holy One, blessed be He, blew upon Mount Sinai." See Midrash Haggadol, *loc. cit.*

[4] The Oxford MS. and the first editions quote Ex. xix. 19.

[5] The first editions add: "at the ingathering of the exiles."

[6] The inference here is derived from the word "great," implying the right side. On the subject of the Messianic trump, see Abḳath Rochel i., and cf. 1 Cor. xv. 52.

[7] The Midrash Samuel (ed. Buber) iii. 7 contains a good parallel text, which is much fuller than our MS. It adds here: "The Israelites were redeemed from Egypt only in consequence of worship, as it is said: 'And the people bowed the head and *worshipped*' (Ex. xii. 27). The Torah was given only through the merit of worship, because it is said: 'And *worship* ye afar off'" (*ibid.* xxiv. 1). See Jalḳuṭ, Gen. § 100.

[8] The Midrash Samuel, *loc. cit.*, adds here: "The dead also will only be quickened through the merit of worship, as it is said: 'O come, let us worship and bow down' (Ps. xcv. 6). The exiles will only be gathered in again owing to the merit of worship, as it is said: 'And it shall come to pass in that day, that a great trumpet shall be blown; and they shall come which were lost in the land of Assyria, and they that were outcasts in the land of Egypt; and they shall *worship* the Lord in the holy mountain at Jerusalem'" (Isa. xxvii. 13). See also Gen. Rab. lvi. 2, and Midrash Haggadol, c. 320 f. On the entire chapter see the Book of Jashar xxiii.; Tanchuma (ed. Buber), Gen. p. 57a, b; Tanchuma, Vayêra, § xxiii.; and Midrash Agadah, Gen. pp. 50 ff.

CHAPTER XXXII

THE DEATH OF SARAH AND THE STORY OF ISAAC AND REBECCA [39B. i.]

SIX (people) were called by their names before they were created,[1] and they are: Isaac, Ishmael, Moses,[2] Solomon, Josiah, and King Messiah.[3]

Whence do we know about Ishmael? Because it is said, "And the angel of the Lord said unto her, Behold, thou art with child,[4] . . . and thou shalt call his name Ishmael" (Gen. xvi. 11). Why was his name || called Ishmael?[5] Because in the future the Holy One, blessed be He, will *hearken* to the cry[6] of the people arising from (the oppression) which the children of Ishmael will bring about in the land in the last (days);[7] therefore was his name called Ishmael.[8]

[1] In Mekhilta, Bô, xvi. p. 19a; only Isaac, Solomon, and Josiah are mentioned. See Agadath Bereshith, 65, and Midrash Haggadol, c. 246. In T.J. Berakhoth i. 8 four names are mentioned, the three as in the Mekhilta and, in addition, Ishmael; cf. Gen. Rab. xlv. 8. In T.B. Chullin, 139b, the name of Moses is mentioned, as also the names of Mordecaï, Esther, and Haman, all these names being hinted at in the Torah. Luria observes that Cyrus (Is. xliv. 28 and xlv. 1) should have been mentioned in the list of people named before their birth. This fact would not warrant the inference that all these people were pre-existent. This reasoning is, however, often applied to the name of the Messiah, as though it meant that the Messiah pre-existed because his name was named before his birth; see *Hellenism and Christianity*, p. 17.

[2] The first editions add: "our Rabbi," or "our teacher."

[3] The first editions read: "the name of the Messiah." The Amsterdam edition reads: "our Messiah." The first editions add: "May the Holy One, blessed be He, cause him to come speedily in our days."

[4] The first editions omit this part of the verse, and give the second half only.

[5] Ishma-*el* is interpreted as meaning "*God* will hear"; cf. Gen. xvi. 11.

[6] The first editions read: "the voice of the cry."

[7] The MS. omits "days." It occurs in the first editions. The reference is to the time of woe preceding the coming of the Messiah. See *supra*, pp. 221 f., and cf. Matt. xxiv. 3 ff. for the Messianic woes.

[8] The first editions add: "as it is said, '*God shall hear* and answer them'" (Ps. lv. 19). The Hebrew for "God shall hear" contains the same letters as the Hebrew word *Ishmael*.

How do we know (this with reference to) Isaac? Because it is said, "And God said, Sarah thy wife shall bear thee a son indeed; and thou shalt call his name Isaac" (*ibid.* xvii. 19). Why was his name called Isaac?[1] Because Yad (the first Hebrew letter of Isaac indicates) the *ten* trials[2] wherewith our father Abraham was tried; and he withstood them all. Zaddi (the second letter indicates) the *ninety* (years), for his mother was ninety years (at the birth of Isaac), as it is said, "And shall Sarah, that is ninety years old, bear?" (*ibid.* 17). Cheth (the third letter points to) the *eighth* (day), for he was circumcised on the eighth day, as it is said, "And Abraham circumcised his son Isaac, being eight days old" (*ibid.* xxi. 4). Ḳuf (the fourth letter of the name marks) the *hundred* (years), for his father was an hundred years old (at Isaac's birth), as it is said, "And Abraham was an hundred years old" (*ibid.* 5).

Whence do we know about Moses?[3] Because it is said, "And the Lord said, My spirit shall not abide in man for ever in their going astray" (*ibid.* vi. 3). What is the implication (of the expression), "In their going astray"?[4] Retrospectively his name was called Moses.[5] For the life of Moses was one hundred and twenty years, as it is said, "His days shall be an hundred and twenty years" (*ibid.*).

Whence do we know concerning Solomon? Because it is said, "Behold, a son shall be born to thee, who shall be a man of rest, . . . for his name shall be *Solomon*"

[1] See Midrash Haggadol, c. 256; Agadath Bereshith, 53; Gen. Rab. liii. 7; and Tanchuma (ed. Buber), Gen. 54a. Jubilees xvi. 3 says: "And we told her (Sarah) the name of her son, as his name is ordained and written in the heavenly tables, (*i.e.*) Isaac."

[2] The Agadath Bereshith, *loc. cit.*, refers to the Ten Commandments. The context in our author agrees with Tanchuma, Ḳorah, § xii.

[3] See T.B. Chullin, 139b. The name of Moses is said to be hinted at in Ps. xviii. 16: "*He drew me out* (ימשני) of many waters." The word Moses is connected with the root "to draw out" in Hebrew.

[4] The first editions read: "The word 'in their going astray' has the same numerical value as (the name) Moses" (משה=MShH). See R.V. *in loc.*

[5] B=2, Sh=300, G=3, M=40=345.
M=40, Sh=300, H=5 =345.
This system is known as Gemaṭria, and was also known to and used by some of the Church Fathers; see Irenæus, *adv. Hær.* v. xxx. 1 ff., where he speaks of the number of the name of the Antichrist; see also Clement of Alexandria, *Strom.* vi. ch. xi. According to Jastrow, *T.D.* 239a, this word is a transposition of the word γραμμάτια, "accounts"; see also 'Arukh, ed. Kohut, ii. p. 309b.

(1 Chron. xxii. 9).[1] Why was his name called Solomon? Because his name was called Solomon in the Aramaic language, as it is said, "I will give *peace* (Shalom) and quietness unto Israel in his days" (*ibid.*).[2] ||

Whence do we know about Josiah? Because it is said, "Behold, a child shall be born unto the house of David, Josiah by name" (1 Kings xiii. 2). Why was his name called Josiah? (Because he was as acceptable)[3] as an offering upon the altar; she[4] said: A worthy offering let him be before Thee.[5] Therefore was his name called Josiah, as it is said, "And he cried against the altar," etc. (*ibid.* 2).

Whence do we know concerning King Messiah? Because it is said, "His name shall endure for ever. Before the sun his name shall be continued (Yinnon)" (Ps. lxxii. 17).[6] Why was his name called Yinnon? For he will *awaken*[7] those who sleep at Hebron out of the dust of the earth, therefore is his name called Yinnon, as it is said, "Before the sun his name is Yinnon" (*ibid.*).

When Abraham returned from Mount Moriah in peace, the anger of Sammael[8] was kindled, for he saw that the desire of his heart to frustrate the offering of our father Abraham

[1] The Venice edition reads: "and thou shalt call his name Solomon, because." See Midrash Haggadol, c. 246.

[2] The name שלמה (Solomon) is connected with שלום (peace). See also 2 Sam. xii. 24, with Kimchi's commentary thereon. The Aramaic Sh'lama (peace) is somewhat similar to the Hebrew name Sh'lomoh (=Solomon). The printed texts omit the words "his name was called Solomon in the Aramaic language."

[3] The words in brackets do not occur in the MS., but they are found in the first editions.

[4] The reference is probably to the mother. The first editions omit this.

[5] See Jalkuṭ on 1 Kings xiii. § 200. The name Josiah (יאשיהו) is interpreted as though it were אי' שי הוא, "he is worthy like a lamb." The next sentence is found only in the MS.

[6] See 'Arukh, ed. Kohut, iv. p. 141a, *s.v.* נין, in the sense of "offspring"; cf. Gen. xxi. 23. Gesenius (Oxford edition) renders Ps. lxxii. 17: "Let his name have increase." See Parchon's *Heb. Dict. s.v.*, and note Jalkut, *loc. cit.*, which says: "He will stir up all the evil ones of the earth (in the future)"; cf. Jalkuṭ, Gen. § 45, and Midrash Haggadol, *loc. cit.*

[7] See Ibn Ezra on this verse of Ps. lxxii. See also T.B. Synhedrin, 95a, and *supra*, p. 230. 'Arukh, *loc. cit.*, reads: "in the future he will bring to life those who sleep in the dust, therefore is his name called Yinnon." See also *supra*, p. 12.

[8] Midrash Haggadol, c. 324, reads, "Satan." On Sammael's discomfiture see Jubilees xviii. 9 and 12. The name Sammael (*i.e.* the Devil) occurs in Christian books, *e.g.* in the Acts of Andrew and Matthew (in *A.N.C.L.* xvi. p. 362).

had not been realized. What did he do? He went and said to Sarah: Hast thou not heard what has happened in the world? She said to him: No. He said to her: Thy husband, Abraham,[1] has taken thy son Isaac and slain him and offered him up as a burnt offering upon the altar.[2] She began to weep and to cry aloud three times,[3] corresponding to the three sustained notes (of the Shophar),[4] and (she gave forth) three howlings corresponding to the three disconnected short notes[5] (of the Shophar), and her soul fled, and she died.[6]

Abraham came and found that she was dead. Whence did he come? From Mount Moriah,[7] as it is said, "And Abraham came to mourn for Sarah" (Gen. xxiii. 2).

Rabbi José said: Isaac observed mourning during three years[8] || for his mother. After three years he married Rebecca, and forgot the mourning for his mother.[9] Hence thou mayest learn that until a man marries a wife his love centres in his parents. When he marries a wife his love is bestowed upon his wife, as it is said, "Therefore shall a man leave his father and his mother, and he shall cleave unto his wife" (*ibid.* ii. 24). Does a man then *leave*[10] his father and mother with reference to the precept, "Honour"?[11] But the love of his soul cleaves unto his wife, as it is said, "And his soul clave (unto Dinah)" (*ibid.* xxxiv. 3); and it says, "And he shall cleave unto his wife" (*ibid.* ii. 24).

[1] See Tanchuma (ed. Buber), Gen. 57b; Pesiḳta Rabbathi xl.; Jalḳuṭ, Gen. § 98; T.B. Giṭṭin, 57b, and the Book of Jashar xxiii. 77. The first editions omit Abraham and read "the old man."

[2] The first editions add: "And the lad wept, and cried aloud because he could not be saved."

[3] Lit. "weepings."

[4] *i.e.* the Teḳi'oth.

[5] This is the "Teru'a"; cf. Mishnah, Rosh Ha-Shanah (iv. 9), p. 16a.

[6] See Lev. Rab. xx. 2, and Eccles. Rab. to Eccles. ix. 1. According to these Midrashim it is Isaac who tells Sarah the story of the 'Aḳedah. See Tanchuma, *in loc.* According to this version Satan, in the guise of Isaac, tells the tale. See also Midrash Haggadol, *loc. cit.*

[7] See Pal. Targum, Gen. *in loc.* According to the Book of Jashar xxiii. 84, Sarah went to look for Abraham, but died at Hebron. Also according to Jubilees xix. 2, Sarah died at Hebron.

[8] At the 'Aḳedah, Isaac was 37 years old, and when he married Rebecca he was 40 years. For an instance of three years of mourning see 2 Sam. xiii. 38 f. See Midrash Haggadol, c. 388.

[9] "Sarah his mother" is the reading in the first editions.

[10] Or "forsake."

[11] "Honour thy father and thy mother" (Ex. xx. 12).

Rabbi Jehudah said: Rebecca[1] was barren for twenty years. After twenty years (Isaac) took Rebecca and went (with her) to Mount Moriah, to the place where he had been bound, and he prayed on her behalf concerning the conception of the womb; and the Holy One, blessed be He, was entreated of him,[2] as it is said, "And Isaac intreated the Lord" (*ibid.* xxv. 21). The children were contending with one another[3] within her womb like mighty warriors, as it is said, "And the children struggled together within her" (*ibid.* 22). The time of her confinement came round, and her soul was nigh unto death owing to her pains.[4] And she went to pray in the place[5] whither she and Isaac had gone, as it is said, "And she went to inquire of the Lord" (*ibid.*). What did the Holy One, blessed be He,[6] do? Jacob took hold of the heels of Esau to make him fall, as it is said, "And after that came forth his brother, and his hand had hold on Esau's heel" (*ibid.* 26). Hence thou mayest learn that the descendants of Esau will not fall until a remnant || from Jacob will come and cut off the feet of the children of Esau from the mountain of Seir, as it is said, "Forasmuch as thou sawest that a stone was cut out of the mountain without hands" (Dan. ii. 45).[7] Another Scripture text says, "Vengeance is mine, and a recompence,[8] at the time when their *foot* shall slide" (Deut. xxxii. 35).

Rabbi Tanchuma[9] said: The two lads grew up; the one went by the way of life, and the other went by the way of death,[10] as it is said, "And the boys grew, and Esau was a cunning hunter" (Gen. xxv. 27). Jacob went on the way

[1] The Book of Jashar xxvi. 5 says: "And Isaac and his wife rose up and went to the land of Moriah to pray there and to seek the Lord." See also T.B. Jebamoth, 64a, and Pal. Targum, Gen. xxv. 21.

[2] According to the Midrash Agadah, Toledoth, p. 21, God hearkened to his prayer because "he was righteous and the son of a righteous man."

[3] See Gen. Rab. lxiii. 6 for the cause of the struggle. Cf. Pal. Targum, Gen. xxv. 22.

[4] See Book of Jashar xxvi. 9; Jalkuṭ, Gen. § 110.

[5] The Book of Jashar xxvi. 10 says: "And she went to the land of Moriah to seek the Lord on account of this."

[6] The first editions omit the words: "the Holy One, blessed be He."

[7] The first editions quote here Dan. ii. 34. See Josephus, *Ant.* x. 10. 4.

[8] The MS. only quotes thus far, the first editions continue the verse.

[9] The first editions read: "R. Acha."

[10] See *supra*, p. 102, for the "two ways."

of life, for he was dwelling in tents,[1] and he studied the Torah all his days.[2] Esau went on the way of death, because he slew Nimrod and his son Chavir, and he almost sought to kill Jacob his brother, as it is said, " The days of mourning for my father are at hand, and I will slay my brother Jacob " (*ibid.* xxvii. 41).

Rabbi Simeon said: In the hour when Isaac was bound, he lifted up his eyes heavenwards and saw the glory of the Shekhinah, as it is written, " For man shall not see me and live " (Ex. xxxiii. 20). Instead of death his eyes grew dim [3] in his old age, as it is said, " And it came to pass, that when Isaac was old, that his eyes were dim, so that he could not see " (Gen. xxvii. 1). Hence thou mayest learn that the blind man is as though he were dead.[4]

The night-fall of the festival day of Passover came,[5] and Isaac called unto Esau his elder son, and said: O my son! To-night the heavenly ones [6] utter songs,[7] on this night the treasuries [8] of dew [9] are opened; on this day the blessing of the dews (is bestowed). Make me savoury meat whilst I am still alive, and I will bless thee. || The Holy Spirit rejoined, saying to him: " Eat thou not the bread of him that hath an evil eye,[10] neither desire thou his dainties " (Prov. xxiii. 6). He went to fetch it, and was delayed there.[11] Rebecca said to Jacob his (other) son:[12] On this night the treasuries of dew

[1] According to the Targumim, *in loc.*, the " tents " are the " academies." See Jalkuṭ, Gen., *loc. cit.*

[2] The first editions read: " And Esau the wicked was going the way of death to slay our father Jacob, as it is said: ' The days of mourning for my father are at hand; then will I slay my brother Jacob ' " (Gen. xxvii. 41).

[3] See *Rabbinic Philosophy and Ethics*, pp. 78 f., and cf. Jalkut, Gen. § 114.

[4] See T.B. Nedarim, 64a, and Gen. Rab. lxv. 10.

[5] See *supra*, p. 153. See also the Vilna Gaon on Orach Chayyim, 583 (108). Cf. Heb. xi. 20 on the theme in our text.

[6] Jalkuṭ, Gen., *loc. cit.*, reads: " All the heavenly ones sing a song "; see Pal. Targum, Gen. xxvii. 1.

[7] Pss. cxiii.–cxviii.

[8] Cf. Slavonic Enoch vi. and Eth. Enoch lx. 20, and *supra*, p. 17, for this expression; and see T.B. Chagigah, 12b; and T.B. Ta'anith, 4b.

[9] The text is in the plural, " dews " here and throughout the chapter. The prayer for dew forms part of the liturgy for the first day of Passover.

[10] In the MS. the quotation ends here.

[11] See *Rabbinic Philosophy and Ethics*, p. 82.

[12] The first editions read: " Rebecca said to Jacob, O my son! "

will be opened, and on this night the angels utter a song.[1] Make savoury meat for thy father, that he may eat and whilst he still lives he may bless thee.

Now (Jacob) was skilled in the Torah,[2] and his heart dreaded the curse of his father. His mother said to him: My son! If it be a blessing, may it be upon thee and upon thy seed; if it be a curse, let it be upon me[3] and upon my soul, as it is said, "And his mother said to him, Upon me be thy curse, my son" (Gen. xxvii. 13). He went and brought two kids of the goats. Were two kids of the goats the food for Isaac? But he brought one as a Paschal offering,[4] and with the other he prepared the savoury meat to eat; and he brought it to his father,[5] and he said to him: "Arise, I pray thee, sit and eat of my venison" (*ibid.* 19).[6] Isaac said: "The voice is the voice of Jacob" (*ibid.* 22). Jacob (declares) the unity of God. "The voice is the voice of Jacob"[7] (*ibid.*) in the meditation of the Torah. "And the hands are the hands of Esau" (*ibid.*), in all shedding of blood and in every evil death. Not only this, but also when they proclaim in heaven, "The voice is the voice of Jacob," the heavens tremble.[8] And when they proclaim on earth, "The voice is the voice of Jacob" (*ibid.*), every one who hears

[1] The first editions add: "On this night in the future thy children will be redeemed from the power of bondage; on this night in the future they will sing a song." See T.B. Soṭah, 12b, and Wisdom xviii. 6.

[2] He should have fulfilled the desire of his father; see T.B. Ḳiddushin, 31a, and Pal. Targum, Gen. xxvii. 6, 11.

[3] So also Pal. Targum, Gen. xxvii. 13.

[4] The first editions read: "Would not one (goat) have been sufficient for him? As it is said: 'The righteous eateth to the satisfying of his soul' (Prov. xiii. 25). But one (goat) corresponded to the Paschal Lamb."[1]

[5] The first editions add here: "For we are taught in a Mishnah: the Paschal Lamb is brought only when one is satisfied with food. He entered," etc.

[6] See Rashi, *in loc.*; Ẓohar, Gen. 154a; and cf. Derekh Erez Ẓuṭṭa v. on the rule as to eating in a sitting posture.

[7] The unity of God proclaimed by the "voice of Jacob" is applied to the declaration of the children of Israel who exclaim: "Hear, O Israel, the Lord is our God, the Lord is one" (Deut. vi. 4).

[8] See *infra*, p. 282; Gen. Rab. lxvi. 4; Pesiḳta Rabbathi xxi. p. 99b; Roḳeach, 362. The 1st ed. reads here: "And when they proclaim on earth, 'The voice is the voice of Jacob' (Gen. xxvii. 22), every one who hears and does not obey, his portion is with 'the hands which are the hands of Esau'" (*ibid.*).

---

[1] See Pal. Targum, Gen. xxvii. 9, and Rashi on Gen., *in loc.*, and T.B. Pesachim, 114b.

will make his portion with "The voice which is the voice of Jacob." And every one || who does not hear and does not act (obediently), his portion is with "The hands, which are the hands of Esau."

Rabbi Jehudah said: Isaac blessed Jacob with ten blessings concerning the dews of heaven and the corn of the earth, corresponding to the ten words [1] whereby the world was created, as it is said, "And God give thee of the dew of the heaven" (*ibid.* 28); "Let peoples serve thee, . . ." (*ibid.* 29). When Jacob went forth from the presence of his father Isaac, he went forth crowned like a bridegroom, and like a bride in her adornment,[2] and the quickening dew from heaven descended upon him, and refreshed his bones,[3] and he also became a mighty hero; therefore it is said, "By the hands of the mighty Jacob, from thence is the shepherd, the stone [4] of Israel" (*ibid.* xlix. 24).

[1] Ma'amaroth; see Lev. Rab. xxxiv. (end); Deut. Rab. i. 14.
[2] See *supra*, pp. 40, 112 f.; and cf. Isa. xlix. 18.
[3] The words are based on Prov. xv. 30.
[4] See *infra*, p. 268. The R.V. should be noted.

CHAPTER XXXIII

ELISHA AND THE SHUNAMMITE WOMAN[1] [41A. i.]

"AND[2] Isaac sowed in that land" (Gen. xxvi. 12). Rabbi Eliezer said: Did Isaac sow the seed of corn?[3] Heaven forbid! But he took all his wealth,[4] and sowed it in charity to the needy, as it is said, "Sow to yourselves in righteousness, reap according to love" (Hos. x. 12).[5] Everything which he tithed, the Holy One, blessed be He, sent him (in return) one hundred times (the value) in different kinds of blessings, as it is said, "And he found in the same year an hundredfold: and the Lord blessed him" (Gen. xxvi. 12).

Rabbi Simeon said: Owing to the power of || charity the dead will be quickened[6] in the future. Whence do we learn this? From Elijah the Tishbite.[7] For he betook himself

[1] This chapter seems to be the Midrash to the Haphṭarah of Vayêra (Gen. xvii.–xxii.), illustrating the resurrection experienced by Isaac at the 'Aḳedah. The Book of Jonah, which formed the contents of Chapter X., is the Haphṭarah in the afternoon service on the Day of Atonement.

[2] The first editions read: "It is written: 'And Isaac sowed,'" etc.

[3] The patriarchs were not to settle in Canaan; therefore they did not devote themselves to the agricultural life. Their wealth was in their flocks, which could be easily removed as occasion demanded. See Pal. Targum, Gen. xxvi. 12; Jalḳuṭ, Gen. § 111; and *infra*, p. 289.

[4] Lit. "his mammon"; see *Jewish Sources of the Sermon on the Mount*, p. 169. The tithe had been observed by Abraham; see Gen. xiv. 20, and therefore Isaac also gave a tithe. See Num. Rab. xii. 11. The first editions read: "But he took a tithe of all his wealth."

[5] See Tanna de bê Elijahu Ẓuṭṭa (ed. Friedmann), i. p. 167.

[6] See Prov. xi. 4. Isaac's charity and righteousness are assumed here to have been the cause of his resurrection; another cause was the "'Aḳedah"; see *supra*, p. 228. The first benediction of the Shemoneh 'Esreh, as we have already seen, refers to Abraham; the second benediction refers to the resurrection, and therefore to Isaac, the *first* to experience this.

[7] The dead son of Elijah's hostess was quickened by God at the request of the prophet. The first editions add here: "For he was going from mountain to mountain, and from cave to cave." This is based on 2 Kings ii. 1 ff.

to Zarephath, and a woman (who was) a widow received him with great honour.[1] She was the mother of Jonah,[2] and they were eating and drinking[3] his[4] bread and oil; he, she, and her son, as it is said, "And she did eat, and he also" (1 Kings xvii. 15).[5]

"He and she" (indicate that it was) by the merit of Elijah that they had to eat. After (a period of) days, the son of the woman fell sick and died,[6] as it is said, "And it came to pass after these things that the son of the woman fell sick" (*ibid.* 17). The woman said to him (Elijah): Thou didst come unto me[7] for coition, and thou wilt bring my sin to remembrance against me, and my son is dead. Now take away all that which thou hast brought[8] to me, and give me my son. Elijah, may he be remembered for good, arose and prayed before the Holy One, blessed be He, and said before Him: Sovereign of all the worlds! Is it not enough (to endure) all the evils which have befallen me,[9] but also this woman; for I know[10] that out of sorrow for her son has she spoken of a matter which has not occurred, which she has brought against me to vex me.[11] Now let all the generations learn[12] that there is a resurrection of the dead, and restore the soul of this lad within him; and He

[1] By giving him the little she possessed and trusting in his word. See Tanna de bê Elijahu Rab. xviii. p. 97.

[2] See T.J. Sukkah v. 1. 55a; Gen. Rab. xcviii. 11; and see also *J.E.* vii. 226.

[3] The Jalḳuṭ, 1 Kings, § 209, omits the words "and drinking"; see T.B. Berakhoth, 35b. People did not drink oil, it was eaten with bread, etc.

[4] The first editions read "her" here.

[5] The first editions add: "Rabbi Levi said: It is written, 'He and she,' but we read, 'She and he.'" The Massorites afford numerous examples of this variation in the reading of the written text. See Berliner, Midrash Ḳeri and Kethib; see also Cant. Rab. ii. 4; and Ḳimchi on 1 Kings xviii. 15; and cf. *J.E.* viii. 368.

[6] The text does not state that the child died; see Maimonides, *Moreh Nebukhim*, i. 42; Ḳimchi, *in loc.*; cf. T.B. Niddah, 70b, and T.B. Chullin, 7b.

[7] The MS. and first editions add: "for coition." The text reads: "Thou art come unto me to bring my sin to remembrance and to slay my son" (1 Kings xvii. 18). The Midrash connects ביאה ("coition") with באת ("thou art come"); see Gesenius (Oxford ed.) p. 98a.

[8] The blessing on the meal and oil.

[9] Lit. "which have come over my head."

[10] Luria holds that the text should read: "For Thou knowest"; cf. Jalḳuṭ, *loc. cit.*

[11] The printed editions read: "to provoke me"; cf. Job ix. 20.

[12] From the resurrection of her son.

was entreated of him, as it is said, " And the Lord hearkened unto the voice of Elijah " (*ibid.* 22). Another Scripture text says, " And Elijah || took the child . . . See, thy son liveth " (*ibid.* 23).[1]

Rabbi Joshua ben Ḳorchah said: Art thou astonished at this?[2] Do not be astonished, come and see, (learn) from Elisha, the son of Shaphat, for no woman was able to gaze at his face without dying; and he went from mount to mount, and from cave to cave, and he went to Shunem, and a great woman received him with great honour. She was a sister of Abishag,[3] the Shunammite, the mother[4] of Oded, the prophet, as it is said, " And it fell on a day, that Elisha passed to Shunem " (2 Kings iv. 8), and the woman said to her husband: This man of God is (holy),[5] no woman is able to gaze at his face without dying; but,[6] " Let us make, I pray thee, a little chamber on the wall; and let us set for him there a bed, and a table, and a stool, and a lampstand " (*ibid.* 10). And every time that he passes he can turn thither into the chamber,[7] as it is said, " And it fell on a day, that he came thither, and he turned into the chamber " (*ibid.* 11). And he called for the Shunammite, as it is said, " And he said, Call her. And when he had called her, she stood at the door " (*ibid.* 15). Why did she stand at the door? Because she was unable to gaze at his face,[8] so that she should not die. He said to her:

[1] This concludes the exposition of R. Simeon on the Resurrection and Charity. The second quotation is not given in the printed texts.

[2] That charity causes the dead to be quickened.

[3] Abishag lived at the close of David's reign; see *J.E.* i. 66.

[4] The first editions read: " the wife of Iddo." Iddo lived in the reign of Jeroboam. See Seder 'Olam Rab. xx.; and cf. T.B. Synhedrin, 89b and 104a; Tanchuma, Toledoth, § xii. Jalḳuṭ, 2 Kings § 228, reads: "The mother of Iddo the prophet." Luria, with fine judgment, suggested that Iddo of the printed texts should be corrected into " Oded," the prophet who lived in the reign of Asa. See 2 Chron. xv. 8; see also Rashi on 2 Kings iv. 8, where our *P.R.E.* is mentioned.

[5] " Holy " is not in the MS., but it occurs in the first two editions.

[6] " As it is said " is added by the first editions; it does not occur in the parallel context in Jalḳuṭ, Kings, *loc. cit.*, which reads as our MS., " But 'Let us make,' " etc.

[7] The first editions and Jalḳuṭ, *loc. cit.*, add: " They built it, and prepared and arranged it. After some time[1] he passed by Shunem and turned in to the chamber."

[8] See Lev. Rab. xxiv. 6, and Sepher Chassidim (ed. Frankfort, 1724), 178.

---

[1] Lit. " days."

"At this season, when the time cometh round, thou shalt embrace a son" (*ibid.* 16), the fruit of thy womb. She said to him: My lord is very old, and the way of women has departed from me, || and it is impossible to do this thing.[1] "Nay, my lord, thou man of God, do not lie unto thine handmaid" (*ibid.*).[2]

Rabbi Zechariah said: "He will fulfil the desire of them that fear him" (Ps. cxlv. 19).[3] The Holy One, blessed be He, fulfilled the desire of the prophet. She conceived and bare, and the child grew. He went forth to refresh[4] himself, and to look at the reapers. A mishap overtook him,[5] and he died, as it is said, "It fell on a day, that he went out to his father to the reapers" (2 Kings iv. 18); this restrained them (from work) until he came (among them),[6] and he died, as it is said, "And he sat on her knees till noon, and then died" (*ibid.* 20).

The woman went to Mount Carmel, and fell on her face to the ground before Elisha, saying to him: Would that my vessel[7] had remained empty! But it was filled, and now its contents are spilt. The prophet answered: Everything which the Holy One, blessed be He, doeth, He telleth to me, but He has hidden this matter, as it is said, "And when she came to the man of God[8] . . . and Gehazi came near to thrust her away"[9] (*ibid.* 27). What is the meaning of "to thrust her away"? To teach us that he put his hand upon (her) pride, which was upon her breasts,[10] as it is said, "And the man of God said, Let her alone[11] . . . and the Lord hath hid it from me, and hath not told me" (*ibid.*).

[1] Luria's reads: "This thing cannot possibly be."

[2] See Kimchi, *in loc.*, who uses the same words as our author, based on the quotation in our context in connection with Ps. cxlv. 19.

[3] Cf. T.B. Megillah, 27a.

[4] See 'Arukh, ed. Kohut vi. p. 288b, *s.v.* נב; cf. Lam. ii. 18.

[5] See T.J. Jebamoth xv. 2, 14d.

[6] The phrase, "this restrained them until he came," is in Aramaic and occurs only in our MS. Its meaning is doubtful. Is it an old Targum?

[7] See 2 Kings iv. 3; כלי (vessel) is used euphemistically here, meaning "womb."

[8] In our MS. the quotation ends here.

[9] The Midrash here has a play on the word "lehadphah," interpreting it as though it were "lehôd japhjah," "the glory of her beauty," *i.e.* the breasts; see T.B. Berakhoth, 10b, and T.J. Jebamoth ii. 4. 3d.

[10] See Lev. Rab., *loc. cit.*

[11] The rest of the verse given by our MS. is omitted in the printed editions.

He took the staff which was in his hand, and gave it to Gehazi, saying to him: Do not speak with thy mouth any word at all; know that[1] thou goest and placest the staff upon the face of the lad, that he may live.

Now as for Gehazi, the matter was laughable in his eyes,[2] and to every man whom he met || he said: Dost thou believe that this staff will bring the dead to life? Therefore he did not succeed[3] until (Elisha) went on foot and put his face[4] upon the face (of the child), and his eyes upon his eyes, and his hands upon his hands, and he began to pray before the Holy One, blessed be He: Sovereign of all the worlds! Just as Thou didst perform miracles by the hand of Elijah, my master, and brought the dead to life, likewise let this child live; and He was entreated of him, as it is said, "Then he returned, and walked in the house once to and fro; and went up, and stretched himself upon him" (*ibid.* 35); "and the child sneezed seven times" (*ibid.*).

Rabbi Azariah[5] said: Know thou the efficacy of charity.[6] Come and see from the instance of Shallum,[7] son of Tikvah, who was one of the important men of his generation, giving charity every day. What did he do? He filled the bottle with water, and sat at the entrance of the city, and he would give water to every person who came on the way, restoring his soul to him.[8] On account of the charity which he did, the Holy Spirit rested upon his wife,[9] as it is

[1] The first editions read here "whilst" and omit "know that."

[2] Lit. "before him." On Gehazi see *J.E.* v. 580 f.

[3] His want of faith led to his failure to restore the child. Moreover, he did not believe that he was dead, because he told Elisha "the lad is not *awaked*" (2 Kings iv. 31).

[4] Jalkut, *loc. cit.*, reads: "His mouth"; this agrees with the text in 2 Kings iv. 34. Perhaps Luria's suggestion that the reading should be: "his face . . . and his hands" is correct. John of Damascus, *op. cit.* iv. 34, refers to the virginity of Elisha; this idea occurs also in Ambrose and other Christian writers. See also Clement, "Two Epistles concerning Virginity," xiv. (*A.N.C.L.* xiv. p. 393).

[5] The Prague edition reads: "Rabbi Zechariah"; this is also Brode's reading.

[6] To cause the dead to be quickened.

[7] See Siphrê, Num. § 78, and *J.E.* xi. 227.

[8] To feed the hungry is to restore his soul; cf. Lam. i. 11.

[9] As to whether it also rested on him see *J.E.*, *loc. cit.*, and cf. Jalkut, *loc. cit.*, which reads "upon him"; see T.B. Megillah, 14b, and Kimchi on 2 Kings xxii. 14, who quotes the entire passage from our *P.R.E.*; he does not, however, read "upon him." The reason why the Holy

said,[1] "So Hilkiah the priest . . . went unto Huldah the prophetess, the wife of Shallum, the son of Tikvah" (*ibid.* xxii. 14). Originally his name was "the son of Sachrah";[2] just as thou dost say, "Merchandise is better[3] than the circulation of money" (Prov. iii. 14). One Scripture text || says, "The son of Sachrah."[4] When her husband died, the charitable deeds of her husband ceased,[5] and all Israel went forth to show loving-kindness to Shallum, son of Tikvah. But they spied the band,[6] and they cast the man into the sepulchre of Elisha,[7] and he came to life, as it is said, "And as soon as the man touched the bones of Elisha, he revived" (2 Kings xiii. 21); and afterwards he begat Chanameel,[8] as it is said, "Behold, Chanameel the son of Shallum thine uncle shall come unto thee" (Jer. xxxii. 7).

Rabbi Eliezer[9] said: Know thou the power of charity.[10] Come and see from (the instance of) Saul, the son of Kish, who removed the witches and the necromancers from off the earth, and once again he loved that which he had hated.[11] He went to En Dor, to the wife[12] of Zephaniah, the mother of Abner, and he inquired of her for himself by the familiar spirit, and she brought for him Samuel the prophet, and

Spirit rested upon Huldah is probably suggested by the special manner of her husband's charity in pouring out water for the thirsty; cf. Isa. xliv. 3, and Joel ii. 28.

[1] Insert שנאמר.

[2] See 1 Chron. xxxiv. 22: "the son of Hasrah," *i.e.* "*Ch*asrah"—this becomes "*Sach*rah" by interchanging the first two letters of the name, just as the Massorites have done with the name "Tikvah" in this verse. "Sachrah" means "merchandise." See also 2 Kings xxii. 14.

[3] In the MS. the quotation ends here; it is continued in the Venice edition.

[4] This quotation is unknown to me; see, however, previous note (2).

[5] The Hebrew word for ceased, is "Chasrah." The Jalkuṭ, *in loc.*, reads: "The charity of her husband failed that righteous woman"; cf. T.B. Synhedrin, 47a, and T.B. Chullin, *loc. cit.*

[6] The first editions add: "that was coming against them."

[7] Cf. Ecclus. xlviii. 13.

[8] See *J.E.* vi. p. 203, *s.v.* Hanameel, son of Shallum and Huldah.

[9] The first editions read: "Chananiah ben Teradion."

[10] The text here is probably corrupt. Instead of reading, "the power of charity," we should perhaps read, "the power of righteous people." Luria thinks that the whole phrase is out of place. The narrative fits in better at the end of Chapter XXXI.

[11] See Targum on 1 Sam. xxviii. 7 ff.; Lev. Rab. xxvi. 7; Midrash Samuel xxiv.

[12] Ḳimchi, on 1 Sam. xxviii. 7, reads: "to a woman who had a familiar spirit, Zephaniah." See also Midrash Samuel, *loc. cit.*, and Lev. Rab., *loc. cit.*

the dead saw Samuel ascending, and they ascended with him,[1] thinking that the resurrection of the dead had come,[2] and the woman beheld, and she became very much confused, as it is said, "And the king said unto her, Be not afraid: for what seest thou?" (1 Sam. xxviii. 13).[3] Some say: Many righteous men like (Samuel) came up with him in that hour.[4]

Rabbi Eliezer said: All the dead will arise at the resurrection of the dead, dressed in their shrouds.[5] Know thou that this is the case. Come and see from (the analogy of) the one who plants (seed) in the earth. He plants naked [6] (seeds) || and they arise covered with many coverings; and the people who descend into the earth dressed (with their garments), will they not rise up dressed (with their garments)?[7] Not only this, but come and see from Chananiah, Mishael, and Azariah, who went down into the fiery furnace dressed in their garments,[8] as it is said,[9] "And the satraps . . . being gathered together, saw these men, that the fire had no power upon their bodies . . . neither were their hosen changed" (Dan. iii. 27). Learn [10] from Samuel, the prophet, who came up clothed with his

[1] See T.B. Chagigah, 4b, and cf. Ascension of Isaiah ix. 17.

[2] Jalkuṭ, ii. § 140, adds that Samuel brought Moses with him. Thinking it was the great Day of the Last Judgment, Moses would testify on behalf of Samuel; see Midrash Samuel, *loc. cit.*

[3] "For what dost thou see?" is added by Luria.

[4] Perhaps this sentence is a gloss added by some copyist, taken from Midrash Samuel or Lev. Rab., *loc. cit.*

[5] The first editions read: "and they will ascend in their garments. From what dost thou learn this?" Luria reads: "When all the dead arise," etc. On the analogy employed by our author, see 1 Cor. xv. 36 ff., where the same thought occurs, and cf. T.B. Kethuboth, 111b; T.B. Synhedrin, 96b; and Jalkuṭ, *loc. cit.*, which reads: "clothed in their shrouds."

[6] The first editions read: "From the seed in the earth, by an inference *a minori ad majus* with reference to wheat. What happens to the (seed of) wheat? It is buried in a naked condition and it comes forth."

[7] The first editions read: "how much more so will this apply to the righteous who were buried with their garments." See 1 Cor. xv. 42 ff. for a similar discussion. See Gen. Rab. xcvi. 6; T.B. Sabbath, 114a; Semachoth ix. on the question as to whether the garments used at the burial will be the garments of the resurrection.

[8] The first editions add: "and they came out in their garments, as it is said, 'Nor was the hair of their head singed'" (Dan. iii. 27).

[9] See T.B. Synhedrin, 92b; and Sepher Chassidim, § 1129.

[10] The first editions read: "And again, from whom canst thou learn this."

robe, as it is said, "And she said, An old man cometh up; and he is covered with a robe" (1 Sam. xxviii. 14).

Rabbi Jochanan [1] said: All the prophets prophesied in their lifetime, and Samuel prophesied in his lifetime, and after his death, because Samuel said to Saul: If thou wilt hearken to my advice to fall by the sword, then shall thy death be an atonement for thee,[2] and thy lot [3] shall be with me in the place where I abide.[4] Saul harkened to his advice, and fell by the sword, he and all his sons,[5] as it is said, "So Saul died, and his three sons" (*ibid.* xxxi. 6). Why? So that his portion might be with Samuel the prophet in the future life, as it is said, "And to morrow shalt thou and thy sons be with me" (*ibid.* xxviii. 19). What is the meaning of "with me"? Rabbi Jochanan said: With me in my division in heaven.[6]

Hillel, the Elder, said: Samuel spake to Saul, saying, Was it not enough for thee that thou didst not hearken || unto His voice, neither didst thou execute His fierce anger upon Amalek,[7] but thou dost also inquire [8] through one possessed of a familiar spirit,[9] and thou seekest (to know the future). Woe is the shepherd, and woe is his flock! For on thy account has the Holy One, blessed be He, given Israel thy people into the hands of the Philistines, as it is said, "Moreover, the Lord will deliver Israel also with thee into the hand of the Philistines" (*ibid.*).

[1] The first editions read: "Nathan."

[2] Death as an atonement is discussed by Schechter, *Aspects*, pp. 304, 307 f. See also T.B. Synhedrin, 44b, on this theme.

[3] See Dan. xii. 13 for a parallel expression.

[4] See Midrash Samuel, *loc. cit.*; and compare the words which are said to have been spoken by the Founder of Christianity to the penitent thief, Luke xxiii. 43.

[5] The text quoted in support of this continues: "and his armour-bearer, and all his men." In 1 Chron. x. 6 the reading is: "So Saul died, and his three sons; and all *his house* died together." The Targum to this passage renders "his house" by "the men of his house." The first editions read: "he and all his house."

[6] See Lev. Rab., *loc. cit.*, and T.B. Berakhoth, 12b, which is probably the source of the Midrash, and cf. Midrash Samuel, x.

[7] See *infra*, p. 388.

[8] Lit. "to inquire through one possessed of a familiar spirit and to seek." The first editions read: "Thou art come to inquire for thyself through one possessed of a familiar spirit."

[9] See Gesenius (Oxford edition), *s.v.* אוב.

Rabbi Tachanah[1] said: Israel was exiled[2] to Babylon, and did not forsake their evil deeds. Ahab, son of Kolaiah, and Zedekiah, son of Maaseiah,[3] became lying healers,[4] and they healed the wives of the Chaldeans, and came unto them for coition.[5] The king heard thereof, and commanded that they should be burnt. They both said: Let us say that Joshua, the son of Jehozadak, was with us, and he will save[6] us from the burning with fire. They said to him: O our lord, O king, this man was with us in every matter. The king commanded that the three should be burnt by fire. And the angel Michael[7] descended and saved Joshua from the fiery flames, and brought him up before the throne of glory, as it is said, "And he shewed me Joshua,[8] the high priest" (Zech. iii. 1); and the other two were burnt by fire, as it is said, "And of them shall be taken up a curse. . . . The Lord make thee like Zedekiah and like Ahab, whom the king of Babylon roasted in the fire" (Jer. xxix. 22). It is not written here "whom the king of Babylon burnt with fire," but "whom he roasted,"[9] hence we learn || that his[10] hairs were singed on account of their sins, as it is said, "In the pride of the wicked the poor is *hotly* pursued" (Ps. x. 2). Whence do we know that he was delivered? Because it is said, "And the Lord said unto Satan, The Lord rebuke thee, O Satan. . . . Is not this a brand plucked out of the fire?" (Zech. iii. 2).

Rabbi Jehudah said: When Nebuchadnezzar brought a

[1] The first editions read "Jochanan." This is also the reading in the Jalkuṭ Makhiri on Zech. iii. 1, p. 35 (ed. Greenup).

[2] The first editions read "went up." This story is one of the versions of the Susanna narrative; see Brüll's *Jahrbücher*, iii. pp. 8 ff., where Origen is quoted, who knew the story and refers to Zedekiah and Ahab.

[3] See Jer. xxix. 21, 23.

[4] See T.B. Synhedrin, 93a; Tanchuma, Vajiḳra, § vi. The incident may be based on Job xiii. 4. Cf. Ezek. xiii. 6, and xxii. 28.

[5] See also Jalkuṭ ii. § 309; Pesiḳta de R. Kahana xxv. pp. 164b.

[6] See T.B. Chullin, 7a. The first editions read: "Let Joshua, the son of Jehozadak, a righteous man, come with us and we shall be saved through his merit."

[7] Cf. Ẓohar, Gen. 104a.

[8] The MS. reads "Jehozadak"; the verse is correctly quoted in the first editions.

[9] Jalkuṭ Makhiri, Zech., *loc. cit.*, adds: "like these ears of corn he roasted them." Is this part of the original text?

[10] *i.e.* Joshua's.

false accusation [1] against Israel to slay them, he set up an idol in the plain of Dura, and caused a herald to proclaim: Any one who does not bow down to this idol shall be burnt by fire. Israel did not trust in the shadow [2] of their Creator, and came with their wives and sons and bowed down to the idolatrous image [3]—except Daniel, whom they called by the name of their God,[4] and it would have been a disgrace to them to burn him [5] in fire, as it is said, "But at the last Daniel came in before me" [6] (Dan. iv. 8). And they took Chananiah, Mishael, and Azariah, and put them into the fiery furnace, and the angel Gabriel [7] descended and saved them from the fiery furnace.[8] The king said to them: [9] Ye knew that ye had a God who saves and delivers; why have ye forsaken your God and worshipped idols which have no power to deliver? But just as ye did in your own land and destroyed it, so do ye attempt to do in this land, (namely) to destroy it. The king commanded, || and they slew all of them. Whence do we know that they were all slain by the sword? Because it is said, "Then said he unto me, Prophesy . . . O breath, and breathe upon these *slain*, that they may live" (Ezek. xxxvii. 9).[10]

Rabbi Phineas said: After twenty years, when all of them had been slain in Babylon,[11] the Holy Spirit rested upon

[1] Lit. "wantonness of words"; baseless charges. Cf. Deut. xxii. 14, 17.

[2] See *supra*, p. 62, for this expression.

[3] See T.B. Megillah, 12a; Cant. Rab. vii. 6. The image is discussed in T.B. Berakhoth, 58b.

[4] See Luria's reading. Daniel was called Belteshazzar. "Bel" is, of course, a name of a Babylonian image or god.

[5] *i.e.* Daniel.

[6] The verse continues: "whose name was Belteshazzar, according to the name of my God."

[7] In Jalkuṭ, on Ezek. xxxvii. § 375, the reading is Michael; see Gen. Rab. xliv. 13. Our reading agrees with T.B. Pesachim, 118a; Pesiḳta Rabbathi, p. 160b; Ex. Rab. xviii. 5; and see Jalkuṭ on Dan., *in loc.*, and T.B. Synhedrin, 95b. It is noteworthy that Daniel is not mentioned here; he was therefore not cast into the furnace.

[8] See *Rabbinic Philosophy and Ethics*, p. 55, note 1.

[9] The Hebrews who had worshipped his image.

[10] See Tanna de bê Elijahu Rab. v. p. 24, and *J.E.* ix. 202 f.

[11] See T.B. Synhedrin, 92b, and Tanchuma, Noah, § x.: "On the day when the three companions were delivered Ezekiel quickened the dead in the valley of Dura." See Pal. Targum, Ex. xiii. 17, on the sons of Ephraim, who were slain for attempting to leave Egypt before the appointed time. See also Shibbolê Ha-Leḳeṭ, 219. According to one authority in T.B. Synhedrin, *loc. cit.*, "the whole incident was indeed a parable."

Ezekiel, and brought him forth into the plain of Dura, and called unto him very dry bones, and said to him: Son of Man! What dost thou see? He answered: I see here dry bones. (The Spirit) said to him: Have I power to revive them? The prophet did not say:[1] Sovereign of all the worlds! Thou hast power to do even more than (this) here; but he said: "O Lord God, thou knowest" (*ibid.* 3), as though he did not believe;[2] therefore his own bones were not *buried* in a pure land,[3] but in an unclean land, as it is said, "And thou shalt die in a land that is unclean" (Amos vii. 17).[4] "Prophesy over these bones" (Ezek. xxxvii. 4). He said before Him: Sovereign of all the worlds! What! will the prophecy bring upon them flesh and sinews and bones?[5] Or will the prophecy bring upon them all the flesh and bones which cattle, beast, and bird have eaten, and they (also) have died in the land?[6] Immediately the Holy One, blessed be He, caused His voice to be heard, and the earth shook, as it is said, "And as I prophesied there was a thundering, and behold an earthquake" (*ibid.* 7), || and every animal, beast, and bird which had eaten thereof and died in another land[7] the earth brought together, "bone to his bone" (*ibid.*).[8]

Rabbi Joshua ben Ḳorchah said: There came down upon them the quickening dew[9] from heaven, which was

[1] The first editions omit the negative. The later editions (*e.g.* Amsterdam and Prague) read: "he should have said."

[2] See Gen. Rab. xix. 11; Ẓohar, Num. 200a; Jalḳuṭ, Kings, § 244.

[3] *i.e.* the land of Israel.

[4] This quotation from Amos is very strange, inasmuch as it is applied to Ezekiel as a prophecy concerning his *burial.* Moreover, the prophet refers to death, which might be quite distinct from the burial of the prophet. See Tanna de bê Elijahu Rab., *loc. cit.*, and cf. *J.E.* v. 315 f., for further parallels to this story.

[5] Read here "skin," as in the text of Ezek. xxxvii. 8.

[6] The first editions read: "in another land." This is probably the correct reading, as it occurs again in this section, and, therefore, what was missing would have to be miraculously restored by God. The prophet had his doubts as to whether this would or could be accomplished. Interesting parallels to this discussion are to be found in the writings of the Church Fathers; see Athenagoras, "Resurrection of the Dead," ch. iv., and Tertullian, mentioned *infra*, p. 251, note.

[7] The words from "every animal" till "another land" occur only in our MS.

[8] See Jalḳuṭ, Ezek. § 375: "He caused His voice to be heard from between the two Cherubim"; see *supra*, p. 228, and cf. Ps. xcix. 1.

[9] See *infra*, p. 260.

like a fountain,[1] which was bubbling and bringing forth water; so likewise (the bones) were moving and bringing forth upon themselves flesh, (other) bones [2] and sinews, as it is said, "And I beheld, and lo, there were sinews upon them, and flesh came up, and *skin* covered them above" (*ibid.* 8). He said to him: Prophesy unto the wind, as it is said, "Then said he unto me, Prophesy unto [3] the wind. . . . Come from the four winds, O breath, and breathe upon these slain, that they may live" (*ibid.* 9). In that hour the four winds of the heaven went forth, and opened the treasure-house of the souls, and each spirit returned to the body of flesh of man, as it is said, "So I prophesied as he commanded me, and the breath came into them, and they lived, . . . an *exceeding* great army" (*ibid.* 10); and it is written about Egypt, "And the children of Israel were fruitful, . . . and waxed *exceeding* mighty" (Ex. i. 7). What is the meaning of "exceeding"? Just as in the latter case there were 600,000 (men), so in the former case there were 600,000 (men), and they all stood upon their feet except one man. The prophet said: Sovereign of all the worlds! What is the nature of this man? He answered him: He gave out money for usury,[4] and he took with interest. || As I live, he shall not live. In that hour the Israelites were sitting and weeping, and saying: We hoped for light, and darkness came. We hoped to stand up with *all* Israel at the resurrection of the dead, and now "our hope is lost" (Ezek. xxxvii. 11). We hoped to arise so as to be gathered with *all* Israel, and now "we are clean cut off" (*ibid.*). In that hour the Holy One, blessed be He, said to the prophet: Therefore, say to them, As I live, I will cause you to stand at the resurrection of the dead in the future that is to come, and I will gather you with all Israel [5] to the land, as

[1] This is also the reading in Jalkuṭ, Ezekiel, *loc. cit.*

[2] Instead of "bones" we should probably read "skin"; see *supra*, p. 249, note 5.

[3] The MS. reads incorrectly "against."

[4] See Jalkuṭ on Ezekiel, *loc. cit.*, which reads: "And he took usury and he shall not live (eternally)." This is based on Ezek. xviii. 8. See Ex. Rab. xxxi. 3, and see Tosaphoth T.B. Baba Mezi'a, 70b, catchword, "Thou mayest lend"; cf. Pal. Targum, Ex. xiii. 17. See also Tosaphoth Soṭah, 5a.

[5] The Venice edition reads here: "for the ingathering of the exiles to the land of Israel." On the vision in Ezek. xxxvii. see Cant. Rab. vii. 9. Maimonides, *Moreh Nebukhim*, ii. 46, regarded the

it is said, " Behold, I will open your graves, and cause you to come up out of your graves . . . and I will bring you into the land of Israel. . . . And I will put my spirit in you, and ye shall live" (*ibid.* 12, 14).

" resurrection " as a prophetic vision; see T.B. Synhedrin, *loc. cit.*, for the Talmudic account. The doubt of Ezekiel is noted by Tertullian, *On the Resurrection of the Flesh*, xxx. In this passage the Church Father interprets the vision in a literal sense, rejecting the allegorical meaning which was given to the vision in his day. Justin Martyr (*First Apology*, lii.) refers to this prophecy as pointing to the resurrection to be brought about by the Christian Messiah at his second coming; his words are: " By Ezekiel the prophet it was said: ' Joint shall be joined to joint, and bone to bone, and flesh shall grow again; and every knee shall bow to the Lord, and every tongue shall confess Him ' " (Ezek. xxxvii. 7, 8, and Isa. xlv. 23). This may serve as a fair illustration of the method of quoting the Hebrew Scriptures by the Church Fathers.

CHAPTER XXXIV

THE RESURRECTION OF THE DEAD [43B. ii.]

"SEE now that I, even I, am he,[1] and there is no God with me" (Deut. xxxii. 39). Only the Holy One, blessed be He, said: "*I am*" in this world, and "*I am*" in the world to come; *I am* the one who redeemed Israel from Egypt, and *I am* the one who, in the future, will redeem them at the end of the fourth kingdom; therefore it is said, "I, even I, am he, and there is no God with me" (*ibid.*). Every nation who say that there is a second God, I will slay them as with a second death[2] || which has no resurrection; and every nation who say that there is no second God, I will quicken them for the eternal life. And in the future I will slay those (first mentioned) and quicken these, therefore it is said, "I kill, and I make alive" (*ibid.*). I have wounded[3] Jerusalem and her people on the day of My anger, and in great mercy[4] I *will* heal them,[5] therefore it is said, "I have wounded, and I *will* heal" (*ibid.*). Neither any angel nor any seraph[6] will deliver the wicked from the judgment of Gehinnom, as it is said, "And there is none that can deliver out of my hand" (*ibid.*).

Rabbi Jochanan[7] said: All the dead will arise at the

[1] In the MS. the quotation ends here, in the first editions the verse is continued and the first editions add: "What purpose has the text in saying twice 'I, even I'?" See Pal. Targum, *in loc.*, and Othijoth de R. 'Aḳiba (*B.H.M.* iii. p. 17), letter א: "I was before the world, and I am after the world." See also T.B. Berakhoth, 9b, Jalkuṭ, Deut. § 946, and cf. Methodius, "On the Resurrection," v. (*A.N.C.L.* xiv. p. 141).

[2] This is based on Dan. xiii. 2. Cf. Rev. xx. 6, 14, xxi. 8, and see Midrash Tannaïm, ed. Hoffmann, p. 202, and Siphrê, Deut. § 329.

[3] God destroyed Jerusalem, and He will rebuild it; cf. Lam. i. 17.

[4] Cf. Isa. liv. 7, 11 f., and Jer. xxxiii. 6, 9.

[5] See Isa. xxx. 26, and cf. Shocher Ṭob, Ps. cxlvii. (end).

[6] "'I, even I,' says God, 'I will deliver them, I alone.'"

[7] The first editions read "Jonathan."

resurrection of the dead, except the generation of the Flood,[1] as it is said, "The dead shall not live, the deceased (Rephaim) [2] shall not rise" (Isa. xxvi. 14). "The dead (who) shall not live" refer to the heathens, who are like the carcase of cattle; [3] they shall arise for the day of judgment,[4] yet they shall not live; but the men of the generation of the Flood, even for the day of judgment they shall not arise, as it is said, "The Rephaim shall not rise" (*ibid.*). All their souls become winds,[5] accursed, injuring [6] the sons of men, and in the future world the Holy One, blessed be He, will destroy them out of the world, so that they should not do harm to a single Israelite, as it is said, "Therefore hast thou visited and destroyed them,[7] and made all their memory to perish" (*ibid.*).[8]

Rabbi Zechariah said: The sleep at night is like this world, and the awakening of the morning [9] is like the world to come. And just as || in the sleep of the night a man lies down and sleeps, and his spirit wanders over all the earth, and tells him in a dream [10] whatever happens, as it is said, "In a dream, in a vision of the night . . . then he openeth the ears of men" (Job xxxiii. 15, 16), likewise (with) the dead, their spirit wanders over all the earth, and tells them all things [11] that happen in the world, but they are silent and (yet) they give song and praise to God, who will quicken them in the future, as it is said, "Let the saints exult in glory" [12] (Ps. cxlix. 5). The awakening in the morning

[1] Cf. T.B. Synhedrin, 107b, and Aboth de Rabbi Nathan (*a*) xxxvi. pp. 53b ff.

[2] The Rephaim (giants) are the men of the generation of the Flood. See *supra*, pp. 160 f., 167, and Gen. Rab. xxxi. 12.

[3] *i.e.* doomed to destruction. Cf. the directions laid down for the conduct of Christians towards heathens, in Clement, "Two Epistles concerning Virginity," vi. (*A.N.C.L.* xiv. pp. 387 f.). See *supra*, p. 208, n. 7.

[4] In the Messianic age, or, rather, at the close of the reign of Messiah.

[5] Or, "spirits who injure."

[6] Or, "Demons unto man"; see Jalkuṭ, Isa. *in loc.*

[7] The quotation ends here in the MS., it is continued in the first editions.

[8] See Ẓohar, Gen. 25b.

[9] This is based on Isa. xxvi. 19. Cf. Hippolytus (ed. Achelis), p. 107.

[10] See Eccles. x. 20, and see Midrash Rab. thereon; cf. T.B. Berakhoth, 18b, Gen. Rab. xiv. 9, and *supra*, p. 87.

[11] This is also the reading of the Venice edition.

[12] Even in the grave the saints continue to glorify God. See Ps. cxlix. 5; Jalkuṭ, 1 Kings, § 169; and Shocher Ṭob on Ps. xxx. p. 117b.

is like the future world. A parable[1]—unto what is the matter to be likened? To a man who awakens out of his sleep, in like manner will the dead awaken in the future world, as it is said, "O satisfy us in the *morning* with thy loving-kindness"[2] (*ibid.* xc. 14).

The voices of five (objects of creation)[3] go from one end of the world to the other, and their voices are inaudible.[4] When people cut down the wood of the tree[5] which yields fruit, its cry goes from one end of the world to the other, and the voice is inaudible. When the serpent sloughs off its skin,[6] its cry goes from one end of the world to the other and its voice is not heard.[7] When a woman is divorced from her husband,[8] her voice goeth forth from one end of the world to the other, but the voice is inaudible.[9] When the infant || comes forth from its mother's[10] womb.[11] When the soul departs from the body,[12] the cry goes forth from one end of the world to the other, and the voice is not heard. The soul does not go out of the body until it beholds the Shekhinah, as it is said, "For man shall not see me and *live*" (Ex. xxxiii. 20).[13]

[1] The parable is only found in our MS. Cf. 1 Cor. xv. 20, 51; 1 Thess. iv. 14; and Eph. v. 14.

[2] The verse continues: "and let us sing and rejoice *all* our days." See Jalkuṭ Makhiri on Ps. xc. p. 44a; T.B. Berakhoth, 18b. "The wicked sleep the eternal sleep, never to awaken in the future." Cf. Jer. li. 39 and Targum, *in loc.*

[3] Brode and Luria read "six." In fact there are "six" cases enumerated according to the text of the first printed editions. The MS. has five instances only.

[4] See T.B. Joma, 20b, where four examples only are given. Jalkuṭ, Psalms, § 743, has used our author. See Gen. Rab. vi. 7. The first editions add: "and they are."

[5] This may be based on Deut. xx. 19. See also Jer. xlvi. 22 and Targum thereon.

[6] See *supra*, p. 99, Gen. Rab. xx. 5. Cf. The Baraitha of the 32 Middoth, No. 14, ed. Reifmann, pp. 33f.

[7] The first editions omit: "The voice goeth forth from one end of the world to the other." It occurs in the Amsterdam edition. Cf. Jer. xlvi. 22.

[8] See Mal. ii. 14–16.

[9] The first editions add: "When a wife is with her husband at the first coition, her voice goeth forth from one end of the world to the other, but the voice is inaudible."

[10] See Isa. xxvi. 17, and xlii. 14; T.B. Joma, *loc. cit.*, and Lev. Rab. xxvii. 7.

[11] The first editions add: "the cry goeth forth from one end of the world to the other, and the voice is not heard."

[12] See T.B. Joma, *loc. cit.*

[13] See Siphrê, Num. § 103; Siphra (beg.), and *infra*, p. 430.

Rabbi Ẓe'era[1] said: All the souls go forth and are gathered, each man's soul to the generation of his fathers and to his people.[2] The righteous with the righteous,[3] and the wicked with the wicked, for thus spake the Holy One, blessed be He, to Abraham: "But thou shalt go to thy fathers in peace" (Gen. xv. 15).[4] And when the soul goes forth from the body,[5] then the righteous come to meet them,[6] and say to them: Come unto peace! One verse says, "Therefore, behold, I will gather thee to thy fathers, and thou shalt be gathered to thy grave in peace" (2 Kings xxii. 20).[7]

Rab Huna[8] said: All Israel[9] who die outside the land (of Israel), their souls[10] are gathered into the land (of Israel), as it is said, "Yet the soul of my lord shall be bound in the bundle of the living"[11] (1 Sam. xxv. 29). All the heathens who die[12] in the land of Israel have their souls cast outside the land (of Israel[13]), as it is said, "And the souls of thine enemies, them shall he sling out, as from the hollow of a sling" (*ibid.*), (even) beyond the land (of Israel).

In the future world the Holy One, blessed be He, will

[1] The first editions read "'Azariah."

[2] Death reunites, whereas in life separation and dispersion are frequent experiences. See Ps. xlix. 19.

[3] See Jalkuṭ, Gen. § 77, and Eccles. Rab. to Eccles. iii. 9.

[4] The first editions read here: "When the soul goes forth from the body, is this peace? But the angels come to meet (it) and say to it: Peace, as it is said: 'He entereth into peace; they rest in their beds' (Isa. lvii. 2). Another verse says: 'Thou shalt be gathered to thy grave in peace'" (2 Kings xxii. 20).

[5] Luria suggests that the text should read: "What is the peace?" (Is there any peace for the body when the soul leaves it?) See also T.B. Sabbath, 152b. See the Book of the Bee lvi. pp. 131 ff. for a parallel to our text.

[6] *i.e.* the souls. See Roḳeach, 313, which has used *P.R.E.*; the reading here is: "The righteous come before the souls." See also T.B. Kethuboth, 104a, and Num. Rab. xi. 7.

[7] Cf. 2 Chron. xxxiv. 28. Our MS. has omitted part of the verse, the first editions read the latter part only.

[8] The first editions read "Rabbi Chanina."

[9] The later editions read: "All the righteous."

[10] Immediately after death.

[11] The land of the living is the Holy Land; when David was an exile from the Holy Land he cries that he cannot worship God. See 1 Sam. xxvi. 19.

[12] Some of the later editions read: "All the dead (bodies) of the wicked." The Amsterdam and Prague editions read: "All the dead (bodies) of the idolaters."

[13] This is the reading of the Amsterdam and Prague editions.

take hold of the corners of the land of Israel, and shake it (free) from all unclean (things),[1] as it is said, "That it might take hold of the ends of the earth,[2] and the wicked be shaken out of it" (Job xxxviii. 13).

A man has three friends ‖ in his lifetime, and they are: his sons and his household;[3] his money, and his good deeds. At the hour of a man's departure from the world he gathers his sons and his household, and he says to them: I beg of you to come and save me from the judgment of this evil death.[4] They answer him, saying to him: Hast thou not heard that there is no one who can prevail over the day of death? and is it not written thus, "None of them can by any means redeem his brother" (Ps. xlix. 7)?[5] "For the redemption of their soul is costly"[6] (*ibid.* 8). And he has his money fetched, and says to it:[7] I beseech thee, save me from the judgment of this evil death. It answers him, saying: Hast thou not

[1] The first editions add: "like a man shakes a garment and casts out all that is therein and throws this away."

[2] In the MS. the quotation ends here; it is continued in the first editions.

[3] Cf. Aboth vi. 9, Jalkuṭ, Isa. § 494; Jalkuṭ, Ps. § 834, reads "household." Bachja in Kad Ha-Ḳemach, *s.v.* אבל, pp. 12a–b, quotes *P.R.E.* and reads: "his wife and his sons." The latter reading is to be found in the first editions. Cf. also Menorath Ha-Maor, 278. See Israel Lévi's article on this passage in *R.É.J.* xviii. pp. 83 ff., where he discusses the influence of "Barlaam and Josaphat" in this parable. "Barlaam and Josaphat" was written in the seventh century probably, and was known to the author of *P.R.E.* in its Greek or Arabic or Syrian version. See also Geiger, *Was hat Mohammed*, etc., p. 93, and *J.E.* ii. pp. 536 f.

[4] This is an explanation of Ps. xlix. 5, "Why should I fear in the days of evil?" (*i.e.* death).

[5] "The first editions read here: "Even his money which he loves cannot redeem him, as it is said: 'Nor give to God a ransom for him' (Ps. xlix. 7). Why?"

[6] Siphrê, Deut. § 329, says: "If they give to Him all the money in the world they would not be able to give Him his ransom." The first editions add here the following: "And this thing must be let alone 'for ever' (Ps. xlix. 8), but go towards peace and rest on thy couch, and stand for thy lot at the end of days, and may thy lot be with the pious of the world.[1] When he sees (things) in this way."[2]

[7] The first editions add: "For thee have I toiled very much by night and by day." See Eccles. v. 10–15 on the folly of heaping up wealth.

---

[1] Note here the universalism of this wish. The pious of the world, not merely the pious of Israel, are the denizens of Paradise. On the "pious of the world," see Tosephta Synhedrin xiii. p. 434. The latter part of the paragraph is based on Dan. xii. 13.

[2] How his family are powerless to help him.

heard, "Riches profit not in the day of wrath"[1] (Prov. xi. 4)? He (then) has his good deeds fetched, and he says to them: I beseech you, come and deliver me from the judgment of this evil death.[2] And they answer him and say to him:[3] Before thou goest, verily, we will go in advance of thee, as it is said, "And charity delivereth from death" (*ibid.*). Does then charity deliver from death? (This refers) to an evil death only. Another Scripture says, "And thy righteousness shall go before thee,[4] the glory of the Lord shall be thy rearward" (Isa. lviii. 8).[5]

All the seven days of mourning the soul goeth forth and returneth from its (former) home to its sepulchral abode, and from its sepulchral abode to its (former) home.[6] After the seven days of mourning the body || begins to breed worms,[7] and it decays and returns to the dust,[8] as it originally was, as it is said, "And the dust returns to the earth as it was"[9] (Eccles. xii. 7). The soul goes forth and returns to the place whence it was given, from heaven, as it is said, "And the soul[10] returns unto God who gave it" (*ibid.*). And whence do we learn that the soul has been given from heaven?[11] Come and see. When the Holy One, blessed be He, formed

[1] *i.e.* the day of death. The text might be rendered "the day of passing away" (from this life). Cf. Eccles. viii. 8.

[2] The first editions add here: "and strengthen yourselves with me,[1] and do not leave me to depart from the world, for ye still have hope for me that I may be saved."[2]

[3] The first editions add: "Go towards peace."

[4] The quotation ends here in the MS., it is continued in the first editions.

[5] In Jalkuṭ, Isa. *loc. cit.*, the verse: "And righteousness delivereth from death" (Prov. x. 2) is quoted. This is also to be found in the Kad Ha-Ḳemach, *loc. cit.*

[6] This sentence is omitted in the printed editions. See 4 Ezra vii. 31.

[7] See Roḳeach, 313, based upon our author; cf. T.B. Sabbath, 152a, and T.J. Mo'ed Kaṭan iii. 5. 82b.

[8] See T.B. Niddah, 69b, and T.B. Sabbath, 152b. The return to dust is considerably later than the first seven days after death.

[9] The next sentence is not found in the printed editions.

[10] The MS. text does not agree with the M.T. "Nephesh," which we have rendered soul, should be "ruach," spirit.

[11] *i.e.* by God.

---

[1] Because all my relatives and friends have forsaken me. For the phraseology, cf. Dan. x. 19.

[2] The next verse (9) in Ps. xlix. says: "and let him live for ever." This is the petition of one's good deeds, the only true and lasting friend of man.

man, he did not have in him the spirit.[1] What did the Holy One, blessed be He, do? He breathed with the spirit of the breath of His mouth, and cast a soul [2] into him, as it is said, "And he breathed into his nostrils the breath of life" (Gen. ii. 7).[3]

Rabbi Ishmael [4] said: All the bodies crumble [5] into the dust of the earth, until nothing remains of the body except a spoonful of earthy matter.[6] In the future life, when the Holy One, blessed be He, calls [7] to the earth to return all the bodies deposited with it,[8] that which had become mixed with the dust of the earth, like the yeast which is mixed with the dough, improves and increases, and it raises up all the body.[9] When the Holy One, blessed be He, calls to the earth to return all the bodies deposited with it, that which has become mixed with the dust of the earth, improves and increases and raises up all the body without water.[10] Forthwith the earth quakes and the mountains tremble,[11] and the graves are opened,[12] and the stones of the graves are scattered about one from the other, as it is said, "And the Lord God shall save them || in that day as the flock of his people: [13] for they shall be as the stones of a crown, lifted on high over his land" (Zech. ix. 16).

Rabbi Azariah said: All the souls are in the hands of

[1] The first editions read: "the spirit of the soul." See *supra*, p. 78, n. 2. Cf. Tertullian, *On the Resurrection*, v.

[2] Or, "breath."

[3] The breath of life came from God and returns to Him.

[4] The first editions read "Simeon."

[5] Read נגועין, and cf. *supra*, p. 77.

[6] Or, "rottenness." See T.J. Naẓir vii. 2, 56b, and Lev. Rab. xviii. 1. The Venice edition adds here: "And it becomes mixed with the dust of the earth like yeast, which is mixed with the dough."

[7] The Voice of God will usher in the resurrection, see *supra*, p. 249; see also Othijoth de R. 'Aḳiba; *B.H.M.* iii. p. 60. Cf. 4 Ezra vii. 32; Apoc. Baruch xi. 4; 1 Thess. iv. 13, 15; and 2 Pet. iii. 4.

[8] Cf. *infra*, p. 335. The earth holds the bodies until the resurrection. The day of death is called the "day of Account" (Isa. x. 3); cf. Num. xvi. 29, "the visiting of every man."

[9] The first edition adds: "without water." This became in the Venice edition: "without a blemish." See T.B. Synhedrin, 91a, and Gen. Rab. xcv. 1.

[10] This sentence is not in the printed texts. It is practically a repetition of the previous sentence. The first editions read instead: "like the leaven which improves and increases the dough."

[11] See T.B. Soṭah, 36b. See Arabic version of 4 Ezra vii. 32 (ed. Box, p. 119).

[12] See Ezek. xxxvii. 13.

[13] In the MS. the quotation ends here.

the Holy One, blessed be He, as it is said, "In whose hand is the soul of every living thing"[1] (Job xii. 10). A parable—to what is the matter like? To a person who was going in the market with the key of his house in his hand. As long as the key is in his hand, all his money is in his hand. Likewise the Holy One, blessed be He, has the key of the graves,[2] and the key of the treasure-houses of the souls;[3] and He will restore every spirit to the body of flesh of man, as it is said, "Thou sendest forth thy spirit,[4] they are created;[5] and thou renewest the face of the ground"[6] (Ps. civ. 30).

The soul is like its Creator.[7] Just as the Holy One, blessed be He, sees and is not visible, so the soul sees and is not visible.[8] Just as the Holy One, blessed be He, has no sleep in His presence,[9] so the soul does not sleep.[10] Just as the Holy One, blessed be He, bears His world,[11] so the soul bears all the body.[12] All souls are His, as it is said, "Behold, all souls are mine" (Ezek. xviii. 4).

Rabbi Jehudah said: From the day when the Temple was destroyed, the land (of Israel) is *broken down* on account of the wickedness of those who dwell therein; like a man who is sick and has no power to stand, so is the land broken down and is without power to yield her fruits, as it is said, "The earth also is polluted under the inhabitants thereof" (Isa. xxiv. 5).[13]

In the future life the Holy One, blessed be He, will cause

[1] After death. The parable illustrates this idea. This does not agree with the interpretation given in Siphrê, Num. § 139, quoted in Jalkuṭ on Job, *in loc.*

[2] See T.B. Ta'anith 2b, "For I am the Lord, when I open your graves."

[3] The first editions add here: "In the future life the Holy One, blessed be He, will open the graves, and He will open the treasure-houses of the souls." See 4 Ezra iv. 35, vii. 32; T.B. Chagigah, 12b; and Siphrê Deut. § 344.

[4] Thereby reviving the spirit of man. Cf. Athenagoras, *Resurrection of the Dead*, xxv.

[5] In the MS. and the first editions the quotation ends here.

[6] The earth will be renewed after the resurrection.

[7] Luria adds: if one may so without irreverence." On this expression, see Bacher, *Terminologie*, i. pp. 72 f.

[8] See T.B. Berakhoth, 10a, and Deut. Rab. ii. 37, where six points of similarity are enumerated; cf. Lev. Rab. iv. 8. On God's seeing, cf. Jer. xxiii. 24; on God's invisibility, see Ex. xxxiii. 20 and Isa. xlv. 15. See similar theories in Tertullian, *de Anima*, xlv.; and Methodius, *Banquet*, vi. 1.

[9] See Ps. cxxi. 4; and Gen. Rab. xiv. 9.

[10] See *supra*, p. 86.

[11] See Isa. xlvi. 4.

[12] Cf. Luria's reading.

[13] See the earlier part of the verse.

the reviving dew to descend, and He will quicken the dead and renew all things, as it is said, "*Thy* dead shall live" (*ibid.* xxvi. 19). They are the Israelites, who died trusting in His name. || "*My* dead bodies shall arise" (*ibid.*). They are the heathens, who are like the carcase of the beast;[1] they shall arise for the day of judgment, but they shall not live. "Awake and sing, ye that dwell in the dust" (*ibid.*). They are the righteous, for they dwell[2] in the dust. "For thy dew is as the dew of light" (*ibid.*). The dew of the righteous is not the dew of darkness,[3] but (it is) the dew of light, as it is said, "For thy dew is as the dew of light" (*ibid.*); and it gives healing to the earth, as it is said, "And the earth shall cast forth the dead"[4] (*ibid.*). And what is the meaning of "And the earth shall cast forth the dead"?[5]

Rabbi Tanchum said[6]: On account of the seed of the earth, when it is commanded, (it) discharges the dew for the resurrection of the dead.[7] From what place does it descend? From the head of the Holy One, blessed be He; for the head of the Holy One, blessed be He, is full of the reviving dew. In the future life the Holy One, blessed be He, will shake His head[8] and[9] cause the quickening dew to descend,[10] as it is said, "I was asleep,[11] but my heart waked[12] . . . for my head is filled with dew, my locks with the drops of the night" (Cant. v. 2).

[1] A similar statement occurs in Tertullian, *On the Resurrection*, *A.N.C.L.* xv. p. 311.

[2] The righteous dead are called "living." See T.B. Soṭah, 5a, and T.B. Berakhoth, 18a. Cf. 4 Ezra vii. 35, 36, 61 to illustrate the preceding part of the paragraph.

[3] The dew of nature descends at night (see Job xxix. 19), and is called "the dew of darkness." There is also "the dew of light," which is the heavenly or spiritual dew.

[4] Rephaim; the root of this word means "to heal." See Cant. Rab. on Cant. v. 2.

[5] The first editions read: "What is the meaning of 'it giveth healing to the earth'?"

[6] This is probably a gloss, copied from T.J. Berakhoth v. 2. 9b. It is only this sentence which belongs to Rabbi Tanchum. Perhaps the saying is merely that the earth will disgorge the dead entrusted to its keeping.

[7] See Luria's reading, and Jalḳuṭ, 1 Kings, § 207.

[8] See Ẓohar, Gen. 130a, and Singer, p. 79, for the "dew of light," based on Isa. xxvi. 19.

[9] See Luria's reading.

[10] The first editions add: "and He will revive the dead."

[11] The righteous sleeps in death, but his heart is ever awake; his soul is fed by the Divine dew which will effect the resurrection.

[12] The quotation ends here in our MS.

CHAPTER XXXV

THE VISION OF JACOB AT BETHEL [45B i.]

" BETTER is the end of a thing than the beginning thereof " (Eccles. vii. 8). The first blessings wherewith Isaac blessed Jacob were concerning the dews of heaven, and concerning the corn of the earth,[1] as it is said, " And God give thee of the dew of heaven,[2] and of the fatness of the earth " (Gen. xxvii. 28). The final blessings were the blessings of the foundation of the world, and in them there is no (interruption),[3] either in this world or in the world to come, as it is said, " And God Almighty bless thee " (*ibid.* xxviii. 3). And he further added unto him the blessing of Abraham, || as it is said, " And may he give thee the blessing of Abraham,[4] to thee and to thy seed with thee " [5] (*ibid.* 4). Therefore (say) [6]: " Better is the end of a thing [7] than the beginning thereof " (Eccles. vii. 8). " Better is the patient in spirit than the proud in spirit " (*ibid.*).[8] " Better is the patient in spirit "—this (saying) is applicable [9] to our father Jacob, for every day he was patient in spirit, and he spake all kinds of words of

[1] *i.e.* material blessings of this earthly life.

[2] In the MS. and the first editions the quotation ends here.

[3] There is a lacuna in the MS.; the space is just sufficient for the word which occurs in the Oxford MS. or in the first editions, and which means " interruption."

[4] In the MS. the quotation ends here; it is continued in the first editions.

[5] The verse continues: " that thou mayest inherit the land of thy sojournings."

[6] This occurs in the first editions, and is missing in the MS.

[7] The reference is to the final blessing of Jacob. The blessings which he received instead of Esau were but a cause of anguish and sorrow to him as far as material benefits were concerned; cf. Job viii. 7.

[8] The first editions read: " 'Better is slowness to anger than the proud in spirit.' 'Better is slowness to anger,' this (saying)," etc. The Oxford MS. agrees with our text.

[9] Read אמור ביעקב.

entreaty.[1] (The words) "than the proud in spirit" (*ibid.*) refer to the wicked Esau, because every day he was eating the flesh of that which he had hunted. Owing to his pride he did not give any of his food to Jacob. Once he went out to hunt but he did not meet with any success. He saw Jacob eating lentil food, and he desired this in his heart, and he said to him: "Let me gulp down, I pray thee, some of that red pottage" (Gen. xxv. 30). Jacob said to him: Thou camest forth red at thy birth from thy mother; (now) thou dost desire to eat (this) *red* food; therefore he called his name "Edom" (red), as it is said, "And Esau said to Jacob" (*ibid.*).

Rabbi Eliezer said: Lentils are the food of mourning[2] and sorrow. Know thou that this is so, for when Abel had been killed, his parents were eating lentil food (as a sign) of their mourning for him in mourning and sorrow.[3] And Jacob was eating lentil food in mourning and sorrow[4] because the kingdom, the dominion, and the birthright belonged to Esau. Moreover, on that day Abraham, his grandfather, died.[5] The Israelites eat lentil food in mourning and sorrow on account of the mourning || and sorrow for the Temple,[6] and on account of the exile of Israel. Hence thou mayest learn that the children of Esau will not fall until a remnant from Israel shall come and give to the children of Esau lentil

[1] The MS. reads "Pangeoth," so also in first editions. Jastrow corrects this and reads Pagneoth (entreaty); see *T.D.* 1135a; his reference to our book on 1186a must be corrected so as to read Chapter XXXV. According to Luria the reading should be: "Every day he ate plain food." The Oxford MS. has: "Every day he ate food which was disqualified" (for the altar).

[2] See T.B. Baba Bathra, 16b; Pal. Targ. Gen. xxv. 29, and Gen. Rab. lxiii. 14. Cf. Jerome, Epist. xxii. *ad Paulam*, quoted in *J.Q.R.* vi. 227, and Brüll in Kobak's *Jeschurun*, viii. 31 ff.

[3] The first editions add: "And when Haran was burned in the furnace of the Chaldees, his parents ate lentil food (as a sign) of their mourning for him in mourning and sorrow."

[4] The Venice edition adds: "because of the kingdom and the dominion and the birthright of Esau."

[5] Luria thinks that since Jacob was wont to eat lentils, there was no special reason to connect this circumstance with the death of Abraham. See Pesiḳta Rabbathi xii. p. 48a.

[6] The custom of eating lentils on the eve of the Fast of Ab obtained formerly; see Ṭur Orach Chayyim, 552, and cf. Gen. Rab., *loc. cit.*, which says that lentils are a suitable repast for mourners because they have no mouth (*i.e.* slit), like the mourner who in his grief is struck dumb. Moreover, the lentils by their round form typify the going around of trouble and loss in this world. (See *J.E.* vii. 682.)

food in mourning and sorrow, and will take away from them the dominion of the kingdom and the birthright, which Jacob acquired from (Esau) by oath, as it is said, "And Jacob said, Swear to me this day; and he sware unto him" (*ibid.* 33).

Rabbi 'Aḳiba said: Every place where our forefathers went, the well went in front of them, and they[1] dug three times and found it before them.[2] Abraham dug three times and found it before him, as it is said, "And Isaac digged again the wells of water, which they had digged in the days of Abraham" (*ibid.* xxvi. 18). And Isaac dug in the land (of Canaan) four times,[3] and found it before him, as it is said, "And Isaac's servants digged in the valley" (*ibid.* 19).[4] And it is written about Jerusalem, "And it shall come to pass in that day, that living waters shall go out from Jerusalem" (Zech. xiv. 8). This refers to the well which will arise in Jerusalem in the future,[5] and will water all its surroundings. Because they found (the well) seven[6] times, he[7] called it Shib'ah (seven).[8]

Jacob was seventy-seven years old[9] when he went forth from his father's house, and the well went before him.[10] From Beer-Sheba as far as Mount Moriah is a journey of two days, || and he arrived there[11] at midday, and the Holy One, blessed be He, met him, as it is said, "And he met in the

[1] Luria thinks that "they" should be deleted, and that instead of this word we should read "Abraham."

[2] Three times in connection with Abraham is the digging of a well mentioned. Isaac also had to dig for water. The Midrashim differ as to the number of wells; see Gen. Rab. lxiv. 8. The next sentence in our text occurs only in our MS.

[3] The first editions read: "three times."

[4] The first editions quote the preceding verse and add the following: "He dug twice in the ground, and found it before him, as it is said, 'And Isaac's servants digged in the valley'" (Gen. xxvi. 19).

[5] The Messianic age.

[6] Three times by Abraham and four times by Isaac.

[7] Isaac.

[8] The first editions add here: "as it is said, 'And he called it Shib'ah' (Gen. xxvi. 33). By the name of the well (Beer) was a city called 'Beer-Sheba unto this day'" (*ibid.*).

[9] See T.B. Megillah, 17a, and Seder 'Olam Rab. ii. p. 5a. Jacob was 63 years when he was blessed in place of Esau; he spent 14 years in the "tents" of Shem and Eber; and therefore he was 77 years old when he went to Beer-Sheba.

[10] On the well in Jewish theology, cf. *Hellenism and Christianity*, p. 87; see also *Rabbinic Philosophy and Ethics*, pp. 81 and 263.

[11] Mount Moriah; see 'Arukh, ed. Kohut, v. p. 227a, *s.v.* "Maḳom."

place,[1] and tarried there all night, because the sun was set" (Gen. xxviii. 11). Why is the name of the Holy One, blessed be He, called Maḳom ? [2] Because in every *place* where the righteous are [3] He is found with them [4] there, as it is said, "In every *place* (Maḳom) where I record my name [5] I will come unto thee, and bless thee" (Ex. xx. 24). The Holy One, blessed be He, said to him: Jacob! The bread is in thy bag,[6] and the well is before thee, so that thou mayest eat and drink [7] and sleep in this place. He said before Him: Sovereign of all the worlds! Till now the sun has still fifty degrees to set,[8] and I am lying down in this place. And (thereupon) the sun set in the west, although not in its proper time. Jacob looked and saw the sun setting in the west, and he tarried there, as it is said, "And he tarried there all night, because the sun was set" (Gen. xxviii. 11).

Jacob took twelve stones [9] of the stones of the altar, whereon his father Isaac had been bound, and he set them for his pillow in that place,[10] to indicate to himself that twelve tribes were destined to arise from him. And they all became one stone, to indicate to him that all (the tribes) were destined to become one people [11] on the earth, as it is said, "And who is like thy people Israel, *a nation that is alone* on the earth" (1 Chron. xvii. 21).

[1] Maḳom is used also as a title of God. The quotation from Gen. xxviii. 11 might be rendered in the sense of our Midrash, thus: "And he met the Omnipresent" (*i.e.* God). In the MSS. the quotation ends here.

[2] *i.e.* "Place." The 'Arukh, *loc. cit.*, reads as our MS. The first editions read: "Why was the place called Maḳom ?"

[3] Jalḳuṭ, Gen. § 119, reads: "where the righteous stand" (in prayer).

[4] Cf. Hos. xii. 4: "He found him in the House of God" (Bethel).

[5] In the MSS. the quotation ends here.

[6] See Jalḳuṭ, Gen. *loc. cit.*; the words are based on 2 Kings iv. 42: "fresh ears of corn in his *sack*." The Targum on this verse renders this last word "garments." Perhaps the best word in our context would be "knapsack."

[7] The first editions omit: "and sleep." It occurs in Jalḳuṭ, Gen. *loc. cit.*

[8] This is also the reading of Jalḳuṭ, Gen. *loc. cit.*, and agrees with the text preserved by Nachmanides, Com. *in loc.* (Gen.); see T.B. Synhedrin, 95b, and Gen. Rab. lxviii. 10.

[9] See Shocher Ṭob on Ps. xci. 6; Gen. Rab. lxviii. 11; Leḳach Ṭob, Gen. xxviii. 11.

[10] Jalḳuṭ, *loc. cit.*, reads: "The Omnipresent came to make known to him," etc.

[11] Or "nation" (גוי), which is used not only of the heathens but also of Israel. Luria reads עם (people); the Venice edition has גוי; this is also the reading of the Amsterdam and Prague editions.

Rabbi Levi said: In that night the Holy One, blessed be He, showed him all the signs. He showed him a ladder standing from the earth to the heaven, as it is said, "And he dreamed, and behold || a ladder[1] set up on the earth, and the top of it reached to heaven" (Gen. xxviii. 12). And the ministering angels were ascending and descending thereon, and they beheld the face of Jacob, and they said: This is the face[2] like the face of the Chayyah,[3] which is on the Throne of Glory.[4] Such (angels) who were (on earth) below were ascending to see the face of Jacob among the faces of the Chayyah, (for it was) like the face of the Chayyah, which is on the Throne of Glory. Some (angels) ascended and some descended,[5] as it is said, "And behold the angels of God were ascending and descending on it" (*ibid.*).[6] The Holy One, blessed be He, showed him the four kingdoms, their rule and their destruction, and He showed him the prince of the kingdom of Babylon ascending [seventy rungs, and descending; and He showed him the prince of the kingdom of][7] Media ascending fifty-two rungs and descending; [and He showed him the prince of the kingdom of Greece ascending 180 ascents and descending;][7] and He showed him the prince of the kingdom of Edom ascending, and he was not descending, but was saying, "I will ascend above the heights of the clouds; I will be like the Most High" (Isa. xiv. 14). Jacob replied to him: "Yet thou shalt be brought down to Sheol,[8] to the uttermost parts of the pit" (*ibid.* 15). The Holy One, blessed be He, said to him: Even "though thou shouldest make thy nest as high as the eagle" (Jer. xlix. 16).

Jacob rose up early in the morning in great fear, and said:[9] The house of the Holy One, blessed be He, is in this place, as it is said, "And he was afraid, and said, How

[1] In the MS. the quotation ends here. On the theme cf. Wisdom x. 10.

[2] Cf. Pal. Targum, Gen. *in loc.*; and see T.B. Chullin, 91b; Gen. Rab. lxviii. 12, lxxviii. 3; and liturgy for the second day of New Year, ed. Heidenheim, p. 36a.

[3] *i.e.* the face of a man; cf. Ezek. i. 10, also T.J. Joma v. 3. 42c.

[4] The next sentence does not occur in the printed texts.

[5] See Pal. Targum, Gen. *in loc.* Note that the text says that the ladder was set up towards the earth, *i.e.* from heaven to earth.

[6] See Gen. Rab. lxviii. 12.

[7] The words in square brackets are wanting in the MS., but they occur in the first editions.

[8] The quotation ends here in the MS.

[9] Cf. Jalḳuṭ Makhiri, Ps. xci. p. 46b.

dreadful is this place![1] this is none other but the house of God" (Gen. xxviii. 17). Hence thou canst learn that every one who prays in Jerusalem[2] is (reckoned) as though he had prayed before the Throne of Glory,[3] for the gate of heaven is there, and it is open to hear the prayers of Israel, as it is said, "And this is the gate of heaven" (*ibid.*).

And Jacob returned to gather the stones, and he found them all (turned into) one stone, and he set || it up for a pillar in the midst of the place, and oil descended for him from heaven,[4] and he poured it thereon, as it is said, "And he poured oil upon the top of it" (*ibid.* 18).[5] What did the Holy One, blessed be He, do? He placed (thereon)[6] His right foot,[7] and sank the stone to the bottom of the depths, and He made it[8] the keystone of the earth, just like a man who sets a keystone in an arch;[9] therefore it is called the *foundation* stone,[10] for there is the navel of the earth, and therefrom was all the earth evolved, and upon it the Sanctuary of God[11] stands, as it is said, "And this stone, which I have set up for a pillar, shall be God's house" (*ibid.* 22).

And Jacob fell upon his face to the ground before the foundation stone, and he prayed before the Holy One, blessed be He, saying: Sovereign of all worlds! If Thou wilt bring me back to this place in peace, I will sacrifice before Thee offerings of thanksgiving and burnt offerings,[12] as it is said, "And Jacob vowed a vow, saying" (*ibid.* 20). There

[1] See Shocher Ṭob on Ps. xci. 7, which has used our book.
[2] Cf. 1 Kings viii. 42.
[3] See Menorath Ha-Maor, 100.
[4] Cf. *Rabbinic Philosophy and Ethics*, p. 88, and see Matt. iii. 16 for the Spirit of God descending like a dove from heaven in the narrative of the baptism of the Founder of Christianity. See Books of Adam and Eve in *A. and P.* ii. pp. 143 f.
[5] See T.J. Joma v. 4. 42c; Lev. Rab. xx. 4; and cf. T.B. Joma, 53b.
[6] Lit. "planted." Late eds. read, "stretched forth."
[7] According to the words of Isaiah the earth is God's footstool, and our Midrash employs this bold imagery in speaking of the right foot of God. The stone became the centre stone of the earth, called "Eben Shethiyah." See the Assumption of Moses i. 17, with Charles' note, *in loc.*, and cf. Ẓohar, Gen. 131a, and T.J. Joma, *loc. cit.*
[8] The MS. reads "them"; the first editions read "it."
[9] See Ẓohar, Gen. 122a.
[10] See *J.E.* iv. 275b; Pal. Targum on Ex. xxviii. 30, and Siphrê, Num. 76b. "Shethiyah" may mean "God has set (or fixed) it."
[11] See *supra*, p. 71.
[12] See Pal. Targum, Gen. xxviii. 22, and Shocher Ṭob on Ps. xci. 7, p. 200b.

he left the well,[1] and thence he lifted up his feet, and in the twinkle of the eye he came to Haran, as it is said, "And Jacob went on his journey,[2] and came to the land of the children of the east" (*ibid.* xxix. 1); and the (text) says, "And Jacob went [2] from Beer-Sheba, and went to Haran" (*ibid.* xxviii. 10). "And the Holy God is sanctified in righteousness"[3] (Isa. v. 16). The angels answered and said: Blessed art Thou, O Lord, the Holy God.[4]

[1] See Shocher Ṭob on Ps. xci., *loc. cit.*

[2] The quotation ends here in the MS.

[3] The divine righteousness or charity experienced by Jacob caused him to sanctify God.

[4] This is the third benediction of the Shemoneh 'Esreh; see Singer, p. 45. This benediction of the sanctification should remind us of Jacob, according to the teaching of our Midrash.

CHAPTER XXXVI

JACOB AND LABAN [46B. ii.]

"WHEN thou goest, thy steps shall not be straitened; and if thou runnest, || thou shalt not stumble" (Prov. iv. 12).

Jacob's steps were not straitened,[1] and his strength did not fail,[2] and like a strong hero he rolled away the stone from the mouth of the well, and the well came up, and spread forth water outside itself,[3] and the shepherds saw and they all wondered, for all of them were unable to roll away the stone[4] from the mouth of the well; but Jacob alone rolled the stone from off the mouth of the well,[5] as it is said, "And Jacob went near, and rolled the stone from the well's mouth" (Gen. xxix. 10).

Rabbi 'Aḳiba said: Anyone who enters a city,[6] and finds maidens coming forth before him, his way will be prosperous (before him). Whence dost thou know this? Know that it is so. Come and see from Eliezer, the servant of our father Abraham, who, whilst he had not yet entered the city, found maidens coming out before him, as it is said, "Behold, I stand[7] by the fountain of water," etc.[8] (Gen. xxiv. 43). And He prospered his way.[9]

[1] This refers to the extraordinary speed of his journey mentioned in the previous chapter of our book; cf. also *supra*, pp. 108, 110.

[2] In spite of his excessive speed; cf. *supra*, p. 213.

[3] Cf. Pal. Targum, Gen. xxix. 10; Gen. Rab. lxx. 8; and Ẓohar, Exodus, 13a.

[4] See Shocher Ṭob on Ps. xci. 1, which reads: "And they wondered, because all of them were unable to roll away the stone."

[5] The rest of the sentence is wanting in the printed texts.

[6] For the purpose of finding a wife. This was the purpose of the journey of Eliezer, Jacob, and Moses. See Gen. Rab. lix. 11, and *supra*, p. 108.

[7] The quotation ends here in our MS.

[8] See the rest of the verse for the reference to the maiden.

[9] The first editions add: "As it is said, 'The Lord hath prospered my way'" (Gen. xxiv. 56).

Whence again dost thou learn this? Know that it is so. Come and see from Moses, for, although he had not yet entered the city, he found maidens coming out before him, as it is said, "Now the priest of Midian had seven daughters; and they came" (Ex. ii. 16). And He prospered his way, and he redeemed Israel from Egypt.[1] Whence dost thou know this? Know that it[2] is so. Come and see from Saul, for whilst he had not yet entered the city, he found maidens coming forth before him, as it is said, "As they went up the ascent[3] to the city, they found young maidens going out" (1 Sam. ix. 11).[4] And He prospered his way and he acquired the sovereignty. || And whence do we know this? Know thou that it is so. Come and learn from Jacob, for whilst he had not yet entered the city, he found maidens coming forth before him, as it is said, "And, behold, Rachel his daughter cometh" (Gen. xxix. 6).

Rab Huna said: Everything is revealed and foreseen before the Holy One, blessed be He. Before Jacob came to Haran, what did the Holy One, blessed be He, do? He sent a plague among the sheep of Laban, and few were left out of many, and Rachel was tending[5] these, as it is said, "Rachel came with her father's sheep;[6] for she kept them" (*ibid.* 9). Whence do we know that few remained of the many? Because it is said, "And Jacob fed the *rest* of Laban's flocks" (*ibid.* xxx. 36), "the rest" (which remained) after the plague, in order to increase and multiply Laban's flocks at the feet of Jacob.[7] Hence (the sages) said: Sometimes the foot of man destroys the house, and sometimes

[1] The Venice edition and MS. Gaster read: "And he advanced to kingship." On the kingship of Moses see the Book of Jashar lxxii. 34 ff.; T.B. Ẓebachim, 102a; cf. Jalḳuṭ, Gen. § 107.

[2] That one's way will be prosperous if he meet maidens when he enters a city.

[3] Our MS. reads: "in the gate." This does not agree with M.T., which reads: "up the ascent."

[4] This section is wanting in the printed texts; cf. Jalḳuṭ, *loc. cit.*

[5] See Pal. Targum, *in loc.*

[6] This part of the quotation is omitted by our MS.

[7] The first editions add here: "'And the Lord hath blessed thee at my foot'[1] (Gen. xxx. 30). The feet of Jacob were worthy[2] to increase and multiply the sheep of Laban. Did the feet of Jacob increase and multiply?"

---

[1] Where I turned I obtained God's blessing on thy behalf.

[2] Luria reads וכו; the Venice edition and MS. Gaster read וכי, "and were then the feet of Jacob," etc.

the foot of man blesses the house,[1] as it is said, "And the Lord hath blessed thee at my foot" (*ibid.* 30). Likewise Laban[2] said to Jacob: "I have divined[3] that the Lord hath blessed me for thy sake" (*ibid.* 27).

When Laban heard the tidings of Jacob, the son of his sister, and the power of his might which he had displayed at the well, he ran to meet him, to kiss him, and to embrace him, as it is said, "And it came to pass, when Laban heard the tidings of Jacob, his sister's son" (*ibid.* xxix. 13). "And Laban said unto Jacob, Because thou art my brother" (*ibid.* 15). Was he then his brother? Was he not the son of his sister? This teaches thee that the son of a man's sister is like his son,[4] and the son of a man's brother || is like his brother. Whence do we learn (this)? From Abraham, our father, because it is said, "And Abram said to Lot, Let there not be strife[5] . . . for we are brethren" (*ibid.* xiii. 8). Another verse (says), "And when Abram[6] heard that his brother was taken captive" (*ibid.* xiv. 14). Was he his brother?[7] Was he not the son of his brother? But it teaches thee that the sons of a man's brother are like his own brothers.

The sons of a man's sons are like his own sons. Whence do we learn (this)? From Jacob, because it is said, "Ephraim and Manasseh, even as Reuben and Simeon, shall be mine" (*ibid.* xlviii. 5). Were they his sons? Were they not the sons of his son? But it teaches thee that the sons of a man's sons are as his own sons. And the sons of one's daughters are as one's own sons. Whence do we learn (this)? From Laban, because it is said, "And

[1] The first editions read: "And Jacob's foot brought blessing, as it is said," etc. See Tanna de bê Elijahu Rab. xxiv. p. 125.

[2] The MS. reads: "Jacob said to Laban." This does not agree with M.T. The Oxford MS., the first editions, and MS. Gaster read: "Laban said to Jacob."

[3] Laban relied on divination and the Teraphim; see T.J. 'Abodah Ẓarah iii. 2. 42d.

[4] This is the reading of our MS., but the margin has: "it seems that one should read, 'like his brother.'" The printed texts also read: "the son of a man's sister is called his *son*." The Oxford MS. reads: "like his brother." Luria reads also "like his brother." MS. Gaster reads, "is called his son."

[5] The quotation ends here in our MS.

[6] Luria's text reads "Abraham"; this should be "Abram" in accordance with the Bible text.

[7] See T.B. Jebamoth, 17b.

Laban answered and said unto Jacob, The daughters are my daughters, and the sons are my sons" (*ibid.* xxxi. 43).[1] Were they then his sons? Were they not the sons of his daughters? But it teaches thee that the sons of a man's daughters are like his own sons.

Jacob began to serve for a wife[2] for seven years. He[3] made a banquet and rejoicing for seven days,[4] and married Rachel,[5] as it is said, "Fulfil the week of this one" (*ibid.* xxix. 27). "And Jacob did so, and fulfilled the week of this one"[6] (*ibid.* 28).[7] All the men of the place were gathered together to show loving-kindness to our father Jacob, as it is said, "And Laban gathered together all the men of the place, and made a feast" (*ibid.* 22).

The Holy One, blessed be He, said: Ye have shown loving-kindness to Jacob, My servant, I also will give || you and your sons your reward[8] in this world, so that there be no reward for the wicked in the future world, as it is said, "Now Naaman, captain of the host of the king of Aram[9] . . . because by him the Lord had given victory unto Aram" (2 Kings v. 1).

(Laban) took his two handmaids, and gave them to his two daughters. Were they his handmaids? Were they not his daughters?[10] But according to the law of the

[1] See T.B. Jebamoth, 62b, and T.B. Baba Bathra, 143b. For an opposite view see Gen. Rab. xciv. 6; and cf. T.B. Soṭah, 49a.

[2] This is based on Hos. xii. 12; see Gen. Rab. lxx. 17.

[3] Jacob. The Oxford MS. and the first editions read: "After seven years he made a banquet." The Bible text says that "*Laban* gathered together all the men of the place, and made a feast" (Gen. xxix. 22).

[4] See *supra*, p. 112, and Pal. Targum, *in loc.*

[5] The Oxford MS. and the first editions read "Leah."

[6] Jubilees xxviii. 8 says: "And Laban said to Jacob, 'Let the *seven days* of the feast of this one pass by, and I will give thee Rachel, that thou mayst serve me another seven years'"; cf. Gen. xxix. 27–29 and cf. Josephus, *Ant.* i. 19. 7.

[7] The Oxford MS. and the first editions add here: "Again he kept another seven days of banquet and rejoicing, and he married Rachel,[1] as it is said: 'And he gave him Rachel his daughter to wife'" (Gen. xxix. 28).

[8] The whole of this paragraph is omitted in the Oxford MS.

[9] In the MS. the quotation ends here. *Aram* suggests to our author Laban, who was an Aramæan.

[10] The legend that Zilpah and Bilhah were sisters occurs in Jubilees xxviii. 9 and in Test. XII Pat., Naph. i. 9, 11; see also Pal. Targ. Gen. xxix. 24, 29, Gen. Rab. lxxiv. 13; and Singer, *Das Buch der Jubiläen*, i. p. 118.

---

[1] See Gen. Rab. lxx. 20.

land the daughters[1] of a man by his concubines are called handmaids, as it is said, "And Laban gave to Rachel his daughter[2] Bilhah his handmaid to be her handmaid" (Gen. xxix. 29).[3]

Rabbi Levi said: The Holy One, blessed be He, saw the sorrow of Leah, and He gave her power to conceive, (bringing) consolation to her soul;[4] and she bare a male child, goodly in appearance, and wise; and she said: *See ye a son*[5] which the Holy One, blessed be He, has given me, as it is said, "And Leah conceived, and bare a son, and she called his name Reuben; for she said, Because the Lord hath looked *upon my affliction*" (*ibid.* 32). Therefore he[6] called his name Reuben.

Rabbi Eliezer said: Leah bare her sons after seven months,[7] and in seven years there were born unto Jacob eleven sons[8] and one daughter.[9] And all of them were born, each with his partner[10] with him, except Joseph, whose partner was not born with him, for Asenath, the daughter of Dinah, was destined to be his wife,[11] and (also) except

[1] Read here שבנותיו.

[2] In the MSS. the quotation ends here.

[3] See Gen. Rab., *loc. cit.* The Midrashic reading of Gen. xxix. 29 seems to be: "And Laban gave to Rachel his daughter Bilhah (by) his handmaid (to be) her handmaid."

[4] *i.e.* the joy of motherhood; see Gen. xxix. 31: "And the Lord saw that Leah was hated."

[5] ראו בן (Reuben). This is not the explanation of the Biblical text (Gen. xxix. 32); see T.B. Berakhoth, 6b, and Gen. Rab. lxxi. 4; cf. *J.E.* x. 386.

[6] The MS. reads "he called." This reading agrees with Jubilees xxviii. 11. The first editions agree with the Oxford MS. and read: "she called."

[7] Of gestation.

[8] The first editions read here "tribes."

[9] See Seder 'Olam Rab. ii. p. 5a: "All the tribes and Dinah were born within 7 years, each one after 7 months." See T.B. Rosh Ha-Shanah, 12a. For a different view see Jalḳuṭ, Ex. § 1, and cf. R. Bechai on Gen. xxix., where the explanation is given as to the month in which each tribe was born, each one being born in a different year. See also the Book of Jashar xxxi. 15 ff., and Jubilees xxviii. 9 ff., according to which the eleven sons were born within ten years; see Charles' note on p. 171 of *Jubilees*, and cf. Schürer, iii.³ 349 (on Demetrius).

[10] *i.e.* future wife. They were twins, male and female; cf. *infra*, p. 304. According to Jubilees xxviii. 23, Leah bare two children, "a son and a daughter," Zebulun and Dinah.

[11] On Asenath see Hastings' *D.B.* i. 162 f.; *J.E.* ii. 172 ff.; see also Pal. Targum on Gen. xli. 45 and xlvi. 20; Midrash Agadah, Gen. p. 97; Jalḳuṭ, Gen. § 146 (in name of Midrash Abkhir). See also *infra*, pp. 287 f.; and cf. the Book of Jashar xlix. 36 f.

Dinah, whose partner was not born with her. She[1] said: This child is (according to) justice and judgment,[2] therefore she called her name Dinah.[3]

Rabbi Eliezer also said: Jacob fled in order to come to Laban, and he fled to get away from Laban. Whence do we know that he fled in order to come to Laban? Because it is said, "And Jacob *fled* || into the field of Aram" (Hos. xii. 12). (Whence do we know that)[4] he fled in order to get away from Laban? Because it is said, "And it was told Laban on the third day that Jacob was fled" (Gen. xxxi. 22). Why did he flee? Because the Holy One, blessed be He, said to him: Jacob! I cannot suffer My Shekhinah to dwell with thee outside the land,[5] but "return unto the land of thy fathers, and to thy kindred; and I will be with thee" (*ibid.* 3).[6] Therefore he fled. And Laban took all the men of his city, mighty men, and he pursued after him, seeking to slay him. The angel Michael descended, and drew his sword behind him,[7] seeking to slay him. He said to him: Do not speak to Jacob, either good or bad, as it is said, "And God came to Laban the Aramæan in a dream of the night,[8] and said unto him, Take heed to thyself that thou speak not to Jacob either good or bad" (*ibid.* 24). Laban rose up early in the morning, and saw all that Jacob had, and he said (to him):[9] All these are mine, and since thou hast taken all these, yet wherefore hast thou stolen my Teraphim, which I worshipped?[10]

What are the Teraphim? They slay a man, a firstborn,

[1] Leah.

[2] "Din" ("justice"). The idea here is probably the same as *supra*, p. 152, that the world was originally developed by the primitive instincts of nature. See Ẓohar, Lev. 77b. There may also be a reference to the coming events in Shechem.

[3] See T.B. Berakhoth, 60a, and Pal. Targum, Gen. xxx. 21.

[4] The Oxford MS. and the first editions read: "Whence do we know?" The expression is wanting in our MS.

[5] The reference is to the land of Israel. The Oxford MS. reads: "I do not desire to let My Glory dwell with thee in this place"; the later editions read: "in the house of Laban."

[6] God promises to be with Jacob in his birthplace, and not in the house of Laban. See *supra*, pp. 54 f.

[7] *i.e.* Laban; see Pal. Targum, Gen. xxxi. 24, and cf. *supra*, p. 191.

[8] In the MSS. the quotation ends here.

[9] "To him" occurs in the first editions, but not in the MSS.

[10] Have we in the description of the Teraphim a protest against the worship of relics? See also Wisdom xiv. 15.

and he is red (in colour). All that a man requires (to know) is not written here. This is impossible, since the men who dispute about the knowledge of making (the Teraphim) have increased. Everyone who follows that knowledge will ultimately go down to Gehinnom.[1] And they pinch off his head, and salt it with salt,[2] and they write upon a golden plate [3] the name of an unclean (spirit),[4] and place it under his tongue,[5] and they put it in the wall, and they kindle lamps [6] || before it, and bow down to it, and it [7] speaks unto them. Whence do we know that the Teraphim speak? Because it is said, "For the Teraphim have spoken vanity" (Zech. x. 2).[8] On that account had Rachel stolen them, so that they should not tell Laban that Jacob had fled, and not only that, but also to remove idolatrous worship from her father's house.[9]

Now Jacob knew nothing of all this, and he said: Anyone who has stolen thy Teraphim shall die before his proper

[1] The preceding words (from "he is red") occur in our MS. only.

[2] For text see Buxtorf, *Lexic. Chald. Talm. Rabb.* (ed. 1640), *s.v.* תרפים; 'Arukh, ed. Kohut, viii. p. 285b, *s.v.* תרף adds: "and spices." This addition agrees with the text of the first editions. The Oxford MS. reads: "And they burn incense before him, and offer spices before him."

[3] On קמיע, (charm) written on golden plates, see Tosephta Kelim (Baba Mezi'a) i. 12, p. 579. See also Origen, *c. Cels.* vi. 31; and M. Friedländer, *Antichrist*, p. 164, note 1, for other references and literature.

[4] The Oxford MS. adds "spirit." This is also the reading of the first editions.

[5] 'Arukh, *loc. cit.*, has "head."

[6] Schwally, *Das Leben nach dem Tode*, pp. 4[illegible] f., sees here a reference to the "lamp of the dead"; and cf. Perles in *Monatsschrift*, x. (1861), p. 382.

[7] 'Arukh, *loc. cit.*, has: "and Laban was speaking with them (the Teraphim)."

[8] This section occurs also in Midrash Tanchuma, Vayezê, § xii.; Jalkuṭ, Gen. § 130, Jalkuṭ, Zechariah, § 578, the Book of Jashar xxxi. 41; Pal. Targum on Gen. xxxi. 19, and see *J.E.* xii. 109; also Athanasius Kircher, *Œdipus Ægyptiacus*, i. p. 261, and cf. Selden, *de Dis Syriis Syntagma*, i. ii. pp. 96 ff. On the Teraphim see Blau, *Altjüd. Zauberwesen*, p. 120; Bacher, T. ii. pp. 164 f.; and cf. Mekhilta pp. 67a, b; Siphrê, Deut. § 43, p. 81b.

[9] The first editions read here: "not only that, but also to cut away the name of idolatry from the house of her father." See also Gen. Rab. lxxiv. 5, and Pal. Targum, Gen. xxxi. 32. 'Arukh, ed. Kohut, viii. p. 285b, reads: "and further to destroy idolatry from her father's house." Jubilees xxix. 5 fixes Nisan 21st as the day of Jacob's departure from Laban. This date corresponds to the day when the Israelites crossed the Reed Sea. Jubilees does not mention the Teraphim, but has a good deal to say about the wickedness of the Rephaim. Are the "Rephaim" purposely substituted for the Teraphim?

time;[1] and the utterance[2] of a righteous person is like the speech from the mouth of an angel,[3] and (Rachel) bare and died, as it is said, "And it came to pass, as her soul was in departing, for she died" (Gen. xxxv. 18).

Rabbi Jehudah said: Three forefathers made covenants with the people of the land.[4] (With reference to) Abraham (the circumstances were as follows).[5] When the angels were revealed unto him, he thought that they were travellers (from among) the people of the land,[6] and he ran to meet them, and he wished to prepare for them a great banquet,[7] and he told Sarah to prepare cakes for them. When Sarah was kneading, she perceived that the manner of women was upon her,[8] therefore he did not hand them any of the cakes. He ran to fetch a calf. But the calf fled from before him, and went into the Cave of Machpelah, and he went in there after it, and he found Adam and his help-meet[9] lying there upon their beds,[10] and they slept, and lights were kindled above them,[11] and a sweet scent was upon them like a sweet savour, therefore he desired to have the Cave of Machpelah as a burial possession. He spoke to the sons of Jebus, in order to purchase from them the Cave of || Machpelah by a purchase with gold,[12] and by a perpetual deed for a possession

[1] The text says: "Let him not live" (Gen. xxxi. 32); *P.R.E.* gives the paraphrase of this, so also the Pal. Targum, *loc. cit.*

[2] Lit. "that which cometh out of the mouth."

[3] This may be an illustration of the verse: "Suffer not thy mouth to cause thy flesh to sin; neither say thou before the *angel*, that it was an error: wherefore should God be angry at thy voice, and destroy the work of thine hands?" (Eccles. v. 6).

[4] Of Canaan. The first editions add: "And they were: Abraham, Isaac, and Jacob."

[5] The words in brackets have been supplied to show the connection of thought. The first editions read: "Abraham made a covenant with the people of the land."

[6] See T.B. Baba Mezi'a, 86b. "The angels looked like Arabs," who travel from land to land, see Jalḳuṭ, Gen. § 82.

[7] See Aboth de R. Nathan (*a*) xiii. p. 29a; Gen. Rab. xlviii. 12; and Jalḳuṭ, Gen. *loc. cit.*

[8] See T.B. Baba Mezi'a, 87a.

[9] See Ẓohar, Gen. 127a, and Midrash Haggadol, c. 348.

[10] See *supra*, p. 148, and cf. *J.E.* viii. 248. According to the Book of Adam and Eve (ed. Malan) II. ix., Adam was "laid on the eastern side of the inside of the cave, the side of the incense, and (Seth) placed in front of him a lampstand kept burning." This was the "Cave of Treasures." The legend occurs in Jalḳuṭ, Gen. *loc. cit.*

[11] Cf. *supra*, previous page, note 6.

[12] See Jalḳuṭ, Gen. *loc. cit.*; here and in Jalḳuṭ, Joshua, § 28, the expression is: "with a purchase by gold." Luria thinks that our text should read: "with a perpetual purchase by gold."

of a burying-place. Were they Jebusites? Were they not Hittites? But they were called Jebusites according to the name of the city of Jebus.[1] The men did not accept (this request).[2] He began to bow down and prostrate himself unto them, as it is said, "And Abraham bowed himself down before the people of the land" (*ibid.* xxiii. 12).

They said to him: We know that the Holy One, blessed be He, will give to thee and to thy seed in the future all these lands; make a covenant with us by an oath that thy seed shall not take possession of the cities [3] of Jebus, and we will sell unto thee the Cave of Machpelah by a purchase with gold and by a perpetual deed and for a perpetual possession. He made with them a covenant with an oath that the Israelites would not take possession of the city of Jebus [4] save by the consent of the sons of Jebus, and afterwards he bought the Cave of Machpelah by a purchase with gold, and a perpetual deed, for a perpetual possession,[5] (as it is said), "And Abraham hearkened unto Ephron; [6] and Abraham weighed to Ephron the silver, which he had named in the hearing of the children of Heth, four hundred shekels of silver, current money with the merchant" (*ibid.* 16).

What did the men of Jebus do? They made images of copper, and set them up in the street of the city, and wrote upon them the covenant of the oath of Abraham. When the Israelites came to the land (of Canaan), they wished to enter the city of the Jebusites,[7] but they were

[1] See I Chron. xi. 4: "Jerusalem, the same is Jebus, and the Jebusites the inhabitants of the land, were there." These inhabitants were Hittites by descent; moreover, the text quoted (Gen. xxiii. 16) speaks of them as the "children of Heth."

[2] At first they only consented to permit him to bury Sarah with their own dead.

[3] See Midrash Haggadol, c. 350. The first editions read: "The city of Jebus except by the consent of the children of Jebus."

[4] The preceding words of this sentence up to "save by the consent" are omitted in the first editions. See Jalḳuṭ, Joshua, *loc. cit.* For a variant reading see 'Arukh, ed. Kohut, vi. p. 180a, *s.v.* עיר.

[5] Cf. Jer. xxxii. 7 ff. for the method of purchasing land. The MS. omits "as it is said"; this reading is found in the first editions.

[6] The quotation ends here in the MS.

[7] See Josh. xv. 8, and Judg. i. 8: "And the children of Judah fought against Jerusalem, and took it, and smote it with the edge of the sword, and set the city on fire"; and cf. verse 19: "for he could not drive out the inhabitants of the valley." What is the political significance of the legend?

not able (to enter),[1] because of the sign of the covenant of Abraham's oath,[2] as it is said, " And the children of Benjamin did not drive out [3] the Jebusites that inhabited Jerusalem " (Judg. i. 21). || When David reigned [4] he desired to enter the city of the Jebusites, (but) they did not allow him, as it is said, " And the king and his men went to Jerusalem against the Jebusites, the inhabitants of the land; which [5] spake unto David, saying, Thou shalt not come in hither " (2 Sam. v. 6).

(Although) the Israelites were like the sand of the sea,[6] yet it was owing to the force of the sign of the covenant of Abraham's oath.[7] David saw (this) and turned backwards, as it is said, " And David dwelt in the stronghold " (*ibid.* 9).[8] They said to him: Thou wilt not be able to enter the city of the Jebusites until thou hast removed all those images upon which the sign of the covenant of Abraham's oath is written,[9] as it is said, " Except thou take away the blind and the lame " (*ibid.* 6). " The lame " refers to the images, as it is said, " Wherefore they say, The blind and the lame shall not come into the house " (*ibid.* 8). Lest thou shouldst say, The blind and the lame did not enter the Sanctuary, Heaven forbid (that we should say this), but these " blind and lame " refer to the images which have eyes and see not, feet and they walk not, (as it is said),[10] " That are hated of David's soul " (*ibid.*). Because David hated to hear of and to see idolatry, as it is said, " Wherefore they say, The blind and the lame shall *not* come into the house " (*ibid.*).

David said to his men: Whoever will go up first, and remove those images upon which the sign of the covenant

[1] The MS. omits " to enter "; it is found in the first editions.

[2] See Midrash Agadah, Gen. p. 56; and Rashi, *in loc.*

[3] The MS. and the first editions omit this first part of the verse.

[4] See Siphrê, Num. § 42; T.B. Ẓebachim, 114b; and cf. 1 Chron. xi. 4 and Ps. cxxxii. 2-5. David desired to conquer Jerusalem and to build the Temple.

[5] Our MS. reads: "The men of Jebus said, Thou shalt not come in hither." The last words occur also in 1 Chron. xi. 5, which reads: " the *inhabitants* of Jebus said to *David*, Thou shalt not come in hither." The first editions have followed the text of 2 Sam. v. 6.

[6] In number; cf. 2 Sam. xvii. 11.

[7] That they were unable to capture the city of the Jebusites.

[8] But not in the city.

[9] Cf. 1 Macc. viii. 22.

[10] " As it is said " is omitted by the MS.; it occurs in the first editions.

of Abraham's oath [1] is written, he shall be the chief.[2] And Joab, the son of Zeruiah, went up,[3] and he became the chief, as it is said, " And Joab the son of Zeruiah went up first, || and was made chief " (1 Chron. xi. 6). Afterwards he [4] bought the city of the Jebusites for Israel by a purchase with gold and with a perpetual deed for a perpetual possession. What did David do ? He took from each tribe fifty shekels; verily all of them amounted to six hundred shekels,[5] as it is said, " So David gave to Ornan [6] for the place six hundred shekels of gold by weight " (*ibid.* xxi. 25).

Isaac [7] made a covenant with the people of the land, when he sojourned in the land of the Philistines. He noticed that they turned their faces away from him. He went away from them in peace, and Abimelech and all his magnates [8] came after him. He said to them : Ye turned aside your faces from me, and now ye come unto me, as it is said, " And Isaac said unto them, Wherefore are ye come unto me,[9] seeing ye hate me ? " (Gen. xxvi. 27). " And they said, We saw plainly that the Lord was with thee " (*ibid.* 28). They said: We know that the Holy One, blessed be He, will give to thy seed in the future all these lands; make a covenant of an oath with us, that thy seed will not take possession of the land of the Philistines. He made a covenant of an oath with them.[10] What did Isaac do ? He cut off one cubit [11] of the bridle of the

[1] According to Rashi and Ḳimchi, *in. loc.*, the sign was the effigy of Abraham.

[2] Lit. " the head."

[3] The first editions add : " first."

[4] David.

[5] See T.B. Ẓebachim, 116b; Siphrê, Num. *loc. cit.*; Deut. § 62, and Baraitha of the 32 Middoth, 15. Our text is referred to by Tosaphoth on T.B. Kethuboth, 99a; catchword, " He gave."

[6] In the MS. and the first editions the quotation ends here.

[7] See Gen. Rab. lxviii. 7.

[8] See Pal. Targum on Gen. xxvi. 26.

[9] The quotation ends here in our MS.; the first editions read as far as " Wherefore." As usual, " etc." is added in all the texts.

[10] This sentence is not in the printed texts.

[11] See Pal. Targum, Gen. xxvi. 28 ff., for this legend. According to the Midrash Agadah (Gen. *in loc.*), p. 66, Isaac was riding upon his ass when he made the covenant with the Philistines. He cut off the measure of a cubit from the bridle of the ass, so that it should be a proof to the Philistines that Isaac had sworn that his children should not take the land of the Philistines.

ass upon which he was riding, and he gave it to them that it might be in their hands [1] for a sign of the covenant of the oath.

When David reigned, he desired to enter the land of the Philistines, but he was unable (to do so) because of the power of the sign of the covenant [2] oath of || Isaac, until he had taken from them the sign of the covenant of Isaac's oath, as it is said, "And David took the bridle of the cubit [3] out of the hand of the Philistines" (2 Sam. viii. 1),[4] as it is written, "So the Philistines were subdued, and they came no more within the border of Israel" (1 Sam. vii. 13).[5]

Jacob made a covenant with the people of the land, because Laban said to him: I know that the Holy One, blessed be He, will give to thy seed in the future all these lands; make a covenant of an oath with me, that the Israelites will not take possession of the land of Edom.[6] He [7] made with him a covenant with an oath, as it is said, "And Jacob said unto his brethren, Gather ye stones" (Gen. xxxi. 46). Were they his brethren? Were they not his sons? But this teaches thee that a man's sons are like his brethren.[8] Laban said to him: If the Israelites obtain possession of the land (of Canaan), then they must not come into the land of Edom [9] for an evil purpose,[10] and if Edom obtain possession they must not come into the land of Israel for evil, as it is said, "That I will not pass

[1] The first editions read here: "And he gave it to him as a sign that there should be between them a covenant of an oath."

[2] See Ex. Rab. xx. 1; and Gen. Rab. lii. 7.

[3] See Shocher Ṭob, Ps. lx. 1, p. 152b, and cf. T.B. Chullin, 60b, for the covenant of Abraham.

[4] See Ḳimchi on this text, where the entire passage from *P.R.E.* is quoted. See also 'Arukh, ed. Kohut, v. p. 286b.

[5] Luria reads: "And he subdued them." See Tosephta Soṭah, xi. 13, p. 316.

[6] The first editions read "Aram" (Syria). They add the following: "And he erected for himself a pillar and (a heap of) stones,[1] and brought his sons with him in the covenant of the oath."

[7] Jacob.

[8] Cf. *supra*, p. 270, and see Rahmer, *op. cit.* p. 41.

[9] See note 6, above.

[10] The next clause up to "as it is said" occurs only in the MS.

---

[1] See the Book of Jashar xxxi. 52 f.; and read in this context: מצבה ואבנים.

over this heap to thee,[1] and that thou shalt not pass over this heap and this pillar unto me, for harm " (*ibid.* 52).

When David reigned, he wished to come into the land of Edom,[2] but he was unable on account of the power of the covenant of Jacob's oath until he had broken that pillar. Concerning this, Solomon [3] said: " And break in pieces their pillars " (Ex. xxiii. 24). Afterwards he conquered the land of Edom,[2] as it is said, " David smote also Hadadezer the son of Rehob, king of Zobah,[4] as he went to recover his dominion at the river " [5] (2 Sam. viii. 3).[6]

[1] The quotation ends here in the MS.; the first editions read: " That I will not pass over this heap," not quoting exactly as in M.T.

[2] See *supra*, p. 279, note 6, first sentence.

[3] This is an error. It should be "Moses." The first editions read "Moses."

[4] The MS. concludes the quotation here and omits "the son of Rehob." The first editions read: "as it is written, 'And David smote Hadadezer, king of Aram.'" This is not to be found in the Hebrew Bible. See 1 Chron. xviii. 3.

[5] The river Euphrates, which flows through the land of Syria. Zobah was an Aramæan kingdom; see Gesenius (Oxford ed.), p. 844a, b, and cf. 2 Sam. x. 6, 8, and Ps. lx. 1.

[6] See Shocher Ṭob, Ps. lx. 1, p. 152b.

CHAPTER XXXVII

JACOB AND THE ANGEL [49A. ii.]

"As if a man did flee from a lion || and a bear met him" (Amos v. 19). The "lion" means Laban, who pursued (Jacob) like a lion to destroy[1] his life. The "bear" refers to Esau, who stood by the way like a bear bereaved by man,[2] to slay the mother with the children. The lion is shamefaced, the bear is not shamefaced.[3] Jacob arose and prayed before the Holy One, blessed be He, saying: Sovereign of all the Universe! Hast Thou not spoken thus unto me, "Return unto the land of thy fathers, and to thy kindred, and I will be with thee"? (Gen. xxxi. 3).

And behold, Esau, the evil one, has now come to slay me; but I fear him and he does not fear Thee. Hence (the sages) say: Do not fear an executive officer or a ruler, but (fear) a man who has no fear of Heaven. (Esau) stood by the way like a bear bereaved by man, to slay mother and child.

What did the Holy One, blessed be He, do? He sent an angel[4] to him to deliver him, and to save him from the hand[5] of Esau; and he appeared unto him like a man, as it is said, "And there wrestled *a man* with him[6] until the breaking of the day" (*ibid.* xxxii. 24). As soon as

[1] In Jalkuṭ, Amos, *in loc.*, the reading is "to tear in pieces"; cf. Ps. vii. 2, and see Midrash Haggadol, c. 524.

[2] The first editions read: "like a bereaved bear, he came."

[3] Laban not only did not molest Jacob, but admitted that he was unable to do so. Esau made no such admission.

[4] See Gen. Rab. lxxviii. 1, as to whether the angel was Gabriel or Michael, see also *Rabbinic Philosophy and Ethics*, 95 f.; for a parallel see Pal. Targum, Gen. xxxii. 25.

[5] For the wording see Jer. xlii. 11.

[6] *i.e.* Jacob. The quotation ends here in the MS.; it is continued in the first editions.

the dawn appeared, the angel said to him: Let me go, for the time has arrived when I must stand[1] to sing[2] and to chant praises before the Holy One, blessed be He. But Jacob did not wish to let him go. What did the angel do? He began to sing and to chant praises from the earth, || and when the angels (on high) heard the voice of the angel who was singing and praising from the earth, they said: Because of the honour of the righteous (one) do we hear[3] the voice of the angel who is singing and praising from the earth; and concerning him the verse says, "From the uttermost part of the earth have we heard songs,[4] glory to the righteous" (Isa. xxiv. 16).

Again the angel said to him: "Let me go" (Gen. xxxii. 26). Jacob answered him: I will not let thee go until thou hast blessed me;[5] and he blessed him, as it is said, "And he blessed him there" (*ibid.* 29). Again he said to him: "Let me go" (*ibid.* 26). He answered him: I will not let thee go until thou tellest me what thy name[6] is. And (the angel) called his name Israel[7] like his own name, for his own name was called Israel.[8] Jacob wished to prevail over the angel, and to throw him down upon the earth. What did the angel do? He took hold of the sinew of the hip, which was upon the hollow of Jacob's thigh, and he lifted the sinew

[1] In Heaven; cf. Isa. vi. 3 for the song of the angels. The same idea occurs in the New Testament; see Luke ii. 13. See also Midrash Haggadol, c. 511 f.

[2] The first editions read: "to minister."

[3] The MS. reads: "stand." The first editions read: "hear."

[4] The quotation ends here in the MS.

[5] The first editions add: "as it is said: 'I will not let thee go except thou bless me'" (Gen. xxxii. 26).

[6] See also Hos. xii. 4.

[7] The second half of this sentence is omitted by the Prague edition.

[8] See Gen. Rab. lxxviii. 3, and Tosaphoth on T.B. Synhedrin, 37b, catchword "From the corner"; cf. Num. Rab. x. 6. The idea of this Haggadah seems to be: the angel is named according to the mission entrusted to him by God. Here it was to announce the ideal for Jacob to pursue, namely, that he was to live as Israel, the warrior of God, destined in his seed to do battle with everything which opposes the establishment on earth of the Kingdom of God. Therefore the angel is named Israel. Israel must fear neither man nor angel; he has prevailed over the powers above man, and need fear only God. See Judg. xiii. 3 ff. for the case of the angel and Manoah, where the same principle obtains. The angel is called פלאי, which suggests הפלאה, "the separation" involved in the Nazirate of Samson. It may also be that the angel was the guardian angel of Israel and therefore bore the name "Israel."

of his hip (out of its place), and it became like the fat[1] of the dead. Therefore the children of Israel are forbidden to eat of the sinew of the hip which is upon the hollow of the animal's thigh, as it is said, "Therefore the children of Israel eat not the sinew of the hip which is upon the hollow of the thigh" (*ibid.* 32).

Jacob wished to cross the ford of the Jabbok, and he was detained[2] there. The angel said to him: Didst thou not speak thus[3]—"Of all that thou shalt give me[4] I will surely give a tenth unto thee" (*ibid.* xxviii. 22)? What did our father Jacob do? He took || all the cattle in his possession which he had brought from Paddan-Aram, and he gave a tithe of them amounting to 550 (animals).[5] Hence thou mayest learn that all the cattle in the possession of our father Jacob, which he had brought from Paddan-Aram, amounted to 5500 (animals).[6] Again Jacob wished to cross the ford of the Jabbok, but he was hindered here. The angel said: Didst thou not speak thus—"*Of all* that thou shalt give me[7] I will surely give a tenth unto thee" (*ibid.*)? Behold, thou hast sons. Thou hast not given a tithe of them. What did Jacob do? He put apart the four firstborn[8] children of the four mothers, and eight children remained. He began (to count) from Simeon, and finished with Benjamin, who was still in his mother's womb.[9]

[1] The fat around the sinew of the thigh is prohibited to the Israelite; see T.B. Chullin, 89b, 92b, and 100b, and Maimonides, *Maakhaloth Asuroth*, viii. 1.

[2] The first editions read: "and to stay there."

[3] The first editions add: "unto me." The Jalkuṭ, Gen. § 132, omits "unto me."

[4] The MS. and the first editions omit the first part of the verse.

[5] Jubilees xxxii. 4 refers to the separation of the tithe of Jacob's cattle, 119 animals being offered: "This was his offering, in consequence of the vow which he had vowed that he would give a tenth."

[6] The Jalkuṭ, *loc. cit.*, reads: "He took all his cattle and gave a tithe amounting to 550 (animals); hence we learn that all his cattle amounted to 5500 animals."

[7] The quotation ends here in the MS.

[8] The first-born are excluded from the operation of the law of tithe; see T.B. Bekhoroth, 53b.

[9] That means, eight children. Two more were required, and starting to count *ab initio* we find that Levi is the tenth. See Jubilees xxxii. 3, where Levi is chosen as the tithe: "Jacob counted his sons from (Benjamin), and Levi fell to the *portion of the Lord*." Pal. Targum, *loc. cit.*, agrees with our author, but Gen. Rab. lxx. 7, and Tanchuma, Re'êh, § xiv., offer another calculation. Both Jubilees and our author fix the choice of Levi at the time when "Rachel became pregnant with her son Benjamin" (Jubilees xxxii. 3).

Again he began (to count) from Simeon, and he included Benjamin, and Levi was reckoned as the tithe, holy to God, as it is said, " The tenth shall be holy unto the Lord " (Lev. xxvii. 32).

Rabbi Ishmael said: All firstborns are required to have a tithe taken (only) when they fall under the observation [1] of the eye.[2] Only Jacob observed the law of tithe in advance; he began with Benjamin, who was in his mother's womb, and Levi was reckoned as holy to the Lord,[3] and concerning him the Scripture says, " The tenth shall be holy unto the Lord " (*ibid.*).

Michael, the angel, descended and took Levi, and brought him up before the Throne of Glory,[4] and he spake before Him: Sovereign of all || the universe! This is Thy lot,[5] and the portion [6] of Thy works.[7] And He put forth His right hand and blessed him, that the sons of Levi should minister on earth [8] before Him, like the ministering angels in heaven.[9] Michael spake before the Holy One, blessed be He: Sovereign of all worlds! Do not such who serve the king have provision of their food given to them? Therefore He gave to the sons of Levi all holy things which accrue to His Name,[10] as it is said, " They shall eat the offerings of the Lord made by fire, and his inheritance " (Deut. xviii. 1).

[1] According to Luria we should read: " When they do *not* fall under the observation of the eye."

[2] *i.e.* guarded so that the owner derives no benefit from them; see T.B. Bekhoroth, 9b, and T.B. Baba Mezi'a, 6b.

[3] This is exactly the same method of reckoning which occurs in Jubilees xxxii. 3. Dr. Charles' note on p. 192 of *Jubilees* must be modified accordingly. See also Jalkuṭ, Gen. § 133.

[4] See Test. Levi ii. 6: " And behold the heavens were opened, and an angel of God said to me, Levi, enter."

[5] See *supra*, p. 177.

[6] So also in Jubilees xxxii. 3.

[7] Instead of " Thy works " (מעשיך) read: " Thy tithe " (מעשרך); see R. Bechai on Num. xviii. 20, p. 200a, and Jalkuṭ, *loc. cit.*

[8] See Deut. x. 8, and cf. Test. Levi ii. 10 ff., which forms a close parallel to our Midrash.

[9] The priests are called " angels "; see Mal. ii. 7, which the R.V. renders " messenger "; see also Ps. ciii. 21, and cf. Gen. Rab. lxx. 7.

[10] Jubilees xxxii. 15 reads: " And all the tithes of the oxen and sheep shall be holy unto the Lord, and shall belong to His priests." Our author and Jubilees agree in ascribing the law of the tithe and the choice of Levi to the priesthood to Jacob's fulfilment of his vow to give a tithe " of all that came with him, both of men and cattle " (Jubilees xxxii. 2).

When Jacob passed to come into the land of Canaan, Esau came to him from Mount Seir in violent anger, contriving to slay him, as it is said, "The wicked plotteth against the just, and gnasheth upon him with his teeth" (Ps. xxxvii. 12). Esau said: I will not slay Jacob with bow and arrows, but with my mouth and with my teeth will I slay him, and suck his blood, as it is said, "And Esau ran to meet him, and embraced him, and fell on his neck, and kissed him; and they wept" (Gen. xxxiii. 4). Do not read *vayishakêhu* (and he kissed him), but (read) *vayishkêhu* (and he bit him). But Jacob's neck became like ivory, and concerning him the Scripture says, "Thy neck is like the tower of ivory" (Cant. vii. 4). The wicked (Esau's) teeth became blunt,[1] and when the wicked one saw that the desire of his heart was not realized he began to be angry, and to gnash with his teeth, as it is said, "The wicked shall see it, and be grieved; he shall gnash with his teeth, and melt away" (Ps. cxii. 10).

Jacob took all the tithe of his possessions and sent it by the hand of his servants, and gave it to Esau, saying to them: Say ye || to him, "Thus saith thy servant Jacob" (Gen. xxxii. 4). The Holy One, blessed be He, said to him: Jacob! That which was holy hast thou made profane? He replied to Him: Sovereign of all worlds! I flatter the wicked, so that he should not slay me. Hence the (wise men) say, we may flatter the wicked in this world for the sake of the ways of peace.[2] Esau said to him: O my brother, I have enough; as it is said,[3] "And Esau said, I have enough" (Gen. xxxiii. 9). And because he gave honour to Jacob,[4] therefore the sons of Jacob paid honour to the sons of Esau with the same

[1] See Cant. Rab. to Cant. vii. 5, Gen. Rab. liv. 9, and Midrash Haggadol, c. 517. The New Testament speaks of Esau as "a fornicator or profane person" (Heb. xii. 16): "For ye know that even when he afterward desired to inherit the blessing, he was rejected, for he found no place of repentance, though he sought it diligently with tears" (*ibid.* 17).

[2] See T.B. Soṭah, 41b, and Midrash Haggadol, c. 508. On the "ways of Peace" see Lazarus, *Ethik*, i. pp. 179 ff. The Sermon on the Mount says: "Resist not him that is evil" (Matt. v. 39). The disciples of the Founder of Christianity are commanded to be "wise as serpents and harmless as doves" (*ibid.* x. 16), as they were being sent forth "as sheep in the midst of wolves" (*ibid.*).

[3] See Jalkuṭ, *loc. cit.*

[4] The first editions read: "Because Jacob gave honour to Esau."

expression;[1] as it is said, "Ye have compassed this mountain long *enough*" (Deut. ii. 3). The Holy One, blessed be He, said to him: Jacob! Is it not enough for thee that thou hast made profane that which is holy? Nay, but I have said, "And the *elder*[2] shall serve the younger" (Gen. xxv. 23); and yet thou hast said, "Thy servant Jacob" (*ibid.* xxxii. 4). By thy life! it shall be according to thy words; he shall rule over thee in this world, and thou shalt rule over him in the world to come. Therefore Jacob said to him (Esau): "Let my lord, I pray thee, pass over before his servant" (*ibid.* xxxiii. 14). Hence thou mayest learn that the sons of Esau will not fall until a remnant from Jacob shall come, and cut off the feet of the children of Esau from Mount Seir,[3] and the Holy One, blessed be He, will descend.[4] "And there shall not be any remaining to the house of Esau;[5] for the Lord hath spoken it" (Obad. 18).

[1] "Rab" (enough), also signifying "Rabbi" or "Master"; cf. the N.T. use of Rabbi, as a title of honour, Matt. xxiii. 7. See also Deut. Rab. xi. 10, and Midrash Haggadol, c. 517.

[2] This in Hebrew is "Rab."

[3] Seir was the territory of Esau.

[4] This phrase, "and the Holy One, blessed be He, will descend," occurs only in the MS. The first editions quote Num. xxiv. 19.

[5] The quotation ends here in the MS.

CHAPTER XXXVIII

JOSEPH AND HIS BRETHREN [50B. i.]

"Or went into the house and leaned his hand on the wall, and the serpent bit him"[1] (Amos v. 19). When Jacob went into his house in the land of Canaan[2] the serpent bit him. || And who was the serpent? This was Shechem, the son of Chamor.[3] Because the daughter of Jacob was abiding in the tents, and she did not go into the street;[4] what did Shechem, the son of Chamor, do? He brought dancing girls who were (also) playing on pipes[5] in the streets.[6] Dinah went forth to see those girls who were making merry; and he seized her,[7] and he slept with her, and she conceived and bare Asenath.[8] The sons of Israel said that she should be killed, for they said that now people would say in all the land[9] that there was an immoral daughter[10] in the tents of Jacob.

[1] The preceding chapter in our book began with the first half of this verse of Amos. Was the Haphtarah for the portion of Vajishlach (Gen. xxxii. 3–xxxvi. 43) Amos v., instead of Obadiah, which is now read in the Synagogues of the Sephardim?

[2] The first editions read: "land of his possession, which was in the land of Canaan."

[3] Add "the Hivite"; this emendation is based on the reading in Eccles. Rab. to Eccles. x. 8; cf. T.B. Sabbath, 85a, and Midrash Haggadol, c. 524 and c. 527. See Jubilees xxx. 2. The Targum of נחש (serpent) is חוי, which suggests "Hivite."

[4] See the Book of Jashar xxxiii. 5 ff., and Pal. Targum, Gen. xxxiv. 1; see also Gen. Rab. lxxx. 5, Leḳach Ṭob, *in loc.*, and Midrash Haggadol, c. 524.

[5] See Luria's commentary *in loc.*, and Sopherim xxi. 8.

[6] The MS. text could be rendered: "outside his (house)"; the first editions read: "outside her (house)."

[7] See Jalḳuṭ, Gen. § 134; Leḳach Ṭob, *in loc.*; Rashi, *in loc.*

[8] See *supra*, pp. 272 f.

[9] The first editions read: "for now would all (the people of) the land say that there was a house of ill-fame in the tents of Jacob."

[10] The reading in Jalḳuṭ, *loc. cit.*, is "daughter" (בת). The 1st ed. reads "house" (בית).

What did (Jacob)[1] do? He wrote the Holy Name upon a golden plate,[2] and suspended it about her[3] neck and sent her away. She went her way. Everything is revealed before the Holy One, blessed be He, and Michael the angel descended[4] and took her, and brought her down to Egypt to the house of Potiphera; because Asenath was destined to become the wife of Joseph.[5] Now the wife of Potiphera was barren, and (Asenath) grew up with her as a daughter.[6] When Joseph came down to Egypt he married her, as it is said, "And he[7] gave him[8] to wife Asenath[9] the daughter of Potiphera priest of On" (Gen. xli. 45).

Simeon and Levi were moved by a great zeal on account of the immorality, as it is said, "And they said, Should he deal with our sister as with an harlot?" (*ibid.* xxxiv. 31). And each man[10] took his sword and slew all the men of Shechem. When Jacob heard thereof, he became sorely afraid.[11] For he said: Now all the people of the land will hear, and they will gather together against me || and smite me. He began to curse the wrath of his sons, as it is said, "Cursed be their anger, for it is fierce" (*ibid.* xlix. 7); and he also cursed their sword[12] in the Greek language,

[1] The MS. omits "Jacob"; the first editions insert this word.

[2] The first editions read: "He brought a plate and wrote upon it," see T.B. Ḳiddushin, 73b.

[3] Asenath's.

[4] See Sopherim, *loc. cit.*

[5] The Midrash Agadah, Gen. p. 97, has copied our book in giving the legend of Asenath. The narrative is also given in the book Raẓiel, p. 7a; see also Jalḳuṭ, Gen. § 146.

[6] As to the sterility of the wife of Potiphera see Koran, Joseph Sura, and cf. Gen. Rab. lxxxvi. 3; Midrash Haggadol, c. 579; Leḳach Ṭob, Gen. p. 98b, note 9; Jalḳuṭ to Pss., § 732; and cf. T.B. Soṭah, 13b. The legend that Potiphera was impotent passed from the Jews to Jerome. See Schapiro, *Die Haggadischen Elemente im erzählenden Teil des Korans*, p. 34 f.; and A. Marmorstein, *Studien zum Pseudo-Jonathan Targum*, pt. i. pp. 31 ff.

[7] Pharaoh.

[8] Joseph; see Sopherim (ed. Müller), p. 309 (49), and J. Perles, *R.É.J.* xxi. p. 254.

[9] The quotation ends here in the MS.; it is continued in the first editions.

[10] Simeon and Levi.

[11] The phraseology is based on Neh. ii. 2. Luria reads here: "as it is said: 'Ye have troubled me, to make me of bad repute among the inhabitants of the land . . . and, I being few in number, they will gather themselves together against me and smite me'" (Gen. xxxiv. 30).

[12] This agrees with the reading preserved in 'Arukh, ed. Kohut, v. p. 139; see *Rabbinic Philosophy and Ethics*, p. 119.

for he said: "Weapons of violence are their *swords*"[1] (*ibid.* 5).[2] All the kings[3] of the earth heard (thereof) and feared very much, saying: If two sons of Jacob have done all these great things, if they all band themselves together, they will be able to destroy the world.[4] And the dread of the Holy One, blessed be He, fell upon them, as it is said, "And the terror of God[5] was[6] upon the cities, . . . and they did not pursue after the sons of Jacob" (*ibid.* xxxv. 5).

Jacob took his sons and his grandsons,[7] and his wives, and he went to Kirjath Arba (so as to be) near Isaac his father. And he found there Esau and his sons and his wives dwelling in the tents of Isaac.[8] And he spread his tent apart from him;[9] and Isaac saw Jacob, his wives,[10] his daughters, and all that belonged to him, and he rejoiced in his heart exceedingly. Concerning him the Scripture saith, "Yea, thou shalt see thy children's children, *peace be upon Israel*"[11] (Ps. cxxviii. 6).

Rabbi Levi said: In the hour of the ingathering[12] of Isaac, he left his cattle and his possessions, and all that he had, to his two sons; therefore they both rendered loving-kindness (to him), as it is said, "And Esau and Jacob his sons buried him" (Gen. xxxv. 29).

Esau said to Jacob: Divide all that my father has left into two portions, and I will choose[13] (first), because I am the elder.[14] || Jacob said: This wicked man has not satisfied

[1] The Amsterdam and Prague editions add: "For thus do the Greeks call the sword," מכיר (μάχαιρα, "daggers"); cf. Tanchuma, Vayechi, § ix. This addition is also given by the 'Arukh (ed. Kohut), v. p. 139b, *s.v.* מכר. Jerome uses this version. See Steinschneider's *Festschrift*, p. 158, article by Krauss.

[2] See Gen. Rab. xcix. 6.

[3] Later editions read: "All the inhabitants."

[4] Later editions read: "us."

[5] R.V. renders here: "a great terror."

[6] In the MS. and the first editions the quotation ends here.

[7] "Grandsons" is probably an error; see Seder 'Olam Rab. ii. 6a; Gen. Rab. *loc. cit.*; and the Book of Jashar xxxi. 38.

[8] But Jacob's home was at Migdal Eder; cf. Pal. Targum, Gen. xxxv. 21, and Mic. iv. 8.

[9] *i.e.* apart from Esau; cf. the Book of Jashar xxxii. 72.

[10] The first editions add: "his sons."

[11] "Israel" is interpreted here as pointing to Jacob.

[12] *i.e.* at his death. See Midrash Haggadol, c. 541.

[13] See T.B. Soṭah, 13a.

[14] The first editions read: "the first-born."

his eye with wealth, as it is said, "Neither are his eyes satisfied with riches" (Eccles. iv. 8). What did Jacob do? He divided all that his father had left as the one part, and the other part was to be the land of Israel and the Cave of Machpelah.[1] What did Esau do? He went to Ishmael[2] in the wilderness in order to consult him, as it is said, "And Esau went unto Ishmael" (Gen. xxviii. 9). Ishmael said to Esau: The Amorite and the Canaanite[3] are in the land, and Jacob trusts (in God) that he will inherit the land, therefore take all that thy father has left, and Jacob will have nothing.[4]

And Esau took all that his father had left, and he gave to Jacob the land of Israel, and the Cave of Machpelah, and they wrote a perpetual deed between them.[5] Jacob said to Esau: Go from the land of my possession, from the land of Canaan. Esau took his wives, and his sons, and his daughters, and all that he had, [as it is said, "And Esau took his wives . . . and all his possessions which he had gathered in the land of Canaan],[6] and went into a land[7] away from his brother Jacob" (*ibid.* xxxvi. 6). And as a reward[8] because he removed all his belongings on account of Jacob his brother, He gave him one hundred provinces from Seir unto Magdiel, and Magdiel is Rome, as it is said, "Duke Magdiel, Duke Iram" (*ibid.* 43).[9]

Then Jacob dwelt safely and in peace in the land of

[1] This is also the reading in Jalkuṭ, Gen. § 138, and in Midrash Haggadol, *loc. cit.*; cf. Ex. Rab. xxxi. 17, and *infra*, pp. 291, 309. The first editions omit "and the Cave of Machpelah." The rest of the paragraph is wanting in Midrash Haggadol.

[2] Luria thinks that we should read "the sons of Ishmael" instead of "Ishmael" both here and in the next sentence. The first editions agree with the text of our MS. See Seder 'Olam Rab. ii. p. 5a.

[3] See Gen. xii. 6. The Jalkuṭ, Gen. *loc. cit.*, reads "The Canaanite," without mentioning the Amorite.

[4] Cf. Test. XII Pat., Gad vii. 4: "For though a man become rich by evil means, even as Esau, the brother of my father, be not jealous; but wait for the end of the Lord."

[5] On the written agreement between them see *infra*, p. 309.

[6] The words in brackets are not in the MS., but they occur in the first editions.

[7] The MS. adds here "etc.," clearly indicating that the words "and went into a land" belong to a quotation from Scripture. The quotation is continued in the first editions.

[8] See Jalkuṭ, Gen. § 76 (quoting the Tanna de bê Elijahu), and see also Tanna de bê Elijahu Rab. xiii. p. 65, note 49.

[9] See Gen. Rab. lxxxiii. 4.

his possession,[1] and in the land of his birth, and in the land of the sojournings of his father.[2]

Rabbi Ishmael said: Every son of the old age || is beloved of his father, as it is said, "Now Israel loved Joseph[3] more than all his children, because he was the son of his old age" (*ibid.* xxxvii. 3). Was he then the son of his old age? Was not Benjamin the son of his old age?[4] But owing to the fact that (Jacob) saw by his prophetic power that (Joseph) would rule[5] in the future, therefore he loved him more than all his sons. And they envied him with a great envy, as it is said, "And his brethren saw that[3] their father loved him more than all his brethren; and they hated him" (*ibid.* 4). Further, because he saw in his dream that in the future he would rule, and he told his father, and they envied him yet more and more, as it is said, "And they hated[3] him yet the more" (*ibid.* 8). Moreover, he saw the sons of his father's concubines[6] eating the flesh of the roes and the flesh of the sheep whilst they were alive,[7] and he brought a reproach[8] against them before Jacob their father, so that they could not see his face any more (in peace), as it is said, "And they could not speak peaceably unto him" (*ibid.* 4). Jacob

[1] The first editions read: "in the land of Canaan."

[2] The first editions add here: "as it is said: 'And Jacob dwelt in the land of his father's sojournings'" (Gen. xxxvii. 1).

[3] The quotation ends here in the MS.; it is continued in the first editions.

[4] According to Rashbam (comm., *in loc.*), Jacob called his youngest child "Son of days"—Ben-jamin; Judah also referred to him as "the child of old age." Onḳelos renders: "Son of wisdom," *i.e.* a wise child; see T.B. Megillah, 16b; Leḳach Ṭob, Gen. xxxv. 18, p. 91a, notes 46 and 47. The interpretation given by *P.R.E.* agrees with the Arabian legend quoted by Schapiro, *op. cit.* p. 19. The same explanation is also given by Ephraim of Syria, *Hist. of Joseph*, p. 16 (quoted by Schapiro).

[5] In Egypt, and there he would sustain the entire family in Jacob's old age. The reference to kingship may also refer to the ascendancy of the house of Joseph in Jewish history, and perhaps to the rule of the Messiah ben Joseph.

[6] See Test. XII Pat., Gad i. 6, and cf. Gen. Rab. lxxxiv. 7.

[7] This was one of the seven precepts of the "Sons of Noah"; see Pal. Targum, Gen. ix. 4. On the mutilation of the flock see T.B. Bekhoroth, 39b; T.B. Kethuboth, 5b, and 37a; and cf. T.B. Chullin, 121b. They are said to have taken of the flesh of the ear of the sheep, although the animals were alive. See Test. of the XII Pat., Gad, *loc. cit.*, where a "lamb" incident is mentioned; and cf. Pal. Targ. on Gen. xxxvii. 2.

[8] דבי, "reproach"; cf. Ps. l. 20, where LXX renders the word by σκάνδαλον (offence).

said to Joseph: Joseph, my son! Verily I have (waited) many days without hearing of the welfare of thy brethren, and of the welfare of the flock, as it is said, "Go now, see whether it be well with thy brethren,[1] and well with the flock" (*ibid.* 14). And the lad[2] was wandering[3] in the field, and the angel Gabriel[4] met him, as it is said, "And a certain *man* found him, and, behold, he was wandering[5] in the field" (*ibid.* 15). (The word) "man" (here in this context) is Gabriel only, as it is said, "The *man* Gabriel,[5] whom I had seen in the vision" (Dan. ix. 21).

And (Gabriel) said to him: What seekest thou? He said to him: I seek my brethren, as it is said, "And he said, I seek my brethren" (Gen. xxxvii. 16). And he led him to || his brethren, and they saw him and sought to slay him, as it is said, "And they saw him afar off" (*ibid.* 18). Reuben said to them: Do not shed his blood, as it is said, "And Reuben said unto them, Shed no blood;[5] cast him into this pit that is in the wilderness" (*ibid.* 22). And[6] his brethren listened to him, and they took Joseph and cast him into the pit, as it is said, "And they took him, and cast him into the pit" (*ibid.* 24). What did Reuben do? He went and stayed on one of the mountains, so as to go down by night to bring up Joseph out of the pit. And his nine brethren were sitting down[7] in one place, all of them like one man, with one heart and one plan.[8] Ishmaelites passed by them, and (the brethren) said: Come, let us sell him to the Ishmaelites, and they will lead him to the end of the wilderness, and Jacob will not hear any further report concerning him.

(The brethren) sold him to the Ishmaelites for twenty

[1] The quotation ends here in the MS.; it is continued in the first editions.

[2] The MS. repeats the word "lad"; this is due to the scribe's carelessness.

[3] See Pal. Targum, *in loc.*, and the Book of Jashar xli. 22. The first editions read: "was walking and wandering on the way."

[4] See Jalkuṭ, Gen. § 141, and Pal. Targum, *in loc.* This legend was known to Basil (i. p. 19). See Schapiro, *op. cit.*, p. 27, for the legend of the angel Gabriel and Joseph in Arabian literature. Gabriel appears in the New Testament account of the Annunciation of the birth of Jesus; see Luke i. 26.

[5] The quotation ends here in the 1st ed.

[6] The first editions add here: "and he will die there."

[7] To eat bread; cf. Gen. xxxvii. 25.

[8] Tanchuma, Vayesheb, § ii., reads: "As one man with one purpose."

pieces [1] of silver, and each one of them took two pieces of silver (apiece) to purchase shoes for their feet, as it is said, "Thus saith the Lord, . . . Because they have sold [2] the righteous for *silver*, and the needy for a pair of *shoes*" [3] (Amos ii. 6). They said: Let us swear [4] among ourselves that no one of us shall declare the matter to our father Jacob.[5] Judah said to them: Reuben is not here, and the ban cannot be valid through nine (adults).[6] What did they do? They associated the Omnipresent with them and proclaimed the ban.

And Reuben || went down by night to bring up Joseph out of the pit, but he did not find him there.[7] He said to them: Ye have slain Joseph; "and I, whither shall I go?" (Gen. xxxvii. 30). And they told him what they had done, and the ban which they had proclaimed; and Reuben heard of the ban, and was silent; the Holy One, blessed be He, because of the ban, did not tell the matter to Jacob, and (though) concerning Him it is written, "He sheweth his word unto Jacob" (Ps. cxlvii. 19); but this word He did not shew unto Jacob, therefore Jacob did not know what had been done to Joseph, and he said: "Joseph is without doubt torn in pieces" (Gen. xxxvii. 33).

Rabbi Jannai said: The sale of Joseph was not atoned by the tribes [8] until they [9] died, as it is said, "And the

[1] See Test. Gad ii. 3(b), with Charles' note, *in loc.*, Pal. Targ., *in loc.*, and the Book of Jashar xlii. 19. Test. Zeb. i. 5 says: "Nor yet do I remember that I have done any iniquity, except the sin of ignorance which I committed against Joseph; *for I covenanted with my brethren not to tell my father* what had been done." See the next verse also.

[2] The quotation ends here in the MS.

[3] Thereby reducing the needy to the condition of slavery. This legend has been borrowed from Test. Zeb. iii. 2, or from its source; see Pal. Targ. Gen. xxxvii. 28, and Liturgy, Day of Atonement, ed. H. M. Adler, ii. pp. 178 f.

[4] Lit. "Let us put ourselves under the ban" (to prevent our divulging the matter).

[5] The first editions add here: "except it be by the consent of all of us." See *supra*, note 1, quotation from Test. Zeb. i. 5.

[6] The first editions read: "The ban cannot be valid save by ten (adults)." See Midrash Haggadol, c. 564.

[7] Tanchuma, *loc. cit.*, adds: "and he returned to his brethren and said to them." See Test. Zeb. iv. 5.

[8] See Gen. Rab. lxxxiv. 17, and cf. Tosephta Berakhoth iv. 18, p. 11.

[9] *i.e.* Joseph's brethren. The brethren are called "the tribes"; see *supra*, p. 264, and *infra*, p. 376.

Lord of hosts revealed Himself in mine ears, Surely this iniquity shall not be purged [1] from you till ye die" (Isa. xxii. 14).[2] Owing to the sale (of Joseph) a famine came into the land of Israel for seven years, and the brethren of Joseph "went down to buy corn" (Gen. xlii. 3) in Egypt. And they found Joseph (still) living, and they absolved themselves of the ban; [3] and Jacob heard about Joseph that he was living, and his soul and his spirit revived.[4] Did their father Jacob's spirit die, so that it had to be revived? But, owing to the ban, the Holy Spirit had departed from him, and when they had removed the ban the Holy Spirit rested on him as at first; that || is what is written, "The spirit of Jacob their father revived" (*ibid.* xlv. 27).[5]

Rabbi 'Aḳiba said: The ban is as much as the oath, and an oath is as much as the ban; and everyone who violates the ban is as though he had violated the oath, and everyone who violates the oath is as though he had violated the ban. Everyone who knows the matter and does not declare [6] it, the ban falls upon him and destroys his timber and his stones, as it is said, "I will cause it to go forth, saith the Lord . . . and it shall enter into the house of him that sweareth falsely by my name . . . and shall consume it with the timber thereof and the stones thereof" (Zech. v. 4).[7]

Know the power of the ban.[8] Come and see from

[1] The quotation ends here in the MS.; it is continued in the first editions. See Midrash Haggadol, c. 565.

[2] See Tanchuma, *loc. cit.*, in name of R. Mana.

[3] Lit. "they annulled" or "loosened the ban." Cf. the use of "binding and loosing" in the N.T.: "I will give unto thee the keys of the kingdom of heaven: and whatsoever thou shalt bind on earth shall be *bound in heaven*: and whatsoever thou shalt loose on earth shall be *loosed in heaven*" (Matt. xvi. 19).

[4] The first editions add: "as it is said, 'The spirit of Jacob, their father, revived'" (Gen. xlv. 27).

[5] The first editions add: "Onḳelos translates this (passage): 'And the spirit of prophecy rested on Jacob their father.'" Luria thinks that this is a gloss. On Onḳelos see *J.E.* ix. 405, and see Hastings' *D.B.* iv. 679b.

[6] As in the case of Achan's children; see *infra*, p. 296. Cf. Tanchuma, *loc. cit.*, and see T.B. and T.J. Nedarim, Maimonides, Hilkhoth Nedarim, and Shulchan 'Arukh, Joreh Di'ah, § 203 ff., on the laws as to vows.

[7] In the MS. the first part only of the verse is given; in the first editions only the latter part is quoted. See Jalḳuṭ, Zech. (ed. King), p. 34.

[8] See Tanchuma, *loc. cit.*

Joshua, the son of Nun, who put Jericho under the ban; it was to be burnt with all things therein by fire. Achan, son of Carmi,[1] son of Zerach, saw the Teraphim,[2] and the silver which they brought (as offerings) before it, and the mantle which was spread before it, and one tongue of gold in its mouth. And in his heart he coveted them, and went and [3] buried them in the midst of his tent. On account of his trespass which he had committed, thirty-six righteous men died on his account,[4] as it is said, "And the men of Ai smote of them [5] about thirty and six men" (Josh. vii. 5).

Joshua went and rent his garments, and fell upon his face to the ground before the Ark of the Covenant of God, and he sought (to effect) repentance, and the Holy One, blessed be He, was appeased by him, and He said to him: Joshua! Israel has trespassed the sin of trespass in the matter of the devoted things, as it is said, "Israel hath sinned" (*ibid.* 11). Joshua gazed at the twelve || stones which were upon the High Priest, which correspond to the twelve tribes.[6] Every tribe that had done some transgression, the light (of its stone) became dim,[7] and he saw the stone of the tribe of Judah,[8] the light of which became dim. And he knew that the tribe of Judah had transgressed in the matter of the devoted thing. He cast lots, and Achan was taken, as it is said, "And he brought near [9] his household man by man; and Achan, the son of Carmi, was taken" (*ibid.* 18). Joshua took Achan, the son of Zerach,[10] with the silver and the mantle and the tongue of gold, and his sons and his daughters, and all that he had,

[1] The name "Carmi" means vineyard-man; see Josh. vii. 1.

[2] This is inferred from the reference in the Book of Joshua vii. 21 to the "tongue of gold" stolen by Achan; see *supra*, p. 274.

[3] The first editions add: "and he took them."

[4] See T.B. Synhedrin, 44a.

[5] The quotation ends here in the MS.; it is continued in the first editions.

[6] The first editions insert here: "The light of every tribe which had observed the commandments (lit. which had a precept in its hand) shone."

[7] The first editions read: "its light did not shine."

[8] See Rashi, on Josh., *in loc.*, who quotes *P.R.E.*

[9] The MS. omits the words: "his household, man by man."

[10] See Josh. vii. 18: "Achan, son of Carmi, the son of Zabdi, the son of Zerach."

and he brought them up into the valley of Achor.[1] And it is written, "The fathers shall not be put to death for the children,[2] neither shall the children be put to death for the fathers" (Deut. xxiv. 16). But because they were cognizant of the matter, and did not report it,[3] he stoned them and burnt them.[4] If there was a burning, why (was there) a stoning, and if a stoning, why a burning? But the stoning was because they knew of the matter and did not report it; burning (was inflicted) because thirty-six righteous men died through him,[5] as it is said, "And the men of Ai smote of them[6] about thirty and six men" (Josh. vii. 5).

Because (Achan) confessed[7] before the Name of the Holy One, blessed be He, he has a portion in the world to come, as it is said, "And Joshua said, Why hast thou troubled us?[8] The Lord shall trouble thee *this day*" (*ibid.* 25). "This day" thou art troubled, but thou shalt not be troubled in the future world.[9]

Know thou the power of the ban. Come and see from the (story of) the tribes, who were zealous because of immorality against || the tribe of Benjamin.[10] The Holy One, blessed be He, said to them: Ye are zealous because of the immorality,[11] and ye are not zealous because of the image of Micah. Therefore the Benjamites slew some of them a first and a second[12] and a third time, until they went[13] before the Ark of the Covenant of the Lord seeking

[1] See Josh. vii. 24.

[2] The quotation ends here in the MS. and in the first editions. The latter add after the quotation: "If so, for what reason did these (children) die?"

[3] See *supra*, p. 294. for the view of Rabbi 'Aḳiba on this point.

[4] See Targum, Josh. vii. 24 f. Rashi, Gersonides, and other Jewish commentators maintain that the stoning was inflicted only on the beasts, and that Achan's children were there merely to see and to be warned.

[5] Achan.

[6] In the MS. the quotation ends here; it is continued in the first editions.

[7] See Josh. vii. 20.

[8] Thus far is the quotation in the MS.; this part of the verse is omitted in the first editions.

[9] See T.B. Synhedrin, *loc. cit.*, and *J.E.* i. 164 f.; cf. also Num. Rab. xxiii. 6, and Semachoth, ii.

[10] See T.B. Synhedrin, 103b; Tanna de bê Elijahu Rab. xi. pp. 56 f.; and cf. T.B. Baba Bathra, 109b.

[11] The first editions add: "of the tribe of Benjamin."

[12] This reading agrees with Jalḳuṭ, Judg. § 76.

[13] The first editions add: "and fell upon their faces to the ground." See Jalḳuṭ, Joshua, § 18. Cf. Tanna de bê Elijahu Rab. xviii. p. 89.

repentance, and they were forgiven. They decreed [1] that all Israel should (make peace) with them,[2] and they repented [3] both old and young, as it is said, "For they made a great oath [4] concerning him that came not up unto the Lord to Mizpah" (Judg. xxi. 5). Did all Israel take an oath? But the ban is the same as the oath.

The men of Jabesh-Gilead neither went up nor did they go with them in the assembly, and they incurred (the penalty of) death, as it is said, "Concerning him that came not up [5] unto the Lord to Mizpah, saying, He shall surely be put to death" (*ibid.*).

Know thou the power of the ban. Come and see from (the story of) Saul, the son of Kish, who decreed that all people, both young and old, should fast, as it is said, "Cursed be the man that eateth any food [4] until it be evening" (1 Sam. xiv. 24). Jonathan did not hear (of this), and ate a little honey,[6] and his eyes were enlightened,[7] as it is said, "And his eyes [8] were enlightened" (*ibid.* 27). Saul saw the Philistines returning against Israel,[9] and he knew that Israel had trespassed in the matter of the ban. He looked at the twelve stones; [10] for each tribe which performed one of the precepts had its stone || (on the High Priest's breast-plate) shining with its light, and each tribe which transgressed, the light of its stone was dim.[11] He knew that the tribe of Benjamin had trespassed in the

[1] Lit. "They issued the ban" (against all who disobeyed).

[2] The first edition has the same reading here as our MS. The Venice edition reads: "all Israel should go up after them."

[3] The first editions read: "and they made an oath."

[4] The quotation ends here in the MS. and in the first editions.

[5] The MS. omits "unto the Lord to Mizpah" and reads instead "into the assembly." The first editions omit the word "saying." This omission in both texts is a probable indication of the dependence of the 2nd ed. on the 1st.

[6] See Midrash Samuel, *in loc.*, and T.B. Berakhoth, 14a. Jalkuṭ on Samuel, *in loc.*, seems to be based on our Midrash.

[7] According to Luria's emendation we should read "both his eyes."

[8] The MS. and the first editions read "both his eyes." M.T. omits "both." See T.B. Joma, 83a.

[9] See Tanchuma, Vayesheb, *loc. cit.*, which reads: "Saul saw that the Philistines were prevailing over the Israelites"; the Jalkuṭ, *in loc.*, reads: "The Philistines were strengthening themselves against Israel."

[10] The first editions read: "He looked at the twelve tribes." Perhaps we should read: "He looked at the twelve stones of the tribes."

[11] See *supra*, p. 295, note 6.

matter of the ban. He cast lots[1] concerning Benjamin, and Saul and Jonathan were taken, as it is said, "And Jonathan[2] and Saul[3] were taken" (*ibid.* 41). Saul took his sword to slay his son, as it is said, "God do so,[4] and more also: for thou shalt surely die, Jonathan" (*ibid.* 44). The people said to him: Our lord king! It is an error. They brought on his behalf a sacrifice of a burnt offering for his error, and He was entreated of him, and they saved him from an evil death, as it is said, "So the people rescued Jonathan, that he died not" (*ibid.* 45).[5]

The Cutheans[6] are not considered as a nation[7] of the seventy languages, but they were the remnant of the five nations precious to the king,[8] as it is said, "And the king of Assyria brought[9] men from Babylon, and from Cuthah, and from Avva, and from Hamath and Sepharvaim, and placed them in the cities of Samaria instead of the children of Israel" (2 Kings xvii. 24).

Rabbi José said: He added four more nations to them, and they were in all nine nations,[10] as it is said, "The Dinaites, and the Apharsathchites,[11] the Tarpelites, the Apharsites, the Archevites, the Babylonians, the Shushan-

[1] The method of procedure was as follows: The tribe concerned was indicated by the stone of that tribe on the breastplate. Then lots were cast to determine the family (see 1 Sam. xiv. 36–42), and finally the members of the family were placed before the Ark of the Covenant, which caused the transgressor to become paralysed. See Ḳimchi, on Josh. vii. 18, and cf. *J.E.* xii. 385 ff.

[2] In this and the next two quotations our MS. reads "Jehonathan." M.T. has "Jonathan."

[3] Our MS. and the first editions read: "Saul and Jonathan." M.T. reads: "Jonathan and Saul."

[4] The MS. and the first editions add "to me." This is not in M.T. The variant readings of Biblical texts preserved by our MS. are noteworthy.

[5] See Pal. Targum and Nachmanides on Lev. xxvii. 29. See also Targum on 1 Sam., *in loc.*

[6] Or Samaritans. In Talmudic times were proselytes accepted from among the Samaritans?

[7] *i.e.* one of the seventy nations. For a parallel view see Ecclus. l. 26.

[8] See Tanchuma, Vayesheb, *loc. cit.*, which reads: "They were the remnant of the five nations whom the king of Assyria led captive, as it is said: etc."

[9] The quotation ends here in the MS.; the first editions add "from Cuthah," and omit "from Babylon," which is the reading of M.T.

[10] On these nine nations see Seder 'Olam Rab. xxii. (end), p. 50a, note 40, and Bacher, T. ii. 189. 5.

[11] The quotation ends here in the MS. and in the first editions.

chites, the Dehaites, the Elamites, and the rest of the nations . . . set in the city of Samaria" (Ezra iv. 9, 10).

And when the Israelites were exiled [1] from Samaria to Babylon, the king sent his servants, and he caused them to dwell in Samaria, to raise tribute for (his) kingdom. What did the Holy One, blessed be He, do? He sent lions among them, || which killed some of them, as it is said, "And so it was, at the beginning of their dwelling there,[2] that they feared not the Lord: therefore the Lord sent lions among them, which killed some of them" (2 Kings xvii. 25).[3] They sent to the king,[4] saying: Our lord, the king! The land whither thou hast sent us will not receive us, for we are left but a few out of many.[5] The king sent and called for all the elders of Israel, and said to them: All those years during which ye were in your land, the beasts of the field did not bereave you, and now it will not receive my servants. They gave him a word of advice, (thinking) perhaps he would restore them to their land. They said to him: Our lord, O king! That land does not receive a nation who do not study the Torah; behold, that land does not receive a nation who are not circumcised.[6] The king said to them: Give me two of you, who shall go and circumcise them and teach them the book of the Torah; and there is no refusal to the word of the king. They sent Rabbi Dosethai [7] of the Court-House,[8] and Rabbi Micaiah,[9] and they circumcised them, and they taught them the book of the Torah in the Noṭariḳon [10] script, and

[1] The first editions add: "from their place."

[2] In the MS. and the first editions the quotation ends here.

[3] See T.B. Ta'anith, 22b, and cf. Rashi, *in loc.*

[4] The first editions read: "king of Babylon." The Bible speaks here of the king of Assyria.

[5] See Jalḳuṭ, 2 Kings, § 234.

[6] The first editions omit the words: "That land does not receive a nation who do not study the Torah." Tanchuma, Vayesheb, *loc. cit.*, and Jalḳuṭ, *loc. cit.*, read: "Because they do not study the Torah."

[7] On Dosethai see Krauss' article in *J.E.* iv. 643 f. Bacher, T. ii. 385–7, considers that the name was probably suggested by its similarity to that of the Samaritan sect of the Dositheans.

[8] The MS. reads "Bedaynê"; cf. Beth Din, and Jastrow, *T.D.* 140a.

[9] This name occurs only in our MS. The same name occurs in Neh. xii. 35. The first editions read "Zechariah." Krauss, *loc. cit.*, seems to identify Zechariah with Sabbæus (סב״א, as in Tanchuma).

[10] On Noṭariḳon (shorthand) see *J.E.* xi. 339 f., where a reference to *P.R.E.* is made; see Krauss' article in *R.É.J.* xlii. p. 29, note 1, and Bacher, *Terminologie*, i. 125.

they[1] wept. Those nations followed the statutes of the Torah, and they served (also) their own gods.[2]

When Ezra came up[3] (with) Zerubbabel, son of Shealtiel, and Jeshua, || son of Jehozadak, they began to build[4] the Temple of the Lord, as it is said, "Then rose up Zerubbabel, the son of Shealtiel,[5] and Jeshua, the son of Jozadak, *and began to build the house of God*" (Ezra v. 2). And the Samaritans came against them to fight (with) 180,000 (men).[6] Were they Samaritans? Were they not Cutheans?[7] But they were called Samaritans because of the city of Samaria. And further, they sought to kill Nehemiah, as it is said, "Come, let us[8] meet together[9] in one of the villages, . . . but they thought to do me mischief" (Neh. vi. 2). Moreover, they made the work[10] of the Lord to cease[11] for two years[12] ["Then *ceased the work of the house of God*, which is at Jerusalem];[13] and it

[1] The two Rabbis who foresaw the troubles destined to come from the Samaritans. Krauss, *loc. cit.*, suggests that ובוכים, "and they wept," should read וכותים, "and Samaritan" (writing); see Bacher, in *Monatsschrift*, xl. 19. The Karaites employed Noṭariḳon, which was known to the Samaritans (cf. At. BSh, א"ת ב"ש).

[2] The first editions add here: "As it is said: 'They feared the Lord, and served their own gods'" (2 Kings xvii. 33).

[3] The first editions add: "from Babylon."

[4] The MS. reads "Bokhim" (weeping); this agrees with Tanchuma and the first editions. It seems probable that the original reading was "Bonim" (building); this reading is preserved in Jalḳuṭ, *loc. cit.*

[5] In the MS. and the first editions the quotation ends here.

[6] This number as the unit for war is derived from 1 Kings xii. 21; see also 2 Kings xix. 35; and T.B. Synhedrin, 95b.

[7] The Dositheans flourished in Egypt, so much so that the Christian patriarch of Alexandria engaged in polemics against them. The Samaritans were divided into two sects: (1) that of the Kushan (Cuthim) and (2) that of the Dostan (Dositheans). See also Josephus, *Ant.* ix. 14. 3. The subject has been dealt with by Drusius in Trigland's *Trium scriptorum illustrium de tribus Judæorum sectis syntagma*, i. 283. See also Montgomery, *The Samaritans*, pp. 254 ff.

[8] *i.e.* Sanballat and Geshem the Arabian; see Neh. iv. 7 ff. and vi. 1 ff.

[9] The quotation ends here in the MS.; in the first editions "in one of the villages" is added.

[10] *i.e.* the rebuilding of the Temple. The first editions read: "the heavenly work"; for the expression see T.B. Ta'anith, 23a.

[11] Lit. "annulled."

[12] The Venice edition reads: "as it is said: 'And it shall be . . . until the year of Jubilee'" (cf. Lev. xxv. 50); so also in the first edition, which omits "as it is said." In our MS. the portion in brackets is not given.

[13] See Jalḳuṭ on Kings, *loc. cit.*, and Tanchuma, Vayesheb, *loc. cit.*, for this reading; see also Gen. Rab. xciv. 9; Seder 'Olam Rab. xxix. p. 67b; T.B. Megillah, 11b.

ceased unto the second year of the reign of Darius, king of Persia" (Ezra iv. 24).

What did Ezra, Zerubbabel son of Shealtiel, and Jeshua son of Jehozadak, do?[1] They gathered all the congregation to the Temple of the Lord, and they brought 300 priests, 300 children,[2] and 300 scrolls of the Torah in their hands,[3] and they blew[4] (the trumpets), and the Levites sang songs and praises, and they excommunicated the Cutheans with the mystery of the Ineffable Name, and with the script such as was written upon the tables (of the Law), and by the ban of the heavenly Court of Justice, and by the ban of the earthly Court of Justice (decreeing) that no one of Israel should eat the bread of the Cutheans.[5] Hence (the sages) said: Everyone who eats the bread[6] of the Cutheans is as though he had eaten of the flesh of swine.[7] Let no man make a proselyte in Israel from among the Cutheans.[8] They have no || portion in the resurrection of

[1] See Ezra iv. 3.

[2] The first editions add "300 trumpets." Shophar is the term here for "trumpet."

[3] *i.e.* the children's hands; see Sopherim iii. 18.

[4] According to Jalkuṭ, *loc. cit.*, the trumpets were in the hands of the priests.

[5] See T.B. 'Abodah Zarah, 35b and 38a, and Jubilees xxii. 16. The first editions add "for ever."

[6] The first editions read "the meat."

[7] See Mishnah Shebi'ith viii. 10; and cf. Tosaphoth Giṭṭin, 10a, and T.B. Chullin, 4a.

[8] On proselytes see *J.E.* x. pp. 220 ff. and *R.É.J.* xii. p. 318. The form of the ban, and the prohibition of eating the bread of the Samaritans, have been exhaustively considered by Dr. Büchler in *R.É.J.* xliii. pp. 50 ff., where the following results are stated: (1) The form of the ban and its accompanying circumstances—(*a*) children as witnesses, (*b*) scrolls of law to sanctify the pronouncement, and (*c*) sounding of the Shofar—tally with the practice known to the Geonim of Babylon in the ninth century (*e.g.* Paltoi; see Chemdah Genuzah, No. xxii., and cf. 'Arukh, *s.v.* חסה, iii. 229a; see also Hekhaloth Rab., ed. Jellinek, *B.H.M.* iii. p. 84). The prohibition of eating the *bread* of the Samaritans mentioned by our author does not find any support in the Talmudic literature (see T.J. Shebi'ith vii. 38b, line 69), but is "an institution of the Geonic age" (p. 64). The decree says that Samaritans could not be received as proselytes. Where the texts of the Talmud speak of כותי, "Samaritan," we have probably to read נכרי. There was a sect who were put on this footing by the Gaon Naṭronai (Teshuboth Ha-Geonim, Sha'arê Zedeḳ, p. 24a, Nos. 7 and 27). The Halakhoth Gedoloth (ed. Hildesheimer, 443) states that "Cutheans, Seboneans, and *Samaritans* are not to be received as proselytes." This again appears in the Tanna de bê Elijahu Zutta (p. 169). The Karaites in the ninth century mutilated the Bible text, and in their reading agreed with the Samaritans (p. 67). In other words the literature of the Samaritans of the ninth century

the dead,[1] as it is said, "Ye have nothing to do with us[2] to build an house unto our God" (*ibid.* 3), neither in this world, nor in the world to come. So that they should have neither portion nor inheritance in Israel,[3] as it is said, "But ye have no portion, nor right, nor memorial, in Jerusalem"[4] (Neh. ii. 20).

They sent the ban (letter) to the Israelites who were in Babylon. Moreover, they added an additional ban upon them, and King Cyrus ordained it as a perpetual ban upon them, (as it is said,)[5] "And the God that hath caused his name to dwell there[6] overthrow all kings and peoples that shall put forth their hand to alter the same, to destroy this house of God which is at Jerusalem. I, Darius, have made a decree; let it be done with all diligence" (Ezra vi. 12).

exercised a baneful influence in creating sects opposed to orthodox Judaism. Hence the ban against them. Moreover, the word for ban (חרם) does not occur in the Talmud (B. Shebu'oth, 35b–36a), but is common in the Geonic period. On the oath or ban see Eth. Enoch vi. 4 ff., where Mount Hermon is mentioned; Dr. Büchler sees here a reference to חרם. Is there any connection, he asks, between Enoch and our book here? That Jubilees was known to the Geonim has been shown by Epstein, מקדמוניות היהודים, page vii, and also the fact that many of the characteristics of the Enoch literature have their parallels in the Geonic literature (see *Z.D.M.G.* vii. (1853) p. 249) has been established.

[1] The Dositheans, like the Sadducees, denied the future life. The question as to a future life would not have arisen in the time of Ezra. See Mishnah Synhedrin x. 1 and the Baraitha in T.B. Synhedrin, 90a, where, however, heretics only are referred to, and not Samaritans.

[2] In the MS. the quotation ends here; it is continued in the first editions.

[3] The first editions read "Jerusalem."

[4] The MS. reads "Israel"; M.T. has "Jerusalem." Is the M.T. purposely altered so as to justify the decree that no one in *Israel* is to receive a Cuthean as a proselyte?

[5] "As it is said" is wanting in the MS.; it occurs in the first editions.

[6] In the MS. and the first editions the quotation ends here. Our MS. and the first editions read "tamman" (there), whereas M.T. has "tammah." The meaning is, of course, identical.

CHAPTER XXXIX

JOSEPH IN EGYPT [53B. ii.]

THE fourth descent was (when) He descended into Egypt, (as it is said),[1] "I will go down with thee into Egypt" (Gen xlvi. 4). Jacob heard concerning Joseph that he was living, and he was thinking in his heart, saying: Can I forsake the land of my fathers, the land of my birth, the land of the sojournings of my fathers,[2] the land where the Shekhinah of the Holy One, blessed be He, is in its midst, and shall I go to an unclean land in their midst,[3] for there is no fear of Heaven therein?[4] The Holy One, blessed be He, said to him: Jacob, do not fear; "I will go down with thee into Egypt,[5] and I will also surely bring thee up again" (*ibid.*).

Jacob heard this word, and he took his[6] wives,[7] and his sons, and his daughters, and the daughters of his sons.[8] Another Scripture says, "With his daughter Dinah"

[1] "As it is said" is omitted by the MS.; it occurs in the first editions and in the Oxford MS. and in MS. Gaster.

[2] This clause occurs in our MS. only.

[3] The Oxford MS. reads: "among slaves, in the midst of the children of Ham, where there is no fear of Heaven among them." The first editions and MS. Gaster read: "among slaves, the children of Ham, in a land where there is no fear of Heaven in their midst."

[4] Cf. Gen. xx. 11.

[5] The quotation ends here in the MSS.; it is continued in the first editions.

[6] Should the reading be: "their wives"? Did any of Jacob's wives go down into Egypt?

[7] See Gen. Rab. xciv. 6; Pal. Targum on Gen. xlvi. 5; and cf. Jalkuṭ, Gen. § 152.

[8] The Oxford MS. adds: "And he brought them down to Egypt, as it is said, 'His sons, and his sons' sons with him, *his daughters*'" (Gen. xlvi. 7). The first editions agree with this reading except in the first words; their reading is: "And he made them come, as it is said." In our MS. there is considerable confusion owing to the carelessness of the scribe who has repeated the text Gen. xlvi. 15.

(*ibid.* 15). And all that he had, and he brought them to Egypt, as it is said, "His sons, and his sons' sons || with him," etc. (*ibid.* 7). Another Scripture says, "With his daughter, Dinah" (*ibid.* 15). Whereas another text says, "His daughters" (*ibid.* 7), to teach thee that the daughters of Jacob were the wives of his sons.[1] And all the seed of Jacob[2] married their sisters and their blood-relations, so that they should not intermarry with the people of the lands, therefore they were called a true seed, as it is said, "Yet I had planted thee a noble vine,[3] wholly a true seed" (Jer. ii. 21).

When they came to the border of Egypt,[4] all the males were enrolled (in genealogical lists to the number of) sixty-six, Joseph with his two sons in Egypt (made the total) sixty-nine.[5] And it is written, "With seventy persons[6] thy fathers went down into Egypt" (Deut. x. 22).[7] What did the Holy One, blessed be He, do? He entered[8] into the number with them, and the total became seventy, to fulfil that which is said, "I will go down with thee[9] into Egypt" (Gen. xlvi. 4). When Israel came up from Egypt all the mighty men were enrolled, (amounting to) 600,000, less one. What did the Holy One, blessed be He, do? He entered[8] into the number with them, and their total amounted to 600,000, to fulfil that which is said, "I will go down with thee into Egypt,[10] and I will also surely bring thee up again" (*ibid.*).

Rabbi Ishmael said: Ten times[11] did the sons of Jacob

[1] Cf. *supra*, p. 272; Gen. Rab. lxxxiv. 21.

[2] Oxford MS. reads: "Hence thou mayest learn that all the seed of Israel," etc.

[3] The MS. omits the first part of the quotation, and incorrectly reads "Ke" (for), which should be "Kullô" (wholly). The verse is accurately quoted in the Oxford MS. and in the first editions.

[4] Oxford MS. reads: "When Jacob came to Egypt."

[5] The Oxford MS. agrees with our MS.; the first editions read: "seventy less one."

[6] The first part of the quotation is given by our MS.; the first editions, as well as the Oxford MS., continue the verse.

[7] See T.B. Baba Bathra, 123a; Gen. Rab. xciv. 9. The seventieth person was Jochebed.

[8] Luria adds: "If one may say so."

[9] In the MS. the quotation ends here; it is continued in the first editions.

[10] Our MS. omits the first part of the quotation, which is given in the first editions.

[11] It was only five times really, but as Joseph employed an interpreter the expression was repeated. On the age of the Patriarchs see T.B. Berakhoth, 55a; T.B. Sotah, 13b; and R. Bechai on Ex.

say to Joseph, "thy servant, our father." Joseph heard the word, and was silent. Silence gives consent; therefore were ten years deducted from his life.[1] Joseph heard || that his father had come to the border[2] of Egypt, and he took all the men who had intercourse with him,[3] and he went to meet his father. All the people go forth to meet the king, but the king does not go forth to meet any man. But this teaches thee that the father of a man is like his king.

Rabbi Phineas said: The Holy Spirit[4] rested on Joseph from his youth;[5] and it led him in all matters of wisdom like a shepherd who leads his flock, as it is said, "Give ear, O Shepherd of Israel,[6] thou that leadest Joseph like a flock, thou that sittest upon the cherubim" (Ps. lxxx. 1). In all his wisdom a certain woman[7] enticed[8] (him), and when he wished to accustom himself to sin,[9] he saw the image[10] of his father, and repented concerning it.[11]

Three people conquered their passion[12] before their Creator, and they were Joseph, Boaz, and Paltê, son of Laish. It was fit that twelve tribes should have arisen from Joseph,[13] as it is said, "And the *seed* of his hands was active"

(beg.), who quotes the Midrash Tadsheh. Test. Joseph ii. 7 refers to the *ten* temptations of Joseph.

[1] Joseph died at the age of a hundred and ten years. The full life of man is a hundred and twenty years.

[2] *i.e.* Goshen.

[3] Luria suggests that the reading should be: "who were with him."

[4] See Test. Joseph vi. 7: "The God of my fathers and the angel of Abraham be with me," and cf. Wisdom x. 13 f

[5] The first editions add: "until the day of his death."

[6] In the MS. the quotation ends here.

[7] The first editions read: "the wife of Potiphera."

[8] See T.B. Chullin, 4b, and Siphrê, Deut. § 87, on "enticement."

[9] See T.B. Sabbath, 49b, and T.B. Soṭah, 36b.

[10] איקון=דיוקנו (εἰκών), image, likeness; see T.B. Soṭah, *loc. cit.*; cf. Jubilees xxxix. 6, 7; Gen. Rab. lxxxvii. 7; *Rabbinic Philosophy and Ethics*, p. 110; Midrash Samuel v.; Jalkuṭ, Gen. § 146, quoting Midrash Abkhir; see also Schapiro, *op. cit.*, p. 41, and Grünbaum, *op. cit.* pp. 148 ff., and *J.E.* vii. 249.

[11] The first editions add: "And he conquered his passion." See Test. Joseph ii. 2 ff.

[12] See T.B. Synhedrin, 19b, and Midrash Haggadol, c. 585. We have a play here on the word "Jezer"—יצרן לפני יוצרן; cf. T.B. Berakhoth, 61a.

[13] This is based on T.B. Soṭah, *loc. cit.* Our MS. has a mutilated text. The first editions add here: "The seed of ten tribes exuded from the tips of his fingers (euphemistic expression for membrum), as it is said: 'And the *seed* of his hands was active' (Gen. xlix. 24), and there remained these two (tribes), Manasseh and Ephraim." The R.V. reads: "The *arms* of his hands." See Coptic Apoc., p. 279.

(Gen. xlix. 24), but there remained two (tribes), Manasseh and Ephraim. The woman brought grave charges against him to vex him, and he was confined in prison [1] for ten years. There he interpreted the dreams of the servants of Pharaoh, (he interpreted for) each one according to his dream just as though the events were taking place before him, as it is said, "And it came to pass, as he interpreted to us, so it was" (*ibid.* xli. 13).

And he interpreted the dream of || Pharaoh when the Holy Spirit rested upon him, as it is said, "And Pharaoh said unto his servants, Can we find such a one as this,[2] a man in whom the spirit of God is?" (*ibid.* 38).

All the nations came to Joseph to purchase food from Joseph. And Joseph spoke to each people according to their different tongue. And he knew what they were speaking. Therefore his name was called Jehoseph,[3] as it is said, "For Joseph understood them, for there was an interpreter between them" [4] (*ibid.* xlii. 23).

Moreover, when he went into the market-place he saw the people forming themselves into various companies and groups, and each one would speak in his own tongue, and he knew what they were saying,[5] as it is said, "He appointed it in Joseph for a testimony,[6] when he went out over the land of Egypt, when I heard the speech of one that I knew not" [7]

[1] See Seder 'Olam Rab. ii. p. 6a, according to which he was in prison twelve years. This agrees with the Book of Jashar xliv. 14 and xlvi. 20; see also Ex. Rab. vii. 1. One year was passed in the service of Potiphar; and as he was thirty years old when he stood before Pharaoh, he had spent thirteen years in Egypt, for he was seventeen years old when he was taken from his brethren. See Jubilees xxxix. 8 for the year in the service of Potiphar, the *eunuch*. After two years the chief baker and butler are thrown into prison with Joseph; and after ten years Pharaoh has his dreams, for "on the day that Joseph stood before Pharaoh he was thirty years old" (*ibid.* xl. 11). See Test. Joseph ii. 7–iii. 1 ff. On Joseph's chastity see Pal. Targum to Gen. xlix. 22, T.B. Soṭah, *loc. cit.*, and Test. Joseph (chs. iii.–vi.).

[2] The quotation ends here in the MS.; it is continued in the first editions.

[3] The first editions read instead Turgoman, (*i.e.*) Dragoman, interpreter = "Milez" of Gen. xlii. 23. On Turgoman see Jastrow, *T.D.* 1657.

[4] The MS. reads "bethokham" (in their midst). This is not the reading of M.T. The section which now follows is printed in the first editions before the words: "all the nations came."

[5] We had this phrase in the preceding paragraph.

[6] In the MS. and the first editions the quotation ends here.

[7] The legend is based on T.B. Soṭah, *loc. cit.*, which is translated in *Rabbinic Philosophy and Ethics*, pp. 103 f.

(Ps. lxxxi. 5). Further, when he was riding in the chariot, and passed through all the borders of the land of Egypt, the Egyptian girls were climbing[1] up the walls for his sake, and they threw to him rings of gold, so that perchance he might look at them, and (they could) see the beauty of his[2] figure, but nobody's eye degraded[3] him, for he was highly esteemed[4] in the eyes of everyone, as it is said, "Joseph is a *fruitful* bough[5] . . . his daughters run over the wall" (Gen. xlix. 22).[6]

All the nations came to purchase food. And they brought to Joseph their tribute (and) a present (and money) to purchase (food). And he spoke to each people according to their different tongue; || therefore was his name called Turgeman,[7] as it is said, "For there was an *interpreter* between them"[8] (*ibid.* xlii. 23), therefore was he speaking.[9]

Some of them were buying grain on account of the famine in their houses, and they went forth, and others came to buy food; and one asked his fellow as to the price in the market. From their reply they opened the price of the market.[10] When they came to Joseph he said to them: Just as ye have heard, so it is; in order that the market should not be scarce (and prices dear). Hence (the sages) said: He who makes a corner in the market will never see a sign of blessing.[11]

[1] "Mez'adoth"; see Targumim on Gen. xlix. 22, and *Rabbinic Philosophy and Ethics*, pp. 122 f., where the parallel version of the legend from the Midrash Haggadol is translated.

[2] The first editions read: "and see them and the beauty of their figure."

[3] The word שזפתו ("degraded") recalls Cant. i. 6 and Job xxviii. 7.

[4] Lit. "fruitful and increasing."

[5] The expression "a *fruitful* bough" is expanded by our author. There is a play upon the word "Porath." The legend is based on T.B. Soṭah, *loc. cit.*, which is translated in *Rabbinic Philosophy and Ethics*, pp. 103 f.

[6] See Pal. Targum on this verse. Here, again, we have a play on the word "Za'adah" ("run"). This word is identified with "Az'adah" (Num. xxxi. 50), "chains," hence the "rings" of our Midrash.

[7] This entire paragraph is practically a repetition of what has gone before. See notes on previous two paragraphs.

[8] The MS. quotes the correct reading here, according to M.T.

[9] The point is in the name *Turgeman*, which means "interpreter," *i.e.* Joseph. The verse Gen. xlii. 23 therefore means: For there was Joseph (an interpreter) between them.

[10] This sentence occurs in our MS. only. It might be rendered: From their reply they revealed the price of the merchandise. Joseph did not wish to make a corner in the market, neither did he wish the price to fall.

[11] See T.B. Ta'anith, 10a; T.B. Baba Mezi'a, 60a; T.B. Megillah, 17b. The scarcity in the market would involve a sudden rise in the

Rabbi Tanchum [1] said: Joseph commanded and they built the treasure-houses in each city, and he gathered all the produce of the lands into the treasure-houses. The Egyptians were scoffing at him, saying: Now the worms will eat the stores of Joseph. But no worm had any power over them; neither did the (stores) diminish until the day of his death.[2] And he supported [3] the land in the famine of bread, therefore was his name called Kalkol.[4] And Kalkol is Joseph, as it is said, "And Joseph nourished" [5] (*ibid.* xlvii. 12). Moreover, he nourished his father, and his brethren, and all his father's house, in the famine with bread to their satisfaction. "And Joseph nourished his father, and his brethren, and all his father's household, with bread, according to their families" (*ibid.*).[6] ||

Rabbi Eliezer said: In the hour of the death of Jacob he called to his son Joseph, and said to him: O my son! Swear to me by the covenant of circumcision that thou wilt take me up to the burial-place of my fathers in the land of Canaan to the Cave of Machpelah. The [7] ancients used to swear by the covenant of circumcision prior to the giving of the Torah, as it is said, "Put, I pray thee, thy hand under my thigh" (*ibid.* 29), and "he sware unto him" (*ibid.* 31). He kept (the oath) and did (accordingly), as it is said, "And he said, Swear unto me" (*ibid.*). And all the mighty men

market prices. See also T.B. Baba Bathra, 90b; Derekh Erez Rabba ii., and Tanna de bê Elijahu Rab. xv. p. 75.

[1] A Palestinian Amora of the third century. His name is mentioned again in Chapter XLIX. p. 392; see Bacher, P. iii. 627 ff., and *J.E.* xii. pp. 42 f.

[2] See T.B. Baba Mezi'a, 40a. Luria thinks that the word חסרו (diminish) should be corrected so as to read סרחו (they became foul), by analogy with the Manna; see Ex. xvi. 20. Perhaps we should retain the reading "diminish" by analogy with the barrel of meal mentioned in 1 Kings xvii. 14 ff. On the question as to whether there was a famine after Jacob's death see Siphrê, Deut. § 38, and Nachmanides on Gen. xlvii. 18.

[3] In spite of supporting the land, the stores did not diminish.

[4] See Lev. Rab. ix. 1, Eccles. Rab. to Eccles. vii. 23. "Kalkol" is based on 1 Kings iv. 31. "Kalkol" is referred to Joseph, about whom the text says, "Vayekhalkêl," "and Joseph nourished" (Gen. xlvii. 12); see T.B. Synhedrin, 44b. This explanation of our book is also given by Jerome, *Comm. in loc.* (ed. Vall. iii. 850, quoted by Grünbaum, *op. cit.* p. 28).

[5] See also 1 Chron. ii. 6.

[6] This paragraph occurs in our MS. only; "as it is said" is omitted before the quotation.

[7] The first editions read: "Originally the ancients," etc.

of the kingdom went up with him to bury him, and to show loving-kindness to Jacob his father, as it is said, "And Joseph went up to bury his father" (*ibid.* l. 7). The camp of Israel numbered 5040 (people). All the (people of the) land were bringing food on account of the famine to the camp of Joseph.[1] The Holy One, blessed be He, said to them: Ye have shown loving-kindness [2] to Jacob, My servant, I also will give you your reward, and also unto your children in this world. When the Egyptians died in the Reed Sea they did not die in the water,[3] but they were deemed worthy to be buried in the earth. The Holy One, blessed be He, said to them: Ye have submitted yourselves [4] to the divine punishment; I also will give you a place of burial, as it is said, "Thou stretchedst forth thy right hand, the earth swallowed them" (Ex. xv. 12).[5]

When they came to the Cave of Machpelah, Esau came against them || from Mount Horeb [6] to stir up strife,[7] saying: The Cave of Machpelah is mine.[8] What did Joseph do? He sent Naphtali to subdue the constellations,[9] and to go down to Egypt to bring up the perpetual deed which was between them,[10] therefore it is said, "Naphtali is a hind let loose" (Gen. xlix. 21). Chushim, the son of Dan, had defective hearing and speech,[11] and he said to them: Why are

[1] "All the people, who were taking food home on account of the famine, were in the camp of Joseph." This is the emended reading suggested by Luria. The people of Canaan were there to pay respect to Jacob; see Gen. l. 11; according to Gen. Rab., *in loc.*, and Tanchuma, Vayechi, § xvii., even the kings of Canaan joined in this mark of respect.

[2] See *supra*, Chapter XVII.

[3] See *infra*, p. 332. The first editions read: "they did not remain in the water."

[4] Pharaoh said: "The Lord is righteous, but I and my people are evil" (Ex. ix. 27); see Mekhilta, Beshallach, Proem, 33b; and cf. T.B. Pesachim, 118a.

[5] See *Rabbinic Philosophy and Ethics*, pp. 169 f., where the passage from the Mekhilta (referred to in the previous note) is translated.

[6] The first editions read: "Esau came against them from Mount Seir." See also Wisdom x. 12.

[7] The expression is based on Prov. xxvi. 17.

[8] See T.B. Soṭah, 13a; this passage is translated in *Rabbinic Philosophy and Ethics*, pp. 125 ff.

[9] "To hasten like a hind." This is Luria's emendation. On Naphtali's fleetness see Gen. xlix. 21, T.B. Soṭah, *loc. cit.*; and cf. Test. Naph. ii. 1.

[10] Jacob and Esau; see *supra*, p. 290. The Prague and Brode's editions read "in their hand" instead of "between them."

[11] See the Book of Jashar, ch. lvi., for a parallel account of the legend, which practically agrees with *P.R.E.* According to Charles the legend in the Book of Jashar "has borrowed its materials from the

we sitting here? He was pointing (to Esau) with his finger. They said to him: Because this man will not let us bury our father Jacob. What did he do? He drew his sword and cut off Esau's head with the sword, and took the head into the Cave of Machpelah. And they sent his body to the land of his possession, to Mount Seir.

What did Isaac do? He grasped the head of Esau and prayed before the Holy One, blessed be He, and said: Sovereign of all the universe! Let mercy be shown [1] to this

Midrash in Josippon"; see *Jubilees*, ed. Charles, p. 215, note. Charles refers to Bousset, *Z.f.N.T. Wissensch.*, 1900, p. 205. In this connection the legend of the wars between the sons of Jacob and Esau with his sons in Jubilees xxxvii., xxxviii., the Testament of Judah (Test. XII Pat.) ix., and Jeraḥmeel, pp. 80–87, must be considered very briefly. According to Charles, "the oldest form of the legend is found in Jubilees and in the Test. Jud. ix.; the next oldest is the Jalkuṭ and Chronicles of Jeraḥmeel, and the latest is the Book of Jashar" (*Jubilees*, p. 215). The account in the Book of Jashar contains two parts: (1) the death of Esau by the hands of Chushim, son of Dan, at the burial of Jacob. This part of the legend is taken directly from our book, which was also the source used by Pal. Targum on Gen. l. 13. The source of our Midrash was T.B. Soṭah, *loc. cit.* Then (2) the account of the wars between the sons of Esau and the sons of Jacob which the Book of Jashar gives is undoubtedly connected with the account of Zepho, son of Eliphas, and Æneas of Africa, given in the history of Josippon. Now the Chronicles of Jeraḥmeel agree with the Book of Jubilees in making Jacob the slayer of his brother Esau, and they agree in fixing the occasion of the conflict at the mourning for Leah. According to Beer, *Das Buch der Jubiläen*, pp. 4 ff., the original form of the legend was that Judah slew Esau at the burial of Isaac. The death of Esau at the hands of Judah is mentioned in T.J. Kethuboth I. 5 (p. 25c); T.J. Giṭṭin v. 6 (p. 47a); Siphrê, Deut. § 348; Shocher Ṭob, Ps. xviii. 40 (sect. 32); see also Jalkuṭ, Gen. § 162; and Jalkuṭ, Samuel, § 163. The later form of the legend is preserved in T.B. Soṭah, *loc. cit.*, which attributes the death of Esau to Chushim, who was deaf and dumb, at the burial of Jacob. Jalkuṭ, Gen. *loc. cit.*, combines both forms of the legend. Jalkuṭ, Pss. § 776, agrees with our book in the details of the death of Esau. Beer draws attention to the fact that the Jews of Palestine in the time of Hadrian (*c.* 135 C.E.) attributed the fierce hatred on the part of the Romans to the belief that Judah, the forefather of the Jews, had slain Esau, the forefather of the Romans, who were identified with the Edomites descended from Esau. In order to remove the "historical" foundation for this hostility, later forms of the legend transferred the deed to an irresponsible person, Chushim, whose descendants, the tribe of Dan, had long since disappeared from the land of Israel, having been carried away into exile, and, as some of the Rabbis taught, lost for all time. Jubilees holds to the original legend, owing to the opposition which it represents to the orthodox Rabbinic traditions of Palestine obtaining in the period prior to and following the rise of Christianity. Pirkê de R. Eliezer is aware of the teaching of Jubilees, and tries to correct and refute it on all fundamental points of controversy. This is sometimes done as strikingly by omission as by a variant doctrine, or story.

[1] The words are borrowed from Isa. xxvi. 10.

wicked one, for he had not learnt all the precepts of the Torah, as it is said, " Let favour be shewed to the wicked,[1] yet will he not learn righteousness " (Isa. xxvi. 10). He was speaking in iniquity concerning the land of Israel and the Cave of Machpelah, as it is said, " In [2] the land of uprightness will he deal wrongfully " (*ibid.*).

The Holy Spirit answered him, saying: As I live! he shall not see the majesty of God.[3]

[1] The MS. and the first editions omit the first part of the verse.

[2] Our MS. reads: "and in the land." This is not the reading in M.T. which is given by MS. Gaster. The reading in the Venice edition is also faulty.

[3] The first editions add here: "as it is said, 'And he will not behold the majesty of the Lord'" (Isa. xxvi. 10).

CHAPTER XL

MOSES AT THE BURNING BUSH [55A. ii.]

THE fifth descent [1] was when He came down to the thorn-bush, as it is said, " And I am come down || to deliver them out of the hand of the Egyptians " (Ex. iii. 8). He abandoned the entire mountain,[2] and descended into the thorn-bush, and He abode therein. And the thorn-bush was (an emblem of) grief and distress,[3] and it was [4] full of thorns and thistles. Why did He abide in the midst of the thorn-bush which was (an emblem of) grief and distress? Because He saw Israel in great grief and He also dwelt with them,[5] thus fulfilling that which is said, " In all [6] their affliction He was afflicted " (Isa. lxiii. 9).[7]

Rabbi Levi said: That rod [8] which was created in the twilight [9] was delivered to the first man [10] out of the garden of Eden. Adam delivered it to Enoch, and Enoch delivered

[1] See *supra*, p. 97, for the fourth descent. These "descents" are connecting links in the narrative. This accounts for the apparent disorder in the chapters which now follow, for we have the " Revelation " in the thorn-bush and at Sinai before the narrative of the birth of Moses. On the " descent " see Pal. Targum, Ex. iii. 8.

[2] *i.e.* Sinai.

[3] See Tanchuma, Shemoth, § xiv.; Jalkut, Pss. § 843, and Ex. Rab. ii. 5.

[4] Luria reads: " The thorn bush was (full of) sorrow and distress because it was all thorns and thistles."

[5] The Venice edition reads: " And He dwelt also with them in the midst of grief."

[6] See *Rabbinic Philosophy and Ethics*, pp. 144 f., note 1 on p. 145.

[7] Cf. T.B. Ta'anith, 16a.

[8] See *supra*, p. 14, and cf. p. 124, and the Book of the Bee, pp. 24, 50.

[9] On the first Sabbath eve in the Creation week, see references given in the previous note.

[10] See the Book of Jashar lxxvii. 39 ff. The Jalkuṭ, Ex. §§ 168, 173, quotes this book as " the Book of the Chronicles of Moses," according to which Adam took the rod from Eden when he was driven forth, at the time when the rod had been made; he tilled the ground therewith. See also *R.É.J.* lxxviii. p. 150.

it to Noah,[1] and Noah [handed it on] [2] to Shem. Shem passed it on to Abraham, Abraham [transmitted it] [2] to Isaac, and Isaac [gave it over] [2] to Jacob,[3] and Jacob brought it down into Egypt and passed it on to his son Joseph,[4] and when Joseph died and they pillaged his household goods, it was placed in the palace of Pharaoh. And Jethro [5] was one of the magicians of Egypt, and he saw the rod and the letters which were upon it, and he desired in his heart (to have it), and he took it and brought it, and planted it [6] in the midst of the garden of his house.[7] No one was able to approach it [8] any more.

When Moses came to his house he went into the garden of Jethro's house, and saw the rod and read the letters [9] which were upon it, and he put forth his hand and took it. Jethro watched || Moses, and said: This one in the future will redeem Israel from Egypt. Therefore he gave him Zipporah his daughter to wife, as it is said, "And Moses was content to dwell with the man; [10] and he gave Moses Zipporah, his daughter" (Ex. ii. 21).

[1] Should this be: "Enoch handed it to Methuselah, and Methuselah handed it to Noah"? See *supra*, p. 53.

[2] The first editions have the words in brackets; the MS. omits same.

[3] Jalkut, Ex. § 168, and the Book of Jashar lxxvii. 46 agree that Jacob received it when he fled to Paddan-Aram. He declares: "For with my *staff* I passed over this Jordan" (Gen. xxxii. 10). See Gen. Rab. lxxvi. 5, and Agadath Bereshith on this verse. The rod divided the Jordan for Jacob and the Reed Sea for Moses and Israel; see Jalkut, Num. § 763. The rod passed on to David and his successors, and will belong to the Messiah.

[4] See the Book of Jashar, *loc. cit.*; and cf. Ezek. xxxvii. 19: "the stick of Joseph."

[5] "Reuel" is the reading in Jeraḥmeel xlvi. 4 and 12; Jalkut, Ex. § 173, reads "Jethro." "Pharaoh" of the printed texts is a mistake; for although he was a magician (cf. Ex. Rab. ix. 6 ff.) he would not take the rod which "he desired in his heart" and plant it in Jethro's garden.

[6] For full details as to the various legends about the rod, see Grünbaum, *op. cit.* pp. 161 ff. Jalkuṭ, *loc. cit.*, omits the words "and he saw the rod" which occur in *P.R.E.*

[7] The first editions read: "in the house of Jethro."

[8] According to the Book of Jashar lxxvii. 49, 51, and the Jalkut, *loc. cit.*, Jethro resolved to give his daughter to the man who was able to remove the rod.

[9] See Ex. Rab. viii. 3; see also *infra*, p. 329, n. 8, and Pal. Targum, Ex. iii. 21. Cf. the Book of Jashar, *loc. cit.*, which appears to have used *P.R.E.* in the account of the "rod" (ch. lxxvii. 39–51). The letters on the rod were the Ineffable Name of God or the initials of the ten plagues.

[10] In the MS. and the first editions the quotation ends here.

Moses was keeping the sheep of Jethro for forty years,[1] and the beasts of the field did not consume them, but they increased and multiplied exceedingly,[2] and concerning them the Scripture saith, "As the flock of holy things" (Ezek. xxxvi. 38).[3]

And he led the flock until he came to Horeb, as it is said, "And he led the flock to the back of the wilderness,[4] and came to the mountain of God, unto Horeb" (Ex. iii. 1). There the Holy One, blessed be He, was revealed unto him from the midst of the thorn-bush. Moses saw the bush burning with fire, and the fire did not consume the bush, and the bush did not extinguish the flames of fire.[5] Now the bush does not grow in the earth unless it has water beneath it. Moses saw and was wondering very much in his heart, and he said: What kind of glory [6] is there in its midst? He said: I will now turn aside and see this great sight, why the thorn-bush is not burnt. The Holy One, blessed be He, said to him: Moses! Stand where thou art standing, for there in the future will I give the Torah to Israel, as it is said, "And he said, Draw not nigh hither; [7] put off thy shoes from off thy feet,[8] for the place whereon thou standest is holy ground" (*ibid.* 5). The Holy One, blessed be He, said to him: Go.[9] Hence (the sages) said: Anyone who enters the Temple [10] must remove || his shoe, for thus spake the Holy One, blessed be He, to Moses: "Put off thy shoes from off thy feet" (*ibid.*).

The Holy One, blessed be He, said to him: "Come and I

[1] See Siphrê, Deut. § 357; and Midrash Tannaim, ed. Hoffmann, p. 226.

[2] See Cant. Rab. iii. 5.

[3] Applied to Jethro's flock because Moses led them to graze near the Mount of God. The first editions add the next two words of the quotation.

[4] In the MS. and the first editions the quotation ends here.

[5] See Pal. Targum, Ex. iii. 2.

[6] Or "mystery" of God; see Lev. Rab. xi. 5. The sentence is in Aramaic and is unusual in our book. The translation might be: "whose glory," etc.

[7] In the MS. the quotation ends here.

[8] In the first editions the quotation ends here.

[9] This sentence occurs in our MS. only. The reference should probably be Ex. iii. 16.

[10] See Mishnah Berakhoth ix. 1; T.B. Berakhoth, 62b; T.B. Soṭah, 40a. The Book of Jashar, *loc. cit.*, omits the reference to the removal of the shoes. See Pal. Targum, *in loc.* The first editions read: "Any one who stands in a holy place."

will send thee unto Pharaoh" (*ibid.* 10). He answered before Him: Sovereign of all worlds! Have I not spoken thus to Thee three or four times, that I have no power, for I have a defective tongue, as it is said, "And Moses said unto the Lord, O Lord, I am not eloquent (*ibid.* iv. 10). Not only this, but moreover Thou dost send me into the power of my enemy who seeks my hurt.[1] For this reason I fled from him, as it is said, "But Moses fled from the face of Pharaoh" (*ibid.* ii. 15). He answered him: Do not fear him,[2] for all the men who sought thy life are already dead.

Were they dead? Were they not alive? Only they had diminished [3] their wealth. Hence thou mayest learn that all who lose their wealth are as though they were dead, therefore it is said, "For all the men are dead who sought thy life" (*ibid.* iv. 19). (God) said to him: "Come and I will send thee unto Pharaoh" (*ibid.* iii. 10). He replied to Him: Sovereign of all worlds! "Send by the hand of him whom thou wilt send" (*ibid.* iv. 13)—that is to say, by the hand of that man whom Thou wilt send in the future.[4] He said to him: I have not said, "Come and I will send thee to Israel," but "Come and I will send thee unto Pharaoh" (*ibid.* iii. 10). And as for that man of whom thou sayest that I should send him to Israel in the future that is to come, so it is said, || "Behold, I will send you Elijah the prophet [5] before the great and terrible day of the Lord come" (Mal. iv. 5). "And he shall turn the heart of the fathers to the children, and the heart of the children to their fathers" (*ibid.* 6).

(Moses) spake before Him: Sovereign of all worlds! Give me a wonder or a sign.[6] He said to him: Cast thy staff to the ground. He cast his staff to the ground, and it became

[1] The first editions read: "enemies, and of them who seek my hurt. Was it not for this reason that I fled from them?"

[2] The first editions read: "them."

[3] Lit. "They had descended from their wealth"; see T.B. Nedarim, 64b and 65a.

[4] Elijah; or, perhaps, the reference is to Phineas the son of Aaron, who is identified by our author with Elijah; see *infra*, p. 371, and Pal. Targum, *in loc.*: "By the hand of Phineas." On Elijah see T.B. 'Erubin, 43b.

[5] In the MS. the quotation ends here and then follows the next verse, of which the first three words in the Hebrew are quoted. The first editions do not have the second quotation, but continue the first verse.

[6] See Ex. Rab. iii. 12, and Siphrê, Deut. § 83. Moses wished to have a sign in heaven and a wonder on earth.

a fiery serpent. Why did the Holy One, blessed be He, show unto Moses (a sign) with a fiery serpent,[1] and why did He not show it to him with something else? But just as the serpent bites and kills the sons of man, likewise Pharaoh and his people bit and slew the Israelites. Afterwards it became again like a dry stick. Thus He spake: Likewise Pharaoh and his people shall become like this dry stick,[2] as it is said, "And the Lord said unto Moses: Put forth thine hand,[3] and take it by the tail" (Ex. iv. 4). He spake before Him: Sovereign of all worlds! Give me a wonder. He said to him: "Put now thine hand into thy bosom" (*ibid.* 6). And he put his hand into his bosom, and he brought it out leprous like snow. Why did the Holy One, blessed be He, show unto Moses (a sign) by means of an unclean thing, and (why) did He not show it by means of a clean thing? But just as the leper is unclean and causes uncleanliness, likewise Pharaoh and his people were unclean, and they caused Israel to be unclean.[4] Afterwards (Moses) became clean again,[5] and He spake to him: Likewise shall Israel become clean from the uncleanliness of the Egyptians, as it is said, "And he said, Put now thine hand into thy bosom" (*ibid.*).

Why did He show unto Moses the fire in the midst of the thorn-bush? || But the fire refers to Israel, who are compared to fire,[6] as it is said, "And the house of Jacob shall be a fire" (Obad. 18). The thorn-bush refers to the nations of the world,[7] who are compared to thorns and thistles. He said to him: Likewise shall Israel be in the midst of the nations. The fire of Israel shall not consume the nations, who are compared to thorns and thistles; but the nations of the world shall extinguish the flames of Israel—(these flames) are the words of the Torah. But in the future that is to come the fire of Israel will consume all the nations, who are

[1] The first editions read: "like a fiery serpent by (means of) the rod and (why) did He not show him something else?"

[2] The preceding part of this sentence occurs in the MS. only.

[3] In the MS. the quotation ends here, in the first editions it is continued.

[4] See *infra*, p. 382.

[5] Luria adds: "as it is said: 'And He said, Restore thy hand.'" Cf. Ex. Rab. iii. 13. The MS. repeats the quotation (Ex. iv. 6).

[6] Because the Shekhinah abides among them, and because they possess the Torah, the "Law of fire." Cf. Mekhilta de R. Simeon, p. 1 ff.

[7] The Amsterdam and Prague editions read: "the idolaters"; later editions read "the wicked."

compared to thorns and thistles,[1] as it is said, " And the peoples shall be as the burnings of lime " (Isa. xxxiii. 12).

Moses said before the Holy One, blessed be He: Sovereign of all worlds! Make known to me Thy great and holy Name, that I may call on Thee by Thy Name,[2] and Thou wilt answer me, as it is said, " And God said unto Moses, I am that I am " (Ex. iii. 14). " And God further said [3] (to Moses) " (*ibid.* 15).

The angels saw that the Holy One, blessed be He, had transmitted the secret of the Ineffable Name [4] to Moses, and they rejoined: Blessed art thou, O Lord, who graciously bestoweth knowledge.[5]

[1] See the rest of the verse quoted from Isaiah.

[2] Cf. *supra*, pp. 129, 264. See Shocher Tob on Ps. xcii. 1, p. 198b, and 8, p. 200b; cf. Isa. lii. 6. The first editions add: " And He made it known to him."

[3] The MS. ends the quotation here. The first editions continue the next two words in the Hebrew text. The verse continues: " Thus shalt thou say unto the children of Israel, The Lord, the God of your fathers, the God of Abraham, the God of Isaac, and the God of Jacob, hath sent me unto you: this is my name for ever, and this is my memorial unto all generations."

[4] See Othijoth de R. 'Akiba, letters ו, ה, א; *B.H.M.* iii. pp. 12 ff.; and cf. Grünbaum, *Z.D.M.G.* xl. p. 245. The rod with the Ineffable Name was transmitted by Moses to his successor Joshua, who conquered the Canaanites by its aid.

[5] This is the fourth benediction of the Shemoneh 'Esreh; see Singer, p. 46. Our Midrash attempts to associate Moses with its origin, see *supra*, p. 267.

CHAPTER XLI

THE REVELATION ON SINAI [56B. i.]

The sixth descent [1] was when He came down on Sinai, as it is said, " And the Lord came down upon Mount Sinai " (Ex. xix. 20). On the sixth of Sivan [2] the Holy One, blessed be He, was revealed unto Israel [3] on Sinai,[4] and from His place was He revealed (on) Mount Sinai,[5] and the heavens were opened, || and the summit of the mountain entered into the heavens. Thick darkness covered the mountain, and the Holy One, blessed be He, sat upon His throne, and His feet stood on the thick darkness, as it is said, " He bowed the heavens also, and came down ; [6] and thick darkness was under his feet " (2 Sam. xxii. 10).[7]

Rabbi Ṭarphon said : The Holy One, blessed be He, rose and came from Mount Sinai [8] and was revealed unto the sons of Esau, as it is said, " And he said, The Lord came from Sinai, and rose [6] from Seir unto them " (Deut. xxxiii. 2). And " Seir " means only the sons of Esau, as it is said, " And Esau dwelt in Mount Seir " (Gen. xxxvi. 8). The Holy One, blessed be He, said to them : Will ye accept

[1] See *supra*, pp. 97, 312.

[2] See *infra*, p. 359. Jubilees fixes the 15th of Sivan as the Festival of the Giving of the Law (see i. 1) and as the Feast of Weeks (vi. 17, 18); see Charles' notes on pp. 52, 106. *P.R.E.* in following Rabbinic tradition opposes this here.

[3] According to the Mekhilta, p. 63b, Moses received the Divine Revelation on the 6th of Sivan.

[4] The first editions read : " Mount Sinai."

[5] The first editions read : " and Mount Sinai was torn from its place." See T.B. Sabbath, 88a ; Jalḳuṭ, Ex. § 284 ; Pal. Targum, Ex. xix. 1 ; and Mekhilta, p. 65a.

[6] The quotation ends here in the MS. ; in the first editions it is continued.

[7] See T.B. Sukkah, 5a, and T.B. Joma, 4a, on the Revelation on Mount Sinai.

[8] The first editions read : " rose from Mount Seir."

for yourselves the Torah? They said to Him: What is written therein? He answered them: It is written therein, "Thou shalt do no murder" (Ex. xx. 13). They replied to Him: We are unable to abandon the blessing with which Isaac blessed Esau, for he said to him, "By thy sword shalt thou live" (Gen. xxvii. 40). Thence He turned and was revealed unto the children of Ishmael, as it is said, "He shined forth from Mount Paran" (Deut. xxxiii. 2). "Paran"[1] means only the sons of Ishmael, as it is said, "And he dwelt in the wilderness of Paran" (Gen. xxi. 21). The Holy One, blessed be He, said to them: Will ye accept for yourselves the Torah? They said to Him: What is written therein? He answered them: "Thou shalt not steal" (Ex. xx. 15) is written therein. They said to Him: We are not able to abandon the usage which our fathers observed, for they[2] brought Joseph down into Egypt, as it is said, "For indeed I was stolen away[3] out of the land of the Hebrews" (Gen. xl. 15).[4] Thence[5] He sent || messengers to all the nations of the world. He said unto them: Will ye receive for yourselves the Torah? They said to Him: What is written therein? He said to them: "Thou shalt have no other gods before me" (Ex. xx. 3). They said to Him:[6] We have no delight in the Torah, therefore let Him give His Torah to His people, as it is said, "The Lord will give strength[7] unto his people; the Lord will bless[8] his people with peace" (Ps. xxix. 11).[9] Thence He returned and was revealed unto the children of Israel, as it is said, "And *he came from the ten thousands* of holy ones" (Deut.

[1] Paran was the abode of Ishmael, Gen. xxi. 21.

[2] The first editions read: "for they stole Joseph and brought him down," etc.

[3] The quotation ends here in the MS.; in the first editions it is continued.

[4] Joseph's statement that he was stolen out of the land of the Hebrews refers to the transaction between his brethren and the Ishmaelites as recounted in Gen. xxxvii. 28. On this section see *Rabbinic Philosophy and Ethics*, pp. 193 ff.

[5] The MS. reads: "And Moses." This is due to an error on the part of the copyist, "Umosheh" standing for "Umesham."

[6] The first editions add: "We are unable to abandon the law of our fathers who served idols."

[7] Strength ('Ôẓ) is identified by the Midrash with the Torah.

[8] The quotation ends here in the MS.; it is continued in the first editions.

[9] See T.B. Ẓebachim, 116a.

xxxiii. 2). The expression "ten thousands" means the children of Israel, as it is said, "And when it rested, he said,[1] *Return*, O Lord, *unto the ten thousands* of the thousands of Israel" (Num. x. 36). With Him were thousands twice-told of chariots, even twenty thousand [2] of holy angels,[3] and His right hand was holding the Torah, as it is said, "At his right hand was a fiery law unto them" (Deut. xxxiii. 2).

Hence thou mayest learn that the words of the Torah are like coals of fire.[4] Why was it "at his right hand"? Whence do we know (that it was given to them) with expression of love? Because it is said, "The Lord hath sworn by his right hand,[5] and by the arm of his strength" (Isa. lxii. 8).[6]

Rabbi Eliezer said: From the day when the Israelites went forth from Egypt, they were journeying and encamping in smoothness,[7] they were journeying in smoothness and

[1] The quotation ends here in the MS.; it is continued in the first editions.

[2] Cf. Ps. lxviii. 17: "The chariots of God are twenty thousand, even thousands upon thousands: the Lord is among them, as in Sinai, in the sanctuary."

[3] Jubilees i. 27 teaches that the "law was given through the ministry of angels." According to Dr. Charles (*Jubilees*, p. 8, note 27) the text in Jubilees i. 27 "forms apparently the earliest testimony" to this idea. In the N.T. we have it also; see Gal. iii. 19, Acts vii. 53, and Heb. ii. 2. The idea is not Palestinian, but seems to be Alexandrian. This is perhaps an indication pointing to Alexandria as the home of Jubilees, just as Hebrews, Acts, and Paul's teaching are all representative of Alexandrine teaching. Our Midrash combats the notion that the Torah was given to Israel by the angels: God Himself gives His law to His people.

[4] Cf. Aboth ii. 10: "for all the words of the Sages are like coals of fire." The first editions add here: "And He gave it to them with an expression of love, as it is said: 'His left hand is under my head' (Cant. ii. 6), and with an expression of an oath, as it is said: 'The Lord hath sworn,'" etc. The quotation from Cant. ii. 6 continues: "and his *right hand* doth embrace me."

[5] The quotation ends here in our MS.

[6] The first editions add: "'His right hand'[1] is nought else save an oath, as it is said, 'The Lord hath sworn by his right hand'"[2] (Isa. lxii. 8).

[7] Of tongue. Luria thinks that the text should read "Machalôḳeth," "strife." This is also the reading in the Mekhilta, p. 62a, Lev. Rab. ix. 9, and Lam. Rab. Proem. The next words, up to "as it is said," occur in the MS. only.

---

[1] The "right hand" is the word used in the two texts to justify the analogy and the inference drawn by our Midrash. In Deut. xxxiii. 2 the "right hand" occurs in connection with the giving of the Law. See *infra*, p. 335.

[2] Here "right hand" occurs in connection with swearing.

they were encamping in smoothness, as it is said, "And they journeyed (from Rephidim, and they came to the wilderness of Sinai),[1] and they encamped in the wilderness" (Ex. xix. 2); until they all came to Mount Sinai, and they all encamped opposite the mountain, like one man with one heart, as it is said, "And there Israel encamped[2] before the mount" (*ibid.*). The Holy One, blessed be He, spake to them: Will ye receive for yourselves || the Torah? Whilst the Torah had not yet been heard they said to Him: We will keep and observe all the precepts which are in the Torah, as it is said, "And they said, All that the Lord hath spoken will we do, and be obedient"[3] (*ibid.* xxiv. 7).

Rabbi Elazar of Modein said: From the day when the heavens and the earth were created, the name of the mountain was Horeb.[4] When the Holy One, blessed be He, was revealed unto Moses out of the thorn-bush, because of the word for the thorn-bush (*S'neh*) it was called Sinai (*Sinai*), and that is Horeb. And whence do we know that Israel accepted the Torah at Mount Horeb? Because it is said, "The day that thou stoodest before the Lord thy God in Horeb" (Deut. iv. 10).[5]

Rabbi Phineas said: On the eve of Sabbath[6] the Israelites stood at Mount Sinai, arranged with the men apart and the women apart.[7] The Holy One, blessed be He, said to Moses: Go, speak to the daughters of Israel, (asking them) whether they wish to receive the Torah. Why were the women asked (first)? Because the way of men is to follow the opinion of women,[8] as it is said, "Thus shalt thou say to the *house of Jacob*" (Ex. xix. 3); these are the women. "And tell the children of Israel" (*ibid.*); these are the men. They all replied (as) with one mouth, and they said: "All that

[1] The MS. and the first editions read: "they journeyed and they encamped."

[2] The verb here is in the singular number; the Israelites were united as though they were a single man, see Pal. Targum, Ex. xix. 2.

[3] The first editions quote Ex. xxiv. 3.

[4] See Ex. iii. 1 and xxxiii. 6; cf. 1 Kings viii. 9.

[5] This is followed by the words: "And he drew near and stood at the foot of the mountain"; and there the Torah was given.

[6] See *infra*, p. 359.

[7] See T.B. Sukkah, 52a. The separation of the sexes was observed in the ark of Noah according to Jewish and Christian legend (see *supra*, p. 169), and it is observed to this day in some of the churches as well as in the synagogue.

[8] See Ex. Rab. xxviii. 2; T.B. Sabbath, 87a, and Mekhilta, p. 62b.

the Lord hath spoken we will do, and be obedient" (*ibid.* xxiv. 7). (The Scripture also says,) "They that sing[1] as well as they that dance[2] (shall say), All my fountains are in thee" (Ps. lxxxvii. 7).[3]

Rabbi Chanina[4] said: || In the third month the day is double the night,[5] and the Israelites slept until two hours of the day, for sleep on the day of the (feast of) 'Azereth[6] is pleasant,[7] the night being short. And Moses went forth and came to the camp of the Israelites, and he aroused the Israelites from their sleep, saying to them: Arise ye from your sleep,[8] for behold, your God desires to give the Torah to you. Already the bridegroom wishes to lead the bride and to enter the bridal chamber. The hour has come for giving you the Torah,[9] as it is said, "And Moses brought forth the people[10] out of the camp to meet God" (Ex. xix. 17). And the Holy One, blessed be He, also went forth to meet them; like a bridegroom who goes forth to meet the bride, so the Holy One, blessed be He, went forth to meet them to give them[11] the Torah, as it is said, "O God, when thou wentest forth before thy people" (Ps. lxviii. 7).

Rabbi Joshua ben Ḳorchah said: The feet of Moses stood on the mount,[12] and all (his body) was in the midst of the

[1] *i.e.* the men. [2] *i.e.* the women.

[3] See Shocher Ṭob. *in loc.*, p. 190b, and Cant. Rab. to Cant. i. 12.

[4] The first editions read "Chakhinai."

[5] This is one of the most interesting expressions in the whole of our book. The longest day is twice as long as the shortest in latitude 49° in Northern Asia; see Eth. Enoch lxxii. 14, and see Charles' note on p. 153 of the second edition of this book. Can we locate the place where this fact applies in connection with *P.R.E.*? Or is it merely a further instance of the dependence of *P.R.E.* upon the Pseudepigrapha?

[6] Pentecost. Jubilees uses the term for the day following the seven days of Tabernacles; see Jubilees xxxii. 27, with Charles' note *in loc.*

[7] The reading "pleasant" agrees with the reading in Cant. Rab., *loc. cit.*: "sleep at 'Azereth is pleasant and the night is long"; see T.B. Sabbath, 147a, and cf. Tosephta 'Arakhin i. 9, p. 543. Luria reads: "for the period of the days at 'Azereth is long and the night is short."

[8] The first editions omit the rest of the sentence.

[9] The first editions add here: "The best man[1] came and led forth the bride just like a man who acts as best man to his companion."

[10] In the MS. the quotation ends here; it is continued in the first editions.

[11] The Amsterdam edition omits "them."

[12] Sinai.

---

[1] שושבין (best man). "In Judea they used to put up two groomsmen (as guards); one appointed by the family of the groom, and one by the bride's family" (Tosephta Kethuboth i. 4).

heaven, like a tent [1] which is spread out, and the children of men stand [2] inside it, but their feet stand on the earth,[3] and all of them are inside the tent; so was it with Moses, his feet stood on the mountain, and all his (body) was in the heavens, beholding and seeing everything that is in the heavens. The Holy One, blessed be He, was speaking with him like a man who || is conversing with his companion, as it is said, " And the Lord spake unto Moses face [4] to face " (Ex. xxxiii. 11).[5] The Holy One, blessed be He, said to Moses: Go and sanctify the Israelites for two days, as it is said, " And the Lord said unto Moses,[6] Go unto the people, and sanctify them to-day and to-morrow " (*ibid.* xix. 10). What then was the sanctity of Israel in the wilderness? There were no uncircumcised people [7] in their midst; the manna descended from heaven for them; they drank water out of the Well;[8] clouds of glory surrounded them. What then was the sanctity of Israel in the wilderness? It refers to their avoidance of sexual intercourse.

Moses argued with himself. Moses said: A man of Israel may have gone to his wife, and they will be found to be prevented from receiving the Torah.[9] What did he do? He added one day (more) for them on his own account, so that if a man of Israel went to his wife [10] they would be found to be clean for two (complete) days; therefore he added one day for them on his own account.

The Holy One, blessed be He, said to him: Moses! How many souls of the children of men would have come

[1] Our MS. reads " Denda." The first editions read " Ṭendos." Jastrow, T.D. 541a, suggests that the reading should be " Ṭorus " (bolster or sofa). The word in our printed editions is taken by the 'Arukh, ed. Kohut, iv. p. 47b, to be the late Latin *tenta*; Greek *τέντα*. The word occurs in Pal. Targum, Lev. xxv. 31. See *supra*, p. 16, note 6.

[2] 'Arukh, *loc. cit.*, reads " stand "; the first editions read " sit."

[3] 'Arukh, *loc. cit.*, reads " stand outside."

[4] In the MS. the quotation ends here; it is continued in the first editions.

[5] " Face to face " means that the Divine word was as a man's speech as far as Moses was concerned.

[6] This part of the verse is omitted by our MS.; it occurs in the first editions.

[7] Luria reads: " people with uncircumcised hearts."

[8] On the Well see *supra*, pp. 124 and 218.

[9] See *The Clementine Homilies*, xi. 30.

[10] On the eve preceding the day before the two days of prohibition; see T.B. Sabbath, *loc. cit.*; T.B. Jebamoth, 62a; and Aboth de R. Nathan (*a*) ii. p. 5a.

forth from Israel in that night? What thou hast done has been (rightly) accomplished.[1] The Holy One, blessed be He, approved his action.[2]

(The Holy One, blessed be He, said: [3]) Let Moses descend to the camp, and afterwards will I cause My Torah to be proclaimed.[4] He said to him: "Go down, charge the people" (*ibid.* 21). Moses was wishing to be || there,[5] and he said to Him: I have already charged the people. He said to him: Go, and call thy Rabbi.[6] Moses descended to the camp to call Aaron, and the Holy One, blessed be He, proclaimed His Torah unto His people, as it is said,[7] "So Moses went down unto the people,[8] and told them" (*ibid.* 25). What is written after this? "And God spake all these words, saying, I, the Lord, am (to be) thy God,[8] who brought thee out of the land of Egypt, out of the house of bondage" (*ibid.* xx. 1, 2).

The voice of the first (commandment) went forth,[9] and the heavens and earth quaked thereat,[10] and the waters and rivers fled,[11] and the mountains and hills were moved,[12] and

[1] The first editions read: "Thou hast done well."

[2] The first editions add here: "as it is said, 'And let them be ready against the third day'" (Ex. xix. 11). See Mekhilta, p. 64a; Tanna de bê Elijahu Rab. xviii. p. 101; and cf. Jalkuṭ, Ex. § 282. Luria reads in place of "as it is said," etc., "Be ready for three days and do not touch any man his wife."

[3] The words in brackets are found in the first editions and are needed. They are wanting in our MS.

[4] The first editions add here: "to Israel, so that one should not say: Moses was speaking to us out of the midst of the cloud."

[5] See T.B. Joma, 4b; Lev. Rab. i. 1; T.B. Berakhoth, 45a; and Mekhilta, p. 66a.

[6] Or "teacher." The first editions read: "Call Aaron."

[7] The first editions add: "And the Lord said to him, Go, get thee down" (Ex. xix. 24).

[8] In the MS. the quotation ends here; in the first editions it is continued.

[9] See Pal. Targum on Ex. xx. 2.

[10] Cf. Judg. v. 4.

[11] Luria reads "dried up" (cf. Nahum i. 4, and see Ex. Rab. xxix. 3) instead of "fled."

[12] See Hab. iii. 6 and Nahum i. 5. These prophets recall the revelation at Sinai, believing firmly in this fundamental fact of the history of Israel. They would have smiled at some of the latest theories of the Higher Critics, who propose to date the Pentateuch as a production of the times of Hezekiah. They would have ridiculed the notion that some late writer had "invented" the Sinaitic theophany in order to account for the Decalogue, which he held to be divinely inspired. One is tempted to ask, Why is not Lev. xix. also set in a theophanic background?

all the trees fell prostrate,[1] and the dead who were in Sheol revived, and stood on their feet till the end of all the generations,[2] as it is said, " But with him that standeth here with us this day " (Deut. xxix. 15),[3] and those (also) who in the future will be created, until the end of all the generations, there they stood with them at Mount Sinai, as it is said, " And also with him that is *not* here [4] with us this day " (*ibid.*).[5] The Israelites who were alive (then) fell upon their faces and died.

The voice of the second (commandment) went forth, and they were quickened,[6] and they stood upon their feet and said to Moses : Moses, our teacher ! We are unable to hear any more the voice of the Holy One, blessed be He, for we shall die even as we died (just now), as it is said,[7] " And they said unto Moses, Speak thou with us,[4] and we will hear : but let not God speak with us, *lest we die* " (Ex. xx. 19). And now, why should we die as we died (just now) ? The Holy One, blessed be He, heard the voice of Israel, and it was pleasing to Him, and He sent for Michael || and Gabriel, and they took hold of the two hands of Moses against his will,[8] and they brought him near unto the thick darkness, as it is said, " And Moses drew near unto the thick darkness where God was " (*ibid.* 21).

It is only written here (in the text concerning) Moses (that) " he drew near." [9] The rest of the commandments He spake through the mouth of Moses,[10] and concerning him the text

[1] Cf. Ps. xxix. 5 : " The voice of the Lord breaketh the cedars." This Psalm is interpreted by the Midrash as referring to the Giving of the Law. Luria thinks that we should read " hinds " in *P.R.E.* instead of " trees " ; cf. Job xxxix. 1.

[2] The words " till the end of all generations " do not occur in all the texts.

[3] See the rest of the verse.

[4] The quotation ends here in the MS. ; in the first editions it is continued.

[5] See Ex. Rab. xxviii. 8, and cf. Tanchuma Nizabim, § ii.

[6] See Ex. Rab. xxix. 4, and *Rabbinic Philosophy and Ethics*, pp. 196 ff.

[7] The first editions add here : " ' My soul went forth when he spake ' (Cant. v. 6), and it is written : "

[8] Cf. T.B. Joma, *loc. cit.*

[9] According to Luria, the Midrashic text is to be explained thus : " He drew near " is not written here, but " He was drawn near." The first editions seem to have the correct reading : " ' was approaching ' is not written, but ' he approached.' "

[10] See Mekhilta, p. 71b, as to whether the children of Israel heard the first two Commandments of the Decalogue, or more. Cf. Cant. Rab. on Cant. i. 2.

says, "As the cold of snow in the time of harvest,[1] so is a faithful messenger to them that send him" (Prov. xxv. 13).

And it came to pass, "When ye hear the sound of the trumpet"[2] (2 Sam. xv. 10). Why did the Holy One, blessed be He, cause His voice to be heard out of the midst of the[3] darkness, and not out of the midst of the light? A parable: to what is the matter to be likened? To a king[4] who was having his son married to a woman, and he suspended in the wedding chamber of his son black curtains,[5] and not white curtains.[6] He said to them: I know that my son will not remain with his wife except for forty days; so that on the morrow they should not say the king was an astrologer, but he did not know what would happen to his son. So with the King, who is the Holy One, blessed be He, and His son is Israel, and the bride is the Torah.[7] The Holy One, blessed be He, knew that Israel would not remain (loyal) to the commandments except for forty days, therefore the Holy One, blessed be He, caused them to hear His voice out of the midst of[8] darkness, and not out of the midst of light, therefore it is said, "And it came to pass, when ye heard the voice" (Deut. v. 23).

Rabbi Jehudah said: When a man speaks with his companion, he || hears the sound of his voice, but he does not see any light with it;[9] the Israelites heard the voice of the Holy

[1] The quotation ends here in our MS.; it is continued in the first editions.

[2] The first editions read: "And it came to pass, when ye heard the voice out of the midst of the darkness" (Deut. v. 23).

[3] The first editions read here: "fire and darkness."

[4] The first editions add: "who was an astrologer." See Tosephta 'Arakhin i. 10, p. 543. Cf. Ziegler's *Die Königsgleichnisse des Midrasch*, p. 353. See also Jalkuṭ, Deut. § 831. אסטרלגום, ἀστρόλογος, astronomer or astrologer. The reading, as emended by Luria, is based on the Jalkuṭ, *loc. cit.* Ziegler's remarks on p. 352 (*op. cit.*) on astrology and marriage are interesting.

[5] See 'Arukh, ed. Kohut, vii. p. 427a, *s.v.* פרכיות.

[6] The first editions add here: "The officials of the palace said to him: Our lord, O king! Nobody suspends in his son's wedding chamber anything except white curtains."

[7] Our book is noteworthy here in referring to God as the "Father" of Israel assisting at the wedding of *His Son* "Israel" and the bride "the Torah." The usual poetry of the Midrashim is to unite God with Israel, His bride.

[8] The first editions read here: "fire and darkness."

[9] Our text agrees with Jalkuṭ, Ex. § 299. The first editions read: "When a man speaks with his companion he is visible, but his voice is invisible."

One, blessed be He, on Mount Sinai, and saw [1] the voice [2] going forth from the mouth of the Almighty [3] in the lightning and the thunder,[4] as it is said, "And all the people saw the thunderings and the lightnings" (Ex. xx. 18). All the precepts which are in the Torah [5] number 611, and two, which the Holy One, blessed be He, spake,[6] as it is said, "God has spoken once,[7] *two* have I heard thus" (Ps. lxii. 11).[8]

Rabbi Phineas said: All that generation who heard the voice of the Holy One, blessed be He, on Mount Sinai, were worthy to be like the ministering angels,[9] so that insects had no power over them.[10] They did not experience pollution in their lifetime, and at their death neither worm nor insect prevailed over them. Happy were they in this world and happy will they be in the world to come,[11] and concerning them the Scripture says, "Happy is the people, that is in such a case" (*ibid.* cxliv. 15).

[1] See Ex. xx. 18.

[2] Our MS. reads Hakkol, "everything"; it should be Haḳḳol, "the voice."

[3] On "Gebburah" see *Rabbinic Philosophy and Ethics*, p. 177.

[4] But otherwise they saw nothing.

[5] The first editions add here: "Therefore is this code called Torah.[1] And whence do you know (this)? Because Torah has the value of 611 and the two (precepts) which the Lord spake."

[6] The first editions read: "number 613 precepts, and two, which the Holy One, blessed be He, spake."

[7] The quotation ends here in the MS. The first editions read: "He has spoken once, *two* have we heard." This is a mutilated form of the quotation Ps. lxii. 11, and clearly proves that the Venice edition copied the first edition (the Constantinople text). After the quotation the first editions add "behold 613."

[8] See Num. Rab. xi. 7; Jalḳuṭ, *in loc.*, Pss. § 783. According to the Midrash the Decalogue was proclaimed in one utterance; see also Mekhilta, 41b, and cf. Ex. Rab. xxviii. 4.

[9] Cf. Ps. lxxxii. 6. According to the Book of Jubilees ii. 17–21, Israel is like the "angels of the presence and the angels of sanctification," chosen to observe the Sabbath with God "in heaven and on earth."

[10] See T.B. Baba Bathra, 15a; and cf. Ezek. xxxiv. 25 and Prov. i. 33; these two verses are applied by the Midrash to the generation of those who received the Torah in the wilderness.

[11] See T.B. Synhedrin, 90a ff., for discussion on the "future life."

---

[1] תורה = 400 plus 6 plus 200 plus 5, *i.e.* 611. This Torah was given to Israel by Moses, and indicates the 611 precepts contained therein. There are two more, namely, the first two Commandments of the Decalogue given by God. This brings up the total to 613. The Torah is called the "Law of Moses" by Mal. iv. 4, and the name Torah is suggested by the word formed by the letters representing this number of 611, namely Taria (תריא); see Jalḳuṭ Makhiri, Ps. lxii. p. 157a.

CHAPTER XLII

THE EXODUS [58B. i.]

"AND it came to pass, when Pharaoh had let the people go" (Ex. xiii. 17). This is what the Scripture says, "Thy shoots[1] are a garden of pomegranates" (Cant. iv. 13). Just as this garden is full of (various) kinds of trees, each one bearing[2] according to its kind, so the Israelites, when they went forth from Egypt, were full of all good, (endowed with) the various kinds of blessings, as it is said, "Thy shoots are (like) a garden of pomegranates" (*ibid.*).

Rabban Gamaliel said: The Egyptians pursued after the children of Israel as far as the Reed Sea, and encamped behind them. The enemy was behind them[3] and the sea || was in front of them. And the Israelites saw the Egyptians, and feared very greatly, and there they cast away from themselves all the Egyptian abominations,[4] and they repented very sincerely, and called upon their God, as it is said, "And when Pharaoh drew nigh, the children of Israel lifted[5] up their eyes" (Ex. xiv. 10). Moses beheld the anguish of Israel, and arose to pray on their behalf.[6] The Holy One, blessed be He, said to him: "Speak unto the children of Israel, that they go forward" (*ibid.* 15).

[1] "Thy shoots" is to be interpreted as though it implied "thy coming forth." In the Midrash here the word שלחיך is also taken to mean, "those of thee who went forth."

[2] The first editions add "fruit."

[3] *i.e.* Israel. The first editions read instead of this sentence: "The Israelites were between the Egyptians and the sea, which was in front of them, whilst the enemy was behind them."

[4] See Ezek. xx. 7; Siphrê, Num. § 84; T.J. Sukkah iv. 3. 54c; Ex. Rab. xxiv. 1; Mekhilta, Bô, 5a and 15a. The authority for the tradition is R. Eliezer ben Hakkapar (*c.* 200 C.E.). See also T.B. Synhedrin, 103b, as to whether the Israelites took any idols with them across the Reed Sea.

[5] MS. Gaster reads: "cried unto the Lord."

[6] See Ex. Rab. xxi. 1.

Moses spake before the Holy One, blessed be He, saying: Sovereign of all worlds! The enemy is behind them, and the sea is in front of them, which way shall they go forward? What did the Holy One, blessed be He, do? He sent[1] Michael,[2] and he became a wall of fire[3] between (Israel and[4]) the Egyptians. The Egyptians desired[5] to follow after Israel, but they are unable to come (near) because of the fire. The angels beheld the misfortune of Israel all the night, and they uttered neither praise nor sanctification[6] to their Creator,[7] as it is said, "And the one came not near the other all the night" (*ibid.* 20).

The Holy One, blessed be He, said to Moses: Moses! "Stretch out thine hand over the sea, and divide it" (*ibid.* 16). "And Moses stretched out his hand over the sea" (*ibid.* 21), but the sea refused to be divided.[8] What did

[1] See Pal. Targum, Ex. xiv. 19, and cf. Num. xx. 16 for the sending of the angel to save God's people. A parallel occurs in the Acts of Andrew and Matthias in *A.N.C.L.* xvi. p. 366.

[2] The first editions add: "the great prince." See Dan. xii. 1 for reference to Michael, and cf. Gen. Rab. l. 2 (and see Reitzenstein, *Poimandres*, 294); Ex. Rab. ii. 5; and *supra*, p. 247. Our text is, perhaps, criticizing the Book of Jubilees, which says: "notwithstanding all signs and wonders the *prince of the Mastema* was *not* put to shame because he took courage and cried to the Egyptians to pursue after them with all the powers of the Egyptians" (xlviii. 12). On the opposition between Mastema (Sammael) on the one hand and Michael on the other, see *Archiv für Religionswissenschaft*, vol. xvi. p. 166, Marmorstein's article, note 5. See Tanchuma (Buber), Gen. 48b; and Ex. Rab. xviii. 5, where Michael and Sammael are contrasted. See also T.B. Sotah, 10b.

[3] See Zech. ii. 5; Nachmanides on Ex., *in loc.*, and *supra*, p. 325.

[4] The words in brackets are missing in our MS.; they occur in the first editions.

[5] Perhaps the text should be rendered "ran."

[6] Cf. Siphrê, Num. § 58, based on Isa. lxii. 6. The first editions read "thanksgiving."

[7] See R. Bechai, *in loc.*; Ex. Rab. xxiii. 7; Shocher Ṭob on Ps. cv. 1, p. 277b; and T.B. Megillah, 10b, which says that the angels did not sing to God because the work of His hands (*i.e.* the Egyptians) were perishing. The quotation is given by our MS. only.

[8] The first editions add here: "He then showed it the covenant of circumcision and the coffin of Joseph, and the staff on which the Ineffable Name was engraved,[1] but it did not consent. Moses returned before the Holy One, blessed be He, saying: Sovereign of all worlds!

---

[1] See *supra*, p. 313; Ex. Rab. xxi. 6; Mekhilta, p. 30b; Pal. Targum, Ex. xiv. 21; Tanchuma, Nasso, § xxx.; and Jalḳuṭ, Isa. § 474 (end); on the staff, see *supra*, pp. 14, 312 f., and note Bacher, *Agada der Tannaiten*, ii. p. 273, where the tradition is recorded in the name of R. Nehemiah, a disciple of R. 'Aḳiba (*c.* 130 C.E.).

the Holy One, blessed be He, do? He looked at the sea, and the waters saw the face of the Holy One, blessed be He, and they trembled and quaked,[1] and descended into the depths, as it is said, "The waters saw thee, O God;[2] the waters saw thee, they were afraid: the depths also trembled" (Ps. lxxvii. 16).

Rabbi Eliezer said: || On the day when He said, "Let the waters be gathered together"[3] (Gen. i. 9), on that very day were the waters congealed, and they were made into twelve valleys,[4] corresponding to the twelve tribes, and they were made into walls of water[5] between each path,[6] and (the people) could see one another,[7] and they saw the Holy One, blessed be He, walking before them, but the heels of His feet[8] they did not see,[9] as it is said,[10] "Thy way was in the sea,[11] and thy paths in the great waters, and thy footsteps were not known" (Ps. lxxvii. 19).

Rabbi 'Aḳiba said: The Israelites advanced to enter the Reed Sea, but they turned backwards, fearing lest the waters would come over them.[12] The tribe of Judah sanctified His

The sea will not listen to me. Forthwith was the Holy One, blessed be He, revealed before him in His glory at the sea. And the sea fled." This is wanting in MS. Gaster.

[1] See Ps. cvi. 9, and Midrash thereon; and see also Jalḳuṭ Makhiri, Ps. cxiv. p. 98a.

[2] In the MS. the quotation ends here; it is continued in the first editions.

[3] *i.e.* on the third day, see *supra*, p. 63. Cf. Gen. Rab. v. 5.

[4] The first editions read "paths." The word in our MS. might mean "streams." On the subject, see Wisdom of Solomon xix. 7 ff., which contains the oldest extant Midrash on the Exodus. The twelve paths may be due to the idea of the twelve tribes; cf. Hab. iii. 9. See also Aboth de R. Nathan (*a*) xxxiii. p. 48b.

[5] See Pal. Targum, Ex. xiv. 21.

[6] The first editions read: "Between each path were windows." See 'Arukh, ed. Kohut, i. p. 124a, b, *s.v.* אמפומיות.

[7] See Wisdom xix. 8; Pesiḳta, Beshallach, p. 86b; Jalḳuṭ on 2 Sam. xx. § 152.

[8] See *supra*, p. 27.

[9] The first editions read: "were neither seen nor known."

[10] The first editions read here: "'They have seen thy goings, O God' (Ps. lxviii. 24); and it is written."

[11] In the MS. the quotation ends here; in the first editions it is continued.

[12] See T.B. Pesachim, 118b; T.B. Soṭah, 36b, 37a; and Shocher Ṭob, Ps. lxxvi. 1, p. 170b. The first editions add here: "The tribe of Benjamin wished to enter therein, as it is said: 'There is little Benjamin, their ruler'[1] (Ps. lxviii. 27). They went down (into the

---

[1] רודם seems to be associated by the Midrash with ירד, "to go down."

great Name, and entered the sea first, and under the dominion of the hand likewise of the sons of Judah[1] (did all Israel enter the sea after them), as it is said, "Judah became his sanctuary,[2] Israel his dominion"[3] (*ibid.* cxiv. 2). The Egyptians desired[4] to follow after Israel, but they turned backwards,[5] fearing lest the waters would return over them. What did the Holy One, blessed be He, do? He appeared before them like a man riding on the back of a mare, as it is said, "To a steed in Pharaoh's chariots" (Cant. i. 9). The horse on which Pharaoh rode saw the mare (of God), and it neighed and ran and entered the sea after it.[6]

The Egyptians saw that Pharaoh had entered the sea, and all of them entered the sea after him, as it is said, "And the Egyptians pursued[7] after them" (Ex. xiv. 9). Forthwith the waters returned, and covered them, as it is said, "And the waters returned, and covered[8] || the chariots, and the horsemen" (*ibid.* 28).[9]

Ben 'Azzai said: Everything is (judged according to the principle of) measure (for measure); just as the Egyptians were proud, and cast the male children into the river,[10] so

sea),[1] and the tribe of Judah began to stone them, as it is said, 'The princes of Judah cast stones[2] at them' (*ibid.*); and Nachshon[3] sprang into the sea first, and he sanctified His great name in the eyes of all." See also *Rabbinic Philosophy and Ethics*, pp. 176 ff.

[1] The first edition and MS. Gaster read: "Under the dominion of the hand of the son of Judah, Nachshon." The words in brackets occur in the first editions but not in our MS., which reads: "under the dominion of the hand likewise the sons of Judah entered first." The second edition reads: "under the dominion of the hand of the sons of Judah."

[2] "His sanctuary," in order to sanctify Him.

[3] The first editions and MS. Gaster add: "of Judah." See Shocher Ṭob, *in loc.*, Gen. Rab. lxxxiv. 17.

[4] See note 5 on p. 329.

[5] See Mekhilta, p. 32a.

[6] See Agadath Shir Ha-Shirim ix. (ed. Schechter, p. 17); Mekhilta, p. 33a; Tanchuma, Shopheṭim, § xiv.; and Jalkuṭ Makhiri, Ps. cxiv., *loc. cit.*

[7] The MS. has in the margin "and they came." Pharaoh is not mentioned here; cf. next chapter, p. 341.

[8] In the MS. the quotation ends here; it is continued in the first editions.

[9] See Tanna de bê Elijahu Rab. vii. p. 43, and cf. *ibid.* xxiii. p. 123.

[10] See Jubilees xlviii. 14: "And all the peoples whom he brought to pursue after Israel, the Lord our God cast them into the midst of the sea, into the depths of the abyss beneath the children of Israel,

[1] This is the reading in the Prague edition and MS. Gaster.

[2] See *Rabbinic Philosophy and Ethics*, p. 177, note 1.

[3] See Num. Rab. xiii. 7.

the Holy One, blessed be He, cast them into the sea, as it is said, " I will sing unto the Lord, for he hath triumphed triumphantly [1]; the horse and his rider hath he thrown into the sea " (*ibid.* xv. 1).

Rabbi Shela said: All the children (of the Israelites) whom the Egyptians cast into the river did not die, for the river cast them up, and threw them into the desert of Egypt.[2] The Holy One, blessed be He, brought a rock to the mouth of each one, and a rock to the side of each one. The rock which was at his mouth was feeding him with honey and milk, and the rock which was at their side was anointing [3] them with oil, like a lying-in woman who anoints [4] her son,[5] as it is said, " And he made him to suck honey out of the rock,[6] and oil out of the flinty rock " (Deut. xxxii. 13). When Israel came to the sea, they saw the Holy One, blessed be He, and they recognized Him, and praised Him, and sanctified Him, as it is said, " This is my God, and I will praise him " (Ex. xv. 2).

Rabbi Simon said: On the fourth day the Israelites encamped by the edge of the sea, and to the south [7] of the sea. The Egyptians were floating like skin-bottles upon the surface of the waters,[8] and a north wind went forth and cast them opposite the camp of Israel, and the Israelites went and saw them, and they recognized them, and they

even as the people of Egypt had cast their children into the river." See also Wisdom xi. 16. Charles refers also to the following parallels illustrating the *lex talionis*: Wisd. xi. 7, xii. 23, xvi. 1, xviii. 4, 5; Philo, *Adv. Flacc.* 20; Josephus, *Contra Ap.* ii. 13.

[1] Just as the Egyptians *triumphed* over the Israelites by casting their children into the *sea*, so God *triumphed* over the Egyptians by casting them into the *sea*. This seems to be the meaning read into the double expression of " triumphing " in Ex. xv. 1. The quotation ends here in the MS. and in the first editions.

[2] See Deut. xxxii. 10, and cf. Ezek. xvi. 5 with the Midrashic interpretation thereon.

[3] The first editions read " feeding."

[4] The first editions read " feeds." See Jastrow, *T.D.* 963b, l. 18.

[5] See Jalkuṭ, Ex. § 165, and Pal. Targum, Deut. xxxii. 13; T.B. Soṭah, 11b; Ex. Rab. xxiii. 8, and Aboth de Rabbi Nathan, *loc. cit.*

[6] The quotation ends here in the MS.; it is continued in the first editions.

[7] Luria thinks that מנגב should be מנגד, " opposite," because the Israelites were encamped towards the east of the sea. See Tosaphoth, ʿArakhin, 15a; catchword: " Just as."

[8] See T.B. Synhedrin, 108a; Tanna de bê Elijahu Rab. xxxi. p. 158, based on Job xxiv. 7, referring to the generation of the Flood. See also Wisdom x. 19 and Josephus, *Ant.* ii. 16. 6.

said:[1] These (here) were the officials of the palace of Pharaoh, and those (there) were the taskmasters, and they recognized every one, as it is said, "And Israel saw the Egyptians[2] || dead upon the sea shore" (*ibid.* xiv. 30).

Rabbi Reuben said: The entire body follows the head,[3] and when[4] the shepherd goes astray the sheep go astray after him, as it is said, "For the sins of Jeroboam which he sinned,[5] and wherewith he made Israel to sin" (1 Kings xv. 30). When the shepherd is good, all follow after him.[6] Moses began to sing, and to utter praises before the Holy One, blessed be He, and all Israel followed him,[7] as it is said, "Then sang Moses and the children of Israel" (Ex. xv. 1). Miriam began to sing and to utter praises, before the Holy One, blessed be He, and all the women followed her, as it is said, "And Miriam the prophetess, the sister of Aaron,[8] took a timbrel . . . and all the women went out after her" (*ibid.* 20). Whence did they have timbrels and chorus in the wilderness?[9] But the righteous always know and conciliate (God), and are assured that the Omnipresent, blessed be He, performs for them miracles and mighty deeds. Before (the time of) their departure from Egypt they prepared for themselves timbrels and chorus.

Israel spake before the Holy One, blessed be He: Sovereign of all worlds! These (Egyptians) who have arisen to come against us to destroy us from Thy world,[10] as well as all who

[1] The first editions read: "and they recognized them, and they said, 'These are the children of Israel.'" We should read: "and the children of Israel said." This is another instance how the Venice edition (1544) has thoughtlessly copied the Constantinople edition (1514).

[2] The quotation ends here in the MS. The next word in the verse, "dead," is in the singular number, hence the Midrashic inference.

[3] See T.B. 'Erubin, 41a.

[4] Luria's text reads: "When the shepherd is good, and goes on the right way, the sheep follow him." This is practically the reading of the first editions in the next sentence.

[5] The quotation ends here in our MS.

[6] The first editions and MS. Gaster add: "Our teacher Moses was a faithful shepherd." Cf. Num. xxvii. 17. The expression "faithful shepherd" in Aramaic is the title of part of the Zohar.

[7] See T.B. Sotah, 30b, and Midrash on Prov., ed. Buber, p. 38a.

[8] The quotation ends here in the MS.

[9] So also in Mekhilta, p. 44a; see also Rashi on Ex. *in loc.*

[10] The first editions and MS. Gaster read here: "And all who rise up against us are as though they rose up against Thee. (Destroy them) all in the majesty of Thy might, and in Thy fierce anger they shall be consumed like stubble."

rise up against us, are as though they had risen up against Thee. Let the majesty of Thy might and Thy fierce anger consume them like stubble, as it is said, "And in the greatness of thine excellency thou overthrowest *them that rise up* against thee:[1] thou sendeth forth thy wrath, it consumeth them as stubble" (*ibid.* 7).

Israel spake before the Holy One, blessed be He: Sovereign of all worlds! There is none like Thee among the ministering angels,[2] and therefore all their descriptive names (contain part of the word) *El*ohim ("God"); *e.g.* Micha*el* || and Gabri*el*.[3] "Who is like unto thee among the divine creatures,[4] O Lord?" (*ibid.* 11). Pharaoh[5] replied after them[6] with the tongue,[7] saying: "Who is like thee, glorious in holiness,[8] fearful in praises, doing wonders?" (*ibid.*). "Fearful in praise"[9] is not written here, but "fearful in praises"; for the praises of the ministering angels are on high, and the praises of Israel are (uttered on earth) below. "Fearful in praises, doing wonders" (*ibid.*), and thus Scripture says, "But thou art holy, O thou that inhabitest the praises of Israel" (Ps. xxii. 3).

"Thou stretchedst out thy right hand,[10] the earth swallowed them" (Ex. xv. 12). The Holy One, blessed be He, told the earth to bury the slain.[11] (The earth) said unto Him: Sovereign of all worlds! The waters have killed them, let the waters swallow[12] them. He answered (the

[1] The quotation ends here in the MS.; it is continued in the first editions. See Ps. lxviii. 34.

[2] This is the explanation of the word אלם in the verse: "Who is like unto thee, O Lord, among the Elim (באלם)?" (Ex. xv. 11).

[3] See *Rabbinic Philosophy and Ethics*, p. 65, note 1; and Shocher Ṭob on Ps. lxviii. p. 160a, Ex. Rab. xxix. 2, and Pesiḳta, p. 108b; and cf. *supra*, p. 88.

[4] "Elim."

[5] See *infra*, p. 341.

[6] *i.e.* the Israelites.

[7] The first editions and MS. Gaster read: "with song and praise in the Egyptian language."

[8] The quotation ends here in the MS.

[9] Our MS. reads, incorrectly, "praises"; the first editions have the right reading, "praise."

[10] The quotation ends here in the MS.; it is continued in the first editions.

[11] See Job xxvi. 5. The first editions read: "The Holy One, blessed be He, said to the earth: Receive thy hosts,[1] the slain."

[12] *i.e.* bury them. Cf. T.B. Pesachim, *loc. cit.*

---

[1] "'Ochlos" (host) may be connected with ὄχλος, "multitude."

earth) saying: On this occasion receive them; on another occasion such that be killed by thee in the future will I cast into the sea, namely, Sisera and all his host, these will I cast into the sea, as it is said, "The river Kishon swept them [1] away,[2] that ancient river" (Judg. v. 21).[3] (The earth) continued, saying to Him: Give me the oath by Thy right hand, that Thou wilt not claim them at my hand.[4] The Holy One, blessed be He, put forth His right hand, and swore to the earth that He would not claim them, as it is said, "Thou stretchedst out thy right hand, the earth swallowed them" (Ex. xv. 12).[5] All the kings [6] of the earth heard of the departure from Egypt, and the dividing of the Reed Sea; they trembled and feared,[7] and fled from their place, as it is said, "The peoples have heard, they tremble" (*ibid.* 14).

Moses spake before the Holy One, blessed be He: Sovereign of all worlds! Put Thy dread || and Thy fear upon them, that their heart may be as stone, until Israel has passed through the Jordan,[8] as it is said, "Till thy people pass over [9] . . . thou shalt bring them in, and plant them in the mountain of thine inheritance" (*ibid.* 16, 17).[10] Thou shalt bring them in to Thy holy mountain. The Holy One, blessed be He, said to Moses: Moses! Thou hast not said, "Bring *us* in [9] and plant *us*,"

[1] Sisera's army.

[2] The quotation ends here in the MS.; it is continued in the first editions.

[3] The first editions add here: "The earth spake before Him: Sovereign of the world! Just as in the hour when only one person was slain [1] I was cursed for his sake, and if I receive all these hosts, how much more so will I be cursed!" MS. Gaster reads almost the same text.

[4] See Lam. Rab. on Lam. i. 9, and Shocher Ṭob, Ps. xxii. p. 90b.

[5] The first editions and MS. Gaster add here: "The 'right hand' is only an oath, as it is said: 'The Lord hath sworn by his right hand, and by the arm of his strength' (Isa. lxii. 8). Forthwith the earth opened her mouth and swallowed them."

[6] The Amsterdam edition has misread the word "kings" and gives "angels."

[7] See T.B. Synhedrin, 37b; and cf. Josh. ii. 9 and ix. 24.

[8] The first editions read "sea." The reading in our MS., "the Jordan," is in agreement with the version of Onḳelos on Ex. xv. 16. See *Liturgy for New Year,* Singer, p. 239. MS. Gaster adds: "until Israel has crossed the fords of Arnon."

[9] In our MS. the quotation ends here; it is continued in the first editions.

[10] See Pal. Targum, *in loc.*

---

[1] And I received Abel's blood and body.

but (thou hast said), " Thou shalt bring *them* in[1] and plant *them.*" The One who brings in, He also brings out. By thy life! According to thy words so shall it be.[2] In this world I shall[3] bring them[4] in, and in the world to come I will plant them as a true plant[5] which shall not be plucked up out of their land,[6] as it is said, " And I will plant them upon their land, and they shall no more be plucked up out of their land which I have given them, saith the Lord thy God " (Amos ix. 15); and it (also) says, " The Lord shall reign for ever and ever " (Ex. xv. 18).[7]

[1] In our MS. the quotation ends here; it is continued in the first editions.

[2] Cf. Deut. Rab. ii. 9, and Num. Rab. xix. 13.

[3] The first editions read : " thou shalt." MS. Gaster agrees with our MS. here.

[4] This was promised to Moses, but by striking the rock at Massah this privilege was forfeited. Luria suggests a variant reading : " Thou hast not said, 'I will bring them in and I will plant them,' but, 'Thou wilt bring them in and plant them.' The one who brings them in is the one who brings them out; so shall it be in this world, and in the future world thou wilt bring them in and I will plant them."

[5] See Jer. xxxii. 41.

[6] From " as it is said " to the end of the quotation from Amos ix. 15 is missing in the MS., which reads " etc." The first editions read as far as " their land."

[7] See *Rabbinic Philosophy and Ethics*, pp. 182–184, for the parallel version from the Talmud.

CHAPTER XLIII

THE POWER OF REPENTANCE [60A. i.]

REPENTANCE and good deeds[1] are a shield against punishment. Rabbi Ishmael[2] said: If repentance had not been created,[3] the world would not stand. But since repentance has been created, the right hand of the Holy One, blessed be He, is stretched forth to receive the penitent[4] every day, and He says, Repent, ye children of men. "Repent, ye children of men" (Ps. xc. 3).[5] Know thou the power of repentance.[6] Come and see from Ahab, king of Israel,[7] for he had robbed, coveted,[8] and murdered,[9] as it is said, "Hast thou killed, and also taken possession?" (1 Kings xxi. 19). He sent and called for Jehoshaphat, king of Judah,[10] who gave him thrice daily forty stripes, and in fasting and with prayer he rose up early and retired late, before the Holy One, blessed be He,[11]

[1] See Aboth iv. 11 in the name of R. Eliezer ben Jacob. תריס = θυρεός, shield.

[2] The first editions read: "Rabbi 'Akiba said: 'Repentance was created and the right hand,'" etc.

[3] See *supra*, Chapter III., p. 10.

[4] See T.B. Pesachim, 119a; Tanna de bê Elijahu Zutta, xxii. p. 37, xxiii. p. 40; and cf. Ezek. i. 8, with the interpretation in Pesachim, *loc. cit.* See Jalkut and Targum on Ps. xc. 3.

[5] See *supra*, pp. 104 f.

[6] The first editions read "charity and repentance"; see next note.

[7] See T.B. Synhedrin, 102b; *J.E.* i. 281; and also Menorath Ha-Maor, § 284. The word Zedakah (Charity) should be omitted. The first editions add: "who repented sincerely." See also Jalkut, 1 Kings xxi. § 222; and T.B. Ta'anith, 25b.

[8] The first editions read "oppressed."

[9] See T.B. Synhedrin, 113a, according to which he introduced idolatry; and cf. T.B. Synhedrin, 48b. Menorath Ha-Maor, *loc. cit.*, reads: "he coveted and murdered"; see Tanna de bê Elijahu Rab. xxvi. p. 130, and Num. Rab. xiv. 1.

[10] See Jalkuṭ on 1 Kings xxi. *loc. cit.*; Menorath Ha-Maor, *loc. cit.*; T.J. Sotah, iii. 4. 18d, which refers to three years of penitence.

[11] The first editions add here: "and he studied the Torah all his days."

and he did not return any more to his evil deeds. His repentance was accepted, as it is said, || "Seest thou how Ahab humbleth himself[1] before me? Because he humbleth himself before me, I will not bring the evil in his days" (*ibid.* 29).

Rabbi Abbahu said: Know thou the power of repentance. Come and see from David, king of Israel.[2] For the Holy One, blessed be He, had sworn to the forefathers that He would multiply their seed like the stars of the heavens. And David came to count their number. The Holy One, blessed be He, said to him: David! I have sworn to the forefathers that I would multiply their seed as the stars of the heavens. And thou comest to annul My word. For thy sake the flock is given over to destruction;[3] and in three hours there fell seventy thousand men,[4] as it is said, "And there fell of Israel seventy thousand men" (1 Chron. xxi. 14). Rabbi Simeon said: Only Abishai, son of Zeruiah, fell amongst the Israelites, for he was equal in his good deeds and his knowledge of the Torah to the seventy thousand men,[5] as it is said, "And there fell of Israel seventy thousand men" (*ibid.*). "Men" is not written here, only "man."[6] And David heard and rent his garments, and clothed himself in sackcloth and ashes, and he fell upon his face to the ground before the ark of the covenant of God.[7]

He sought (to do) penitence, and spake before the Holy One, blessed be He: Sovereign of all worlds! It is I who have sinned; forgive me, I beseech Thee, my sin. His repentance was accepted, and He said to the angel who had destroyed many (*Rab*) among the people: "Stay thine hand"[8] (*ibid.* 15). What is the meaning of || "many" (*Rab*)? He said to him: *Rab* (the teacher) has fallen in Israel.[9] What did the angel do? He took his sword

[1] In the MS. the quotation ends here.

[2] See Jalḳuṭ on 2 Samuel, § 165, and Menorath Ha-Maor, *loc. cit.*

[3] See 2 Sam. xxiv. 17, and *infra*, p. 400. The Pesiḳta, pp. 160b ff., has used *P.R.E.*

[4] See T.B. Berakhoth, 62b.

[5] See Midrash Samuel xxxi. (end); T.B. Berakhoth, *loc. cit.*; Shocher Ṭob on Ps. xvii. p. 64a; and *J.E.* i. p. 66.

[6] The MS. has "70,000 men," and above this the letter כ, "as" or "like," has been added by a later writer.

[7] The first editions regard this sentence as a quotation and add: "as it is said." The text is based on Josh. vii. 6.

[8] The first editions read: "Now stay thine *hands*."

[9] See 2 Sam. iii. 38: "for a prince and a great man has fallen this day in Israel."

and cleaned it with the garment[1] of David. David saw the sword of the angel,[2] and he trembled in all his limbs until[3] his death[4] (as it is said,[5]) "But David could not go before it[6] to inquire of God; for he was afraid because of the sword of the angel of the Lord" (*ibid.* 30).

Rabbi Joshua said: Know thou the power of repentance. Come and see from Manasseh,[7] son of Hezekiah, who perpetrated all the evil abominations much more than all the nations.[8] He made his son to pass through the fire to Baal outside Jerusalem, causing (doves) to fly,[9] and sacrificing to all the host of heaven. The princes of the troops of the king of Babylon came,[10] and they caught him by the hair of his head, and brought him down to Babylon, and they put him

[1] טלית, garment, also "Ṭallith."

[2] The first editions add "of death."

[3] The first editions add "the day of."

[4] See Tanna de bê Elijahu Rab. vii. p. 39, and Shocher Ṭob, Ps. xvii. p. 63b.

[5] The MS. omits "as it is said"; the first editions have the expression.

[6] The quotation ends here in the MS.

[7] See *J.E.* viii. 281 on the Prayer of Manasseh. The legend dealing with his punishment and repentance occurs in the Apocalypse of Baruch lxiv. 8. Traces of this legend are to be found in the Apostolic Constitutions, ii. 22; also in Anastasius on Ps. vi., quoted by Charles in his Note on Apoc. Baruch, p. 107, where the Targum of 2 Chron. xxxiii. 12 f. is given. See also T.B. Synhedrin, 103a.

[8] The first editions add here: "of the world, and wrought much evil, and sacrificed to idols,[1] as it is said: 'He also made his children to pass through the fire in the valley of the son of Hinnom: (and he practised augury, and used enchantments, and practised sorcery, and dealt with them that had familiar spirits, and with wizards): he wrought much evil in the sight of the Lord, to provoke him to anger' (2 Chron. xxxiii. 6).[2] He went to Jerusalem dedicating doves[3] to all the host of heaven." MS. Gaster has almost the same reading.

[9] See Mishnah Synhedrin, iii. 3. The dove-flying was an occasion for betting.

[10] See 2 Chron. xxxiii. 11, and Menorath Ha-Maor, *loc. cit.* The first editions read: "The princes of the troops of Assyria came."

---

[1] Venice edition reads: "strange gods." The Targum, 2 Chron. xxxiii. 7, refers to Manasseh's image of himself, which he set up in the Temple. The Talmud (B. Synhedrin, 103b) holds that the image had originally one face, but ultimately it had four faces to provoke God. Apoc. Baruch, lxiv. 3, says: "And he made an image with *five* faces; four of them looked to the four winds, and the fifth on the summit of the image as an adversary of the zeal of the Mighty One," see also Assumption of Moses, ii. 8.

[2] See also 2 Kings xxi. 2 ff.

[3] "He filled Jerusalem with the blood which he shed, and he sacrificed to all the host of heaven" is the reading suggested by Luria, based on 2 Kings xxiv. 4.

in a pan (over) a fire,[1] and there he called upon all the other gods[2] to whom he had sacrificed, and not one of them either answered him or saved him. He said: I will call on the God of my fathers with all my heart; perhaps He will do unto me according to all His wonders which He did unto my father. And he called on the God of his fathers with all his heart, and He was entreated of him, and He heard his supplication, as it is said, "And he prayed unto him; and he was intreated of him,[3] and heard his supplication . . . then Manasseh knew that the Lord he was God" (2 Chron. xxxiii. 13). In that hour Manasseh said: There is both judgment as well as a judge.

Ben Azzai[4] said: Know thou the power of repentance. Come and see from (the story of) Rabbi Simeon, son of Laḳish. He with two || of his friends[5] in the mountains, were robbing[6] all who passed them on the way. What did he do? He forsook his two companions who were plundering on the mountains, and he returned to the God of his fathers with all his heart. Fasting and praying he arose early and retired late,[7] before the Holy One, blessed be He, and he was studying the Torah all (the rest of) his days, and (giving) gifts to the needy. He did not return any more to his evil deeds, and his repentance was accepted. On the day when he died, his two companions, who were plundering on the mountains, also died. And they gave a portion in the treasury of the living[8] to Rabbi Simeon, son of Laḳish, but his two companions (were put) in the lowest Sheol.

[1] Luria reads: "in copper fetters," according to the Targum on 2 Chron. xxxii. 11; see Ruth Rab. v. 6, and the Note in Lightfoot's Hor. Heb. et Tal. in *Acta Apost.* xii. 7. See T.B. Synhedrin, 101b; Targum, 2 Chron., *loc. cit.*; Deut. Rab. ii. 13. The reading במולות, the "hollow brazen horse," occurs in the Targum as well as in Apoc. Baruch; see 'Arukh, *s.v.* מולתא. Luria offers a variant reading: דודא דנחשת; see 'Arukh, *s.v.* מליאר—an iron barrel with apertures around which a fire was kindled. See also Agadath Bereshith, ix. (end), and Bacher in *R.É.J.* xlv. 291 ff.

[2] Or "strange gods"; the later editions read "idols."

[3] The quotation ends here in the MS.

[4] The chronology is hopelessly at fault here. Ben 'Azzai was dead long before the time of Simeon ben Laḳish.

[5] See T.B. Gittin, 47a, and cf. *J.E.* xi. 354 f.

[6] The first editions add: "and oppressing."

[7] See Menorath Ha-Maor, *loc. cit.*

[8] See the reading in the Menorath Ha-Maor, *loc. cit.*, which has used our book. Our text might be rendered: "They put Rabbi Simeon, son of Laḳish, in the treasury of the living."

The two companions spake before the Holy One, blessed be He: Sovereign of all the universe! There is before Thee respect for certain persons. This one was plundering with us on the mountains, and he is in the treasury of the living, whilst the other men are[1] in the lowest Sheol. He said to them: This one repented in his lifetime, but ye have not repented. They said to Him: Give us the opportunity, and we will repent very sincerely. He said to them: Repentance is only possible until one's death.[2]

A parable—To what is the matter comparable? To a man who wished to take a voyage at sea. If he did not take with him bread and water from an inhabited land, he will not find anything to eat or to drink on the sea. Again, || if a man wish to go to the end of the wilderness, unless he take from some inhabited place bread and water, he will not find anything to eat or to drink in the wilderness. Likewise, if a man did not repent in his lifetime, after his death he cannot repent.[3] But (God) gives to a man according to his ways, as it is said, "I[4] the Lord search the heart,[5] I try the reins, even to give every man according to his ways, according to the fruit of his doings" (Jer. xvii. 10).

Rabbi Nechunia, son of Haḳḳanah, said: Know thou the power of repentance. Come and see from Pharaoh, king of Egypt, who rebelled most grievously against the Rock, the Most High,[6] as it is said, "Who is the Lord, that I should hearken unto his voice?" (Ex. v. 2).[7] In the same terms of speech in which he sinned, he repented, as it is said

[1] The first editions read: "whilst we are."

[2] See Midrash on Prov. vi. (ed. Buber, p. 28a), and cf. Eccles. ix. 10 with Midrash thereon.

[3] The first editions add: "as it is said, 'He will not regard any ransom;[1] neither will he rest content, though thou givest many gifts'"[2] (Prov. vi. 35).

[4] Our MS. reads: "For I the Lord." This does not agree with M.T.

[5] In the MS. the quotation ends here; it is continued in the first editions as far as "reins."

[6] Luria suggests another reading: "the Rock of Eternity." The Menorath Ha-Maor, *loc. cit.*, reads: "Sovereign of Eternity."

[7] See the preceding chapter of our book, p. 331.

---

[1] The quotation ends here in the first editions.

[2] See Midrash on this verse. Luria reads: "But He will give to a man according to his ways and according to the fruit of his deeds, as it is said, 'He will not regard,'" etc. A parallel reading is given by Menorath Ha-Maor, *loc. cit.*

"Who is like thee, O Lord, among the mighty?" (*ibid.* xv. 11). The Holy One, blessed be He, delivered him from amongst the dead. Whence (do we know) that he died?[1] Because it is said, "For now I had put forth my hand,[2] and smitten thee" (*ibid.* ix. 15).[3] He went and ruled in Nineveh. The men of Nineveh were writing fraudulent deeds, and everyone robbed his neighbour, and they committed sodomy,[4] and such-like wicked actions. When the Holy One, blessed be He, sent for Jonah, to prophesy against (the city) its destruction, Pharaoh hearkened and arose from his throne, rent his garments and clothed himself in sackcloth and ashes, and had a proclamation made to all his people, that all the people should fast for two[5] days, || and all who did these (wicked) things[6] should be burnt by fire. What did they[7] do? The men were[8] on one side, and the women on the other, and their children were by themselves; all the clean animals were on one side,[9] and their offspring were by themselves. The infants saw the breasts of their mothers,

[1] In the Reed Sea. The first editions read: "that he did not die."

[2] The quotation ends here in the MS. and in the first editions.

[3] The 1st ed. and Gaster MS. read here: "But in very deed, for this cause have I made thee to stand" (Ex. ix. 16). The 2nd ed. adds: "And the Holy One, blessed be He, raised him up from amongst the dead[1] to declare the might of His power.[2] Whence (do we know) that He raised him up? Because it is said: 'But in very deed for this cause have I made thee to stand, for to shew thee my power, and that my name may be declared throughout all the earth'" (Ex. ix. 16).[3]

[4] Cf. Pesiḳta, p. 161a, and Jalḳuṭ, Jonah, § 550.

[5] The first editions read: "three days."

[6] The first editions read: "All who did *not* do these things."

[7] The first editions read: "he."

[8] The first editions read: "He made the men stand on one side."

[9] The first editions add: "and all the unclean animals were on the other side." Luria thinks that "male animals" and "female animals" would be a more appropriate reading. See the reading in the Menorath Ha-Maor, *loc. cit.* Jalḳuṭ Jonah, *loc. cit.*, omits it.

---

[1] We have here a conflate text arising from two different versions of the legend. In Jalḳuṭ on Jonah (§ 550) we have one reading: "And He delivered him from death to declare the power of His might, as it is said: 'But in very deed for this cause have I made thee to stand'" (Ex. ix. 16). The other reading is preserved in the Menorath Ha-Maor, *loc. cit.* See also the rest of the verse (Ex. ix. 16) in Pal. Targum, which refers to Pharaoh, who is to recount the Divine praise.

[2] The Amsterdam edition reads: "His might and His power."

[3] See Mekhilta, Beshallach vi. p. 33a, and Shocher Ṭob on Ps. cvi. p. 228a. The Rabbis differ as to whether Pharaoh escaped; see Eccles. Rab. to Eccles. x. 5, and Pal. Targum on Ex. xiv. 27.

(and they wished[1]) to have suck,[2] and they wept. The mothers saw their children, (and they wished[1]) to give them suck. By the merit of 4123 children more than twelve hundred thousand men (were saved), as it is said, "And should not I have pity on Nineveh,[3] that great city; wherein are more than six score thousand persons that cannot discern between their right hand and their left hand; and also much cattle?" (Jonah iv. 11); "And the Lord[4] repented of the evil,[5] which he said he would do unto them"[6] (*ibid.* iii. 10). For forty years was the Holy One, blessed be He, slow to anger with them, corresponding to the forty days during which He had sent Jonah.[7] After forty years they returned to their many evil deeds, more so than their former ones, and they were swallowed up like the dead, in the lowest Sheol, as it is said, "Out of the city of the dead[8] they groan" (Job xxiv. 12).

The Holy One, blessed be He, sent by the hand of His servants, the prophets, to Israel[9] (saying), "O Israel, return unto the Lord thy God" (Hos. xiv. 1).[10] (Even) unto Him whose voice ye heard at Mount Sinai, saying, "I, the Lord, am to be thy God" (Ex. xx. 2).

"For thou hast fallen by thine iniquity" (Hos. xiv. 1).

[1] The words in brackets, which are missing in our MS., occur in the first editions.

[2] The Menorath Ha-Maor, *loc. cit.*, reads: "To have suck and they did not permit it, and they wept, and the mothers saw their offspring and they wished to give them suck, and they were unable and they wept." See T.B. Ta'anith, 16a, and T.J. Ta'anith ii. 1. 65b.

[3] The quotation ends here in the MS.; in the first editions it concludes with the word "city." The preceding part of the sentence reads in the first editions: "By (their) merit there were more than twelve hundred thousand men."

[4] The MS. and the first editions read "the Lord"; M.T. has "God."

[5] The quotation ends here in the MS.; in the first editions it concludes with the word "said."

[6] See the reading in the Menorath Ha-Maor, *loc. cit.*

[7] Menorath Ha-Maor, *loc. cit.*, reads: "when He spake to Jonah."

[8] R.V. has "populous," but in margin, "city of men." Nineveh was destroyed by Nebuchadnezzar; see T.B. Megillah, 11b.

[9] The first editions read: "to prophesy against Israel and He said."

[10] The use of these verses from Hosea seems to suggest that this entire chapter on Repentance was originally a homily for the Sabbath of Repentance, *i.e.* the Sabbath before the Day of Atonement. This suggestion seems to be reasonable, because the reference to Jonah would be appropriate on the Sabbath before it was read. The Book of Jonah is the Haphṭarah at Minchah on the Day of Atonement; see *supra*, Chapter X.

"And thy wealth"[1] is not written here, but "For thou hast fallen by thine *iniquity*." It is not written here, "Take with you silver and gold," || but "Take with you words" (*ibid.* 2). It is not written here, "And we will render silver and gold," but "And we will render as bullocks (the offering of) our lips" (*ibid.*).[2]

Rabbi Jehudah said: If Israel will not repent they will not be redeemed.[3] Israel only repents because of distress,[4] and because of oppression, and owing to exile, and because they have no sustenance. Israel does not repent quite sincerely[5] until Elijah[6] comes, as it is said, "Behold, I will send you[7] Elijah, the prophet,[8] before the great and terrible day of the Lord come. And he shall turn the heart of the fathers to the children, and the heart of the children to their fathers" (Mal. iv. 5, 6).

Blessed art thou, O Lord, who delightest in repentance.[9]

[1] The first editions read: "By thy glory and thy wealth."

[2] See Menorath Ha-Maor, § 279; Tanna de bê Elijahu Zutta ix. p. 189; T.B. Synhedrin, 96b; and cf. 4 Ezra iv. 39.

[3] See T.B. Synhedrin, 93a, and T.J. Ta'anith, *loc. cit.*

[4] See Tanna de bê Elijahu Rab. xxi. p. 116; and Tanna de bê Elijahu Ẓuṭṭa iv. p. 180, and xiv. p. 196. See also Assumption of Moses, i. 18.

[5] Lit. "Does not do a great repentance."

[6] The first editions add: "Of blessed memory," or, "May his memory be a blessing"; see *supra*, p. 2, note 7. Cf. Luke i. 16 f.

[7] In the MS. the words from "Elijah" to "come" are omitted. In the first editions the entire verse is given.

[8] See Seder 'Olam Rab. xvii. p. 36a, b.

[9] See Singer, p. 46. This is the fifth benediction of the Shemoneh 'Esreh. Does our Midrash wish to associate Elijah with this benediction?

CHAPTER XLIV

AMALEK AND ISRAEL [61B. i.]

RABBI JOCHANAN, son of Nuri, said: (After)[1] all the mighty deeds and wonders which the Holy One, blessed be He, did unto Israel in Egypt, and at the Reed Sea, they repeatedly tempted the Omnipresent[2] ten times,[3] as it is said, "Yet have they tempted me these ten times" (Num. xiv. 22). Moreover, they slandered the Holy One, blessed be He, saying: He[4] has forsaken us in this wilderness, and His Shekhinah is not in our midst, as it is said, "Is the Lord among us,[5] or not?" (Ex. xvii. 7).[6]

Rabbi Joshua,[7] son of Ḳorchah, said: After this section what is written? "Then came Amalek" (*ibid.* 8). Amalek came against them to punish them. He who comes from || a journey should be met on the way with food and drink. (Amalek) saw them faint and weary, owing to the Egyptian bondage and the affliction of the journey, and he did not take to heart[8] the precept of "Honour,"[9]

1 "After" is wanting in our MS.; it occurs in the first editions.

2 The first editions read: "The Holy One, blessed be He."

3 Read עד, instead of עוד. See Aboth, v. 4, and Aboth de R. Nathan (*b*) xxxiv. p. 49b.

4 The first editions read: "The Lord."

5 In the MS. the quotation ends here.

6 See Ps. lxxviii. 22; and cf. *infra*, pp. 436 f.

7 The MS. reads incorrectly: "Ishmael, son of Ḳorcha." MS. Gaster reads: "Simeon."

8 To have pity on them, or to fear God, so as not to afflict them. See Tanna de bê Elijahu Rab. xxiv. p. 126: "Eliphaz the father of Amalek advised his son to go and dig wells for Israel, but he met them with the sword."

9 The fifth commandment is probably referred to here; see previous note, 8. The MS. alone reads: "the precept of 'Honour.'" The Book of Jubilees offers a parallel to this idea in the disobedience of the children of *Esau*, who forced him against his will to attack Jacob; see Jubilees xxxvii. 1 ff.

but he stood by the way like a she-bear, bereaved by man [1] (and eager) to slay mother and children,[2] as it is said, "How he met thee by the way" (Deut. xxv. 18).

Rabbi Azariah [3] said: Amalek was a descendant [4] of Esau, and because of his ancestor's [5] enmity he came against them to punish them. The cloud [6] was surrounding [7] the camp of Israel like a city surrounded by a wall.[8] The adversary and enemy [9] were unable to touch them, but (when) anyone needed a ritual bath [10] the cloud excluded him from the camp of Israel, because the camp of Israel was holy, as it is said, "Therefore shall thy camp be holy" (*ibid.* xxiii. 14), and (then) Amalek was smiting and slaying [11] the hindmost of those who were beyond the cloud,[12] as it is said, "And he smote the hindmost of thee,[13] all that were feeble behind thee" (*ibid.* xxv. 18).

Moses said to Joshua: Choose men for us, houses [14] of the fathers,[15] men who are mighty in strength and valour,[16] and go forth and do battle with Amalek. Moses, Aaron, and Hur stood on a high place,[17] in the camp [18] of Israel, one on his right hand, and one on his left. Hence thou mayest learn that the precentor [19] is prohibited to officiate unless

[1] "By man" occurs in the MS only.

[2] See *supra*, p. 281; cf. 1 Sam. xv. 33.

[3] The first editions and MS. Gaster read: "Zechariah."

[4] Lit. "grandson."

[5] Lit. "grandfather's." See Pal. Targ. Ex. xvii. 8, and Targum on Cant. ii. 15.

[6] The first editions read: "The Pillar of Cloud."

[7] Cf. Deut. xxxii. 10 and Pal. Targum, Deut. xxv. 18. See also Mekhilta, p. 53a: "The clouds surrounded the Israelites on all four sides."

[8] Cf. Zech. ii. 5.

[9] Cf. Lam. iv. 12 for phraseology.

[10] Cf. T.B. Pesachim, 68a; T.B. Giṭṭin, 60a; Num. Rab. vii. 1; and see *J.E.* viii. 588 on the "Ritual Bath."

[11] The MS. reads: "vehôlekh," "and going"; the first editions read: "vehôreg," "and slaying." The latter seems to be the more correct reading.

[12] For another interpretation, see Tanchuma, Ki Têzê, § ix., and Pesiḳta, p. 27b. See *infra*, p. 389.

[13] In the MS. the quotation ends here; it is continued in the first editions.

[14] The first editions read: "sons."

[15] See T.B. Ḳiddushin, 76b.

[16] The first editions add: "who fear Heaven." See Mekhilta, p. 53b: "Amalek did not fear Heaven." Cf. Ex. Rab. xxvi. 3.

[17] See Nachmanides on Ex. xvii. 9.

[18] The first editions read: "in the midst of the camp."

[19] The MS. has an abbreviation: "Sheshaz"; lit. "that the Messenger of the Congregation." The 1st ed. agrees.

there are two (men) standing with him,[1] || one on his right hand and one on his left.

All the Israelites (were standing[2]) outside (their tents[3]); they had gone forth from their tents, and saw Moses kneeling on his knees, and they were kneeling on their knees.[4] He fell on his face to the ground, and they fell on their faces to the ground. He spread out the palms of his hands towards the heavens, and they spread out their hands to heaven.[5] Just as[6] the precentor officiates, in like manner all the people answer[7] after him.

The Holy One, blessed be He, caused Amalek and his people to fall into the hand of Joshua,[8] as it is said, "And Joshua discomfited[9] Amalek and his people with the edge of the sword" (Ex. xvii. 13).[10]

Rabbi Shela said: The Holy One, blessed be He, wished to destroy, to cut off all the seed of Amalek. What did the Holy One, blessed be He, do? He put forth His right hand and took hold of the throne of His glory, and swore that He would destroy and cut off all the seed of Amalek,[11] as it is said, "And he said, Because there is a hand against the throne[9] of the Lord, the Lord will wage war against Amalek" (*ibid.* 16).

Rabbi Phineas said: (After[12]) forty years Moses wished to say to Israel: Do ye remember that which ye said in the wilderness—"Is the Lord among us,[13] or not?"

[1] See Mekhilta, p. 54b, Pesiḳta, p. 22a, and Tanchuma Beshallach, § xxviii. Was the custom mentioned in our book applicable only to public prayer on Fast Days (for rain or when war arose)? See Ṭur, Orach Chayyim, 566; and Beth Joseph, 566. 7.

[2] The MS. omits "were standing." The first editions have this reading.

[3] This is missing in the MS., but occurs in the first editions; the next words up to "tents" are found in the MS. only.

[4] Cf. Jalḳuṭ, Ex. § 264.

[5] The first editions read: "to their Father who is in Heaven." See T.B. Rosh Ha-Shanah, 29a.

[6] The first editions read: "Hence thou mayest learn."

[7] The first editions add: "Amen." See Jalḳuṭ (*loc. cit.*), which omits "Amen"; see also T.B. Berakhoth, 49b.

[8] The first editions read: "to fall by the edge of the sword."

[9] In the MS. the quotation ends here; it is continued in the 1st ed.

[10] See Targum on Cant. ii. 16, and cf. Pal. Targum on Num. xxi. 1.

[11] The first editions add: "from this world and from the world to come."

[12] The MS. omits: "after"; it occurs in the first editions.

[13] The MS. omits: "or not"; it occurs in the first editions.

(*ibid.* 7).[1] But Moses said: If I speak[2] thus to Israel, behold I will put them to shame, and whosoever puts (his fellow) to shame will have no portion in the world to come.[3]

A parable—To what is the matter to be compared? To a king[4] who had || a garden and a dog chained at the entrance to the garden. The king was sitting in his upper room, watching and looking at all that (transpired) in the garden. The friend of the king entered to steal (fruit) from the garden, and he incited the dog against him, and it tore his garments. The king said: If I say to my friend, Why didst thou enter my garden? behold I will put him to shame; therefore, behold, I will say to him: Didst thou see that mad dog, how it tore thy clothes?[5] And he will understand what he has done. Likewise spake Moses: Behold, I will tell Israel the story of Amalek, and they will understand what is written before it; therefore Moses said: "Remember what Amalek did unto thee[6] by the way, as ye came forth out of Egypt" (Deut. xxv. 17).

The Israelites said to our teacher Moses: Moses! One Scripture text says, "Remember the Sabbath day, to keep it holy" (Ex. xx. 8); and it is written, "Remember what Amalek did unto thee" (Deut. xxv. 17). How can these two texts be fulfilled?[7] He said to them: The cup of spiced wine[8] is not to be compared to the cup

[1] See T.B. 'Abodah Zarah, 5b.

[2] The MS. adds: "not"; this is probably an error; it does not occur in the first editions.

[3] See Aboth iii. 12; T.B. Megillah, 25b, and Pal. Targum on Deut. vi. 16. The first editions add: "But I will tell them the story of Amalek, and they will understand[1] what is written (immediately) preceding this story.

[4] The legend is also given by Tanchuma, Ki Têzê, § ix., translated in *Rabbinic Philosophy and Ethics*, pp. 190 f.

[5] The first editions add: "not knowing that thou art my friend."

[6] In the MS. the quotation ends here; it is continued in the first editions.

[7] Or: "established." See Tanchuma, Ki Têzê, *loc. cit.* The first editions add: "this 'Remember' and that 'Remember.'"

[8] "קונדיטון" (*conditum*, κονδῖτον); cf. *Rabbinic Philosophy and Ethics*, p. 101.

---

[1] See T.B. Baba Mezi'a, 58b; T.B. Pesachim, 33b; and Tanchuma, Jethro, § iii. This Midrashic piece is translated in *Rabbinic Philosophy and Ethics*, pp. 188 f.

of vinegar.[1] This "Remember" is in order to observe and to sanctify the Sabbath day,[2] and the other "Remember" is in order to destroy and to cut off all the seed of Amalek, as it is said, "Therefore it shall be, when the Lord thy God hath given thee rest [3] from all thine enemies . . . thou shalt not forget" (*ibid.* 19).[4] || Israel forgot to destroy and to cut off all the seed of Amalek, but the Holy One, blessed be He, did not forget.[5] When Saul reigned, Samuel said to him: "Thus saith the Lord of hosts, I have marked that which Amalek did to Israel. . . . Now go and smite Amalek, and utterly destroy all that they have" (1 Sam. xv. 2, 3). What is the meaning of "all that they have"? Even all the living male creatures.[6] "Spare them not, but slay" (*ibid.*). Saul took the men of war, and he went out to meet Amalek. When Saul came to the crossing of the ways, he stood still, and thought in his heart,[7] as it is said, "And Saul came to the city of Amalek,[8] and argued [9] in the valley" (*ibid.* 5). Saul said: If the men have sinned, what [10] have the beasts done amiss? A Bath Kol [11] came forth, saying to him: Saul! Be not

[1] The MS. reads "sumin," the first editions have "chomez," and then add: "this is a 'cup,' and that is a 'cup.'" The precept to "remember" the Sabbath is explained by the Rabbis to refer to the Kiddush, or sanctification of the Sabbath over the cup of wine; see Singer, p. 124.

[2] See *supra*, p. 138.

[3] In the MS. the quotation ends here. The first editions read: "'Remember what Amalek did unto thee' (Deut. xxv. 17), and when thou comest to the land 'thou shalt not forget'" (*ibid.* 19).

[4] See T.B. Synhedrin, 20b. Amalek was to be punished, and this Divine decree was not to be forgotten when Israel had their own land and king. This duty of executing Divine justice devolved upon Saul as the first king of the Israelites.

[5] See Tanchuma, Ki Têzê, *loc. cit.*; Pesikta (Zachor), p. 26a, and Lam. Rab. v. 1.

[6] On משתין בקיר see Lexica.

[7] See T.B. Joma, 22b: Midrash Samuel (ed. Buber), xviii. p. 50a.

[8] In the MS. the quotation ends here; in the first editions the verse is continued.

[9] וירב might be interpreted in the sense of meditating. See R.V.

[10] The first editions add here: "Have the women done amiss? If the women have sinned, what have the children done amiss? [1] If the children have sinned."

[11] The text in 1 Samuel xv. 19 says: "Why hast thou not hearkened unto the *voice* of the Lord?" The Bath Kol was a Heavenly voice; see *supra*, p. 225.

---

[1] They and their children failed to bring bread and water to the Israelites.

more righteous than thy Creator,[1] as it is said, "Be not righteous overmuch" (Eccles. vii. 16).

Rabbi said: When Saul came to the camp of Amalek he saw the children of Israel tarrying[2] in the midst of Amalek.[3] He said to them: Separate yourselves from the midst of Amalek, as it is said, "And Saul said unto the Kenites, Go, depart, get you down[4] from among the Amalekites, lest I destroy you with them" (1 Sam. xv. 6). Did Jethro show loving-kindness to all Israel? But did he not show loving-kindness to Moses our teacher alone? Hence thou mayest learn || that whosoever shows loving-kindness unto one of the great men of Israel is considered as though he had shown loving-kindness unto Israel.[5] Because of the loving-kindness which he showed, his children were saved from among the Amalekites.[6]

Rabbi José said: When Sennacherib came to the land (of Israel), all the nations who were in the regions round about the land of Israel saw the camp of Sennacherib, and feared greatly, and every man fled from his place, as it is said, "I have removed the bounds of the peoples,[4] and have robbed their treasures" (Isa. x. 13). They went into the wilderness, and intermixed with the children of Ishmael,[7] and all of them were (composed of) ten peoples, as it is said, "The tents of Edom, and the Ishmaelites;[8] Moab, and the Hagarenes; Gebal, and Ammon, and Amalek; Philistia, with the inhabitants of Tyre; Assyria also is joined with them" (Ps. lxxxiii. 6, 7, 8).[9] All of them are destined to fall by the hand of the Son of David, as it is said, "O my God, make them like the whirling dust"

[1] Cf. 4 Ezra viii. 47; T.B. Joma, *loc. cit.*; and Eccles. Rab. to Eccles. vii. 16.

[2] The first editions read: "Jethro mixed up in the midst"; this reading is probably the correct text.

[3] The Kenites dwelt among the Amalekites.

[4] In the MS. the quotation ends here; in the first editions it is continued.

[5] See T.B. Berakhoth, 63b; Midrash Samuel, *loc. cit.*, and Cant. Rab. on Cant. ii. 5.

[6] The first editions add here: "as it is said, 'So the Kenites departed from among the Amalekites'" (1 Sam. xv. 6).

[7] The Ishmaelites dwelt hard by the Amalekites; see *supra*, p. 220.

[8] In the MS. the rest of the verses up to the word Assyria are omitted; as usual, "etc." replaces the part left out.

[9] See T.B. Sukkah, 52b.

(*ibid.* 13).[1] "As the fire that burneth the forest,[2] and as the flame that setteth the mountains on fire" (*ibid.* 14). "So pursue them with thy tempest,[2] and terrify them with thy storm" (*ibid.* 15).

[1] This Messianic passage is omitted in the modern editions owing to the fear of the censor. The ten nations mentioned in the Psalm are, of course, only memories of the past. The MS. adds "etc." at the end of its quotation; the verse continues: "As stubble before the wind."

[2] Thus far the MS. quotes this verse.

CHAPTER XLV

THE GOLDEN CALF [62B. ii.]

RABBI SIMEON BEN JOCHAI said: When the Holy One, blessed be He, was revealed to Moses out of the thorn-bush, in order to send him to Egypt, Moses spake before the Holy One, blessed be He (saying): Sovereign of all the worlds![1] Swear to me that all things which I desire to do,[2] Thou wilt do, so that I should not speak words before Pharaoh, and Thou wilt not fulfil them, for then will he slay me. And He swore unto him that "whatsoever thou || desirest to do, I will do, except with reference to two things," (namely,) to let him enter the land (of Canaan),[3] and (to postpone) the day of (his) death. Whence do we know that He swore unto him? Because it is said, "By myself have I sworn, saith the Lord, the word is gone forth from my mouth in righteousness" (Isa. xlv. 23).[4] When Israel received the commandments they forgot their God[5] after forty days, and they said to Aaron: The Egyptians were carrying their god, and they were singing and uttering hymns[6] before it, and they saw it before them. Make unto us a god like the gods of the Egyptians, and let us see it before us, as it is said, "Up, make us a god" (Ex. xxxii. 1).

They betook themselves to the one who carried out

[1] This is also the reading of the Prague edition. The Venice edition omits "all."

[2] Just as God agreed to comply with the request of Moses in Ex. viii. 13 and xxxiii. 17, and Num. xvi. 31.

[3] Cf. Deut. iv. 21.

[4] The quotation from Genesis (xxii. 16) given in the printed texts is hardly applicable to Moses. The quotation as in our text does not quite agree with M.T., which omits "saith the Lord."

[5] Cf. Ps. cvi. 21.

[6] See *supra*, p. 333; Pal. Targum on Ex. xxxii. 5; T.J. Soṭah iii. 4. 19a; and see also Num. Rab. ix. 49.

the words of Moses,[1] (to) Aaron his brother, and Hur, the son of his sister. Whence (do we know) that Hur was the son of (Moses') sister? Because it is said, "And Caleb took unto him Ephrath,[2] which bare him Hur" (1 Chron. ii. 19). Why was Miriam's name called Ephrath?[3] Because she was a daughter of the palace,[4] a daughter of kings, one of the magnates of the generation; for every prince and great man who arose in Israel had his name called an Ephrathite, as it is said, "And Jeroboam, the son of Nebat, an Ephrathite"[5] (1 Kings xi. 26); and it says, "And David was the son of that Ephrathite" (1 Sam. xvii. 12). Was he then an Ephrathite? Was he not of the tribe of Judah? But he was a nobleman,[4] a son of kings, one of the magnates of the generation. But since Hur was of the tribe of Judah, and one of the magnates of the generation, he began to reprove Israel with harsh words,[6] and the plunderers[7] who were in Israel arose against him, and slew him.

Aaron arose || and saw that Hur, the son of his sister, was slain; and he built for them an altar, as it is said, "And when Aaron saw this,[8] he built an altar before it" (Ex. xxxii. 5).

Aaron argued with himself, saying: If I say to Israel, Give ye to me gold and silver, they will bring it immediately;

[1] The Venice text reads: "to the companions of Moses."

[2] The quotation ends here in the MS.; it is continued in the first editions.

[3] See T.B. Soṭah, 11b; and Ex. Rab. i. 17.

[4] פלטיני (*palatinus*; παλατῖνος, παλατίνη), a palatina, a daughter of a nobleman. See Midrash Agadah, Ex. p. 122.

[5] R.V. has: "Ephraimite." Jeroboam was of the tribe of Ephraim; he was not an inhabitant of the city of Ephrath, but of Zeredah. See 1 Kings xi. 26.

[6] See Num. Rab. xv. 7; Ex. Rab. xli. 7, xlviii. 4; and Lev. Rab. x. 3.

[7] The first editions read: "despised ones." See Tanchuma Tezavveh, § x. Whilst Moses ascended Mount Sinai, Aaron and Hur were left in charge of the Israelites; and when Moses descended the Mount he refers to Aaron only. Hence the inference that Hur was dead. See *Rabbinic Philosophy and Ethics*, pp. 205 f.; parallels to Rabbinic literature are given there, p. 206, note 1.

[8] MS. omits this first part of the quotation. The first editions read: "And Aaron saw (what had happened) to Hur, for he was slain; and he built an altar, as it is said, 'And Aaron saw' (Ex. xxxii. 5). What did he see? (He saw) that Hur, the son of his sister, had been slain, and he built an altar, as it is said, 'And he built an altar'" (*ibid.*). See Rashi, *in loc.*, and Midrash Agadah, Ex. p. 181.

but behold I will say to them, Give ye to me the earrings of your wives, and of your sons,[1] and forthwith the matter will fail,[2] as it is said, "And Aaron said to them, Break off the golden rings" (*ibid.* 2). The women heard (this), but they were unwilling[3] to give their earrings to their husbands; but they said to them: Ye desire to[4] make a graven image and a molten image without any power in it to deliver. The Holy One, blessed be He, gave the women their reward in this world and in the world to come. What reward did He give them in this world? That they should observe the New Moons[5] more stringently than the men, and what reward will He give them in the world to come? They are destined to be renewed like the New Moons, as it is said, "Who satisfieth thy years with good things;[6] so that thy youth is renewed like the eagle" (Ps. ciii. 5).

The men saw that the women would not consent to give their earrings to their husbands. What did they do? Until that hour the earrings were (also) in their own ears, after the fashion of the Egyptians, and after the fashion of the Arabs.[7] They broke off their earrings which were in their own ears, and they gave (them) to Aaron, as it is said, "And all the people brake off || the golden rings which were in their ears" (Ex. xxxii. 3). "Which were in the ears of their wives" is not written here, but "which were in *their* ears." Aaron found among the earrings one plate of gold upon which the Holy Name was written, and engraven thereon was the figure of a calf, and that (plate) alone did he cast into the fiery furnace,[8] as it is said, "So they gave *it* me:[9] and I cast it into the fire, and there came out this calf" (*ibid.* 24). It is not written here, "And I cast them in," but "And I cast *it* in the fire, and there came out this

[1] The first editions add: "and of your daughters."

[2] See Tanchuma, Ki Thissa, § xix., and Ẓohar, Ex. 192a.

[3] The first editions add: "and they did not consent."

[4] The "addition" (Tosaphoth) to Rashi on T.B. Megillah, 22b, reads as in our MS., but the first editions read: "To make an idol, and an abomination without power in it to deliver—we will not listen to you."

[5] This custom is referred to in T.J. Pesachim iv. 1. 30d; T.J. Ta'anith i. 6. 64c; see "addition" (Tosaphoth) to Rashi on T.B. Megillah, *loc. cit.*; Jarchi's Manhig, 43, and Roḳeach, 228, and cf. *infra*, p. 410.

[6] The quotation ends here in the MS. and in the first editions.

[7] See Judg. viii. 24, which speaks of the earrings of the Ishmaelites.

[8] See Pal. Targum on Ex. xxxii. 24.

[9] This first part of the verse is given by the first editions, the MS. omits the quotation here, although "as it is said" is given.

calf." The calf came out lowing, and the Israelites saw it,[1] and they went astray after it.

Rabbi Jehudah said: Sammael[2] entered into it, and he was lowing to mislead Israel, as it is said, "The ox knoweth his owner"[3] (Isa. i. 3).

The Holy One, blessed be He, said to Moses: Israel has forgotten the might of My power, which I wrought for them in Egypt and at the Reed Sea,[4] and they have made an idol for themselves. He said to Moses:[5] Go, get thee down from thy greatness.[6] Moses spake before the Holy One, blessed be He: Sovereign of all the worlds! Whilst Israel had not yet sinned before Thee, Thou didst call them "My people," as it is said, "And I will bring forth *my* hosts, *my* people" (Ex. vii. 4). Now that they have sinned before Thee, Thou sayest unto me, "Go, get thee down, for *thy* people have corrupted themselves" (*ibid.* xxxii. 7). They are Thy people, and Thine inheritance, as it is said, "Yet they are thy people and thine inheritance" (Deut. ix. 29).

Moses took ‖ the tables (of the law),[7] and he descended, and the tables carried their own weight[8] and Moses with them; but when they beheld the calf and the dances,[9] the writing fled from off the tables,[10] and they became heavy in his hands,[11] and Moses was not able to carry himself and

[1] "And they went astray after it" is omitted by the first editions, but it is preserved by R. Bechai in his comm. on Ex. *in loc.*

[2] The later editions read: "Satan." See Introduction, p. li.

[3] The owner is Satan according to the Midrash; see T.B. Berakhoth, 32a, and cf. Ps. cvi. 19, 20. The first editions add here: "All Israel saw it, and kissed it, and bowed down to it, and sacrificed to it."

[4] See Ps. cvi. 22.

[5] The first editions and MS. Gaster read: "as it is said, 'Go, get thee down: for thy people have corrupted themselves' (Ex. xxxii. 7). He spake to Moses: 'Go, get thee down, for thy people have corrupted themselves.'"[1]

[6] See *Rabbinic Philosophy and Ethics*, p. 207.

[7] See T.J. Ta'anith iv. 4. 68b, and Ex. Rab. xxviii. 1. Moses took them against the will of the heavenly host.

[8] See *Rabbinic Philosophy and Ethics*, p. 212; cf. T.B. Soṭah, 35a, with reference to the ark of the Covenant and its transportation. MS. Gaster reads: "When Moses came to the camp and saw the calf."

[9] The first editions read: "the cymbals, the dances, and the calf."

[10] Cf. Aboth de R. Nathan (*a*) xli. p. 67a; T.B. Pesachim, 87b; Leḳach Ṭob, Ex. p. 102a, and see Pal. Targum on Ex. xxxii. 19. The first editions read: "fled and flew away from off the tables."

[11] See T.B. Nedarim, 38a, and Deut. Rab. iii. 12.

---

[1] With idolatry, see Ibn Ezra, *in loc.*

the tables, and he cast them from his hand,[1] and they were broken beneath the mount, as it is said, " And Moses' anger waxed hot,[2] and he cast the tables out of his hands, and brake them beneath the mount "[3] (Ex. xxxii. 19).

Moses said to Aaron : What hast thou done to this people ? Thou hast made them unruly, like a woman who is unchecked[4] owing to immorality. He said to Moses : I saw what they did to Hur, and I feared very greatly.

Rabbi said : All the princes were not associated in the affair of the calf, as it is said, " And upon the nobles[5] of the children of Israel[6] he laid not his hand " (*ibid.* xxiv. 11). The word (" Azilê ") means the " princes," therefore they were accounted worthy to gaze upon the glory[7] of the Shekhinah, as it is said, " And they saw the God of Israel " (*ibid.* 10).[8]

Rabbi Jehudah said : The tribe of Levi[9] also did not associate itself in the affair of the calf, as it is said, " Then Moses stood in the gate of the camp,[6] and said, Whoso is on the Lord's side (let him come) unto me. And all the sons of Levi gathered themselves together unto him " (*ibid.* xxxii. 26). Moses saw that the tribe of Levi was with him.[10] He became strengthened with his might, and he burnt the calf with fire,[11] and powdered it, like the dust[12] of the earth, and he cast its dust upon the face of the waters, as it is said, " And he took the || calf which they had made " (*ibid.* 20). He made Israel drink the water (with the dust of the calf). Everyone who had kissed the calf with all

[1] See T.B. Sabbath, 87b.

[2] Thus far the quotation in the MS. ; the printed texts give the latter part of the verse only.

[3] See Rashbam's comm. *in loc.*

[4] For the phrase cf. Num. v. 18 with Pal. Targum thereon. See also *supra*, p. 100, and cf. Num. Rab. ix. 49.

[5] " Azilê." See T.B. Megillah, 10b ; Tanna de bê Elijahu Rab. ix. p. 52, and cf. Kallah i. (end).

[6] Thus far the quotation in the MS. ; in the first editions it is continued.

[7] The first editions read : " the presence."

[8] *P.R.E.* identifies here the Shekhinah with the Deity.

[9] See T.B. Joma, 66b, and T.B. Chagigah, 6b.

[10] The first editions read : " had not associated itself with them."

[11] The first editions and MS. Gaster read : " Forthwith was he strengthened and endowed with might, that he took the calf and burnt it with fire."

[12] Read כעפר, as in MS. Gaster and the Venice edition.

his heart, his upper lip and his bones [1] became golden,[2] and the tribe of Levi slew him,[3] until there fell of Israel about three thousand men,[4] as it is said, " And the sons of Levi did according to the word of Moses " (*ibid.* 28).

The Holy One, blessed be He, sent five angels to destroy Israel. (The angels were) Wrath, Anger, Temper, Destruction, and Glow of Anger.[5] Moses heard,[6] and he went to invoke Abraham, Isaac, and Jacob [7] at the Cave of Machpelah, and he said : If ye be of the children of the world to come, stand ye before me in this hour, for behold your children are given over like sheep to the slaughter.[8] Abraham, Isaac, and Jacob stood there before him. Moses spake before the Holy One, blessed be He (saying) : Sovereign of all the worlds ! Didst Thou not swear to these (forefathers) thus to increase their seed like the stars of the heaven, as it is said, " Remember Abraham, Isaac, and Israel,[9] thy servants, to whom thou swarest by thine own self, and saidst unto them, I will multiply your seed as the stars of heaven " (*ibid.* 13).

By the merit of the three patriarchs, the three angels, Wrath, Anger, and Temper, were restrained from (doing harm to) Israel. But two (angels) remained. Moses spake before the Holy One, blessed be He: Sovereign of all the universe ! For the sake of the oath which Thou didst swear unto them, keep back (the angel) Destruction || from Israel, as it is said, " To whom thou swarest by thine own self " (*ibid.*); and Destruction was kept back from Israel, as it is said, " But he, being full of compassion, forgave

[1] The first editions read : " his lips became golden."
[2] Cf. the legend of Midas in Ovid's *Metam.* xi. See also Pal. Targum, Ex. xxxii. 20, and cf. Jalkut Makhiri on Ps. lxxviii. p. 15a.
[3] See Tanna de bê Elijahu Rab. iv. p. 17, and cf. T.B. Joma, *loc. cit.*
[4] The quotation does not appear in the printed editions.
[5] See Ex. Rab. xli. 5 (end) ; Shocher Tob on Ps. vii. p. 33b ; Tanchuma (ed. Buber), Ex. pp. 57a, b ; Deut. Rab. iii. 11 ; and cf. T.B. Sabbath, 55a ; T.B. Nedarim, 32a ; and T.B. Berakhoth, *loc. cit.*
[6] God's threat to destroy Israel ; see Ex. xxxii. 10.
[7] See Jalkut on Ps. vii. § 637 : "He went to the cave of Machpelah," as in our MS. ; this phrase does not occur in the printed editions of our book. See also Midrash Agadah, Ex. p. 182. For a parallel in Christian literature see the Acts of Andrew and Matthias (*A.N.C.L.* xvi. p. 356) ; cf. also 4 Ezra vii. 106 f., and Assumption of Moses, xii. 6.
[8] For this phrase see Jer. xii. 3. Cf. T.B. Sabbath, 129b.
[9] The quotation ends here in the MS. and the first editions.

their iniquity,[1] and *destroyed*[2] (them) not" (Ps. lxxviii. 38). Moses spake before the Holy One, blessed be He: Sovereign of all worlds! For the sake of Thy great and holy Name, which Thou didst make known unto me,[3] hold back from Israel (the angel called) Glow of Anger, (as it is said,[4]) "Turn away from thy *fierce*[5] *anger*" (Ex. xxxii. 12). What did Moses do? He dug in the earth in the possession of Gad,[6] as (though for the foundation of) a large dwelling, and he buried "Fierce Anger" in the earth,[7] like a man who is bound in the prison.[8] Every time Israel sins it arises and opens its mouth to bite[9] with its breath, and to destroy Israel. Moses pronounced against it the (divine) Name,[10] and brought it down beneath the earth. Therefore is its name called Peor (the one who opens). When Moses died, what did the Holy One, blessed be He, do? He put his burial-place opposite to it. Every time Israel sins[11] it opens its mouth to bite with its breath, and to destroy Israel, but (when) it sees the burial-place of Moses opposite to it, it[12] returns backward, as it is said, "And he buried him in the valley,[13] in the land of Moab, over against the house of Peor" (Deut. xxxiv. 6).[14]

[1] In the MS. the quotation ends here, it is continued in the first editions. See Wisdom xviii. 22, 25 for a parallel.

[2] *i.e.* there was no "Destruction." Cf. Deut. x. 10.

[3] The first editions and MS. Gaster read: "For the sake of the oath which thou didst swear unto me."

[4] "As it is said" is wanting in the MS.; it occurs in the first editions.

[5] חרון, fierce; also used as the name of the angel here.

[6] See Tosaphoth to T.B. Soṭah, 14a. The first editions and MS. Gaster read: "the children of Gad."

[7] Cf. Job xl. 13 with Targum thereon, and Lev. Rab. x. (end).

[8] Cf. Jubilees xlviii. 15: "the prince of the Mastema was bound and imprisoned."

[9] Einhorn suggests the reading לנשוף, "to blow," instead of לנשוך, "to bite." See T.B. Synhedrin, 64a. MS. Gaster reads: "to blow."

[10] The New Testament speaks of the invocation of the name of Jesus in order to exorcise demons; see Mark ix. 38 and Acts iv. 10.

[11] See Tosaphoth to T.B. Soṭah, *loc. cit.*: "Every year at that season when they sinned with the daughters of Moab, it arises to accuse them."

[12] The first editions and MS. Gaster add: "it becomes afraid."

[13] The quotation ends here in the MS.; it is continued in the first editions.

[14] See Pal. Targum, *in loc.*, and Jalkuṭ, Deut. § 965.

CHAPTER XLVI

MOSES ON THE MOUNT [64A. ii.]

RABBI ELAẒAR, son of 'Aẓariah, said: On Friday, || on the 6th of the month,[1] at the sixth hour of the day, Israel received the Commandments.[2] At the ninth hour of the day they returned to their tents, and the Manna was prepared for them for two days,[3] and Israel rested on that Sabbath full of joy as (with) the joy of the festival, because they were worthy to hear the voice of the Holy One, blessed be He, as it is said, "For who is there of all flesh,[4] that hath heard the voice of the living God speaking out of the midst of the fire, as we have, and lived?" (Deut. v. 26). The Holy One, blessed be He, said to Moses in a pure expression of speech:[5] Go, tell the children of Israel, that for My sake they should return to their tents, (as it is said,[6]) "Go, say to them, Return ye to your tents" (*ibid.* 30). It is possible that even thou (Moses) shouldst return. Hence thou mayest learn that from the hour when Moses brought down the Torah to Israel, he did not approach his wife,[7] as it is said, "But as for thee, stand thou *here by me*" (*ibid.* 31).

Rabbi Joshua, son of Ḳorchah, said: Forty days was Moses on the mountain, reading the Written Law by day, and

[1] See *supra*, p. 318; and cf. Mekhilta, Jethro iii. p. 63b; T.B. Sabbath, 86b and 88a; Book of Jashar lxxxii. 6; Pal. Targum to Ex. xix. 16; and cf. Roḳeach, 296.

[2] *i.e.* at 12 o'clock noon; the day begins at 6 a.m.; see Tosephta 'Arakhin i. 9, p. 543.

[3] For Friday and Sabbath.

[4] The quotation ends here in the MS.; in the first editions it is continued up to "living God."

[5] *i.e.* an elegant expression, euphemism. "Tent" signifies the wife who is to be found in the *tent*. This is wanting in MS. Gaster.

[6] "As it is said" is wanting in the MS.; it occurs in the first editions.

[7] See *Rabbinic Philosophy and Ethics*, p. 270, where in note 2 it is pointed out that the Church Father Aphraates knew this legend.

studying the Oral Law[1] by night. After the forty days he took the tables (of the Law) and descended into the camp on the 17th of Tammuz,[2] and he broke in pieces the tables, and slew the sinners[3] in Israel. He then spent forty days in the camp, until he had burnt the calf, and powdered it like[4] the dust of the earth,[5] and he had destroyed the idol worship from Israel,[6] and he instituted every tribe in its place. And on the New Moon of Ellul[7] the Holy One, blessed be He, said to him: "Come up || to me on the mount" (Ex. xxiv. 12), and let them sound the Shophar (trumpet) throughout the camp, for, behold, Moses has ascended the mount, so that they do not go astray again after the worship of idols. The Holy One, blessed be He, was exalted[8] with that Shophar, as it is said, "God is exalted[9] with a shout,[10] the Lord with the sound of a trumpet" (Ps. xlvii. 5).

Therefore the sages instituted that the Shophar should be sounded on the New Moon of Ellul every year.[11]

Rabbi Tachanah[12] said: The tables (of the Law) were not created out of the earth but out of the heavens, the handicraft[13] of the Holy One, blessed be He, as it is said, "And the tables, the work of God were *they*" (Ex. xxxii. 16).

[1] Lit. "Mishnah." See Shocher Tob on Ps. xix. 7, p. 83b.

[2] See Mishnah Ta'anith, 26b.

[3] See Nachmanides, Commentary on Ex. xxxiii. 7. Asheri at end of T.B. Rosh Ha-Shanah reads: "the Levites slew the Israelites." The first editions read ל"ט'.

[4] See *supra*, p. 356, n. 12. The first editions read: "in the dust." Luria's text reads: "like the dust."

[5] The first editions and MS. Gaster add: "and he had slain everyone who had kissed the calf."

[6] Cf. T.B. 'Abodah Ẓarah, 44a.

[7] Asheri (*loc. cit.*) considers the reading in our text to be faulty. Moses was three times on Mount Sinai, each time forty days. On the 18th of Tammuẓ he ascended the second time and descended on the 29th of Ab. See Ṡeder 'Olam Rab. vi. p. 15a; Midrash Agadah, Ex. p. 185; Tanchuma, Ki Thissa, § xxxi.; Lekach Tob, Ex. p. 103b; and cf. Tosaphoth on T.B. Baba Kamma, 82a, catchword, "In order that." Nachmanides, Comm. Ex. *loc. cit.*, also disputes our author. See also Rokeach, 208; Tanna de bê Elijahu Zutta, iv. p. 178; and Jalkut, Ex. § 391.

[8] The first editions read: "on that day and with that Shophar."

[9] R.V. gives "gone up."

[10] The quotation ends here in the MS.; in the first editions it is continued.

[11] See Ṭur, Orach Chayyim, 581, which reads: "every year and during all the month." See Menorath Ha-Maor, § 290, and Jarchi's Manhig, 24.

[12] Cf. *infra*, p. 430.

[13] Cf. Ps. cii. 25, for phraseology. See Lekach Tob, Ex. p. 102a, and Jalkut, Ex. § 392.

They are the tables which were of old,[1] "*and the writing*" was divine writing; that was the writing which was of old, "*graven*[2] *upon the tables.*" Do not read Charuth, "graven," but (read) Chêruth, "liberty."[3] When the Holy One, blessed be He, said to Moses: "Hew thee two tables of stone[4] like unto the first" (*ibid.* xxxiv. 1), a quarry of sapphires[5] was created for Moses in the midst of his tent,[6] and he cut them out (thence), as it is said, "And he hewed two tables of stone like unto the first" (*ibid.* 4). Moses descended with the tables, and spent forty days on the mountain, sitting down before the Holy One, blessed be He, like a disciple who is sitting before his teacher,[7] reading the Written Law, and repeating the Oral Law which he had learnt.

The ministering angels said to him: Moses! This Torah has been given only for our sakes.[8] Moses replied to them: It is written in the Torah, "Honour thy father[9] || and thy mother" (*ibid.* xx. 12). Have ye then father and mother? Again, it is written in the Torah, "When a man dieth in the tent" (Num. xix. 14). Does death happen among you?[10] They were silent, and did not answer anything further.[11]

Hence (the sages) say: Moses went up to the heavenly regions with his wisdom, and brought down the might of the trust[12] of the ministering angels, as it is said, "A wise man[13]

1 "Mikkedem" probably refers in our book to premundane creation; see *supra*, p. 11. The text of the verse Ex. xxxii. 16 continues: "And the writing was the writing of God, graven upon the tables."

2 This word only is given in the MS.; the first editions continue the quotation.

3 See T.B. 'Erubin, 54a. The meaning of the Haggadah is: You are free if you observe the Torah. See Aboth vi. 2; and Aboth de R. Nathan (*a*) ii. p. 5b.

4 Thus far the quotation in the MS. and in the first editions.

5 See T.B. Nedarim, 38a.

6 See Siphrê, Num. § 101; Lev. Rab. xxxii. 2; Eccles. Rab. to Eccles. ix. 11, and x. (end).

7 See T.B. Megillah, 21a.

8 See T.B. Sabbath, 88a, with reference to the first tables; here in our book the second tables are considered.

9 Thus far our MS. text; the first editions read till "mother." See Pesikta Rabbathi, p. 98a.

10 The first editions add: "(The Torah) has been given for our sake only." See *Rabbinic Philosophy and Ethics*, pp. 198 ff., where the legend as told by the Talmud B. Sabbath, 88b and 89a, is translated. See also T.B. Chagigah, 16a.

11 The phrase is borrowed from Job xxxii. 15.

12 *i.e.* the great trust.

13 *i.e.* Moses.

scaleth the city of the mighty,[1] and bringeth down the strength[2] of the confidence thereof" (Prov. xxi. 22). When the ministering angels saw that the Holy One, blessed be He, gave the Torah to Moses, they also arose and gave unto him presents and letters[3] and tablets[4] for healing the sons of man, as it is said, "Thou hast ascended on high, thou hast led thy captivity captive;[5] thou hast received gifts among men" (Ps. lxviii. 18).

The Son of Bethera said: Moses spent forty days on the mount, expounding the meaning of the words of the Torah, and examining its letters.[6] After forty days he took the Torah, and descended on the tenth of the month,[7] on the Day of Atonement, and gave it as an *everlasting* inheritance to the children of Israel, as it is said, "And *this* shall be unto you an *everlasting* statute" (Lev. xvi. 34).[8]

Rabbi Zechariah said: They read in the Torah[9] and found written therein, "And ye shall afflict your souls" (*ibid.* 29), and on the Day of Atonement[10] they caused a Shophar to be sounded throughout all the camp and proclaimed a fast for all Israel,[11] old and young.[12] Were it not for the Day of Atonement the world could not stand,[13] because the Day of Atonement is[14] in this world and in the world to

[1] *i.e.* Heaven. The angels are called mighty heroes; see Ps. ciii. 20, and cf. Aboth de R. Nathan (*a*) xxiii. p. 38a; Lev. Rab. xxxi. 5. The angels according to the Midrash are male creatures, "Gibborim." They have no females in their company. In the MS. the quotation ends here; it is continued in the first editions.

[2] *i.e.* the Torah. See *supra*, p. 319, on "'Ôẓ" (might) as a term used to denote the Torah.

[3] The Prague edition reads: "bound together" instead of "letters." This is an error.

[4] See T.B. Ḳiddushin, 73b; "Pittaḳin," πιττάκιον, tablet. See *infra*, p. 399, and *Rabbinic Philosophy and Ethics*, p. 260.

[5] The quotation ends here in the MS. and in the first editions.

[6] See T.B. Menachoth, 29b.

[7] The first editions read: "the seventh month."

[8] See Leḳach Ṭob, Ex. p. 103b. "This" (Ẓôth) refers to the Torah in the Midrash. Here it also refers to the institution of the Day of Atonement. See Seder 'Olam Rab. vi. p. 15a, note 17; and Tanna de bê Elijahu Ẓuṭṭa iv. p. 181.

[9] See T.B. Giṭṭin, 60a, on the public reading of the Torah. The section referred to is Lev. xxi.–xxiv.

[10] The first editions read: "on that selfsame day."

[11] The first editions read: "all the people, both men and women."

[12] See T.B. Sukkah, 28a, b.

[13] See my sermon on "Judaism: the Religion of Life" (1913), p. 4.

[14] The Venice edition reads: "effects atonement." MS. Gaster omits till "effects reconciliation" (p. 363).

come,[1] || as it is said, "It is a sabbath of sabbaths unto you" (*ibid.* 31). "A sabbath" refers to this world, "sabbaths" refers to the world to come. Moreover, if all the festivals pass away,[2] the Day of Atonement will not pass away, for the Day of Atonement effects reconciliation for serious offences[3] as well as for slight offences. Whence do we know that the Day of Atonement effects reconciliation? Because it is said, "For on this day shall atonement be made[4] for you, to cleanse you; *from all* your sins shall ye be clean" (*ibid.* 30). "From your sins" is not written here, but "from *all* your sins shall ye be clean before the Lord" (*ibid.*).

Sammael[5] said before the Holy One, blessed be He: Sovereign of all the universe! Thou hast given me power[6] over all the nations of the world, but over Israel Thou hast not given me power. He answered him, saying: Behold, thou hast power over them on the Day of Atonement if they have any sin, but if not, thou hast no power over them. Therefore they gave him a present[7] on the Day of Atonement, in order that they should not bring their offering,[8] as it is said, "One lot for the Lord, and the other lot for *Azazel*"[9] (*ibid.* 8).

The lot for the Holy One, blessed be He, was the offering of a burnt offering, and the lot for Azazel was the goat as a sin offering, for all the iniquities of Israel were upon it, as it

[1] See T.B. Joma, 86a, and T.B. Kethuboth, 103b.

[2] According to one opinion all the festivals except Purim will pass away in the future; cf. T.J. Megillah, i. 7. 70d.

[3] See Mishnah Shebu'oth i. 1; Maimonides, Hilkhoth Teshubah i. 2. Cf. T.B. Kerithoth, 26a.

[4] The quotation ends here in the MS.; it is continued in the first editions.

[5] The first editions read: "On the day when the Torah was given, Sammael," etc.

[6] See T.B. Joma, 20a. The New Testament has a parallel idea. See the expression "son of the devil," Acts xiii. 10, and cf. Matt. iii. 7, and John viii. 44.

[7] Or "bribe."

[8] To Sammael. The first editions read: "in order not to annul the offering of Israel." Luria suggests an alteration in the text: "that he should not come nigh to accuse them." See 'Arukh, ed. Kohut, vi. p. 182a, *s.v.* עזא, and cf. R. Bechai, *in loc.*, and T.B. Joma, 67b, for the only reference in the Talmud to 'Aẓẓa (or, 'Uẓẓa) and *Azazel* as angels. See also Jastrow, T.D. 1049a, and cf. T.B. Nedarim, 32b, and Lev. Rab. xxi. on "Satan," and see Roḳeach, 216.

[9] Azazel is to be identified with Satan or Sammael. See Zunz, *Gesammelte Schriften*, i. p. 236.

is said, "And the goat shall bear upon him[1] all their iniquities" (*ibid.* 22). Sammael saw that sin was not to be found among them on the Day of Atonement. He said before the Holy One, blessed be He: Sovereign of all the universe! Thou hast one people like the ministering angels who are in heaven. Just as the ministering angels || have bare feet,[2] so have the Israelites bare feet on the Day of Atonement.[3] Just as the ministering angels have neither food nor drink,[4] so the Israelites have neither food nor drink on the Day of Atonement. Just as the ministering angels have no joints, in like wise the Israelites stand upon their feet. Just as the ministering angels have peace obtaining amongst them,[5] so the Israelites have peace obtaining amongst them on the Day of Atonement.[6] Just as the ministering angels are innocent of all sin on the Day of Atonement, so are the Israelites innocent of all sin on the Day of Atonement. The Holy One, blessed be He, hears the prayers[7] of Israel rather than (the charges brought by) their accuser,[8] and He makes atonement for the altar, and for the sanctuary, and for the priests,[9] and for all the people of the congregation both great and small, as it is said, "And he shall make atonement for the holy place" (*ibid.* 16).

Moses said: On the Day of Atonement I will behold the glory of the Holy One, blessed be He, and I will make atonement for the iniquities of Israel.[10] Moses spake before the Holy One, blessed be He: Sovereign of all the universe! "Shew me, I pray thee, thy glory" (Ex. xxxiii. 18). The Holy One, blessed be He, said to him: Moses! Thou art

[1] Thus far the quotation in the MS.

[2] The first editions read: "have no joints," *i.e.* in the feet and legs, and therefore they cannot sit down. See T.J. Berakhoth i. p. 2c; Gen. Rab. lxv. 21; Ruth Rab. i. (beg.); and 'Arukh, *s.v.* קפץ.

[3] The custom still obtains. See Orach Chayyim, 124.

[4] The first editions add: "on the Day of Atonement."

[5] See T.B. Chagigah, 15a; Shocher Ṭob on Ps. i. p. 1b.

[6] See T.B. Joma, 58b. The Day of Atonement effects atonement only between God and man; in order for man to be fully pardoned he must be reconciled with his fellow-creature. Cf. T.B. Ta'anith, 22a.

[7] The Prague edition reads: "their testimony." MS. Gaster reads: "the misfortunes of Israel."

[8] "Ḳatêgôr," κατήγορος, accuser. See *Rabbinic Philosophy and Ethics*, p. 74. Should the line read: "rather than the testimony of Israel from the accuser"?

[9] See Mishnah Shebu'oth i. 1, and T.B. Shebu'oth, 14b.

[10] Moses stood in the cleft of the rock and beheld the Divine Vision on the Day of Atonement, when God pardoned Israel.

not able to see My glory lest thou die, as it is said, "For men shall not see me and live" (*ibid.* 20); but for the sake of the oath which I have sworn unto thee[1] I will do thy will. Stand at the entrance of || the cave,[2] and I will make all the angels[3] who move[4] before Me pass before thy face. Stand in thy might, and do not fear, as it is said, "And he said, I will make all my goodness pass before thee" (*ibid.* 19). When thou dost hear the Name which I have spoken to thee,[5] there am I before thee, as it is said, "And he said, I will make all my goodness pass before thee" (*ibid.*).[6]

The ministering angels said: Behold, we serve before Him by day and by night, and we are unable to see His glory,[7] and this one born of woman[8] desires to see His glory. And they arose[9] in wrath and excitement[10] to slay him, and his soul came nigh unto death.[11] What did the Holy One, blessed be He, do? He revealed Himself unto him in a cloud,[12] as it is said, "And the Lord descended in the cloud" (*ibid.* xxxiv. 5). This was the seventh descent.[13]

The Holy One, blessed be He, protected him[14] with the hollow of His hand that he should not die, as it is said, "And it shall come to pass, while my glory passeth by,[15] that I will put thee in a cleft of the rock, and I will cover thee with my hand" (*ibid.* xxxiii. 22). When the Holy

[1] See *supra*, p. 358. The first editions add: "and the Name which I have made known unto thee."

[2] See Pal. Targum, Ex. xxxiii. 22. Cf. 1 Kings xix. 9; Elijah stood at the entrance of the cave. Cf. T.B. Megillah, 19b.

[3] Where do we find this idea? See Midrash Agadah, Ex. p. 185.

[4] The first editions read: "who minister."

[5] See Ex. Rab. xxiii. 15.

[6] Instead of this part of the verse, the first editions read here: "'And I will be gracious to whom I will be gracious, and I will shew mercy on whom I will shew mercy'" (Ex. xxxiii. 19).

[7] See Siphrê, Num. § 58, and Num. Rab. xiv. 21. Cf. *supra*, p. 25. The first editions have all the pronouns referring to God in the second person.

[8] Who sleeps by night. Cf. *Rabbinic Philosophy and Ethics*, pp. 198 f., and Aboth de R. Nathan (*a*) ii. p. 5b, note 39.

[9] Against "him" is added by the first editions and MS. Gaster.

[10] The wording is borrowed from 2 Chron. xxvi. 20. See T.B. Megillah, 29a.

[11] Cf. Dan. iii. 28.

[12] To protect him. See T.B. Chullin, 91b.

[13] See *supra*, p. 97.

[14] Cf. Ps. xci. 4: "He shall cover thee with his pinions, and under his wings shalt thou take refuge." See Pesikta Rabbathi, p. 37b; and Tanchuma (ed. Buber), Ex. p. 57a.

[15] The quotation ends here in the MS.

One, blessed be He, had passed by, He removed the hollow of His hand from him, and he saw the traces of the Shekhinah, as it is said, " And I will take away mine hand,[1] and thou shalt see my back " (*ibid.* 23). Moses began to cry with a loud voice, and he said : [2] " O Lord, O Lord, a God full of compassion and gracious . . ." (*ibid.* xxxiv. 6).

Moses said before the Holy One, blessed be He : Sovereign of all worlds ! Pardon now the iniquities of this people.[3] He said to him : Moses ! If thou hadst said, Pardon now the iniquities of all Israel, even to the end of all generations (He would have done so).[4] It was an acceptable time. || But thou hast said : Pardon, I beseech Thee, the iniquities of this people with reference to the affair of the calf. He said to him : Moses ! Behold, let it be according to thy words, as it is said, " And the Lord said, I have pardoned according to thy word " (Num. xiv. 20).[5]

[1] In the MS. and the first editions the quotation ends here.

[2] Moses is the one who declares the thirteen divine attributes. See T.B. Joma, 36b.

[3] The first editions and MS. Gaster read : "the iniquities of Israel in connection with the affair of the (golden) calf. But if Moses had said : Pardon," etc.

[4] The words : " He would have done so," do not occur in our MS. ; but the first editions and MS. Gaster have this reading, and they add : " because it was an acceptable time ; and thus it says : 'In an acceptable time have I answered thee' " (Isa. xlix. 8). See T.B. Berakhoth, 8a, and T.B. Jebamoth, 72a.

[5] See Ex. Rab. li. 4, and Deut. Rab. iii. 17.

CHAPTER XLVII

THE ZEAL OF PHINEAS [66A. i.]

RABBI ELAZAR, son of 'Arakh, said: When the Holy One, blessed be He, descended upon Mount Sinai to give the Torah to Israel, sixty myriads [1] of the ministering angels descended with Him, corresponding to the sixty myriads of the mighty men of Israel, and in their hands were swords and crowns,[2] and they crowned the Israelites with [3] the Ineffable Name.[4] All those days, whilst they had not done that deed,[5] they were as good as [6] the ministering angels before the Holy One, blessed be He. The Angel of Death did not hold sway over them, and they did not discharge any excretions [7] like the children of man; but when they did that deed the Holy One, blessed be He, was angry with them, and He said to them: I thought that ye would be [8] like the ministering angels, as it is said, "I said, Ye are angels,[9] and all of you sons of the Most High" (Ps. lxxxii. 6). But now, "Nevertheless, ye shall die like men" (*ibid.* 7).

Rabbi Jehudah said: As long as a man is dressed in

[1] רבוא, "ten thousand." See T.B. Sabbath, 88a; and cf. Cant. Rab. on Cant. iii. 7.

[2] Cf. Wisdom xviii. 16; Cant. Rab. on Cant. viii. 4; Ex. Rab. xxix. 2; Ẓohar, Ex. 193b; Pesiḳta, pp. 107b, 124b; and the Targumim on Ex. xxxiii. 5. See 'Arukh, *s.v.* ויינאות, וניאות, ויינות, and Pesiḳta Rabbathi, pp. 98b, 154a.

[3] The first editions add: "with the diadem of."

[4] See *supra*, p. 22, and Bacher, T. ii. 118.

[5] The making of the golden calf.

[6] The first editions read: "They were better than the ministering angels."

[7] See T.B. Joma, 75b; and cf. Num. Rab. vii. 4. The gnostics held similar views with reference to Jesus; see F. C. Conybeare, *Myth, Magic, and Morals*, p. 232.

[8] The first editions add: "before Me."

[9] "Elohim"; cf. Judg. xiii. 22. The quotation in our MS. ends here, but it is continued in the first editions.

his garments of glory, he is beautiful in his appearance[1] and in his honour;[2] so were the Israelites when they apparelled themselves with that Name—they were good before the Holy One, blessed be He, like the ministering angels. But when they did that deed (of the golden calf), the Holy One, blessed be He, was angry with them.[3] || In that night the same[4] sixty myriads of ministering angels[5] descended,[6] and they severally took from each one of them what they had put upon them, and they became bare,[7] not according to their own wish, as it is said,[8] "And the children of Israel stripped themselves" (Ex. xxxiii. 6). It is not written here,[9] "the children of Israel took away," but "the children of Israel stripped themselves." Some say by itself (their adornment) was stripped off.[10]

Rabbi said: At every place where Israel *sat down*[11] in the wilderness, they made idols[12] for themselves, as it is said, "And the people *sat down* to eat and to drink" (*ibid.* xxxii. 6). What is written here? "And they rose up to play" (*ibid.*); they commenced to worship idols. One verse says, "And Israel *abode* in Shittim" (Num. xxv. 1). What is written here? "And the people began to commit whoredom[13] with the daughters of Moab" (*ibid.*). They commenced to be immoral.[14]

[1] This reminds one of the English proverb: "Fine feathers make fine birds."

[2] The first editions add: "and in his glory."

[3] The first editions add: "and He said to them: 'Put off thy ornaments from thee, that I may know what to do unto thee'" (Ex. xxxiii. 5).

[4] "The same" is in the MS. only.

[5] See the different account in T.B. Sabbath, *loc. cit.*; according to this version, "One hundred and twenty myriads of ministering angels" were present at the Revelation at Sinai.

[6] The first editions add: "Corresponding to the sixty myriads of the strong men of Israel."

[7] Cf. *supra*, p. 98.

[8] The quotation is wanting in the MS.; it occurs in the first editions.

[9] The first editions read: "'They were stripped off,' but 'they stripped themselves' with all their strength." The later editions modify the last words and read: "against their will."

[10] Or, "it peeled off."

[11] The verb here means "to sit down" or "to abide."

[12] See Ex. Rab. xli. 11: "wherever you find a reference to sitting down you find some stumbling block" (occurring to the Israelites). Cf. also T.B. Synhedrin, 107a.

[13] In the MS. the quotation ends here: it is continued in the first editions.

[14] The first editions add: "This is idolatry."

Rabbi Jehudah said: "The counsel of the wicked is far from me" (Job xxi. 16). This (text) refers to the counsel of Balaam, the wicked, who advised Midian, and there fell of Israel twenty-four thousand men. He said to them: You will not be able to prevail against this people, unless they have sinned before their Creator. They made for themselves booths[1] outside the camp of Israel, and they sold all kinds of merchandise of the market. The young men of Israel went beyond the camp of Israel and they saw the daughters of Midian, who had painted[2] their eyes like harlots, and they took wives of them, and went astray || after them, as it is said, "And the people began to commit whoredom with the daughters of Moab" (Num. xxv. 1).[3]

Simeon and Levi were exceedingly zealous because of the immorality, as it is said, "And they said, As with an harlot[4] should he deal with our sister?" (Gen. xxxiv. 31). Each man took his sword and they slew the men of Shechem. The prince of the tribe of Simeon[5] did not remember that which his ancestor[6] had done, and he did not rebuke the young men of Israel, but he himself came[7] publicly[8] to the Midianitish woman for an immoral purpose, as it is said, "Now the name of the man of Israel that was slain,[4] who was slain with the Midianitish woman, was Zimri . . . a prince of a fathers' house among the Simeonites" (Num. xxv. 14).

[1] Or "shops"; cf. *Rabbinic Philosophy and Ethics*, p. 242; Num. Rab. xx. 23; T.B. Synhedrin, 82b; and T.J. Synhedrin x. 2. 28d.

[2] In the Book of Jashar (lxxxv. 54) we read: "The children of Moab took all their daughters and wives of beautiful appearance and comely form and dressed them in gold and silver and costly raiment." See T.B. Synhedrin, 106a; Siphrê, Num. § 131; T.J. Synhedrin, *loc. cit.*; cf. T.B. Synhedrin, 82b; Num. Rab., *loc. cit.*; Tânchuma, Balaḳ, § xxvii., and Jalḳuṭ, Num. § 771; Pal. Targum to Num. xxv. 1; Midrash Agadah, Num., p. 147. Twelve miracles were connected with Phineas' deed; see Ginzberg, *Legends of the Jews*, vol. iii. p. 387, and Pal. Targum, Num. xxv. 8.

[3] In the 1st ed. the entire section is wanting; in the 2nd ed. the words "they sold . . . camp of Israel" are omitted.

[4] Thus far the quotation in the MS.; it is continued in the first editions. The next sentence occurs in our MS. only.

[5] See T.B. Synhedrin, *loc. cit.*

[6] Simeon, son of Jacob, was zealous for the honour of his sister Dinah.

[7] The Venice edition adds: "with immorality."

[8] פרהסיא, παρρησία, "openly."

All the princes with Moses, Eleazar, and Phineas saw the angel who was to destroy the people,[1] and they sat down and wept, and they did not know what to do. Phineas saw how Zimri went publicly to the Midianitish woman for an immoral purpose, and he was moved by a great zeal,[2] and he snatched the spear out of the hand of Moses, and ran after (Zimri) and pierced him through the back, through the pudenda, and the spear went into the belly of the woman. Therefore the Holy One, blessed be He, gave a good reward to him and to his sons with the food of the shoulder.[3] And the jaws were separated, the jaws of the man (from) the jaws of the woman; therefore the Holy One, blessed be He, gave him and his sons a good reward with the food of the cheeks,[4] as it is said, "And they shall give unto the priest the shoulder,[5] and the two cheeks, and the maw" (Deut. xviii. 3).

He arose like a great spiritual leader[6] and he judged Israel,[7] as it is said, "Then stood up Phineas, || and he executed *judgment*" (Ps. cvi. 30). What is the meaning of this expression, "And he executed judgment"? Like a great judge. Just as thou dost say,[8] "And he shall pay as the judges determine" (Ex. xxi. 22). And he smote the young men of Israel[9] so that all Israel should see and fear, as it is said, "And all Israel shall hear, and fear" (Deut. xxi. 21).[10] The Holy One, blessed be He, saw what Phineas had done, and forthwith was He filled

[1] The first editions read: "the angel of death."

[2] To slay a prince, chief of one of the tribes.

[3] The first editions read: "gave him the food of the maw. Moreover He strengthened his arms (so that) he fixed the spear in the earth, and they were found hanging from the top of the spear, the one above the other, the man above the woman." See Pal. Targum, Num., *loc. cit.*

[4] The first editions read: "Gave him for food the cheeks." The gifts referred to were portions of certain sacrifices.

[5] In the MS. the quotation ends here; it is continued in the first editions. For the Biblical account of the narrative see Num. xxv. 8. On this section see Gaster, *Jeraḥmeel*, p. xcvii and lv. 10–12, and Ginzberg, *op. cit.* p. 389.

[6] דיין, "judge" or spiritual leader. See Ex. Rab. xxxiii. 5 and T.B. Synhedrin, *loc. cit.*

[7] The first editions read: "a judge for Israel."

[8] This is an unusual form of introducing a quotation from the Bible in this book.

[9] The first editions add here: "and they drew them throughout all the corners of the camp of Israel."

[10] The quotation is given by the MS. only.

with compassion; the plague was stayed, as it is said, "And so the plague was stayed" (Num. xvi. 50).

Rabbi Eliezer said: He called[1] the name of Phineas by[2] the name of Elijah[3]—Elijah of blessed memory,[4] (who was) of those who repented in Gilead, for he brought about the repentance of Israel[5] in the land of Gilead. The Holy One, blessed be He, gave him the life of this world and the life of the world to come,[6] as it is said,[7] "My covenant was with him[8] of *life* and *peace*" (Mal. ii. 5). He gave to him and to his sons a good reward,[9] in order that (he might have) the everlasting priesthood, as it is said, "And it shall be unto him, and to his seed[10] after him, the covenant of an everlasting priesthood" (Num. xxv. 13).

Rabbi Elazar of Modein said: Phineas arose, and pronounced the ban[11] upon Israel by the mystery of the Ineffable Name, and with the script which was written on the tables (of the Law), and by the ban of the celestial Court of Justice,[12] and by the ban of the terrestrial Court of Justice, that a man of Israel should not drink the wine

[1] The first editions read: "The Holy One, blessed be He, changed." See Jalkuṭ, Num., *loc. cit.*

[2] The text literally means "like." Phineas flies in the heavens (see Pal. Targum to Num. xxxi. 8) by invoking the Ineffable Name. This is also done by Elijah; cf. Basset, *Les Apocryphes éthiopiens*, vii. p. 26; a parallel story occurs in the conflict between Peter and Simon Magus (see Hastings' *D.B.* iv. p. 523).

[3] According to the Midrash Elijah was from Jerusalem of the tribe of Benjamin; see Ex. Rab. xl. 4; Gen. Rab. lxxi. 9; Tanna de bê Elijahu Rab. xviii. pp. 97 f. and note 57; and Tanna de bê Elijahu Ẓuṭṭa xv. p. 199 (end). Cf. Tosaphoth on T.B. Baba Mezi'a, 113b.

[4] See *supra*, p. 2.

[5] See T.B. Synhedrin, 106b, and Siphrê, Num., *loc. cit.*

[6] See T.B. Mo'ed Ḳaṭan, 26a, "Elijah lives on"; cf. Ps. cvi. 30, where Phineas is spoken of by the Psalmist.

[7] "'Behold, I give my covenant of peace,' and it is written: 'My covenant was with him.'" This is the reading in the Jalkuṭ, Num., *loc. cit.*, and is probably the most correct version preserved. "My covenant was with him" refers to Elijah, who is called the "angel." Phineas is also called the "angel"; see Lev. Rab. i. 1.

[8] The quotation ends here in the MS.; it is continued in the first editions.

[9] The first editions add: "between the righteous and the wicked."

[10] The MS. reads "sons" instead of "seed after him," which is the MT. and the reading in the first editions.

[11] On the ban and the bread of the Cutheans see *supra*, p. 301.

[12] Cf. Liturgy of Evening of Day of Atonement, introduction to כל נדרי.

of the nations [1] unless it had been trodden by the feet, as it is said, "And as for my sheep, that which ye have trodden with your feet [2] they eat, and they drink that which ye have fouled with your feet" [3] (Ezek. xxxiv. 19). Because all the wine of the nations was devoted to idolatry and immorality, for they took the first of their new wine for idolatry and immorality,[4] as it is said, "Whoredom and wine [5] || and new wine take away the heart" (Hos. iv. 11).

Rabbi Phineas said: The Holy One, blessed be He, said to Moses: Do ye remember what those Midianites did to you, for twenty-four thousand men fell in Israel? But before "thou art gathered in," [6] arise, execute vengeance,[7] (as it is said,[8]) "Avenge the children of Israel of the Midianites; afterwards shalt thou be gathered unto thy people" (Num. xxxi. 2).[9]

What did Moses do? He took a thousand men [10] (and) a prince [11] from each tribe of the tribes of Israel. Behold, (there were) twelve thousand (men), and he who had been zealous because of the immorality, was the prince [12] over them. The [13] holy vestments and the trumpets of alarm [14]

[1] For the parallel in the New Testament see 1 Cor. viii. 1 ff. and *ibid.* x. 20 f., and the parallel passages.

[2] The quotation ends here in the MS.; it is continued in the first editions.

[3] The Venice edition adds here: "For all the wine of the heathens is poured out for idolatrous purposes and for immoral purposes."

[4] The orgies in connection with the Bacchic rites illustrate this statement.

[5] The quotation ends here in our MS. The first editions continue thus: "Another verse says: 'Be not among winebibbers; among gluttonous eaters of flesh'" (Prov. xxiii. 20).

[6] *i.e.* before thy death.

[7] The first editions add: "on them."

[8] The MS. omits "as it is said," and reads only the first two words of the verse; the first editions have: "as it is said."

[9] The command to punish the Midianites on account of the Peor idolatry was not put into execution immediately. Moreover, the punishment of the Amalekites was to be deferred until the Israelites had possession of the Holy Land.

[10] See Siphrê, Num. § 157, and cf. Tanchuma (Buber), Maṭṭoth, p. 79b, for the meaning: "two thousand from each tribe."

[11] "a prince" occurs in the MS. only; it is apparently an error.

[12] Phineas, see T.B. Soṭah, 43a; Siphrê, Num., *loc. cit.*; and cf. 1 Chron. ix. 20.

[13] The first editions read: "They took the holy vestments."

[14] תרועה, "alarm."

were in his hand,[1] and they went, and they took captive the daughters of Midian, and they brought them (to the camp).[2] (Moses) said to (Phineas): Because of these did not twenty-four thousand men of Israel fall? as it is said, "Behold, these[3] caused the children of Israel, through the counsel of Balaam,[4] to commit trespass against the Lord in the matter of Peor" (*ibid.* 16); and he began to be angry with them, as it is said, "And Moses was wroth with the officers of the host" (*ibid.* 14).[5] During his anger the Holy Spirit departed from him. Hence thou mayest learn that the impetuous[6] man destroys his wisdom.[7] Eleazar saw[8] and he heard (the voice) behind (Moses),[9] as it is said, "And Eleazar the priest said[10] unto the men of war ... This is the statute of the Law which the Lord hath commanded Moses" (*ibid.* 21). He[11] said to them: He[12] commanded Moses and He did not command me.

[1] The first editions read: "in their hand."
[2] The first editions read here: "And Moses heard, and he went forth to meet them, and he saw them."
[3] The preceding verse says: "And Moses said unto them: Have ye saved all the women alive?"
[4] The quotation ends here in the MS. and in the first editions.
[5] See Jalkuṭ, Num. § 785, which quotes the Siphrê Ẓuṭṭa; see also Siphrê, Num., *loc. cit.*
[6] קפדן, "hot-tempered," "impatient."
[7] Cf. Eccles. vii. 7, and see Eccles. Rab. on Eccles. vii. 7.
[8] The first editions read: "He (*i.e.* God) called to Eleazar."
[9] It passed by Moses, who failed to hear the Divine message.
[10] In the MS. the quotation ends here; it is continued in the first editions.
[11] Eleazar; see Siphrê, Num., *loc. cit.*, and cf. T.B. Pesachim, 66b, and Aboth de R. Nathan (*a*) i. p. 2a.
[12] God.

CHAPTER XLVIII

THE EGYPTIAN BONDAGE [67A. i.]

RABBAN JOCHANAN, son of Ẓakkai, opened (his exposition with the text): "In that day the Lord made a covenant with Abram,[1] saying, Unto thy seed will I give this land, from the river of Egypt unto the great river, the river Euphrates" (Gen. xv. 18). Abram said before the Holy One, blessed be He, Sovereign of all the universe! Thou hast not given me seed, yet dost Thou say, "Unto thy seed will I give[2] || this land" (*ibid.*). He said: "Whereby shall I know that I shall inherit it?" (*ibid.* 8). The Holy One, blessed be He, said to him: Abram! The entire world stands by My word,[3] and thou dost not believe in My word, but thou sayest, "Whereby *shall I know*[4] that I shall inherit it?" (*ibid.*). By thy life! In two ways shalt thou surely know, as it is said, "And he said to Abram, Know of *a surety*[5] that thy *seed* shall be a *stranger* in a land which is not theirs, . . . and *they shall afflict them*" (*ibid.* 13).

Rabbi Elaẓar, son of 'Aẓariah, said: Is it not so that the Israelites did not dwell in Egypt except for 210[6] years?

[1] The quotation ends here in the MS. and in the first editions.

[2] The MS. reads: "I have given." The first editions have: "will I give this land," and the following is added: "as it is said, 'Behold to me thou hast given no seed'" (Gen. xv. 3).

[3] The first editions read "command" (*Dibbur*) = λόγος. See Shocher Ṭob on Ps. cxix. 89; cf. Jer. xxxi. 3 ff. on the eternity of Israel.

[4] In the MS. the quotation ends here; it is continued in the first editions.

[5] The double form of the verb in the Hebrew text suggests the Haggadic interpretation in our book. One form of the verb is taken to refer to the promise of seed; the other refers to the affliction of Abraham's seed. In the MS. the quotation ends with the word "surety"; in the first editions it is continued.

[6] רד״ו = 200 plus 4 plus 6; *i.e.* 210.

But in order to teach thee, know that this is so, come and see; for when Joseph went down to Egypt he was seventeen years old, and when he stood before Pharaoh he was thirty years old, as it is said, "And Joseph was thirty years old when he stood[1] before Pharaoh, king of Egypt" (*ibid.* xli. 46). And the seven years of plenty, and the two years of famine, behold, they are nine-and-thirty years (in all). And Levi, the son of Jacob, was six years older than Joseph,[2] and when he went down to Egypt he was forty-five years,[3] and the years of his life in Egypt were ninety-two years;[4] behold, all of them (amount to) 137 years, (as it is said,[5]) "And the years of the life of Levi were an hundred thirty and seven years" (Ex. vi. 16). On his going down to Egypt, his wife bare unto him Jochebed, his daughter,[6] as it is said, "And the name of Amram's wife was Jochebed" (Num. xxvi. 59), and she was 130 years[7] when she bare Moses, (as it is said,[8]) "And Moses was fourscore years old when he stood before Pharaoh" (Ex. vii. 7). || Behold, (the total is) 210 years in all.[9] And thus it says, "And they shall serve them; and they shall afflict them[10] four hundred years" (Gen. xv. 13).

Rabbi Elazar, son of 'Arakh, said to them:[11] The Holy One, blessed be He, said this to Abraham only at the hour when he had seed, as it is said, "Thy *seed* shall be a

[1] The quotation ends here in the MS.

[2] See *supra*, p. 272. There was seven months' interval between the birth of each child; Reuben, Simeon, and Levi. The last-named was born in the twenty-first month. Joseph was the last son born in the first seven years of Rachel's married life.

[3] See Pal. Targum to Ex. vi. 16; Levi lived so long that he knew of Moses and Aaron standing before Pharaoh, and see T.B. Baba Bathra, 121b.

[4] See Seder 'Olam Rab. iii. p. 8a: "One hundred and sixteen years elapsed between the death of Levi and the Exodus." See Ratner's note (14), *in loc.* Cf. *Jubilees* (ed. Charles), p. 172.

[5] The MS. and the first edition omit "as it is said"; it occurs in the Venice edition.

[6] See Num. xxvi. 59: "who was born to Levi." Jochebed was called "daughter of Levi" when Amram was married to her.

[7] According to the Book of Jashar lxvii. 2, Jochebed was one hundred and twenty-six years old at her marriage. See Seder 'Olam Rab. iii. p. 7b; Pal. Targum, Ex. ii. 1; T.B. Baba Bathra, 120a; T.B. Megillah, 8a, and Midrash Agadah, Ex. pp. 122 f.

[8] The MS. omits "as it is said"; it occurs in the first editions.

[9] The first editions add: "and the mnemonic is 'Rdu.'" "Descend" is the literal meaning of this word; the numerical value is 210, as above.

[10] In the MS. the quotation ends here.

[11] The first editions read: "said to him," *i.e.* R. Jochanan.

stranger [1] in a land that is not theirs" (*ibid.*). From the time when Isaac was born until Israel went forth from Egypt 400 years (elapsed).[2] (Rabban Jochanan, son of Ẓakkai [3]) said to him: Verily it is written, "Now the sojourning of the children of Israel,[4] which they sojourned in Egypt, was four hundred and thirty years" (Ex. xii. 40). He answered him, saying: 210 [5] years Israel abode in Egypt, and five years before Jacob came to Egypt there were born unto Joseph (the fathers of) two tribes, Manasseh and Ephraim,[6] and they belonged to the Israelites.[7] Behold, (we have) 215 years of days and nights,[8] (this equals) 430 years; for the Holy One, blessed be He, reduced [9] the time for the sake of the merit of the Patriarchs, for they are the mountains of the world,[10] and for the sake of the merit of the Mothers,[11] for they are the hills of the world, and concerning them the Scripture says, "The voice of my beloved! Behold, he

[1] The quotation ends here in the MS. and in the first editions; the latter add: "and it is written, 'For in Isaac shall thy *seed* be called'" (Gen. xxi. 12). And not through Ishmael; see *supra*, p. 215, and cf. T.B. Nedarim, 31a, and Seder 'Olam Rab., *loc. cit.*

[2] Sixty years from the birth of Isaac to the birth of Jacob, plus 130 years when Jacob stood before Pharaoh and 210 years of bondage in Egypt, give a total of 400 years; cf. Seder 'Olam Rab. iii. p. 7a.

[3] The words in brackets are wanting in the MS., but occur in the first editions.

[4] In the MS. the quotation ends here; it is continued in the first editions.

[5] The MS. reads "220 years." The first editions have "210 (Rdu) years." The MS. text is corrupt. This can be proved by the fact that the next sentence speaks of 215 years as the total—210 years plus 5 years. In the previous pages our text mentions "210 years," and this same figure reappears *infra*, p. 391.

[6] See the Book of Jashar l. 15; they were born when Joseph was thirty-four years old, *i.e.* in the fourth year of plenty, for he was thirty years old when he stood before Pharaoh and foretold the seven years of plenty which were to be followed by the years of famine.

[7] The first editions read: "they belonged to the tribes, as it is said, Ephraim and Manasseh, even as Reuben and Simeon, shall be mine'" (Gen. xlviii. 5).

[8] The bondage was by day and night. See Ex. Rab. xviii. 11. The Egyptians prevented the Israelites from living in peace and comfort when the day's work was done. See Haggadah for the Passover (ed. Landshuth), p. 18.

[9] Lit. "skipped."

[10] See *Rabbinic Philosophy and Ethics*, pp. 248 f. The Jalkuṭ, Cant. § 986, reads: "the fathers, who are the mountains of the world; and for the merit of the sons of Jacob, who are the hills of the world"; cf. T.B. Rosh Ha-Shanah, 11a, and Pal. Targum, Gen. xlix. 26.

[11] Sarah, Rebecca, Rachel, and Leah.

cometh,[1] leaping upon the mountains, *skipping* over the hills" (Cant. ii. 8).

Rabbi Eliezer said: During all those years, when the Israelites abode in Egypt, they dwelt securely and peacefully at ease [2] until Ganoon,[3] one of the grandchildren of Ephraim, came and said to them, The Holy One, blessed be He, has revealed Himself to me,[4] to lead you out of Egypt. The children of Ephraim, in the pride of their heart, for they were of the royal seed,[5] and mighty men in battle,[6] took their wives and their sons, || and they went forth from Egypt.[7] The Egyptians pursued after them, and slew of them 200,000, all of them mighty men,[8] as it is said, "The children of Ephraim,[9] being armed and carrying bows, turned back in the day of battle" (Ps. lxxviii. 9).

Rabbi Jannai said: The Egyptians did not enslave the Israelites but for one hour of the day [10] of the Holy One, blessed be He, (that is to say, for) 83⅓ years. Whilst [11] yet Moses was not born, the magicians said to Pharaoh: In the future a child will be born, and he will take Israel out of Egypt.[12] Pharaoh thought, and said: [13] Cast ye all the male

[1] The MS. omits the first part as well as the latter part of the quotation, reading: "leaping upon the mountains." The first editions give the first part of the verse.

[2] As long as they trusted in God and kept faith in His promises. The phrase is borrowed from Prov. i. 33. Cf. *supra*, p. 182.

[3] The printed text of *P.R.E.* reads "Jagnoon." MS. Gaster omits the name. See Introduction, p. l. For the legend see the Book of Jashar, ch. lxxv. For further references in Rabbinical literature see *J.E.* v. 189, and *Rabbinic Philosophy and Ethics*, pp. 256 f.

[4] Cf. Ps. lxxviii. 8, 9. See also Mekhilta Beshallach, p. 24a; Cant. Rab. to verse of Cant. ii. 7; and T.B. Kethuboth, 111a.

[5] Of Joseph, according to Jacob's blessing.

[6] The first editions read: "arose and took their wives, their sons, and their daughters."

[7] This was thirty years before the Exodus. This vain attempt to hasten the Divine Deliverance was the cause of the harsh bondage which began then. See also Seder 'Olam Rab. iii. 7b, for another opinion.

[8] The text is not correct. See Pal. Targum on Ex. xiii. 17 and *ibid.* note 7. Luria reads: "The Egyptians pursued them and slew 200,000, all mighty men, as it is said," etc. MS. Gaster reads: "The Egyptians arose and slew them, as it is said," etc.

[9] In the MS. the quotation ends here.

[10] God's day equals 1000 years, and reckoning 12 hours to the day the hour of God's day equals 83⅓ years. On God's day see *supra*, p. 128

[11] Luria reads: "Three years and a third before Moses was born."

[12] See the Book of Jashar lxvii. 19.

[13] The first editions read: "He thought and said in his heart."

children into the river, and he[1] will be thrown in with them,[2] and thereby the word (of the magicians) will be frustrated; therefore they cast all the (male) children into the river.

Three years (elapsed) until[3] the birth of Moses. When Moses was born they said (to Pharaoh): Behold, he is born, and he is hidden from our vision. (Pharaoh) said to them: Since he is born, henceforth ye shall not cast the male children into the river, but put upon them a hard yoke[4] to embitter the years of their lives with hard labour,[5] as it is said, "And they made their lives bitter" (Ex. i. 14).

Rabbi Nathaniel said: The parents of Moses saw the child, (for) his form was like that of an angel of God.[6] They circumcised him on the eighth day,[7] and they called his name Jekuthiel.[8]

Rabbi Simeon said: They called him Ṭob (good), as it is said, "And when she saw him that he was *good*" (*ibid.* ii. 2). They concealed him in a house || of[9] the earth for three months. After three months[10] she put him in an ark of bulrushes, and she cast him upon the bank of the river. All things are revealed before the Holy One, blessed be He. Now Bithyah,[11] the daughter of Pharaoh, was[12] smitten sorely with leprosy and she was not able to bathe

[1] Moses. See Leḳach Ṭob, Ex. p. 3b; and Pal. Targum, Ex. i. 15.

[2] The first editions add: "as it is said, 'Every son that is born ye shall cast into the river'" (Ex. i. 22).

[3] See Jalḳuṭ, Exodus, § 165, which reads: "For three years and a third of a year they cast them in until Moses was born." The first editions read: "Three years and a third of a year (elapsed) until Moses was born." See also 'Arukh, *s.v.* אהרן, and cf. the Book of Jashar lxviii. 3.

[4] See Deut. xxvi. 6.

[5] The first editions read: "to embitter the lives of their fathers."

[6] See T.B. Soṭah, 12a.

[7] See T.B. Soṭah, *loc. cit.*, and cf. Jalḳuṭ, Gen. § 16.

[8] See the Book of Jashar lxviii. 24 ff. and Jalḳuṭ, Ex. § 166, quoting the Book of Chronicles of Moses on the various names of Moses. See also 1 Chron. iv. 18, where Jekuthiel is spoken of as the son of Bithyah, the daughter of Pharaoh. See the Targum to this verse and cf. T.B. Megillah, 13a. Clement of Alexandria, *Strom.* i. 23, gives Joachim and Melchi as names of Moses.

[9] The first editions read: "beneath the earth for three months, as it is said, 'She hid him three months'" (Ex. ii. 2).

[10] The first editions add: "she could hide him no longer."

[11] See *J.E.* iii. p. 231a.

[12] The Venice edition reads: "Was smitten with sore leprosy." According to the Book of Jashar lxviii. 15, the reason why Bithyah went down to bathe was because God had sent a consuming heat which oppressed the Egyptians.

in hot water,[1] and she came to bathe in the river, and she saw the crying child. She put forth her hand and took hold of him, and she was healed.[2] She said: This child is righteous, and I will preserve his life. Whosoever preserves a life [3] is as though he had kept alive the whole world. Therefore was she worthy to (inherit) the life in this world and the life in the world to come.

All the household of Pharaoh's palace were (helping) to educate (Moses), as it is said, "And it came to pass in those days, when Moses was grown up, that he went out unto his brethren" (*ibid.* 11).[4] Moses went into the camp of Israel, and saw one of the taskmasters of Pharaoh smiting one of the sons of Kohath, the Levites, for they were his brethren, as it is said, "And he saw an Egyptian smiting an Hebrew, *one of his brethren*" [5] (*ibid.*). He began to rebuke him with the sword of his lips,[6] and he slew him, and buried him in the midst of the camp, as it is said, "And he smote the Egyptian, and hid him in the sand" (*ibid.* 12). The word Chôl (sand) signifies (here) Israel only, as it is said, "Yet the number of children of Israel shall be as the *sand* of the sea" (Hos. i. 10).

He went forth on the second day, and saw two Hebrew

[1] See Tanna de bê Elijahu Rab. vii. p. 42; Ex. Rab. xi. 5; Pal. Targum to Ex. ii. 5, and Jalkuṭ, Ex. *loc. cit.*

[2] See T.B. Soṭah, 12a–b. This seems to be a Jewish-Hellenistic Midrash, as it occurs in Ezekiel's drama, "The Exodus," quoted by Clement of Alexandria, *loc. cit.*

[3] The first editions read: "a single life in Israel." See T.B. Synhedrin, 37a, and T.B. Baba Bathra, 11b. The first editions add: "And whosoever destroys a single life in Israel is as though he had destroyed the whole world. Therefore was the daughter of Pharaoh worthy to take shelter beneath the wings of the Shekhinah, and she was called the daughter of Omnipresent." Jalkuṭ, Ex. *loc. cit.*, reads: "She was worthy to have the life of the future world"; cf. Derekh Erez Ẓuṭṭa i., where we read that "Bithyah entered Paradise in her lifetime," *i.e.* without experiencing death. See also *J.E.* iii. 231 for further details as to the Rabbinical legends concerning Bithyah, "Daughter of God."

[4] See Rashi on Ex. ii. 11; see also Jalkuṭ, Ex. *loc. cit.*

[5] The *brethren* of Moses would be of the tribe of Levi.

[6] Cf. Ps. lix. 7: "swords are in their lips," and also Isa. xi. 4. See *supra*, p. 156, and cf. Jalkuṭ, Ex. *loc. cit.* As a parallel to our text see Pss. of Solomon xvii. 27: "He shall destroy the ungodly nations with the word of his mouth." Probably the reference is to the invocation of the Ineffable Name. See Ex. Rab. i. 29, and Leḳach Ṭob, Ex. p. 7a, notes 78 and 80. Cf. Fürst, *Z.D.M.G.* xxxiii. p. 299; Lev. Rab. xxxii. 4, and Bacher, T. ii. p. 252. Clement of Alexandria, *loc. cit.*, says: "And the mystics say that he slew the Egyptian by a word only." This is also probably a Jewish-Hellenistic Midrash.

men striving. Who were they? || Dathan and Abiram, as it is said, "And he said to him that did the wrong,[1] Wherefore smitest thou thy fellow?" (Ex. ii. 13).[2] Dathan said to him: What! Dost thou wish to kill me with the sword of thy mouth as thou didst kill the Egyptian yesterday, as it is said, "Who made thee a prince and a judge over us?[3] Speakest thou[4] to kill me, as thou killedst the Egyptian?" (*ibid.* 14). "Seekest thou to kill me" is not written (in the Scripture) here, but "Speakest thou to kill me."

When Moses and Aaron came to Pharaoh, they said to him: "Thus saith the Lord,[1] the God of Israel, Let my people go" (*ibid.* v. 1), that they may serve Me.[5] He said: I know not the Lord. "Who is the Lord,[1] that I should hearken unto his voice to let Israel go? I know not the Lord, and moreover I will not let Israel go" (*ibid.* 2).[6] Aaron cast down his rod,[7] and it became a fiery serpent. The[8] magicians also cast down their rods, and they became fiery serpents. The rod of Aaron ran and swallowed them up with their rods, as it is said, "And Aaron's rod swallowed up their rods" (*ibid.* vii. 12).

(Moses) put his hand into his bosom, and brought it forth leprous like snow, and the magicians also put their hands in their bosoms, and brought them forth leprous like snow. But they were not healed till the day of their

[1] The quotation ends here in the MS.; it is continued in the first editions.

[2] Ex. Rab., *loc. cit.*, adds: "even though thy neighbour be an evil-doer." Dathan and Abiram are cited because they vexed Moses in the wilderness. See Num. xvi. 1. Our Midrash has been used by the Pal. Targum on Ex. ii. 13 f., which reads thus: "And he went out (on) the second day, and looked, and behold, Dathan and Abiram, men of the (tribe of) Judah, contended; and seeing Dathan put forth his hand against Abiram to smite him, he said to him: Wherefore dost thou smite thy companion? And Dathan said to him: Who is he who hath appointed thee a chief man and a judge over us? Speakest thou to kill me as thou didst kill the Egyptian?"

[3] This part of the quotation is wanting in the MS. The entire verse is given in the first editions.

[4] Lit. "sayest thou," *i.e.* by the word of thy mouth wilt thou kill me? See Midrash Agadah, Ex. pp. 125 f., n. 43.

[5] This translation agrees with the Venice edition text. The modern editions read according to the Scripture: "That they may keep a festival (offering) unto me" (ויחגו לי). Our translation is a paraphrase of the Bible text. See T.B. Chagigah, 6b.

[6] See Mekhilta Beshallach, 23b.

[7] The first editions read: "Forthwith Aaron cast down his rod before Pharaoh."

[8] The first editions read: "Immediately Pharaoh called the magicians."

death.[1] Every plague which the Holy One, blessed be He, brought upon them,[2] they also produced every plague until He brought upon them the boils, and they were not able to stand and to do likewise,[3] as it is said, "And the magicians could not [4] stand before Moses because of the boils" (*ibid.* ix. 11).

Rabbi 'Aḳiba said: The executioners [5] of Pharaoh used to strangle the Israelites in the walls of the houses,[6] || and the Holy One, blessed be He, heard their cry, as it is said, "And God heard their groaning,[4] and God remembered his covenant with Abraham, with Isaac, and with Jacob" (*ibid.* ii. 24). Further, they burnt their children in the furnace of fire,[7] as it is said, "But the Lord hath taken you,[4] and brought you forth out of the iron *furnace*, out of Egypt" (Deut. iv. 20).

When [8] Israel went forth,[9] what did the Holy One,

[1] This sentence occurs in the MS. only. Cf. Pal. Targum, Ex. viii. 14.

[2] The first editions read: "brought upon the Egyptians in Egypt, they also performed."

[3] See T.B. Synhedrin, 67b; Ex. Rab. ix. 6; and Jalḳuṭ, Ex. § 183.

[4] In the MS. the quotation ends here.

[5] This word is the Latin *speculator*, executioner. See Jalḳuṭ, Ex. § 169, and Deut. § 826, and cf. *Rabbinic Philosophy and Ethics*, p. 144, note 1.

[6] The first editions add: "between the layers of bricks, therefore they cried out of the walls." The Bible text says: "The Egyptians *oppressed* the Israelites." "To oppress" (לחץ) suggests to the Haggadist writer the word which occurs in the story of Balaam, Num. xxii. 25: "And the ass saw the angel of the Lord and she *thrust* herself unto the *wall*, and *crushed* Balaam's foot against the *wall*." Hence the inference that the Egyptians oppressed Israel in connection with the walls. See T.B. Synhedrin, 111a.

[7] Jalḳuṭ, *loc. cit.*, adds: "a sacrifice to their gods; therefore, when Israel left Egypt, God executed judgment on their gods." Cf. Jer. xi. 4, where we read of the "iron *furnace*." See also Book of Jashar lxix. 7.

[8] The first editions insert before this word: "And the Holy One, blessed be He, measured to them by that measure (which they had used), and slew their firstborn, as it is said, 'To him that smote Egypt in their firstborn'" (Ps. cxxxvi. 10). Israel was called God's firstborn. When God bade Pharaoh to send forth His firstborn son Israel, he refused. In return God smote his firstborn. The Jewish teaching as to the Divine method of retribution is well expressed by the Book of Wisdom xi. 16, which refers to the plagues thus: "That they might know that by what things a man sinneth, thereby he is punished." Cf. Revelation of Peter, 7 and 9, for a parallel view of retribution. As a parallel to our text, the following verse from Wisdom xviii. 5 seems appropriate: "But them who plotted to slay the infants of the holy ones (and when a single child had been exposed and saved) Thou to convict them didst deprive of the multitude of their children, and all together didst destroy them in a mighty flood." Jubilees xlviii. 14 says: "A thousand strong and brave men perished for one infant whom they had cast into the river." For further illustrations see Goodrick, *Wisdom*, p. 352.

[9] The first editions add: "from Egypt."

blessed be He, do ? He cast down all the idols of their abominations, and they were broken,[1] as it is said, " Upon their gods also the Lord executed judgments " (Num. xxxiii. 4).

Rabbi Joseph [2] said : The Egyptians defiled the Israelites and their wives with them.[3] Bedijah, the grandson of Dan, married a wife from his tribe, Shelomith, daughter of Dibri,[4] and in that night the taskmasters of Pharaoh came in unto her, for they slew him and came in unto her, and she conceived and bare a son. In every case the offspring follows the (nature of) the seed :[5] if it be sweet, it will be due to the sweet (seed); if it be bitter, it will be due to the bitter (seed). And when Israel went forth from Egypt, he [6] began to blaspheme and revile the Name of the God of Israel, as it is said, " And the son of the Israelitish woman blasphemed the [7] Name, and cursed " (Lev. xxiv. 11).

Rabbi Ishmael said : The five fingers of the right hand of the Holy One, blessed be He, all of them appertain to the mystery [8] of the Redemption.[9] He showed the little finger of the hand to Noah,[10] (pointing out) how to make the ark, as it is said, " And *this* [11] is how thou shalt make it " (Gen. vi. 15). With the second finger, which is next to the little one, He smote the firstborn of the Egyptians,[12] as it is said, " The magicians said unto Pharaoh, || This is

---

[1] See Mekhilta, 7b.

[2] The first editions read : " José."

[3] For another opinion see Mekhilta, 5a, and Lev. Rab., *loc. cit.* Israel was redeemed because of four virtues, which included the merit of not being suspected of immorality. See also Jalḳuṭ, Lev. § 657.

[4] See Lev. xxiv. 11, Midrash Agadah, Ex. p. 125, and Leḳach Ṭob, Ex. p. 7a.

[5] Cf. *supra*, p. 150, and T.B. Niddah, 31a. The reference here is to the intellect which rules one's life.

[6] The son of Shelomith.

[7] The quotation ends here in the MS.

[8] Read לסוד, which is the reading preserved by the 'Arukh, ed. Kohut, iv. p. 439a, *s.v.* חמש. Later editions read : " are the foundations." On the " hand " of God see Passover Haggadah, p. 22. See also Jalḳuṭ, Ex. § 183, and Jalḳuṭ to Micah, § 653. Cf. Orach Chayyim, 473. 28.

[9] Of Israel.

[10] 'Arukh, *loc. cit.*, reads : " The little finger, therewith He shewed the ark to Noah." See *supra*, p. 164, n. 2.

[11] The word " this " in the text is the basis for the Haggadic inference that God's finger pointed out to Noah what he was to do in making the ark. Cf. Ex. xxx. 13.

[12] See T.B. Synhedrin, 93b : " The Egyptians and Sennacherib were smitten by the entire hand." Cf. Shocher Ṭob, Ps. lxxviii. pp. 177b f.

the finger of God" (Ex. viii. 19). With how many (plagues) were they smitten with the finger? With ten plagues.[1] With the third finger, which is the third (starting from) the little finger, He wrote the tables (of the Law), as it is said, "And he gave unto Moses, when he had made an end[2] of communing with him . . . tables of stone, written with the finger of God" (*ibid.* xxxi. 18). With the fourth finger, which is next to the thumb, the Holy One, blessed be He, showed[3] to Moses what the children of Israel should give for the redemption of their souls,[4] as it is said, "*This* they shall give[5] . . . half a shekel for an offering to the Lord" (*ibid.* xxx. 13). With the thumb and all the hand the Holy One, blessed be He, will smite in the future all the children of Esau, for they are His foes,[6] and likewise (will He smite) the children of Ishmael, for they are His enemies, as it is said, "Let thine *hand* be lifted up above thine adversaries, and let all thine enemies be cut off" (Mic. v. 9).

Rabbi Eliezer said: The five letters of the Torah, which alone of all the letters in the Torah are of double (shape),[7] all appertain to the mystery of the Redemption.[8] With "Khaph" "Khaph" our father Abraham was redeemed from Ur of the Chaldees, as it is said, (Le*kh* Le*kh*a) "Get thee out of thy country, and from thy kindred[9] . . . unto the land that I will shew thee" (Gen. xii. 1). With "Mem" "Mem"

[1] The MS. alone has this sentence. Cf. Passover Haggadah, pp. 21 f.

[2] The MS. gives the first part of the verse; the latter part only is given by the first editions.

[3] The half-shekel.

[4] See the Commentary "Tosaphoth" to the Torah, p. 43b (ed. Warsaw, 1876): "With the fourth finger He showed to Moses the moon, and with the thumb He showed to him the half-shekel."

[5] The MS. and the first editions end the quotation here.

[6] The first editions read: "the foes of the children of Israel."

[7] M, N, Z, P, Kh,—the five letters which have a different shape when they are the final letters in words. The reading of our MS. is supported by the text preserved in the 'Arukh, ed. Kohut, iv. p. 439b. On these letters see T.B. Sabbath, 104a; T.B. Megillah, 2b; T.J. Megillah, i. 9. 71d; and Num. Rab. xviii. 21.

[8] See Gen. Rab. i. 11; Tanchuma, Ḳorach, § xii. The term "mystery of the redemption" might also be rendered by "the secret of the redemption." The idea in the Midrash here seems to be that the Israelites had a tradition or secret concerning the redemption. This is brought out in the legend of Serach and Moses. The Book of Wisdom says: "That night (of redemption) was known *beforehand* to our fathers, that knowing surely on what oaths they trusted they might be cheered" (xviii. 6).

[9] The MS. and first editions end quotation here.

our father Isaac was redeemed from the land[1] of the Philistines, as it is said, "Go from us:[2] for thou art much mightier (*M*emennu *M*'ôd) than we" (*ibid.* xxvi. 16). With "Nun" "Nun" our father Jacob was redeemed from the hand of Esau,[3] as it is said, "Deliver me, I pray thee,[2] (Hazilê*ne* *na*) from the hand of my brother, from the hand of Esau" (*ibid.* xxxii. 11). With "Pê" "Pê" Israel[4] was redeemed from Egypt, as it is said, "I have surely visited you,[5] (*P*aḳôd *P*aḳadti) and (seen) that which is done to you in Egypt, and I have said, I will bring you up out of the affliction of Egypt" (Ex. iii. 16, 17). With "Zaddi" "Zaddi" the Holy One, blessed be He, in the future will redeem Israel from the oppression of the kingdoms,[6] and He will say to them, I have caused a branch to spring forth for you, as it is said, "Behold, the man whose name is (Zemach) the Branch;[7] and he shall grow up (yi*z*mach) || out of his place,[2] and he shall build the temple of the Lord" (Zech. vi. 12).[8] These letters were delivered only to our father Abraham. Our father Abraham delivered them to Isaac, and Isaac (delivered them) to Jacob, and Jacob delivered the mystery of the Redemption to Joseph, as it is said, "But God will surely visit (*P*aḳôd yi*p*hḳôd) you" (Gen. l. 24). Joseph his son delivered the secret of the Redemption to his brethren. Asher, the son of Jacob, delivered the mystery of the Redemption to Serach[9] his daughter. When Moses and Aaron came to the elders of Israel and performed the signs in their sight, the elders of Israel went to[10] Serach, the daughter of Asher, and they said to her: A certain man has come, and he has performed

[1] 'Arukh, *loc. cit.*, reads: "from the land of the Philistines," as in our MS. The first editions read: "from the *hand* of the Philistines."

[2] The quotation ends here in the MS.

[3] This is also the reading of the Venice edition, and agrees with the text in the 'Arukh, *loc. cit.*

[4] The first editions read: "our fathers."

[5] The MS. and first editions end the quotation here. See Leḳach Ṭob, Ex. p. 10b, n. 3.

[6] The first editions read: "at the end of the four kingdoms."

[7] The verse, Jer. xxiii. 5: "I will raise unto David a righteous Branch," is quoted by Tanchuma, *loc. cit.* See also Tanchuma (ed. Buber), Ex. p. 7, n. 107.

[8] For the Messianic interpretation of this verse in Philo see my *Hellenism and Christianity*, pp. 119 f.

[9] See T.B. Soṭah, 13a; Gen. Rab. xciv. 9; Eccles. Rab. to Eccles. ix. 18; Derekh Erez Rab. i. See also *J.E.* xi. 200 f.

[10] The first editions add: "our ancestress."

signs in our sight, thus and thus.[1] She said to them: There is no reality in the signs. They said to her: He said "*Paḳôd yiphḳôd*"—"God will surely visit you" (*ibid.*).[2] She said to them: He is the man who will redeem Israel in the future from Egypt, for thus did I hear,[3] ("*Paḳôd Paḳadti*") "I have surely visited you" (Ex. iii. 16). Forthwith the people believed[4] in their God and in His messenger, as it is said, "And the people believed,[5] and when they heard that the Lord *had visited*[6] the children of Israel" (*ibid.* iv. 31).[7]

Rabbi 'Aḳiba said: The taskmasters of Pharaoh were beating the Israelites in order that they should make[8] the tale of bricks, and it is said, "And the tale of the bricks,[9] which they did make heretofore, ye shall lay upon them" (*ibid.* v. 8).[10] The Israelites were gathering the straw of the wilderness, and they were carrying it on their asses and (also on) their wives,[11] and their sons. The straw of the wilderness pierced their heels,[12] and the blood was mingled[13] with the mortar. Rachel, the granddaughter || of Shuthelach,[14] was near childbirth, and with her husband she

[1] The first editions add: "She said to them: There is no reality in those signs[1] of Moses. They said to her: Did they not say to us 'Paḳôd Paḳadti'—'I have surely visited you?'"[2] (Ex. iii. 16).

[2] The next two sentences are written on the margin of the MS.

[3] The first editions read: "from my father, 'Pê Pê,' as it is said, 'Paḳôd Paḳadti.'"

[4] The first editions read: "in God and in Moses."

[5] The quotation ends here in the MS.; it is continued in the first editions.

[6] The people believed when they heard that God had *visited* them. This was the secret or mystery of the redemption.

[7] See Ex. Rab. v. 19, which has used *P.R.E.* See also Midrash on 2 Sam. xx. 19.

[8] The first editions add: "for them."

[9] The quotation ends here in the MS. and in the first editions.

[10] The first editions add: "The Egyptians did not give straw to the Israelites, as it is said: 'There is no straw given unto thy servants, and they say to us, Make brick'" (Ex. v. 16).

[11] MS. Gaster and Jalḳuṭ, Ex. § 176, read: "They were treading it in the mortar, they and their wives, their sons and their daughters." The first editions read: "they were treading it down with their asses, their wives, and their sons and their daughters."

[12] See Jalḳuṭ, Ex. *loc. cit.*

[13] Cf. Ezek. xvi. 6, and Zech. x. 5.

[14] See Num. xxvi. 36. Shuthelach was of the tribe of Ephraim.

---

[1] See Cant. Rab. on Cant. ii. 7; Pesiḳta Rabbathi, p. 94a, on the Egyptian exile decreed by God, and the actual period of the bondage.

[2] Joseph also, in his last message to his relatives, said: "God will surely visit you (פקד יפקד) and bring you up from this land" (Gen. L. 24).

was treading the mortar, and the child was born (there) and became entangled in the brick mould.[1] Her cry ascended before the Throne of Glory.[2] The angel Michael[3] descended and took the brick mould with its clay, and brought it up before the Throne of Glory.[4] That night the Holy One, blessed be He, descended,[5] and smote the firstborn of the Egyptians, as it is said, "And it came to pass at midnight[6] that the Lord smote all the firstborn in the land of Egypt" (*ibid.* xii. 29).[7]

Rabbi José[8] said: All that night the Israelites were eating and drinking, rejoicing and taking wine and praising[9] their God with a loud voice,[10] whilst the Egyptians were crying with a bitter soul,[11] because of the plague[12] which came upon them suddenly,[13] as it is said, "And there was a great cry in Egypt;[14] for there was not a house where there was not one dead" (*ibid.* 30).

The Holy One, blessed be He, said: If I bring forth the Israelites by night, they[15] will say, He has done His deeds like a thief.[16] Therefore, behold, I will bring them forth when the sun is in his zenith at midday.[17]

1 See Pal. Targum to Ex. xxiv. 10.

2 See Jalḳuṭ, Ex. *loc. cit.*, which has used *P.R.E.*

3 In Pal. Targum, *loc. cit.*, Gabriel is the angel.

4 See Pal. Targum, *loc. cit.*, which reads: "A memorial of the bondage wherein the Egyptians made the children of Israel to serve in clay and bricks, (when) there were women treading the mortar with their husbands. The delicate young woman with child was also there and made abortive by being crushed with the mortar. And thereof did Gabriel, descending, make brick, and ascending to the heavens on high, set it (as) a footstool under the throne of the Lord of the world." Cf. 3 Baruch iii. 5 for a parallel.

5 The first editions read: "was revealed, and smote all the firstborn."

6 The quotation ends here in the MS.

7 The first editions read here the paragraph beginning, "The Holy One."

8 The first editions read: "Jehudah."

9 See Shocher Ṭob on Ps. cxiii. p. 235a, and cf. T.B. Pesachim, 95b.

10 Cf. Ps. cv. 43.

11 Cf. Isa. lxv. 14 for the expression; see also Ezek. xxvii. 30.

12 The slaying of the firstborn.

13 Cf. Job xxxiv. 20.

14 The MS. omits the first part of the quotation.

15 The first editions read: "The Egyptians will say: Now hath He done His deeds according to the way of thieves." See Midrash Agadah, Ex. p. 142.

16 See the Book of Jashar lxxx. 60 and cf. T.B. Berakhoth, 9a.

17 This day was also the middle of the month, at the time of full moon. The time of the deliverance was believed to be appointed at

By the merit of three things[1] Israel went forth from Egypt: (1) They did not change their language; (2) they did not change their names;[2] (3) and they did not slander one another. In the unity of (God's) Name Israel went forth from Egypt full of all good things, comprising (all) blessings,[3] because He remembered the word which He spake to our father Abraham,[4] as it is said, "And also that nation, whom they shall serve,[5] will I judge, and afterwards shall they come out with great substance" (Gen. xv. 14).

that time in order to show the Egyptians that their gods, including the heavenly host, were powerless and unable to save them. The first editions add here: "as it is said, 'And it came to pass the *selfsame*[1] day, that the Lord did bring the children of Israel out of the land of Egypt by their hosts'" (Ex. xii. 51).

[1] See Mekhilta, Bô, v. p. 5a; Lev. Rab. xxxii. 5; Cant. Rab. on Cant. iv. 12, Leḳach Ṭob, Ex. p. 16a, note 10.

[2] See Mekhilta, Bô, *loc. cit.* The first editions omit this clause.

[3] See *supra*, p. 328.

[4] Cf. Ps. cv. 42: "For he remembered his holy word, and Abraham his servant."

[5] The quotation ends here in the MS.; it is continued in the first editions.

---

[1] בעצם refers to the *essential* part of the day: cf. Ps. cxxxvi. 7–11.

CHAPTER XLIX

THE SEED OF AMALEK [69B. i.]

|| RABBI SIMEON, son of Jochai, said: The Holy One, blessed be He, wished to destroy and to cut off all the seed of Amalek.[1] He sent to Saul, the son of Kish, to destroy and to cut off all the seed of Amalek. Saul and the people heard, and did not spare any vile man except Agag, as it is said,[2] "But Saul and the people spared[3] Agag, and the best of the sheep, and of the oxen" (1 Sam. xv. 9). Samuel heard (thereof), and he went to meet them, and he said to them: Ye have spared Amalek, and ye have left over a remnant of him.[4] They said to him: The sheep and the oxen are for sacrifices[5] unto thy God. (Samuel) said to (Saul): The Omnipresent hath no delight in burnt offerings and sacrifices, but only in obeying His voice and in doing His will, as it is said, "And Samuel said, Hath the Lord as great delight[3] in burnt offerings and sacrifices, as in obeying the voice of the Lord? Behold, to obey is better than sacrifice, and to hearken than the fat of rams" (*ibid.* 22).

Rabbi Phineas said: The Holy One, blessed be He, saw that in the future there would arise from Agag a man, a great enemy and adversary of the Jews.[6] Who was this? This was Haman, as it is said, "Because Haman,

[1] See *supra*, p. 346.

[2] The verse reads: "But Saul and the people spared Agag, and the best of the sheep, and of the oxen, and of the fatlings, and the lambs, and all that was good, and would not utterly destroy them."

[3] The quotation ends here in the MS.; it is continued in the first editions.

[4] See Lev. Rab. xxv. 8 and xxvi. 7.

[5] See T.B. 'Abodah Ẓarah, 24b.

[6] See *supra*, p. 384; Ex. Rab. xxxviii. 4; T.B. Megillah, 12a and 19a; and cf. *infra*, p. 399.

the son of Hammedatha,[1] the *Agagite*, the enemy of all the Jews" (Esth. ix. 24). From the seed of Saul (arose) an avenger and a redeemer for Israel, (who delivered them) out of the hand of Haman. Who was this? This was Mordecai, as it is said, "There was a certain Jew[1] in Shushan, the capital, whose name was Mordecai . . . the son of Kish, a Benjamite" (*ibid.* ii. 5).

And there stood Samuel before the Holy One, blessed be He, and he said: Sovereign of all the Universe! Do not forget the sin[2] which Esau did to his father, || for he took strange women (for his wives), who offered sacrifices and burnt incense to idols, to embitter the years of the life of his parents.[3] Remember his sin unto his sons and unto his grandsons unto the end of all generations, as it is said, "Let the iniquity of his fathers be remembered[1] with the Lord" (Ps. cix. 14). Samuel heard the voice of Agag muttering with his mouth, saying: Perhaps the bitterness of the evil death has passed from me, as it is said, "And Agag said, Surely the bitterness of death is past" (1 Sam. xv. 32). Samuel said to him:[4] Just as the sword of Amalek thy ancestor consumed the young men of Israel who were outside the cloud,[5] so that their women dwelt (as) childless women and widows,[6] so by the prayer of the women[7] all the sons[8] of Amalek shall be slain, and their women shall dwell (as) childless women and widows. And by the prayer of Esther and her maidens all the sons of

[1] The quotation ends here in the MS.

[2] The first editions and MS. Gaster read: "The sorrow which the wicked Esau caused his father."

[3] The first editions and MS. Gaster add: "as it is said, 'and they were a bitterness of spirit unto Isaac and unto Rebecca'" (Gen. xxvi. 35). The Book of Jubilees offers a parallel here; see ch. xxvii. 7 ff. and ch. xxv. 1, which reads: "My son, do not take thee a wife of the daughters of Canaan, as Esau, thy brother, who took him two wives of the daughters of Caanan, and they have embittered my soul with all their unclean deeds: for all their deeds are fornication and lust, and there is no righteousness with them, for (their deeds) are evil."

[4] The first editions add here: "Just as thy sword made women childless, so shall thy mother be childless among women."

[5] See *supra*, p. 346.

[6] The Prague edition adds: "so shall thy mother be childless." MS. Gaster omits the rest of the paragraph, except the quotation.

[7] This idea is due to the Midrashic interpretation of the words in 1 Sam. xv. 33, *i.e.* "*by women* (Esther and her maidens) shall thy mother be made childless."

[8] The first editions read: "every son." The Prague edition has "every male."

Amalek were slain and their women remained childless and widowed, as it is said, "And Samuel said, As thy sword hath made women childless,[1] so shall thy mother be childless among women" (*ibid.* 33).

The prayer of Samuel destroyed[2] the power of the children of Agag against Israel,[3] as it is said, "And Samuel broke[4] Agag before the Lord in Gilgal" (*ibid.*).

The Holy One, blessed be He, said: He has made his attack against the heavenly beings,[5] (and God) will send against them insignificant things, to teach them that the power of their might is nought. When Titus,[6] the wicked, entered the Holy of Holies, he said: No adversary || or enemy can prevail against me. What did the Holy One, blessed be He, do to him? He sent a single gnat,[7] and it went into his nostril, and it ate its way into his brain. That gnat became like a young pigeon, weighing two pounds,[8] to teach him that there was nothing at all in the might of his power. When Israel[9] walked in the Holy of Holies with a proud heart, and said: No adversary or enemy[10] is able to stand before us. What did the Holy One, blessed be He, do to them? He sent against them a man, proud and like one sifting the sea, Nebuchadnezzar, whose name was Kabbīr Mayim (like one sifting the sea),[11]

[1] The quotation ends here in the MS. and in the first editions.

[2] The Prague edition reads: "diminished" (חסר).

[3] The first editions add: "in Gilgal." MS. Gaster reads "Amalek" instead of "Agag."

[4] *i.e.* destroyed the power of Amalek. The Targum renders וישסף by ופשח (cf. Targum to Ps. vii. 3): "and he flayed"; see also 2 Chron. xiv. 13: "for they were broken before the Lord." In the MS. the quotation ends here; it is continued in the first editions.

[5] The first editions read: "Everyone who acts with the pride of the mighty." See Gen. Rab. x. 7. The point here is that Haman's pride was punished by the hand of a woman. On God's ways with man, see Num. Rab. xviii. 19 (on Num. xvi. 35).

[6] See Lam. iv. 12 with Midrash Rab. thereon. See Aboth de R. Nathan (*b*) vii. p. 11a; T.B. Giṭṭin, 56b; and cf. *J.E.* xii. p. 164a.

[7] The first editions add: "against him."

[8] ליטרין (λίτρα), *litra*; the Roman libra or pound weight.

[9] Represented by the High Priest.

[10] See Lam., *loc. cit.*

[11] Cf. Tanna de bê Elijahu Rab. xxxi. p. 158; Shocher Ṭob on Ps. cxxxvii. p. 262b; and Pesiḳta Rabbathi, p. 144a. The first editions read: "He sent against them Nebuchadnezzar the wicked, who was a very proud enemy against them." Kabbīr Mayim might mean "the mighty one of the waters." According to Kebra Nagast (G.T.), p. 79, Nebuchadnezzar was the one who "escaped from the water" at his birth; cf. Ex. ii. 10.

to teach; "For by strength shall no man prevail" (*ibid.* ii. 9).[1]

Rabbi Chakhinai[2] said: The Holy One, blessed be He, set[3] no limit to the kingdoms, except to the Egyptian bondage,[4] and to the kingdom of Babylon. Whence do we know this about the Egyptian bondage? Because it is said, "And they shall serve them; and they shall afflict them four hundred years" (Gen. xv. 13). The Holy One, blessed be He, dealt according to the abundance of His tender mercy,[5] and He shortened (this time limit) by its half,[6] 210 years.[7] Whence do we know about the Babylonian kingdom? Because it is said, "For thus saith the Lord,[8] After seventy years be accomplished for Babylon, I will visit you, and perform my good word toward you, in causing you to return to this place" (Jer. xxix. 10).

Rabbi Abbahu said: Forty-five years did Nebuchadnezzar reign. Know that it is so. In the year[9] when he began to reign, he went up to Jerusalem, and conquered Jehoiakim, king of Judah, as it is said, "In the third year of the reign of || Jehoiakim, king of Judah,[10] came Nebuchadnezzar, king of Babylon, unto Jerusalem, and besieged it" (Dan. i. 1). For eight years he ruled over the kingdom of Jehoiakim, and eleven years Zedekiah ruled.[11] (Behold,) nineteen years before he destroyed the

[1] See Ezek. vii. 20: "As for the beauty of his ornament, he turned it to pride"; see also *ibid.* xxiv. 21. On Nebuchadnezzar, see *J.E.* ix. pp. 201 ff.

[2] The Prague edition and Brode's edition read: "Chaninah."

[3] The first editions omit: "and to the kingdom of Babylon. Whence do we know this about the Egyptian bondage?"

[4] Cf. T.B. Joma, 9a and 9b.

[5] The first editions add: "and according to His abounding love." As Isa. lxiii. 7 says: "I will make mention of the loving-kindnesses of the Lord, and the praises of the Lord, according to all that the Lord hath bestowed upon us; and the great goodness toward the house of Israel, which he hath bestowed on them according to his mercies, and according to the multitude of his loving-kindnesses."

[6] The first editions read: "in the number of 'Rdu' 210 years."

[7] Cf. *supra*, p. 376.

[8] The MS. and the first editions omit this part of the verse; the MS. reads: "After seventy years be accomplished"; the first editions add "for Babylon."

[9] Luria's emendation reads: "In the second year."

[10] The quotation ends here in the MS.; it is continued in the first editions.

[11] The first editions read: "he ruled over the kingdom of Zedekiah."

Temple. (Thereafter he ruled) twenty-six years.[1] Know that it is so. Come and see from the exile of Jehoiachin until his son Evil-Merodach[2] reigned thirty-seven[3] years elapsed, as it is said, " And it came to pass in the seven and thirtieth year of the captivity of Jehoiachin,[4] king of Judah, in the twelfth month, on the seven and twentieth day of the month, that Evil-Merodach, king of Babylon, in the year that he began to reign, did lift up the head of Jehoiachin, king of Judah, out of prison " (2 Kings xxv. 27).

Rabbi Jonathan said: The last of the kings of Media[5] was Artaxerxes,[6] king of Babylon, and he reigned thirty-two years, as it is said, " But in all this time I was not in Jerusalem;[7] for in the two and thirtieth year of Artaxerxes, king of Babylon, I went unto the king " (Neh. xiii. 6).[8]

Rabbi Tachanah[9] said: Come and see how wealthy Ahasuerus was, for he was wealthier than all the kings of Media and Persia, and concerning him the Scripture saith, " And the fourth shall be far richer than they all " (Dan. xi. 2). What was the wealth of Ahasuerus? He erected couches of gold and silver in the streets[10] of the city, to show all the peoples[11] how rich he was, as it is said, " The couches were of gold and silver " (Esth. i. 6). All the vessels

[1] The first editions read: " Behold nineteen years (elapsed) before the Temple was destroyed." The Venice edition and MS. Gaster add: " After the Temple had been destroyed (he reigned) twenty-six years." This is omitted in the 1st ed. See T.B. Megillah, 11b, and Rashi, who quotes Seder 'Olam Rab.

[2] Son of Nebuchadnezzar.

[3] Deduct from these thirty-seven years the eleven years of Zedekiah's reign prior to the destruction of Jerusalem, and we have twenty-six years, mentioned in our book.

[4] The quotation ends here in the MS.; it is continued in the first editions.

[5] The first editions add: " and Persia."

[6] He is apparently identified by R. Tachanah in the next paragraph of our book with the " fourth king " of Dan. xi. 2.

[7] The quotation ends here in the MS. and in the first editions.

[8] See Seder 'Olam Rab. xxviii. p. 65a and xxx. p. 68b, note 10. According to some Jewish traditions (see T.B. Rosh Ha-Shanah, 4a) Artaxerxes II. is Darius II., who sanctioned the rebuilding of the Temple. This king appears to have reigned thirty-six years; see Esth. Rab. viii. 3, and Lev. Rab. xiii. 5. See also *J.E.* iv. p. 442, and cf. Josephus, *Ant.* xi. 6. 1.

[9] The first editions and MS. Gaster read: "Tanchum." See *supra*, p. 308.

[10] This is the paraphrase of Esth. i. 5: " in the court of the garden of the king's palace."

[11] The first editions read: " to let all the world know."

used by Ahasuerus were not vessels of silver, but vessels of gold.[1] He brought the vessels of the Temple, and all the vessels of his palace were changed in appearance,[2] so that they became like lead, as it is said, "The vessels being *diverse* one from another" (*ibid.* 7).

All the pavement of his palace consisted of precious stones and pearls, || as it is said, "Upon a pavement of porphyry, and white marble,[3] and alabaster, and *stone* of blue colour" (*ibid.* 6).

Rabbi Eliezer said: For half the year Ahasuerus made great banquets for all the peoples, as it is said, "Many days, even an hundred and eighty days" (*ibid.* 4). Every people[4] who ate its food in impurity,[5] had its food provided in impurity, and every people who ate its food in purity[6] had its food provided (according to the regulations of) purity,[7] as it is said,[8] "That they should do according to every man's pleasure" (*ibid.* 8).[9]

Rabbi José[10] said: It was the universal custom of the kings of Media[11] when they were eating and drinking to cause their women to come before them stark naked, playing and dancing, in order to see the beauty of their figures. When the wine entered the heart of Ahasuerus, he wished to act in this manner[12] with Vashti the queen. She was

[1] Cf. 1 Kings x. 21, and Assumption of Moses iii. 2.

[2] Because they became dim in splendour when brought together with the beautiful sacred vessels of the Temple. This constituted the diversity referred to in the text (Esth. i. 7); see Targum 1. thereon, which is probably the source of *P.R.E.* s version.

[3] The quotation ends here in the MS.; it is continued in the first editions.

[4] The first editions read: "Everyone."

[5] *i.e.* this food lacked the characteristics which marked the levitically pure food.

[6] The Jewish Law determines the kind of food which may be eaten by its adherents. Such food is pure. The expression used here in our author, "Every people who ate its food in purity," points to priestly regulations and conditions. The subject has been dealt with exhaustively by Dr. Büchler in his *Der Galiläische 'Am-ha 'Areṣ des Zweiten Jahrhunderts.*

[7] The first editions reverse the order of the clauses.

[8] The first editions read: "to fulfil that which is written."

[9] See Esth. Rab., *in loc.*; Jalkuṭ, Esth. § 1056; T.B. Megillah, 12a; and cf. Jalkuṭ, Esth. § 1048.

[10] The first editions read: "Simeon."

[11] Although Ahasuerus was the king of Persia he was apparently a Mede by race. On the morals of the Medes see T.B. Berakhoth, 8b.

[12] For other instances of the evil effect of too much wine see Gen. ix. 21, and *supra*, p. 170; see also Hos. iv. 11, and cf. T.B. Soṭah, 7a.

the daughter of a king,[1] and she was not willing to do this.[2] He decreed concerning her, and she was slain. When the wine had passed from the heart of Ahasuerus, he sought after Vashti, but he did not find her. They told him of the deed which had been done,[3] and (also) of the decree which had been ordained concerning her. Why was the decree passed against her? Because she used to make the daughters of Israel come [4] and toil for her on Sabbaths, therefore was the decree ordained against her that she should be slain naked on the Sabbath,[5] as it is said, "He remembered Vashti,[6] and *what she had done*, and what was decreed against her" (*ibid.* ii. 1).

Rabbi Zechariah said: || Merit is transmitted by the hand of the worthy. By the hand of Daniel [7] the sovereignty was transferred to Esther, because he said to the king, Let not the king weep, since all that thou hast done [8] thou hast done according to the Torah. And whosoever keeps the Torah,[9] the Holy One, blessed be He, preserves his kingdom; for thus the Torah says that the man shall rule his wife, as it is said, "And he shall rule over thee" [10] (Gen. iii. 16). The king sent in all the provinces to do

[1] Belteshazzar; see T.B. Megillah, 9b, and Jalkuṭ, Esth. § 1050.

[2] The first editions and MS. Gaster read: "that she should come naked before him," and then add: "She sent to him saying: Foolish drunkard! If I come they may see that I am ugly, (then) they will despise thee at thy table; and if they see that I am beautiful, one of thy princes will kill thee [1] in the hour of (his taking) wine. The king heard her words and commanded that she should be slain."

[3] The first editions read: "His princes told him of the decree which he had ordained against her."

[4] The first editions add: "naked."

[5] In the first editions the words "on the Sabbath" follow the words "ordained against her."

[6] The quotation ends here in the MS.; it is continued in the first editions. On the theme see Esth. Rab., *in loc.*, and Targum I. to Esth. ii. 1.

[7] The first editions and MS. Gaster add: "who was Memucan." See the Targum II. to Esth. i. 16, and cf. Esth. Rab. iv. 2 and 6. The latter does not, however, identify Memucan with Daniel. In Targum I. to Esth. i. 16 he is compared with Haman; cf. T.B. Megillah, 12b. *P.R.E.* is the source used by Targum II. in identifying Memucan with Daniel. Memucan means the "establisher."

[8] The first editions add: "to Vashti."

[9] The first editions read: "the precepts of the Torah." See Ezra vi. 11, 12 for a parallel to the expression in our text.

[10] This was said to the first woman, and is one of the nine afflictions imposed upon womankind. See *supra*, p. 100.

---

[1] The Targum II. to Esther i. 12 has used here *P.R.E.*

according to his words,[1] as it is said, "That every man should[2] bear rule in his own house" (Esth. i. 22). He also said to the king: "Let there be sought for the king[2] fair young virgins" (*ibid.* ii. 2). Not[3] "all young virgins," but "fair young virgins."[4] "And let the maiden which pleaseth[2] the king be queen instead of Vashti" (*ibid.* 4); and it is written elsewhere, "And the maiden pleased him" (*ibid.* 9). This refers to Esther. The Holy One, blessed be He, invested her with grace and love[5] in the eyes of all who saw her.[4] "And Esther obtained favour[2] in the sight of all them that looked upon her" (*ibid.* 15).[6]

[1] The first editions read: "the words of Memucan."

[2] The quotation ends here in the MS.; it is continued in the first editions.

[3] The first editions and MS. Gaster read: "Young virgins" and not "all young virgins."

[4] The first editions add: "as it is said."

[5] Cf. Targum II. to Esth. ii. 17: "and she was rewarded by (the king) with more grace and favour than all the virgins."

[6] The 1st ed. adds: "for the sake of the merit that was to be (accomplished) at her hands."

CHAPTER L

HAMAN [70B. ii.]

"THERE was a certain Jew in Shushan, the capital,[1] whose name was Mordecai" (Esth. ii. 5). Rabbi Shema'iah said: Was there then no other Jew in Shushan, the capital, except Mordecai alone? Lo! it is written, "And the Jews that were in Shushan" (*ibid.* ix. 15). But because he was a Jew,[2] and a direct descendant of the patriarchs and also of the royal seed, and he was engaged in (the study of) the Torah all his days, and he was not defiled by any forbidden[3] food in his mouth, therefore was his name called "a Jew."[4]

"Whose name was Mordecai" (*ibid.* ii. 5), because his prayer || ascended before the Holy One, blessed be He, like the scent of *pure myrrh*[5] (מר דכי). "The son of Jair" (*ibid.*), because he enlightened (*Mair*) the faces (of the scholars) in Halakhah.[6] "The son of Shimei" (*ibid.*), who went forth to curse David.[7] "The son of Kish" (*ibid.*),[8] of the seed of

[1] The quotation ends here in the MS.; it is continued in the first editions.

[2] The first editions read: "a righteous Jew."

[3] The first editions read: "anything of unclean food did not pass into his mouth." See *supra*, p. 393, note 6.

[4] The first editions read: "a certain Jew." Cf. Ps. lx. 7 and Jalkuṭ, Esth. § 1052 (end). See also T.B. Megillah, 12b.

[5] A play on the word Mordecai; see Targum II. to Esth. ii. 5. T.B. Chullin, 139b, translates the words מר דרור of Ex. xxx. 23 by מירא דכיא, clear (liquid) myrrh; cf. T.B. Megillah, 10b. Prayer is compared with incense; see Ps. cxli. 2.

[6] As a member of the Synhedrion, he brought light to Israel in the hour of darkness; see Esth. viii. 16: "The Jews had light and joy."

[7] Shimei was of the royal house of Saul, and therefore Mordecai as his descendant belonged also to the royal house. See Targum II. to Esth., *loc. cit.*

[8] The first editions read: "Because he knocked (*shêhiḳḳish*) upon the doors of mercy and they were opened unto him." See Sheḳalim v. 1: "Petachiah is Mordecai, because God opened to him the gates of prayer."

those who could use both the right hand and the left,[1] as it is said, "The children of Ephraim, being armed and carrying bows" (Ps. lxxviii. 9).

Rabbi Simeon said: Come and see the wisdom of Mordecai, for he knew seventy languages,[2] as it is said, "Which came with Zerubbabel, Jeshua[3] . . . Mordecai, Bilshan"[4] (Ezra ii. 2), and he sat in the gates of the king to see that Esther and her maidens should not become defiled by any kind of unclean[5] food. He heard the two eunuchs of the king speaking in the language of the Chaldees,[6] saying:[7] Now will the king take the afternoon sleep, and when he arises[8] he will say, Give me a little water; let a deadly poison[9] be given to him in the golden vessel,[10] and he will drink thereof and die. Mordecai[11] went in and told Esther. Now Esther told the king in the name of Mordecai, as it is said, "And Esther told the king in Mordecai's name" (Esth. ii. 22). Hence (the Wise Men) have said: Whosoever tells a matter in the name of its author brings redemption into the world.[12]

When the king arose from his sleep, he said to his servants, his eunuchs, who were wont to give him something to drink: Give me a little water. They brought him the golden jug, and a deadly poison || was therein. He said to them: Pour out the water before me. They said to him: O our lord, O king, this water is excellent, good, even choice. Why should we pour it out before thee? He said to them: Thus have I resolved to have it poured out before me. They poured

[1] For phraseology see I Chron. xii. 2.

[2] The first editions read: "and his name was Mordecai Bilshan."

[3] The quotation ends here in the MS.

[4] See T.B. Menachoth, 65a; T.B. Megillah, 13b. Bilshan (="linguist") is mentioned in this verse (Ezra ii. 2) as a separate person.

[5] See T.B. Megillah, *loc. cit.*

[6] According to T.B. Megillah, *loc. cit.*, the language was that of Tarsus (טורסים).

[7] The first editions add: "one to the other."

[8] The first editions read: "and when he gets up from his sleep he will say to us."

[9] The Targum II. to Esth. ii. 21 speaks of "a poisonous snake in the golden cup" out of which Ahasuerus would drink.

[10] Our MS. reads "Ḳesibath." The first editions read "Ḳitôn" (jug); see *Rabbinic Philosophy and Ethics*, p. 24. See also Targum II. to Esth., *loc. cit.*: "Keepers of the *vessels*." See also Zech. xii. 2 for the word סף.

[11] The first editions add: "heard their speech."

[12] See Aboth vi. 6, T.B. Chullin, 104b, and T.B. Megillah, 15a.

it out before him, and he found therein the deadly poison,[1] and he commanded that they should be hanged, as it is said, "They were both hanged on a tree" (*ibid.* 23). They were both hanged on one tree, one after the other,[2] as it is said, "Upon a tree" (*ibid.*); it is not written, "Upon trees." All affairs which were enacted before the king they wrote before him, and they placed it in the king's box,[3] and when the king wished to discover what had happened to him they read the documents, and he knew what had happened to him. So they wrote in the book the word which Mordecai had told, as it is said, "And it was written in the book of the chronicles" (*ibid.*).

Rabbi Phineas said: Two wealthy men arose in the world, one in Israel and one among the nations of the world,[4] Korah in Israel,[5] and Haman among the nations of the world,[6] who took the treasures of the kings of Judah.[7] (When) the king[8] saw his wealth and his ten sons[9] keeping guard before him, he exalted him, and aggrandized him, as it is said, "After || these things did king Ahasuerus promote[10] Haman, the son of Hammedatha" (*ibid.* iii. 1). The king commanded concerning him that all the people should

[1] See T.B. Megillah, 13b, according to which there was a serpent in the king's cup. See also Jalkuṭ, Esth. § 1053, quoting Abba Gorion.

[2] This sentence occurs in our MS. only.

[3] Our MS. reads "Achmetha" (pot or vessel); see Targum I. to Esth. i. 4. The word in the first editions and in Luria's edition should probably be "G'loosḳoma" (γλωσσόκομον), which occurs in the LXX to 2 Chron. xxiv. 8, meaning case, chest, or coffin.

[4] "And their wealth brought them only trouble," says Esth. Rab. vii. 4; see T.B. Pesachim, 119a; Ex. Rab. xxxi. 3; and Eccles. Rab. to Eccles. v. 12.

[5] The first editions add: "for he found the treasures of gold belonging to Joseph." Esth. Rab., *loc. cit.*, says: "treasures of silver and gold which Joseph hid"; see T.B. Pesachim, *loc. cit.*

[6] "In Shushan" is inserted by the later editions instead of "among the nations of the world." This is due to the censor.

[7] The first editions add: "and all the treasures of the Holy of Holies." Haman was supposed by the Haggadist to have been in the army of Nebuchadnezzar at the capture of Jerusalem, and to have appropriated the treasures of the palace and Temple. Cf. Shocher Ṭob on Ps. xxii. p. 99a and on Ps. lxxviii. p. 173b.

[8] Ahasuerus.

[9] Perhaps the text should read "the wealth of his sons," cf. *infra*, p. 408. See Esth. Rab., *loc. cit.*, which adds, after the word "sons": "who were princes before him; he arose and exalted him and he aggrandized him."

[10] The quotation ends here in the MS.; it is continued in the first editions.

bow down and show reverence to him.[1] What did Haman do? He made for himself an image of an idol, and had it embroidered upon his dress, above his heart, so that everyone who bowed down to Haman also bowed down to the idol which he had made. Mordecai[2] saw this, and did not consent to bow down to the idol,[3] as it is said, "But Mordecai bowed not down, nor did him reverence" (*ibid.* 2); and (Haman) was full of wrath against him, and said: These Jews hated my forefathers from of old, and now will I say to the king that he should destroy them from the world. Haman entered before Ahasuerus, and said to him: O my lord, O king, "There is a certain people scattered abroad and dispersed among the peoples[4] in all the provinces of thy kingdom" (*ibid.* 8), and they are of no benefit to thee and do not obey thee, and they do not perform thy will, and it is not for the king's profit to suffer them. If it please the king, accept half of my wealth and give me power[5] over them, as it is said, "If it please the king, let it be written that they be destroyed" (*ibid.* 9). (The king) said to him: Behold, they are given into thy hand for nought, as it is said, "And the king said to Haman, The silver is given to thee, the people also" (*ibid.* 11). The Holy Spirit cried out, saying: "Thus saith the Lord, Ye were sold for nought,[4] || and ye shall be redeemed without money" (Isa. lii. 3).[6]

Rabbi José said: Haman was an astrologer,[7] and he wrote letters on slips,[8] and cast lots by the constellations to know the distinction between one day and another, and between one month and another, and between one constellation and another, as it is said, "They cast Pur, that is, the

[1] The first editions read: "to Haman."

[2] Luria suggests another reading: "(Haman) saw that Mordecai did not consent to bow down and to prostrate himself before him, and he became full of wrath."

[3] The first editions read: "to his abomination." See Jeraḥmeel, lxxix. 1.

[4] The quotation ends here in the MS.; it is continued in the first editions.

[5] Lit. "permission," or "control."

[6] The two previous quotations are not given by the first editions.

[7] The first editions read: "a great astrologer." The Targum II. to Esth. iii. 7 gives the reasons why the various days of the week and the months (except Adar) were unpropitious for Haman.

[8] פתקין, slips; see above, p. 362, note 4.

lot,[1] before Haman from day to day, and from month to month" (Esth. iii. 7). He wrote and sent throughout all the provinces to destroy and to slay and to exterminate all the Jews[2] on the thirteenth day of[3] the month Adar, on the third day in the constellation Leo.[4] Mordecai heard (thereof), and rent his garments,[5] and put on sackcloth with ashes, and he went forth into the midst of the city, as it is said, "And Mordecai knew all that was done" (*ibid.* iv. 1); and he cried before the Holy One, blessed be He, saying: Sovereign of all the worlds! Thou didst swear to our forefathers to multiply their seed like the stars of the heaven, and now hast Thou given them like sheep to the slaughter.[6] "Remember Abraham,[7] Isaac, and Israel . . . to whom thou swarest . . . I will multiply your seed as the stars of heaven" (Ex. xxxii. 13). Esther heard (thereof), and her strength failed, as it is said, "And the queen was exceedingly enfeebled"[8] (Esth. iv. 4). She sent and called for Hathach, the trusty (servant) of her household, to know what had been done[9] to Mordecai. Hathach went forth to Mordecai, who told him the words.[10] (Hathach) went in and told Esther. Haman saw Hathach coming and returning, and he slew him,[11] and Esther did not find another

[1] The quotation ends here in the MS.; it is continued up to "Haman" in the first editions.

[2] The first editions add: "both young and old, little children and women."

[3] The first editions add: "the twelfth month which is."

[4] The constellation of Adar is Pisces; see *supra*, p. 33, as to the constellations. It is Tuesday which is said to be connected with the constellation Leo. See T.B. Megillah, *loc. cit.*; Esth. Rab. vii. 11. On the subject of the horoscope see Cassel's *Esther*, pp. 104 f. This book contains an English version of the Second Targum.

[5] On the custom of rending the garments see T.B. Mo'ed Ḳaṭan, 26a. The MS. adds here "etc."

[6] See *supra*, p. 357. On the Prayer of Mordecai cf. the prayer in the Apocrypha and in the Targum II.; see T.B. Megillah, 11a; and cf. Siphra, p. 112b.

[7] The quotation ends here in the MS.

[8] R.V. renders: "grieved." For the meaning of חלחלה as "weakness" see Isa. xxi. 3 and Nahum ii. 11 (Heb.).

[9] What sin had brought about this dire misfortune. See T.B. Megillah, 15a.

[10] Of the decree against the Jews.

[11] The text in Esther (iv. 12) says: "and *they* told Mordecai"; see Targum I. thereon; Jalḳuṭ, Esther, § 1056; and cf. T.B. Megillah, *loc. cit.*, which identifies Hathach with Daniel. Targum II. to Esth. iv. 11 says: "And because Hathach was a messenger between Esther and Mordecai, Haman was very wroth against him and

man faithful enough to send to Mordecai. She said that it was her || desire to return answer to Mordecai.[1] *She* said to him, " Go, gather together all the Jews [2] that are present in Shushan, and fast ye for me, and neither eat nor drink three days " (*ibid.* 16). These (days) were the thirteenth, the fourteenth, and the fifteenth of Nisan.[3] Mordecai said to her: Is not the third day [4] (of the fast) the day of Passover? She said to him: Thou art the elder in Israel.[5] If there be no Israel, wherefore is the Passover? Mordecai hearkened to her words, and he [6] agreed with her. " So Mordecai transgressed " [7] (*ibid.* 17). What is the meaning of the expression, " So he transgressed "? That he transgressed the festivals and Sabbaths.[8] On the third day (of the fast) Esther put on the royal apparel, and sent and invited the king and Haman to the banquet which she had prepared on the fifteenth of Nisan.[9] When they had eaten and drunk, Haman said:[10] The king exalts me, and his wife aggrandizes me, and there is none greater than I am in all the kingdoms;

killed him. The words of Esther were then reported by writing to Mordecai."

[1] The first editions read: " She said that she would go to Mordecai, as it is said, 'And Esther *spake* to return answer unto Mordecai'" (Esth. iv. 15). This was her intention. See Jalkuṭ, Esther, *loc. cit.*: "The Holy Spirit carried her message to Mordecai."

[2] The quotation ends here in the MS.; it is continued in the first editions.

[3] See T.B. Jebamoth, 121b; T.B. Megillah, *loc. cit.*; Seder 'Olam Rab. xxix. p. 66b; Lev. Rab. xxviii. 4; Pesiḳta, 71b. The first banquet was on the 16th of Nisan, and the second on the following day.

[4] *i.e.* the 15th of Nisan.

[5] The first editions read: " Thou art the head of the Synhedrion and thou sayest this word! If there be no Israel, for whom is the Passover? " The " word " refers to Mordecai's objection to fast on the Passover. The rule was not to fast on Sabbath or festival. The only exception was the Day of Atonement on a Sabbath, when the fast was duly kept thereon. See Shulchan 'Arukh i. 288 (8).

[6] The first editions read: "and he did all that she commanded, as it is said."

[7] ויעבר (Esth. iv. 17). R.V. renders: "And he went his way." The word עבירה, "transgression," is from the same root as the verb ויעבר; see Tanna de bê Elijahu Rab. i. p. 3.

[8] The first editions read: " Teaching that he transgressed the law of the first day of Passover, by not eating" the unleavened bread, as prescribed by the Torah (Ex. xiii. 6).

[9] Should we read " on the 16th of Nisan"? The printed texts as well as the MS. read " on the 15th." This would mean that Esther had prepared the banquet on the first day of Passover, and that the king dined with her on the evening of that day, which was the 16th day of Nisan at night.

[10] The first editions read: " in his heart."

26

and Haman rejoiced very much in his heart, as it is said, "Then went Haman forth that day, joyful[1] and glad of heart" (*ibid.* v. 9).

"On that night the king's sleep fled" (*ibid.* vi. 1). That night the throne[2] of the King who is King of kings, the Holy One, blessed be He, became unsteady,[3] because He saw that Israel was in great distress. The sleep of the king[4] on earth fled, for he had seen in his dream Haman taking the sword to slay him;[5] || and he became agitated and arose from his sleep,[6] and he told the sons of Haman, the scribes,[7] to read in the books so as to see what had happened to him. They opened the books, and found the incident which Mordecai had told,[8] but they did not wish to read this, and they rolled up the scrolls. The king said to them: Read ye what is written before you. But they were unwilling to read, and the writing was read (of its own account)[9] by itself, as it is said, "And they were read before the king" (*ibid.*). It is not written here, "They were reading," but "They were read."[10] The king spake to his servants: Call ye Haman to me. They said to him: Behold, he is standing outside. The king said: The thing is

[1] The quotation ends here in the MS.; it is continued in the first editions.

[2] The first editions read: "the sleep."

[3] The first editions read: "fled."

[4] See T.B. Megillah, 15b, which reads: "the sleep of the king of the world." There is no reference to the sleep of God in our MS.; this agrees with the Targum II. on Esth. vi. 1; cf. Esth. Rab. x. 1, and Jeraḥmeel lxxxiii. 1.

[5] Ahasuerus.

[6] The Targum II. on Esth., *loc. cit.*, reads: "(God) commanded the angel, who is in charge of confusion, to confound Ahasuerus and to deprive him of sleep." See Eccles. Rab. v. on Eccles. v. 3, and Jalḳuṭ, Esther, § 1057.

[7] The 'Arukh, ed. Kohut, v. p. 385a, *s.v.* נקראין, quotes *P.R.E.*: "They were the readers of the books of the king." See also Esth. Rab., *loc. cit.*, which has used our book.

[8] The first editions add: "concerning Bigthan and Teresh." See Esth. ii. 21–23; cf. T.B. Megillah, 15a.

[9] By a miracle. The Targum II., *loc. cit.*, says: "When Shimshê the scribe saw what was told concerning Mordecai in the affair of Bigthan and Teresh, he turned over the leaves and did not want to read them. But it was the will of the Lord of the world that the leaves should open and *read of themselves* the record written on them." This passage illustrates how this Targum has used *P.R.E.*

[10] Jalḳuṭ, Esth., *loc. cit.*, adds: "Do not be surprised, because the reading was due to the (power of) the lot (גורל); for the script had flown away from the various narratives and came to the lap of the king."

true which I saw in my dream;[1] he has come only in this hour to slay me. He said: Let him come in. He entered before the king. The king said to him: I wish to exalt and aggrandize a certain man; what shall be done to him? Haman said in his heart, for the seed of Esau[2] speak in their hearts, but never reveal their secret with their mouths, as it is said, "And Haman said in his heart" (*ibid.* 6). Haman said in his heart: He does not desire to exalt any other man except me.[3] I will speak words so that I shall be a king just as he is. He said to him: Let[4] them bring the apparel ‖ which the king wore on the day of the coronation,[5] and (let them bring) the horse upon which the king rode on the coronation day, and the crown which was put upon the head of the king on the day of coronation.[6] The king was exceedingly angry because of the crown. The king said: It does not suffice this villain, but he must even desire the crown which is upon my head.[7] Haman saw that the king was angry because of the crown; he said: "And let the apparel and the horse be delivered[8] to the hand of one of the king's most noble princes" (*ibid.* 9).[9] (The king) said to him: Go, and do thus to Mordecai.[10] As soon as Haman heard this he became greatly agitated,[11] and he said to him: My lord, O king! There are very

[1] See Eccles. Rab., *loc. cit.*; the Targumim on Esther, *in loc.*; I.C.C. Esther, p. 244, and Gelbhaus, *Das Targum Scheni zum Buche Esther*, for Midrashic parallels.

[2] The first editions read: "All the seed of Amalek." See T.B. Megillah, 7a, which infers that the Book of Esther was inspired, as otherwise we could not know what Haman thought in his heart.

[3] The first editions read: "To whom should the king desire to do honour more than to me."

[4] The first editions omit the previous sentence and read here: "My lord, O king! if thou desirest to do honour to the man in whom thou takest delight."

[5] See Targum II. on Esth. vi. 7 for the dream and its fulfilment by Haman's words. Targum I. on Esth. vi. 8 adds: "on the day of his accession to the throne."

[6] This is probably due to the text: "And the royal crown which is set upon his head" (Esth. vi. 8).

[7] The first editions add: "if so, what hast thou left me?"

[8] In the MS. the quotation ends here.

[9] No reference is now made to the crown.

[10] The first editions add: "the Jew, who sitteth at the king's gate."

[11] The first editions read: "he became confused and agitated." See Targum II. on Esth. vi. 10: "When Haman heard these words he was in great trouble, his countenance was changed, his sight became dim, his mouth became distorted, his thoughts confused, his loins languid, and his knees beat one against the other."

many named Mordecai. The king answered: "The Jew." (Haman) said to him: There are very many Jews.[1] The king said to him: "He who sits at the king's gate" (*ibid.* 10).[2]

Haman took the apparel and the horse and went to Mordecai.[3] (Haman) said to him: Arise, and put on the purple of the king. (Mordecai) said to him:[4] Villain! Dost thou not know that for three days I have put on sackcloth with ashes,[5] sitting on the ashes,[6] because of that which thou hast done to me? Now take me to the bath-house,[7] and afterwards will I put on the purple of the king. And he washed him and dressed him. (Haman) said to him: Mount and ride upon the horse. He said to (Haman): On account of the affliction of the fast I have no strength to mount and ride upon the horse. What did Haman do? He lowered himself, || and Mordecai put his foot upon his

[1] The first editions add: "who are named Mordecai."

[2] The first editions add here the following: "He said to him: My lord, O king! I did not think when thou didst speak but that it was for one greater than this man. As for this man, give him fields and vineyards and it will suffice for him; as for these other (honours), how will they benefit him? The king said to him: Go, do as thou hast spoken. I also am able to give him all that which thou hast decreed with thy mouth.[1] The king said to him: By the life of my head and my kingdom! It is becoming for thee to do thus."[2]

[3] The Venice edition adds here: "And he inquired after his welfare (lit. peace). Mordecai replied: 'There is no *peace,* saith the Lord, unto the wicked'" (Isa. xlviii. 22). This passage is wanting in the Oxford MS.

[4] The Venice edition adds: "Fool of the world!"

[5] See Esth. iv. 1. Targum II. on Esth. vi. 11 reads: (Haman says): "Now arise from your sackcloth and ashes, and put on the royal garment."

[6] See Esth. iv. 3.

[7] The first editions add here: "What did Esther do? She ordained that any person who should stand (about) in the baths (the same) should not live. And if (Haman) should tell anyone to kindle lights, they should not hearken unto him. Haman went and (by) himself kindled the lights against his will. He sent his eldest son to call Mordecai into the baths. Mordecai received (him) and struck him with his foot, saying to him: Why did not thy father come himself? Is he not my servant? He returned to his father and told him, and he went against his will to take (Mordecai) to the baths, and he shaved his head and divested him (of his garments) and dressed him."

---

[1] See T.B. Megillah, 16a, and Targum II. to Esth. vi. 10.

[2] See Targum II. to Esth., *loc. cit.*, and Jalkut, Esth. § 1058, which adds: "How long wilt thou continue to talk before me."

neck, and he mounted and rode upon the horse.[1] Mordecai[2] said: Blessed be the Omnipresent, who hath not let aught of His words fall to the earth, to fulfil that which is said, "But thou shalt tread upon their high places" (Deut. xxxiii. 29). Mordecai[3] betook himself to his seat of honour at the king's gate, whilst Haman was hurried along, and he went[4] "to his house mourning and having his head covered" (Esth. vi. 12),[5] because of that which had happened to him.[6]

Zeresh his wife and all his astrologers[7] said to him: Hast thou not heard what was done unto Pharaoh?[8] as it is said, "And Zeresh his wife said unto him, If Mordecai, before whom thou hast begun to fall, be of the seed of the Jews,[9] thou shalt not prevail against him" (*ibid.* 13).

In that hour the pages of Esther came and took Haman

[1] The first editions add here: "And as he lifted up one leg, he struck him with the other foot. (Haman) said to him: Is it not written in the Torah (*i.e.* Bible): 'Rejoice not when thine enemy falleth' (Prov. xxiv. 17)? (Mordecai) said to him: These words apply to Israel, but concerning the nations of the world (the text says): 'But thou shalt tread upon their high places'" (Deut. xxxiii. 29). The Amsterdam and Prague editions read "idolaters" instead of "nations of the world" just before the quotation from Deuteronomy. This long section is undoubtedly a later expansion of the simple original narrative which we have probably preserved in our MS. and in the Targum II. The Venice text contains several Aramaic words which are quite alien to the language of the *P.R.E.*

[2] See Targum II. to Esth., *loc. cit.*

[3] The first editions read: "Mordecai came before the king, and Haman was proclaiming before him: 'Thus shall it be done unto the man whom the king delighteth to honour' (Esth. vi. 11). 'But Haman hasted to his house'" (*ibid.* 12), etc.

[4] See T.B. Megillah, *loc. cit.*

[5] The covered head was a sign of disgrace and mourning among the Jews (see *supra*, p. 100); also among the Persians (see Q. Curtius, v. 10 and x. 5).

[6] See T.B. Megillah, *loc. cit.*, for the legend of Haman's daughter, who killed herself when she discovered her father's disgrace.

[7] The first editions read: "friends."

[8] The first editions add: "in Egypt." See Targum I. to Esth. vi. 13, which seems to have preserved the original text of *P.R.E.*; or is the real fact *vice-versa*? See Posner's dissertation on Targum I. p. 47. The version in the Targum I., *loc. cit.*, reads: "Before whom thou hast begun to fall, as the kings fell before Abraham in the Plain of the Field, as Abimelech fell before Isaac, as the angel was vanquished by Jacob, and as by the hands of Moses and Aaron Pharaoh and all his host sank in the Reed Sea, and as all kings and princes, who did them harm, were delivered by God into their hand, so also wilt thou accomplish nothing harmful against him." See also Targum II. to Esth. vi. 13.

[9] The quotation ends here in the MS. and in the first editions.

to the banquet which she had prepared on the sixteenth[1] of Nisan. When they had eaten and taken (wine) the king said to Esther: "What is thy petition,[2] queen Esther? and it shall be granted thee; and what is thy request?" (*ibid.* vii. 2). She said to him: My lord, O king![3] I ask nought of thee, except my life, and my people. Because one man has come and has bought us to destroy, to slay, and to cause to perish.[4] "But if we had been sold for bondmen and bondwomen, I had held my peace" (*ibid.* 4). The king said to her:[5] Who is this man? She answered him: This one is the wicked Haman,[6] as it is said, "And Esther said, An adversary and an enemy, even this wicked Haman" (*ibid.* 6). "The king arose in his wrath" (*ibid.* 7).[7] What did the angel Michael[8] do? He began to cut down the plants in his presence.[9] || Intense wrath was kindled within him, and the king returned from the palace garden to the place of the banquet of wine. What did the angel Michael do? He lifted up Haman[10] from Esther. The king ex-

[1] The first editions and MS. Gaster read: "the 17th of Nisan."

[2] The quotation ends here in the MS.; it is continued in the first editions.

[3] The first editions read here: "'If it please the king, let my life be given me at my petition, and my people at my request'" (Esth. vii. 3). See Targum I., *in loc.*, which paraphrases this verse thus: "If I have found grace in thy sight, O king": "If I have found mercy before Thee, O High King," referring to God. Our author also only quotes the second half of the verse as referring to Ahasuerus.

[4] See Esth. Rab. Proem.

[5] The first editions read: "Who is he and where is he?" (Esth. vii. 5).

[6] The first editions read: "This wicked Haman" (Esth. vii. 6). See Targum I., *in loc.* In the MS. the quotation which follows ends with the word "enemy." Then the first editions add: "Forthwith they covered his face."

[7] The first editions add: "from the banquet of wine, and he went into the palace garden."

[8] See Targum II. to Esth. vii. 7, and cf. Targum I. to Esth. vii. 7, which speaks of the "ten angels in the guise of the ten sons of Haman cutting down the king's plants." Josephus should be compared with our Midrash in connection with his account of the story of Esther.

[9] The first editions add here: "The king saw and asked him: Who is this? He answered him: I am the son of Haman, for thus did my father command me.[1] Immediately was his wrath kindled." See T.B. Megillah, *loc. cit.*, and Esth. Rab. x. 9.

[10] Against Esther, see Esth. vii. 8; and cf. Targum II. to Esth. vii. 8. The Venice edition reads: "He lifted Haman up from Esther, as though he had wished to come to her."

---

[1] This Midrash seems to be designed to express the attempt of Haman to cut off the Jews by the use of the figure of the cutting off of the plants in the king's garden.

claimed:[1] As for this villain, he is not satisfied with having purchased the people of Esther to destroy, to slay, and to cause to perish, but he must needs come upon her! "Will he even force the queen before me in the house?" (*ibid.* 8).[2] Haman heard this word and his countenance fell, as it is said, "They covered Haman's face" (*ibid.*).[3] And the king commanded that he should be hanged on the gallows.[4] What[5] did Elijah, his memory be a blessing, do? He assumed the guise of Harbonah,[6] one of the chamberlains of the king. He said to him: My lord, O king! There is a tree[7] in Haman's house (taken) from the Holy of Holies,[8] fifty cubits high. Whence do we know that it was from the Holy of Holies? Because it is said, "And he built the house of the forest of Lebanon" (1 Kings vii. 2).[9] Forthwith the king commanded that he should be hanged thereon, as it is said, "And (the king[10]) said, Hang him thereon" (Esth. vii. 9), so as to fulfil that which is said, "Let a beam be pulled out from his house,[11] and let him be lifted up and fastened thereon; and let his house be made a dunghill for this" (Ezra vi. 11). And it says, "So they hanged Haman[12] on the gallows that he had prepared for Mordecai" (Esth. vii. 10). The king took all that belonged to Haman[13] and gave it to Mordecai and to Esther.[14] He[15] said to them: Write

[1] The rest of this sentence occurs in the MS. only.

[2] Josephus, *Ant.* xi. 6. 11, adds: "as he had fallen upon the queen's bed."

[3] This sentence occurs in the MS. only.

[4] The first editions add: "as it is said, 'And the king said, Hang him thereon'" (Esth. vii. 9).

[5] The first editions read: "In that hour what did Elijah," etc.

[6] See Hagahoth of Maimonides, Hilkhoth Megillah, i. 7; *J.E.* vi. 231, also Esth. Rab. x. 9.

[7] "'*Ez*," tree, wood, or gallows. See also Targum II. to Esth. vii. 9; Josephus, *loc. cit.*, and cf. Jerahmeel lxxxii. 6.

[8] Luria thinks that we should read here: "from the house of the forest of Lebanon." This is very likely correct.

[9] The first editions vary the quotation and read:- "'And he made the porch of pillars; the length thereof was fifty cubits'" (1 Kings vii. 6).

[10] The MS. omits "the king."

[11] The quotation ends here in the MS. and in the first editions.

[12] In the MS. the quotation ends here; it is continued in the first editions.

[13] "and his house" is added by Luria.

[14] The first editions add the following: "to fulfil that which is said: 'And let his house be made a dunghill for this'" (Ezra vi. 11).

[15] The first editions read: "The king commanded the Jews to do as seemed good in their eyes."

concerning the Jews as seems good in your eyes [1] in the name of the king. They wrote official letters, and they sent throughout all the provinces [2] to destroy, to slay, || and to cause all the enemies of the Jews to perish on the thirteenth of the month of Adar, on the third day in the constellation of Leo.[3] Just as the lion [4] is the king [5] over all the beasts, and he turns his gaze towards any place as he wishes; likewise did he [6] think fit, and he turned his face to destroy and to slay all the enemies of Israel, as it is said, "In the day that the enemies of the Jews hoped to have rule over them" (*ibid.* ix. 1).[7]

Rabbi Eliezer said: Haman had forty sons; [8] ten of them were the scribes of the books of the king, and thirty were ruling in all the provinces, as it is said, "And the ten sons of Haman, in the rest of the king's provinces" (*ibid.* 12). They were all hanged upon the gallows of their father, as it is said, "And they hanged Haman's ten sons" (*ibid.* 14) upon the gallows. Another Scripture text says, "And they hanged Haman's ten sons" (*ibid.*).[9]

Rabbi Phineas said: Mordecai ruled [10] over the Jews. Just as the king is dressed in purple, so was Mordecai dressed in purple, as it is said, "And Mordecai went forth from the presence of the king [11] in royal apparel" (*ibid.* viii. 15).[12] Just as the king has a crown upon his head, so Mordecai had a crown upon his head, as it is said, "And Mordecai went forth [13] . . . with a great crown of gold"

[1] The king had told Haman to do with the Jews as seemed good in his eyes; this was the sequel. "Measure for measure."

[2] The first editions add: "of the king."

[3] See Jalkuṭ, Esth. § 1059, and the note at the end of the Warsaw (1877) edition of the Jalkuṭ.

[4] *i.e.* the constellation Leo.

[5] Jalkuṭ, *loc. cit.*, reads: "And the lion is the king."

[6] The constellation Leo.

[7] The first editions read: "Just as he thought and he turned his face to destroy and to slay and to exterminate all the Jews, so was it reversed to their enemies, as it is said, 'Whereas it was turned to the contrary, that the Jews had rule'" (Esth. ix. 1).

[8] In the Book of Esther the ten sons of Haman are referred to four times.

[9] The previous quotation does not contain the words "upon the gallows"; probably Esth. ix. 25 was intended to be the quotation.

[10] The first editions read: "reigned over all the Jews."

[11] The quotation ends here in the MS.

[12] The later editions omit part of this section.

[13] This part of the quotation is not given by the MS.

(*ibid.*). Just as the king's fear obtains in all the land, so was the fear of Mordecai upon them, as it is said, "Because the fear of Mordecai was fallen upon them . . ." (*ibid.* ix. 3).[1] Just as the king's money is current throughout the land, || so was Mordecai's money current in all the land, as it is said, "For Mordecai was great" (*ibid.* 4).[2] What was the money of Mordecai? On the one side was (the face of) Mordecai and on the other (the face of) Esther. Wherefore? Because he was a good man, and a man of peace and seeking the peace of his people, as it is said, "For Mordecai the Jew was next unto king Ahasuerus, and great among the Jews" (*ibid.* x. 3); concerning him the Scripture saith, "Mark the perfect man, and behold the upright: [3] for the latter end of (that) man is peace" [4] (Ps. xxxvii. 37).[5]

[1] The first editions add: "And his fame went forth throughout all the provinces" (Esth. ix. 4).

[2] The first editions quote the next phrase in the verse: "And his fame went forth."

[3] The quotation ends here in the MS.; it is continued in the first editions.

[4] The R.V. has in the margin: "For there is a reward for the man of peace."

[5] See the Midrashim to this Psalm, which could be applied to the fall of Haman; see also Esth. Rab. x. 12. The Midrash Abba Gorion, as well as the other Midrashim to Esther edited by Buber in Siphrê d'Agadatha, should be compared with this chapter. Munk's edition of Targum II. should also be consulted.

CHAPTER LI

THE NEW HEAVENS AND EARTH [73B. i.]

RABBAN GAMALIEL said: Just as the New Moons are renewed [1] and sanctified in this world, so will Israel [2] be sanctified [3] and renewed in the future world just like the New Moons, as it is said, "Speak unto all the congregation of the children of Israel, and say unto them, Ye shall be holy: [4] for I the Lord your God am holy" (Lev. xix. 2). The sages say: The heavens and the earth are destined to pass away and to be renewed. What is written concerning them? "And all the host of the heaven shall be dissolved,[5] and the heavens shall be rolled together as a scroll" (Isa. xxxiv. 4). Just as when a man reads in a scroll of the Torah and he rolls it,[6] and again he opens it to read therein and he rolls it (together), likewise in the future will the Holy One, blessed be He, roll together the heavens like a scroll, as it is said, "And the heavens shall be rolled together

[1] The first editions read: "are sanctified and renewed." The reference is to the "Benediction pronounced at the beginning of every lunar month." See T.B. Synhedrin, 42a; Sopherim xxv. 1, p. 280; Ex. Rab. xv. 24; and cf. T.B. Rosh Ha-Shanah, 24a, and *supra*, p. 354.

[2] It is only natural that the authors of the Midrashim should think of Israel in the same way as the Christian writers in all ages think of Christians. Thus Justin Martyr, in his *Second Apology*, vii., declares that the whole world is preserved only for the sake of Christians.

[3] Cf. Ezek. xxxvi. 23, and T.B. Synhedrin, 90b, on the future life. The Church Fathers also discuss the passing away of the heavens and their renewal, see Methodius, *On the Resurrection*, viii. f.

[4] The quotation ends here in the MS.

[5] This part of the verse is omitted by the MS. and the first editions.

[6] R.S. b. Adereth in his Responsa, i. ix, and R. Bechai on Gen. i. 22, add here: "again he opens it and reads therein and rolls it together." This agrees with the reading of our MS. The first editions omit this. The opening of the scroll the first time might be for the purpose of airing the parchment, the second time to find the place which was to be read.

as a scroll"[1] (*ibid.*); "And the earth shall wax old like a garment" (*ibid.* li. 6); just as a man spreads out his garment and folds it[2] up, and again he unfolds it ‖ and puts it on and renews it (thereby), likewise the Holy One, blessed be He, in the future will fold up the earth and again will He spread it out and put it in its place like a garment, as it is said, "And the earth shall wax old like a garment" (*ibid.*).

All its inhabitants shall taste the taste of death[3] for two days, when there will be no soul of man or beast upon the earth, as it is said, "And they that dwell therein shall die in like manner" (*ibid.*). On the third day He will renew them all and revive the dead, and He will establish it[4] before Him, as it is said, "On the third day he will raise us up, and we shall live before him" (Hos. vi. 2).

Rabbi Eliezer said: All the host of heaven in the future will pass away and will be renewed. What is written concerning them? "And all the host of heaven shall be dissolved"[5] (Isa. xxxiv. 4). Just as the leaves fade[6] from off the vine and the fig tree, and the latter remain standing as a dry tree, and again they blossom afresh and bear buds and produce new leaves and fresh leaves. Likewise[7] in the future will all the host of heaven fade away like a vine and a fig tree, and they will again be renewed before Him to make known that there is passing away (which) does not (really) pass away. No more shall there be evil, and no

[1] R.S. b. Adereth, *loc. cit.*, and R. Bechai, *loc. cit.*, agree here also with the reading in our MS. The text is corrupt in the first editions.

[2] Unless we adopt this reading, which is probably the correct text, we should read: "and shakes it." The first editions have an abbreviated text.

[3] But they will not really die. Cf. T.B. Synhedrin, 91b.

[4] The first editions and R.S. b. Adereth read: "them."

[5] The MS. reads: "yibbôlu" (shall fade away); this does not agree with M.T. The first editions quote from the same verse: "And all their host shall fade away, as the leaf fadeth from off the vine."

[6] R.S. b. Adereth and R. Bechai agree herewith. The first editions read somewhat differently.

[7] The 1st ed. reads: "Likewise all the hosts of heaven in the future will pass away and blossom again, bearing buds and sprouting afresh, and they shall become renewed in their place; to make known that He maketh everything to pass away. Never again will there be famine or plague, as it is said, 'For, behold, I create new heavens and a new earth'" (Isa. lxv. 17). The Venice edition agrees on the whole with this text, but adds: "there will not be any more new misfortunes." R.S. b. Adereth reads "evil" instead of "plague." In the Messianic Kingdom there will be neither sin nor misfortune.

more shall there be plague,[1] and (there shall) not be the former misfortunes, as it is said, " For, behold, I create new heavens " (*ibid.* lxv. 17).

Rabbi Jannai said : || All the hosts of heaven pass away and are renewed every day.[2] What are the hosts of heaven? The sun, the moon, the stars, and the constellations.[3] Know that it is so. Come and see, for when the sun turns in order to set in the west, it bathes in the waters of the Ocean[4] and extinguishes the flames of the sun, and no light is left, and it has no flame all night long until it comes to the east. When it arrives at the east it washes itself in the river of fire,[5] like a man who kindles his lamp in the midst of the fire. Likewise the sun kindles its lamps and puts on its flames and ascends to give light upon the earth, and it renews every day the work of the Creation.[6] And thus (it is) until even comes.[7] At evening-time the moon and the stars and the constellations wash themselves in the river of hail,[8] and they ascend to give light upon the earth. In the future that is to come, the Holy One, blessed be He, will renew them and add to their light a sevenfold light,[9] as it is said, " Moreover, the light of the moon shall be as the light of the sun, and the light of the sun[10] shall be sevenfold, as the light of seven days " (*ibid.* xxx. 26). " In the day " (*ibid.*).[11] Like which day? In the day of the redemption of Israel, as it is said, " In the day that the Lord bindeth up the hurt of his people " (*ibid.*).

[1] And then all misfortunes, even death, will cease. See Gen. Rab. xxvi. 6, cf. Assumption of Moses, x. 2, and Methodius, *op. cit.* ix.

[2] See Singer, p. 128: "Who reneweth in His goodness every day continually the work of the Creation."

[3] This line occurs in the MS. only.

[4] See *supra*, p. 39; Jalkuṭ, Isa. § 513; T.B. Pesachim, 94b, and the Pal. Targum to the verse Gen. xix. 23. The first editions add here: " like a man who extinguishes his lamp in the midst of the waters, so by the waters of the Ocean the flames of the sun are extinguished."

[5] See T.B. Chagigah, 13b; Ex. Rab. xv. 6, and cf. *supra*, p. 25.

[6] See note 2 above.

[7] The first editions read: " until it comes to the west."

[8] *e.g.* the light of the moon and stars, which lacks heating power. See Jalkuṭ on Isa., *loc. cit.*

[9] The first editions add: " like the light of seven days."

[10] The quotation ends here in the MS.; in the first editions it ends with the words, "as the light of the sun," mentioned previously.

[11] The verse continues: " *in* the day that the Lord bindeth up the hurt of his people, and healeth the stroke of their wound." The MS. reads: "*as* the day."

Rabban Gamaliel said: **The Sabbath** burnt offering which they brought || every **Sabbath** (consisted of) two he-lambs, and the burnt offering **for the** New Moon which **they** brought every New **Moon consisted** of two young **bullocks.** Two for each occasion,[1] **corresponding** to what? **Corresponding** to the two worlds, **this world** and the world to come. "One ram and one **he-goat**":[2] just as they[3] are a single nation, their God is (likewise) *one*. "*Seven* **he-lambs** of the first year **without blemish**" (**Num.** xxviii. **11**), **corresponding** to those **who bring their offerings**,[4] to Him who renews them[5] **like the New Moons**, as it is said, "**This is the burnt offering** of **every month**[6] throughout the **months of the year**" (***ibid.*** **14**).

Rabbi Zechariah said: After[7] (the words) "the burnt **offering** of every **month**[8] **throughout** the months of the **year**" (***ibid.***), **what is written?** "**And one**[9] **he-goat for a sin offering unto the Lord**" (***ibid.*** **15**). For what purpose was **the sin offering? When the Holy One, blessed** be He, **created His world, He created two great luminaries**,[10] as it is said, "**And God made the two great lights**"[11] (Gen. i. 16). **The** one **He** made **larger** and the other smaller, and the moon **obstinately** refused[12] to do the will of its Creator so as to be **made smaller**; **therefore Israel offered** on its behalf

[1] Lit. "These two and those two," *i.e.* Sabbath and New Moon.

[2] See Num. xxviii. 11, 15.

[3] The Israelites. Our MS. text agrees with that of the Amsterdam and Prague editions. The first editions read: "Just as He is one, so are they one and their God is one." This seems to be a conflate text.

[4] The seven occasions when additional offerings (the Mussaphim) were brought, namely, Passover, Pentecost, Tabernacles, New Year, Atonement, Sabbath, and New Moon. Perhaps the reference is to the seven planets.

[5] "In the future" is added by Luria.

[6] The quotation ends here in the MS. and in the first editions.

[7] Our MS. reads "one"; it should be "after (the words) the burnt offering of every month." The Venice edition reads: "After 'the New Moon' what is written?"

[8] The quotation ends here in the MS.

[9] The MS. omits in this quotation, which is repeated a little lower down, the word "one."

[10] See *supra*, p. 31.

[11] In Luria's text the word for "lights" is inaccurate as a quotation from the Bible. In the MS. the quotation ends with the word "made." In the first editions the quotation is continued.

[12] On the Midrash see T.B. Chullin, 60b; Midrash Kônen, p. 26; and *Rabbinic Philosophy and Ethics*, p. 13, and note 1; and cf. Midrash Agadah on Gen. i. 16.

the he-goat for a sin offering heavenwards as one of the burnt offerings of the New Moon, as it is said, "And one [1] he-goat for a sin offering unto the Lord" (Num. xxviii. 15). What is the meaning of "unto the Lord"? The Holy One, blessed be He, said: This he-goat shall be an atonement for Me,[2] because I have diminished the (size of the) moon.[3]

Rabbi Eliezer said: In the future the Temple will be raised up and renewed, as it is said, "Behold, I will do a new thing; now shall it spring forth; [4] shall ye not know it?" (Isa. xliii. 19). || And its gates [5] which are buried in the earth will be renewed in the future and arise every one in its place, and the gate of the inner court which turned to the east.[6] On the six days of work its doors shall be closed, and on the Sabbath day they are opened by themselves, as it is said, "Thus saith the Lord God: The gate of the inner court [7] that looketh toward the east shall be shut the six working days; but on the Sabbath day it shall be opened, and in the day of the new moon it shall be opened" (Ezek. xlvi. 1).[8]

Rabbi Jehudah said: On Sabbath and New Moons Israel stood there,[9] (and they perceived) that the Sabbath day had come, and they sanctified the Sabbath day;[10] and

[1] The MS. omits again the word "one" in this quotation.

[2] The interpretation is due to the fact that only in connection with the sin offering for the New Moon does the Torah say: "A sin offering to the Lord." See T.B. Shebu'oth, 9a; T.B. Chullin, *loc. cit.*; and Gen. Rab. vi. 3; and cf. Jalkuṭ, Gen. § 44, quoting Midrash Abkhir.

[3] Perhaps the idea underlying this Haggadah is not only the fact that the moon is much smaller than the sun, but also the fact that, unlike the sun, the moon is never constant in its phases as seen from the earth. Perhaps the waxing and waning are referred to in our Midrash. See Singer, p. 129, and *supra*, p. 31.

[4] The quotation ends here in the MS.; it is continued in the first editions.

[5] Of the Temple; cf. Isa. lxi. 4 and Zech. vi. 12, 13; Jalkuṭ, Ezek. § 383.

[6] The MS. adds: "shall be, etc."

[7] The quotation ends here in the MS. and in the first editions.

[8] See Ẓohar, Gen. 75b.

[9] In the inner court of the Temple. The first editions add: "and they saw the doors open by themselves and they knew."

[10] The first editions add here: "and afterwards the heavenly (ones, *i.e.* angels) do likewise." This reading is exceedingly interesting, as it seems to be a parallel to the Book of Jubilees ii. 18: "And all the angels of the presence, and all the angels of *sanctification*, these two great classes—He hath bidden us to keep the Sabbath with Him

so also on the New Moons the Israelites were standing there and saw the doors opening by themselves,[1] and they knew that in that hour it was New Moon, and they sanctified the New Moon,[2] and afterwards (this was done) among the heavenly ones. Therefore Israel sanctifies the New Moons first in the lower regions (on earth) and afterwards (it is sanctified) in the heavenly regions, because they[3] have defined the beginning of the Molad of the Moon in the presence of Israel, who saw the doors open by themselves, and they knew that the Shekhinah of the Holy One, blessed be He (was therein[4]), as it is said, "For the Lord, the God of Israel, hath entered in by it"[5] (*ibid.* xliv. 2). Forthwith they[6] fall down and prostrate themselves before their God. So it was in the past and so will it be in the future that is to come, as it is said, "And the people of the || land shall worship[7] at the door of that gate before the Lord in the Sabbaths and in the New Moons" (*ibid.* xlvi. 3).[8]

Rabbi[9] said: Is it not written, "There is no *new* thing under the sun" (Eccles. i. 9)? The (sages) said to

in heaven and on earth." The sanctification of the Sabbath is not the same as the sanctification of the New Moon. See T.B. Bezah, 17a; and T.B. Ḳiddushin, 37a.

[1] See Jalḳuṭ, *loc. cit.*: "Israel *will stand*." There is no tradition to support the saying of R. Jehudah as to the part attributed to the people in proclaiming the New Moon. This function was in the hands of the Synhedrion or the Nasi. See *supra*, Chapter VIII., on the intercalation of the month.

[2] The first editions read here: "They sanctified the New Moon, and afterwards in the heavenly regions, because the sign of the beginning of a New Moon (was known) to the children of Israel." The Venice text continues: "Since they stood there and saw the doors open by themselves they knew that the Shekhinah of the Holy One, blessed be He, was therein, as it is said, 'O Lord God of hosts, who is a mighty one like unto thee, O Lord?' (Ps. lxxxix. 8); (and it is said: 'And the Lord) said unto me, This gate shall be shut' . . . 'for the Lord, the God of Israel, hath entered in *by it*; therefore it shall be shut'" (Ezek. xliv. 2). The first editions have a corrupt text here, the portions in brackets are wanting.

[3] The doors moved by the presence of the Shekhinah.

[4] In the MS. there is a lacuna; the first editions read: "was therein."

[5] The Hebrew for "by it" might be rendered "therein."

[6] The people of Israel.

[7] The quotation ends here in the MS.; it is continued in the first editions.

[8] There were thirteen gates in the Temple, and the people prostrated themselves thirteen times. See Sheḳalim vi. 1.

[9] The first editions read: "Rabbi Jonathan."

him:[1] The righteous and all their works will be *renewed*, but the wicked will not be renewed and "no new thing" shall be given to them, (even) to all who worship and trust *under* the sun, therefore it is said, "There is no new thing under the sun" (*ibid.*).

Rabbi Phineas said: In the future the waters of the well will ascend from under the threshold of the Temple, and they will overflow and bubble[2] over and issue forth and become twelve streams corresponding to the twelve tribes, as it is said, "And he brought me back unto the door of the house; and[3] behold, waters issued out[4] from under the threshold of the house eastward, for the forefront of the house was toward the east: and the waters came down from under, from the right side of the house, on the south of the altar" (Ezek. xlvii. 1). Three (streams) towards the south to pass through them up to the ankles, and three (streams) towards the west to pass through them up to the knees, as it is said, "When the man[5] went forth eastward with the line in his hand, he measured a thousand cubits, and he caused me to pass through the waters, waters that were to the ankles. Again he measured a thousand, and[6] he caused me to pass through the waters, waters that were to the knees" (*ibid.* 3, 4).[7] And

[1] The Venice edition and Luria's text read: "He said to him." It should be: "the sages said to him," that there was an exception to the saying of Solomon that "there was nothing new under the sun," namely, the righteous, who were destined to be *renewed*.

[2] The first editions read: "and will fructify." Jalkuṭ, Ezek., *loc. cit.*, reads "umephakin": "The waters of the well in the future shall rise up from under the threshold of the Temple, and shall ooze and bubble and go forth in twelve streams." See also Jalkuṭ, Josh. § 15, and Jalkuṭ, Zech. § 579. Jalkuṭ, Ezek., *loc. cit.*, says that this water of the well "will go forth in *three* parts." See Wisdom xix. 7 on the narrative of the Exodus. Cf. *supra*, pp. 70, 330, on the twelve paths in the Reed Sea.

[3] The quotation commences here in the MS.; in the first editions the preceding clause is given.

[4] The quotation ends here in the MS.; in the first editions the quotation ends with the word "house," and they add the concluding part beginning with the words: "from the right side."

[5] The first editions read here "the sun"; the M.T. has "the man"; both editions omit "and he caused me to pass," which occurs in the M.T. and in the MS. This variation of the texts proves the dependence of the Venice text upon that of the first edition.

[6] In the MS. the quotation begins here.

[7] The first editions add here: "There were three (streams) towards the north to pass through them up to the loins, as it is said, 'And he measured a thousand *cubits* and caused me to

three (streams) towards the east to pass through them up to the neck, for the neck is the extremity of the body, as it is said, "And he measured a thousand cubits, and [1] he caused me to pass through the waters that were to the extremity" [2] (*ibid.* 3). And (the waters) descended to the brook of Kidron, and they rose higher than in "the stream,[3] that I could not pass through" (*ibid.* 5), as it is said, "For the waters were risen, waters to swim in, a stream that could not be passed through" [4] (*ibid.*). And the waters are drawn (thence), and they flow down to the fords of the Jordan,[5] as it is said, "And they shall go down into || the Arabah" (*ibid.* 8).

Every field and vineyard which did not yield fruit, people water [6] them with those waters and they yield fruit, as it is said, "And it shall come to pass, that every living creature which swarmeth, in every place whither the rivers come, shall live [7] . . . for these waters are come thither, that all things may be healed and live" (*ibid.* 9). Then (the waters) enter the Salt Sea and they heal it.[8] And [9] the waters "shall go towards the sea, . . . and the waters shall be *healed*" (*ibid.* 8). And there they generate all kinds (of fish). The Scripture text (here) gives a general rule concerning the fish, that they will be as sweet as

pass through *the waters*, waters that were to the loins'" (Ezek. xlvii. 4). In this verse also there are two variations of the M.T., and both occur alike in the first edition. The variations are printed in *italics*.

[1] In the MS. the quotation begins here.

[2] אפסים, R.V. renders "ankles." See Tosephta Sukkah iii. 3, pp. 195 f.; cf. T.B. Joma, 77b; and Targum on Ezek. xlvii. 3, which also renders this word by קרסולים.

[3] See Jalkuṭ on Ezek. *loc. cit.*

[4] The last word in the quotation in our MS. differs from the M.T.

[5] Jalkuṭ, Ezek. *loc. cit.*, reads: "to the fords of Jericho."

[6] The entire chapter seems to refer to the future, therefore the verb should be rendered as though it were the future tense: "will water."

[7] The quotation in the MS. begins with the words "for these waters," and ends with the word "thither"; the first editions begin the verse and end with the word "swarmeth."

[8] See Sheḳalim vi. 3. Another reading is given by Jalkuṭ, Ezek. *loc. cit.*, "and they extract from them" (the salt thereof); the first editions read: "and they cover it."

[9] The first editions read: "as it is said: 'Then said he unto me, These waters issue forth from the eastern regions.'" The whole verse might be read with advantage in order to follow the trend of the Midrash.

Manna.[1] They ascend in the stream as far as Jerusalem, and there they are caught in its nets,[2] as it is said, " And it shall come to pass that [3] fishers shall stand by it " (*ibid.* 10). It is written, " They shall stand by it." [4]

There upon the bank of the stream grow all kinds of trees bearing according to their kind.[5] By the river they shall stand, " upon the banks thereof on this side and on that side " (*ibid.* 12). Every month they bring forth new fruit, as it is said, " It shall bring forth new fruit every month " (*ibid.*).[6] Some of them are for food and others are growing, as it is said, " Because [7] the waters thereof issue out of the sanctuary: and the fruit thereof shall be for meat, and the leaf thereof for healing " (*ibid.*).

Every man who is ill and bathes in those waters, will be healed, as it is said, " In every place whither the rivers come, he shall live [8] . . . and every thing shall live whithersoever the river cometh " (*ibid.* 9). Every man who has a wound will be healed by taking of their leaves [9] and applying

[1] Perhaps the MS. reads: " like Manna." The first editions read for this sentence: " And they produce all kinds of fish in the great sea (ocean), as it is said: ' Their fish shall be after their kinds, as the fish of the great sea, exceeding many ' (Ezek. xlvii. 10). And they are sweetened." For the last word Luria suggested: " they are moved." In view of the text preserved in our MS. the reading in the first editions is not to be rejected.

[2] The first editions read: " in their nets."

[3] The MS. adds here " Ki," which does not occur in M.T.

[4] "And be caught there." The first editions add: "'From En-gedi [1] even unto Eneglaim [2] shall be a place for the spreading of nets '" (Ezek. xlvii. 10).[3]

[5] The first editions read: " were growing all kinds of trees bearing fruit according to their kind, as it is said, ' By the river upon the banks thereof shall grow '" (Ezek. xlvii. 12).

[6] See Num. Rab. xxi. 22, and Jalkuṭ, Ezek. *loc. cit.*

[7] The quotation in the MS. begins here and ends with the word " sanctuary." The first editions continue to the end of the verse. The idea seems to be: The waters will be drawn from the Dead Sea and flow through the brook Kidron to Jerusalem. The reading in our MS. is considerably shorter than in our printed texts.

[8] The quotation ends here in the MS. and in the first editions.

[9] And by using them as a plaster. See T.J. Sabbath vii. 2. 10c, and Jalkuṭ, Ezek. *loc. cit.*

---

[1] Engedi is near the Dead Sea.

[2] Both editions read " Enreglaim," which does not agree with M.T.

[3] In the future the fish will be caught near Eneglaim, which is near Jerusalem. See Neh. iii. 3 for the " fish gate " in the Holy City.

them to his wound, as it is said, "And the fruit thereof shall be for meat, and the leaf thereof for healing" (*ibid.* 12). What is the meaning of "for healing"? Rabbi Jochanan said: For a laxative; || suck its leaves and one's food is digested.[1]

[1] See Shekalim vi. 5; Cant. Rab. to Cant. iv. 12; and Jalkut, Ezek. *loc. cit.*

CHAPTER LII

THE SEVEN WONDERS OF OLD [75A. ii.]

SEVEN wonderful things have been done[1] in the world, the like of which have not been created.[2] From the day when the heavens and the earth were created no man was ever saved from the fire[3] until our father Abraham[4] came and was delivered from the fiery furnace. All the kings of the earth heard (thereof) and they were astonished, for they had not seen anyone like him from the day when the world was created. And whence do we know that he was delivered from the fiery furnace? Because it is said, "And he said unto him, I am the Lord that brought thee out of the *furnace* of the Chaldees" (Gen. xv. 7).[5] Another text says, "Thou art the Lord the God, who didst choose[6] Abram, and broughtest him forth out of the furnace of the Chaldees" (Neh. ix. 7).

The second wonder (was) about the wives of the sons of Noah.[7] From the day when the heavens and the earth were created there never was a woman who at ninety years of age had a child, until[8] Sarah came and bare (a son) when (she was) ninety years old.[9] All the kings

[1] See Jalkuṭ, Gen. § 77, which also reads: "have been done." The first editions read: "have been created."

[2] The first editions read: "which have no equal. The first wonder (was)."

[3] The first editions read: "fiery furnace."

[4] See *supra*, p. 188.

[5] The next quotation is omitted by the first editions.

[6] The quotation ends here in the MS.

[7] The words: "About the wives of the sons of Noah" occur in the MS. only.

[8] "Our mother" is added by the first editions. See Midrash Haggadol, c. 303.

[9] The first editions add: "as it is said, 'And shall Sarah, that is ninety years old, bear?'" (Gen. xvii. 17).

of the earth heard (thereof), and they did not believe.[1] What did the Holy One, blessed be He, do to them? He dried up [2] the breasts of their wives,[3] as it is said,[4] "And all the trees [5] of the field shall know [6] that I the Lord have brought down the high tree, have exalted the low tree, have dried up the green tree, and have made the dry tree to flourish" (Ezek. xvii. 24).

"All [7] the trees of the field shall know" (*ibid.*); this (expression) refers to the nations of the world.[8] "That I the Lord have brought down the high tree" (*ibid.*) (this refers to Nimrod [9]). "I have exalted the low tree" (*ibid.*); this is Abraham our father. "I have dried up the green tree," refers to the breasts of the wives of the nations of the world.[8] || "I have made the dry tree to flourish"; this refers to the breasts of Sarah, for they brought their children to be suckled by Sarah's breasts, for Sarah gave suck to all their children in peace, as it is said, "And she said, Who would have said [10] unto Abraham, that Sarah should give children suck?" (Gen. xxi. 7).

The third wonder (was): From the day when the heavens and the earth were created there never was a man upon whom grey hairs were sprinkled [11] until Abraham

[1] See Gen. Rab. liii. 9. For phraseology see Ps. xlviii. 5. The first editions read: "All the kings of the earth saw and were astonished, and they did not believe."

[2] The first editions read: "He caused the ducts of the breasts of their wives to become dried up"; cf. Gen. Rab., *loc. cit.*

[3] The first editions add: "and they brought their children to Sarah that she might give them suck"; cf. T.B. Baba Mezi'a, 87a.

[4] The verse is not given as a complete quotation in the MS. or in the first editions.

[5] The identification of human beings with trees has occurred in our book; see *supra*, p. 150; cf. Gen. Rab. liii. 1.

[6] In the MS. the quotation ends here.

[7] The verse (Ezek. xvii. 24) is now expounded allegorically.

[8] The later editions read: "the worshippers of fire."

[9] "This refers to Nimrod" is omitted by our MS., but it occurs in the first editions. The reference is to Nimrod's attempt to destroy Abraham by casting him in the fiery furnace.

[10] The quotation ends here in the MS. The first editions read: "'I have made the dry tree to flourish.' This refers to our mother Sarah, for all of them brought their children to Sarah and she gave them suck, as it is said, 'Should Sarah give children suck?'" (Gen. xxi. 7).

[11] See Hos. vii. 9 for a similar expression; cf. T.B. Baba Mezi'a, *loc. cit.*, and Gen. Rab. lxv. 9.

came.[1] The people were astonished because they had not seen any one like him from the day when the world was created. Whence do we know that grey hairs were sprinkled upon him? Because it is said, "And Abraham was old, well *stricken in age*" (*ibid.* xxiv. 1).[2]

Rabbi Levitas, a man of Jamnia, said:[3] Like a diadem which belongs to the head of the king, so are grey hairs beauty and glory to old men, as it is said, "The glory of young men is their strength,[4] and the beauty of old men is the hoary head" (Prov. xx. 29).[5]

The fourth wonder (was): From the day when the heavens and the earth were created no man was ill, (who) sneezed and lived, but in every place where he happened to be, whether on the way or in the market,[6] and (when he) sneezed, his soul went out through his nostrils; until our father Jacob came and prayed[7] for mercy concerning this, and he said before the Holy One, blessed be He: Sovereign of all the worlds! Do not take my soul from me until I have charged[8] my sons and my household;[9] and He was entreated of him, as it is said, "And it came to pass after these things, that one said to Joseph,[10] Behold, thy father is sick" (Gen. xlviii. 1). || All the kings of the earth heard (thereof), and they wondered because there had been no one like him from the days when the heavens and earth had been

[1] The first editions read: "From the day when the heavens and the earth were created, grey hairs were not sprinkled upon the children of men until our father Abraham came, and upon him were grey hairs sprinkled."

[2] See Gen. xv. 15.

[3] The first editions read: "Like a crown which is the glory on the king's head, so are grey hairs," etc.

[4] In the MS. the quotation begins here; the first editions read the entire verse.

[5] Cf. also Prov. xvi. 31: "The hoary head is a crown of glory; it shall be found in the way of righteousness"; cf. Gen. Rab. lix. 1.

[6] The first editions differ from our text; they read: "no man was ill unless he happened to be on the way or in the market-place." Jalkuṭ on Job, § 927, reads: "Till Jacob's day it had never happened that a man sneezed and recovered from his sickness."

[7] The first editions read: "And he sought for mercy." See T.B. Baba Mezi'a, *loc. cit.* On "sneezing" see *J.E.* ii. 255 f.; a bibliography is appended.

[8] To keep the way of God.

[9] See T.B. Baba Mezi'a, *loc. cit.*; Gen. Rab. lxv. 9; and cf. T.B. Synhedrin, 107b.

[10] The quotation ends here in our MS.; it is continued in the first editions.

created. Therefore a man is in duty bound to say to his fellow: Life![1] when the latter sneezes,[2] for the death of the world was changed into light, as it is said, "His neesings flash forth light" (Job xli. 18).

The fifth wonder (was): From the day when the heavens and the earth were created, the waters of the sea had not been changed into dry land until Israel went forth from Egypt and passed over on dry land in the midst of the sea, as it is said, "But the children of Israel walked on dry land in the midst of the sea" (Ex. xv. 19).[3] All the kings of the earth heard (thereof) and trembled, because there had been nothing like it from the day when the world had been created, as it is said, "The people heard, they trembled" (*ibid.* 14).[4]

The sixth wonder (was): From the day when the heavens and earth were created, the sun,[5] the moon, and the stars and the constellations were ascending to give light upon the earth, and they did not come into contact[6] with one another until Joshua came and fought the battles of Israel. It was the eve of the Sabbath,[7] and he[8] saw the plight of Israel lest they might desecrate the Sabbath, and further, he saw the magicians of Egypt[9] compelling[10] the constellations to come[11] against Israel. What did he[8] do?

[1] The first editions read: "Therefore is a man bound to say when he sneezes, Life! for this death has been changed into light." See the parallels quoted by the 'Arukh (ed. Kohut) vi. 191a. Cf. T.J. Berakhoth iii. 5. 6d; Tosephta Sabbath viii. p. 118, and T.B. Berakhoth, 53b.

[2] Jalkuṭ, Gen. *loc. cit.*, reads: "A man is bound to thank God when he sneezes." To sneeze in times of illness was regarded as a good omen; cf. 2 Kings iv. 35, for the story of the child restored to life. See T.B. Berakhoth, 57b.

[3] The first editions omit the quotation.

[4] See *supra*, p. 330.

[5] The first editions omit: "the sun."

[6] See Jalkuṭ, Josh. § 22, and Shocher Ṭob on Ps. xix. 9, p. 84a.

[7] According to Seder 'Olam Rab. xi. it was the 3rd of Tammuz, the day of the "Teḳuphah."

[8] The first editions read: "Joshua."

[9] The first editions read: "the magicians of the nations."

[10] The Venice edition agrees with our MS. and reads: "compelling." Perhaps the reading should be "Chôshebim" (calculating). Jalkuṭ, Gen. *loc. cit.*, reads: "exciting." See Gen. Rab. xliv. 10, 12. Perhaps the idea is that of casting spells to force the constellations to oppose the enemy; cf. for this notion Judg. v. 20: "They fought from heaven; the stars in their courses fought *against* Sisera." See also Jalkuṭ, Josh., *loc. cit.*

[11] The first editions read: "coming," present participle, and not the infinitive as in the MS.

He stretched forth his hand to the light of the sun and to the light of the moon,[1] and he invoked upon them the || (Divine) Name, and each one stood for thirty-six hours in its place until the termination of the Sabbath day,[2] as it is said, "And the sun stood still, and the moon stayed" (Josh. x. 13).[3] All the kings of the earth [4] heard thereof and they wondered, because there had been none like him from the day when the world had been created, as it is said, "And there was no day like that [5] before it or after it, that the Lord hearkened unto the voice of a man" (*ibid.* 14).

The seventh wonder (was): From the day when the heavens and earth had been created there had never been a sick man who had recovered from his sickness,[6] until Hezekiah, king of Judah, came and fell sick and (yet) he recovered, as it is said,[7] "The writing of Hezekiah, king of Judah, when he had been sick, and was recovered of his sickness" (Isa. xxxviii. 9). He began to pray before the Holy One, blessed be He, saying: Sovereign of all worlds! "Now, O Lord, remember, I beseech thee, how I walked before thee in truth [8] and with a perfect heart, and have done that which is good in thy sight" (2 Kings xx. 3); and He was entreated of him, as it is said, "Behold, I will add unto thy days fifteen years" (Isa. xxxviii. 5).[9] Hezekiah said before the Holy One, blessed be He: Sovereign of all worlds! Give me a sign, as it is said, "And Hezekiah said unto Isaiah, What shall be the sign [10] that the Lord

[1] The first editions add: "and to the light of the stars."

[2] See T.B. 'Abodah Ẓarah, 25a.

[3] The first editions add: "'until the nation had avenged themselves of their enemies' (Josh. x. 13). And it is written, 'And there was no day like that before it or after it, that the Lord hearkened unto the voice of a man'" (*ibid.* 14).

[4] The first editions read: "The kings of the earth heard." The later editions have: "many people heard."

[5] The quotation ends here in the MS. and in the first editions.

[6] See Gen. Rab. lxv. 9. Because of the unprecedented experience of Hezekiah, a sign was given. See T.B. Baba Mezi'a, *loc. cit.*, where Elisha's cure is quoted as the first. Cf. T.B. Synhedrin, 104a, and *ibid.* 107b.

[7] The quotation in the first editions is: "'In those days was Hezekiah sick unto death'" (2 Kings xx. 1).

[8] In the MS. the quotation ends here; in the first editions the last word quoted is "thee."

[9] The text of the quotation in our MS. differs from that printed in the first editions. The M.T. should also be compared.

[10] The quotation ends here in the MS.; it is continued in the first editions. The MS. as well as the first editions differ from the M.T. by omitting "unto Isaiah."

will heal me, and that I shall go up unto the house of the Lord?" (2 Kings xx. 8). He answered him: Ahaz thy father compelled[1] the constellations, and he bowed down[2] to the sun,[3] and the sun fled before him[4] and went down in the west ten steps.[5] If thou desirest, it shall go down ten steps, or it shall ascend ten steps.[6] Hezekiah spake before the Holy One, blessed be He: Sovereign of all worlds! Nay, || but those ten steps which it has (already) gone down let it retrace and stand,[7] as it is said, "Nay, but let the shadow return[8] backward ten steps" (*ibid.* 10). And He was entreated of him, as it is said, "Behold, I will cause the shadow on the steps,[9] which is gone down on the dial of Ahaz with the sun, to return backward ten steps" (Isa. xxxviii. 8). All the kings[10] of the earth saw, and they were astonished, for there had been nothing like it from the day when the world was created, and they[11] sent to behold the wonder,[12] as it is said, "Howbeit[13] in (the business of) the ambassadors of the princes of Babylon[14] who sent unto him to inquire of the wonder that was done in the land" (2 Chron. xxxii. 31).

[1] Should we read "Chôsheb," "was calculating"? Cf. *supra*, p. 423, note 10. The reading in our MS. agrees with the previous reading in this chapter in connection with Joshua. Brode suggests: "paid respect to" or "honoured"; if "compelled" be correct, "through spells" might be added for the purpose of interpretation.

[2] See Jalkuṭ on 2 Kings, § 245.

[3] The first editions add: "moon, stars, and constellations."

[4] Jalkuṭ, *loc. cit.*, agrees practically with this reading. The first editions read: "He fled before the sun."

[5] Should we render the word "steps" or "degrees"?

[6] The first editions read: "If thou desirest, it shall again descend ten steps." See 2 Kings xx. 9. Our MS. reads: "or shall it ascend ten constellations?" (מזלות). This last word should be מעלות, "steps."

[7] The first editions add: "in its place."

[8] The quotation ends here in the MS.; the first editions read also the next word. The Venice edition and the MS. read as a quotation כי לא ישוב instead of לא כי ישוב. The first editions add after the quotation from 2 Kings xx. 10 the words: "on the steps which it had gone down."

[9] The quotation ends here in the MS.; it is omitted in the first editions.

[10] The later editions read: "All the nations of the earth."

[11] *i.e.* the Babylonians.

[12] The first editions read "as it is said," as though it were a Biblical quotation. This is an error.

[13] The MS. reads: "uba," "and he came," instead of "vekhên," "howbeit," which occurs in the M.T. and in the first editions.

[14] The quotation ends here in the first editions; it is continued in the MS. as in our version.

And Hezekiah saw the messengers,[1] and his heart was puffed with pride,[2] and he showed them all the treasures of the kings of Judah, and all the treasures of the Holy of Holies in the Temple,[3] and further, he opened the Ark of the Covenant, and he showed them the tables of the Law,[4] and he said to them: With this do we wage war [5] and conquer, as it is said, "And Hezekiah was glad of them, and shewed them [6] the house of his precious things" (Isa. xxxix. 2). The Holy One, blessed be He, was angry with him, and He said to him: Was it not enough for thee to have shown them all the treasures of the kings of Judah and all the treasures of the Holy of Holies? Moreover, thou hast opened for them the Ark, and hast shown them the tables, the work of My hand. By thy life! They shall come up and take away all the treasures of the kings of Judah, and all the treasures of the Holy of || Holies, as it is said, "Behold, the days come,[7] that all that is in thine house, and that which thy fathers have laid up in store until this day, shall be carried to Babylon" (*ibid.* 6). Instead of the tables of the Law, they shall take of thy sons to be eunuchs in the palace of the king of Babylon, as it is said, "And of thy sons that shall issue from thee,[8] which thou shalt beget, shall they take away; and they shall be eunuchs in the palace of the king of Babylon"

[1] The first edition reads: "And Hezekiah saw the kings of Babylon." The Venice edition corrects this and reads: "And Hezekiah saw the kings (?) of the king of Babylon"; it should be: "the messengers of the king of Babylon."

[2] See 2 Chron. xxxii. 31. See also Tanna de bê Elijahu Rab. viii. p. 46: "He became proud when he saw that God had worked a miracle on his behalf."

[3] This is inferred from the words of the text: "There was nothing in his house, nor in all his dominion, that Hezekiah shewed them not" (2 Kings xx. 13). The king controlled the treasures of the Temple; see Shekalim v. 2.

[4] See Targum to 2 Chron. xxxii. 31; and cf. Num. Rab. v. 9. There may have been in the Temple a second ark containing the broken Tables of the Law; see Tosaphoth to 'Erubin, 63b, which quotes T.J. Soṭah on this point.

[5] See Cant. Rab. to Cant. iii. 4.

[6] The quotation ends here in the MS.; it is continued in the first editions.

[7] The MS. adds: "saith the Lord." This does not occur in the M.T. or in the printed editions. The quotation ends in the MS. with the word after "come" in the Hebrew text; in the first editions the quotation is continued up to "house."

[8] The quotation ends here in the MS. and in the first editions.

(*ibid.* 7). These were [1] Hananiah, Mishael, and Azariah, who were made eunuchs in the palace of the king of Babylon, and they did not beget children. Concerning them the Scripture says, " For thus saith the Lord to the eunuchs that keep my sabbaths,[2] . . . Unto them will I give in mine house and within my walls a memorial [3] and a name [4] better than of sons and of daughters ; I will give them an everlasting name, that shall not be cut off " (*ibid.* lvi. 4, 5).

[1] The first editions insert " Daniel."

[2] Cf. Tanna de bê Elijahu Rab. xxvi. p. 134. The MS. omits " my sabbaths " ; the first editions give this.

[3] See T.B. Synhedrin, 104a.

[4] The quotation ends here in the MS. ; in the first editions one word more of the text is added.

CHAPTER LIII

THE SIN OF SLANDER [76B. i.]

EVERYONE[1] who secretly slanders[2] his fellows has no remedy,[3] as it is said, "Whoso privily slandereth his neighbour,[4] him will I destroy: him that hath an high look and a proud heart will I not suffer" (Ps. ci. 5). Another Scripture text says, "Cursed be he that smiteth his neighbour in secret" (Deut. xxvii. 24).[5] Know that it is so. Come and see from the (narrative of) the serpent which uttered slander concerning the Holy One, blessed be He, to Adam and his helpmate.[6] The Holy One, blessed be He, cursed it, so that its food became the dust, as it is said, "And dust shalt thou eat all the days of thy life" (Gen. iii. 14).

Rabban Gamaliel said: Israel also slandered[7] the Holy One, blessed be He, (by) saying: Wilt thou say that He has power[8] to feed us in the wilderness? as it is said, "Yea, they spake against God; they said, Can God prepare a table in the wilderness? Behold, he smote the rock,[9]

[1] The first editions read: "All who slander a man in secret." This chapter is numbered lii. in the MS. referred to by Wertheimer; see *infra*, p. 436, note 5.

[2] This leads on to the narrative of Miriam and Aaron, who slandered Moses; see Num. xii. 1 ff.

[3] The first editions read: "has no portion in the world to come." See T.B. 'Arakhin, 15b. The Menorath Ha-Maor, § 52, reads: "He has no remedy," as in our MS. text. See also Derekh Erez Rab. xi.; and cf. Maimonides, Hilkhoth Teshubah, iii. 6, vii. 4; Tosephta Peah i. 1; and Aboth de R. Nathan (*a*) xl. p. 60b.

[4] The quotation ends here in the MS.

[5] See T.B. Soṭah, 37a. The quotation from Deuteronomy is interpreted as though it meant that one must not slander.

[6] See *supra*, p. 94; and cf. Gen. Rab. xix. 4.

[7] See Jalḳuṭ, Lev. § 524.

[8] The first editions read: "Has the Lord power."

[9] The quotation ends here in the MS.

that waters gushed out, and streams overflowed" (Ps. lxxviii. 19, 20). The Holy One, blessed be He, heard[1] that they slandered His Glory, || and from His Glory,[2] which is a consuming fire, He sent against them a fire which consumed them round about, as it is said, "And the people were as murmurers[3] . . . and the fire of the Lord burnt among them, and devoured in the uttermost part of the camp" (Num. xi. 1). The Israelites betook themselves to our teacher Moses, and they said to him: Moses, our lord![4] Let these be given like sheep to the slaughter,[5] but not to the fire which is consuming fire. Moses saw the plight of Israel, and he arose to pray on their behalf,[6] and He was entreated of him, as it is said, "And the people cried unto Moses" (*ibid.* 2).[7]

Rabbi Judah[8] said: That fire which descended from heaven settled on the earth, and did not again return to its (former) place in heaven,[9] but it entered the Tabernacle. That fire came forth and devoured all the offerings which they[10] brought in the wilderness,[11] as it is said.[12] "And there descended fire from heaven" is not written here, but "And there came forth fire from before the Lord" (Lev. ix. 24).[13]

[1] The first editions read: "saw."

[2] Jalkut, *loc. cit.*, reads: "And He sent against them from His Glory, which is a fire that consumes fire, a fire to devour them." This is the correct text according to Luria. See also T.B. Joma, 21b.

[3] Thus far the quotation in the MS.; in the first editions the latter part only of the quotation beginning with "and the fire" is given.

[4] The first editions read: "Moses, our Rabbi! Give us like sheep."

[5] See *supra*, p. 357.

[6] See Siphrê, Num. § 85.

[7] The first editions cite the next verse: "And Moses prayed unto the Lord, and the fire abated."

[8] The first editions read: "Jehudah."

[9] See Siphrê, Num. § 86, and Tanna de bê Elijahu Rab. i. p. 6.

[10] The first editions read: "Israel."

[11] See T.B. Zebachim, 61b; Siphra, pp. 44b f.; Lev. Rab. vii. 5. The fire was kindled for 116 years—39 years in the wilderness, 24 years in Gilgal, and 53 years in Nob and Gibeon; see, however, Luria's note, *in loc.*

[12] The first editions add: "'And there came forth fire from before the Lord'" (Lev. ix. 24).

[13] See T.B. Sabbath, 87b. It was on the 1st of Nisan that the fire descended upon the altar. The people revolted at the end of Iyar; see T.B. Ta'anith, 29a; Jalkut, Num. § 732 and § 752, and Deut. § 813: "That fire came down and devoured the (two) sons of Aaron, as it is said, 'And fire came forth from the Lord' (Num. xvi. 35); and that fire also consumed the company of Korah."

This was the fire which came forth and consumed the sons of Aaron,[1] as it is said, "And there came forth fire from before the Lord" (*ibid.*). That fire came forth and consumed the company of Korah, as it is said, "And fire came forth from the Lord" (Num. xvi. 35).

No man departs from this world until some of that fire,[2] which rested among the sons of man,[3] passes over him, as it is said, "And the fire rested" (*ibid.* xi. 2). ||

"And Miriam and Aaron spake against Moses[4] because of the Cushite woman whom he had married" (*ibid.* xii. 1). Was she then a Cushite woman?[5] Was she not Zipporah? But just as this Cushite[6] is different as regards his body from all other people,[7] so was Zipporah different from all other women by her words[8] and by her good deeds; therefore was she called a Cushite, as it is said, "For he had married a Cushite woman" (*ibid.*).

Rabbi Tachanah[9] said: The Israelites also are called Cushites, as it is said, "Are ye not as the children of the Cushites unto me,[10] O children of Israel?"[11] (Amos ix. 7). Just as the body of this Cushite is different from all creatures, so do the Israelites differ from all the nations of the world in their ways and by their good deeds; therefore are they called Cushites. One Scripture saith, "And Ebedmelech,

[1] The first editions read: "That was the fire which consumed the company of Korah," and omit the reference to Nadab and Abihu, the sons of Aaron.

[2] The inference is probably based on Deut. xviii. 16: "Neither let me see this great fire any more, that I die not." At the hour of death the fire, which symbolizes the Shekhinah, is seen. For man cannot see God and live, but he beholds the Vision Divine when he ceases to live. See *supra*, p. 254, and cf. Siphra, p. 4a.

[3] The first editions read: "which rested upon the earth."

[4] The quotation ends here in the MS.; it is continued in the first editions.

[5] See T.B. Mo'ed Ḳaṭan, 16b; Siphrê, Num. § 99; Shocher Ṭob, Ps. vii. p. 35b; and see Siphrê, Ẓuṭṭa, p. 33, in the last instalment in *Monatsschrift*, vol. 54.

[6] Or "Ethiopian."

[7] The first editions read: "is different in his skin."

[8] The first editions read: "by her good deeds."

[9] The later editions read: "Tanchum."

[10] The quotation ends here in the MS. and in the first editions.

[11] For a Christian Midrashic parallel see "The Arabic Gospel of the Saviour's Infancy," 40 (in *A.N.C.L.* xvi. p. 119).

the Cushite, said" (Jer. xxxviii. 12). Was it Ebed?[1] Was he not Baruch, son of Neriah?[2] But just as this Cushite is different in his body from all other people, so was Baruch, son of Neriah, different in his deeds and good ways from the rest of the sons of men.[3] Therefore was he called a Cushite.

One Scripture text says, "Then said Joab to the Cushite, Go, tell the king[4] what thou hast seen" (2 Sam. xviii. 21). Was he a Cushite? Was he not a Benjamite?[5] But just as this Cushite is different from all creatures, so was the Benjamite || different by his ways and his good deeds;[6] therefore was his name called "Cushite."

Rabbi Eliezer said: Come and see the integrity and perfection of that man, for he said to Joab, Even if thou wouldst give me gold and silver[7] I would not transgress the king's commands which he commanded thee, as it is said, "And the man said unto Joab,[8] Though I should receive a thousand (pieces of) silver in mine hand" (*ibid.* 12). Joab said to him: I beseech thee, show me the place where Absalom is hanging. But he did not consent. Joab began to bend the knee, and to prostrate himself before him, as it is said, "Then said Joab, Shall I not entreat[9] thee in this wise?" (*ibid.* 14). Then he took (Joab) by his arm, and showed him the place where Absalom was hanging.[10] Everyone who transgresses the commandment "Honour thy father"[11] is accounted as though he had transgressed the Decalogue. Therefore was (Absalom) pierced by ten

[1] See Pesiḳta Rab. p. 130b; Jalḳuṭ, Jeremiah, § 326, where the title of Cushite is given to Ebed; see also T.B. Mo'ed Ḳaṭan, *loc. cit.*, and Targum on Jer. xxxviii. 7, where the title is referred to the king Zedekiah. The first editions read: "Was Ebed a Cushite?"

[2] See Jer. xxxix. 15 and xlv. 1.

[3] The words following till "Then" do not occur in the first editions.

[4] The quotation ends here in the MS. and in the first editions.

[5] See Ps. vii. 1: "Cush a Benjamite."

[6] The first editions add: "from all Israel."

[7] The first editions read: "a thousand pieces of silver."

[8] The quotation ends here in the MS.; the first editions begin with the next word. The text of the quotation in the M.T. differs from that cited in the first editions.

[9] R.V. renders: "I may not tarry thus with thee."

[10] See Mishnah Soṭah, 9b.

[11] The MS. reads: "Honour"; this is the Fifth Commandment. The first editions omit this sentence.

spears, as it is said, "And ten young men that bare Joab's armour compassed about[1] and smote Absalom; and slew him" (*ibid.* 15).

Six people were similar to the first man,[2] and they were all slain. They were: Samson with his[3] might, and he was slain;[4] Saul with his stature, and he was slain;[5] Asahel with his swiftness, and he was slain;[6] Josiah with his nostrils,[7] and he was slain through his nostrils; Zedekiah with his eyes, and he was slain through his eyes;[8] Absalom with his hair, and he was killed through his hair. Absalom was a mighty hero in battle, and his sword was bound upon his loins.[9] Why || did he not draw his sword and cut the hair of his head, and get down? But he saw that Gehinnom was open beneath him, and he said: It is better for me to hang by my hair[10] and not to descend into the fire; therefore he was hanging,[11] as it is said, "Behold, I saw Absalom[12] hanging in an oak" (*ibid.* 10).

Rabbi José said: There are seven doors to Gehinnom. Absalom entered as far as the fifth door,[13] and David heard (thereof), and began to weep, to lament, and to mourn, and he called[14] Absalom! My son! five times,[15] My son, my son, my son! "And the king was much moved, and he

[1] The quotation ends here in the MS.; the text of the verse in the first editions differs from the M.T.

[2] See T.B. Soṭah, 10a; five people were created with some likeness to the nature of the heavenly bodies. Because before his sin Adam was a perfect image of the heavenly bodies. In the legend of the Talmud, the third and fourth instances enumerated by our Midrash are omitted, and instead Asa of fleet foot is mentioned.

[3] *i.e.* the might of Adam at his creation.

[4] The first editions add: "in his might."

[5] The first editions add: "in his stature."

[6] The first editions add: "in his swiftness."

[7] The inference is probably based on Lam. iv. 20: "The breath of our *nostrils*, the anointed of the Lord"; cf. T.B. Ta'anith, 22b, and T.B. Synhedrin, 93b.

[8] The Babylonians put out his eyes; see 2 Kings xxv. 7.

[9] Cf. 2 Sam. xx. 8, and T.B. Soṭah, 9b.

[10] The first editions read: "by the hair of my head."

[11] The first editions read: "in an oak," and omit the quotation.

[12] The quotation ends here in our text.

[13] The first editions add: "of Gehinnom." Cf. 4 Ezra vii. 80–87.

[14] The first editions read: "for Absalom five times, 'My son,' 'My son,' as it is said."

[15] At five doors of Gehenna; cf. T.B. Soṭah, *loc. cit.*, and T.B. Synhedrin, 102b.

went up to the chamber over the gate,[1] and wept: and as he went, thus he said, O my son Absalom, my son, my son Absalom! would God I had died for thee, O Absalom, my son, my son!" (*ibid.* xviii. 33). And they[2] brought him back from the five doors of Gehinnom, and he began to praise and laud and to glorify his Creator, saying: "Shew me a token for good;[3] that they which hate me may see it, and be ashamed: because thou, Lord, hast helped me, and comforted me" (Ps. lxxxvi. 17). "Thou hast helped me" out of the war of Absalom, and "thou hast comforted me" in my mourning for him.[4]

The eighth descent[5] was when He[6] descended into the Tabernacle, as it is said, "And the Lord came down in a pillar of cloud,[7] and stood at the door of the Tent, and called Aaron and Miriam;[8] and they both came forth" (Num. xii. 5). The Holy One, blessed be He, said to them:[9] Whosoever speaketh slander against his fellow in secret, hath no cure; if he slander his brother, the son of his father or the son of his mother,[10] how much more so[11] is this the case? The Holy One, blessed be He, was angry with them, and He departed from the Tent, as it is said,[12] "And the anger of the Lord was kindled against them; and he departed" (*ibid.* 9). || "And the cloud removed from over

[1] The MS. adds "etc.," indicating that this is a quotation; the first word differs from the M.T. and the text in the first editions, which continue the quotation from the words, "O my son."

[2] The words of David; by his intercession and merit Absalom was saved from Gehenna. The first editions read: "And *he* brought him back."

[3] The quotation ends here; it is continued in the first editions.

[4] The MS. continues the chapter with the material of the fifty-fourth chapter in the printed editions.

[5] See *supra*, p. 97, and Introduction, p. xv.

[6] The first editions read: "The Holy One, blessed be He."

[7] The quotation ends here in our MS.; it is continued in the first editions.

[8] According to the Biblical record the eighth descent was at the appointment of the seventy elders; so that the descent in our chapter is really the ninth.

[9] The first editions read: "to him," *i.e.* Aaron.

[10] Cf. Ps. l. 20: "Thou sittest and speakest against thy brother; thou slanderest thine own mother's son." See also Siphrê, Num. §§ 25 and 99; Aboth de R. Nathan (*a*) ix. pp. 20b f., note 35; and cf. Deut. Rab. vi. 8 ff. The first editions read: "the son of his father and mother."

[11] *i.e.* is the punishment an incurable disease?

[12] The first editions read: "as it is written"; this is unusual in our book.

the Tent" (*ibid.* 10).[1] Forthwith Miriam became leprous. The Holy One, blessed be He, said: If Aaron also be leprous,[2] the High Priest, who is afflicted with a blemish, will not be able to bring an offering upon My altar; [3] but he shall look upon his sister and become astonished,[4] as it is said, "And Aaron looked upon Miriam, and, behold, she was leprous" (*ibid.*).[5] Aaron went to Moses, and said to him: O our lord, Moses! Brethren do not suffer themselves to be separated one from the other except through death, as it is said, "Though he be fruitful among his brethren" [6] (Hos. xiii. 15). Our sister, while still among the living, is separated from us,[7] as it is said, "Let her not, I pray, be as one dead" (Num. xii. 12). Not only this, but now all Israel will hear and say that the sister of Moses and Aaron is leprous. Half of this infamous report concerns thee.[8] Moses was appeased by the words, and he arose and prayed for her,[9] and He was entreated of him, as it is said, "And Moses cried unto the Lord, saying,[10] Heal her, O God, I beseech thee" (*ibid.* 13).

Rabbi Levitas, a man of Jamnia, said: Unless the father [11] of a leprous person spit [12] in his face, he will not be healed,[13]

[1] This quotation occurs only in the MS.

[2] See T.B. Sabbath, 97a.

[3] See Tosaphoth to Ẓebachim, 102a; Mo'ed Ḳaṭan, 8a; and Bechoroth, 45b.

[4] The first editions read: "and become distressed." See Siphrê, Num. § 105: "As long as he beheld her (the leprosy) was spreading over her"; see also Aboth de R. Nathan (*a*) ix. p. 21a.

[5] In the Fragments from the lost writings of Irenæus (xxxii.) we find a parallel Midrash to our author; see "Ante-Nicene Christian Library," vol. ix. p. 173.

[6] The text in Hosea reads: "he be fruitful," but the first editions read: "he be separated"; this is probably to be interpreted as an instance of "Do not read" . . . "but read . . ."

[7] The first editions add: "by death," and omit the quotation.

[8] This sentence occurs in our MS. only.

[9] The Prague edition reads: "he prayed for them."

[10] The quotation ends here in our MS.; it is continued in the first editions.

[11] The MS. reads: "mother," but as the verb belonging to this word is masculine, it is an error due to the scribe's carelessness, and we should read "father," as in the first editions.

[12] The reading agrees with the Venice edition. Cf. Lev. xv. 8; and Aboth de R. Nathan, *loc. cit.*

[13] See Aboth de R. Nathan, *loc. cit.*: "Moses drew a small circle about him, and said: I will not move until Thou hast healed Miriam my sister." The New Testament affords a parallel to the practice of healing by spitting; see Mark vii. 33, where it is said that Jesus cured a man who was deaf and who had an impediment in his speech: "And

as it is said, "And the Lord said unto Moses, If her father had but spit in her face,[1] would she not be ashamed seven days?" (*ibid.* 14). Hence (the sages) say: A male afflicted with unclean issue (needs) seven (days for his purification [2]); a woman with an issue (requires) seven (days' separation); a menstruant (needs) seven (days of purification); [3] one made unclean through a corpse [4] (needs) seven (days of purification); a mourner (mourns for) seven (days); the wedding feast (lasts) seven (days); [5] and a leprous person (requires) seven (days' separation). (Whence do we know that [6]) a male with an unclean issue (requires) seven days (for his purification)? || (Because it is said,[6]) "And when he that hath an issue is cleansed [7] of his issue, then he shall number to himself seven days for his cleansing" (Lev. xv. 13). Whence do we know that a woman with an issue (requires) seven (days of purification)? Because it is said, "But if she be cleansed of her issue,[7] then she shall number to herself seven days, and after that she shall be clean" (*ibid.* 28).[8] Whence do we know that a menstruant (requires) seven (days of separation)? Because it is said, "She shall be in her separation seven days" (*ibid.* 19). "Her separation" [9] (or impurity) thou dost not read, but "*in* her impurity";

he took him aside from the multitude privately, and put his fingers into his ears, and he spat, and touched his tongue." See also Mark viii. 23: "When he had spit on his eyes." See Preuss, *Medizin des Talmuds: Speichel als Heil-Mittel*, pp. 321 f.

[1] The quotation ends here in the MS.

[2] Or, "cleansing."

[3] This and the next instance are omitted in the first editions. On the subject see Aboth de R. Nathan (*b*) i. p. 1b.

[4] See Num. xix. 11. On mourning customs see *supra*, p. 115.

[5] This clause occurs in the MS. only; the reference is to the marriage banquet, see *supra*, p. 112.

[6] This is wanting in the MS.; it occurs in the first editions.

[7] The quotation ends here in the MS.; it is continued in the first editions.

[8] In the printed editions there is a lacuna here. The MS. has probably some of the missing text. The Tanna ḍe bê Elijahu Ẓuṭṭa has also part of the lost chapters of the *P.R.E.*, according to Friedmann.

[9] The MS. reads the exact letters of the word in Lev. xv. 19 ("B'niddathah"), which is translated by the R.V. "in her separation," or "impurity." The fact that the same letters are repeated as the word which has to be read suggests either that this word with the same letters was read differently to the M.T., or that some other form of the word, such as the same word less the first letter ("Niddathah"), *i.e.* "Her separation," as we have assumed in our version, was before the copyist. The Midrashim on this theme are to be found in Horowitz' edition of the Baraitha dealing with Niddah, of which there are several recensions.

because Rabbi Ẓe'era said: The daughters of Israel have made the Law exceptionally stringent for themselves, so that if they see a blood stain of the size of a mustard seed[1] they observe on its account seven days, after that they are cleansed[2] (of their issue of blood[3]). Whence do we know that one made unclean through a corpse (needs) seven (days of purification)? Because it is said, "And whosoever in the open field toucheth one[4] that is slain with a sword, or a dead body . . . shall be unclean seven days" (Num. xix. 16). Whence do we know that the mourner (mourns for) seven (days)? Because it is said, "And he made a mourning for his father seven days" (Gen. l. 10). Whence[5] do we know that the (bridal) banquet (lasts) seven days? Because it is said, "Fulfil the week of this one. . . . And Jacob did so, and fulfilled[4] her week" (*ibid.* xxix. 27, 28). Whence do we know that a leper (keeps) seven (days of purification)? From Miriam, as it is said, "And Miriam was shut up[4] without the camp seven days" (Num. xii. 15).

Rabbi said: They[6] slandered God again and said, We were dwelling in the land of Egypt in ease and contentment, but the Holy One, blessed be He, and Moses have brought us forth from Egypt to die in the wilderness, as it is said, "And the people spake against God, and against Moses, Wherefore have ye brought us up[4] out of Egypt to die in the wilderness?" (*ibid.* xxi. 5). What did the Holy One, blessed be He, do unto them? He sent against them fiery serpents which bit and killed them, as it is said, "And the Lord sent among the people fiery serpents,[4] and they bit the people; and much people of Israel died" (*ibid.* 6). Moses beheld the misfortune of Israel, and he arose and prayed on their behalf. The Holy One, blessed be He, said to him: Moses! Make thee a serpent of copper like that serpent[7] || which spoke slander betwixt Adam and his help-mate, and place it on a high place. Let every man who

[1] See T.B. Berakhoth, 31a; and cf. T.J. Berakhoth, v. 1. 8d.
[2] Lit. "clean."
[3] See Lev. xv. 19.
[4] The quotation ends here in the MS.
[5] The rest of the paragraph is wanting in the text of this last chapter of *P.R.E.* published by Wertheimer in *Bottê Midrashoth*, iii. pp. 29–34.
[6] The Israelites.
[7] See *supra*, p. 428, and cf. Tanchuma (ed. Buber), Num. p. 63 f.

has been bitten direct his heart to his Father[1] who is in heaven, and let him gaze at that serpent, and he will be healed. Moses made a serpent of copper and set it up in a high place, and every man who had been bitten turned his heart to his Father who is in heaven, and gazed at that serpent, forthwith he became restored to health, as it is said, "And it came to pass, that if a serpent had bitten[2] any man, when he looked at the serpent of copper, he lived" (*ibid.* 9); and it also says, "If the serpent bite without enchantment, then is there no advantage in the master of the tongue" (Eccles. x. 11).[3]

Rabbi Meir said: If a doctor visit one whom a serpent has bitten, and cure him, verily will goodness be shown to this one.[4]

Rabbi José said: If a man hire a workman who is zealous, and (when) he discharges him should he give him his wages in full; what favour does he give him?[5] But if he hire a workman who is lazy, (when) he discharges him should he give him his wages in full, verily he is giving him a real favour.[6] Likewise spake Solomon before the Holy One, blessed be He[7]: Sovereign of all the worlds! Abraham, Isaac, and Jacob were zealous workmen. Thou gavest to them wages in full, of their own (earnings) Thou didst give them. But we are lazy workmen, and when Thou wilt give us our wages in full, and wilt heal us; verily, every one will praise Thee and bless (Thee).[8]

It is finished. Praise be to God!

[1] See T.B. Rosh Ha-Shanah, 29a, and Wisdom, xvi. 7.
[2] The quotation ends here in the MS.
[3] The expression, "the master of the tongue," seems to point to the slanderer, whose condemnation forms the theme of our chapter. See Bacher, P. i. 402 and 485, for Midrashic interpretations of this verse.
[4] The doctor.
[5] The labourer who has fully earned his wages. Cf. Matt. xx. 1–16.
[6] For the lazy workman has not earned his wages, and therefore is receiving more than his due.
[7] Wertheimer's text omits the following two sentences.
[8] In acknowledging that all we receive is due to the boundless love and grace of our Heavenly Father. See T.B. Baba Mezi'a, 86b.

Immediately following the *P.R.E.* in the MS. comes the well-known Aboth de R. Nathan, the text of which corresponds to the Recension "A" in Dr. Schechter's edition. In a future work, I hope to translate the chapters claimed to belong to *P.R.E.*, and published by Horowitz, and later by Friedmann in his edition of the Tanna de bê Elijahu.

I have a very humble favour to ask at the hands of my readers. Will they kindly let me know whether they can suggest any variations in my translation and offer any parallels from Jewish and Christian and Mohammedan, as well as from classical literature, in illustration of the various points arising out of this Midrash? I am painfully aware that this work is in a very crude condition, and that there are many errors, but in spite of all its blemishes I sincerely hope that something of value may be found in this volume, which has cost the author very many hours of toil snatched away from leisure and holiday.

NOTE[1]

Dr. Büchler's essay, "*Das Schneiden des Haares als Strafe der Ehebrecher bei den Semiten*," which appeared in the *Wiener Zeitschrift für die Kunde des Morgenlandes*, xviii. pp. 91–138, demonstrates that the punishment of cutting the hair of one guilty of adultery arose under Arabian influence. This penalty is unknown in the Talmud and Midrash. The custom was known to R. Simon b. Zemach Duran, *c.* 1440, who quotes the ***Pirḳê de R. Eliezer***, xiv., as his authority. The punishment was already known in the Geonic age. Naṭronai Gaon (857–867) is said to have been the authority when this form of punishment was discussed (cf. *Halakhoth Pesuḳoth*, ed. Müller, p. 53, No. 94, and *Sha'arê Zedeḳ*, p. 25, No. 13). The earliest reference is in *Halakhoth Ḳezuboth*, attributed to the Gaon Jehudai of Sura, *c.* 760 (in Horowitz, תורתן של ראשונים, i. 29). On the basis of these facts Dr. Büchler infers that the curse pronounced upon Eve that a woman should not have her hair cut save for adultery arose in the Schools of Sura and Pumbaditha. This fact may point to the home and date of the ***Pirḳê de R. Eliezer***, which was probably written after the introduction of this penalty; but see Perls in ***Magyar-Zsidó Szemle***, vol. xxiii. p. 124, who suggests as the correct reading מגלה אותו for מגלחתו.

[1] Cf. *supra*, p. 100, note 4.

INDEX OF SUBJECTS AND NAMES

Hor, Mount, 114.
Horeb, Mount, 213, 309, 314, 321.
Horn of Isaac's ram, 230.
Horns of Menachem, 131.
Horns of reëm, 131.
"Horror," 201.
Host of heaven daily renewed, 412.
Host of heaven to pass away, 411.
Host of heaven to be renewed, 411.
Hosts of heaven coming into contact with one another, 423.
Hour of God's day, 49, 377.
Hours, large, 48.
Hours, service of, 32.
House of Abimelech, 191 f.
House of Abraham, 184.
House of Peor, 358.
Houses of study, 123.
Huldah, 244.
Human life, indifference to, at Tower of Babel, 176.
Huna, R., 255, 269.
Hur, 346, 353.
Hur slain by Israelites, 353.
Hur, son of Caleb and Miriam, 353.
Husband and wife, 394 f.
Hyrḳanos, 1 ff.
Hyrḳanos, sons of, 5 ff.

Ice, 40.
Idol in plain of Dura, 248.
Idolaters, 129 f.
Idolaters slain by sword, 248.
Idolatrous worship of Teraphim, 274 f.
Idolatry, 118 f.
Idolatry, sin of, 194.
Idolatry of Israel, 248.
Idolatry and David, 277.
Idolatry and Israel, 360, 368.
Idolatry and wine, 372.
Ignorance, 129.
Ignorance, sins of, 191.
Image for idolatry, 148.
Image of Micah, 296.
Images = the "blind," 277.
Images = the "lame," 277.
Images of copper inscribed with Abraham's covenant, 276 f.
Immorality, 119, 159 ff.
Immorality of Israel, 369 ff.
Immorality of tribe of Benjamin, 296 f.
Immorality and wine, 372.
Impetuosity and wisdom, 373.
Inaudible voices, 254.
Incomplete state of north quarter, 17.
Indestructible portion of body, 258.
Indifference to human life at Tower of Babel, 176.
Ineffable Name, 22, 58, 367, 371.
Ineffable Name, secret of, 301.
Ineffable Name revealed to Moses, 317.
Infant, birth of, 254.
Influence of constellations, 48 f.
Ingathering of Israel, 117 f.
Inheritance in Israel, 302.
Inheritance of Noah's sons, 172 f.
Iniquity of Esau, 311.
Iniquity of Sodom, 181 ff.
Insignificant things and the powerful oppressors, 390 f.
Intercalation, 47, 52 ff., 57 ff.
Intercalation ceremony, 58.
Intercalation delivered to Adam, 52.
Intercalation in Holy Land, 54, 56.
Intercalation, principle of, 56 f.
Intercalation and Israelites in Egypt, 55.
Intercalation and the patriarchs, 54 f.
Intercalation and its three signs, 56 f.
Intercession and the dead, 310 f.
Iram, 290.
Isaac, R., 230.
Isaac, 54, 108 ff., 111, 178, 313, 319.
Isaac blesses Jacob, 261.
Isaac, bound by Abraham, 227.
Isaac circumcises Jacob and Esau, 209.
Isaac dies on altar, 228.
Isaac digs for water, 263.
Isaac intercedes for Esau, 310 f.
Isaac invoked by Moses, 357.
Isaac marries Rebecca, 234.
Isaac mourns for Sarah, 234.
Isaac prays for Rebecca, 235.
Isaac revived, 228.
Isaac sees glory of Shekhinah, 236.
Isaac, birth of, 376.
Isaac, children of, 235 ff.
Isaac, circumcision of, 207 f.
Isaac, covenant of, 278 f.
Isaac, eyesight of, impaired, 236.
Isaac, name of, 231 f.
Isaac, possessions of, 289 f.
Isaac, ram of, 125, 229 f.
Isaac, redemption of, 384.
Isaac, sowing of, 239.
Isaac, tithe of, 239.
Isaac and Abimelech, 278 f.
Isaac and Esau, 236 ff., 389.
Isaac and Holy Spirit, 311.
Isaac and Ishmael, 215.
Isaac and Jacob, 237, 289.
Isaac and mystery of redemption, 384.
Isaac and the Philistines, 278 f.
Isaac and Rebecca, 110 f., 148, 234 f.
Isaac and his sons, 289.
Isaac as offering, 227 f.
Ishmael, R., 41, 211, 221, 258, 284, 304, 337, 382.

INDEX OF OLD TESTAMENT PASSAGES

GENESIS—*continued*

GENESIS—*continued*

EXODUS

EXODUS—*continued*

EXODUS—*continued*